Political Culture in the Latin West, Byzantium and the Islamic World, *c.700–c.*1500

T0382164

This comparative study explores three key cultural and political spheres – the Latin west, Byzantium and the Islamic world from Central Asia to the Atlantic – roughly from the emergence of Islam to the fall of Constantinople. These spheres drew on a shared pool of late antique Mediterranean culture, philosophy and science, and they had monotheism and historical antecedents in common. Yet where exactly political and spiritual power lay, and how it was exercised, differed. This book focuses on power dynamics and resource-allocation among ruling elites; the legitimisation of power and property with the aid of religion; and on rulers' interactions with local elites and societies. Offering the reader route-maps towards navigating each sphere and grasping the fundamentals of its political culture, this set of parallel studies offers a timely and much-needed framework for comparing the societies surrounding the medieval Mediterranean.

Catherine Holmes is Professor of Medieval History at the University of Oxford. Her books include *Basil II and the Governance of Empire 976–1025* (2005) and she co-edited *Literacy, Education and Manuscript Transmission in Byzantium and Beyond* (2002) with Judith Waring, *Between Byzantines and Turks* (2012) with Jonathan Harris and Eugenia Russell, and *The Global Middle Ages* (2018) with Naomi Standen.

Jonathan Shepard was Lecturer in History at the University of Cambridge. He is the author of *The Emergence of Rus* (1996) with Simon Franklin, with whom he co-edited *Byzantine Diplomacy* (1992). His edited volumes include *The Cambridge History of the Byzantine Empire* (2008; 2019), *Byzantium and the Viking World* (2016) with Fedir Androshchuk and Monica White, *Imperial Spheres and the Adriatic* (2018) with Mladen Ančić and Trpimir Vedriš, and *Viking-Age Trade* (2020) with Jacek Gruszczyński and Marek Jankowiak.

Jo Van Steenbergen is Professor of Arabic and Islamic Studies at Ghent University. He is the author of *Order out of Chaos* (2006), *Caliphate and Kingship in a Fifteenth-Century Literary History of Muslim Leadership and Pilgrimage* (2017), *A History of the Islamic World, 600–1800: Empires, Dynastic Formations, and Heterogeneities in Islamic West-Asia* (2020), and editor of *Trajectories of State Formation across Fifteenth-Century Islamic West-Asia: Eurasian Parallels, Connections and Divergences* (2020).

Björn Weiler is Professor of Medieval History at Aberystwyth University. He is the author of *Paths to Kingship in Medieval Latin Europe, 950–1200* (2021) and *Kingship, Rebellion and Political Culture: England and Germany, c.1215–c.1250* (2007; 2011), and co-editor of *How the Past was Used: Historical Cultures, c.750–2000* (2017) with Peter Lambert, *Authority and Resistance in the Age of Magna Carta* (*Thirteenth Century England* XV) (2015) with Janet Burton and Phillipp Schofield, and *Representations of Power in Medieval Germany* (2006) with Simon MacLean.

Political Culture in the Latin West, Byzantium and the Islamic World, *c.*700–*c.*1500

A Framework for Comparing Three Spheres

Edited by

Catherine Holmes
University of Oxford

Jonathan Shepard
University of Oxford

Jo Van Steenbergen
Ghent University

Björn Weiler
Aberystwyth University

CAMBRIDGE
UNIVERSITY PRESS

Shaftesbury Road, Cambridge CB2 8EA, United Kingdom

One Liberty Plaza, 20th Floor, New York, NY 10006, USA

477 Williamstown Road, Port Melbourne, VIC 3207, Australia

314–321, 3rd Floor, Plot 3, Splendor Forum, Jasola District Centre, New Delhi – 110025, India

103 Penang Road, #05–06/07, Visioncrest Commercial, Singapore 238467

Cambridge University Press is part of Cambridge University Press & Assessment, a department of the University of Cambridge.

We share the University's mission to contribute to society through the pursuit of education, learning and research at the highest international levels of excellence.

www.cambridge.org
Information on this title: www.cambridge.org/9781009011136

DOI: 10.1017/9781009022231

© Cambridge University Press & Assessment 2021

First published 2021
First paperback edition 2023

A catalogue record for this publication is available from the British Library

Library of Congress Cataloging-in-Publication data
Names: Holmes, Catherine, 1968– editor. | Shepard, Jonathan, editor. | Steenbergen, J. van, editor. | Weiler, Björn K. U., editor.
Title: Political culture in the Latin west, Byzantium and the Islamic world, c.700-c.1500 : a framework for comparing three spheres / edited by Catherine Holmes, Jonathan Shepard, Jo Van Steenbergen, Björn Weiler.
Description: Cambridge ; New York, NY : Cambridge University Press, 2021. | Includes bibliographical references and index.
Identifiers: LCCN 2021008453 (print) | LCCN 2021008454 (ebook) | ISBN 9781316519769 (hardback) | ISBN 9781009022231 (ebook)
SSubjects: LCSH: Political culture. | Comparative government. | Civilization, Medieval. | Europe – Politics and government – 476–1492. | Byzantine Empire – Politics and government. | Islamic countries – Politics and government.
Classification: LCC JA75.7 .P657 2021 (print) | LCC JA75.7 (ebook) | DDC 306.2094/0902–dc23
LC record available at https://lccn.loc.gov/2021008453
LC ebook record available at https://lccn.loc.gov/2021008454

ISBN   978-1-316-51976-9   Hardback
ISBN   978-1-009-01113-6   Paperback

Contents

Figures and Maps

Figures

Maps

Contributors

ERIC HANNE is Associate Professor at Florida Atlantic University, specialising in medieval Islamic history. He is the author of *Putting the Caliph in His Place: Power, Authority and the Late Abbasid Caliphate* (Madison, NJ, 2007).

JUDITH HERRIN is Emeritus Professor of Byzantine History at King's College London. Her books include *The Formation of Christendom* (London, 1987); *Women in Purple* (London, 2000); *Byzantium: The Surprising Life of a Medieval Empire* (London, 2007); *Margins and Metropolis* (Princeton, 2013); *Unrivalled Influence* (Princeton, 2013) and *Ravenna: Capital of Empire, Crucible of Europe* (London, 2020).

CATHERINE HOLMES is Professor of Medieval History at the University of Oxford. Her books include *Basil II and the Governance of Empire (976–1025)* (Oxford, 2005); (co-ed. J. Waring) *Literacy, Education and Manuscript Transmission in Byzantium and Beyond* (Leiden, 2002); (co-ed. J. Harris and E. Russell) *Between Byzantines and Turks* (Oxford, 2012); and (co-ed. N. Standen) *The Global Middle Ages* (Oxford, 2018).

R. STEPHEN HUMPHREYS is Professor Emeritus at the University of California Santa Barbara. His books include *From Saladin to the Mongols: The Ayyubids of Damascus, 1193–1260* (Albany, NY, 1977); *The History of al-Tabari, XV: The Crisis of the Early Caliphate* (Albany, NY, 1990); *Islamic History: A Framework for Inquiry* (Princeton, 1991); and *Between Memory and Desire: The Middle East in a Troubled Age* (Berkeley, 1999; 2005).

ANDREW MARSHAM is Reader in Classical Arabic Studies at the University of Cambridge. He is the author of *Rituals of Islamic Monarchy: Accession and Succession in the First Muslim Empire* (Edinburgh, 2009) and (co-ed. A. George) *Power, Patronage, and Memory in Early Islam: Perspectives on Umayyad Elites* (Oxford, 2018).

ROSEMARY MORRIS was Reader in History at the University of Manchester. Her books include *Monks and Laymen in Byzantium, 843–1118* (Cambridge, 1995); (ed.) *Church and People in Byzantium* (Birmingham, 1995); and (with R. Jordan), *The Hypotyposis of the Monastery of the Theotokos Evergetis, Constantinople* (Farnham, 2012); *The Life and Death of Theodore of Stoudios* (Cambridge, MA, 2021).

DANIEL POWER is Professor of Medieval History at Swansea University. He is the author of *The Norman Frontier in the Twelfth and Early Thirteenth Centuries* (Cambridge, 2004); (ed.) *The Central Middle Ages 900–1250* (Oxford, 2006); and (co-ed. N. Standen) *Frontiers in Question: Eurasian Borderlands, 700–1700* (Basingstoke, 1999).

LEN SCALES is Professor of Late Medieval History at Durham University. His publications include *The Shaping of German Identity, c.1250–c.1380* (Cambridge, 2012); (co-ed. O. Zimmer) *Power and the Nation in European History* (Cambridge, 2005); and (co-ed. C. Given-Wilson and A. Kettle) *War, Government and Aristocracy in the British Isles, c.1150–1500* (Woodbridge, 2008).

JONATHAN SHEPARD was Lecturer in History at the University of Cambridge. His books include (with S. Franklin) *The Emergence of Rus* (London, 1996) and (co-ed.) *Byzantine Diplomacy* (Aldershot, 1992); (ed.) *The Cambridge History of the Byzantine Empire* (Cambridge, 2008; 2019); (co-ed. F. Androshchuk and M. White) *Byzantium and the Viking World* (Uppsala, 2016); (co-ed. M. Ančić and T. Vedriš) *Imperial Spheres and the Adriatic* (Abingdon, 2018); and (co-ed. J. Gruszczyński and M. Jankowiak) *Viking-Age Trade* (Abingdon, 2020).

JO VAN STEENBERGEN is Professor of Arabic and Islamic Studies at Ghent University. He is the author of *Order out of Chaos* (Leiden, 2006); *Caliphate and Kingship in a Fifteenth-Century Literary History of Muslim Leadership and Pilgrimage* (Leiden, 2017); *A History of the Islamic World, 600–1800: Empires, Dynastic Formations, and Heterogeneities in Pre-Modern Islamic West-Asia* (London, 2020); and editor of *Trajectories of State Formation across Fifteenth-Century Islamic West-Asia: Eurasian Parallels, Connections and Divergences* (Leiden, 2020).

BJÖRN WEILER is Professor of Medieval History at Aberystwyth University. His books include *Paths to Kingship in Medieval Latin Europe, 950–1200* (Cambridge, 2021); *Kingship, Rebellion and Political Culture: England and Germany, c.1215–c.1250* (Basingstoke, 2007; 2011); (co-ed. P. Lambert) *How the Past was Used: Historical Cultures, c.750–2000* (Oxford, 2017); and (co-ed. J. Burton and P. Schofield) *Authority and Resistance in the Age of Magna Carta* (*Thirteenth Century England* XV) (Woodbridge, 2015).

Preface and Acknowledgements

We have thought long and hard about how to present political culture across the Latin west, Byzantium and the Islamic world during a period of many centuries to as wide an audience as possible. For that reason, we have tried to make proper names and technical terms accessible wherever practicable. Greek has been transliterated without diacritics. Greek forms of proper names have generally been adopted, but not where the names of people and places are very well known in their Latinised form (Nicaea instead of Nikaia, for example); familiar English forms have been preferred out of the same consideration – Athens not Athenai. Arabic diacritics have been discarded in proper names, including the opening ayn ('), and only the ayn and hamza (') retained for technical terms. To help orientate the reader, reign-dates have been given after the names of key individuals. There is a brief Glossary at the end of the book: this offers a selection of technical terms and other unfamiliar words, although in general we have tried to explain these in the chapter(s) in which they are introduced. To facilitate comparisons within and between the spheres, there are extensive cross-references throughout the book. These internal references are distinguished by the use of p./pp. and occasionally n. for a footnote within the same chapter.

We have tried to limit the use of quotation marks to signal words or phrases of particular significance – or which are particularly problematic – to specialists. These range from the archaic to those which are, for scholarly or political reasons, contentious or open to misunderstanding. Thus inverted commas are generally used only on the first mention in a chapter, alerting the reader that there is uncertainty around, or dispute about the legitimacy of, such terms as barbarian/barbarous/pagan, Berber, church/state, civilising, classical/medieval Islam, the dark ages, empire/imperial, the establishment, family confederations, feudal, gunpowder empires, law/justice, Orientalism, outsider/foreign, peace/violence, the poor/the powerful and successor states. Although it may be argued that each of these terms requires exegesis or justification, if it is not to be avoided altogether, repeated disclaimers in the form of quotation marks tend to distract or unnecessarily confuse the newcomer, even if placating the expert eye.

The running order across sections is one which is shaped by our anticipated readership. The Latin west comes first in each section, not because we deem it more important than the Islamic world or Byzantium but simply because we choose to start with the sphere which we think will be most familiar to most readers. We do not regard that sphere as the benchmark against which the other two spheres should be compared. The chapters are all self-contained, stand-alone items and can be read in any order.

Many thanks are due to Liz Friend-Smith of Cambridge University Press, for her unfailing patience and support; to Ruth Boyes at the Press and Gayathri Tamilselvan at Integra for their help in seeing this volume through to print; to Barbara Hird, our indefatigable and eagle-eyed indexer; to Wade Guyitt and Beth Hamer for their copy-editing and proofreading skills; to David Cox for his superlative maps; to Ryan Kemp for his editorial assistance; and, above all, to Nicola Sigsworth for all her help with organisation and copy-editing. For help in obtaining images, thanks go to Florian Kugler of the Kunsthistorisches Museum Vienna; to Jonathan Shea and Lucy Ruowan at Dumbarton Oaks Research Center, Washington, DC; to Adele West at the Ashmolean Museum, Oxford; to Muge Kuleli and Barlas Özden Çağlayan in Oxford and Istanbul; to Anne-Catherine Biedermann and Barbara Van Kets of the Réunion des Musées Nationaux Grand Palais Agence Photo; to Ulrike Polnitzky of the Österreichische Nationalbibliothek; to Vera Schulz of the Universitätsbibliothek Heidelberg; and to the Département Images at the Bibliothèque Nationale de France. We thank the three anonymous readers for their responses to our initial publishing proposal: their suggestions impelled us to focus and refine our ideas. Immense thanks are also due to our extremely long-suffering authors, both for their fine contributions to this volume and for their infinite patience.

Abbreviations

BBOL	N. Necipoğlu, *Byzantium between the Ottomans and the Latins: Politics and Society in the Late Empire* (Cambridge, 2009)
BCC	H. Maguire (ed.), *Byzantine Court Culture from 829 to 1204* (Washington, DC, 1997)
BDI	J. Donohue, *The Buwayhid Dynasty in Iraq 334 h./ 945 to 403 h./1012: Shaping Institutions for the Future* (Leiden, 2003)
BMFD	J. Thomas and A. C. Hero (eds), *Byzantine Monastic Foundation Documents: A Complete Translation of the Surviving Founders' Typika and Testaments*, 5 vols (Washington, DC, 2000)
BMGS	*Byzantine and Modern Greek Studies*
BSOAS	*The Bulletin of the School of Oriental and African Studies*
BZ	*Byzantinische Zeitschrift*
Cal	H. Kennedy, *The Caliphate* (London, 2016)
CCCM	*Corpus christianorum, continuatio mediaevalis*
CCSL	*Corpus christianorum, series latina*
CFHB	*Corpus fontium historiae byzantinae*
CHBE	*The Cambridge History of the Byzantine Empire, c.500– 1492*, ed. J. Shepard (Cambridge, 2008; 2019)
CHC 5	*The Cambridge History of Christianity, V: Eastern Christianity*, ed. M. Angold (Cambridge, 2006)
CHI 5	*The Cambridge History of Iran, V: The Saljuq and Mongol Periods*, ed. J. A. Boyle (Cambridge, 1968)
CHMPT	*The Cambridge History of Medieval Political Thought, c.350–c.1450*, ed. J. H. Burns (Cambridge, 1988)
CHS 1	*The Cambridge History of Scandinavia, I: Prehistory to 1520*, ed. K. Helle (Cambridge, 2003)
CSHB	*Corpus scriptorum historiae byzantinae*

DAI	Constantine VII, *De administrando imperio*, ed. and tr. G. Moravcsik and R. J. H. Jenkins (Washington, DC, 1967)
DC	Constantine VII, *De cerimoniis aulae byzantinae*, ed. J. J. Reiske, 2 vols (Bonn, 1829); repr. in and tr. A. Moffatt and M. Tall, *The Book of Ceremonies*, 2 vols (Canberra, 2012)
DOP	*Dumbarton Oaks Papers*
EHB	*The Economic History of Byzantium: From the Seventh through the Fifteenth Century*, ed. A. E. Laiou *et al.*, 3 vols (Washington, DC, 2002)
EHR	*The English Historical Review*
EI²	*Encyclopaedia of Islam*, ed. P. Bearman *et al.*, 2nd edn, 12 vols (Leiden, 1960–2004) (available online https://referenceworks.brillonline.com/browse/ency clopaedia-of-islam-2)
EI³	*Encyclopaedia of Islam*, ed. K. Fleet *et al.*, 3rd edn (Leiden, 2007–) (available online https://reference works.brillonline.com/browse/encyclopaedia-of-isla m-3)
EME	*Early Medieval Europe*
EMK	P. Magdalino, *The Empire of Manuel I Komnenos, 1143–1180* (Cambridge, 1993)
GC¹	Wipo, *Gesta Chuonradis II. imperatoris*, ed. and tr. W. Trillmich, *Quellen des 9. und 11. Jahrhunderts zur Geschichte der hamburgischen Kirche und des Reiches* (Darmstadt, 1961), 505–613
GC²	Wipo, 'The Deeds of Conrad II', tr. T. E. Mommsen and K. F. Morrison, in *Imperial Lives and Letters of the Eleventh Century* (New York, 1962), 52–100
GOB	H. C. Evans and W. D. Wixom (eds), *The Glory of Byzantium: Art and Culture of the Middle Byzantine Era, AD 843–1261* (New York, 1997)
GSE	A. C. S. Peacock, *The Great Seljuk Empire* (Edinburgh, 2015)
IHFI	R. S. Humphreys, *Islamic History: A Framework for Inquiry*, rev. edn (Princeton, 1991)
IIPTB	D. G. Angelov, *Imperial Ideology and Political Thought in Byzantium, 1204–1330* (Cambridge, 2007)
IJMES	*International Journal of Middle Eastern Studies*
INTI	I. E. Binbaş, *Intellectual Networks in Timurid Iran: Sharaf al-Din ʿAli Yazdi and the Islamicate Republic of Letters* (Cambridge, 2016)
JAL	*Journal of Arabic Literature*

JAOS	*Journal of the American Oriental Society*
JESHO	*Journal of the Economic and Social History of the Orient*
JNES	*Journal of Near Eastern Studies*
JÖB	*Jahrbuch der Österreichischen Byzantinistik*
JRAS	*Journal of the Royal Asiatic Society*
JSAI	*Jerusalem Studies in Arabic and Islam*
KI	A. F. Broadbridge, *Kingship and Ideology in the Islamic and Mongol Worlds* (Cambridge, 2008)
LPIB	M. C. Bartusis, *Land and Privilege in Byzantium: The Institution of Pronoia* (Cambridge, 2012)
MGH	*Monumenta Germaniae historica*
MGH SRG	*MGH Scriptores rerum Germanicarum in usum scholarum*, 78 vols to date (Hanover, 1871–)
MGH SRG n.s.	*MGH Scriptores rerum Germanicarum* n.s., 24 vols to date (Berlin, Weimar and Hanover, 1922–)
MGH SS	*MGH Scriptores*, 39 vols to date (Hanover, 1826–)
MLIB	R. Morris, *Monks and Laymen in Byzantium* (Cambridge, 1995)
MOB	M. Whittow, *The Making of Orthodox Byzantium, 600–1025* (London, 1996)
MPMM	T. Reuter, *Medieval Polities and Modern Mentalities*, ed. J. L. Nelson (Cambridge, 2006)
MSR	*Mamluk Studies Review*
MW	*The Muslim World*
NCHI 1	*The New Cambridge History of Islam, I: The Formation of the Islamic World, Sixth to Eleventh Centuries*, ed. C. F. Robinson (Cambridge, 2010)
NCHI 2	*The New Cambridge History of Islam, II: The Western Islamic World, Eleventh to Eighteenth Centuries*, ed. M. Fierro (Cambridge, 2010)
NCMH 4	*The New Cambridge Medieval History, IV: c.1024–c.1198*, ed. D. Luscombe and J. Riley-Smith, 2 vols (Cambridge, 2004)
NCMH 5	*The New Cambridge Medieval History, V: c.1198–c.1300*, ed. D. Abulafia (Cambridge, 1999)
NCMH 6	*The New Cambridge Medieval History, VI: c.1300–c.1415*, ed. M. Jones (Cambridge, 2000)
NCMH 7	*The New Cambridge Medieval History, VII: c.1415–c.1500*, ed. C. Allmand (Cambridge, 1998)
ODB	*The Oxford Dictionary of Byzantium*, ed. A. P. Kazhdan *et al.*, 3 vols (Oxford and New York, 1991)
ODNB	*Oxford Dictionary of National Biography*, ed. D. Cannadine *et al.*, 60 vols to date (Oxford, 2004–) (available online www.oxforddnb.com/)

OHBS	*The Oxford Handbook of Byzantine Studies*, ed. E. Jeffreys *et al.* (Oxford, 2008)
P&P	*Past & Present*
PG	*Patrologia cursus completus: series graeca*, ed. J.-P. Migne, 161 vols (Paris, 1857–66)
PL	*Patrologia cursus completus: series latina*, ed. J.-P. Migne, 221 vols (Paris, 1841–64)
PmbZ[1]	*Prosopographie der mittelbyzantinischen Zeit*, ed. R.-J. Lilie *et al., I: (641–867)*, *Prolegomena*, 5 vols and list of abbreviations (Berlin and New York, 1998–2002) (available online www.degruyter.com/view/db/pmbz)
PmbZ[2]	*Prosopographie der mittelbyzantinischen Zeit*, ed. R.-J. Lilie *et al., II: (867–1025)*, *Prolegomena*, 7 vols and indices (Berlin and New York, 2009–11) (available online www.degruyter.com/view/db/pmbz)
REB	*Revue des études byzantines*
REMMM	*Revue des mondes musulmans et de la Méditerranée*
RIM	A. Marsham, *Rituals of Islamic Monarchy: Accession and Succession in the First Muslim Empire* (Edinburgh, 2009)
RPCMC	J. Van Steenbergen, 'Ritual, politics, and the city in Mamluk Cairo: the Bayna l-Qasrayn as a Mamluk "lieu de mémoire", 1250–1382', in A. Beihammer *et al.* (eds), *Court Ceremonies and Rituals of Power in Byzantium and the Medieval Mediterranean* (Leiden, 2013), 227–76
SGMI	A. K. S. Lambton, *State and Government in Medieval Islam: An Introduction to the Study of Islamic Political Theory: The Jurists* (Oxford, 1981)
SOE	M.-F. Auzépy, 'State of emergency (700–850)', in *CHBE*, 251–91
SOH	P. Crone, *Slaves on Horses: The Evolution of the Islamic Polity* (Cambridge, 1980)
TBA	M. Angold (ed.), *The Byzantine Aristocracy, IX to XII Centuries* (Oxford, 1984)
TBAMF	J.-C. Cheynet, *The Byzantine Aristocracy and its Military Function* (Aldershot, 2006)
TIT	M. E. Subtelny, *Timurids in Transition: Turko-Persian Politics and Acculturation in Medieval Iran* (Leiden, 2007)
TM	*Travaux et mémoires*
TRHS	*Transactions of the Royal Historical Society*

General Maps

These maps are intended to help orient readers and to locate some of the key places and areas mentioned by our authors. Absolute consistency is difficult to achieve, and readers may find modern place-names alongside ancient ones. It goes without saying that the historical boundaries depicted are approximate and, in some cases, highly speculative or controversial.

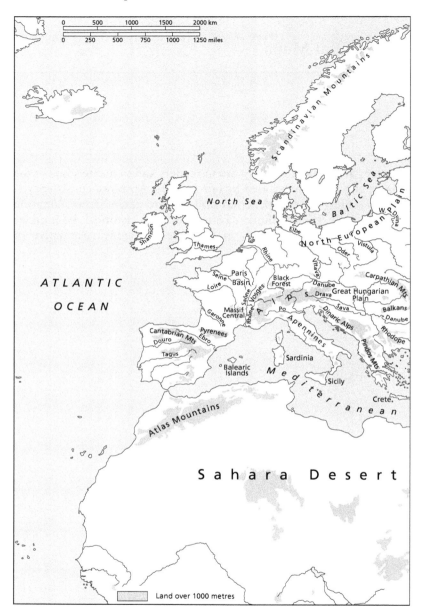

Map 1 The physical geography of western Eurasia, with inset extending
to the Pacific

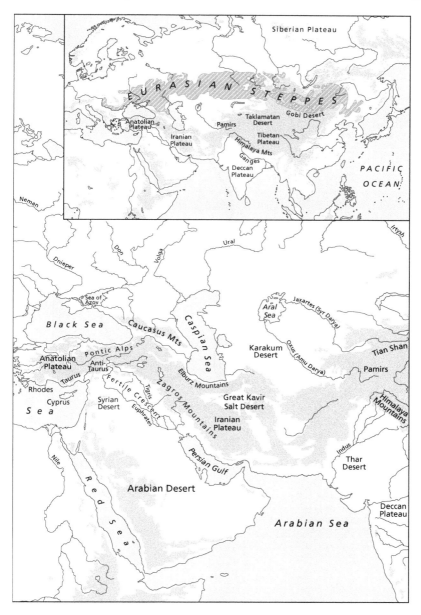

Map 1 (cont.)

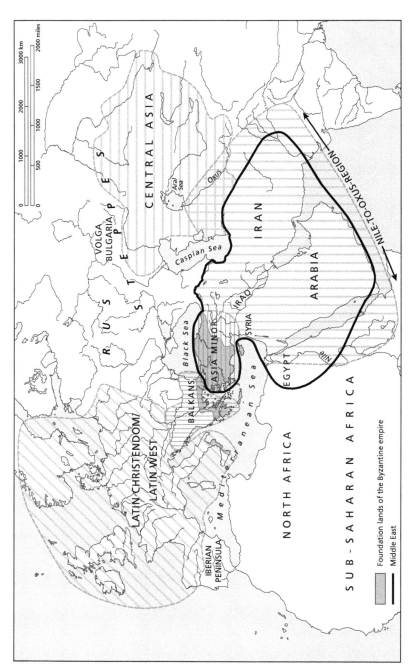

Map 2 A guide to some of the main geographical terminology used in this volume

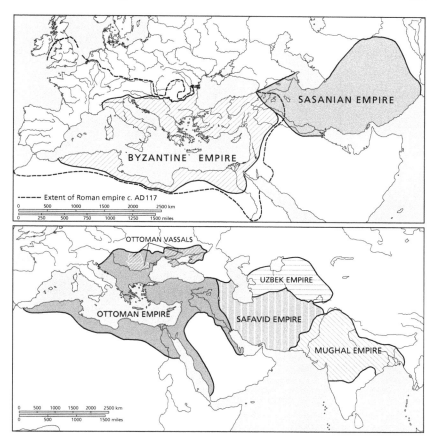

Map 3 Empires before and after: a sketch of the pre-eminent polities preceding and following this book's timespan: (top) Rome in its heyday, also showing Byzantium and the Sasanian empire in the sixth century; (bottom) the 'gunpowder empires' in the sixteenth century

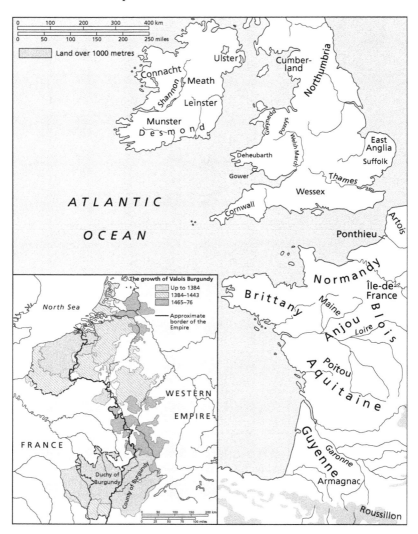

Map 4 Regions of the Latin west mentioned in this volume, with inset showing the growth of Valois Burgundy in the fourteenth and fifteenth centuries

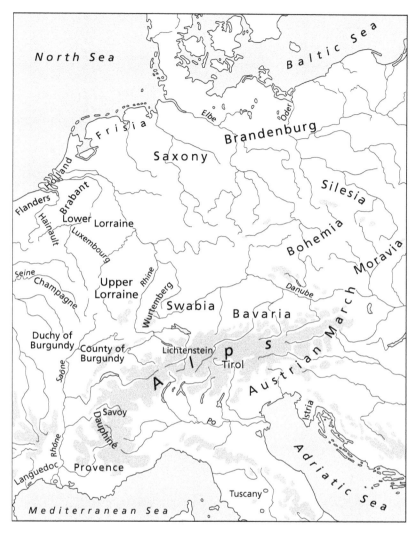

Map 4 (cont.)

Map 5 Places in the Latin west mentioned in this volume, with inset showing the progress of the Spanish Reconquista

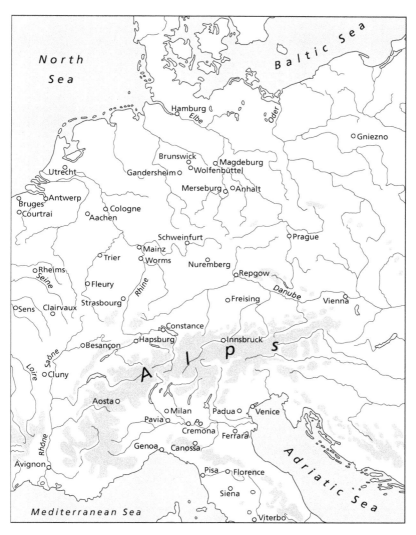

Map 5 (cont.)

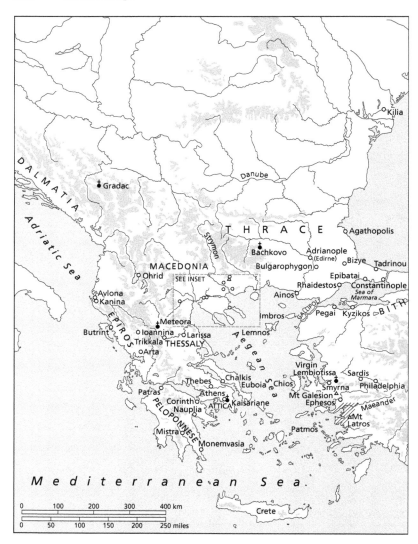

Map 6 Byzantine places and regions mentioned in this volume, with inset showing the Chalcidike peninsula

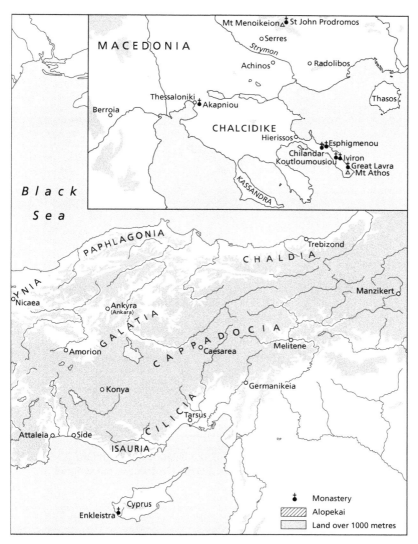

Map 6 (cont.)

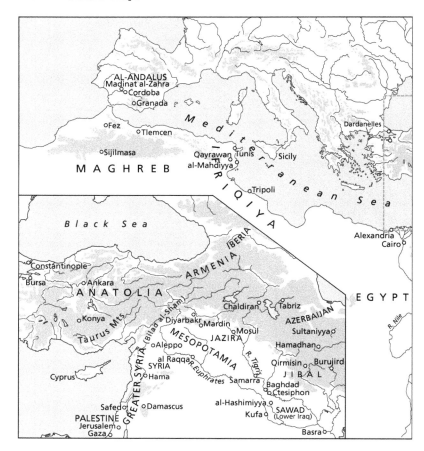

Map 7 Regions and places of the Islamic world mentioned in this volume, with inset showing the Fertile Crescent in more detail

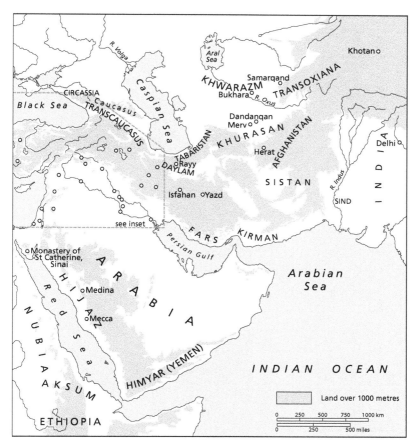

Map 7 (cont.)

Map 8a The Carolingian empire

Map 8b The Latin west *c*.1250

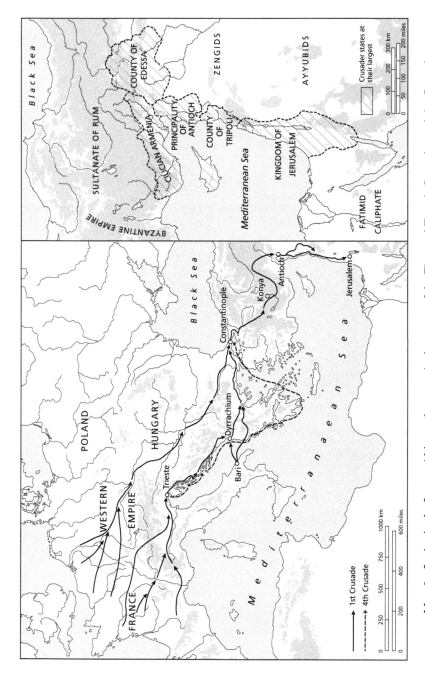

Map 8c Latins in the Levant (thirteenth century): the routes of the First and Fourth Crusades and the Crusader states

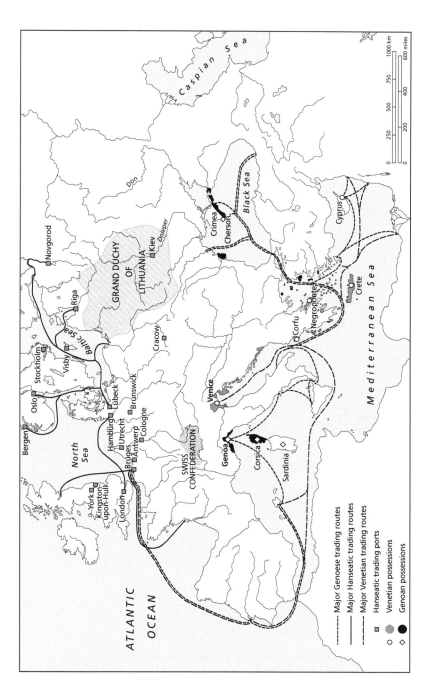

Map 8d Commercial ties (fourteenth and fifteenth centuries): major trading routes of the Genoese, Venetians and the Hanseatic League

Major Genoese trading routes

Major Hanseatic trading routes

Major Venetian trading routes

Hanseatic trading ports

Venetian possessions

Genoan possessions

ATLANTIC
OCEAN

North
Sea

Baltic Sea

Bergen

Oslo

Stockholm

Visby

Riga

Novgorod

GRAND DUCHY
OF
LITHUANIA

Kiev

Dnieper

Don

Caspian Sea

York

Kingston-
upon-Hull

London

Bruges

Antwerp

Utrecht

Hamburg

Lübeck

Brunswick

Cologne

Cracow

SWISS
CONFEDERATION

Genoa

Corsica

Sardinia

Venice

Corfu

Negroponte

Crete

Cyprus

Black Sea

Crimea

Cherson

Mediterranean Sea

0   250   500   750   1000 km

0   200   400   600 miles

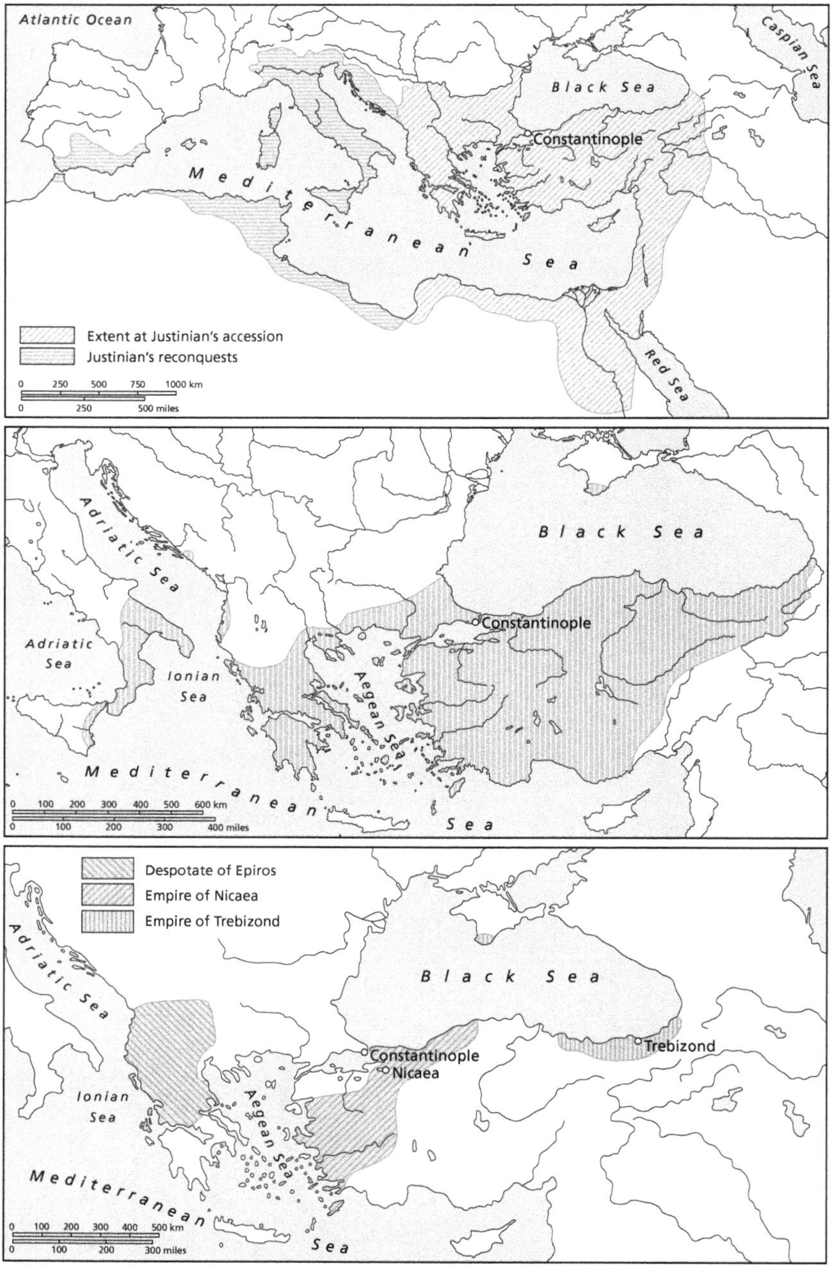
Atlantic Ocean
Caspian Sea
Black Sea
Constantinople
Mediterranean Sea
Red Sea
Extent at Justinian's accession
Justinian's reconquests
0 250 500 750 1000 km
0 250 500 miles
Adriatic Sea
Black Sea
Constantinople
Adriatic Sea
Ionian Sea
Aegean Sea
Mediterranean Sea
0 100 200 300 400 500 600 km
0 100 200 300 400 miles
Despotate of Epiros
Empire of Nicaea
Empire of Trebizond
Adriatic Sea
Black Sea
Trebizond
Constantinople
Nicaea
Ionian Sea
Aegean Sea
Mediterranean Sea
0 100 200 300 400 500 km
0 100 200 300 miles

Maps 9a, 9b and 9c Byzantium's variable geometry: (a, top) The empire at the accession of Justinian, and his reconquests; (b, centre) Middle Byzantium; (c, bottom) the Greek-speaking polities after the Fourth Crusade

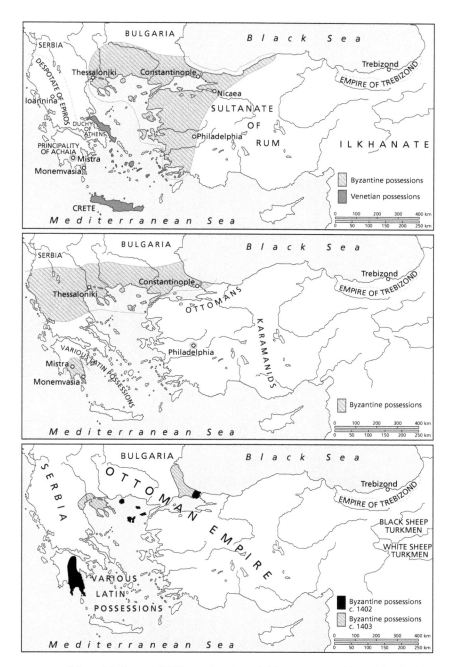

Maps 9d, 9e and 9f Byzantium's variable geometry: (d, top) in the late thirteenth century; (e, centre) in the mid-fourteenth century; (f, bottom) c.1402/3

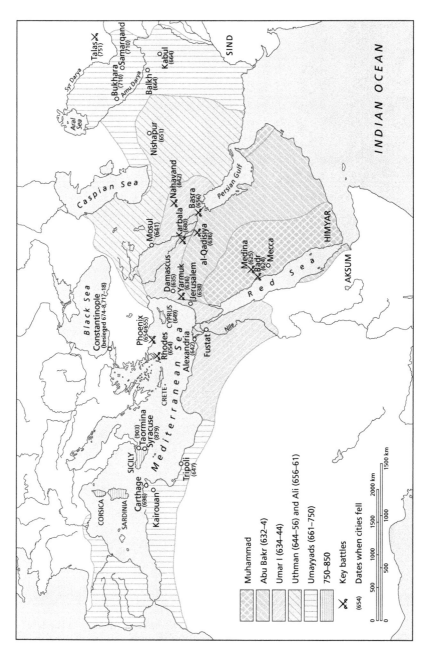

Map 10a The expansion of Islam (seventh to ninth centuries)

SIND

INDIAN OCEAN

Talas✗
(751)
oSamarqand
(710)
Syr Darya
oBukhara
(710)
oKabul
(664)
Balkh o
(664)
Aral
Sea
Amu Darya

Nishapur
o
(651)

Caspian Sea

✗Nahavand
(642)
✗Basra
(656)
Persian Gulf

o Mosul
(641)
Karbala✗
(680)
✗
al-Qadisiya
(636)

Medina
(625)
Badr
(624)
o Mecca

HIMYAR

Black Sea

Constantinople
(besieged 674–8, 717–18)

Damascus
o (635)
✗Yarmuk
(636)
oJerusalem
(638)

Red Sea

AKSUM

Phoenix
(654/655)
✗
Rhodes
(654)
CYPRUS
(649)
Alexandria
(642)

Fustat o

Nile

Mediterranean Sea

CRETE

SICILY
(903)
o Taormina
(879)
Syracuse

Tripoli
(647)

CORSICA

SARDINIA

Carthage
(698) o
Kairouan o

	Muhammad
	Abu Bakr (632–4)
	Umar I (634–44)
	Uthman (644–56) and Ali (656–61)
	Umayyads (661–750)
	750–850
✗	Key battles
(654)	Dates when cities fell

0   500   1000   1500   2000 km
0   500   1000   1500 km

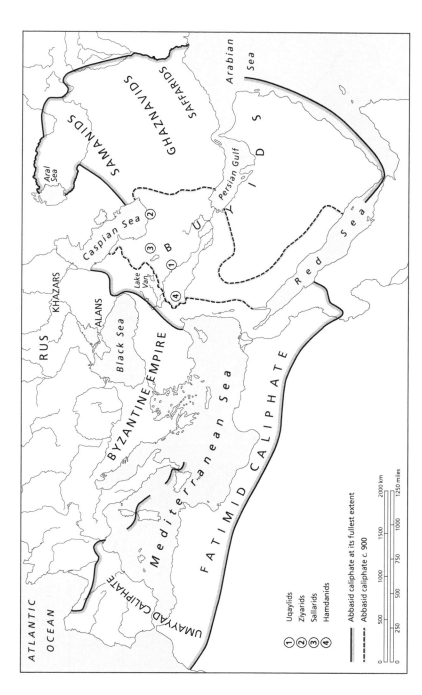

Map 10b Islamic successor polities around the year 1000

ATLANTIC
OCEAN

RUS

KHAZARS

ALANS

Black Sea

BYZANTINE EMPIRE

Mediterranean Sea

UMAYYAD CALIPHATE

FATIMID CALIPHATE

Aral
Sea

SAMANIDS

GHAZNAVIDS

SAFFARIDS

Arabian
Sea

Persian Gulf

B U Y I D S

Caspian Sea

Lake
Van

Red Sea

① Uqaylids
② Ziyarids
③ Sallarids
④ Hamdanids

Abbasid caliphate at its fullest extent
Abbasid caliphate c. 900

0   250   500   750   1000   1250 miles
0   500   1000   1500   2000 km

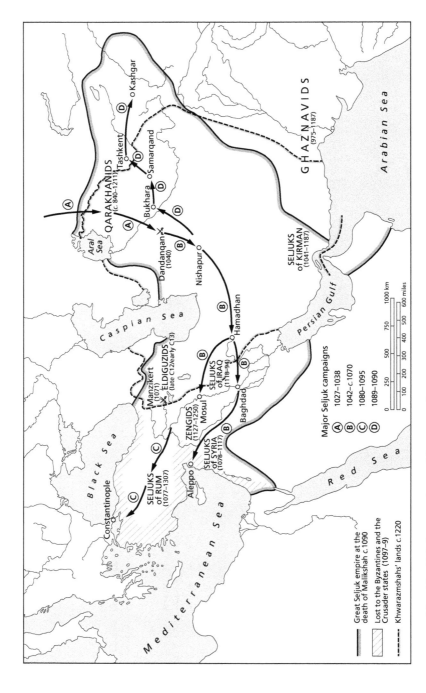

Map 10c Seljuk expansion and fragmentation

Major Seljuk campaigns

- (A) 1027–1038
- (B) 1042–c.1070
- (C) 1080–1095
- (D) 1089–1090

0 100 200 300 400 500 600 miles
0 250   500   750   1000 km

— Great Seljuk empire at the death of Malikshah c.1090

▨ Lost to the Byzantines and the Crusader states (1097–9)

---- Khwarazmshahs' lands c.1220

QARAKHANIDS (c. 840–1211)

GHAZNAVIDS (975–1187)

SELJUKS of KIRMAN (1041–1187)

SELJUKS of IRAQ (1118–94)

SELJUKS of SYRIA (1078–1117)

SELJUKS of RUM (1077–1307)

ELDIGUZIDS (late C12/early C13)

ZENGIDS (1127–1250)

Kashgar

Tashkent

Samarqand

Bukhara

Dandanqan (1040)

Nishapur

Hamadhan

Baghdad

Manzikert (1071)

Mosul

Aleppo

Constantinople

Aral Sea

Caspian Sea

Black Sea

Mediterranean Sea

Persian Gulf

Arabian Sea

Red Sea

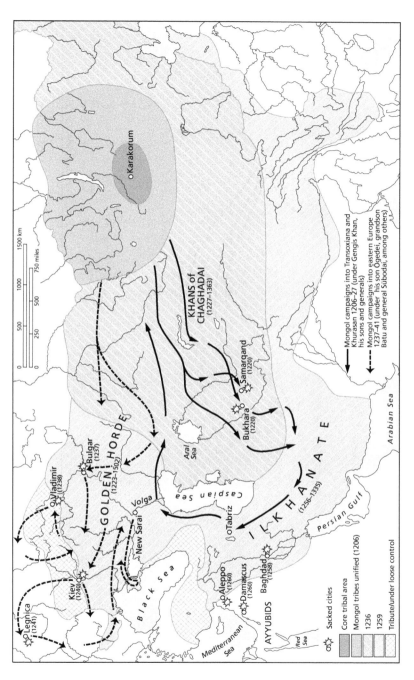

Map 10d The Mongols' campaigns in the west (1206–59) and subsequent polities

KHANS of
CHAGHADAI
(1227–1363)

GOLDEN HORDE
(1223–1502)

ILKHANATE
(1256–1335)

AYYUBIDS

oKarakorum

oVladimir
(1238)

oLegnica
(1241)

Kiev
(1240)

Bulgar
(1237)

New Sarai

Volga

oTabriz

Samarqand
(1220)

Bukhara
(1220)

Aleppo
(1260)
Damascus
Baghdad
(1258)

Black Sea

Caspian Sea

Aral Sea

Mediterranean Sea

Red Sea

Persian Gulf

Arabian Sea

0   250 500   1000
0   500   1000 1500 km
      750 miles

Mongol campaigns into Transoxiana and
Khurasan 1206–27 (under Gengis Khan,
his sons and generals)

Mongol campaigns into eastern Europe
1237–41 (under his son Ögedei, grandson
Batu and general Sübödai, among others)

☆ Sacked cities

    Core tribal area
    Mongol tribes unified (1206)
    1236
    1259
    Tribute/under loose control

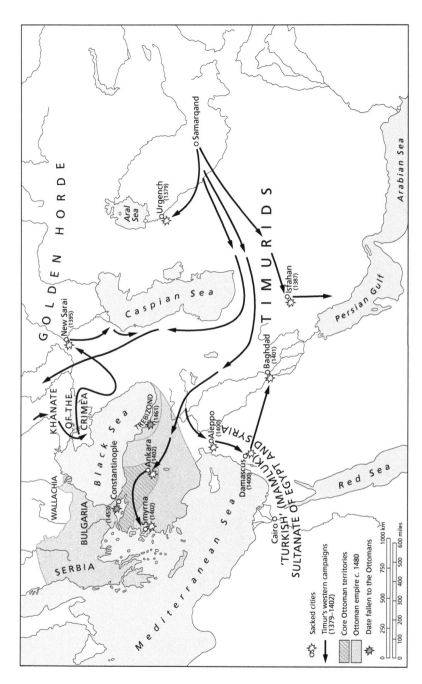

Map 10e The rise of the Ottomans, the 'Turkish' (Mamluk) sultanate of Egypt and Cairo, and Tīmūr's campaigns

GOLDEN HORDE

Aral Sea

Urgench (1379)

Samarqand

TIMURIDS

Caspian Sea

Iṣfahān (1387)

Arabian Sea

Persian Gulf

New Sarai (1395)

Baghdad (1401)

KHĀNATE OF THE CRIMEA

Black Sea

TREBIZOND (1461)

Ankara (1402)

Aleppo (1400)

TURKISH (MAMLUK) AND SYRIA

WALLACHIA

Constantinople

Damascus (1400)

BULGARIA

(1453)

Smyrna (1402)

Red Sea

SERBIA

Cairo

'TURKISH' (MAMLUK)
SULTANATE OF EGYPT

Mediterranean Sea

Sacked cities

Tīmūr's western campaigns (1379–1402)

Core Ottoman territories

Ottoman empire c. 1480

Date fallen to the Ottomans

0   100 200 300 400 500 600 miles
0 250   500   750   1000 km

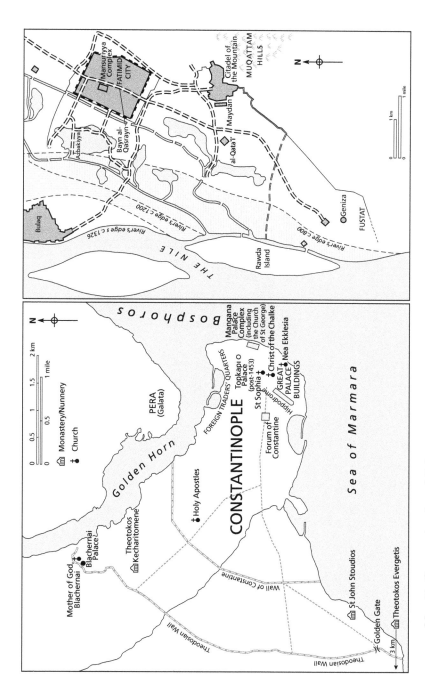

Map 11 Constantinople and Cairo

1 Political Culture in Three Spheres
Introduction

Catherine Holmes, Jonathan Shepard, Jo Van Steenbergen and Björn Weiler

This book appears at a time when our understanding of the scope of the medieval world and the ways in which we should approach it are changing fast. With the globalising of historical studies across all periods, medievalists are eager to explore broader trans-regional contexts and to break out of long-standing disciplinary and area-studies silos. This enthusiasm is burgeoning into publications which sketch the contours of a middle ages extending far beyond western Europe and which treat Europe as just one region among many.[1] Underpinning this new focus is a desire to compare and to connect: to examine what different world regions had (or did not have) in common; and to establish if and how they were connected. But while the drivers for such global study are strong, most medievalists, including the editors and contributors to this volume, are regional specialists. If we are to extend lines of sight and engage in productive trans-regional and trans-cultural investigation, we need practical tools to help us survey broadly without losing specificity and nuance. This volume is an attempt to provide one such set of tools.

It focuses on the political culture of the Latin west, Byzantium and the Islamic world between around 700 and 1500, three entities we have

---

[1] J. Abu-Lughod, *Before European Hegemony: The World System AD 1250–1350* (Oxford and New York, 1989); V. Lieberman, *Strange Parallels: Southeast Asia in Global Context, c.800–1830*, 2 vols (Cambridge, 2003); P. Boucheron *et al.* (eds), *Histoire du monde au XVe siècle* (Paris, 2009); B. Z. Kedar and M. E. Wiesner-Hanks (eds), *The Cambridge World History, V: Expanding Webs of Exchange and Conflict, 500 CE–1500 CE* (Cambridge, 2015); J. Coatsworth *et al.*, *Global Connections: Politics, Exchange, and Social Life in World History, I: To 1500* (Cambridge, 2015); C. Holmes and N. Standen (eds), *The Global Middle Ages, P&P Supplement* 13 (Oxford, 2018); K. B. Berzock (ed.), *Caravans of Gold, Fragments in Time: Art, Culture, and Exchange across Medieval Saharan Africa* (Philadelphia, 2019); see also important single-author studies including A. Haour, *Rulers, Warriors, Traders and Clerics: The Central Sahel and the North Sea* (Oxford, 2007); E. Lambourn, *Abraham's Luggage: A Social Life of Things in the Medieval Indian Ocean World* (Cambridge, 2018), as well as several journals with global or transregional foci: *Al-Masaq*; *Medieval Worlds*; *Medieval Encounters*; *The Medieval Globe*; *The Medieval History Journal*. See also n. 4.

termed 'spheres'.[2] Although the book's remit is chronologically and geographically broad, we do not claim that these three spheres are synonymous or coterminous with a 'global middle ages'. Nor do we claim any special status for them: much of the medieval world, particularly in Africa, the Americas, South and East Asia, and Australasia, lay beyond them, and any fully global history of medieval political culture would include these regions, too. Because our chapters are largely intended as tools for comparative study, our focus is neither on connections nor on those zones where inter-sphere contact was particularly intense, such as the western Eurasian reaches of the land and maritime Silk Roads or the Mediterranean. Thus we do not offer deep investigation of mobility and exchange, both important themes in global medieval history. And while our time frame and geographical range is substantial, we do not offer systematic comparison between spheres, nor do we attempt an overarching grand narrative.[3] Even within the fraction of the medieval world that we cover, our focus is partial: our primary concern is with the political culture of elites and especially with those elites whose power was sustained in a relationship with monarchy. But, as we hope to make clear, there are good reasons for adopting this particular geographical and thematic focus; and, to the best of our knowledge, no such introduction to the political cultures of these three spheres over such a time span currently exists.[4]

Our main aim is to provide a set of parallel studies to enable readers with experience in the history and historiography of one sphere to gain grounding in the fundamentals of the political cultures of the other two. We hope to provide a framework, or set of starting points, for those keen

---

[2] For 'political culture': pp. 5–16; also pp. 17–18, 506–9.

[3] On the desirability of medieval historians engaging with large-scale comparison and grand narrative as a much-needed contribution to global history: A. Strathern, 'Global early modernity and the problem of what came before', in Holmes and Standen (eds), *Global Middle Ages*, 317–44.

[4] Although note the integration of medieval materials pertaining to our three spheres into volumes concerned with rule and governance in Eurasia and beyond over a wider time frame, e.g. P. Fibiger Bang and C. A. Bayly (eds), *Tributary Empires in Global History* (Basingstoke, 2011); P. Fibiger Bang and D. Kołodziejczyk (eds), *Universal Empire: A Comparative Approach to Imperial Culture and Representation in Eurasian History* (Cambridge, 2012); the series *Rulers & Elites: Comparative Studies in Governance*, especially in the later medieval and early modern centuries, e.g. J. Duindam *et al.* (eds), *Royal Courts in Dynastic States and Empires: A Global Perspective* (Leiden, 2011); L. G. Mitchell and C. P. Melville (eds), *Every Inch a King: Comparative Studies on Kings and Kingship in the Ancient and Medieval Worlds* (Leiden, 2013); J. Duindam *et al.* (eds), *Law and Empire: Ideas, Practices, Actors* (Leiden, 2013); R. van Leeuwen, *Narratives of Kingship in Eurasian Empires, 1300–1800* (Leiden, 2017); J. Duindam and S. Dabringhaus (eds), *The Dynastic Centre and the Provinces: Agents and Interactions* (Leiden, 2014); M. van Berkel and J. Duindam (eds), *Prince, Pen and Sword: Eurasian Perspectives* (Leiden, 2018).

to work at a comparative level across spheres or to explore overlaps and entanglements between them. Individual chapters refer to current specialist scholarship and may be of interest to subject specialists, but our overriding concern is to make these spheres accessible to non-specialists. Indeed, it is those chapters that lie *outside* a given reader's specialist knowledge that are likely to be of greatest interest and utility to that reader. For this reason, a glossary of some specialist terms and proper names is also provided (see pp. 510–16).

In presenting these parallel studies we are conscious that comparative history on a broad geographical scale poses methodological challenges. Most immediately, it calls for an approach that recognises conceptual and linguistic boundaries but also allows scholars to transcend them. Timothy Reuter pointed to the rather different meanings that, even within a fairly limited geographical area in the Latin west, were attached to terms such as lordship, *seigneurie* and *Herrschaft*. Each described an economic system based on the extortion of surplus from agricultural labour by elites who were themselves normally defined by their military or religious expertise. Yet each also reflected distinctive academic traditions of engaging with the medieval past, the type and nature of evidence surviving in a given region and the conceptual toolkits developed for interpreting it.[5] So comparative study needs appropriate points for comparison but also questions that are informed by what makes each topic or region distinctive.[6] It also requires an understanding of the contexts from which discourses, practices and conventions emerged; and of the cultural, political and socio-economic horizons of expectation and practice with which people in the past engaged. Thus, in order to make meaningful comparisons as to how power was exercised and thought about in the Latin west, Byzantium and the Islamic world, we need to speak a shared conceptual language. If lordship, *seigneurie* and *Herrschaft* can have widely divergent meanings, how much greater is the room for misunderstanding when comparing terms such as *imperator*, *basileus* and caliph? Used to describe emperors in the Latin west, the rulers of Byzantium (or east Rome) and the leaders of the Islamic *umma*, all three could be translated as 'monarch'. But defaulting to such a generalisation does little

[5] T. Reuter, 'Kings, nobles, others: "base" and "superstructure" in the Ottonian period', in *MPMM*, 300–24 at 304–8. See also N. Vincent, 'Sources and methods: some Anglo-German comparisons', in T. Huthwelker *et al.* (eds), *Princely Rank in Late Medieval Europe: Trodden Paths and Promising Avenues* (Ostfildern, 2011), 119–38; C. Wickham, 'Problems in doing comparative history', in P. J. Skinner (ed.), *Challenging the Boundaries of Medieval History: The Legacy of Timothy Reuter* (Turnhout, 2009), 5–28.
[6] As Bruce Lincoln has shown, asking about apples and oranges and why they are different – even if both are fruits – can be revealing: B. Lincoln, *Apples and Oranges: Explorations In, On, and With Comparison* (Chicago, 2018).

to illuminate the wider cultural signifiers that attach to these specific terms; nor would it accommodate the rather different conceptualisations of the religious and secular in each of the three spheres.

Thus we aim not only to present a set of parallel studies but also to attempt discussions within a shared conceptual framework. We present that framework not as a rigid strait-jacket into which the three spheres must be squeezed at all costs. Rather, these chapters have been shaped by a series of basic preliminary questions about the components of political culture which we asked our authors to bear in mind when writing. These questions are listed in the Appendix to this volume. Developed during a series of prepublication workshops held in Aberystwyth, Oxford and York, the questions were meant to encourage our authors to think about similar structures and processes across the three spheres while also allowing them scope to highlight areas of distinctiveness within and between their broader geographical specialisms. Our inspiration for this approach was the question-led methodology underpinning Nora Berend's project on Christianisation in Scandinavia, central Europe and Rus, albeit revised to take account of the much wider cultural and geographical range of the present volume.[7] Just as our efforts build on Berend's work, so we hope that this book will contribute to current thinking about how medievalists should tackle comparisons on even broader, perhaps even global, scales. We would argue that our approach sidesteps two widely acknowledged risks in the practice of global history: first, the presentation of a cacophony of voices which never quite tune into a composite whole; and second, the flattening and homogenising of the specific and the local, the individual and the particular.[8] Our approach offers one route out of such dilemmas: by developing a series of framing questions, fleshed out and tested by our various contributors, each of whom was in communication with the others but who nonetheless focused primarily on their own area of expertise, we have sketched out a framework to facilitate comparison.[9]

---

[7] N. Berend (ed.), *Christianization and the Rise of Christian Monarchy: Scandinavia, Central Europe and Rus', c. 900–1200* (Cambridge, 2007).

[8] R. Drayton and D. Motadel, 'Discussion: the futures of global history', *Journal of Global History* 13 (2018), 1–21; M. Tamm, 'Interview with Sebastian Conrad', www .academia.edu/37795184/The_Aims_and_Achievements_of_Global_History_Interview_ with_Sebastian_Conrad (accessed 1 December 2019); see also S. Conrad, *What Is Global History?* (Princeton, 2016). Recent methodological debates among medievalists interested in global history have focused on how to avoid these dangers: e.g. C. Holmes and N. Standen, 'Introduction: towards a global middle ages', in Holmes and Standen (eds), *Global Middle Ages*, 1–44 at 20–5.

[9] Just as easily, it lends itself to a more pointillist approach where specific case studies are used to sketch a broader picture that combines the general with the specific: see e.g.

So what are the fundamental premises of this book? What do we mean by 'political culture' and why does this matter? Why have we chosen to focus primarily on elites and monarchy? And why, when monarchy was a type of political organisation shared by many cultures beyond the Latin west, Byzantium and the Islamic world, do we focus on these three spheres? Why conceptualise these worlds as 'spheres' at all? And why choose to start around 700 and end around 1500, when some formations we are describing can be identified in the early medieval centuries before 700 as well as those which come after 1500?[10] In the rest of these introductory remarks, we summarise what we mean by key terms, justify the parameters we have imposed and outline the contours of the book as a whole.

The main anchor to this volume is 'political culture'. We have chosen to frame our shared concern with the theory and practice of power in this way, conscious that 'political culture' is itself a contested notion.[11] Aware of the challenges, we have chosen a pragmatic approach, recognising that any concept used to examine medieval theories and practices of power is open to debate. 'Political culture' is adopted here as an umbrella term for the many different dimensions of elite power relations in the three spheres. It is a formulation that offers some very basic interpretative space within which the three spheres can be discussed in parallel – a space broad enough to allow us to overcome, or at least accommodate, different

---

P. Lambert and B. Weiler (eds), *How the Past was Used: Historical Cultures, 700–2000* (Oxford, 2017).

[10] 'Pre-modern' can, after all, cover virtually any period of human history up to the eighteenth century. On the problems of defining 'modernity' and demarcating the 'pre-modern', see D. L. Smail and A. Shryock, 'History and the "pre"', *American Historical Review* 118 (2013), 709–37, esp. 713–17. For more on whether 'medieval' is a helpful term to describe anything other than the western middle ages, and perhaps not even to describe those: T. Reuter, 'Medieval: another tyrannous construct', in *MPMM*, 19–37; D. M. Varisco, 'Making "medieval" Islam meaningful', *Medieval Encounters* 13 (2007), 385–412. Similar methodological concerns have been raised in connection with the study of late medieval and early modern Eurasia: J. Duindam, 'Prince, pen and sword: Eurasian perspectives', in van Berkel and Duindam (eds), *Prince, Pen and Sword*, 542–66, esp. 542–4.

[11] For its oft-debated genealogy in wider humanistic and social sciences scholarship, see e.g. G. Almond and S. Verba, *The Civic Culture: Political Attitudes and Democracy in Five Nations* (Princeton, 1963); R. Welch, *The Concept of Political Culture* (Basingstoke, 1993); G. Gendzel, 'Political culture: genealogy of a concept', *Journal of Interdisciplinary History* 28 (1997), 225–50; G. Steinmetz (ed.), *State/Culture: State-Formation after the Cultural Turn* (Ithaca, NY, 1999); R. Barker, *Legitimating Identities: The Self-Presentation of Rulers and Subjects* (Cambridge, 2001); R. Formisano, 'The concept of political culture', *Journal of Interdisciplinary History* 31 (2001), 393–426; S. Welch, *The Theory of Political Culture* (Oxford, 2013); P. Crooks and T. H. Parsons (eds), *Empires and Bureaucracies in World History: From Late Antiquity to the Twentieth Century* (Cambridge, 2016).

conceptualisations of power among medieval contemporaries in those spheres and among modern scholars who work on them.

We are conscious that this approach may already be familiar to many scholars working on political history in the Latin west, particularly those who have moved away from looking at top-down administrative structures and events to focus on the ideas, assumptions and practices which shaped the conduct of political life. Yet 'political culture' is a term that has been less frequently invoked by scholars working on Byzantine and Islamic political societies. Of course, there have been landmark studies which take a largely political culture approach or which reflect on component parts of what might be construed as political culture.[12] But there is relatively little scholarship on either Byzantium or the Islamic world which provides an extensive framework for thinking about medieval political culture in the manner that Gerd Althoff's *Family, Friends and Followers* does for the medieval Latin west between the sixth and twelfth centuries.[13] Systematic comparisons of the three spheres' political cultures have also been rare, other than in German scholarship.[14] Nonetheless, some recent volumes suggest that much can be gained by putting the three spheres' political cultures into conversation with one another. Although with a shorter time frame than ours, *The 'Abbasid and Carolingian Empires*, edited by Deborah Tor, offers rich and suggestive comparisons between the concepts and modes of rulership of these vast political orders and the ways in which they both reflected and inflected their respective social contexts.[15] And despite some wariness about 'culture', *Diverging Paths?*, edited by John Hudson and Ana Rodríguez, yields valuable perspectives on political culture in its approach to jurisprudence

---

[12] For Byzantium, e.g. J.-C. Cheynet, *Pouvoir et contestations à Byzance (963–1210)* (Paris, 1990); G. Dagron, *Empereur et prêtre: étude sur le 'césaropapisme' byzantin* (Paris, 1996); English tr. J. Birrell, *Emperor and Priest: The Imperial Office in Byzantium* (Cambridge, 2003); for the Islamic world, R. P. Mottahedeh, *Loyalty and Leadership in an Early Islamic Society* (Princeton, 1980); *IHFI*; M. Chamberlain, *Knowledge and Social Practice in Medieval Damascus, 1190–1350* (Cambridge, 1994); W. W. Clifford, 'Ubi sumus? Mamluk history and social theory', *MSR* 1 (1997), 45–62.

[13] G. Althoff, *Family, Friends and Followers: Political and Social Bonds in Medieval Europe*, tr. C. Carroll (Cambridge, 2004).

[14] J. R. Österle, *Kalifat und Königtum: Herrschaftsrepräsentation der Fatimiden, Ottonen und frühen Salier an religiösen Hochfesten* (Darmstadt, 2009); A. Höfert, *Kaisertum und Kalifat: der imperiale Monotheismus im Früh- und Hochmittelalter* (Frankfurt, 2015). A classic Anglophone study of rulership in the early medieval west and Byzantium is M. McCormick, *Eternal Victory: Triumphal Rulership in Late Antiquity, Byzantium, and the Early Medieval West* (Cambridge, 1986). Ceremonial cultures in the Mediterranean which draw on Byzantine, Islamic and Latin traditions are considered in parallel in A. D. Beihammer *et al.* (eds), *Court Ceremonies and Rituals of Power in Byzantium and the Medieval Mediterranean: Comparative Perspectives* (Leiden, 2013).

[15] D. G. Tor (ed.), *The 'Abbasid and Carolingian Empires: Comparative Studies in Civilizational Formation* (Leiden, 2017).

in the three spheres, on the workings of legal systems, and on fiscal exactions and other such mechanisms of governance, all set against the symbols and places whereby power was expressed or concretised.[16] Perhaps closer still to the themes that we explore is *Visions of Community in the Post-Roman World*, edited by Walter Pohl, Clemens Gantner and Richard Payne, which, in examining the transformation of the Roman and Iranian worlds of late antiquity, deals with the interplay of power, belief and religious organisation.[17] A key feature of this study is the ways in which, following the Roman empire's demise in the west, subsequent regimes merged regional or ethnic rallying calls with Christian ideals of all-embracing community; and there are illuminating comparisons with Islam, where no attempt was made to enforce religious unanimity, and tribal affiliations (actual or adopted) continued to count for the holders or seekers of high office.

Important as issues such as identity are for getting at the texture of politics, we would suggest that any broad enquiry into the political cultures of the three spheres should start with some rather more basic questions. As Stephen Humphreys argues in his chapter, there is something to be said for narrowing one's scope to Harold Lasswell's question: 'Who gets what, when and how?' In answering this, Humphreys identifies and develops some clear and compelling coordinates for an understanding of political culture across our three spheres. The chapters which follow build in different ways on Humphreys' thinking in their exploration of political culture as the interplay between context, norm and practice. Thus after Humphreys' chapter and a general survey of those primary sources most germane to political culture in the three spheres, we have three sections, each of three chapters, one for each sphere. The first section, entitled 'Historical Contexts', sets the geopolitical scene. Without essaying blow-by-blow accounts, the chapters in this section set out the developments and happenings that gave each sphere its characteristics, as well as its potential for fissures. The next section, 'Norms, Values and Their Propagation', covers the justifications for those wielding power or aiming for predominance, along with the rites, theories and formulae denoting legitimate authority before which all should defer. The third section, 'Practice and Organisation', attends not only to matters of administration but also the practical rules and tangible resources shaping the conduct of political life. As in any study of political culture, the interplay between the holding of office purportedly for general benefit

---

[16] J. Hudson and A. Rodríguez (eds), *Diverging Paths? The Shapes of Power and Institutions in Medieval Christendom and Islam* (Leiden, 2014).
[17] W. Pohl *et al.* (eds), *Visions of Community in the Post-Roman World: The West, Byzantium and the Islamic World, 300–1100* (Abingdon, 2012).

and the pursuit of personal, familial or factional gain looms large. As noted earlier, this book is not in itself a work of comparative history. However, in the spirit of providing guidance, throughout the volume we provide some cross-references between chapters so that readers can follow up on potential inter-sphere comparative leads, and in the final chapter of the book we offer a glance at some striking parallels and differences in political culture between the three spheres.

We have chosen to focus above all on self-styled worldwide empires – or on polities emerging within or near the vestiges of such an empire or in its aftermath. This approach foregrounds monarchy and elites of various types, as well as the sweeping powers they were able to gain and subsequently sought to retain. Empires and other polities with grandiose pretensions could not have gained momentum without nurturing some sense of manifest destiny, visions of truth and duty revealed from higher powers. For this reason, our chapters pay considerable attention to professions of piety and justifications for the use of power; and to hegemonial ideologies bolstered by religious doctrine. But this public face of admirable ideals is barely half the story. This volume therefore also aims to set out, as Humphreys puts it, the 'rules of the game', whether the goal was the topmost, monarchical, seat; lesser posts in the hierarchy; or simply the acquisition or retention of position and possessions amongst regional elites and local powerbrokers. These rules comprised the ways in which rulers were expected to conduct themselves; the expectations placed upon them by fellow members of political elites but also by the population at large; along with the fouls that might cost a ruler his or her throne or other players their position in the power game. Practical matters of organisation and administration are presented in their essentials, and attention is given to the smaller-scale or looser-knit polities. But the modus operandi of those playing for high stakes in great empires or amidst their remnants takes centre stage.

As will become clear, the types of elite varied between polities. In some, power was widely diffused, the principles of pluralism, consultation and representation being proclaimed positive virtues, with everbroader cross sections of society drawn into political life. Nonetheless, the power-play at imperial or royal courts remains a crucial coordinate, along with the activities of various other kinds of political heavyweights: the churchmen, provincial aristocrats, military commanders and other leaders of hierarchies which underpinned the political leadership but were not always synonymous with it. Some may question an emphasis on overarching authority and on the nodal points and elites it fostered. Marginal groupings and subaltern societies should, however, themselves come into sharper focus through a survey of the power dynamics of self-styled centres and over-rulers. Studying political culture involves assessing how its tentacles reach out, as well the conditions under which they are embraced, refined, refocused, resisted or simply deemed irrelevant.

In some periods, the empires and realms at the heart of this book were almost coterminous with the geographical extent and political elite of a particular sphere. In others, the spheres may be characterised in part or whole by smaller units, including kingdoms (in the Latin west), alternative caliphates and emirates (in the Islamic world), and (especially in formerly Byzantine lands) pocket empires which arose from the detritus of grander structures, many of them aspiring to the former empire's majesty or using aspects of that empire's political culture for the purposes of their self-legitimisation. All three spheres are richly documented, partly because of a feature they shared: the prominence – more or less all-encompassing – of monotheistic religion and the value it placed on the written word. It is striking that Islamic writers from the seventh century onwards singled out the Christians and the Jews from other unbelievers and polytheists. These were 'the Peoples of the Book', who set store by divine truths put down in their scriptures, albeit now failing to see that the Qur'an contained the ultimate truth about the one true God, as revealed to the Prophet Muhammad. It was the belief that they were carrying out God's instructions that drove armies across swathes of territory in the early centuries of Islam. And their faith in a single God, shared with the proponents of Christianity and Judaism, put a premium on monarchical power.

Not, of course, that upholding monotheism meant a guarantee of vast or long-lasting empire. Thus, the adherence of the Jews to monotheism and their regard for kingship did not translate into territorial empire, with the ninth-century adoption of Judaism by the semi-nomadic polity of the Khazars constituting only a partial exception.[18] Conversely, one should not suppose that monotheism was a precondition of extensive imperial power or of the privileging of written culture. The empires of East Asia serve to illustrate this caveat. Although the emperors of China styled themselves the 'heaven-born', signalling their special bond with the cosmos and supernal powers, the imperial order was not geared to a divine plan for mankind in the manner of its Islamic and Christian counterparts. The philosophy of Confucianism envisioned a hierarchy culminating with the emperor, but not one committed to monotheism. Rather, the emperor

---

[18] A much earlier instance of conversion to Judaism and the growth of a polity defined by that faith is provided by the Himyarite kingdom in the southwest of the Arabian peninsula during the fifth and early sixth centuries.

presided over sundry cults and ethical codes, holding the benevolent command over earthlings that his 'Mandate of Heaven' entailed.[19]

So, although the Chinese empire is very well-documented, and although its ideology was adopted as a model by other East Asian polities, including Japan, it lacked the stance of monotheism taken up by the rulers of the three spheres considered here together with the religious interpreters and exegetes who were integral to those monotheisms. Not that rulers were always committed to evangelising or even to enforcing monotheism. Conversely, claims to be expanding the faith were sometimes a mask for aggression. Still less did a general commitment to monotheism bring about political harmony within a sphere. As the following chapters will show, bitter conflict arose within single spheres over whose was the correct interpretation of the sacred writings or which was the best way to define or worship the one true God. Even so, the focus on monotheism did yield coordinates, points of tension and a kind of envelope for containing conflicts. The religions of Christianity and Islam alike were all-encompassing in their provision of doctrine, cosmology and ethical code along with the apparatus for worship. At the same time, their insistence on monotheism put a premium on monarchy – that is, on he (sometimes she) who convincingly laid claim to be interpreter of God's testament (as revealed through the scriptures and the Qu'ran) and enactor of God's will on earth. This, of course, opened the door to disputations and critiques of rulers' performance. No monarch could, in practice, pay regard to interpretation and enforcement singlehandedly. In all three spheres, a separate, clerical, organisation arose to interpret scriptures and doctrine and to oversee the faithful. Indeed, in the Latin west the clergy came under the care of the papacy, which was, from the eleventh century on, taking a robust alternative line to that offered by the western emperors.[20] The pope's blueprint for clerical authoritarianism made him God's representative on earth, replete with imperial symbols. While Latin Christendom became characterised by the more or less standing confrontation between their two visions, they see-sawed on the relative weight of emperor and pope rather than on their right to exist. In other words, these antagonisms played out within a conceptual framework that held even after the development of urban federations and other

[19] C. K. Yang, *Religion in Chinese Society: A Study of Contemporary Social Functions of Religion and Some of Their Historical Factors* (Berkeley, 1961), 104–23, 127–43; C. A. Hucker, *China's Imperial Past: An Introduction to China's History and Culture* (Berkeley, 1975), 54–7, 69–82, 87–92, 193–202; R. L. Nadeau (ed.), *The Wiley-Blackwell Guide to Chinese Religions* (Oxford, 2012), esp. K. Knapp, 'The Confucian tradition in China', 147–69 and J. Miller, 'Nature', 349–68; A. Strathern, *Unearthly Powers: Religious and Political Change in World History* (Cambridge, 2019), 20–6, 129–34.
[20] See pp. 53, 146, 387.

alternative forms of polity, as well as the changes unleashed by printing and by Martin Luther.[21]

Besides their commitment to monotheism along with monarchical ideals, the Latin west, Byzantium and the Islamic world shared what amounted to a common past. They had all come under the sway of the superpowers of late-antique western Eurasia: Iran and Rome. Indeed, a fundamental tenet of Byzantine ideology was that the Roman empire was still in place; its ruler continued to style himself 'Roman emperor' until the fall of the capital, Constantinople, to the Ottomans in 1453, a title which was then adopted by the new ruler Mehmed II, together with many of the conceptual underpinnings. Having been under Roman rule in its heyday, Byzantium and many of the Christian powers of the Latin west benefited from its apparatus for control: the road networks, urban centres (chosen partly to foster trade) and imposing monuments, most spectacular of which was the city of Rome itself. Texts and variants of Roman law remained in use in Byzantine law-courts and across the Christian Mediterranean. And even to the north of the Alps, the literate classes – mainly churchmen, before the thirteenth and fourteenth centuries – drew on a common stockpile deriving from Greco-Roman culture, including the natural sciences and mathematics. Such skills were often in high demand at the courts of Islamic rulers, where works of literature, philosophy, science and treatises on kingship from ancient Iran as well as Greece were translated. Muslim and Jewish intellectuals, along with scholars from the Christian populations living under Islamic rule, mobilised this storehouse of ancient knowledge in the development of new bodies of knowledge, which were in turn transmitted to the Latin west and back to Byzantium.[22]

The combination of monotheism and monarchy provided coordinates for each sphere, laying down markers for their internal conflicts. But it also laid down a sort of mutually competitive agenda. This stance of antagonism itself prompted many types of writings in all three spheres, not least those which formatted the past in the cause of religious and political authority.[23] But this cultural repertoire encompassed a broader

---

[21] See pp. 144–6, 171–6, 268–73, 288–9.

[22] See p. 341. On Islamic co-opting of aspects of Iranian symbols and ideals of rulership: p. 19; on the transmission of late antique knowledge in Greek to the Islamic world: D. Gutas, *Greek Thought, Arabic Culture: The Graeco-Arabic Translation Movement in Baghdad and Early 'Abbasid Society (2nd–4th/8th–10th Centuries)* (London, 1998); and then back again to Byzantium: M. V. Mavroudi, *A Byzantine Book on Dream Interpretation: The Oneirocriticon of Achmet and its Arabic Sources* (Leiden, 2002).

[23] For the way in which opposing communities could couch their claims within shared coordinates: T. Sizgorich, 'Religious history', in S. Foot and C. F. Robinson (eds), *The Oxford History of Historical Writing, II: 400–1400* (Oxford, 2012), 604–27 at 624. See also Höfert, *Kaisertum und Kalifat*.

band of issues involving hierarchy, ethics and social behaviour. Not coincidentally, the formatting of the past, whether to forge a collective identity or to promote or indict a particular regime or school of thought, was integral to political culture within all three of our spheres. This emerges from our chapters in this volume;[24] and the fruitfulness of such an approach can also be seen from another multi-authored work focused on the Latin west but offering glances at the broader 'monotheistic world, stretching from the Atlantic to the Arabian Sea'.[25]

Such overlap raises the question of how far the spheres were separate, self-contained, entities and, indeed, of what is really meant by 'sphere'. Addressing the former question, one should note that Islam was conceived in opposition to the imperial order of Byzantium and Iran, with every expectation of replacing it. Moreover the Byzantines' sense of their own identity was sharpened by closer encounters with traders and warriors of the Latin world from the eleventh century on. This is not to claim that lines of demarcation between the spheres were clear-cut. Broad swathes of the Latin as well as the Islamic world, for instance, continued to be receptive to cultural tropes and religious cults emanating from Byzantium, while in the process of reception transforming purposes and meanings.[26] Many polities in Mediterranean regions, including Iberia, Sicily, and even the Latin kingdom and principalities which grew up in Syria and Palestine after the First Crusade (1099), often fused aspects of the political culture from at least two of the spheres under consideration here, even when their rulers professed allegiance to only one.[27] Indeed, one way of thinking about spheres of political culture is as force fields: zones of activity exerting powerful magnetism and diverting particles from their former trajectories.[28]

---

[24] See pp. 77, 80–2, 105–7, 124–5, 148–9, 240, 265–6, 268–9, 292–3, 302–4, 334, 351. See also P. Geary, *Phantoms of Remembrance; Memory and Oblivion at the End of the First Millennium* (Princeton, 1996), esp. 134–57; M. Kempshall, *Rhetoric and the Writing of History, 400–1500* (Manchester, 2011); Lambert and Weiler (eds), *How the Past was Used.*

[25] M. Borgolte, 'A crisis of the middle ages? Deconstructing and constructing European identities in a globalised world', in G. A. Loud and M. Staub (eds), *The Making of Medieval History* (York, 2017), 70–84 at 78. The proven benefits of a comparative approach, encompassing Byzantium and the Middle East besides the west and utilising other disciplines, are highlighted by J. L. Nelson, 'Why reinventing medieval history is a good idea', in *ibid.*, 17–36 at 26–33.

[26] See pp. 191–3.

[27] On Sicily: J. Johns, *The Arabic Administration of Norman Sicily* (Cambridge, 2002); on the early thirteenth-century Latin Empire of Constantinople, S. Burkhardt, *Mediterranes Kaisertum und imperiale Ordnungen: das lateinische Kaiserreich von Konstantinopel* (Berlin, 2014); on the Latin states in the east: C. H. MacEvitt, *The Crusades and the Christian World of the East: Rough Tolerance* (Philadelphia, 2008).

[28] J. Shepard, 'Byzantium's overlapping circles', in E. Jeffreys (ed.), *Proceedings of the 21st International Congress of Byzantine Studies, London, 21–26 August 2006, I: Plenary Papers* (Aldershot, 2006), 15–55; *idem*, ' Superpower to soft power, within overlapping circles:

Yet for all its attractions, the image of a force field does not quite capture the connotations of a sphere as an entity possessing some sort of magnetic centre – potentially more than one – whilst allowing for multi-directional traffic and free-willed adherence on the part of outsiders. The workings of such a sphere underwrote Byzantium's claims to worldwide leadership. Known simply as 'the City', Constantinople stood at the hub of imperial power, high society and culture, ecclesiastical administration, and commerce until its sack by the Fourth Crusaders in 1204. This amounted to a conjunction of interest groups rather than explicitly harmonious agreement about the merits of empire. Indeed, many monks (and some churchmen, too) were more preoccupied with the heavenly kingdom and their 'spiritual father' along with centres like Mount Athos ('the Holy Mountain').[29] But the powers of attraction were all the greater for often being consensual. Constantinople drew in multifarious outsiders, becoming a place of pilgrimage for such believers as Anthony of Novgorod and his fellow Rus whose ancestors had adopted Byzantium's brand of Christianity.[30] The term 'sphere' also befits the dynamics of Islam, whose ideology was (like Byzantium's) universalist, deeming the caliph 'God's shadow on earth' and the Abbasid court at Baghdad the measure of all things. Many other places were sacred, but care of the holiest pilgrimage centres, Mecca and Medina, was the duty of the supreme ruler.[31] Emperors and other potentates in the Latin west lacked a physical locus of authority of the stature enjoyed by the Byzantine *basileus* and the caliph. But in the west lay a city whose very name had long been synonymous with worldwide rule, and the papal elite ensconced in Rome was, from the eighth century onwards, invoking its right to bestow earthly authority on deserving candidates in the west.[32]

Byzantium and its place in twenty-first-century international history', in B. Haider-Wilson *et al.* (eds), *Internationale Geschichte in Theorie und Praxis / International History in Theory and Practice* (Vienna, 2017), 81–122.

[29] See pp. 315–16, 426. The term 'imperial-ecclesiastical complex' seems apt enough to denote the multi-part, negotiable and so not wholly stable, interrelationship between the imperial power, the hierarchies and informal affinities making up the patriarchate, and the webs of monastic communities. See p. 78; see also pp. 311–15.

[30] Anthony of Novgorod, *Die Kniga palomnik des Antonij von Novgorod*, ed. and German tr. A. Jouravel (Wiesbaden, 2019); also G. P. Majeska, *Russian Travelers to Constantinople in the Fourteenth and Fifteenth Centuries* (Washington, DC, 1984).

[31] See pp. 77–80, 105, 166, 340, 353–4.

[32] Its foundation text was, effectively, the 'Donation of Constantine'. Written in the later eighth century in the name of Constantine the Great (d. 337), it purports to grant the pope authority over the empire in the west: *Das Constitutum Constantini (Konstantinische Schenkung): Text*, ed. H. Fuhrmann (Hanover, 1968); tr. in P. E. Dutton (ed.), *Carolingian Civilization: A Reader*, 2nd edn (Peterborough, ON, 2004), 14–22; J. Herrin, *The Formation of Christendom*, rev. edn (London, 2001), 385–9.

The emergence of the Franks as contenders for predominance across the Latin west makes the period spanning the turn of the seventh and eighth centuries an apt starting point for the discussion of our three spheres. It was, after all, the victory of Charles Martel at Poitiers in 732 that served to discourage further Muslim raiding deep into Francia.[33] And his grandson Charlemagne's claim, on the strength of God-given conquests, to be restoring imperial order in the west was solemnised by coronation at the hands of Pope Leo III in St Peter's Church, Rome, in 800. The interrelationship then forged between empire and the papacy along with the city of Rome would set the style for later bids for imperial hegemony in the west, while the zeal for instruction and control which Charlemagne embodied gave rise to precedents and texts still resonant five or six centuries later.[34] The early eighth century was also a time of triumph for Islamic armies, and it was under the Umayyad caliphs that rites and monuments of monarchical rule began to be elaborated, overtaking the more collegiate line taken by Muhammad's immediate successors.[35] In 716–18 Caliph Suleiman sent his brother to capture Constantinople, and, although the encirclement by land and sea ultimately failed, the Byzantines were now on the defensive, with too few territories for their claims to worldwide overlordship to ring true.[36] This era saw the development of an exclusive ideology, casting the Byzantines as a Chosen People, undergoing God's punishment for their sins.[37] The eighth century was, then, a time of two new empires rising and an ancient one reeling.[38]

Despite its fragility in the eighth century, Byzantium persisted in upholding 'Roman' imperium in the eastern Mediterranean for another seven centuries, until its last outcrop, Trebizond, fell to the Ottomans in 1461, eight years after Mehmed II conquered the long-term imperial capital Constantinople. These events take us to our end point. It could be argued that Byzantium's disappearance as a polity in the fifteenth century – more accurately a set of polities, given that Trebizond was governed by a different dynasty from Constantinople – did not spell the

---

[33] Although Muslim enclaves continued in some northern Mediterranean locations, most famously at Fraxinetum, for two centuries or more: S. G. Bruce, *Cluny and the Muslims of La Garde-Freinet: Hagiography and the Problem of Islam in Medieval Europe* (Ithaca, NY, 2016).
[34] See pp. 141, 274–5.   [35] See pp. 103, 235.   [36] See p. 183.   [37] See p. 301.
[38] The multi-authored volume edited by D. G. Tor has also highlighted the importance of this period, drawing attention to the templates for rulership and social order created by the Carolingians and the Abbasids, as well as the ways in which they moulded or inspired not only political cultures but also the broader social forms and ideological claims that would follow: D. G. Tor, 'The ʿAbbasid and Carolingian dynasties in comparative perspective', in *eadem* (ed.), *ʿAbbasid and Carolingian Empires*, 3–10 at 6–7.

end of a Byzantine sphere. Some Eastern Christian polities would thrive throughout the early modern centuries.[39] Nonetheless, the erasure of Byzantine power in the east had such profound consequences – not only for the Byzantine sphere itself but for the other two spheres too – as to make the fifteenth century a crucial watershed in the shared history of these three spheres. Although the empire's demise was hardly unexpected, the repercussions were far-reaching. The imperial order which the Ottomans set about imposing was strongly shaped by the political traditions and formation of earlier Islamic regimes whose origins lay in the Eurasian steppes.[40] But they used their vantage point in Constantinople (Istanbul) to reorganise fiscal and judicial administration across much of the Islamic world.[41] This fuelled a formidable war machine which had taken over swathes of Hungarian territory by 1550 and kept western Europe in its sights for another century or so. One might speak of a geopolitical shift to the Islamic world's advantage, especially as over many centuries it had been gaining converts around the Indian Ocean world, in South and South-East Asia and in Sub-Saharan Africa.[42] The fragmentation of the west, in contrast, was such that the Ottomans found a useful – and willing – ally in one of its foremost powers, France.[43] At the same time, English and other privateers were preying on the merchantmen laden with silver from the New World that bolstered the Hapsburgs' resistance to Ottoman expansion in the Mediterranean, short-term opportunism which found justification in the religious upheavals unleashed by Luther's teachings. So, by the sixteenth century, the outlook for the Latin west was mixed.[44] Its polities, mostly fairly puny compared to the Byzantine or Abbasid empires in their heyday, could not count on withstanding the Ottoman advance.

Between c.700 and c.1500 there was considerable evolution in the political culture of each of the three spheres analysed here. Yet these spheres not only evolved internally: they also existed in a dynamic relationship with each other. As medievalists engage more closely with the global history agendas of comparison and connection-tracing over

---

[39] See p. 490.
[40] D. Kastritsis, 'Conquest and political legitimation in the early Ottoman empire', in J. Harris and C. Holmes (eds), *Byzantines, Latins and Turks in the Eastern Mediterranean World after 1150* (Oxford, 2012), 221–45; *idem*, 'Tales of viziers and wine: interpreting early Ottoman narratives of state centralization', in J. Van Steenbergen (ed.), *Trajectories of State Formation across Fifteenth-Century Islamic West-Asia: Eurasian Parallels, Connections and Divergences* (Leiden, 2020), 224–54.
[41] See pp. 123–4, 231–2, 451–3.   [42] See p. 490.
[43] N. Malcolm, *Useful Enemies: Islam and the Ottoman Empire in Western Political Thought, 1450–1750* (Oxford, 2019), 110–19.
[44] See pp. 176–7.

a variety of geographical scales – local, regional and planetary – we would expect that many of the features of the political cultures highlighted here will be nuanced, refined and even refuted. This will undoubtedly involve integrating research on other, non-monarchical aspects of the political culture of the three spheres; on the geographical zones or areas of cultural production where contact and interaction between spheres was at its most intense; and on zones beyond the Latin west, Byzantium and the Islamic world. We could easily imagine a companion volume whose organising principle is the interaction across spheres rather than their presentation in parallel. Any such volume would necessarily focus more squarely on connection and entanglement (*l'histoire croisée*), especially on the agents and processes of communication, miscommunication, transmission and brokerage. In the process, the cast list of communities and individuals who created and sustained the three spheres' political cultures, and of those in other world regions, would undoubtedly expand. Integrating more inter-sphere connection and interaction into the picture of political culture we present, particularly if that integration were conducted comparatively and not from the perspective of a single region of western Eurasia, could further disrupt the model of heartland and frontier that has been such a dominant paradigm in much medieval scholarship over the past three decades.[45] Paradoxically, it might reinforce the idea that, for all its somewhat nebulous qualities, the term 'sphere' captures with some accuracy both the tangible and intangible elements of medieval political culture. We offer this introductory survey to the history of political culture in three spheres in that dual sense of providing some useful tools for learning, teaching and research in the present but also as an incitement to future study.

[45] R. Bartlett, *The Making of Europe: Conquest, Colonization and Cultural Change, 950–1350* (London, 1993); J. Hudson, 'The making of Europe: a brief summary', in J. Hudson and S. Crumplin (eds), *'The Making of Europe': Essays in Honour of Robert Bartlett* (Leiden, 2016), 5–10 at 6.

2 Reflections on Political Culture in Three Spheres

R. Stephen Humphreys

What should we mean by the term 'political culture'? Is it a powerful concept with (potentially) broad explanatory power, or is it rather a nearly vacuous phrase, which by promising to explain everything winds up explaining nothing? If we want it to be a useful and productive way of thinking about political life, we must ask what concrete problems it helps us identify and spell out what guidance it can provide in framing an analysis of these problems. Politics, as Harold Lasswell said over eighty years ago, is simply who gets what, when and how.[1] Lasswell was a close observer of Chicago politics – a place where the game is taken seriously – and in many ways it is hard to better his definition. We might, however, put it in more formal terms, something like the following: politics is that body of institutions and practices by which a society controls its resources and distributes the power to allocate those resources among its members. If we adopt this definition as a starting point, we need to specify two points. Firstly, resources are both material and symbolic. (In some circumstances it is symbolic resources that are the most important element in play.) Secondly, politics is inherently a struggle for power, but always power with a purpose. Purposes can get lost sight of in the heat of the struggle – at some point antagonists are just fighting to win, never mind why – but they are always lurking in the background.

Culture, the second part of our phrase, is a slippery word, so fluid and all-encompassing that it threatens to become meaningless. We can perhaps avoid that danger, at least in part, by following Clifford Geertz's lead. He argues that culture ought to be understood as all the ways in which a group assigns meaning to its practices and institutions.[2] Or, to put the matter conversely, actions and practices should be viewed from

[1] The title of possibly his most famous book: *Politics: Who Gets What, When, How* (New York, 1936). Lasswell was a complex and many-sided intellect, but he often favoured terse, even gnomic aphorisms as a way of framing his ideas.

[2] C. Geertz, 'Thick description: toward an interpretive theory of culture', in his *The Interpretation of Cultures* (New York, 1973), 3–30.

the perspective of the ideas and values ascribed to and embodied in them. Geertz's approach has undeniably been extremely productive over the last half-century, but for the purposes of this chapter it may be a bit too narrow. I would propose that culture is simply 'what we do'. That is, culture is the body of rules and agreed-upon practices that shape our behaviour, which is to say all the ways in which we deal with one another. The rules which constitute a particular culture might be formally articulated, as in a code of law or moral doctrine, or they might be unspoken and almost unrecognised in any conscious way. Likewise, cultural practices can be embodied in formal institutions and meticulously delineated rituals, or they can be everyday customs that are simply taken for granted as right and proper.

And so at last we come to a definition of political culture: namely, the body of concepts, institutions, rituals and ingrained patterns of behaviour that define the forms of power through which a society controls and allocates its resources and that also identify those members of society who will possess such power and on what terms. In this definition, society stands out as a crucial but so far undefined term; let us then stipulate, as a rough working hypothesis, that a society may be any relatively cohesive and self-conscious grouping of people, ranging from a nuclear family to a street gang to the subjects of a transcontinental empire.

If one prefers the more casual language of Lasswell, political culture is just how we go about deciding who gets what, when and how. Political culture includes everything in this arena, from unspoken assumptions about the 'right' way to behave or what is simple common sense to the most elaborately staged ceremonial and the most convoluted discursive formations.

One last point: political culture is the expression of a detached observer – that is, of someone who maintains some sense of distance even from events in which he or she is intimately involved. The very phrase 'political culture' is a proposition that a certain congeries of words and actions does in fact constitute a definable, structured system of thought and behaviour. But it is the detached observer who decides which words and actions should be included, and which excluded, in this putative system. Thus when the term political culture is applied to some socio-political complex, it is by its very nature a subjective assertion. As such, it is an assertion which a second outside observer might well contest or dismiss altogether.

Now, how can we apply these abstractions to the long period between c.700 and c.1500, over vast stretches of the western Eurasian landmass, with its tumultuous cast of characters who constantly trample one another, overturning the sets as they tumble on and off the stage? If we follow Shakespeare's excellent example and frame politics as a play, we have not one but a multiplicity of dramas, all going on at once, a mad mixture of comedy, tragedy, and (all too rarely) romance.

With so many actors, so many plots, there is no way to tell a single, well-focused story. It is more profitable to search for a few key themes that recur over and over. The problem is how to choose among an infinitude of possibilities. I would propose that we *not* begin with the abstract categories of grand theory: hierarchies of class and status, primordial loyalties, or the bases of political legitimacy. Such categories are indubitably essential to any theory of political culture, but they are abstractions, and we can pursue them endlessly, with ever more subtle distinctions, without ever engaging the concrete realities of any actual society. For historians, at least, that goes against the grain.

I suggest, then, that we begin with tangible and visible elements, ones shared by all the societies discussed in this volume, and deploy abstract analytic categories only as they seem useful in exploring these elements. Among all the elements we might choose, four seem to me to be the heart of the matter: religion, women, property and war. What is history, after all, if not a tale of lust, greed and ambition, all of it thought to be pleasing (or displeasing) to God?

Religion is the odd one out in this group – so all-embracing and all-pervasive that it verges on being a vacuous category. However, we cannot meaningfully discuss political cultures in the world of the eighth to fifteenth centuries without it. As Ardashir, the founder of the Sasanian dynasty, is supposed to have said, religion and kingship are twin brothers: neither can stand without the other. This aphorism was constantly repeated in neo-Sasanian political writing, a genre which begins to emerge as early as the later eighth century and is clearly articulated by the mid-ninth. A classic statement is found in Nizam al-Mulk's *Siyasat-nameh*, composed *c.*1090 for the Seljuk sultan Malikshah by his chief minister.[3] Religious doctrines, practice and institutions are not only embedded in every aspect of political life but even define what the political is. Politics deals with the power to allocate goods: both material ones, such as gold, and symbolic ones, for example sanctity or social rank. When religion enters the political realm, it shapes it in several ways.

First, religion defined what goods truly possess value, and in so doing it proclaimed a divinely ordained hierarchy of values. Such

[3] Nizam al-Mulk, *Siyasat-nameh*, tr. H. Darke, in *The Book of Government, or Rules for Kings*, ch. 8 (London, 1960; rev. edn 1978 on the basis of a new manuscript), 60 (rev. edn). The adoption of aspects of Sasanian political culture by post-Abbasid Islamic polities, 'ranging from the widespread revival of Sasanian titulature, symbols of rulership, and even genealogies, to the adoption of Sasanian rulership as an Islamic political model in Muslim literature and political theory', remains a matter for debate: D. G. Tor, 'The long shadow of pre-Islamic Iranian rulership: antagonism or assimilation', in T. Bernheimer and A. Silverstein (eds), *Late Antiquity: Eastern Perspectives* (Warminster, 2012), 145–63 at 146; see also pp. 110–11, 226, 469–70.

proclamations of value are admittedly not always easy to understand or apply to the messy, complicated realities of life, but they permeate the scriptures of all three cultural zones: the Latin west, Byzantium and the Islamic world.

Second, religion laid out how and to whom a society's goods should be allocated. In this way, it could either legitimise or sharply challenge society's actual distribution of wealth and power. Of course religious texts do not speak for themselves; they acquire meaning only as they are proclaimed, interpreted and enforced by influential spokesmen, and there are inevitably as many meanings as there are spokesmen.

Thirdly, religion defined, or at least strongly implied, how power should be used, who had the right to wield it and what its proper limits were. Here again religious doctrine is protean to say the least – not only ambivalent in itself but vulnerable to shameless manipulation. In the societies under study in this collection, all three core religious traditions proclaimed the ideal of the government of God but were compelled to recognise that, in the absence of Moses, Christ or Muhammad, no such thing was possible. What then was the alternative?

It goes without saying that all three lines of discourse were zones of contestation, often of the most vitriolic sort. Nor was religion the only voice; it was very often not even the decisive or most influential voice. There were always competing and sometimes contradictory value systems in play. Islamic austerity (*zuhd*) had to compete with princely luxury, piety (*taqwa*, *birr*) with the harsh code of manliness (*muruwwa*) of the Bedouin tribesman. But in the final analysis, no statement about the values which underlay the exercise of power and distribution of resources, or about the rules which governed the application of these values, could be made without reference to religion.

The relationship between religion and political culture would be complex enough if each sphere – the Latin west, Byzantium and the Islamic world – had had but a single hegemonic religion possessing a well-defined centre of authority. Plainly that was not the case. Even in the Latin west, the capacity of the pope to speak for the church fluctuated wildly. All three spheres saw major dissident movements – the Cathars, Paulicians and Kharijites, among others – and beyond these we find a host of subtler, more localised differences. In assessing the role of religion in political culture, it is essential to look for the lines of tension, the zones of friction, within larger religious systems. We also need to ask where, when, under what circumstances and in what ways religion became a point of contention in shaping a political culture. Some of these are obvious and much studied, like the long-running and hugely disruptive contest between popes and western rulers in the late eleventh and early twelfth centuries, known as the Investiture Contest,[4] or the imposition of the Inquisition in the south of France in the thirteenth. Others are far subtler and perhaps more revealing, for example the tug of war in early eleventh-century Baghdad between Sunni traditionalists aligned with the Abbasid caliphs and Twelver Shiʻis aligned with the Buyid emirs.

Religion is perhaps so fundamental and pervasive in the medieval world, such an inextricable part of the self-definition of any society of that era, that we should regard it as a substrate of political culture, an essential element in the grammar of political action. How then should we think about the other three elements identified – women, property and war? These are very different in character from religion, for they are what politics is about, the things for which or by which politics is conducted. They are of course major aspects of political action, as concrete objectives or instruments of power, but they are not merely that. All three possess enormous symbolic power, and any political culture is constituted in large part by the ways in which they are conceptualised and articulated.

I begin with women, because their status and roles within a political system provide a remarkably sensitive gauge for determining how that system worked and how its members understood it. Most contemporary sociologists would say that female literacy and education are the best single indicator we have for a society's developmental level. Obviously medieval societies do not yield the sort of data needed for such analysis, and in any case the medieval and modern worlds are very different places. Even so, social indicators in contemporary society do encourage us to scrutinise the sources we do have for all possible information on how women were integrated into a given political culture at every level, from household to empire. I think it fair to say that we now possess a very substantial body of work in this arena for the Latin west,[5] some significant progress for Byzantium[6] and disappointingly little on the societies of the

---

[4] See p. 146.

[5] For a very small sample: A. J. Duggan (ed.), *Queens and Queenship in Medieval Europe* (Woodbridge, 2002); J. L. Nelson, *Courts, Elites, and Gendered Power in the Early Middle Ages: Charlemagne and Others* (Aldershot, 2007); T. Earenfight, *Queenship in Medieval Europe* (Basingstoke, 2013); E. Woodacre (ed.), *Queenship in the Mediterranean* (Basingstoke, 2013); M. Gaude-Ferragu, *Queenship in Medieval France, 1300–1500*, tr. A. Krieger (New York, 2016); S. MacLean, *Ottonian Queenship* (Oxford, 2017); for a useful overview with bibliography: T. Earenfight, 'Medieval queenship', *History Compass* 15 (2017).

[6] See e.g. L. Garland, *Byzantine Empresses: Women and Power in Byzantium, AD 527–1204* (London, 1999); L. Garland (ed.), *Byzantine Women: Varieties of Experience, 800–1200* (Aldershot, 2006); I. Kalavrezou (ed.), *Byzantine Women and their World* (Cambridge, MA, 2003); C. L. Connor, *Women of Byzantium* (New Haven, CT, 2004); A.-M. Talbot, *Women and Religious Life in Byzantium* (Aldershot, 2001); J. Herrin, *Women in Purple: Rulers of Medieval Byzantium* (London, 2001); J. Herrin, *Unrivalled Influence: Women and Empire in Byzantium* (Princeton, 2013).

Islamic Middle East despite the presence of many formidable female scholars in this field. When I published my *Islamic History: A Framework for Inquiry* a generation ago,[7] I believed we were on the verge of a flood of gender and feminist studies, but it has not happened. So far as I can tell, only a few historically grounded full-length studies have really moved the debate along. In addition, the place of women in Islamic jurisprudence (*fiqh*) has at last begun to attract serious study.[8] To these few works we can add a number of good articles, but overall it is a thin harvest.

Dealing with the ways women are situated within political culture is problematic not only because our sources are spotty but also because ideology – statements about how things ought to be – masks the realities of how things actually are. Ideology is controlled by the literate, and in the societies we are studying, the literate were overwhelmingly though never exclusively male. More than that, they were males who represented the irredeemably patriarchal realms of church, synagogue and mosque. In their representations, women are not supposed to be autonomous political actors; it follows that any political action they do take is by definition questionable, if not simply illegitimate. In all three spheres, both official and popular ideology was aggressively misogynistic, though of course in reality women sometimes wielded great power in the public arena, a fact which contemporary observers viewed variously with alarm, grudging respect and (occasionally) admiration. Even outside the explicitly political arena, women were still viewed as a problem, for they were a principal source (for Christianity at least *the* original source) of moral disorder. This is so partly because they embodied erotic temptation, but even more because they symbolised thought and action driven by emotion rather than guided by reason.

Ideology is of course but one element in political culture, and seldom the most important one. Ideology is abstract and based on absolute values. As such it is typically not a dispassionate description of society and politics but rather a harsh critique – or, perhaps less commonly, an ardent defence – of the existing order of things. But in the final analysis, political culture is precisely a society's currently *accepted* practice and

[7] *IHFI*, xii.
[8] E.g. D. Spellberg, *Politics, Gender, and the Islamic Past: The Legacy of 'A'isha bint Abi Bakr* (New York, 1994); L. Peirce, *The Imperial Harem: Women and Sovereignty in the Ottoman Empire* (New York, 1993); L. Peirce, *Morality Tales: Law and Gender in the Ottoman Court of Aintab* (Berkeley, 2003); Y. Rapoport, *Marriage, Money and Divorce in Medieval Islamic Society* (Cambridge, 2005); D. Cortese and S. Calderini, *Women and the Fatimids in the World of Islam* (Edinburgh, 2010); also G. R. G. Hambly (ed.), *Women in the Medieval Islamic World* (New York, 1998); for jurisprudence: J. E. Tucker, *Women, Family, and Gender in Islamic Family Law* (Cambridge, 2008); S. A. Spectorsky, *Women in Classical Islamic Law: A Survey of the Sources* (Leiden, 2012).

institutions – not everything that is actually done, of course, since there are always scoundrels and malefactors among us, but what is considered ordinary, right and proper.

Where do women fit within this pragmatic understanding of political culture? We should start by recognising that the answer varies enormously. We must always focus on the particularities of time and place: Frederick II's Sicily is not the England of Henry I, and Ayyubid Aleppo in the 1230s is not Umayyad Damascus in the early 700s.

Family relationships are a critical variable in any political equations – mother and son, husband and wife, sometimes brother and sister. Examples are legion, but the point is that intimate personal relationships forged within a household shape and sometimes trump normative political structures and values. Obviously there is no Macbeth without Lady Macbeth, but we could say the same about Louis IX without Blanche of Castile, Justinian without Theodora, Kanuni Süleyman without Roxelana (Hürrem Sultan). On a more systemic level, female lineages in the early Islamic community remain almost unstudied, but such lineages were clearly a core element in the politics of that period. One can argue that early Islamic history is a story of the rivalry between closely related families, and alliances and fractures on the female side were a critical aspect of that rivalry. Even in settings where women seem mere pawns, whose chief role was to produce heirs for the reigning dynasty, the way marriages were made reveals much about deep political structures – for example, the long female succession in the Latin kingdom of Jerusalem after the catastrophe of 1187, which both enabled and circumscribed the powers wielded by their consorts from Guy de Lusignan to Frederick II.

As I have already argued, politics is not only a matter of rulership; rather, it addresses the whole spectrum of ways in which a society allocates its resources. For this reason we always need to be on the lookout for actors who do not claim to govern, but who have a large role in the control and distribution of resources. So far as we can see, the Ayyubid princesses of late twelfth- and thirteenth-century Damascus had no direct role in the high politics of that principality, but they did found a surprisingly high percentage of the city's educational and religious institutions and were at the core of charitable giving to the populace at large. These are pre-eminently political acts, and ones that underwrote the Islamic legitimacy of the Ayyubid regime.[9]

---

[9] R. S. Humphreys, 'Women as patrons of religious architecture in Ayyubid Damascus', *Muqarnas* 11 (1994), 35–54. On the other hand, the Ayyubid princess and wife of the emir of Aleppo, Dayfa Khatun, was the widely respected and highly effective regent of Aleppo between 1236 and 1244 on behalf of her grandson: A.-M. Eddé, *La Principauté ayyoubide d'Alep (579/1183–658/1260)* (Stuttgart, 1999), 109–30.

Politics occurs not merely at the state or quasi-state level. Where our sources permit, we need to examine the politics of extended families, urban neighbourhoods and so forth, both as entities in their own right and to see what light they might throw on larger processes. For example, scholarship suggests that fourteenth- and fifteenth-century Mamluk emirs often focused their patronage and property-holdings in particular Cairene neighbourhoods.[10] These emirs were thus both neighbourhood ward bosses and players at the highest level of imperial politics. Women were also property-holders, often very substantial ones, and well-focused family or neighbourhood studies might show whether they were able to convert such holdings into political capital, and if so at what level.

There are other approaches to discuss – such as the theatre of politics, and in what situations women could be openly viewed as performing public functions. Or we might examine women's access to public justice in courts of law, both as a matter of right and a matter of actual practice. The striking differences between Islamic *shari'a*-based courts and common-law courts in England, for example, open up remarkable possibilities for comparative study. In any case, I have said enough to suggest how much can be learned about a given political culture when we focus on a group that was supposed to have at best a subordinate role within that culture.

The second element of political culture to be examined is property. More broadly, the right to hold, exploit, take or distribute property is what politics is all about, at least under Lasswell's definition. Property is the substance of politics. Property and politics constitute a mutual force field, each exerting a powerful influence on the other.

It is the political system that defines property in the first place – what goods (including human beings) count as property, whether it is a collective or private good, whether one has an absolute and untrammelled right to acquire and dispose of it, or whether possession is on the contrary only limited and contingent. It is the political system that guarantees and limits property-rights and protects one property-holder from the greed and violence of others. Conversely, it is the existing body of beliefs, values and rights pertaining to property that defines what a political system is supposed to do and that shapes how institutions are built and operate. Finally, beliefs and values about property give a political system its distinctive flavour.

Though property is a very comprehensive term – it includes almost anything to which some kind of ownership can be asserted – we are here

---

[10] See e.g. J. Van Steenbergen, *Order out of Chaos: Patronage, Conflict and Mamluk Socio-Political Culture, 1341–1382* (Leiden, 2006); also pp. 116–17, 363–4.

dealing with a cluster of medieval societies, and for all of them the kind of property that really counted was land. In using concepts of property to pry open the inner workings of a political culture, therefore, it makes sense to focus on land. So many of the key words that are at the centre of our work refer to rights over land: *emphyteusis, pronoia, beneficium, feudum, allodium, milk, iqta', muqata'a.* Few words reveal more about the core concerns of the political cultures that deployed them. Investing a person with land under one of these headings, or trying to take it away in turn, was an act of great symbolic power, often elaborately staged. However great the practical consequences of such investitures or takings (and these consequences were often immense), they were no mere transfer of goods from X to Y.

So much for lust and greed. We have now to turn to ambition, in the form of war. The three spheres we are discussing were dominated for long periods of time by a military class, and they devoted a very large proportion of their social resources (both material and symbolic) to the care and feeding of this class. That is not to say that the military class had a monopoly of political power in these societies, though it came close to that at certain moments – one thinks of Francia between the Rhine and the Loire in the tenth and early eleventh centuries, or the 'Turkish' (Mamluk) sultanate in Egypt and Syria between 1250 and 1517. In the Latin west the church could challenge and sometimes face down the military class, especially after 1100, and in Byzantium and the Islamic lands before 1100 the civilian bureaucracy was a force to be reckoned with. Even so, the men of the sword fundamentally dictated the shape and content of politics.

In both Byzantium and the Latin west there was plainly some ambivalence about this situation, at least on the part of the church. In the west, there was a concerted effort to vindicate the profession of arms as at least potentially a Christian vocation – the *loci classici* being the crusade sermon of Urban II (insofar as we can reconstruct it) and the treatise 'De laude novae militiae' of Bernard of Clairvaux.[11] The Byzantines were unwilling to go so far, though they recognised the

[11] The exact contents of Urban's speech at Clermont in 1095 are uncertain, although what he is supposed to have said is related by several writers, including Fulcher of Chartres, Robert of Rheims, Guibert of Nogent and Baldric of Bourgueil; for translations: *Crusades: Idea and Reality, 1095–1274,* tr. L. and J. Riley-Smith (London, 1981), 40–53; see also H. E. J. Cowdrey, 'Pope Urban II's preaching of the First Crusade', *History* 55 (1970), 177–88. For the canons issued formally at the Council of Clermont and their connection with Urban's crusade sermon: *The Councils of Urban II, I: Decreta Claromontensia,* ed. R. Somerville (Amsterdam, 1972), 71–82 (text); 101–4 (discussion). For Bernard of Clairvaux's 'Liber ad Milites Templi: de laude novae militiae': *Sancti Bernardi opera, III: Tractatus et opuscula,* ed. J. LeClercq and H. M. Rochais (Rome, 1963), 213–39.

defence of the empire and the Christian people as a necessary evil. In Islam, with its imperative (more often neglected than not) for jihad, ambivalence was less about a military class per se than about the kind of people who made it up and about the relationship between the soldiers and the caliph, the lawful head of the Community of Believers. Muslim jurists were uncomfortable seeing the caliph as the plaything of his troops, and all the more so because many of Islam's defenders were rough frontier tribesmen or slave recruits (*mamluk*s). However, the dominance of the military class was a fact of life. One had to make the best of it, find some way to make them a lawful element of political life and constrain their excesses.

A military class only justified its existence through war. So we need to ask how war itself was imbedded within the political culture. War was after all a critical way through which a polity proclaimed and manifested not only its power (or lack thereof) but also its profoundest sense of identity and purpose. As in most settled societies, war was an activity both honoured and reviled, very much like the men who conducted it. The problem, however, is to identify the mix of reverence and revulsion and to delineate precisely how these attitudes and emotions found expression. All three spheres produced a lot of pictorial art, most commonly in the form of manuscript illustrations. The Islamic lands also produced a host of images on metalwork and ceramics. Much of this pictorial art portrays war either in its heroic guise (the clash of armies or warrior kings laying waste to their opponents) or as a set of technical skills (such as couching a lance and mounted archery). However, so far as I know this military art has never been studied in any systematic way as a form of cultural expression, only as an ancillary source for military history. In literature infinitely more has been done; if the *Chanson de Roland* or the *Shah-nameh* are not about war, what are they? But in this realm too, it is the heroic ideal and its many-layered ironies that have drawn attention, rather than the ways in which war itself is depicted and understood.

A critical issue confronting all three spheres was whether, and under what circumstances, war might be pleasing to God or even mandated by him. Islam proclaimed jihad, the struggle to realise God's rule on earth, as a core mission, and it was developed both as a cultural ideal and an elaborate set of legal doctrines. Our earliest jihad text, compiled *c.*800 by Ibn al-Mubarak (a Khurasani scholar who had taken up residence on the Byzantine frontier in Syria), is more about martyrdom and its rewards than a book about fighting.[12] The Latin west developed an

---

[12] Ibn al-Mubarak (d. 797), *Kitab al-jihad*, ed. N. Hammad (Beirut, 1971). See also C. Melchert, 'Ibn al-Mubarak's *Kitab al-jihad* and early renunciant literature', in

elaborate discourse on holy war, just war and (a curious blend of these and other motifs) the crusade, a war to vindicate Christ and His Church. As for Byzantine discourse, the current consensus sees it as very ambivalent – war was inherently evil, but it was an unavoidable necessity for the defence of the Christian empire of Rome. Victory was celebrated as a sign of divine favour, defeat mourned, but war itself was not glorified.[13] By its very nature, however, consensus invites dissent, and we should expect closer scrutiny to yield a more nuanced if not entirely different picture.

This discussion could be extended indefinitely, but enough has been said to suggest the kinds of insight which the themes of women, property and war might offer for the comparative study of political cultures in the medieval world. In particular, these themes may help us find some fresh things to say about a number of long-established categories in socio-political analysis – such as social hierarchies and pyramids; the cluster of loyalties that bind people together, whether in permanent social groups or momentarily in opportunistic alliances; the endless and never fully resolved quest for political legitimacy (that is, the widely agreed-upon authority to make major collective decisions on behalf of others and to retain that authority when things go awry); and the formation of a political class, a group – sometimes very large, but more often rather small – that can expect to be closely involved in the making of political decisions.[14] The preceding remarks, I hope, will suggest some useful ways to begin a conversation on political culture in the three spheres of the Latin west, Byzantium and the realm of Islam.

I. Kristó-Nagy and R. Gleave (eds), *Violence in Islamic Thought from the Qur'an to the Mongols* (Edinburgh, 2015), 49–69.

[13] See e.g. J. Koder and I. Stouraitis (eds), *Byzantine War Ideology between Roman Imperial Concept and Christian Religion* (Vienna, 2012); Y. Stouraitis (ed.), *A Companion to the Byzantine Culture of War, ca. 300–1204* (Leiden, 2018).

[14] For example, in Saladin's vast empire, stretching from the upper Nile deep into northern Mesopotamia, the political class probably comprised no more than 500 men – and Saladin was a famously consultative ruler.

Part I

Sources

3 Comparing the Three Spheres through the Prism of the Sources

Jonathan Shepard

The notion of devoting a whole section to the sources for political culture is perhaps oxymoronic. After all, reading between the lines of documents is key to understanding the power politics in play within a society. The presuppositions and working methods of its more potent or propertied elites generate the political culture. And unwritten moral understandings, rules of the game and undeclared ways of working the system are at least as important as laws, much-touted codes of behaviour, or authority symbols and visual imagery, telling though these can be. Indeed, what is not put in writing and goes unsaid constitutes the quintessence of political culture. This may be a matter of core beliefs and expectations too routine to be thought worth mentioning. But it can also involve the mores, attitudes and modus operandi that form part of the socio-political fabric yet are largely left unspoken, for fear of political disgrace, charges of deviancy, heresy or worse. So far as the middle ages are concerned, our chances of gaining an inkling of what was taken for granted or lay too near the bone to be voiced in words may look slim.

Our oxymoron may seem to be aggravated by the unevenness of this part's chapter lengths. The chapter devoted to the Latin west is almost twice that of the Byzantine one, and it deals with goings-on at grassroots in closer detail than is attempted for the other two spheres. The imbalance is in part a reflection of the survival pattern of our sources. Far more written materials, many fairly humdrum or household in nature, have survived for the Latin west than they have for Byzantium or the Islamic world, despite the fact that, before the later middle ages, only a relatively small proportion of the west's population possessed functional literacy. Unevenness of survival rates is explained by a variety of factors such as the destruction of Byzantium's state archives and the paucity of extant eastern monastic archives beyond Mount Athos. But the superabundance also registers a characteristic of the Latin west brought out by all the chapters dedicated to this sphere: its variegated polities. They encompassed republics, loose-knit confederations of clans, closely regulated

realms and numberless 'lordships', all lesser structures aiming to collect –
and often to maximise – tolls, rents and dues in return for maintenance of
order. Many of these microstructures' archives survive, as do records of
English manorial court proceedings and petitions to the crown, even
occasional family collections. These documents reveal something of the
interaction between a district's propertied notables, supra-regional elites
and the royal court, besides shedding medieval sidelights on US Speaker
Tip O'Neill's dictum that 'all politics is local'. The contentiousness
intermingled with consensus which such records convey raises a key
question: do they illustrate peculiarly western fragmentation and want
of any overarching authority, or is this all an illusion, generated by the
accidents of survival? In other words, would a similar picture emerge from
Islamic and Byzantine court or family sources, had they survived?

Fairly extensive treatment of the western sources may help to answer
these questions, accidents of survival notwithstanding. One cannot rule
out, on the basis of extant Byzantine sources, the likelihood of some
sort of jurisdiction being exercised by great landlords. But there is nothing
for the period before 1204 to suggest the motley assortments of regional
customs or seigneurial courts with rights of capital punishment found in,
say, contemporaneous Francophone lands. Nor was such a combination
of landownership and sweeping rights of justice a feature of rulership in
the Islamic world: after all, many matters involving law were not the prime
responsibility of its secular leaders.[1] Furthermore (and paradoxically),
the profusion of records about the west brings out what might well
indicate its economic and bureaucratic weaknesses in relation to the
other two spheres. Most obvious is the lack of governmental apparatuses
capable of supra-regional supervision before the twelfth century (later still
in many areas). Without major resource centres doling out money, robes
and similar status symbols, would-be rulers had to fall back on, essentially, land, granting it out together with rights over those who worked on
it. Or they had to recognise the powerful families and individuals already
ensconced there. For elites, therefore, conservation of their rights over
land and its workers was of higher priority than when service of the state or
access to its fiscal machinery brought utmost wealth and status, as was the
case in our other two spheres.[2] This, in turn, put a premium on ways of
vindicating property-rights, and one such was charters and other documents amounting to title-deeds. Given the interconnections between
the landed families and ecclesiastical institutions, it is not surprising

---

[1] See pp. 104–5, 127, 362.

[2] For state service in Byzantium: pp. 201, 309–10, 419–21, 432–4; on the importance of
controlling the fiscal apparatus and of revenue from land grants in the Islamic world:
pp. 241, 461–4.

that churches and monasteries made useful – although not the only – repositories of documents. And the acquisitiveness of some religious houses led to many records of transactions originally between lay parties ending up in their archives, thereby surviving into modern times.

The paperwork, then, marks out western political culture's concern with land, interwoven with (oft self-serving) pious professions and prayers for the soul, rather than special regard for legality or the written word. In a sense, the documentation is the reputable face of a culture whose other side accommodated violence and saw in it a fair means of dispute settlement, while prizing martial prowess and, in the later middle ages, a cult of chivalry. To some extent the plethora of documentation, along with the Mirrors for Princes and injunctions against private warfare from monarchs such as Louis IX, obscures the routineness of violent acts. Only scrutiny of court records reveals how acclimatised French nobles were to fighting it out, clashes too habitual to earn much coverage in narrative sources.[3] From this perspective, the documentation can be deceptive, skirting hard facts of everyday life. In contrast, study of Byzantine sources, visual as well as literary, suggests that neither coats-of-arms nor fortified residences loom large in even the military elite's culture.[4] Neither were these prominent in Muslim urban centres before the thirteenth century. So something of the west's idiosyncracy emerges from perusing western sources.

Another reason for foregrounding the Latin sources is their capacity to illustrate dynamics and currents of political culture which may have existed in other spheres but are less intensively documented in the surviving record. Take petitions, for example, which involve all of Stephen Humphreys' touchstones of political culture.[5] Airing of individual and communal grievances or seeking redress against neighbours, lords or the ruler's own officials could be done at several removes from the royal court or through entreaties before the ruler, face-to-face. What the petitions have in common is their trust in an ability to override all countervailing parties. Such expectations and demands for 'justice' arose 'from the

---

[3] J. Firnhaber-Baker, *Violence and the State in Languedoc, 1250–1400* (Cambridge, 2014); also *idem*, ' Seigneurial war and royal power in later medieval southern France', *P&P* 208 (2010), 37–76. For the ambivalence enshrouding, and rationale to, collective acts of violence in urban settings: H. Skoda, *Medieval Violence: Physical Brutality in Northern France, 1270–1330* (Oxford, 2013), 232–44.

[4] See pp. 88, 200, 420–1, 423–4; M. Whittow, 'Rural fortifications in western Europe and Byzantium, tenth to twelfth century', *Byzantinische Forschungen* 21 (1995), 63–71; J. Shepard, 'Aspects of moral leadership: the imperial city and lucre from legality', in P. Armstrong (ed.), *Authority in Byzantium* (Farnham, 2013), 9–30.

[5] Religion, women and property came within the scope of petitioning, along with war; see pp. 19–22, 161.

bottom up', rather than being initiated by political leaderships. And so, albeit haphazardly, they shed light on forces making for some sort of coherent polity. It is in the west that one finds the richest mix of forms. Petitioning could, at a personal level, involve the Icelandic lawspeaker (*lögsögumaður*) or the petitions presented to the newly crowned Conrad II.[6] The French and English kings were also targets of petitions and, by the later thirteenth century, elaborate institutions were needed for coping, institutions that were themselves liable to be short circuited by ever more petitions seeking to bypass them.[7] What western examples show are the expectations placed upon some sort of figure, not invariably monarchical, almost regardless of means of enforcement. The tendency is discernible in the case of Conrad II, a newcomer to the throne in 1024 and lacking institutional backup. What might be termed 'demand-driven' pronouncements or adjudication are relatively well-attested for the west even in the earlier medieval period. They are no less important to its political culture than formal acts of law-making or administrative steps towards dispensing justice systematically.[8] Expectations rode high long before institutionalisation.

What is striking from our Byzantine and Islamic evidence is the rather different role of petitioning of the supreme ruler and the questing after access to him or his representatives, as mentioned in court manuals or recounted (albeit fleetingly) in other sources.[9] Undoubtedly, the pattern implies the buoyancy of expectations at grassroots as well as among their elites, an abiding 'faith' in what a monarch could do, his (or sometimes her) ability to override hindrances or underlings and set things to right. One may infer that petitions are addressed to wherever overarching power is thought to lie, or once lay and still potentially resides, with notions of 'power' shading into those of 'authority'. Approaches could be made readily enough to a ruler within hailing distance under open skies, itinerant rulers like Conrad II in the west. But petitions may also be put to rulers emerging only occasionally for processions: their allure may be all the greater for this, as witness the emperor's in Constantinople, where

---

[6] See p. 256.
[7] G. Dodd and S. Petit-Renaud, 'Grace and favour: the petition and its mechanisms', in C. Fletcher *et al.* (eds.), *Government and Political Life in England and France, c. 1300–c. 1500* (Cambridge, 2015), 240–78, esp. 263–9 (on petitioners' recourse to 'intercessors', informal networks of influential contacts).
[8] See pp. 59–61, 63, 68–9, 162, 279.
[9] See pp. 352–3; for petitioning under the Umayyads of al-Andalus: O. Herrero, 'L'intercession (shafaʿa) sous les Omeyyades d'al-Andalus à travers quelques récits historiques', *REMMM* 140 (2016), 165–80; and under the Abbasid caliph al-Muqtadir: M. van Berkel, 'Political intercession at the court of caliph al-Muqtadir', *REMMM* 140 (2016), 181–90.

ceremonial and acclamations highlight the *basileus'* relationship with God and heavenly forces.[10] Yet belief in the supernal powers at a king's disposal was not calibrated to inaccessibility: it was running strong in France and England at the end of the middle ages, with the first of the Tudors, Henry VII, hoping to legitimise his rule through regularising the ritual known as 'the king's touch'.[11]

To this extent, bottom-up expectations of monarchical authority and intimations of sacred kingship constitute a spectrum ranging from remedial action to the application of formal procedures of 'justice' within all three spheres, with a common dynamic behind the petitioning. On the other hand, even allowing for the Byzantine and Islamic sources' sparsity, methods of meeting these expectations really do seem to have varied between spheres. In the Islamic world, legislation was not a prime function of the supreme ruler, and interpreting the *shari'a* became the preserve of the *'ulama'*, while the courts of *qadis* saw to the settlement of many kinds of dispute.[12] Methods of administration stood apart from the west in Byzantium, too, albeit in the court system and the rather stripped-down version of Justinianic law instituted by emperors during the eighth century. These mechanisms for resolving discord seemingly worked well enough. Thus, to the eyes of Constantine VII (945–59), a grand gesture of his grandfather, Basil I, involved taking his seat in the Public Treasury (*Genikon*) and hearing complaints against tax-collectors; once, Basil threw open the doors to all comers, just to be told that 'no one anywhere [. . .] was raising a complaint against anyone'.[13] This hardly means that injustice in Byzantium was rarer. But its rulers inclined more towards channelling petitions through regular courts than their western counterparts, whose procedures for relieving grievances were, until the later middle ages, less well-oiled or comprehensive.

At the same time, the idea of reciprocity and mutual obligations between ruler and subjects underlay most western polities. Inlaid with

---

[10] R. Macrides, 'The ritual of petition', in P. Roilos and D. Yatromanolakis (eds), *Greek Ritual Poetics* (Washington, DC, 2004), 356–70; *Pseudo-Kodinos and the Constantinopolitan Court: Offices and Ceremonies*, ed. and tr. R. Macrides *et al.* (Farnham, 2013), 399–400; also R. Morris, 'What did the epi tôn deêseôn actually do?', in D. Feissel and J. Gascou (eds), *La Pétition à Byzance* (Paris, 2004), 125–40.
[11] S. Brogan, *The Royal Touch in Early Modern England. Politics, Medicine and Sin* (Woodbridge, 2015), 45–51.
[12] See pp. 126–7, 331–2.
[13] The *Life* of Basil was commissioned by Constantine in the mid-tenth century: *Vita Basilii* ch. 31, ed. and tr. I. Ševčenko, *Chronographiae quae Theophanis Continuati nomine fertur liber V quo Vita Basilii imperatoris amplectitur*, CFHB 42 (Berlin and New York, 2011), 122–5; see also pp. 295–7. On the *Ecloga* ('Selection') promulgated in 741: M. G. Humphreys, *Law, Power, and Imperial Ideology in the Iconoclast Era, c. 680–850* (Cambridge, 2015), 81–129.

notions of counsel and aid owed to the king from the great and good, it was crystallised in the coronation-oaths pledging justice.[14] In the case of England, kings coping with ever knottier legal pleas alongside complaints about governance found it politic to engage with large assemblies of magnates and, increasingly, the representatives of other interest-groups, too. The term *parlamentum* (Old French: *parlement*) merged notions of assembly and conversation.[15] Over time, 'parliaments' developed into forums for promulgating royal decrees and enactment of laws, besides channelling protests and petitions. They could also authorise general taxes and, through knights of the shire and burgesses of prosperous towns, facilitate their collection. Comparable processes were under way in the realm of Aragon-Catalonia in the later middle ages. Their origin lies in the shortcomings of governmental machinery, alongside positive regard for counsel and consent.

Quite general assemblies and councils convened at the rulers' behest in our other spheres, too, and for a Byzantine emperor to confer with his senators was not unusual.[16] If these did not burgeon into anything like a western parliament, this has something to do with the efficacy of fiscal apparatuses and bureaucracies in the heyday of the Byzantine and Abbasid empires, with some wheels still turning even in periods of decline. No less relevant to notions of general assembly (as against court) are their ideologies of God-given autocracy and exaltation of top-down hierarchy and obedience. In the Byzantine emperor's case, his subjects were routinely termed *douloi*.[17] In political cultures of this variety, the chances of a ruler's court or council turning into a counterweight to the ruler were slighter. So, too, were the chances of its outcomes being promulgated or having the force of law.

To this extent, the copiousness of our Latin western sources is not simply a fluke of survival. In societies with regard for rights (especially to land) and endemic uncertainty as to where the ultimate locus of authority lay, a tendency to hold on to every scrap of documentation to bolster these rights would be understandable. And this although – sometimes even *because* – so few persons could figure out the Latin of charters; besides, many disputes were in practice sorted out by violence, intimidation or word-of-mouth peer-group pressure, seldom leaving a written word. A great deal of networking, lobbying and defamation went on in the

---

[14] See pp. 63, 74, 161–2, 254–9, 279, 396–8.
[15] J. R. Maddicott, *The Origins of the English Parliament, 924–1327* (Oxford, 2010), 75–6, 96, 157–66, 411–17.
[16] See e.g. Theophanes Continuatus, *Chronographia* VI.8, ed. I. Bekker (Bonn, 1838), 474; see also p. 85.
[17] See pp. 80, 412.

Byzantine and Islamic spheres, too, as witness the letters of Michael Psellos.[18] But the latter presupposes specialised judges and the ultimate redress of provincial wrongs in Constantinople. Meanwhile, in the Islamic world, many issues of material concern were for the *qadi* to determine.[19] There were, in other words, well-known channels leading to accredited sites of adjudication, and those seeking to divert or subvert the channels were likely to have their own means of access to the sources of supreme power: disruptive, arbitrary, probably unjust, making for a handful of wellsprings. In these polities, too, property and local standing counted for much, but fewer parties were confident enough to take, almost literally, the law into their own hands: the proliferation of jurisdictions is a distinguishing characteristic of the west. The latter's relative abundance in data about seigneurial court and out-of-court settlements, along with records from bishoprics and territorial principalities, is, then, a fair enough reflection of the cellular structure of polities in the west, a mirror rather than a prism. The prominence in these sources of matters of landed property and invocations of godliness registers well enough the preoccupations and rules of the game in the west. And in showing how the household was at the heart of the landed elites' modus operandi, they let slip the abiding importance of those often in effective charge: the wives and widows who could provide continuity and, very often, set the tone. They were of no less consequence to western political culture for managing affairs mostly well below the level of royal courts and goings-on around the throne.[20] Here, our written sources are something of a distorting mirror, but not beyond all recognition.

---

[18] See pp. 96–8.   [19] See p. 126.   [20] See pp. 71–2, 175, 502.

4   The Latin West
Sources

Björn Weiler and Jonathan Shepard

Figure 4.1 The king wields his sword over the seas between England and Aquitaine: gold noble of Edward III, possibly treaty series 1363–9, London Mint (32.79mm); © The Portable Antiquities Scheme[1]

Latin, the Written Language of Clergy and Others

In the case of medieval western Europe, a number of features stand out: the dominance of a literary language of communication (Latin) which, for much of the period, was superimposed over the vernaculars; considerable regional variations in the nature, type and amount of written sources; the wealth and richness of administrative evidence and of fiscal and judicial records; and the provenance of much of this material from within a rather narrow elite, defined not in terms of social status but religious function.

In terms of language, Latin remained the dominant medium of instruction, education and administration well into the fourteenth century and in

---

[1] E. Wood, 'SUSS–4078FE: a medieval coin' (2017); https://finds.org.uk/database/arte facts/record/id/833213 (accessed 31 December 2019).

many areas – such as diplomacy – long afterwards. There were exceptions: from the ninth to eleventh centuries, late Anglo-Saxon England
witnessed a flowering of vernacular writings, and from the thirteenth
century regions like Castile, Norway and Iceland employed the vernacular more freely and widely than other parts of the Latin west.[2] Latin owed
its dominance to a diversity of factors: the immense cultural and political
prestige of the Roman empire to which – until the eleventh century – most
of Christian Europe had once belonged; the painstaking educational
reforms and lasting inspiration of Charlemagne and his heirs in the
ninth century, which had codified and implanted as normative the use
of a certain kind of Latin; and the universal role of Latin as language of
ecclesiastical communication, oral and written. Unlike Arabic or the
Greek of the New Testament, however, this was not a language of revelation. Latin may have been the medium for studying the Bible in the west,
but it was not the divine language in which either the Old or New
Testament had originally been written. Nor was it, like Arabic in the
Islamic world or Greek in the Byzantine, the vernacular of a dominant
ethnic or social elite. In fact, the kind of Latin used bore little resemblance
even to the vernacular as spoken in fourth- and fifth-century Italy. The
rhetorical ideal remained classical Latin. For most of the middle ages, an
often wilful conservatism prevailed, in which mastery of arcane Latin was
a mark of cultural sophistication. Both these peculiarities mattered: they
are essential for understanding the place of Latin within contemporary
political culture; and they reinforce some key characteristics in the production of sources in the west.

Latin existed alongside a bedazzling range of vernaculars. Not only
were there distinct language groups – Romance, Germanic, Slavonic,
Celtic, Finnish and Hungarian – but western Europeans were also speaking regionally distinct dialects. Most famously, perhaps, the denizens of
northern France found it almost impossible to communicate with those
from the south. Moreover, political entities could encompass a whole
range of language groups. The rulers of the western empire – modern
Germany, Austria, Switzerland, the Netherlands, Belgium, eastern
France, northern Italy and the Czech Republic – could hardly prioritise
just one vernacular. But even the kings of England ruled over subjects
who communicated in English, French, Welsh, Irish and Scots Gaelic.
Latin provided a means whereby often disparate realms could be governed: thanks to Latin, decisions, initiatives and suchlike could be communicated to the educated elites within the kingdom at large.

[2] T. Ruiz, *From Heaven to Earth: The Reordering of Castilian Society, 1150–1350* (Princeton, 2004); T. M. Andersson, *The Growth of the Medieval Icelandic Saga* (Ithaca, NY, 2006).

Not that Latin was universally spoken or understood. Even within religious communities, daily conversation was often in a range of vernaculars,[3] and many even in the secular elites had little or no grasp of Latin. When Charlemagne's heirs divided their inheritance in 842, the document outlining the division was drawn up in Latin as well as in the respective vernaculars; when in 1157, Emperor Frederick Barbarossa received envoys from the pope at Besançon, papal letters had to be translated into German for him; and when the nobles in England forced the king to agree to reform of the realm under their oversight in 1258, the relevant document was disseminated first in Anglo-Norman, then in Latin. So even when Latin was dominant in written communications, it remained a language rarely used outside specific cultural or procedural contexts. Consequently, students of medieval political culture face the problem of sources written in a language other than the ones in which those discourses were often conducted or in which the institutions featuring in our sources functioned.

Of course, different languages need not denote distinct discourses. Much of the vernacular output of Anglo-Saxon England, for instance, consisted of translations from Latin. Because even literary elites communicated in both Latin and the vernacular, concepts, movements and ideas, stylistic techniques, themes and topics could migrate between languages.[4] Moreover, until almost the end of the middle ages, the ability to commit ideas and concepts to writing remained the preserve of a very specific group within western society. This resulted in a relatively coherent, yet by no means uniform, outlook since most of our surviving texts from before the thirteenth century were written by members of the church. This included vernacular works of fiction. Before the fourteenth century there was barely a western equivalent to Usama b. Munqidh, the twelfth-century Syrian warrior-bureaucrat who once lost a baggage train laden with his library of 400 books.

---

[3] S. G. Bruce, *Silence and Sign-Language in Medieval Monasticism* (Cambridge, 2007).
[4] See e.g. H. Antonsson, 'The present and the past in the Sagas of Icelanders', in P. Lambert and B. Weiler (eds), *How the Past was Used: Historical Cultures, c. 750–2000* (Oxford, 2017), 69–90 at 76–9; *idem*, 'Salvation and early saga writing in Iceland: aspects of the works of the Þingeyrar monks and their associates', *Viking and Medieval Scandinavia* 8 (2012), 71–140; *idem*, 'Christian themes', in Á. Jakobsson and S. Jakobsson (eds), *The Routledge Research Companion to the Medieval Icelandic Sagas* (London, 2017), 279–91; T. H. Tulinius, 'Honour, sagas and trauma: reflections on literature and violence in thirteenth-century Iceland', in A. M. Bjorvand Bjørkøy and T. Norheim (eds), *Literature and Honour* (Oslo, 2017), 81–94; *idem*, '*Skaði kennir mér minni minn*: on the relationship between trauma, memory, revenge and the medium of poetry', in K. Müller-Wille *et al.* (eds), *Skandinavische Schriftlandschaften: Vänbok til Jürg Glauser* (Tübingen, 2017), 129–35; P. Beekman Taylor, '*Njáll grómr*: Christian morality and Norse myth in *Njál's Saga*', *Mediaeval Scandinavia* 13 (2000), 167–80.

In fact, until the twelfth century at least, writing was not the primary means of communication. Western Europe, its sizable textual output notwithstanding, remained a largely oral society. The spoken word mattered, but so did what has been termed symbolic communication: the use of rituals, gestures and ceremonies.[5] They were an easy and visible means of expressing status, claims and power relations. They derived their legitimacy from having a large audience capable of testifying to their occurrence, and participants could call upon these witnesses to verify an agreement that had been visually and symbolically expressed. This makes writing the history of western political culture more difficult. That difficulty is heightened by the complex interrelationship between written, oral and symbolic means of communication, about which no clear scholarly consensus has yet emerged. But we should bear in mind that a lack of written documentation does not denote a lack of political sophistication. The relative scarcity of written evidence for western Europe before the ninth and tenth centuries reflects not so much the barbaric nature of western society in the 'dark ages' as the fact that written communication was largely the preserve of a language and a social group distinct from, perhaps even marginal to, the politically active elites as a whole.[6]

This ecclesiastical predominance remains one of the defining features of western political society, shaping the historian's image of medieval political organisation. Unlike much of the Islamic world, the clergy constituted a distinct legal and institutional category, a group set apart from the overarching structure of society by their religious function. They were not homogeneous. A distinction commonly drawn is between the secular clergy (who engaged with the world, primarily through pastoral care: parish priests, chaplains or bishops, as well as their clerical entourage) and the religious (who were meant to focus on prayer and contemplation of the divine: monks and nuns living in communities secluded from mainstream society). Of course, the two groups overlapped, and in the later middle ages new movements would emerge that further bridged

---

[5] The term 'symbolic communication' was introduced to medieval studies by Gerd Althoff: *Die Macht der Rituale: Symbolik und Herrschaft im Mittelalter* (Darmstadt, 2003); *idem* (ed.), *Formen und Funktionen öffentlicher Kommunikation im Mittelalter* (Stuttgart, 2001); *idem*, 'Zur Bedeutung symbolischer Kommunikation für das Verständnis des Mittelalters', *Frühmittelalterliche Studien* 31 (1997), 370–89.

[6] However, for a more complicated image: M. Aurell, *The Lettered Knight: Knowledge and Behaviour of the Aristocracy in the Twelfth and Thirteenth Centuries* (Budapest and New York, 2016); H. Bainton, *History and the Written Word: Documents, Literacy, and Language in the Age of the Angevins* (Philadelphia, 2020). For literacy and practices of reading in Byzantium and the Islamic world: D. Krallis, *Serving Byzantium's Emperors: The Courtly Life and Career of Michael Attaleiates* (Cham, 2019); K. Hirschler, *The Written Word in the Medieval Arabic Lands: A Social and Cultural History of Reading Practices* (Edinburgh, 2012); see also pp. 427, 126–8, 246–7.

these divides. All of them, however, shared a legal status that clearly set them apart from the majority of western Europeans.

Members of the clergy held privileges, secular courts having only limited jurisdiction over them. But they also had to abide by certain restrictions: they were not meant to shed blood or have jurisdiction in cases of capital punishment. For most of the period, they could not pass on possessions to heirs outside the clerical community and were supposed to remain celibate. In theory, at least, they were excluded from the lineage-based society around them: a distinct group whose membership rested not on social status or bloodline but on the performance of religious duties.

In practice, deviations from these norms were numerous and variegated.[7] In many parts of western Europe, links of protection and patronage tied together members of the local secular and ecclesiastical elites. Nuns, monks and canons, abbots, abbesses and bishops frequently interacted with lay aristocrats who were their own aunts and uncles, nieces and nephews, cousins and other blood relatives. In addition – and this is a key distinguishing characteristic, unlike anything we encounter in the Islamic or Byzantine worlds – many leading members of the secular clergy were secular lords in their own right. Bishops, archbishops and, on occasion, abbots or the heads of nunneries ruled over extensive lands and estates; in some religious orders, this included networks of monasteries. They faced pressures and concerns not unlike those of their secular counterparts and were sometimes, in fact, indistinguishable from them. Western clerical culture, in short, frequently overlapped with, echoed and reflected its secular environs. Byzantine clerics and Islamic scholars could write narratives and pronounce judgements on ethical and religious issues, but they did not have their most prominent Latin counterparts' family connections and resources, nor the firepower of knights residing on their estates.

What does this mean for the sources at our disposal? On an elementary level, there was no uniform clerical perspective. Monks saw things differently from papal officials or those who served as chaplains to the great and powerful. The identity of an author, his function and status, frequently helped to form the views he adopted, the measures he thought worth recording or the kind of evidence he left behind. Even so, members of the

---

[7] B. Schimmelpfennig, 'Zölibat und Lage der Priestersöhne vom 11. bis 14. Jahrhundert', *Historische Zeitschrift* 227 (1978), 1–44; J. Keupp, 'Die zwei Schwerter des Bischofs: von Kriegsherren und Seelenhirten im Reichsepiskopat der Stauferzeit', *Zeitschrift für Kirchengeschichte* 117 (2006), 1–24; T. Reuter, '*Episcopi cum sua militia*: the prelate as warrior in the early Staufen era', in T. Reuter (ed.), *Warriors and Churchmen in the Middle Ages: Essays Presented to Karl Leyser* (London, 1992), 79–94; W.-R. Berns, *Burgenpolitik und Herrschaft des Erzbischofs Balduin von Trier (1307–1354)* (Sigmaringen, 1980); R. A. Fletcher, *God's Catapult: The Life and Times of Diego Gelmírez of Santiago de Compostela* (Oxford, 1984); S. Hamilton, *Church and People in the Medieval West, 900–1200* (Harlow, 2013), esp. 73–98, 129–52.

church shared a common framework within which to view the world. We have already highlighted Latin as the language of communication. Another reference point came from the Bible, not least the Old Testament books recounting the importance of the priesthood. Depending on an individual's level of education and formal training, there was also classical literature (especially Cicero and Suetonius) and, more generally, the Church Fathers. From the eleventh century, Roman and ecclesiastical law, if not formal, university-based instruction in theology, formed part of the intellectual equipment of the abler, more ambitious and better-connected clergy.[8] Naturally, considerable variations persisted – the level of education within a community was dependent on the wealth of an institution, its relative age and its ability either to preserve large numbers of texts or to secure copies of them.[9] Yet, there existed a broad, shared framework within which thinking developed.

Unsurprisingly – and tautologically – religious texts predominate among the written materials left behind by ecclesiastical authors. At the same time, not all of these materials have been edited, and scholars are only beginning to grasp the usefulness of others. A mass of liturgical materials describing and outlining religious services still await modern editions, and close study of the manuscripts (including the make-up of their bindings and insertions) can have wider-ranging implications for political culture and history.[10] Large and extensive sermon collections, especially from the later middle ages, remain virtually an editorial terra incognita;[11] and the collections of historical anecdotes that became a popular preaching aid in the thirteenth century await full exploration

---

[8] For a general overview: C. S. Jaeger, *The Envy of Angels: Cathedral Schools and Social Ideals in Medieval Europe, 950–1200* (Philadelphia, 1994); and a couple of case studies: J. Peltzer, *Canon Law, Careers, and Conquest: Episcopal Elections in Normandy and Greater Anjou between c.1140 and c.1230* (Cambridge, 2008); J. S. Ott, *Bishops, Authority and Community in Northwestern Europe, c.1050–1150* (Cambridge, 2015).

[9] For case studies: M. Mostert, *The Library of Fleury: A Provisional List of Manuscripts* (Hilvershum, 1989); J. G. Clark, *A Monastic Renaissance at St Albans: Thomas Walsingham and his Circle, c.1350–1440* (Oxford, 2004); see also B. Pohl and L. Gathagan (eds), *A Companion to the Abbey of Le Bec in the Central Middle Ages (11th–13th Centuries)* (Leiden, 2017).

[10] For an introduction: E. Palazzo, *Liturgie et société au Moyen Âge* (Paris, 2000); *idem*, *Histoire des livres liturgiques: le Moyen Âge, des origines au XIIIe siècle* (Paris, 1993); also H. Parkes, *The Making of Liturgy in the Ottonian Church: Books, Music and Ritual in Mainz, 950–1050* (Cambridge, 2015); J. H. McCarthy, *Music, Scholasticism and Reform: Salian Germany, 1024–1125* (Manchester, 2009); S. Rankin, *The Winchester Troper: Facsimile Edition and Introduction* (London, 2007); *idem*, *Writing Sounds in Carolingian Europe: The Invention of Musical Notation* (Cambridge, 2018).

[11] G. Donavan (ed.), *Speculum Sermonis: Interdisciplinary Reflections on the Medieval Sermon* (Turnhout, 2004); S. Wenzel, *Latin Sermon Collections from Later Medieval England: Orthodox Preaching in the Age of Wyclif* (Cambridge, 2005); R. Andersson (ed.), *Constructing the Medieval Sermon* (Turnhout, 2007).

for the study of political culture.[12] Apart from a few well-known authors of Biblical exegesis, an immense corpus of commentaries on books of the Bible still exists mostly in manuscript form.[13] Hagiographical texts have fared better thanks to the Bollandists: their compilation of narratives on the cults of all the Catholic saints began in the seventeenth century and is ongoing.[14] But we also have letter collections (many still unedited),[15] texts for the education of monks and clerics, as well as more familiar types of historical narrative such as chronicles and annals. We will consider how these materials have been used later in the chapter, but it is worth recalling just how vast the corpus of surviving sources is. It must not be overlooked in comparison with the administrative materials upon which western scholars have traditionally swooped.

The role of women in the production of narrative materials is also easily overlooked. With notable exceptions such as Hrotsvitha of Gandersheim and, to a lesser extent, Christine de Pisan, this may be because individual women and convents seldom appear to have engaged in producing new historical narratives. Cloistered women seem rather to have been encouraged towards religious treatises, for example Hildegard of Bingen, Elisabeth of Schönau and Margery Kempe. Yet so stark a contrast is misleading. We know, for instance, of active literary traditions involving the copying (as against composing) of texts;[16] of the importance of female

---

[12] See, though, M. Menzel, *Predigt und Geschichte: historische Exempel in der geistlichen Rhetorik des Mittelalters* (Cologne, Weimar and Vienna, 1998).

[13] Henri de Lubac, *Medieval Exegesis: The Four Senses of Scripture*, tr. M. Sebanc, 3 vols (Grand Rapids, MI, 1998–2009); P. Buc, *L'Ambiguïté du livre: prince, pouvoir, et people dans les commentaires de la Bible au Moyen Âge* (Paris, 1994); R. Pletl, *Irdisches Regnum in der mittelalterlichen Exegese. Ein Beitrag zur exegetischen Lexikographie und ihren Herrschaftsvorstellungen (7.–13. Jahrhundert)* (Frankfurt am Main, 2000); J. L. Nelson and D. Kempf (eds), *Reading the Bible in the Middle Ages* (London, 2015); J. Eldevik, 'Saints, pagans and the wonders of the east: the medieval imaginary and its manuscript contexts', *Traditio* 71 (2016), 235–72.

[14] The standard reference work is *Bibliotheca Hagiographica Latina*, 3 vols (Rome, 1949–86).

[15] M. Camargo, *Ars dictaminis, ars dictandi* (Turnhout, 1991); G. Constable, *Letters and Letter Collections* (Turnhout, 1976). For such collections: Anselm of Canterbury, *Letters*, tr. W. Fröhlich, 3 vols (Kalamazoo, MI, 1990–4); S. Niskanen, *The Letter Collections of Anselm of Canterbury* (Turnhout, 2011); Nicholas of Clairvaux, *Letter Collections*, ed. and tr. L. Wahlgren-Smith (Oxford, 2018); M. Garrison, '"Send more socks": on mentality and the preservation context of medieval letters', in M. Mostert (ed.), *New Approaches to Medieval Communication* (Turnhout, 1999), 69–99; G. Signori, 'Letters by and to religious women in light of the rule, single letters, and letter collections: a research survey', *Journal of Medieval Monastic Studies* 6 (2017), 169–94.

[16] S. Vanderputten, *Dark Age Nunneries: The Ambiguous Identity of Female Monasticism, 800–1050* (Ithaca, NY, 2018); A. Beach, *Women as Scribes: Book Production and Monastic Reform in Twelfth-Century Bavaria* (Oxford, 2003); A. Beach (ed.), *Manuscripts and Monastic Culture: Reform and Renewal in Twelfth-Century Germany* (Turnhout, 2007); V. Blanton et al. (eds), *Nuns' Literacies in Medieval Europe* (Turnhout, 2013).

patrons in commissioning and receiving historical works;[17] and of the role that royal women played in facilitating cultural exchanges and contacts across the English Channel.[18] Thus the seemingly marginalised only emerge as active participants in the political process only once we look beyond the male clerical gaze that frames so much of the extant materials.

Medieval clerics and bureaucrats left behind an abundance of sources to do with property disputes, estate administration, court cases and other such everyday affairs. This is not to say that the processes thus documented did not exist (or matter) in an Islamic or Byzantine context. The early caliphate presided over a far more developed administrative apparatus than anything we can trace in the contemporary west, while the flowering of legal scholarship in the Muslim world presupposes a rich soil of paperwork and judicial process. Yet relatively few traces survive from before the fourteenth century. In the case of Muslim Iberia, we only know how extensive its administrative holdings were because the Christian conquerors preserved some of them. It was not so much the documenting of matters of legal and administrative significance as it was the preserving of them that was of greater cultural significance in the west. Documents concerning commercial agreements, wills and other such family matters were also made, and preserved, in the Byzantine world; their disappearances are largely due to the losses inflicted by centuries of shifting control culminating in the Ottoman conquest in the late middle ages.

The Uses of Written Records to Elites

The different approaches to the safeguarding of documents and their divergent survival rates receive attention in this section.[19] Worth highlighting here is the fact that the west's apparent abundance of materials reflects its multiplicity of elites and also, paradoxically, uncertainty as to what made the most reliable testimony. For want of urban centres, monetary economies or fiscal apparatus, its kings cut puny figures in comparison with caliphs, sultans or the Byzantine *basileus*. The means of sustained coercion or policing available to even the most rumbustious being modest, they relied on cooperativeness on the part of local

---

[17] E. van Houts, 'The writing of history and family traditions through the eyes of men and women: the *Gesta Principum Polonorum*', in K. Stopka (ed.), *Gallus Anonymus and his Chronicle in the Context of Twelth-Century Historiography from the Perspective of the Latest Research* (Cracow, 2010), 189–203.

[18] E. Tyler, *England in Europe: English Royal Women and Literary Patronage, c. 1000–1150* (Toronto, 2017).

[19] On the making and preservation of written records in the Byzantine and Islamic worlds: pp. 92–3, 427, 126–8.

landholding elites. Anyway, at grassroots, dispute settlement and questions of ownership were largely in the hands of kinsmen and communities, with some form of feuding or combat an option at most social levels, in practice if not in written law.[20] Moreover, as the documentation of even a relatively orderly realm like England indicates, the principle that 'oral witness deserves more credence than written evidence' was a legal commonplace. As late as the thirteenth century, written evidence was being accepted 'cautiously – and perhaps reluctantly'.[21] Yet there was a certain premium put on records kept by institutions better-proofed against mortality than any ruling family or noble household. And episcopal sees and monasteries were only too willing to draft, copy or forge charters, especially those conferring lands or privileges on themselves. A corollary was that landed families with copious and often impressive-looking textual supports – hagiographical texts featuring forebears and lists of relics donated alongside charters and suchlike legitimisers of possession – had an edge over those lacking them, even if monasteries often had their own acquisitive agendas. In fact, we owe the preservation of deeds concerning earlier medieval lay estates largely to ecclesiastical archives.[22] As other chapters emphasise, extracting surpluses from the land – with the aid of those working it – was the principal means to wealth and power until the later middle ages.[23] Besides force majeure, force of habit and collective

---

[20] P. Hyams, 'Was there really such a thing as feud in the high middle ages?', in S. A. Throop and P. R. Hyams (eds), *Vengeance in the Middle Ages: Emotion, Religion and Feud* (Farnham, 2010), 151–75; B. Stoddard Tuten and T. L. Billado (eds), *Feud, Violence and Practice: Essays in Medieval Studies in Honour of Stephen D. White* (Farnham, 2010); I. Wood, '"The bloodfeud of the Franks": a historiographical legend', *EME* 14 (2006), 489–504; T. Reuter, 'The insecurity of travel in the early and high middle ages: criminals, victims and their medieval and modern observers, repr. in *MPMM*, 38–71.

[21] M. T. Clanchy, *From Memory to Written Record: England 1066–1307*, 3rd edn (Oxford, 2013), 265.

[22] R. McKitterick, *The Carolingians and the Written Word* (Cambridge, 1989), 77–134; J. Jarrett and A. S. McKinley (eds), *Problems and Possibilities of Early Medieval Charters* (Turnhout, 2013); M. Mostert, *Organising the Written Word: Scripts, Manuscripts and Texts* (Turnhout, 2020); A. R. Rumble, 'Anglo-Saxon royal archives: their nature, extent, survival and loss', in G. Owen-Crocker and B. Schneider (eds), *Kingship, Legislation and Power in Anglo-Saxon England* (Woodbridge, 2013), 185–99 at 188–90, 196; S. Keynes, 'Church councils, royal assemblies and Anglo-Saxon diplomas', in *ibid.*, 17–183 at 62 and n. 189. On the hints of family archives in Anglo-Saxon England and the probable reasons why so many of our extant charters and other deeds have survived through the archives of great monasteries: C. Insley, 'Archives and lay documentary practice in the Anglo-Saxon world', in W. C. Brown *et al.* (eds), *Documentary Culture and the Laity in the Early Middle Ages* (Cambridge, 2013), 336–62, esp. 338–42, 253–62; also H. Hummer, 'The production and preservation of documents in Francia: the evidence of cartularies', in *ibid.*, 189–230. On the question of what constitute 'archives' and how they come to be formed: A. Burton, 'Introduction', in A. Burton (ed.), *Archive Stories, Facts, Fiction and the Writing of History* (Chapel Hill, NC, 2005), 1–24.

[23] See pp. 143–4, 149–50, 152, 369–70.

memory,[24] written deeds in church custodianship were invaluable for bolstering landholding and related rights. The entwining of landowner-ship with law and care for the church was tighter and more urgent for socio-political elites in the west than in Middle Byzantium, where offices were (literally) worth their weight in gold, or in the Islamic world, where word-of-mouth attestations (*isnad*) took precedence in law and urban centres long held sway.[25]

While Biblical precedent mattered, long-standing custom and the rediscovery of late antique Roman law were of equal significance. Unlike schools of Islamic law, centred largely on interpretive traditions harking back to the early days of Islam, western legal tradition was far less legitimised by reference to sacred texts.[26] Just because something was written in law did not mean that this was how law was practised. Oral tradition, custom and informal mechanisms still mattered greatly. Nonetheless, what was, for most of the middle ages, the least lettered and poorest of our spheres has left the most abundant records.

This abundance of legal and administrative sources also defines what questions historians of the medieval west can ask about its political practice and organisation. It is possible to investigate the economic bases of power, for instance: evidence survives for the peasant land market, financial organisa-tion, and the administration of royal, baronial and ecclesiastical estates.[27] We also have details of royal bureaucracy and the administration at work, even the process of legislation or on-the-job training of officials and lawyers.[28]

---

[24] M. Innes, 'Memory, orality and literacy in an early medieval society', *P&P* 158 (1998), 108–36.

[25] On the wealth and power of office-holders: pp. 199–202, 414–24; for word-of-mouth attestation: p. 465.

[26] As yet there is no comprehensive history of medieval European law (as opposed to national legal traditions). See *Handwörterbuch zur deutschen Rechtsgeschichte*, 2nd rev. edn (Stuttgart, 2004–); H. Vogt and M. Müller-Swendsen (eds), *Law and Learning in the Middle Ages* (Copenhagen, 2006); A. Harding, *Medieval Law and the Foundations of the State* (Oxford, 2002); P. Wormald, *Legal Culture in the Early Medieval West: Law as Text, Image and Experience* (London, 1999). Matters are somewhat different with church or ecclesiastical law: W. Hartmann (ed.), *The History of Medieval Canon Law in the Classical Period, 1140–1234: From Gratian to the Decretals of Pope Gregory IX* (Washington, DC, 2008); J. A. Brundage, *Medieval Canon Law* (London, 1995).

[27] C. Wickham, *Courts and Conflict in Twelfth-Century Gascony* (Oxford, 2003); M. Wade Labarge, *A Baronial Household of the Thirteenth-Century* (London, 1965); L. Feller and C. Wickham (eds), *Le Marché de la terre au Moyen Âge* (Rome, 2005); P. Fouracre and W. Davies (eds), *Property and Power in the Early Middle Ages* (Cambridge, 1995).

[28] J. A. Brundage, *The Medieval Origins of the Legal Profession: Canonists, Civilians, and Courts* (Chicago, 2008); F. Lachaud, *L'Éthique du pouvoir au Moyen Âge: l'office dans la culture politique (Angleterre, vers 1150–vers 1330)* (Paris, 2010); P. A. Brand, *Kings, Barons and Justices: The Making and Enforcement of Legislation in Thirteenth-Century England* (Cambridge, 2003); idem, *The Origins of the English Legal Profession* (Oxford, 1992); F. Rexroth, *Expertenweisheit: die Kritik an den Studierten und die Utopie einer geheilten Gesellschaft im späten Mittelalter* (Basel, 2008).

There are, however, considerable variations in the spread, type and wealth of such materials. Things changed over time and place, and there are mismatches between the quantity of documents left for a polity and its significance. So much depends on what a church or monastery deemed worth preserving or amassing in cartularies.[29] And, anyway, prolific output of documents is not necessary a reliable index of the effectiveness of administration or the overall significance of a realm. We thus have, at a very rough estimate, 30,000 charters and similar documents surviving from the period *c*.750–*c*.900 and relating to the governance of the Carolingian empire.[30] By contrast, nobody has counted the number of charters and writs (short mandates) issued or recorded by the chancery of the English kings in the later middle ages; a plausible guess would be that, in the 1240s, output reached about 8,000 to 10,000 items per annum. Yet the English case was hardly typical: the combined chanceries of Frederick II (d. 1250), who reigned over the German-speaking and other lands of the western empire and who also was king of Sicily and Jerusalem and overlord of Cyprus, yield only about 3,500 surviving items over his thirty-four-year reign.[31] Similarly, the kind of information collected varied, as did the reasons for storing it and, indeed, the collectors and keepers. The rich archives of late medieval Italian cities contain different types of material from the vast and intertwining collections of the medieval crown of Aragon;[32] and there are contrasts even here between, say, the ordered documentation of the Venetian state councils and the contracts

---

[29] M. Whittow, 'Sources of knowledge; cultures of recording', in C. Holmes and N. Standen (eds), *The Global Middle Ages, P&P Supplement 13* (Oxford, 2018), 45–87, at 58–63; F. Rexroth, *Fröhliche Scholastik: die Wissenschaftsrevolution des Mittelalters* (Munich, 2018); see also pp. 278, 403.

[30] Personal communication Janet Nelson.

[31] For the chancery under Frederick: A. Kiesewetter, 'Il governo e l'amministrazione centrale del regno', in G. Musca (ed.), *Le eredità normanno-sveve nell'età angioina: persistenze e mutamenti nel Mezzogiorno* (Bari, 2004), 25–68. The survival-rate (and output) of the French royal chancery grows higher for the thirteenth century: *Recueil des actes de Philippe Auguste roi de France*, ed. H.-F. Delaborde *et al.*, 6 vols (Paris, 1916–2005); *Les registres de Philippe Auguste*, ed. J. Baldwin *et al.* (Paris, 1992); J. Baldwin, 'Les premiers registres Capétiens de Philippe Auguste à Louis IX', in X. Hermand *et al.* (eds), *Décrire, inventorier, enregistrer entre Seine et Rhine au Moyen Âge: formes, fonctions et usages des écrits de gestion* (Paris, 2012), 15–22. The abundance of materials for St Louis' reign has hindered publication of a full edition: J. Le Goff, *Saint Louis*, tr. C. E. Gollrad (Notre Dame, IN, 2009), 243–51; W. Koch, 'Die Edition der Urkunden Friedrichs II', in W. Koch (ed.), *Das Staunen der Welt: Kaiser Friedrich II. von Hohenstaufen (1194–1250)* (Göppingen, 1996), 40–71.

[32] A. Silvestri, 'Archives of the Mediterranean: governance and record-keeping in the crown of Aragon in the long fifteenth century', *European History Quarterly* 46 (2016), 435–57. For Italian archives in general: A. De Vivo *et al.* (eds), *Archivi e archivisti in Italia tra medioevo ed età moderna* (Roma, 2015).

and deeds of Genoese banks and great families.[33] Accidents of survival compound real differences between societies. Thus the centralised nature of English governance, and the relative stability of political organisation, as well as ready access to a highly trained pool of clerical administrators, not only facilitated an expansion of royal administration but also necessitated the preservation of its output. In Iceland, by contrast, the lack of any administrative apparatus for raising revenues or enforcing the judgements made at the *Thing* and its courts meant that – for all its highly developed legal system, historical writings and law-books such as the *Grágás* ('Grey Goose') – oral tradition predominated into the thirteenth century.[34]

Differences in the survival and production rate of administrative sources were replicated in other sorts of writing. Regions like Catalonia thus stand out for their wealth of charters, yet also for a scarcity of historical and hagiographical texts.[35] While the *Rolls Series* and the *Monumenta Germaniae historica*, collections of predominantly narrative sources for England and Germany respectively, run to hundreds of volumes, the *Scriptores rerum Hungaricarum* has only two.[36] While southern Italy and northern France have a more or less continuous tradition of narrative history going back to the early middle ages,[37] in Sweden

---

[33] For the variegated state of archives, see e.g. *Deliberazioni del maggior consiglio di Venezia*, ed. R. Cessi, 3 vols (Bologna, 1931–50); *Régestes des délibérations du Sénat de Venise concernant la Romanie*, ed. F. Thiriet, 3 vols (Paris and The Hague, 1958–71); *Consiglio dei dieci: deliberazioni miste, registri I–V*, ed. F. Zago *et al.*, 3 vols, Fonti per la storia di Venezia. Sez. I, archivi pubblici (Venice, 1962–93); G. G. Musso, *Navigazione e commercio genovese con il Levante nei documenti dell'Archivio di Stato di Genova (Secc. XIV–XV)* (Rome, 1975); *Inventario dell'archivio del Banco di San Giorgio (1407–1805)*, ed. G. Felloni, 4 vols to date (Rome, 1989–); *Gli archivi Pallavicini di Genoa*, ed. M. Bologna, 2 vols, Atti della Società ligure di storia patria n.s. 34, 35 (Rome, 1994–5); *L'archivio della famiglia Sauli di Genova*, ed. M. Bologna, Atti della Società ligure di storia patria n.s. 40, 41 (Rome, 2000–1).

[34] *Laws of Early Iceland: Grágás, the Codex Regius of Grágás, with Material from Other Manuscripts*, tr. A. Dennis *et al.* (Winnipeg, 1980–2000). W. I. Miller observes, 'There is no reason to believe that Icelandic judges used written texts to inform themselves of the law, but there is good reason to believe that the legal culture of the experts had become intimately connected to reading and writing by the twelfth century': *Bloodtaking and Peacemaking: Feud, Law, and Society in Saga Iceland* (Chicago, 1990), 364 n. 49. See also *ibid.*, 221–32, 235–6, 250–7; S. Bagge, 'Scandinavian historical writing, 1100–1400', in S. Foot and C. F. Robinson (eds), *The Oxford History of Historical Writing, II: 400–1400* (Oxford, 2012), 414–27 at 415–17, 421–2, 424.

[35] A. J. Kosto, *Making Agreements in Medieval Catalonia: Power, Order and the Written Word* (Cambridge, 2007), esp. 16–19, 158–70, 175–7, 289–94; J. Jarrett, *Rulers and Ruled in Frontier Catalonia, 880–1010: Pathways of Power* (Woodbridge, 2010), 5–10, 18–19, 167–76; *idem*, 'Comparing the earliest documentary culture in Carolingian Catalonia', in Jarrett and McKinley (eds), *Problems and Possibilities*, 89–126; Whittow, 'Sources', 60–1.

[36] *Rolls Series* 1–99 (London, 1858–1965); *MGH SS*; *MGH SRG* n.s.; *MGH SRG*; *Scriptores Rerum Hungaricarum*, ed. E. Szentpétery, 2 vols (Budapest, 1937–8).

[37] For southern Italy see e.g. John of Naples, 'Deeds of the Bishops of Naples', in *MGH Scriptores rerum Langobardicarum et Italicarum saec. VI–IX* 1, ed. G. Waitz (Hanover, 1878), 402–36; *Chronicon Salernitanum: A Critical Edition with Studies on Literary and*

narratives only emerged in the fourteenth century in the form of Duke Erik's rhyming chronicle.[38] Moreover, such differences were not only matters of source survival and production: they reflect different expectations and structures of political organisation. Quite well-ordered polities like England or the German realm stand out from the prevailing polyarchy. Yet even they differ as to the role of the written word in royal administration, and as to record-keeping. While English kings relied on the writ – a brief mandate ordering immediate action from their officials, with copies kept in the chancery from the early thirteenth century on – few writs survive from Germany, for want of an overall bureau or confidence that such mandates were worth preserving.[39] This meant that the ruler had no ready record of what he and his counsellors had determined or commanded.

Such fluctuations and black holes in our knowledge crop up across the Latin west: there was no quintessentially Latin kingdom, no normative gold standard against which we might measure convergence and divergence. There were shared frameworks, grand ideas and principles of organisation, fashions, networks that proliferated and individuals who travelled. But what norms and structures meant in practice, how fashions spread and groups and individuals were perceived and integrated (or rejected), depended very much on local circumstances and a particular polity's make-up. It is this diversity – all the regional differences as well as the relative variety and wealth of the surviving evidence – that makes the west so complex and its political culture ultimately more accessible than that of the other two spheres.

Historical Sources and on Languages, ed. U. Westerbergh (Stockholm, 1956); *Annales Barenses*, ed. G. H. Pertz, in *MGH SS* 5 (Hanover, 1844), 51–6; Lupus Protospatharius, in *ibid.* 51–63; *Chronica Monasterii Casinensis*, ed. H. Hofmann, *MGH SS* 34 (Hanover, 1980); T. Brown, 'The political use of the past in Norman Sicily', in P. Magdalino (ed.), *Perceptions of the Past in Twelfth-Century Europe* (Woodbridge, 1992), 191–210; P. Oldfield, *City and Community in Norman Italy* (Cambridge, 2009), 11–13. For northern France: W. Goffart, *The Narrators of Barbarian History (AD 550–800): Jordanes, Gregory of Tours, Bede, and Paul the Deacon* (Princeton, 1988); R. McKitterick, *Perceptions of the Past in the Early Middle Ages* (Notre Dame, IN, 2006); Y. Hen and M. Innes (eds), *The Uses of the Past in the Early Middle Ages* (Cambridge, 2000), esp. M. Garrison, 'The Franks as the New Israel? Education for an identity from Pippin to Charlemagne' (114–61), R. McKitterick, 'Political ideology in Carolingian historiography' (162–74) and Y. Hen, 'The Annals of Metz and the Merovingian past' (175–90); M. Costambeys *et al.*, *The Carolingian World* (Cambridge, 2011), 18–25, 31–3.

38 *The Chronicle of Duke Erik: A Verse Epic from Medieval Sweden*, tr. E. Carlquist and P. C. Hogg (Lund, 2012); Bagge, 'Scandinavian historical writing', 422–3.

39 P. A. Brand, 'Chancery, the justices and the making of new writs in thirteenth-century England', in M. Dyson and D. J. Ibbetson (eds), *Law and Legal Process: Substantive Law and Procedure in English Legal Procedure* (Cambridge, 2013), 17–33; D. A. Carpenter, *The Reign of Henry III* (London, 1996), 20–5, 61–73; on modes of governance in Germany and England: pp. 64–5, 68–9.

Ideals of Kingly and Queenly Virtues, and of Political Order

The upshot of all the variety, and the stand-offs between quite different modes of politico-social structures and scales of values, was a proliferation of works on the subject, from ideal theorising to practical guides, once functional literacy spread and ceased to be the preserve of the clergy from the thirteenth century onwards. One could think – and argue – in terms of *Staatlichkeit* in respect of quite distinct political entities (England against Aragon, for instance) and also in terms of an abstract body capable of existing and persisting in the absence of an individual monarch, prince or other authority. For example, the realm of Bohemia existed independently of the ruler and had its own set of legal norms and customs.[40] Indeed, such issues exercised contemporary observers, who produced a rich literature of *Fürstenspiegel*, of theoretical treatises on royal authority, frequently centring on issues of moral norms[41] but also – and with increasing frequency from the later thirteenth century (spurred by the discovery of Aristotle) – on basic abstract principles of political organisation.[42]

Undeniably, the techniques of rigorous argument and critical enquiry housed in universities and law-schools would serve to prise apart long-standing assumptions and ideologies in the fifteenth century and beyond. But before looking at them further, one must stress that change, even when it came, was still couched in terms of returning to ancient republican virtues, as with Machiavelli's historical writings and advice to princes,[43] or of a traditional *Disputatio*, as with Luther's ninety-five theses, 'On the Power of Indulgences'.[44] Few writers would make a virtue of the endemic polyphony and discord: most still set their sights on Christian unity or antiquity. Whatever else may have been stirring in intellectual hothouses, the economic structures were still overwhelmingly

[40] S. Airlie *et al.* (eds), *Staat im frühen Mittelalter* (Vienna, 2005); J. R. Lyon, 'The medieval German state in recent historiography', *German History* 28 (2010), 85–94; S. Bagge, *From Viking Stronghold to Christian Kingdom: State Formation in Norway, 900–1350* (Copenhagen, 2010); W. Reinhard, *Geschichte der Staatsgewalt: eine vergleichende Verfassungsgeschichte Europas von den Anfängen bis zur Gegenwart* (Munich, 1999); N. Berend *et al.*, *Central Europe in the High Middle Ages: Bohemia, Hungary and Poland c. 900–c. 1300* (Cambridge, 2013), 211–12.
[41] Besides Hans Anton's classic study *Fürstenspiegel und Herrscherethos in der Karolingerzeit* (Bonn, 1968), see pp. 262, 263.
[42] See p. 288.
[43] Niccolo Macchiaveli, *Florentine Histories*, tr. L. F. Banfield and H. C. Mansfield (Princeton, 1988); *idem*, *The Prince*, tr. G. Bull (Harmondsworth, 1961).
[44] Martin Luther, *Disputatio pro declaratione virtutis indulgentiarum*, in *Martin Luther, Werke: Kritische Gesamtausgabe, I: Schriften 1512/18* (Weimar, 1883), 233–8; M. Brecht, *Martin Luther, I: His Road to Reformation, 1483–1521*, tr. J. F. Schaaf (Philadelphia, 1985), 190–202; see also pp. 170, 171, 288.

rural and the modes of communication barely susceptible to change; the same goes for the political landscape, at least until the late middle ages.

Exceptions to the rule of documents being preserved mainly in ecclesiastical holdings bear out our overall impression of interlocking elites of secular and clerical landholders with broadly conservative leanings. Thus the Paston letters and papers, kept in family hands until the eighteenth century, illustrate the preoccupation of East Anglian landholding lawyers with their estates and their zeal to protect, expand and bequeath them with the help of title-deeds and testaments (written *and* unwritten); they also deal with church courts and bishops, whose separate status could redound to their own credit.[45] The order of priorities they convey is not so different from what the documents preserved under ecclesiastical auspices attest. And this gives one greater confidence in trying to reconstruct the workings of political culture in the west, for all the clerical filters of our sources and the multiplicity of regions and polities.

The enduring importance attached to clerical endorsement of property-ownership and power takes us back to broader issues of political thought and ideology, as well as the key role of senior clergy in placing rightful rulership in the hands of one man. For the earlier and central middle ages, our heavily clerical sources leave no room for doubt as to which political order was pleasing to God: monarchy. The Old Testament offered models. It allowed for legitimacy by inheritance through royal descent but also for upstarts like David, whom God had favoured with manifest victories. The concept of the king as Lord's Anointed was brought to life by the story of David's anointing by the priest Samuel. This episode was highlighted by churchmen, their enthusiasm stoked by the role of the bishop (or bishops) responsible for anointing and other elements in the inauguration-ritual.[46] Here was a template for rulers wielding their temporal swords, yet in step with bishops and helping uphold their hierarchy. Legitimisation of the forceful (and, usually, their heirs) in return for their adherence to norms was axiomatic to the medieval church. The rationale for some such 'Dual Control' had been set out in antiquity: Pope Gelasius' conception of the 'Two Swords' distinguished between the earthly ruler and the priesthood, enjoying higher moral authority yet needing the former's blade for enforcement and

---

[45] *Paston Letters and Papers of the Fifteenth Century*, rev. edn N. Davis *et al.*, 3 vols (Oxford, 2004–5); H. Castor, *Blood and Roses: The Paston Family in the Fifteenth Century* (London, 2004).

[46] See e.g. J. L. Nelson, 'Inauguration rituals', repr. in her *Politics and Ritual in Early Medieval Europe* (London, 1986), 283–307 at 293–6, 299–300; *eadem*, 'The Lord's Anointed and the People's Choice: Carolingian royal ritual', repr. in her *The Frankish World, 750–900* (London, 1996), 99–132 at 103–6, 108–11. On David, models of rulership in the Old Testament, and unction: J. Canning, *A History of Medieval Political Thought, 300–1450* (London, 1996), 18, 50–9; see also p. 259.

protection.[47] Church Fathers like Archbishop Ambrose of Milan wrote profusely on the duties of the Christian ruler. Their teachings mattered when the 'blood royal' ran out, opening the succession to competition. What they expected of a ruler could tip the balance. After all, bishops had warriors themselves and ample material resources, besides conducting inauguration-rituals. Events after the childless emperor Henry II's death in 1024 exemplify this. Or rather, the priest Wipo saw it so, devising a narrative around Conrad's accession.[48] The dedicatee of Wipo's *Gesta Chuonradi imperatoris* ('Deeds of Emperor Conrad II') was Conrad's son and heir, Henry III, whose succession went uncontested. It is therefore noteworthy that Wipo chose to play upon the conditional element, personal fitness to rule.[49]

By Wipo's time there was a lengthy tradition of historical writing designed to instruct members of the ruling elite, not just to praise or divert. Models of kingly conduct are, for example, plentiful in Bede's *Ecclesiastical History*, and, writing not long after Charlemagne's death, Einhard offers guidelines for rulers, besides depicting his hero in classical guise, adapted from Suetonius.[50] Soon after Henry III's reign, churchmen became less inclined to depict kings as imitators of Christ. Whereas his contemporary, Edward the Confessor, soon gained a virtual hagiography and Charlemagne formally received sainthood in 1165, perhaps with the help of the keepers of his tomb in Aachen,[51] few male rulers were recognised as saints by near-contemporaries thereafter. The exception constituted by St Louis tends to prove the rule, given his singular combination of irenic and ascetic qualities

[47] Gelasius I, *Epistolae Romanorum pontificum genuinae et quae ad eos scriptae sunt a S. Hilaro usque ad Pelagium II., I: A S. Hilario ad S. Hormisdam*, ann. 461–523, ed. A. Thiel (Brunsberg, 1868), no. 12, 349–58; tr. B. Neil and P. Allen, *The Letters of Gelasius I (492–496): Pastor and Micro-Manager of the Church of Rome* (Turnhout, 2014), 73–80; S. Menache, 'The Gelasian theory from a communication perspective: development and decline', *Edad Media: revista de historia* 13 (2012), 57–76; see also pp. 136–7, 386.

[48] GC¹, chs 2–4, 536–51; GC², 60–9; see also p. 252.

[49] GC¹, ch. 3, 546–51; GC², 66–8; S. Bagge, *Kings, Politics, and the Right Order of the World in German Historiography c. 950–1150* (Leiden, 2002), 189–230; see also pp. 258–9, 261, 271.

[50] Bede, *Historia ecclesiastica gentis Anglorum*, ed. and tr. B. Colgrave and R. A. B. Mynors (Oxford, 1969; repr. 2001), e.g. II.14–16 (Edwin), 186–93; III.6–7 (Oswald), 230–3; Einhard, *Life of Charlemagne*, ed. Oswald Holder-Egger, *Vita Karoli magni, MGH SRG 25* (Hanover, 1911); McKitterick, *Perceptions of the Past*, 78–9; G. Becht-Jördens, 'Einharts "Vita Karoli" und die antike Tradition von Biographie und Historiographie. Von der Gattungsgeschichte zur Interpretation', *Mittellateinisches Jahrbuch* 46 (2011), 335–69, esp. 337–46, 348–56.

[51] *The Life of King Edward who Rests at Westminster*, ed. and tr. F. Barlow, 2nd edn (Oxford, 1992), xxix–xliv. For the circumstances behind Charlemagne's coronation: K. Görich, 'Karl der Große – ein "politischer Heiliger" im 12. Jahrhundert?', in L. Körntgen and D. Wassenhoven (eds), *Religion und Politik im Mittelalter: Deutschland und England im Vergleich* (Berlin, 2013), 117–55; see also p. 259.

with crusading. His *Life*, written by a fellow Crusader, tells of their adventures and many vicissitudes.[52] Even when writers were recounting novel situations, such as the creation of a Latin kingdom of Jerusalem, Anglo-Norman and Italo-Norman kingdoms, or the volatile state of affairs in twelfth-century Bruges, they fell back on quite conventional portrayals of good (and bad) leadership.[53]

What is most striking is how familiar from earlier epochs is the checklist of kingly virtues at the end of the middle ages: personal piety, justness and protection of the church as of the poor and the weak, but also firm leadership and martial prowess, doing justice and correcting sinners as necessary. The regard for justice, extolled by Pseudo-Cyprian in, probably, the seventh century, was still deemed essential in the twelfth, along with the qualities enjoined on Carolingian kings by Hincmar of Rheims and other churchmen.[54] Indeed, Mirrors for Princes were turning out similar injunctions in the later middle ages for rulers from Norway and Scotland to the Iberian peninsula, sometimes in the vernacular.[55]

[52] Joinville, *Vie de Saint Louis*, ed. and tr. J. Monfrin (Paris, 1995); tr. M. R. B. Shaw, in *Chronicles of the Crusades* (Harmondsworth, 1963), 161–353; Le Goff, *Saint Louis*, 120–38, 145–6, 155–7, 377–97, 482–3; see also p. 399. For sainted kings: G. Klaniczay, *Holy Rulers and Blessed Princesses: Dynastic Cults in Medieval Central Europe*, tr. E. Pálmai (Cambridge, 2002), discussing St Louis on 243–5, 296–7.

[53] Fulcher of Chartres, *Historia Hierosolymitana*, ed. H. Hagenmeyer (Heidelberg, 1913); tr. F. R. Ryan and H. S. Fink, *A History of the Expedition to Jerusalem, 1095–1127* (New York, 1969); Galbert of Bruges, *De multro, traditione et occisione gloriosi Karoli comitis Flandriarum*, CCCM 131, ed. J. Rider (Turnhout, 1994); tr. J. Rider, *The Murder, Betrayal, and Slaughter of the Glorious Charles, Count of Flanders by Galbert of Bruges* (New York, 2013); J. Rider, *God's Scribe: The Historiographical Art of Galbert of Bruges* (Washington, DC, 2001). For chronicles as a means of bolstering both regional and regnal identity: J. Gillingham, *The English in the Twelfth Century: Imperialism, National Identity, and Political Values* (Woodbridge, 2000); E. Albu, *The Normans in their Histories: Propaganda, Myth, and Subversion* (Woodbridge, 2001); see also p. 263.

[54] *Vincent of Beauvais: On the Instruction of a Prince; and Pseudo Cyprian: The Twelve Abuses of the World*, tr. P. Throop (Charlotte, VT, 2011), 127–9; see also pp. 262, 275. Hincmar set out the moral duties of a king in *De ordine palatii*, ed. and tr. T. Gross and R. Schieffer, *MGH Fontes iuris Germanici antiqui in usum scholarum* 3 (Hanover, 1980); tr. P. Throop, *Hincmar of Rheims: On Kingship, Divorce, Virtues and Vices* (Charlotte, VT, 2014), 365–88; as also in *De regis persona et regio ministerio*, PL 125, cols 833–56; tr. Throop, *On Kingship*, 1–34. See also Jonas of Orléans, *De institutione regia*, ed. and tr. A. Dubreucq (Paris, 1995); Sedulius Scottus, *De rectoribus christianis*, ed. and tr. R. W. Dyson (Woodbridge, 2010) .

[55] *Konungs skuggsjá*, ed. L. Holm-Olsen, 2nd edn (Oslo, 1983); tr. L. M. Larson, *The King's Mirror (Speculum regale – Konungs skuggsjá)* (New York, 1917); K. G. Johansson and E. Kleivane, '*Konungs skuggsjá* and the interplay between universal and particular', in K. G. Johansson and E. Kleivane (eds), *Speculum septentrionale: Konungs skuggsjá and the European Encyclopedia of the Middle Ages* (Oslo, 2018), 9–34; John Ireland, *The Meroure of Wyssdome: Composed for the Use of James IV, King of Scots, AD 1490*, ed. C. Macpherson et al., 3 vols (Edinburgh and London, 1926–90); Alvarus Pelagius, *Speculum regum*, ed. and Portuguese tr. M. Pinto de Meneses, *Espelho dos reis*, 2 vols (Lisbon, 1955–63). For Mirrors for Princes in the other two spheres: pp. 294–5, 322–3, 107–8, 341.

One change is detectible, starting in the more closely regulated realms. Administration – if merely the ability 'to reflect daily upon the text of divine law' – became worthy of royal concern. In twelfth-century Anglo-Norman England, an 'unlettered king' was 'a crowned ass', while Walter Map saw the Exchequer as relatively free from venality, 'for the glance of the just king seems ever to be fresh there'.[56]

Given the elaboration of bureaucracy, allowing for a less itinerant court and peaceable pursuits, and given the literacy and culture of noblewomen in the later middle ages, one might have expected female rulership to become acceptable. However, signs of drastic change – valuing a queen for more than bearing male heirs and exemplifying feminine virtues – are scant.[57] One looks in vain for full-blown counterparts to the *Encomium Emmae*, a work commissioned by Cnut's widow to press her own claims to queenly power alongside those of her two sons.[58] Some figures do stand out – the striking, strong-minded and well-travelled Eleanor of Aquitaine, for instance, despite clerical writers' coolness (at best).[59] And, reflecting the dynamics of the Francophone courts of her day, Christine de Pisan offered many works of counsel to men and women with power. Among these is her *Livre des Trois Vertus*, written around 1405 for Margaret of Burgundy, newly wed to the dauphin Louis de Guyenne, enjoining diplomacy: the wise queen does 'whatever she can to find a way of peace'.[60]

[56] John of Salisbury, *Policraticus: Of the Frivolities of Courtiers and the Footprints of Philosophers*, tr. C. J. Nederman (Cambridge, 1990), 44; Walter Map, *De nugis curialium: Courtiers' Trifles*, ed. and tr. M. R. James, rev. C. N. L. Brooke and R. A. B. Mynors (Oxford, 1983), 508–9. Full-blooded denunciation of Henry II's regime comes in Gerald of Wales, *Liber de principis instructione (Instruction for a Ruler)*, ed. and tr. R. Bartlett (Oxford, 2018). See also pp. 271–2.

[57] This is not to deny the influence or even agency which these qualities could engender, perhaps particularly in the Scandinavian world: A. J. Duggan, 'Introduction', in A. J. Duggan (ed.), *Queens and Queenship in Medieval Europe* (Woodbridge, 1997), xv–xxii; S. Imsen, 'Late medieval Scandinavian queenship', in *ibid.*, 53–73; more generally: T. Earenfight, *Queenship in Medieval Europe* (Basingstoke, 2012); for writers about tenth- and early eleventh-century queens, such as Liudprand of Cremona, Floduard of Rheims and Hrotsvitha of Gandersheim: S. Maclean, *Ottonian Queenship* (Oxford, 2017).

[58] *Encomium Emmae reginae*, ed. and tr. A. Campbell, intro. S. Keynes, 2nd edn (Cambridge, 1998); P. Stafford, 'Emma: the powers of the queen in the eleventh century', in Duggan (ed.), *Queens*, 3–26, esp. 4–8, 19–20, 22–3.

[59] J. Flori, *Eleanor of Aquitaine: Queen and Rebel*, tr. O. Classe (Edinburgh, 2007), 43–5, 109–10, 146–9, 210–31; M. R. Evans, *Inventing Eleanor: The Medieval and Post-Medieval Image of Eleanor of Aquitaine* (London, 2014), 6–32.

[60] Christine de Pisan, *Le Livre des trois vertus*, ch. 9, ed. C. C. Willard and E. Hicks (Paris, 1989), 35; tr. S. Lawson, *The Treasure of the City of Ladies, or, The Book of the Three Virtues*, rev. edn (London, 2003), 22 ; K. Pratt, 'The image of the queen in Old French literature', in Duggan (ed.), *Queens*, 235–59, esp. 237–42, 258; M. Gaude-Ferragu, *Queenship in Medieval France*, tr. A. Krieger (New York, 2016), 86–7 . See also Christine's *Le Livre du corps de policie*, ed. R. H. Lucas (Geneva, 1967); tr. K. L. Forhan, *The Book of the Body Politic* (Cambridge, 1994); *The 'Livre de la Paix' of Christine de Pisan*, ed. C. C. Willard (Gravenhage, 1958).

But if Christine thought empowerment of women could shore up the monarchy, she still saw forcefulness and martial prowess as prerequisite for princes.[61] Indeed, notions of chivalry and courtly violence were thriving in her time. Among their most consummate exponents was the duke of Burgundy. The Order of the Golden Fleece instituted in 1430 by Philip the Good enlisted paragons of chivalrous virtues from near and afar, and his son Charles commissioned a *History of the Golden Fleece* which included a 'Treatise of Advice' for the duke.[62] Burgundian dominions encompassed many towns, literate and culturally sophisticated, and the dukes' attempt to knit these together by identifying with knighthood and heroes from antiquity reflects the appeal of war-leadership and -fellowship, even – perhaps especially – in societies grown rich from advanced craftsmanship and commerce. In similar vein, God-sent victory at Bosworth Field was integral to Henry Tudor's claim to the throne, and he named his firstborn son after King Arthur.[63]

Inauguration-Rituals and Their Connotations

No less traditional were the symbols of monarchy and inauguration-rituals current in the Latin west around 1500. The crown, sceptre and other insignia used for coronations such as those of Henry VII, Louis XI or even Emperor Frederick III did not differ drastically from those in depictions of their earlier medieval predecessors any more than did the underlying ideas.[64] The same goes for the proceedings for investing

[61] Z. E. Zohr, 'True lies and strange mirrors: the uses and abuses of rumor, propaganda, and innuendo during the closing stages of the Hundred Years War', in Z. E. Zohr *et al.* (eds), *Queenship, Gender, and Reputation in the Medieval and Early Modern West, 1060–1600* (Cham, 2016), 51–75 at 63–4; Gaude-Ferragu, *Queenship*, 5, 87, 96–8; on the exceptional figure of Joan of Arc: p. 164; on chivalry: pp. 267–8.

[62] On this text and its conventional accent on 'good counsel': Guillaume Fillastre, *Le Traittié de conseil*, ed. H. Häyrynen (Jyväskylä, 1994), 1–3, 6, 9–14, 17–20 (introduction); on the Order's statutes: D. J. D. Boulton, 'The Order of the Golden Fleece and the creation of Burgundian national identity', in D. J. D. Boulton and J. R. Veenstra (eds), *The Ideology of Burgundy: The Promotion of National Consciousness, 1364–1565* (Leiden, 2006), 21–97 at 27–9; see also p. 169.

[63] S. J. Gunn, 'Henry VII (1457–1509), king of England and lord of Ireland', *ODNB*; R. Horrox, 'Arthur, prince of Wales (1486–1502)', *ODNB*.

[64] J. M. Bak (ed.), *Coronations: Medieval and Early Modern Monarchic Ritual* (Berkeley, CA, 1990); for England: M. A. Hicks, *English Political Culture in the Fifteenth Century* (London, 2002), 28–9; A. Hunt, *The Drama of Coronation: Medieval Ceremony in Early Modern England* (Cambridge, 2008), 4–7, 13–22, 31, 57–8; for France: P. Demouy, *Le Sacre du roi: histoire, symbolique, cérémonial* (Strasbourg, 2016), 138–49; H. Pinoteau, *La Symbolique royale française Ve–XVIIIe siècles* (Paris, 2003), 279–300, 304–15; on Frederick III's mitre crown and on other imperial and royal crowns: H. Trnek, *Lexikon des Mittelalters* 7 (Munich, 1995), s.v. 'Reichsinsignien', cols 623–6; G. Clark, *Symbols of Excellence* (Cambridge, 1986), 97; P. E. Schramm and F. Müterich, *Denkmale der*

a ruler, rendering his reign unimpeachably legitimate. Coronations could be solemn, and highly visible, yet a crown might be worn before any such ceremony, and crown-wearing predated Christianity. In contrast, anointing by the foremost prelates of the polity consecrated one man as God's choice. Reminiscent of Samuel's anointing of David, unction marked him out from brothers and anyone else whose bloodline might qualify them for kingship. Carolingian clerics such as Archbishop Hincmar of Rheims insisted on the transformative properties of these rites, especially unction. Thus in 869 Hincmar stage-managed ceremonial so as to 'liturgify' through coronation and holy oil Charles the Bald's takeover of his late nephew's realm.[65] Key motifs recur in western inauguration-ritual. They are enshrined in texts that are commonly known as coronation *ordines* but in fact contain formulae, rubrics, descriptive passages and much else. Attempting to systematise procedures for legitimising newly acceded rulers along with other liturgical services, they crystallised at imperial level only gradually.[66] Even so – and allowing for variations upon each regime change, proliferation of regalia and minor details – certain texts attest continuity, England's doing so from the late ninth century onwards.[67] The French royal *ordo* took some while to stabilise. A compilation designed for St Louis went beyond Carolingian and Old Testament traditions in highlighting the role in the proceedings of oil brought from heaven for the baptism of Clovis and still kept in the Holy Ampulla. By 1270 all necessary rites and prayers were contained within a single volume, becoming the standard work, ready-for-use by king and queen, from the coronation of Charles VIII

---

deutschen Könige und Kaiser: ein Beitrag zur Herrschergeschichte von Karl dem Grossen bis Friedrich II. 768–1250 (Munich, 1962); P. E. Schramm, *Herrschaftszeichen und Staatssymbolik: Beiträge zu ihrer Geschichte vom dritten bis zum sechzehnten Jahrhundert*, 3 vols (Stuttgart, 1954–6), esp. ii:403–4, 560–82, 619–35, iii:884–95, 904–7, 1019–20, 1066–76, 1081–3; R. Staats, *Die Reichskrone: Geschichte und Bedeutung eines europäischen Symbols* (Kiel, 2006), esp. 18–30, 53–70.

[65] Hincmar of Rheims, 'Ordo coronationis Karoli II. in regno Hlotharii II. factae', *MGH Capitularia regum Francorum* 2, no. 302, ed. A. Boretius and V. Krause (Hanover, 1897), 456–8. Hincmar wrote several comparable texts: Nelson, 'Lord's Anointed', 103–5, 117–19.

[66] Parkes, *Making of Liturgy*, 19–20, 212–14, 218–22; for a reconstructed master-copy of a collection of liturgical texts for use by a bishop, supposedly made in Mainz after 950: C. Vogel *et al.*, *Le Pontifical romanogermanique du dixième siècle*, 3 vols (Rome, 1963–72).

[67] D. H. Turner (ed.), *The Claudius Pontificals (from Cotton MS. Claudius A. iii in the British Museum)* (Chichester, 1971), 1–88; J. L. Nelson, 'The first use of the Second Anglo-Saxon ordo', in J. Barrow and A. Wareham (eds), *Myth, Rulership, Church and Charters: Essays in Honour of Nicholas Brooks* (Aldershot, 2008), 117–26; D. Pratt, 'The making of the second English coronation ordo', *Anglo-Saxon England* 46 (2017), 147–258; also J. A. Green, *Forging the Kingdom: Power in English Society, 973–1189* (Cambridge, 2017), 80–4.

in 1484 until the French Revolution.[68] In the meantime Charles V had, in 1365, signed off a text he had commissioned. The thirty-eight illuminations of his *Livre du sacre des rois de France* demonstrate how due performance of the rites, especially anointing from the Holy Ampulla (depicted ten times), renders Charles accountable to no earthly superior, a unique blend of the spiritual and the temporal. This did not, however, save the book from captivity during the Hundred Years War; it remains in English hands.[69]

Such an episode serves to warn how reliant we are upon the *ordines* and narratives penned by churchmen for data concerning inauguration-ritual. Churchmen are represented as mediating divine grace and setting the monarch indelibly apart from other laypersons. Evaluation of how these rites were actually carried out or understood is therefore difficult.[70] The clergy framed royal duties, encapsulating them in the oaths kings swore before being crowned. These are akin to what Hincmar – first storyteller of Clovis' heavenly oil – prescribed for Charles the Bald in 869. For example, according to the coronation-oath taken by an English king in the 970s, the church of God and all the people would hold true peace under his rule; he would uphold justice and mercy in all his judgements and 'forbid robbery and all unrighteous things to all orders'. Translated from Latin into Old English, the text was thought worth copying, together with a sermon on kingship, for a book of homilies in the mid-eleventh century.[71]

Texts like this present façades, glassily smooth, of an ecclesiastical-kingly establishment. However, they do not exclude other sources of legitimisation. 'Election' by 'the people' and acclamations by magnates (often tantamount to 'the people'!) generally featured in inauguration-ritual: God's voice was heard this way, and not exclusively through liturgical acts performed by clergymen, especially in default of a strong

[68] J. Le Goff *et al.*, *Le Sacre royal à l'époque de Saint Louis d'après le manuscrit latin 1246 de la BNP* (Paris, 2001); *Ordines coronationis Franciae: Texts and Ordines for the Coronation of Frankish and French Kings and Queens in the Middle Ages*, ed. R. A. Jackson, 2 vols (Philadelphia, 1995), ii:380–418, 469–522; Le Goff, *Saint Louis*, 88–90, 472; Demouy, *Le Sacre du roi*, 80–1, 100.

[69] C. F. O'Meara, *Monarchy and Consent: The Coronation Book of Charles V of France, British Library, Cotton MS Tiberius B. VIII* (London, 2001), 306 (Latin text); Demouy, *Le Sacre du roi*, 100, 102; French tr. of entire text, *ibid.*, 178–89; illuminations, *ibid.* 190–231.

[70] To the point of impossibility, according to P. Buc, *The Dangers of Ritual: Between Early Medieval Texts and Social Scientific Study* (Princeton, 2001). However, that overall assessments are feasible through setting all available evidence (including charters and seals) within context is shown by J. Dale, *Inauguration and Liturgical Kingship in the Long Twelfth Century* (York, 2019); see also pp. 173, 394.

[71] M. Clayton, 'The Old English *Promissio Regis*', *Anglo-Saxon England* 37 (2008), 91–150 at 148–9 (text and tr.), 106–30 (exegesis of contents); C. Breay and J. Story (eds), *Anglo-Saxon Kingdoms: Art, Word, War* (London, 2018), no. 119, p. 300; see also p. 279.

dynastic claimant. The notion of God conveying His choice through multiple means had ancient roots, reinforced by the Franks' self-image of being a Chosen People.[72] It meshed with rulership involving counsel and collaboration, underpinned by oaths. Such a 'discourse of consensus' was characteristic of Carolingian political order and the polities which emerged from it, but also of Anglo-Saxon England.[73] Coronation *ordines* reflect all this: texts like Charles V's *Livre du sacre*, which makes no mention of approbation of the people, are the exception, not the rule.[74]

Another potential constraint on the king arose from his pledging justice in the coronation-oath. Admittedly, justice was quite a malleable concept. Presenting himself as lawmaker, formulator and enforcer of universal norms could set a ruler on an autocratic pedestal comparable to early Christian emperors like Justinian, if not the contemporary *basileus*.[75] Carolingian rulers were apt to cast instructions in normative terms, supplementing such pronouncements as Charlemagne's *Admonitio generalis* of 789.[76] Anglo-Saxon rulers showed similar tendencies, and, soon after seizing control in 1016, the Danish Cnut put his name to a number of sets of laws.[77] Subsequent rulers of fairly tight-knit polities inclined towards grandiose pronouncements. Thus in 1231 the *Liber Augustalis* styled its promulgator, Frederick II: 'we, whom [God] elevated beyond hope of man to the pinnacle of the Roman empire'.[78] And, as noted already, the fifteenth century saw a plethora of codifications. Rulers like Charles VII saw them as means of self-aggrandisement, while statutes of English kings make resounding declarations of concern for their people.

Despite such grandstanding, coronation-oaths in polities like England could bind a king not only to general principles but also to guaranteeing

[72] For the concept of *vox populi* as *vox Dei*: Nelson, 'Lord's Anointed', 105–6, 117–20, 127; for the German election of 1024: p. 258; see also B. Weiler, 'The *rex renitens* and the medieval idea of kingship, ca. 900–ca. 1250', *Viator* 31 (2000), 1–42; *idem*, 'Tales of first kings and the culture of kingship in the west, *c.* 1050–1200', *Viator* 46 (2015), 101–28.
[73] Costambeys *et al.*, *Carolingian World*, 321.   [74] Demouy, *Le Sacre du roi*, 102.
[75] See pp. 264, 281–2, 295. On Justinian: T. Honoré, *Tribonian* (London, 1978), 15–30, 35–9.
[76] *Die Admonitio generalis Karls des Grossen*, ed. H. Mordek *et al.*, *MGH Fontes iuris Germanici antiqui in usum scholarum* 16 (Hanover, 2012); J. L. Nelson, *King and Emperor: A New Life of Charlemagne* (London, 2019), 258–67.
[77] F. Liebermann, *Die Gesetze der Angelsachsen*, 3 vols (Halle, 1898–1916), i:612–19; M. K. Lawson, *Cnut, England's Viking King 1016–35* (Stroud, 2004), 55–65, 188–91; Clayton, 'Old English *Promissio Regis*', 136–47; T. Lambert, *Law and Order in Anglo-Saxon England* (Oxford, 2017), 164–5, 168, 292–3.
[78] *Die Konstitutionen Friedrichs II. für das Königreich Sizilien*, ed. W. Stürner, *MGH Constitutiones et acta publica imperatorum et regum 2, Supplementum* (Hanover, 1996), 147; tr. J. M. Powell, *The Liber Augustalis: or, Constitutions of Melfi, Promulgated by the Emperor Frederick II for the Kingdom of Sicily in 1231* (Syracuse, NY, 1971), 4 . See also A. Romano (ed.), ... *colendo iustitiam et iura condendo ... Federico II legislatore del regno di Sicilia nell'Europa del duecento* (Rome, 1997).

rights and customs, particularly when his succession was contestable. Conrad II undertook to confirm Burgundian laws and even barbarous Saxon customs, while a 'Charter of Liberties' was circulated just after Henry I's crowning at Westminster in 1100; this precedent was of avail to the magnates extracting a 'Magna Carta' from King John in 1215.[79] Codifications can themselves represent responses to petitions coming in from far beyond the royal nucleus in an attempt to channel ever-rolling streams of judgements and pronouncements into some sort of orderly pool. Indeed, codification could take place haphazardly and regionally, unbidden by any ruler. Our knowledge of Charlemagne's capitularies owes much to the manuscripts of tenth-century Ottonian clerical collectors and tabulators, as well as to near-contemporaries in ruling circles.[80]

More ad hoc than formal declarations of law, codifications show how readily instructions might metamorphose into regulations. The collection Abbot Ansegis of Saint-Wandrille made during Louis the Pious' reign has been published,[81] and samples of the output from the milieus of Charlemagne and his successors are available in translation. Many texts offer rulings on particular issues of property-rights or services due. Occasionally, though, one catches Charlemagne's voice in exchanges with distant officials[82] or his vision, extending to repair-work on churches and monasteries in the Holy Land.[83] The Carolingians'

---

[79] Henry I's 'Charter of Liberties', ed. W. Stubbs, *Select Charters and Other Illustrations of English Constitutional History*, rev. H. W. C. Davis, 9th edn (Oxford, 1921), 117–19; *Acta of Henry I*, ed. and tr. R. Sharpe (in preparation) (draft available: https://actswilliam2henry1 .files.wordpress.com/2013/10/h1-a-liberties-2013-1.pdf [accessed 16 February 2020]); J. A. Green, *The Government of England under Henry I* (Cambridge, 1986), 98–106. For an edition and translation of Magna Carta (which had no master copy): J. C. Holt, *Magna Carta*, 3rd edn, rev. J. Hudson and G. Garnett (Cambridge, 2015), 378–98.

[80] C. Leyser, 'Introduction: the transformation of law in the late and post-Roman world', *EME* 27 (2019), 5–11 at 9; S. Patzold, 'Capitularies in the Ottonian realm', *EME* 27 (2019), 112–32 at 115–19, 131–2.

[81] Ansegis, *Collectio capitularium*, ed. G. Schmitz, *Die Kapitulariensammlung des Ansegis*, *MGH Capitularia regum Francorum* n.s. 1 (Hanover, 1996).

[82] In e.g. Charlemagne's answers to written questions put by an agent (*missus*): 'Responsa misso cuidam data', *MGH Capitularia regum Francorum* 1, no. 58, ed. A. Boretius (Hanover, 1883), 145–6; J. L. Nelson, 'The voice of Charlemagne', repr. in her *Courts, Elites and Gendered Power in the Early Middle Ages: Charlemagne and Others* (Aldershot, 2007), no. 13, 76–88 at 80; Nelson, *King and Emperor*, 248–51, 473; J. Davis, *Charlemagne's Practice of Empire* (Cambridge, 2015), 294–8. For some capitularies in translation: *Charlemagne: Translated Sources*, tr. P. D. King (Lancaster, 1987), 202–68; *The Reign of Charlemagne: Documents on Carolingian Government and Administration*, tr. H. R. Loyn and J. Percival (London, 1975), 46–105; *Carolingian Civilization: A Reader*, ed. P. E. Dutton, 2nd edn (Peterborough, ON, 2004), 65–95, 147–52.

[83] See M. McCormick, *Charlemagne's Survey of the Holy Land: Wealth, Personnel, and Buildings of a Mediterranean Church between Antiquity and the Middle Ages* (Washington, DC, 2011). See p. 501.

championing of the written word eclipsed that of their Merovingian predecessors, whose recourse to it for governance may have been extensive.[84] But the Carolingians' assiduousness was such that their texts looked useful to Ottonian churchmen seeking guidelines and data for conducting and settling disputes.[85] Such collections show how much common ground – figuratively and literally – clerical and lay elites shared before and even after fissures deepened in the eleventh century. Issues of property are, as Stephen Humphreys remarks (see pp. 24–5), fundamental to political culture. In Francia and other parts of the west with bishoprics and long-established monasteries, the modus operandi amounted to ongoing review of rights, services and mutual obligations, riven with tensions usually containable, and ultimately consensual. These were too far-reaching for any king to begin to resolve, and mostly they did not revolve around him.[86] Rulers found themselves presiding over configurations of small worlds whose leading protagonists wrangled and made their own arrangements about property, status and power. Numerous texts register their bids at reaching settlements in the French- and German-speaking lands whose rulers' respective ranges of personal intervention were, in the tenth to thirteenth centuries, the confines of the Île-de-France and so stretched that the royal presence was in many areas fitful, if not inconceivable.[87]

General arrangements could gain normative standing and eventually be written down. 'Customs' or 'the good old law' had the advantage of being geared to localities and of adaptability to changing circumstances. Those which made it into writing give us only an inkling of goings-on.[88] Yet there were enough fixed points in the cultural landscape of the Latin west for

---

[84] G. Barrett and G. Woodhuysen, 'Assembling the *Austrasian Letters* at Trier and Lorsch', *EME* 24 (2016), 3–57, esp. 45–9.

[85] Patzold, 'Capitularies in the Ottonian realm', 120, 122–4, 127–32.

[86] Patzold, 'Capitularies in the Ottonian realm', 131–2.

[87] For an example of a settlement in southern France *c.*1212: *Cartulaire de Trinquetaille*, ed. P. Armaguier (Gap, 1972), nos 210–13; for further instances of *concordiae* from southern and western France: F. L. Cheyette, 'Suum cuique tribuere', *French Historical Studies* 6 (1970), 287–99 at 291–3; S. White, '"Pactum ... legem vincit et amor judicium": the settlement of disputes by compromise in eleventh-century western France', *American Journal of Legal History* 22 (1978), 281–308; P. Geary, 'Vivre en conflit dans une France sans État: typologie des mécanismes de règlement des conflits (1050–1200)', *Annales: économies, sociétés, civilisations* 41 (1986), 1107–33; see also pp. 166, 380; for German royal itineraries: J. Bernhardt, *Itinerant Kingship and Royal Monasteries in Early Medieval Germany, c.936–1075* (Cambridge, 1993), 51–75 and maps 4 and 5 on 318, 319. Le Goff observes that, for all his conscientiousness and the vigour of his officials, Louis IX's 'most frequent stays were in the Île-de-France': *Saint Louis*, 428.

[88] For an instance of 'remembered' custom from twelfth-century England: H. Cam, 'An East Anglian shire-moot of Stephen's reign, 1148–53', *EHR* 39 (1924), 568–71 at 570; M. Clanchy, 'Remembering the past and the good old law', *History* 55 (1970), 165–70 at 173–4.

even quite small-scale property-owners to be the subject of formularies that provided for the drawing up of deeds for many kinds of land transactions, besides settlement of disputes. Some early medieval formularies have been edited.[89] There was also sufficient consensus for landholders in Catalonia to draw up elaborate pacts with one another (*convenientiae*), encompassing general matters of order and power as well as property transactions.[90] Agencies of uniform enforcement may have been lacking. But in most societies, brazen flouting of pacts and charters solemnised before assemblies or eminent witnesses was to put at risk one's local standing; and written agreements were most likely to lie in ecclesiastical archives, with clergy (backed up by the saints) acting as conscience-keepers or -prickers.[91] To that extent, such texts together with more general sets of 'good customs' reflect widespread assumptions besides recording details of real estate. So for all the sectional interests and particularism behind these texts, representing constraints on any would-be active king, currents were also running in favour of consensus. And that was, in certain circumstances, what sole rulership could foster and conjoin. It is, after all, an implication of the mutation into law of the rulings of Carolingian decision-makers, at the hands of later churchmen.[92]

Variations of Kingship, Lordship and Partnership among Western Polities

Thus the commitment to peace, justice and order which a king swore at his coronation could mean anything from pious gesture to justification for intervening in far-flung localities. Much depended on his personal qualities, his relations with family members and senior churchmen, and what

[89] A. Rio, *Legal Practice and the Written Word in the Early Medieval Ages: Frankish Formulae, c. 500–1000* (Cambridge, 2009), esp. 21–4, 33–40, 183–6, 206–11.

[90] Kosto, *Making Agreements*, 268–89 (drawing on extensive edited and unpublished texts).

[91] See e.g. W. C. Brown, 'The *gesta municipalia* and the public validation of documents in Frankish Europe', in Brown *et al.* (eds), *Documentary Culture*, 95–124, esp. 116–24; Innes, 'Memory, orality and literacy'; C. Insley, 'Rhetoric and ritual in late Anglo-Saxon charters', in M. Mostert and P. Barnwell (eds), *Medieval Legal Process: Physical, Spoken and Written Performance in the Middle Ages* (Turnhout, 2011), 109–21 at 112–17, 120–1; Keynes, 'Church councils, royal assemblies', 61–8, 102–6, 125–6, 137–9; C. Gauvard and R. Jacob (eds), *Les Rites de la justice: gestes et rituels judicaires au Moyen Âge* (Paris, 2000); B. Lemesle, *Conflits et justice au Moyen Âge* (Paris, 2008), 35–46; Hyams, *Rancor and Reconciliation*; C. Wickham, *Courts and Conflict in Twelfth-Century Tuscany* (Oxford, 2003), 74–85, 281–92. For what may lurk behind written texts – of charters and deeds, as well as those more obviously designed for performance: C. Symes, 'The medieval archive and the history of theatre: assessing the written and unwritten evidence for premodern performance', *Theatre Survey* 52 (2011), 29–58.

[92] P. Wormald, *Lawyers and the State: The Varieties of Legal History: Selden Society Lecture* (London, 2006).

material resources and full-time administrators were at his disposal. Not that all western kings looked to such inauguration-ritual to solemnise their ascendancy or made much of law and justice as paramount duties, especially those whose powers of coercion were limited.[93] But in those realms where the panoply of church-managed rites and ideals of kingship loomed large, certain patterns of behaviour do emerge. Although largely clerically derived until the later middle ages, our sources do bring out the importance of other parts of what amounted to the body politic in the ceremonial process of legitimising a ruler and in governance itself. Indeed, such phrases as 'with the counsel of the barons' recur in the acts and formal declarations of many western kings. These formulae contrast with the self-designations of Byzantine emperors and Muslim caliphs as God-crowned or -sent to take care of 'the common good' or the *umma*.[94] They simultaneously reflect and solemnise the indispensability of collaboration between the king and secular elites, especially the higher nobility. And in England the themes of consultation, access to justice and reciprocal obligations – already manifest at Henry I's accession and formulated in Magna Carta – found expression in the poems, manifestos and reform proposals and counter-proposals accompanying the confrontations of the barons with the king, headed by Simon de Montfort, between 1258 and 1265.[95]

These affirmations and protestations chime in with the overall impression given by a variety of sources: that a kind of partnership in military undertakings and quasi-judicial arbitration was, along with the general exercise of 'lordship' over landed property, the modus operandi of western monarchies. If there are already plenty of signs of this in the earlier medieval period, the evidence only builds up to an imposing mass from the twelfth and thirteenth centuries on, and then only for the few realms that have left quite full traces of their workings. Nonetheless, three sets of phenomena hint at what might be termed popular demand for a monarch's exercise of his authority, demand best-attested on the part of the individuals and groupings of elites but increasingly in evidence among broader sectors of society, too. These are petitions; recourse for justice to royal (or royally authorised) law-courts; and assemblies engaging in matters purportedly of common concern to the ruler and his subjects. These do not constitute

[93] See e.g. the situation implied in T. M. Charles-Edwards, *The Welsh Laws* (Cardiff, 1989); see also pp. 286, 404.

[94] See pp. 116, 348–9, 353–5, 292–4, 297.

[95] E.g. *The Song of Lewes*, ed. C. L. Kingsford (Oxford, 1890); the manifesto of 1264 in *Documents of the Baronial Movement of Reform and Rebellion, 1258–1267*, ed. and tr. R. E. Treharne and I. J. Sanders (Oxford, 1973), 270–3; for the key text making up the reform programme, known as the Provisions of Oxford: *ibid.*, 96–113; Carpenter, *Reign of Henry III*, 80–2, 94–103, 221–37, 261–80; Brand, *Kings, Barons and Justices*, 15–41, 140–6, 161–4.

a checklist for successful polities or a line of development. Indeed, they sometimes illustrate the paradox that a distant figure lacking in material resources could enjoy respect and be sought after as arbiter or tie-breaker when individuals', communities' or grand families' disputes and grievances had gone unresolved.

The variations over place and time are, as ever in the west, vast. Much depended on how sharp a distinction was drawn between the royal family (or families) and other noble houses; on how far leading families engaged directly in royal governance or effectively managed quasi-polities of their own; and also on the constant involvement of more localised elites, the lesser landholders and the gilds and other groupings of substantial burghers in towns.[96] But certain tendencies emerge from the sources, offering variations on the theme of balance between the ruler and other elites, viewed from the perspective of petitions, assemblies and the quest for an ultimate – and singular – locus of judgement and authority. Foremost among what might be termed the confederate model is the German-led empire, whose extent virtually dictated the sharing of power and where the monarch's material resources dwindled to very modest proportions. The Golden Bull of 1356 merely ratified a long-standing state of affairs and provided for the empire's future in the form of conventions of electors drawn from top princely families and bishoprics.[97] From the twelfth century on, it was territorial principalities that began to form complexes of lordships, involving rights to services, castles, revenues and the doing of justice. The variations between them and fluctuations in their forms of development have left their mark in the sources. For example, by 1200 the Babenberger, dominant over the Austrian March, had established an *urbarium* (register of possessions) to facilitate exactions and enshrined their princely lordship in a concession from the emperor, now known as the *Privilegium Minus*.[98] And in the northwest, officials of the counts of Flanders and Hainault and Brabant were defining their lordships and recording their transactions in writing.[99]

---

[96] See pp. 156–65, 280, 281, 384.
[97] *Die goldene Bulle Kaiser Karls IV.*, ed. K. Zeumer (Weimar, 1908), 5–38 (text); see also pp. 169–71, 396.
[98] *MGH Diplomata Friedrich I.* 1: *1152–8*, ed. H. Appelt *et al.* (Hanover, 1975), 259–60 (no. 151); tr. G. A. Loud, 'Appendix', in G. A. Loud and J. Schenk (eds), *The Origins of the German Principalities, 1100–1350* (Abingdon, 2017), 347– 9; for sources concerning the Babenberger from the twelfth century onwards: *Niederösterreichisches Urkundenbuch*, ed. M. Weltin *et al.*, 3 vols to date (St Pölten, 2008–), ii: *1078–1158*; iii: *1156–1182*.
[99] For sources: A. Dierkens and D. Guilardian, 'Actes princiers et naissance des principautés territoriales: du duché de Basse-Lotharingie au duché de Brabant (XIe–XIIIe siècles)', in T. de Hemptinne and J.-M. Duvosquel (eds), *Chancelleries princières et 'Scriptoria' dans les anciens Pays-Bas Xe–XVe siècles* (Brussels, 2010), 243–58; E. de Paermentier, 'La chancellerie comtale en Flandre et en Hainaut sous Baudouin VI/IX (1195–1206) et pendant la régence de Philippe Ier de Namur (1206–1212)', in *ibid.*, 259–84.

But nothing like a chancery with overall responsibility for court proceedings and tax returns is discernible in most principalities before the fourteenth century. There was no clear-cut hierarchy of jurisdiction, and the emperor's judicial court has been described as 'a collective tribunal' convening under his 'presidency': the 'privileges' issued by Frederick I Barbarossa were more manifestos than documents of binding legal authority.[100] This balance of interests and principles is discernible in the declarations issued by rulers, notably the imperial peace (*Reichslandfrieden*) Frederick II issued at Mainz in 1235. Affirming a peace without end across the German lands, Frederick announced the appointment of a new official, a *justiciarius*, complete with staff, to deal with all cases and complaints put before him, but it also confirmed many of the princes' privileges and practices and left feud as a legitimate response to denial of justice.[101] Although far from being implemented to the letter, it enshrined the role of the emperor as senior arbitrator and was the first text of this sort to be issued in German as well as Latin. Indeed, Rudolf of Hapsburg and subsequent claimants to the imperial title renewed Frederick's *Reichslandfrieden*, and a series of *justiciarii* held office.[102] Although the emperor was in no position to enforce his agents' judgements, leaving effective rulership to the princes and counts, petitions continued to roll in, crowds turned out to meet him at city-gates and assemblies convened in his presence – albeit often independently of him, too. The idea of a glorious Romano-German past was kept alive partly by such advocates of empire as Alexander von Roes and Conrad von Megenberg, whose treatises seem to reflect a broader discourse, oral as well as textual.[103] The notion that imperial monarchy was prerequisite for political (and religious) order seems to have remained compelling, transcending princely and regional differences and rivalries and fostering a sense of 'Germanness'.[104] The

[100] T. Reuter, 'Mandate, privilege, court judgement: techniques of rulership in the age of Frederick Barbarossa', repr. in *MPMM*, 413–31 at 423, 419. For the sort of case and documents underpinning Reuter's statement: *MGH Diplomata Friedrich I.* 1, 118–21 (nos 71, 72).

[101] *MGH Constitutiones* 2, ed. L. Weiland (Hanover, 1896), 241–63 (no. 196); *Regesta imperii* 5.3, ed. J. F. Böhmer *et al.* (Innsbruck, 1901), no. 2100.

[102] *Regesta imperii* 6.1, ed. O. Redlich (Innsbruck, 1898), no. 1357; see also p. 279; J. F. Battenberg, *Lexikon des Mittelalters* 7, s.v. 'Reichshofgericht', cols 622–3.

[103] Alexander von Roes, *Memoriale de prerogativa Romani imperii*, in *Alexander von Roes: Schriften*, ed. H. Grundmann and H. Heimpel, *MGH Staatsschriften des späteren Mittelalters* 1.1 (Stuttgart, 1958), 91–148; *idem*, *Noticia seculi*, in *ibid.*, 149–71; Conrad von Megenberg, *De translatione Romani imperii*, in *Unbekannte kirchenpolitische Streitschriften aus der Zeit Ludwigs des Bayern (1327–1354)*, *II: Texte*, ed. R. Scholz (Rome, 1914), 249–345; see also *Politische Lyrik des deutschen Mittelalters*, *I: Von Friedrich II. bis Ludwig dem Bayern*, ed. U. Müller (Göppingen, 1972).

[104] L. Scales, *The Shaping of German Identity: Authority and Crisis, 1245–1414* (Cambridge, 2012), 96–7, 113–25, 204–13, 224–35, 243–59, 289–94, 531–6.

material tatters of the empire were no impediment and may, indeed, have exerted a positive magnetism, as in the case of commonwealths and imperial regimes in our other spheres.[105]

Another example of the confederate model might be the kingdom of Hungary. Although relatively small in territorial terms, its components bear comparison with the western empire in their diversity, comprising substantial Jewish, Islamic and non-Christian (Cuman) groupings and a sizable number of towns. Quite full documentation survives of the privileges and laws kings issued to such groupings in the thirteenth and fourteenth centuries. These offered protection and access to the king's judgement in return for loyalty and rendering of taxes or military service. Although much of the evidence is prescriptive, rather than directly attesting practice, the groupings do seem to have enjoyed a fair degree of legal autonomy in handling their own internal affairs.[106] While the royal insignia came to incorporate a Byzantine crown, the coronation-ritual with its oaths and terminology denoting estates of the realm was unambiguously 'Latin'.[107] The prominence of a few families of 'barons' recalls some other western polities. Indeed, the Golden Bull of 1222, setting out the rights of 'servants of the king' (in effect, lesser nobles and castle warriors) alongside those of barons, is sometimes compared with England's Magna Carta, and it was confirmed in the fourteenth century and subsequently.[108] Other bulls, such as that of 1267, even conceded the right of the representatives of the nobility to meet yearly with the ruler to correct abuses and infringement of their privileges.[109]

[105] See p. 220, but for reservations pp. 195–7.
[106] For a careful review of the sources for the legal position of these groupings: N. Berend, *At the Gate of Christendom: Jews, Muslims and 'Pagans' in Medieval Hungary, c.1000– c.1301* (Cambridge, 2001), 74–101. For the relatively full data (including accounts of cases), see the first five volumes of *Magyar-zsidó oklevéltár (Monumenta Hungariae Judaica)*, ed. S. Scheiber and A. Friss, 18 vols (Budapest, 1903–80).
[107] On the crown: J. Deér, *Die heilige Krone Ungarns* (Vienna, 1966), 72–80, 83–8; C. J. Hilsdale, 'The social life of the Byzantine gift: the royal crown of Hungary re-invented', *Art History* 31 (2008), 602–31 at 613–15, 620–4 (that the crown was purpose-built is overwhelmingly likely: *ibid.*, 608–9, 617–19); on Hungarian coronation-ritual: J. M. Bak, 'Holy lance, holy crown, holy dexter: sanctity of insignia in medieval east central Europe', repr. in his *Studying Medieval Rulers and Their Subjects* (Farnham, 2010), no. 6, 56–65.
[108] For the definitive Latin text of the Golden Bull, with introduction: G. Érszegi, 'Az aranybulla', *Fejér Megyei Történeti Évkönyv* 6 (1972), 5–26. It is reproduced in L. Besenyei *et al.* (eds), *De Bulla Aurea Andreae II Regis Hungariae MCCXXII* (Verona, 1999), 23–9, and in *Online Decreta regni mediaevalis Hungariae (The Laws of the Medieval Kingdom of Hungary)*, ed. and tr. J. M. Bak *et al.* (2019) https://digitalcom mons.usu.edu/lib_mono/4, 156–71; M. Rady, *Customary Law in Hungary: Courts, Texts, and the Tripartitum* (Oxford 2015), 78–81.
[109] *Online Decreta regni mediaevalis Hungariae*, ed. and tr. Bak *et al.*, 183–9; Berend *et al.*, *Central Europe*, 428–9.

From 1277 on, assemblies of the realm were attended by barons and representatives of the nobles and commons. The barons' hold on vast tracts of land made them potentially autonomous, and a chronicle written *c.*1200 set out to depict them as descendants of the conquering heroes of 300 years earlier, whose rights to the lands seized had merely been confirmed by the king.[110] There were, however, enough fertile lands and lucrative commercial exchanges both to sustain numerous lesser landholders and to yield substantial revenues to the king and make service on his behalf worthwhile. The barons' insistence on the *communitas* of the realm found expression in Simon de Kéza's *Gesta Hungarorum*, depicting their past feats as rightful holders of power and electors of the king.[111]

Competition for resources and status and a stake in the polity was less keen in loose-knit structures spread across extensive areas with only limited agrarian potential. Thus Norway's inhabitants were, outside the area of Oslo fjord, scattered, and only a very few noble families disposing of large landed estates are discernible in our sources, at least before the fourteenth century. These sources are, admittedly, quite meagre, consisting to a large extent of prescriptive texts and sagas. But the law-codes offer a coherent picture of local and regional assemblies of mostly lesser landholders, capable of resolving disputes, raising taxes and marshalling levies for ship service in times of war, with peasants obliged to contribute.[112] The king relied on them, having few warriors permanently at his disposal and only a small staff of administrators. Although texts like the thirteenth-century *Konungs skuggsjá* ('King's Mirror') and the *National Law* represent the monarch as the Lord's Anointed and insist on displays of deference at his court, the working assumption of some kind of contract between the king and his people or his men permeates other texts, such as the *Hirðskrá* ('Book of the Retinue [*hirð*]') which regulated the rights and duties of the king's retainers.[113]

---

[110] *Gesta Hungarorum*, ed. A. Jakubovich, *Scriptores rerum Hungaricarum* 1 (Budapest, 1937), 13–117; ed. and tr. M. Rady *et al.*, *Anonymi Bele regis notarii Gesta Hungarorum et Magistri Rogerii Epistola in miserabile Carmen super destructione regni Hungarie per Tartaros facta* (Budapest and New York, 2010), 2–129; see also p. 270.

[111] Simon de Kéza, *Gesta Hungarorum*, ed. and tr. L. Vészpremy and F. Schaer, with J. Sczücs (Budapest, 1999), 1–185.

[112] *Frostatingslagen*, ed. R. Keyser and P. A. Munch, in *Norges gamle Love indtil 1387*, ed. R. Keyser, P. A. Munch *et al.*, 5 vols (Christiania, 1846–95) i:119–258; Norwegian tr. J. R. Hagland and J. Sandnes, *Frostatingslova* (Oslo, 1994); *Den eldre Gulatingslova*, ed. B. Eithun *et al.* (Oslo, 1994).

[113] *Konungs skuggsjá*, ed. Holm-Olsen; tr. Larson, *King's Mirror*; *Hirðskråen: Hirdloven til Norges konge og hans håndgangne menn: Etter AM322 fol.*, ed. and tr. S. Imsen (Oslo, 2000); German tr. R. Meissner, *Das norwegische Gefolgschaftsrecht (Hirðskrá)* (Weimar, 1938). For idealisation of a faraway, pious and powerful ruler in Haakon IV's 'Mirror for Princes': R. Scheel, '"He wanted to meet no one but the mightiest man in the world":

In more than one sense, the tiers of assemblies making up the Norwegian polity speak for themselves, and, although treaties and charters mention a 'council of the realm' (*ríkis ráð*) from 1319 onwards,[114] the king does not seem to have looked to any coterie of aristocratic families to sustain him at court or perform administrative duties in far-flung regions. Ultimately, the compact between ruler and smallholders finds expression – and not simply idealising – in the *National Law* of the 1270s, written in their name:

> In the name of the same Jesus Christ, our rightful Norwegian king, His servant, shall decide over commands and bans and our expeditions and rule by law and not against law, for God's praise and honour, for his own benefit, and for our needs. We shall not deny him *leidang* or mobilisation if he decrees according to the rules which here follow.[115]

Across the North Sea, property-holding and power inclined more in the direction of a limited number of elite families. They vied for possession of extensive landed estates and dealt with the occupant of the throne collectively or individually on near-equal terms, while enjoining loyalty towards him on lowlier orders of society. Much depended on such issues as the fertility of land and its accessibility and scale. Thus lowland England could be treated as a 'community of the realm' liable to Common Law that was, by 1300, distinct from, yet complementary to, statutes of the king made in Parliament, and with potential referral of petitions, grievances and disputes to the King's Bench.[116] Such was the efficacy of this apparatus that the widow of a freeholder murdered near Newark in 1295 was able to bring an appeal directly before the Bench,

---

imagining Byzantium in Norse romance', in J. Shepard *et al.* (eds), *Byzantine Spheres: The Byzantine Commonwealth Re-evaluated* (Oxford, forthcoming).

[114] *Diplomatarium Norvegicum*, ed. C. C. A. Lange *et al.*, 23 vols (Christiana and Oslo, 1847–2011), viii:73–6 (no. 50).

[115] *Nyere Lands-Lov* III.1 (*Landværnsbolk*), in *Norges gamle Love*, ed. Keyser, Munch *et al.* ii:1–178 at 33; tr. from Bagge, *From Viking Stronghold to Christian Kingdom*, 365–77 at 374.

[116] *The Statutes of the Realm, I: 1101–1377*, ed. A. Luders *et al.* (London, 1810); also *Curia Regis Rolls ... Preserved in the Public Record Office*, ed. C. T. Flower *et al.*, 20 vols (London, 1922–2006) (covering the period from 1196 to 1250); *The Earliest English Law Reports*, ed. P. A. Brand, 4 vols to date (London, 1996–2007) (covering the period from 1268 to 1290); J. R. Maddicott, 'Edward I and the lessons of baronial reform: local government 1258–1280', in P. R. Coss and S. D. Lloyd (eds), *Thirteenth Century England* 1 (Woodbridge, 1985), 1–30, esp. 13–16, 27–8; J. R. Maddicott, 'Parliament and the people in medieval England', *Parliamentary History* 35 (2016), 336–51, esp. 341–3; on the development of statutes and the concept of the 'community of the realm': J. R. Maddicott, *The Origins of the English Parliament, 924–1327* (Oxford, 2010), 139–47, 228–32, 282–4, 324–5; also P. A. Brand, 'English thirteenth century legislation', in Romano (ed.), *... colendo iustitiam et iura condendo ...*, 325–44, esp. 339–44; Brand, *Kings, Barons and Justices*, 324–5, 331–2. See also p. 402.

citing three knights of the shire as responsible.[117] Alternative courts of justice were seldom proof against appeals to the King's Bench from dissatisfied parties, eventually not even those of the lords overseeing the Welsh March.[118] The demand for rectification of grievances and supposed wrongs perpetrated by other parties or the king's own agents is attested not only by individual lawsuits but by the number of petitions submitted to the king, his ministers, and the Lords and Commons in Parliament.[119] This governed the priorities of upwardly mobile families like the Pastons (who had first made their fortunes through legal expertise), and their letters pay attention to goings-on at the royal court and Westminster where, by the fifteenth century, Parliament usually convened. The private rhythms of acquisition and retention of property could be geared to the workings of royal governance at local level, as well as to the law-courts. Although great landed families sought, quite successfully, to implant themselves and members of their 'affinities' within these institutions, complete control was elusive, and mutual rivalries kept them from the throne itself.[120] Even the recourse of some of them to war,[121] in the form of the Wars of the Roses, only goes to show the advantages accruing to those contenders able to appeal to interest-groups encompassing lesser gentry, freeholders and burghers: the local elites that manned juries at shire courts and sent representatives to Parliament.[122]

---

[117] For the plea roll from which this case can be partially reconstructed: D. Crook, 'The anatomy of a knightly homicide in rural Nottinghamshire, 1295', *Nottingham Medieval Studies* 57 (2013), 69–88.

[118] R. R. Davies, 'The Law of the March', *Welsh History Review* 5 (1970), 1–30, esp. 28–30; M. Lieberman, *The Medieval March of Wales: The Creation and Perception of a Frontier, 1066–1283* (Cambridge, 2010), 218–19, 227–8, 261–3; W. W. Scott, 'The March Laws: for use or ornament?', in J. Ní Ghrádaigh and E. O'Byrne (eds), *The March in the Islands of the Medieval West* (Leiden, 2012), 261–85 at 278–80, 284; P. Russell, 'The languages and registers of law in medieval Ireland and Wales', in J. Benham *et al.* (eds), *Law and Language in the Middle Ages* (Leiden, 2018), 83–103.

[119] G. Dodd, 'Blood, brains and bay-windows: the use of English in fifteenth-century Parliamentary petitions', in T. W. Smith and H. Killick (eds), *Petitions and Strategies of Persuasion in the Middle Ages: The English Crown and the Church, c.1200–c.1550* (York, 2018), 11–39; W. M. Ormrod *et al.* (eds), *Early Common Petitions in the English Parliament, c.1290–c.1420* (London, 2017); W. M. Ormrod, 'Murmur, clamour and noise: voicing complaint and remedy in petitions to the English crown, c.1300–c.1460', in W. M. Ormrod *et al.* (eds), *Medieval Petitions: Grace and Grievance* (York, 2009), 135–55; G. Dodd and S. Petit-Renaud, 'Grace and favour: the petition and its mechanisms', in C. Fletcher *et al.* (eds), *Government and Political Life in England and France, c.1300–c.1500* (Cambridge, 2015), 240–78, esp. 241–2, 245–6, 249–50, 260–1, 265–6, 274.

[120] C. Carpenter, *The Wars of the Roses* (Cambridge, 1997), 27–66.

[121] One of Stephen Humphreys' benchmarks of political culture: p. 19.

[122] For pamphlets addressing shire gentry, burghers and others, before and during the Wars of the Roses: V. J. Scattergood, *Politics and Poetry in the Fifteenth Century* (London, 1971); D. McCulloch and E. D. Jones, 'Lancastrian politics, the French war, and the

Indeed, the involvement of so many groups in what has been termed 'self-government at the king's command' and the problems arising from a manifestly ineffectual ruler can be linked to England's relative propensity to depositions and regicide, a connection perhaps no less valid (*mutatis mutandis*) for Byzantium in its heyday.[123]

The French kings, too, made appellate jurisdiction – the availability of hearings of those with grievances or with a claim unsatisfied – a cornerstone of their rulership. The volume of cases brought before their courts or agents by *c.*1300 was immense, as witness the records of Philip the Fair's Council functioning as the *Parlement* and also the writings of Paris-based lawyers.[124] The readiness of royal *enquêteurs* – oft of lowly status, yet acting on the king's behalf – to hold 'investigations' both of other officials and of local customs and lordships, to intervene in a seigneurial court's proceedings, or to override their judgements became a running sore, arousing protests from regional grandees.[125] Their sweeping powers could, however, be justified as responses to petitions or interventions in support of the weak. Joinville's depiction of Louis IX hearing petitioners beneath an oak tree at Vincennes accords with Louis' high-minded pronouncements against violence and disorder, including the actions of nobles. He even went so far, in an *ordonnance* issued in 1258, as to declare:

Know that, having taken advice, we have prohibited all wars in the realm (*guerras omnes inhibuisse in regno*), and arson and the disruption of carts. Wherefore we order you, with a stern warning, neither to make wars or arson against our prohibition, nor to disturb farmers (*agricolas*) who work with ploughs.

rise of the popular element', *Speculum* 58 (1983), 95–138 at 103–7, 112–14, 117–25, 135–8; W. Scase, *Literature and Complaint in England, 1271–1553* (Oxford, 2007); C. Oliver, *Parliament and Political Pamphleteering in Fourteenth-Century England* (Woodbridge, 2010), 188–91. See also G. L. Harriss, 'Political society and the growth of government in late medieval England', *P&P* 138 (1993), 28–57, esp. 56–7; C. Barron, 'The political culture of medieval London', in L. Clark and C. Carpenter (eds), *Political Culture in Late Medieval Britain* (Woodbridge, 2004), 111–34.

[123] S. Bagge, 'The decline of regicide and the rise of European monarchy from the Carolingians to the early modern period', *Frühmittelalterliche Studien* 53 (2019), 151–89 at 168–74, 179–84. The phrase 'self-government at the king's command' was coined by A. B White, *Self-Government at the King's Command: A Study in the Beginnings of English Democracy* (Minneapolis, MN, 1933). See also pp. 298, 444.

[124] *Textes relatifs à l'histoire du Parlement de Paris*, ed. C.-V. Langlois (Paris, 1888); *Actes du Parlement de Paris*, ed. E. Boutaric, 2 vols (Paris, 1863–7); *Les Olim, ou registres des arrêts rendus par la cour du roi*, ed. A. Beugnot, 3 vols in 4 pts (Paris, 1839–48); J. R. Strayer, *The Reign of Philip the Fair* (Princeton, 1980), 70, 75, 85–9, 205–36; F. J. Pegues, *The Lawyers of the Last Capetians* (Princeton, 1962); E. A. R. Brown, 'Moral imperatives and conundrums of conscience: reflections on Philip the Fair of France', *Speculum* 87 (2012), 1–26 at 17–26.

[125] Strayer, *Reign of Philip*, 89–93, 96–7, 200–16, 412–15.

Louis seems to have intended his ban to be of general effect, treating breaches of the peace as transgressions which his officials must punish in the name of God and morality.[126]

In practice, however, lordships north of the Loire were too well entrenched, with variegated customary rights and courts behind castle walls, for such royal legislation to prevail. And local officials administering justice long remained attentive to traditions even in conquered regions like Normandy, whose lucrative material resources the crown sought to exploit.[127] As for warfare involving nobles and lesser landholders, local custom implied its licitness.[128] Although royal *ordonnances* continued to inveigh against private wars and profess concern for their innocent victims, the working assumption took it for a fact of life. This applies to Charles V, whose splendiferous *Livre du sacre des rois de France* has already been noted. Among the *ordonnances* issued after an Estates General held at Sens in 1367 is a ban on nobles warring on one another unless the main parties had agreed to do so – in which case they must not harm royal subjects![129] In such a climate, those accused by royal officials or at the Paris *Parlement* of waging private wars felt free to invoke long-standing practice, even if the *Parlement* rejected claims of custom for any region.[130]

In reality, if not in jurisprudence, a convergence of interests was in play, with seigneurial jurisdictions and nobles' armed forces potentially of avail to the king and his officials; conversely, appeals to the crown's courts and networks were an option for landholders at odds with their lords, yet the crown could assist the latter to cope with persistent recalcitrants. Such connivance or cooperation also obtained over issues of landholding itself and of inheritance. Contestations of the king's right to resolve inheritance

---

[126] *Les Ordonnances des rois de France de la troisième race*, ed. E. de Laurière *et al.*, 21 vols and supplement (Paris, 1723–1849), i:84; see also J. Firnhaber-Baker, *Violence and the State in Languedoc, 1250–1400* (Cambridge, 2014), 26–35 (tr. on 27).

[127] Not that Norman customs and assumptions were themselves clear-cut or uniform at the time of Philip Augustus' conquest in 1204: D. Power, *The Norman Frontier in the Twelfth and Early Thirteenth Centuries* (Cambridge, 2004), 143–7, 171–9, 195–6; Z. A. Schneider, *The King's Bench: Bailiwick Magistrates and Local Governance in Normandy, 1670–1740* (Rochester, NY, 2008), 110–18, 147–51; see also p. 403.

[128] See e.g. *Archives administratives de la ville de Reims*, no. 89, ed. P. Varin, 3 vols in 5 pts (Paris, 1839–48), iii:516; Firnhaber-Baker, *Violence and the State*, 66–71, 82, 134–40, 155.

[129] *Ordonnances des rois de France*, ed. de Laurière *et al.*, v:19–22 (article 10).

[130] *Ordonnances des rois de France*, ed. de Laurière *et al.*, iii:646–9 (articles 8, 11); R. Cazelles, 'La réglementation royale de la guerre privée de Saint Louis à Charles V et la précarité des ordonnances', *Revue historique de droit français et étranger* 4th series 37 (1960), 530–48 at 542–4; L. de Carbonnières, 'Le pouvoir royal face aux mécanismes de la guerre privée à la fin du Moyen Âge. L'exemple du Parlement de Paris', *Droits: Revue française de théorie, de philosophie et de cultures juridiques* 46 (2007), 3–17; see also Firnhaber-Baker, *Violence and the State*, 100, 154–5.

questions were rife. Yet a politically deft ruler like Philip Augustus could align significant landholders' interests with his own in judgements that were expressly of 'the magnates of the realm'.[131] Those passing the judgement would disseminate letters patent echoing the king's letter precisely but making plain the collective nature of the judgement, each highlighting his individual relationship with the subject of the judgement. This concept of multiple and pooled authorities in adjudication is expressed in, for example, the documents announcing judgement on the right of the young Theobald IV to inherit the county of Champagne.[132] Documents such as these exemplify the joint-stock nature of political leadership grounded in landholding, for all the surface noise individual objectors generated. They also show how attempts to regularise conventions of homage, inheritance and jurisdiction to the king's advantage could bolster lordship in general, clarifying a lord's rights over his liegemen's holdings.

Detailing any such tendencies in societies where mutual obligations were less grounded in landholding is difficult. This is particularly true of regions where land was infertile and agriculture unremunerative, with even the elites' rights going largely unwritten. Scotland was one such polity, its kings acting as little more than *primus inter pares*, namely heads of noble families and clans. Here, though, from the twelfth century on, the kings came to terms with the Anglo-Norman realm and the aristocratic families emanating from it. They adopted increasingly standardised administrative and judicial practices, issuing charters and using Latin terminology and formulae borrowed from their southern neighbours.[133] Royal authority over magnates was thus asserted, triggering spectacular acts of defiance. Yet the shift brought advantages. The extent of the beneficiaries' territory was clarified, along with their rights to hold courts, on the understanding that their lands and jurisdictional powers were to be held directly or indirectly from the king. They were now embedded more deeply in a particular district with express authorisation to bequeath it to their heirs, so long

---

[131] In 1209, he issued – with 'public assent' – a pronouncement about the inheritance of 'feudal holdings' that was at once broad-brush and supportive of a single hierarchy: *Recueil des actes de Philippe Auguste*, ed. Delaborde *et al.*, iii: no. 1083; A. Taylor, 'Formalising aristocratic power in royal *acta* in late twelfth- and early thirteenth-century France and Scotland', *TRHS* 6th series 28 (2018), 33–64 at 55.

[132] All were thought worth preserving by his mother Blanche and her clerks, who copied each letter patent into their cartularies: *Recueil des actes de Philippe Auguste*, ed. Delaborde *et al.*, iv: nos 1437, 1438; *The Cartulary of Countess Blanche of Champagne*, nos 24, 39–47, 396–401, ed. T. Evergates (Toronto, 2010), 53–5, 64–77, 350–8; Taylor, 'Formalising aristocratic power', 55–9.

[133] A. Taylor, *The Shape of the State in Medieval Scotland, 1124–1290* (Oxford, 2016), 33–5, 37–8, 45–53, 78–83, 102–13, 172–5, 435–55.

as royal officials could attend their courts, even convening courts of their own.[134] The charters and other deeds that become plentiful from the later twelfth century onwards style with terms like *comes* magnates who had formerly enjoyed loose-defined rights, such as 'sea steward' or 'great steward' (Gaelic: *mormaer*), responsible for levying the host across a vast region. What is striking is that *non*-royal charters begin to use formulae denoting their jurisdictional rights, with nobles describing their land as held 'as freely' 'as other lands are held in the kingdom of the Scots/Scotland'.[135] Thus members of elite families were seeing their own interests as bound up with the king's, accepting office from him while tightening their own claims to hold tracts of land and to determine rights and wrongs there.

Conclusion

Several features stand out from this survey of some of the Latin west's polities and realms. First, and most obvious, is the variety of interpretations and actual practices lurking behind the commitment to justice and protection of the church and the weak that so many rulers swore to uphold. Such zealous takers of coronation-oaths as late Anglo-Saxon kings and the de Valois kings of France presided over routine feuds and private war. Yet these practices were already being actively discouraged in Anglo-Norman England. And violence ran not far beneath the surface of all these realms. Arms-bearing was, after all, a mark of nobility and a privilege in most late medieval polities, and not even the elaborate apparatus of the English state could stay rival, ambitious or despairing groups of nobles from marshalling their armed followers and fighting it out.[136] Indeed, very many societies in the west were, in effect, attuned to

---

[134] For early examples of grants specifying a perpetual, heritable grant: *The Charters of King David I; The Written Acts of David I, King of Scots, 1124–53 and of His Son Henry Earl of Northumberland, 1139–52*, ed. G. W. S. Barrow (Woodbridge, 1999), nos 16, 54, 210; for subsequent charters' greater detail: *The Acts of William I, King of Scots, 1165–1214*, ed. G. W. S. Barrow and W. W. Scott, Regesta regum Scotorum 2 (Edinburgh, 1971), nos 49–51, 80, 116, 135–7, 147, 152, 185, 204–5, 302, 334–5, 340, 344–5, 350, 405, 418, 473, 524; M. Hammond, 'The adoption and routinization of Scottish royal charter production for lay beneficiaries, 1124–1195', *Anglo-Norman Studies* 36 (2014), 91–115; Taylor, *Shape of the State*, 157–64, 184–7, 206–10, 271–84; *idem*, 'Formalising aristocratic power', 43–6, 61.

[135] On *mormaer*, see D. Broun, 'Statehood and lordship in Scotland', *Innes Review* 66 (2015), 1–71 at 15–26, 66–8; *idem*, ' Kingdom and identity: a Scottish perspective', in K. J. Stringer and A. J. L. Winchester (eds), *Northern England and Southern Scotland in the Central Middle Ages* (Woodbridge, 2017), 31–85 at 45–53, 64–74; Taylor, *Shape of the State*, 27–33, 37–45, 81–3, 102–13, 172–87, 454–5.

[136] Carpenter, *Wars of the Roses*, 111–12, 126–7, 137–9, 141–50; on arms-bearing, chivalry and violence: pp. 156–8, 377–8, 380.

discord and disputation, and the west has fairly been called 'in its political aspect, an ongoing argument'.[137]

But this brings us to a second feature of the west, the extent to which elite competition and rivalries hinged on land and on their rights not only to allocate and profit from it, but also to adjudicate matters arising and liable to disrupt production. So long as agriculture was labour-intensive and slow-moving, with stock-raising ever prey to disease, landowners' interests were bound up with the rhythm of the seasons, and that, ultimately, meant peaceable conditions and regard for property. It was concern for order that involved substantial landowners in dispute settlement among their tenants, and this, along with intimations of force majeure, underlay their exercise of lordship. Constantly drawn into questions of 'who gets what, when and how' of the sort posed by Harold Lasswell, they needed mechanisms for regulation that might range from their own family traditions or manorial court to a local community's customs and on to the procedures of some higher court, whether a regional grandee's or that of an official (very likely the grandee) acting in the name of generally acknowledged authority, for example a court in the service of the king. All these mechanisms are covered by the general concern for attestation, from living witnesses and written words, as to long-standing practices and past agreements, largely to do with land and those who worked it. It was, above all, the Carolingian Franks who provided a scheme of how things could be done, underpinned by oaths of mutual obligation and with invocations of collective assent and universal values. Their model can be traced, with many permutations, across western Europe. The adaptation of a variant by the Scots is particularly suggestive: it shows the appeal of these arrangements along with the concept of the king presiding over jurisdictions while having a say in allocation of lands. The Scots elites had never been subject to the Roman or Carolingian empires nor found much use for the written word in Latin. Yet the advantages were plain to ruler and magnates alike. The basics of this political culture were stark and simple enough for application in many different societies, allowing for ambiguities, rivalries and divergent local customs. Such flexibility, resting upon common assumptions, facilitated cross-referral between jurisdictions and appeals to overlords and kings against what local lords adjudged or demanded.

This brings out another feature of the Latin west. The modus operandi of the larger lordships and principalities in exercising supra-regional authority was akin to that of kings, as witness their administrative documents along

---

[137] See p. 167.

with oaths of fealty and suchlike devices of mutual obligation.[138] This facilitated the formation, in regions newly won from the Muslims and with heterogeneous populations, of the kingdoms of Jerusalem, Portugal and Norman Sicily.[139] One also observes from towards the mid-twelfth century onwards how ambitious dynasts' alliances could bring about abrupt reconfigurations of polities. The linking of the Anglo-Norman realm with the duchy of Aquitaine through Henry II's marriage to Eleanor is just one of the most spectacular.[140] Several other assortments of lands, cities and islands were brought within the reaches of a royal dynasty: for example, the Balearic islands and Sicily came under the crown of Aragon, while the Angevin kingdom of Naples was instituted by Charles of Anjou, a younger brother of St Louis. And, for some while, the kingdom of Naples was linked with Hungary by dynastic ties, starting with the marriages of Charles II and his sister on the one hand and the Hungarian king Laszlo IV and his sister on the other.[141] If the range and durability of some of these conglomerations is striking, given the diversity of laws and landholding patterns they encompassed, it owes something to the aforementioned blend of personal bonds and professions of a ruler's duties that western coronation rites encapsulated. But the capacity of polities to take the absorption of multiple other lordships in their stride or, conversely, to carry on functioning after losing swathes of territory, also reflects their interconnectedness and that underlying concern not 'to disturb farmers who work with ploughs', which St Louis pronounced upon. One might conceive western political culture in terms of assemblages of the Danish toy Lego. Varying greatly in shapes, sizes and colours, the components have sufficient interlocking parts to form

---

[138] See p. 375; p. 64 on documentation for the Babenberger's governance of the Austrian March. See also G. A. Loud, 'A political and social revolution: the development of the territorial principalities in Germany', in Loud and Schenk (eds), *Origins of the German Principalities*, 3–22, esp. 12–17, 20–1; J. Rogge, 'The growth of princely authority: themes and problems', in *ibid.*, 23–36, esp. 28, 35; W. Paravicini, 'L'embarras de richesses: comment rendre accessible les archives financières de la maison de Bourgogne-Valois', *Académie Royale de Belgique: Bulletin de la Classe des Lettres et des Sciences Morales et Politiques et de la Classe des Beaux-Arts*, 6th series 7 (1996), 17–68 at 21–66.

[139] See pp. 145, 373–4.

[140] B. Weiler, 'Crown-giving and king-making in the west, ca. 1000–ca. 1250', *Viator* 41 (2010), 57–88; see also pp. 147, 375.

[141] Perhaps the most striking instance of the malleability of western modes is the adoption of Christianity by the Lithuanian Grand Duke Jagiello and his marriage to Jadwiga, heiress to the crown of Poland. The Union of Krewo (1385) entailed incorporation of the formerly pagan Lithuanians and the extensive Eastern Christian populations already beneath their sway within a sprawling polity now governed by Latin Christians and housing a Catholic hierarchy: *Acta unji Polski z Litwą, 1385–1791*, nos 1 and 2, ed. S. Kutrzeba and W. Semkowicz (Cracow, 1932), 1–4; D. Baronas and S. C. Rowell, *The Conversion of Lithuania: From Pagan Barbarians to Late Medieval Christians* (Vilnius, 2015), 256–63; N. Nowakowska (ed.), *Remembering the Jagiellonians* (London, 2018).

structures and even, in favourable circumstances and skilful hands, an overarching structure that amounts to a dwelling-house.

Finally, developing Len Scales' description of political life in the west as 'an ongoing argument', one should note the distinctiveness of the west in being geared to differences and conflict. This holds true in the literal sense of elites, families and communities coming to blows. But it also applies to the forms of arbitration and mechanisms for settling disputes surveyed in this chapter. The parties involved might switch between violent and non-violent modes, and the spectacle is volatile and untidy-looking. But one may argue that the disorder was, more often than not, contained: there was a working assumption of consensus, and, however skewed this may have been in favour of the propertied classes, it gained formal expression in royal pronouncements about 'counsel' and, in several major polities, in the attendance at assemblies of representatives of estates of the realm. In this respect, western polities differed from the other two spheres, which upheld the ideal of internal peace and general order attuned to the cosmos with greater ceremonial panache and, in their heyday, possessed the means to enforce it.[142] Perhaps because of this, along with the abundance of law-courts and jurists in Islamic urban centres and the relative efficacy of Byzantine legal procedures, there was less need to provide for endemic low-intensity violence and disorder or competing jurisdictions. And when the central power frayed, as in Byzantium in the late twelfth century, there was no time or tradition for alternative structures to develop. In comparison, the Latin west may be characterised as less ambitious, eschewing the cosmic harmony and communal unity so congenial to cultures familiar with traditions of sacral kingship. Western elites were, literally, more earth-bound, in that the bulk of their resources and power sprang from the land and their rights to it, demonstrable by title-deeds. And that, in turn, meant that the preservation of (and forging or tampering with) documents was of the essence to perpetuation of their advantages. It is this characteristic, in many ways a shortcoming, which makes our sources about them so much richer than is the case for the various Byzantine or Islamic elites for whom landownership was just one of the means to resources, status and power.

---

[142] See pp. 84–9, 293, 303–9, 336–9.

5   Byzantium
Sources

Jonathan Shepard

Figure 5.1 Gold *solidus* of Empress Eirene struck in Constantinople between 797 and 802 (20 mm); © Dumbarton Oaks Byzantine Collection, Washington, DC

Narrative Context

At first sight, Byzantium looks to be the most rounded of all our three spheres. A unitary state until the Fourth Crusaders struck, and showing talent for regenerating itself in various guises thereafter,[1] it had a clear-cut political leadership which paid lip service, at least, to religious and legal traditions. Much of its legitimacy sprang from the unassailable claim to have been functioning thus since the era of Roman antiquity, uplifted by the conversion of Constantine the Great. Taken on its own terms, Byzantium constitutes a mighty 'empire of the Romans' whose ups-and-downs look easily trackable, through narratives emanating largely from the imperial-ecclesiastical complex, the establishment of secular and

---

[1] For fuller treatment of this period: pp. 188–94, 438–55.

ecclesiastical hierarchies whose interests, assumptions and stated values were essentially congruent, despite individual difference of opinion and personal and factional rivalries. These narratives are supplemented by accounts written by outsiders, some of them detailed and accurate. In respect of affairs in the capital and the doings of provincial post-holders and many others looking to Constantinople for advancement or protection, this impression holds true. The imperial grand narrative is sustainable for periods before the City's fall to the Fourth Crusaders.

This is not, however, the full story even for the period before 1204. In fact, the government's abiding attention to foreign affairs reflects its susceptibility to goings-on in scores of other regimes and societies. And so, after their fashion, do accounts in external sources of events in Constantinople along with enemy inroads into the provinces and Byzantine counterattacks. These accounts do more than simply reflect the allure of Constantinople or the geopolitical realities of the world around it. They register the special relationship obtaining between the court and citizens of Constantinople and the elites and economies of other societies – and, more generally, the fact that Byzantium's territorial interests overlapped with our other two spheres to a far greater degree than those spheres did with each other. The Christian west engaged with the Islamic sphere in the Iberian peninsula and Sicily, and commercial exchanges became entangled with military and cultural contacts in the heyday of crusading. Yet their mutual engagement was small-scale compared with Byzantium's overlap with each of them. Moreover, Byzantium's own sphere encompassed those societies and polities intent on acquiring and maintaining correct religious worship with reference mainly (though not exclusively) to Constantinople's example. This received its characterisation and name of the Byzantine Commonwealth from Dimitri Obolensky.[2] His thesis sets the imperial-ecclesiastical complex at the heart of a sphere extending far beyond the emperor's territorial holdings. Kaleidoscopic and yet possessing unmistakable contours, this cultural configuration does not have exact counterparts in our other two spheres.[3]

Byzantium's ambivalent relationship with the polities subscribing to its own sphere receives attention from Catherine Holmes.[4] Whether or not one accepts the term 'Byzantine Commonwealth', one must acknowledge the absence of any contemporary term for it,[5] and no attempt is made here

---

[2] D. Obolensky, *The Byzantine Commonwealth: Eastern Europe 565–1453* (London, 1971).

[3] One can, however, detect the contours of commonwealths and common cultural zones in the Islamic sphere (see p. 220) and even, for all the fractiousness, the Latin west (see pp. 167–9, 174–5).

[4] See pp. 196–8.

[5] The lack of evidence of contemporary terms or formulations of the Commonwealth features prominently in critiques of Obolensky's thesis. See e.g. C. Raffensperger, 'Revisiting the idea of the Byzantine Commonwealth', *Byzantinische Forschungen* 28

systematically to survey the interrelationship between Byzantine elites and political structures ranging from the Balkans to Rus and on to the Alans of the northern Caucasus and the Georgians. The sole vestiges of institutional props for the supra-territorial sphere come from the Constantinopolitan patriarchate, with all its sees beyond the imperial frontier and its registers and formularies for correspondence with, amongst others, the Rus churchmen and potentates coming within its jurisdiction.[6] And, although one can detect patterns of deference towards the imperial and ecclesiastical authorities on the part of the Rus,[7] Constantinople's centrality was not incontestable. Other loci of politico-religious authority such as Mount Athos existed even within the territorial empire, and beyond the borders Jerusalem's patriarch and the Georgian church leadership commanded respect. At the same time, the imperial authorities sought to channel commerce with traders from all three spheres through the markets of Constantinople, generating a kind of greater co-prosperity sphere. And, in practice, their strategy made for a variable geometry empire, relying on networks of peripheral elites, Open Cities, and distant yet complaisant potentates to maintain a presence in areas of economic and strategic concern without heavy military commitments.[8] Ambivalence as to what and who belonged to the empire is conveyed by the Byzantines' own usage: *he basileia* could denote either 'the empire' as a polity or the 'imperial majesty' (embodied in

---

(2004), 159–74; A. Kaldellis, *Ethnography after Antiquity: Foreign Lands and Peoples in Byzantine Literature* (Philadelphia, 2013), 127–39.

[6] For lists of sees of metropolitanates beyond the frontier (and kept up to 1453), see J. Darrouzès, *Notitiae Episcopatuum ecclesiae Constantinopolitanae* (Paris, 1981), no. 17 (appendix 2 and 3), 403; no. 18 (appendix 1), 409 ; no. 20, 416–18 ; no. 21, 419–21. For the patriarchal register extant for the period from 1315 so far published up to 1363, see *Das Register des Patriarchats von Konstantinopel*, ed. H. Hunger *et al.*, 3 vols to date (Vienna, 1981–). For the formulary for correspondence, see J. Darrouzès (ed.), 'Ekthesis nea, Manuel des pittakia du XIVe s.', *REB* 27 (1969), 5–127. See also J. Preiser-Kapeller, 'Eine "Familie der Könige"? Anrede und Bezeichnung "ausländischer" Machthaber in den Urkunden des Patriarchatsregisters von Konstantinopel im 14. Jahrhundert', in C. Gastgeber *et al.* (eds), *The Register of the Patriarchate of Constantinople: An Essential Source for the History and Church of Late Byzantium* (Vienna, 2013), 257–89, esp. Appendix on 273–89; C. Gastgeber, 'Das Formular der Patriarchatskanzlei (14. Jahrhundert)', in C. Gastgeber *et al.* (eds), *The Patriarchate of Constantinople in Context and Comparison* (Vienna, 2017), 197–302.

[7] G. Prinzing, 'Byzantium, medieval Russia and the so-called "family of kings": from George Ostrogorsky to Franz Dölger's construct and its critics', in A. Alshanskaya *et al.* (eds), *Imagining Byzantium: Perceptions, Patterns, Problems* (Mainz, 2018), 15–30.

[8] J. Shepard, 'Bunkers, Open Cities and boats in Byzantine diplomacy', in K. Parry and D. Dzino (eds), *Byzantium, its Neighbours and its Cultures* (Brisbane, 2014), 11–44. Behind the façade of autocracy, the de facto pluralism or diffusion of power in Byzantium can be compared with that of the Islamic world and also with the Latin west: in the latter, in some ways it was a different dynamic, being more hereditary and without the same trappings of autocracy, and with a lot more explicit acknowledgement of reciprocities. See e.g. pp. 142–3, 160–2, 196–8.

the emperor personally); and the term *doulos* – 'subject of the emperor, servant, slave'[9] – was applicable in its milder tone to virtually anyone receiving from him a court-title or other significant privileges, wherever they might reside.[10]

The mists enveloping Byzantine political culture, especially its interaction with the other spheres, do not receive much exposition from Byzantine narrative sources. They were, in fact, themselves integral to that culture. Whether depicting accomplishments and building-projects in the grand manner of earlier Romano-Greek historians or excoriating iconoclast and other 'unorthodox' regimes in plainer prose,[11] the histories and chronicles format matters around the doings and character of the emperor, happenings in Constantinople and warfare against the barbarians. It is largely in a militarised context that relations with the other spheres are covered, if at all. The resultant picture is ill-balanced, focusing on the centre and dealings with barbarians, while treating the provinces sketchily. Such formatting enabled admirers and critics of a regime alike to convey imperial hegemony in momentous if not heroic terms, ever parrying barbarian challenges to Roman majesty and Divine Providence, with the City centre-stage.[12] Contemporaneous with the events they narrate are orations delivered in Constantinople, usually at court. A substantial number survive

[9] See, beside the entries for *douleia, douleuo* and *doulos* in Liddell and Scott's *Lexicon*, entries for *douleo, douleusis* and *doulosynos* in *Lexikon zur byzantinischen Gräzität: besonders des 9.–12. Jahrhunderts*, ed. E. Trapp (Vienna, 1996), fasc. 2, 407, 408. On the habitual use by imperial acts of *basileia* in this abstract yet person-specific sense, and the reception of this usage by elites in Dalmatia and Venice, see I. Basić, '*Imperium* and *regnum* in Gottschalk's description of Dalmatia', in D. Dzino *et al.* (eds), *Migration, Integration and Connectivity on the Southeastern Frontier of the Carolingian Empire* (Leiden, 2018), 170–209, esp. 177–86, 195–7. See also pp. 290–4.

[10] Thus a grant of privileges in 1189 could go so far as to dub the Venetians 'native Romans' by way of rewarding their 'devotion' to the empire and readiness to suffer for it. Emperor Isaac II's warm tone was coloured by fear of an approaching army of German Crusaders, but it illustrates how readily those 'serving' the empire might individually metamorphose into 'Romans'. See G. L. F. Tafel and G. M. Thomas (eds), *Urkunden zur älteren Handels- und Staatsgeschichte der Republik Venedig*, 3 vols (Vienna, 1856–57), i:206–11 at 208; P. Magdalino 'Isaac II, Saladin and Venice', in J. Shepard (ed.), *The Expansion of Orthodox Europe: Byzantium, the Balkans and Russia* (Aldershot, 2007), no. 5, 93–106 at 102.

[11] Foremost among these works of churchmen are: Nikephoros I, *Short History*, ed. and tr. C. Mango, *CFHB* 13 (Washington, DC, 1990); Theophanes Confessor, *Chronicle*, tr. R. Scott and C. Mango (Oxford, 1997); George the Monk, *Chronicle*, ed. C. de Boor, 2 vols (Leipzig, 1904) ; rev. edn P. Wirth (Stuttgart, 1978). For a collection of studies on Theophanes, see M. Jankowiak and F. Montinaro (eds), *Studies in Theophanes [= TM 19]* (Paris, 2015). On Nikephoros' *Short History*, see D. Marjanović, *Creating Memories in Late 8th-Century Byzantium: The Short History of Nikephoros of Constantinople* (Amsterdam, 2018).

[12] See P. Alexander, 'The strength of empire and capital as seen through Byzantine eyes', *Speculum* 37 (1962), 339–57; repr. in Shepard (ed.), *Expansion of Orthodox Europe*, no. 2, 9–28.

from the Middle Byzantine and Palaiologan periods. Using classical names, these compositions in Attic Greek often portray matters as virtual replays of episodes from scripture or the Romano-Greek past. For example, Theodore Daphnopates acclaimed the peace with Bulgaria in 927, recalling that made between the warring rulers 'of Phrygia and Mycenae' whilst likening Tsar Symeon to Goliath.[13] Historical narratives composed under imperial auspices strike classical poses, too, for example the *Life* of Basil, purportedly written by Constantine VII (945–59), and the portrayal of Alexios I's reign (1081–1118) by his daughter, Anna.[14] Even when they are less encomiastic, Middle Byzantine narratives are arranged by emperors' reigns, although some works recount the feats of military commanders, often emperors *manqués*.[15] They essentially project the empire's self-image, Constantinople and its court being the measure of all things civilised. A reliable guide to the main Byzantine historians is now available, and those works with classicising pretentions form a self-consciously continuous sequence.[16] A partial exception is the *History* of George Akropolites, recounting the emergence of Nicaean-based emperors from among rival dynasts after 1204. Significantly, though, his narrative breaks off at 1261, when Michael VIII Palaiologos recovered the City from

[13] The case for Theodore's authorship is very strong, without being absolute: ed. and tr. in I. Dujčev, 'On the treaty of 927 with the Bulgarians', *DOP* 32 (1978), 217–95 at 264–5 (ll.160–1), 278–9 (l. 366).

[14] *Vita Basilii*, ed. and tr. I. Ševčenko, *Chronographiae quae Theophanis Continuati nomine fertur liber V quo Vita Basilii imperatoris amplectitur*, *CFHB 42* (Berlin and New York, 2011); Anna Komnene, *Alexiad*, ed. D. R. Reinsch and A. Kambylis, 2 vols (Berlin and New York, 2001); tr. E. R. A. Sewter, rev. P. Frankopan (Harmondsworth, 2009). Women's voices – albeit mostly elite – are particularly audible in late Byzantine sources, as well as occasionally in medieval western ones. For examples, see pp. 203–4, 55–6.

[15] See A. Markopoulos, 'Roman antiquarianism: aspects of the Roman past in the Middle Byzantine period (9th–11th centuries)', in E. Jeffreys (ed.), *Proceedings of the 21st International Congress of Byzantine Studies, London, 21–26 August 2006: Plenary Papers* (Aldershot, 2006), 277–97; A. Markopoulos, 'From narrative historiography to historical biography: new trends in Byzantine historical writing in the 10th–11th centuries', *BZ* 102 (2009), 697–715. See also contributions to the session on 'How the Byzantines Wrote History' at the 2016 Belgrade International Congress of Byzantine Studies by R. Macrides, 'How the Byzantines wrote history', in S. Marjanović-Dušanić (ed.), *Proceedings of the 23rd International Congress of Byzantine Studies, Belgrade, 22–27 August 2016: Plenary Papers* (Belgrade, 2016), 257–64; L. Neville, 'Why did the Byzantines write history?', in *ibid.*, 265–76; W. Treadgold, 'The unwritten rules for writing Byzantine history', in *ibid.*, 277–92; A. Kaldellis, 'The manufacture of history in the later tenth and eleventh centuries: rhetorical templates and narrative ontologies', in *ibid.*, 293–308. On a hypothetical text that probably made the case for Caesar John Doukas' fitness for the imperial throne, see L. Neville, *Heroes and Romans in Twelfth-Century Byzantium: The Material for History of Nikephoros Bryennios* (Cambridge, 2012), 46–59.

[16] L. Neville, *Guide to Byzantine Historical Writing* (Cambridge, 2018), esp. 14; P. Magdalino, 'Byzantine historical writing, 900–1400', in S. Foot and C. F. Robinson (eds), *The Oxford History of Historical Writing, II: 400–1400* (Oxford, 2012), 218–37.

the Latins, rendering his credentials as 'Roman' emperor unassailable.[17] Akropolites was writing partly in vindication of his own performance as an official in the run-up to the recovery of Constantinople, and other office-holders still saw fit to recount the empire's misfortunes in classicising tones.

Only in the mid-fourteenth century does grandstanding narrative cease, with Nikephoros Gregoras glumly recording the use of glass paste and gilded leather instead of bejewelled vestments and golden diadems at Emperor John V's wedding party in 1347.[18] Subsequent historians like Doukas and Michael Kritoboulos took up the pen to recount Byzantium's last days, but their City now housed a *basileus* of rather different stamp, Mehmed the Conqueror.[19] Other narratives exist, notably the self-justifying memoirs of the emperor John VI Kantakouzenos.[20] And figures aiming to sway policy or make their name could survey events in letters, tracts and orations.[21] However, current affairs showed signs of losing their grip. A member of the senate was too lost in spiritual contemplation to heed a question Andronikos II put to him: far from annoyance, the emperor showed respect. Such, at least, is what an encomium of the senator's son, the spiritual leader Gregory Palamas, maintains.[22] Otherworldliness is at a premium in the *Lives* of such saints, but semi-detachment from imperial concerns was becoming the norm. It could take the form of commercial and social engagement by elite families with external networks and powers, as texts emanating from Italian trading families and Turkish dynasts reveal.[23] Indeed, as Byzantine historical

---

[17] George Akropolites, *The History* XV.11, tr. with intro. and comm. R. Macrides (Oxford, 2007), 383–8.

[18] Nikephoros Gregoras, *Byzantina historia*, ed. L. Schopen and I. Bekker, 3 vols (Bonn, 1829–55), ii:788–9.

[19] Doukas, *Istoria Turco-Bizantina*, ed. V. Grecu (Bucharest, 1958); tr. H. J. Magoulias, *Decline and Fall of Byzantium to the Ottoman Turks* (Detroit, 1975); Michael Kritoboulos, *Historiae*, ed. D. R. Reinsch (Berlin and New York, 1983); tr. C. T. Riggs, *History of Mehmed the Conqueror* (Princeton, 1954).

[20] John Kantakouzenos, *Libri historiarum IV*, ed. L. Schopen, 3 vols (Bonn, 1828–32).

[21] See e.g. Nikephoros Gregoras, *Epistulae*, ed. P. A. M. Leone, 2 vols (Matino, 1982–3); John Kantakouzenos, *Refutationes duae Prochori Cydonii et Disputatio cum Paulo Patriarcha Latino epistulis septem tradita*, ed. F. H. Tinnefeld and E. Voordeckers (Turnhout and Louvain, 1987); Theodore Metochites, *Orationes*, ed. I. Polemis and E. Kaltsogianni (Berlin, 2019); Demetrios Kydones, *Correspondance*, ed. R.-J. Loenertz, 2 vols (Rome, 1956–60); Demetrios Kydones, *Briefe*, ed. and German tr. F. Tinnefeld, 5 vols (Stuttgart, 1981–2003); I. Toth, 'Rhetorical *theatron* in late Byzantium: the example of Palaiologan imperial orations', in M. Grünbart (ed.), *Theatron: Rhetorische Kultur in Spätantike und Mittelalter* (Berlin and New York, 2007), 429–48, esp. 431–2, 436–8; N. Gaul, *Thomas Magistros und die spätbyzantinische Sophistik: Studien zum Humanismus urbaner Eliten in der frühen Palaiologenzeit* (Wiesbaden, 2011), 18–61. See also p. 85.

[22] Philotheos Kokkinos, *Enkomion* chs 4–5, in *Hagiologika erga, I: Thessalonikeis hagioi*, ed. D. G. Tsames (Thessaloniki, 1985), 425–91 at 430–1; S. Runciman, *The Great Church in Captivity* (Cambridge, 1968), 128.

[23] *BBOL*, 15–17.

writing peters out, information about imperial affairs and political culture comes mainly from external sources. Thus, for example, the *Annals of Genoa* along with a Latin copy of a treaty surviving in the Genoese archive offer the background to Michael Palaiologos' recovery of Constantinople in 1261.[24] And much of our knowledge of goings-on in the thirteenth-century Peloponnese comes from a chronicle written in the fourteenth century for the peninsula's Frankish masters, the *Chronicle of Morea*, of which Greek and Old French versions survive.[25]

The importance of such texts reflects the exposure of imperial territories to external elements in this era. Yet even for the period before 1204, non-Byzantine sources shed valuable light on political events and culture alike. Works of the crusading era illuminate imperial affairs, with well-placed writers supplying data for earlier periods, too.[26] In fact, for episodes such as Alexios' involvement with the First Crusaders, external sources are more forthcoming about his negotiations and demarches than anything on offer from the account of his daughter, Anna Komnene.[27] The same goes for earlier periods, such as Basil II's participation in the Armenian church's festival in celebration of Christ's baptism in the Armenian-populated province of Chaldia.[28] Such diplomatic adaptability features only in those Byzantine texts devoted to denigrating an emperor. Thus Leo V's espousal of iconoclasm earned him execration from the author known as Theophanes Continuatus, who also condemned his recourse to pagan

[24] *Annales Ianuenses*, in *Annali Genovesi di Caffaro e de'suoi continuatori dal MXCIX al MCCXCII*, ed. L. T. Belgrano, C. Imperiale di Sant'Angelo *et al.*, 5 vols (Rome, 1890–1929), iv:41–3, 45; D. J. Geanakoplos, *Emperor Michael Palaeologus and the West, 1258–1282: A Study in Byzantine-Latin Relations* (Cambridge, MA, 1959), 75–91; I. Toth with M. Grabačić, 'The narrative fabric of the Genoese *pallio* and the silken diplomacy of Michael VIII Palaiologos', in H. G. Meredith (ed.), *Objects in Motion: The Circulation of Religion and Sacred Objects in the Late Antique and Byzantine World* (Oxford, 2011), 91–109; C. J. Hilsdale, *Byzantine Art and Diplomacy in an Age of Decline* (Cambridge, 2014), 37–41.

[25] A full English translation of the Greek text is given in *Crusaders as Conquerors: The Chronicle of Morea*, tr. H. E. Lurier (New York, 1964); *The Old French Chronicle of Morea: An Account of Frankish Greece after the Fourth Crusade*, tr. A. Van Arsdall and H. Moody (London, 2017); see C. T. M. Shawcross, *The Chronicle of Morea: Historiography in Crusader Greece* (Oxford, 2009).

[26] See, for example, William of Tyre, *Chronique*, ed. R. B. C. Huygens, 2 vols, *CCCM* 63, 63A (Turnhout, 1986); Michael the Syrian, *Chronique*, ed. and French tr. J.-B. Chabot, 4 vols (Paris, 1899–1924). See also M. Whitby (ed.), *Byzantines and Crusaders in Non-Greek Sources, 1025–1204* (Oxford, 2007).

[27] P. Frankopan, *The First Crusade: The Call from the East* (London, 2012), 87–100, 118–36; J. Shepard, 'Man-to-man, "dog-eat-dog", cults in common: the tangled threads of Alexios' dealings with the Franks', in J.-C. Cheynet and B. Flusin (eds), *Autour du Premier humanisme byzantin et des Cinq études sur le XIe siècle, quarante ans après Paul Lemerle* [= *TM* 21/2] (Paris, 2017), 749–88, esp. 759–62, 777–86.

[28] Aristakes of Lastivert, *Récit des malheurs de la nation arménienne*, French tr. M. Canard and H. Berberian (Brussels, 1973), 15.

rites of sacrifice to ratify a peace treaty with the Bulgars in 815. Such indulgence of barbarian sensibilities was probably common for sealing agreements.[29] But keeping up appearances was the task of classicising narratives, as of members of the imperial-ecclesiastical complex in general. None of the U-turns of an emperor's policy, the haggling with or pandering to lesser potentates, must be allowed to detract from his aura or his Roman credentials. An unbroken sheen of decorum was essential. Given this optical illusion generated so sedulously by Byzantine state broadcasting, external sources are not simply useful for filling gaps in our factual knowledge. They offer windows into Byzantine political culture as a whole. Other, invaluable, insights come from the handbook for dealing with outsiders composed by Constantine VII for his son, known as the *De administrando imperio* ('On Governing the Empire'). Here, among much else, are stories to fob off 'brazenly' 'importunate demands' from northern barbarians and miscellaneous origin-myths to be peddled to Croats and others.[30]

Ideology and Ceremonial

In comparison with our other two spheres, sources concerning Byzantine ideology and ceremonial are plentiful, but very few full-scale exegeses of political theory are known. Treatises on political thought peter out in late antiquity, with the tract addressed by the deacon Agapetos to Justinian.[31] Although men of letters learnt their Attic prose style from such denouncers of 'tyranny' as Demosthenes, discussion of alternatives to the imperial order would scarcely enhance anyone's career. From the twelfth century onwards the status quo was sometimes questioned or compared unfavourably with western constitutional arrangements and the ancient Roman past.[32] And after 1204 the rivalries between contending dynasts

[29] Theophanes Continuatus, *Chronographia* I.28, ed. and tr. M. Featherstone and J. Signes Codoñer, *Chronographiae quae Theophanis Continuati nomine fertur libri I–IV*, CFHB 53 (Berlin, 2015), 50–1; D. A. Miller, 'Byzantine treaties and treaty-making: 500–1025 AD', *Byzantinoslavica* 32 (1971), 56–76 at 75; S. A. Ivanov, *'Pearls before Swine': Missionary Work in Byzantium* (Paris, 2015), 89.
[30] *DAI* chs 13, 30, 31, 66–77, 142–5, 146–9; F. Borri, 'White Croatia and the arrival of the Croats: an interpretation of Constantine Porphyrogenitus on the oldest Dalmatian history', *EME* 19 (2011), 204–31 at 209–12, 222–31.
[31] Agapetos, *Mirror for Princes*, ed. R. Riedinger, *Der Fürstenspiegel für Kaiser Iustinianus von Agapetos Diakonos* (Athens, 1995); tr. as 'Advice to the emperor Justinian' in P. N. Bell, *Three Political Voices from the Age of Justinian* (Liverpool, 2009), 99–122; see also p. 294.
[32] P. Magdalino, 'Aspects of twelfth-century *Kaiserkritik*', *Speculum* 58 (1983), 326–46; F. H. Tinnefeld, *Kategorien der Kaiserkritik in der byzantinischen Historiographie: von Prokop bis Niketas Choniates* (Munich, 1971). For comparisons drawn already in the eleventh century, see D. Krallis, '"Democratic" action in eleventh-century Byzantium:

gave rise to disquisitions on the nature of polities, generally in rhetorical form such as a funeral oration.[33] Speeches were now sometimes intended for lively debate rather than sheer panegyric performance before the emperor,[34] and these, too, could float public policy changes with, for example Demetrios Kydones calling for rapprochement with the Latin west.[35] Indeed, there are hints of councils becoming more active, especially when new taxes were involved.[36] A member of the imperial family drew attention to the advantages accruing from conciliar approaches to governance. Theodore Palaiologos was, however, writing on the point of departure back to the west and, tellingly, his treatise survives only in Old French.[37] Rhetoric for court consumption might criticise current policy, even advocating bold changes,[38] but on the assumption that it did not dent the imperial carapace. Here, too, keeping up appearances was all.[39]

Such concern for appearances thrust ceremonial and visual imagery to the fore. Monuments of worldwide empire were strewn across the capital, counterparts to the classicising narratives, rekindling memories of victories and glory. Guidelines for staging triumphs in classical style through

Michael Attaleiates's "republicanism" in context', *Viator* 40 (2009), 35–53; D. Krallis, *Michael Attaleiates and the Politics of Imperial Decline in Eleventh-Century Byzantium* (Tempe, AZ, 2012); C. Mallan, 'The style, method and programme of Xiphilinus' *Epitome* of Cassius Dio's *Roman History*', *Greek, Roman, and Byzantine Studies* 53 (2013), 610–44.

[33] *IIPTB*, 18–19.   [34] *IIPTB*, 64–115; Gaul, *Thomas Magistros*, 74–113, 144–63.

[35] Demetrios Kydones, 'Oratio pro subsidio Latinorum', *PG* 154, cols 961–1008; Demetrios Kydones, 'Oratio de non reddenda Gallipoli', *PG* 154, cols 1009–1036; J. Ryder, *The Career and Writings of Demetrius Kydones: A Study of Fourteenth-Century Byzantine Politics, Religion and Society* (Brill, 2010), esp. 57–67, 70–81, 157–60, 217–20; J. Ryder, 'Byzantium and the west in the 1360s: the Kydones version', in J. Harris *et al.* (eds), *Byzantines, Latins, and Turks in the Late Medieval Eastern Mediterranean World* (Oxford, 2012), 345–66; Toth, 'Rhetorical *theatron*', 437–8.

[36] D. Kyritses, 'The imperial council and the tradition of consultative decision-making in Byzantium (eleventh to fourteenth centuries)', in D. Angelov and M. Saxby (eds), *Power and Subversion in Byzantium* (Farnham, 2010), 57–69, esp. 63–5.

[37] T. Shawcross, '"Thou shalt do nothing without counsel …"', *Al-Masaq* 20 (2008), 89–118 at 89–105. The Old French version was edited by C. Knowles, *Les Enseignements de Théodore Paléologue* (London, 1983). On the murky role of councils in the first half of the fourteenth century, see Kyritses, 'Imperial council and the tradition of consultative decision-making', 63–8. See also pp. 326–7.

[38] For example, John the Oxite pilloried Alexios I's style of governance, but he may well have been speaking with the emperor's connivance: ed. and French tr. P. Gautier, 'Diatribes de Jean l'Oxite contre Alexis Ier Comnène', *REB* 28 (1970), 5–55 (text and tr. 18–55). See J. Ryder, 'The role of the speeches of John the Oxite in Komnenian court politics', in T. Shawcross and I. Toth (eds), *Reading in the Byzantine Empire and Beyond* (Cambridge, 2018), 93–115, esp. 96–106, 110–11, 114.

[39] In the Latin west, in contrast, ritual and formulaic declarations make much more of counsel, assistance and even consent, given to the enactment of a ruler's decisions, and this took on more elaborate and explicit form in the assemblies convened by English, Castillian and in a rather different way, French kings: see p. 492.

the streets, drawn from descriptions of past occasions, feature in the *De cerimoniis* ('Book of Ceremonies') commissioned by Constantine VII.[40] So do prescriptions and memorandums concerning many other ceremonies in Constantinople, some determining the seating arrangements at palace banquets. The seating showed, literally, one's placing in the pecking-order, and savoir faire was a means towards social acceptability and, even, imperial legitimacy.[41] Political considerations underlie Constantine VII's emphasis on his own fitness to adjudge Roman customs, being purple-born and steeped in them, unlike his arriviste rival, the 'common fellow' Romanos I Lekapenos.[42] Contenders for the throne by virtue of military reputation also had need of ritual, as witness the acclamations for the entry of Nikephoros II Phokas (963–9) into the City in 963. These were incorporated into the 'Book of Ceremonies' by the influential grand chamberlain, Basil, along with acclamations for himself as having proved the 'loyal servant and friend of the emperor'.[43] The jockeying for position between leading figures prompted a flurry of pronouncements on ceremonial towards the mid-fourteenth century, crystallised in the treatise known as Pseudo-Kodinos.[44] By then, the City itself was almost tantamount to the empire, presiding over an archipelago of strongholds and principalities. This anomaly made generating imperial aura all the more essential. Pseudo-Kodinos prescribes what form should be maintained while the emperor was campaigning, at a time when his army was

[40] A triumph of Justinian along with others from the ninth century is covered in Constantine VII's *De cerimoniis aulae byzantinae*: *DC*, i:497–508. For an authoritative edition of the relevant texts, see Constantine VII, *Three Treatises on Imperial Military Expeditions*, ed. and tr. J. F. Haldon (Vienna, 1990), 138–51. See also M. McCormick, *Eternal Victory: Triumphal Rulership in Late Antiquity, Byzantium, and the Early Medieval West* (Cambridge, 1986), 146–50 153–7, 189–216,.

[41] The fullest of these prescriptive guides to the order of precedence for banquets was composed by the master of ceremonies, Philotheos, in 899: *Kleterologion*, ed. and tr. in N. Oikonomides, *Les Listes de préséance byzantines des IXe et Xe siècles* (Paris, 1972), 80–235, esp. 80–7. See also p. 310.

[42] *DAI* ch. 13, 72–3. See N. Gaul et al. (eds), *Center, Province and Periphery in the Age of Constantine VII Porphyrogennetos: From* De ceremoniis *to* De administrando imperio (Wiesbaden, 2018), notably the chapters by N. Gaul, 'Zooming in on Constantinople', 1–21, esp. 1–10, 17–18 and I. Marić, 'Lost on reverse? Constantine VII Porphyrogennetos's vying with Romanos I Lekapenos for legitimacy as a tale of coins, seals, and tesserae', 103–23.

[43] *DC* I.96, 97, pp. 438–9, 443. See J. M. Featherstone, 'Basileios Nothos as compiler: the *De cerimoniis* and *Theophanes Continuatus*', in I. Pérez-Martín and J. Signes Codoñer (eds), *Textual Transmission in Byzantium: Between Textual Criticism and Quellenforschung* (Turnhout, 2014), 355–72, esp. 357–60, 363.

[44] See *Pseudo-Kodinos and the Constantinopolitan Court: Offices and Ceremonies*, ed. and tr. R. Macrides et al. (Farnham, 2013). Chapters such as I and VI (26–34, 204–9), highlighting the 'Great Domestic', probably bear fingerprints of the long-term holder of that office, who eventually became co-emperor, John VI Kantakouzenos: *ibid.*, 287–9 ('Studies').

numbered in hundreds rather than thousands. One version of Pseudo-Kodinos' list of titles reflects usage at a rival alternative seat of imperial authority, Trebizond.[45] In this period, the emperor in Constantinople lived mainly at Blachernai and not the Great Palace, whose buildings conjoined with ceremonies and prayers in manifesting the emperor's distance from his subjects and centrality to the cosmos, a heaven on earth.[46] But displays of continuance from an ancient past and special access to divine favour kept alive the sense of imperial order being the one willed by God.[47]

This outlook was not confined to visitors to the palace or citizens of Constantinople. It was propagated by churchmen, one of its most eloquent advocates being Patriarch Anthony IV. Writing to the prince of Moscow in 1393, he urged that prayers be said for the emperor in the liturgy: in effect, it was he that held other rulers up to the orthodox mark.[48] The Byzantine liturgy aligned true religion quite closely with the empire's well-being.[49] Thus ecclesiastical organisation under the patriarchate and integral parts of religious services broadcast ideology far beyond Constantinople and, indeed, the frontiers throughout the Byzantine centuries. Diplomatic gifts of exquisite silks, some showing eagles and other imperial emblems,[50] along with coins depicting Christ or

[45] *Pseudo-Kodinos*, ed. in and tr. Macrides *et al.*, 282–3 ('Studies'); Table IV; N. Gaul, 'The partridge's purple stockings: observations on the historical, literary and manuscript context of Pseudo-Kodinos' Handbook on Court Ceremonial', in Grünbart (ed.), *Theatron*, 69–104 at 101.

[46] J. M. Featherstone, 'Sakrale Raum und Prozessionen im Grossen Palast von Konstantinopel im 10. Jahrhundert', in H. Luchterhand and H. Röckelein (eds), *Palatium Sacrum – Sakralität am Hof des Mittelalters: Orte – Dinge – Rituale* (Regensburg, 2019), 23–37; H. Maguire, 'The heavenly court', in *BCC*, 247–58; M. C. Carile, *The Vision of the Palace of the Byzantine Emperors as a Heavenly Jerusalem* (Spoleto, 2012), 164–80; N. Drocourt, *Diplomatie sur le Bosphore: les ambassadeurs étrangers dans l'Empire byzantin des années 640 à 1204*, 2 vols (Louvain, 2015), ii:487–544, 597–609. See on the interplay of monuments, routes, palaces and ceremonies in Constantinople: pp. 306–9.

[47] Concepts and ceremonial highlighting the ruler as lynchpin of the divine order can be found in all their variations in the Muslim world: for examples, see pp. 337–8, 343–6, 353–64.

[48] *Acta et diplomata graeca medii aevi sacra et profana*, ed. F. Miklosich and J. Müller, 6 vols (Vienna, 1860–90), no. 447, ii:190. See also P. Guran, 'Frontières géographiques et liturgiques dans la lettre d'Antoine IV au grand prince de Moscou', in M.-H. Blanchet *et al.* (eds), *Le Patriarcat oecuménique de Constantinople et Byzance hors frontières (1204–1586)* (Paris, 2014), 81–97; Prinzing, 'Byzantium, medieval Russia and the so-called family of kings', 19, 25.

[49] R. F. Taft, 'At the sunset of the empire: the formation of the final "Byzantine liturgical synthesis" in the patriarchate of Constantinople', in P. Odorico (ed.), *Le Patriarchat oecuménique de Constantinople aux XIVe–XVIe siècles: rupture et continuité* (Paris, 2007), 61–71.

[50] On silks as such gifts, see A. Muthesius, *Studies in Byzantine and Islamic Silk Weaving* (London, 1995); A. Muthesius, *Byzantine Silk Weaving: AD 400 to AD 1200*, ed.

the Cross on one side and the emperor on the other,[51] propounded Byzantium's raison d'être. The manner in which his silver coins bearing the cross or the bust of an emperor were turned into pendants implies a certain cachet as far afield as Viking-Age Scandinavia.[52] On the imperial periphery, adherence to the emperor blended easily with public devotions. In eighth-century Istria, a notable's court-title governed the sequence in which he received Holy Communion, besides the pecking-order at dinners.[53] A century or so later, members of urban elites would regale fellow Venetians and Dalmatians with tales of an audience with the emperor.[54] Such demonstrative affiliation with the court has left traces in the provinces, too. Thus the regulations of an eleventh-century confraternity in Thebes provide for prayers to be said for 'our orthodox emperors [...] [and] the most holy patriarch' amongst others. Some members have court-titles to their name, and laymen and laywomen feature alongside priests, monks and also nuns.[55] Such chance attestations from unofficial sources are rare, yet suggestive. What is clear is that the Byzantine establishment's multimedia presentation of its assets and virtues enjoyed wide circulation – literally so, in the case of the emperor's coins. Moreover, lead seals of office-holders would sometimes list the successive titles held by their issuer, showing what titles did for an individual's standing.[56] Such a compound of God, gold and imperial preferment was attractive, making it difficult for any alternative political order to take hold. However, Nikephoras Gregoras tells of meeting an old

E. Kislinger and J. Koder (Vienna, 1997); Hilsdale, *Byzantine Art and Diplomacy*, 39–48, 82–7.
[51] See e.g. P. Grierson, *Byzantine Coins* (London, 1982), 27–9, 34–7.
[52] F. Audy, 'How were Byzantine coins used in Viking-Age Scandinavia?', in F. Androshchuk et al. (eds), *Byzantium and the Viking World* (Uppsala, 2016), 141–65, esp. 149–59, 162–5. See also S. Jakobsson, 'Scandinavian kings and the Byzantine emperor', *BZ* 110 (2017), 649–72, esp. 658–61.
[53] As often with Byzantine political culture, fullest information comes from an external source, the *Placitum of Rižana*: A. Petranović and A. Margetić (eds), 'Il placito del Risano', *Atti del Centro di ricerche storiche – Rovigno*, 14 (1983/84) (Trieste–Rovigno), 62, ll. 14–17; M. McCormick, 'The imperial edge: Italo-Byzantine identity, movement and integration, AD 650–950', in H. Ahrweiler and A. E. Laiou (eds), *Studies on the Internal Diaspora of the Byzantine Empire* (Washington, DC, 1998), 48–9; F. Borri, 'Gli Istriani e i loro parenti. *Phrangoi*, Romani e Slavi nella periferia di Bisanzio', *JÖB* 60 (2010), 1–25 at 22.
[54] This was witnessed by the Frankish monk Gottschalk: *Oeuvres théologiques et grammaticales de Godescalc d'Orbais*, ed. C. Lambot (Louvain, 1945), 208; Borri, 'Gli Istriani', 8, 20–1.
[55] J. Nesbitt and J. Wiita, 'A confraternity of the Comnenian era', *BZ* 68 (1975), 360–84, esp. 364–73 (text), 381–4 (conclusions). Pious charitable foundations and institutions receiving input from various sectors of society are a feature of the other spheres, too: see p. 501.
[56] See e.g. J.-C. Cheynet, *La Société byzantine: l'apport des sceaux*, 2 vols (Paris, 2008), i:17–18, 326–7; ii:422, 502, 505, 507, 514, 535–6, 568, 575, 635–6.

friend who had just returned to Constantinople by sea. The friend complained that the ten gold pieces' worth of smaller denominations he had acquired upon arrival had fallen in value overnight, and they were now worth only 8 *nomismata*. The government ceased striking gold coins altogether after 1353, and to that extent Byzantium itself was no longer a kind of gold standard of empire, alluring with prospects of preferment.[57]

Practice and Organisation

Evidence about the nuts and bolts of Byzantine administrative procedures is even sparser than for the Islamic sphere. Not that governance was lacking in paperwork, at local or central level. Mentions made in passing presuppose frequent communications between Constantinople and border regions.[58] And the palace-bound Constantine VII was praised for responding immediately to the letters streaming in from the provinces and beyond.[59] The more noteworthy materials arising were, along with deeds and suchlike acts of state, kept in archives of the Great Palace. Nearly all are lost. The main traces of record-taking and -keeping are the finds in Istanbul of tens of thousands of lead seals accompanying provincial officials' letters and other missives.[60] Unfortunately the contents of the latter are unknown, as are most of the judgements at the court of the Hippodrome. We owe much of our knowledge of proceedings there to a single manuscript. This contains an edited collection of the rulings of a senior judge, Eustathios Romaios, formatted to give guidance on general rules and problematic cases.[61] The losses are the more regrettable in that doing justice was, along with the mechanisms for dispensing it,

---

[57] Nikephoros Gregoras, *Byzantina historia* XXV.27, ed. Schopen and Bekker, iii:52.

[58] See e.g. Patriarch Nicholas I's mention of the 'daily' arrival of letters from frontier governors, reporting the moves of Symeon of Bulgaria: *Letters*, ed. and tr. R. J. H. Jenkins and L. G. Westerink (Washington, DC, 1973), 58–9.

[59] Theophanes Continuatus, *Chronographia*, ed. I. Bekker (Bonn, 1838), 448.

[60] For the seals collected on land and from the sea near the site of the imperial archives, see G. Zacos and A. Veglery, *Byzantine Lead Seals*, 2 vols (Basel, 1972), i:vii; *MOB*, 1–3.

[61] *Peira Eustathiou tou Romaiou*, in *Ius graecoromanum*, ed. J. Zepos and P. Zepos, 8 vols (Athens, 1931; repr. Darmstadt, 1962), iv:9–260; N. Oikonomides, 'The "Peira" of Eustathios Romaios: an abortive attempt to innovate in Byzantine law', *Fontes minores* 7 (1986), 169–92; B. Sirks, 'The Peira: Roman law in Greek setting', in *Studi in onore di Remo Martini III* (Milan, 2009), 583–91; Z. Chitwood, *Byzantine Legal Culture and the Roman Legal Tradition, 867–1056* (Cambridge, 2017), 8–10, 77–8, 94–6; J. Howard-Johnston, 'The Peira and legal practices in eleventh-century Byzantium', in M. D. Lauxtermann and M. Whittow (eds), *Byzantium in the Eleventh Century: Being in Between* (London, 2017), 63–76; J. Nilsson, *Aristocracy, Politics and Power in Byzantium, 1025–1081* (unpublished DPhil thesis, University of Oxford, 2017); and contributions to J. Howard-Johnston (ed.), *Social Change in Town and Country in Eleventh-Century Byzantium* (Oxford, 2020).

integral to imperial rulership. The *Ecloga* of Leo III (741) set the tone,[62] and in the tenth century Romanos I provided hostels in the capital for provincials facing prolonged litigation there.[63] Romanos made a point of declaring policy through laws, posing as champion of smallholders – 'the poor' (*penetes*) – against 'the powerful' (*dynatoi*), who were acquiring their lands and taking over whole communities.[64] Romanos' successors reinforced this stand with, for example, Constantine VII promulgating a new law that hindered sales to 'the powerful' of lands with military obligations, all in the name of equitableness.[65] Whether or not such legislation was effective,[66] imperial law-making attended to property- and family-matters, while tax-assessors were supposed to take careful account of a community's ability to pay.[67] This intertwining of everyday administrative matters with the law stood in contrast to the general modus operandi in the Islamic world.[68] In so doing, Byzantium upheld the ways of ancient Rome, and emperors sometimes drew attention to this in grandiose style. A monumental product of the 'Cleansing of the Ancient Laws', a codification project begun by the usurper Basil I, is the redaction of the sixth-century laws of Justinian that became known as the *Basilika* (meaning

---

[62] Leo III, *Ecloga*, ed. and German tr. L. Burgmann (Frankfurt am Main, 1983); M. G. Humphreys, *Law, Power, and Imperial Ideology in the Iconoclast Era, c.680–850* (Cambridge, 2015), 81–129.

[63] Theophanes Continuatus, ed. Bekker, 430; S. Runciman, *The Emperor Romanus Lecapenus and his Reign* (Cambridge, 1929), 75. Not, one should note, that charitable foundations and acts were in any way an imperial monopoly, as witness the seals of charitable institutions: B. Caseau, 'L'exercice de la charité d'après les sceaux et les tessères', in B. Caseau et al. (eds), *Hou doron eimi tas graphas blepon noei: Mélanges Jean-Claude Cheynet* [= *TM* 21/1] (Paris, 2017), 31–52 at 31–43.

[64] N. Svoronos and P. Gounarides, *Les Novelles des empereurs macédoniens concernant la terre et les stratiotes: introduction, édition, commentaires* (Athens, 1994), nos 2, 3, 47–71, 72–92; tr. E. McGeer, *The Land Legislation of the Macedonian Emperors* (Toronto, 2000), 40–8, 53–60.

[65] Svoronos and Gounarides, *Les Novelles des empereurs macédoniens*, no. 5, 104–26; tr. McGeer, *Land Legislation*, 71–6.

[66] C. Holmes, *Basil II and the Governance of Empire, 976–1025* (Oxford, 2005), 20–8.

[67] F. Dölger, *Beiträge zur Geschichte der byzantinischen Finanzverwaltung* (Leipzig, 1927), 114–23 (text of the taxation treatise Cod. Marc. gr 173); J. Karayannopoulos, 'Fragmente aus dem Vademecum eines byzantinischen Finanzbeamten', in P. Wirth (ed.), *Polychronion: Festschrift Franz Dölger zum 75. Geburtstag* (Heidelberg, 1966), 318–34 at 321–4. Translations of these guides are available in C. M. Brand, 'Two Byzantine treatises on taxation', *Traditio* 25 (1969), 35–60. Significantly, ancient treatises on land-measurement were copied and revised along with an assortment of texts on 'agricultural matters' (*Geoponika*): *Géoponiques*, French tr. J.-P. Grélois and J. Lefort (Paris, 2012); *Géométries du fisc byzantin*, ed. and French tr. J. Lefort et al. (Paris, 1991), 223–4, 235, 252–5, 263–5(commentary); J. Lefort, 'The rural economy, seventh-twelfth centuries', in *EHB*, i:231–310 at 272; N. Oikonomides, 'The role of the Byzantine state in the economy,' in *EHB*, iii:973–1058.

[68] See pp. 124, 126–7, 331–2.

imperial lawbooks).[69] What amounted to detailed regulations could be presented in legalistic format, as with those governing Constantinople's guilds, the *Book of the Eparch* issued by Leo VI in 912. The preface likens his law-making to that of Moses.[70] Emperors could also pronounce on issues of ethical and even religious import, as Alexios I Komnenos did. Miniatures in a manuscript of the 'Armoury of Doctrine' commissioned by Alexios himself set him in the company of the Church Fathers, who hand him their various works, and of Christ, to whom Alexios presents a copy of the 'Armoury', which draws on these works.[71] His grandson Manuel Komnenos sought to declare upon doctrine, albeit without gaining widespread support from churchmen. Manuel reportedly took up an interpretation of Christ's statement 'My Father is greater than I' (John 14:28) brought back by an envoy from the west, sparking objections from Constantinopolitan clergymen. Manuel eventually prevailed, a council ruling in support of his line in 1166.[72]

The *Basilika* sparked discussion from eleventh- and twelfth-century commentators,[73] while the *Book of the Eparch* long remained in force. However, direct evidence about governance and enforcement of legislation in the provinces is sparse, paperwork for Middle Byzantium being virtually non-existent. Hints come from peripheral regions. For example, two Armenian-language inscriptions on the cathedral's outside wall at Ani announce public works done and new tax arrangements;[74] and

---

[69] *Basilicorum libri LX*, ed. H. J. Scheltema *et al.*, Series A (Text) 9 vols, Series B (Scholia) 9 vols (Groningen, 1953–88); Chitwood, *Byzantine Legal Culture*, 21–2, 32–5, 43–4. A wide assortment of Byzantine legislation, drawn from various earlier editions, is available in *Ius graecoromanum*, ed. Zepos and Zepos.

[70] Leo VI, *Book of the Eparch*, ed. and German tr. J. Koder, *Das Eparchenbuch Leons des Weisen*, prologue, CFHB 33 (Vienna, 1991), 72–3. See M. L. D. Riedel, *Leo VI and the Transformation of Byzantine Christian Identity: Writings of an Unexpected Emperor* (Cambridge, 2018), 5. See also p. 295.

[71] Codex Vatican. Gr. 666, fols 1 verso and 2 recto and verso; I. Spatharakis, *The Portrait in Byzantine Illuminated Manuscripts* (Leiden, 1976), figs 78–80, with exegesis of the miniatures on 122–8; A. Cutler and J.-M. Spieser, *Byzance médiévale 700–1204* (Paris, 1996), 350 and figs 279, 289; G. R. Parpulov, 'The Dogmatic Panoply', in V. Tsamakda (ed.), *A Companion to Byzantine Illustrated Manuscripts* (Leiden, 2017), 430–1.

[72] Manuel's consultations with the Paris-educated Hugh Eteriano during the controversy flagged up his interpretation's background: A. Dondaine, 'Hugues Ethérien et Léon Tuscan', *Archives d'histoire doctrinale et littéraire du moyen âge* 19 (1952), 67–134 at 124. See John Kinnamos, *Epitome rerum ab Ioanne et Alexio Comnenis gestarum* VI.2, ed. A. Meinecke, CSHB (Bonn, 1836), 251–6; *EMK*, 90–1, 287–91; M. Angold, *Church and Society in Byzantium under the Comneni, 1081–1261* (Cambridge, 1995), 83–5.

[73] D. Penna, 'Hagiotheodorites: the last *antecessor*? Some remarks on one of the "new" *Basilica* scholiasts', *Subseciva Groningana* 9 (2014), 399–427

[74] J.-P. Mahé, 'Ani sous Constantin X d'après une inscription de 1060', in V. Déroche (ed.), *Mélanges Gilbert Dagron [= TM 14]* (Paris, 2002), 403–14 at 405–8, 411–14.

standardised tax exemptions and suchlike devices from archives in Byzantine southern Italy indicate the dissemination of administrative measures.[75] Documents occasionally cast light on governance in other provinces, too. Thus a tax-register records the updating of liabilities of taxpayers near Thebes in the eleventh century; the entries bespeak diligence of the calibre assumed in treatises on land assessment and tax-collecting.[76] Although secular landowners kept archives[77] and clues about private estates emerge from a handful of wills and property-transfers of middling-size landowners,[78] surviving documentation mostly concerns properties that ended up in ecclesiastical or monastic hands. The fullest assortments come from houses still in existence such as St John's on Patmos[79] and, most notably, those on Mount Athos replete with acts concerning properties and privileges.[80] The pattern of evidence is all the more skewed in that Athos enjoyed imperial protection and its estates lay mostly in eastern Macedonia. Far less is known about houses lacking the sort of privileges emperors lavished upon Athos. Among the exceptions are the rules and foundation charters of houses founded by senior office-holders in the late eleventh century. One of these, at

[75] V. Minale, 'Sulla recezione dell'*Ecloga* isaurica nell'Italia bizantina: variazioni sul leit-motiv "alla periferia dell'impero"', in J.-M. Martin *et al.* (eds), *L'Héritage byzantin en Italie (VIIIe–XIIe siècle)*, 4 vols to date (Rome, 2011–), ii:37–49; V. von Falkenhausen, 'Amministrazione fiscale nell'Italia meridionale bizantina (secoli IX–XI)', in *ibid.*, ii:533–56 at 536–52.

[76] N. Svoronos, 'Recherches sur le cadastre byzantin et la fiscalité aux XIe et XII siècles: le cadastre de Thèbes', *Bulletin de Corréspondance Héllenique*, 83 (1959), 1–166, esp. 11–19 (text), 144–5 (conclusion); repr. in his *Études sur l'organisation intérieure, la société et l'économie de l'Empire byzantin* (London, 1973), no. 3. See p. 90.

[77] For indications of individuals keeping copies of title-deeds and tax receipts, see B. Caseau, 'Un aspect de la diplomatique byzantine: les copies de documents', in *L'Autorité de l'écrit au Moyen Âge (Orient-Occident)* [= *Histoire ancienne et médiévale* 102] (Paris, 2009), 159–73.

[78] For such wills, see S. Vryonis, 'The will of a provincial magnate, Eustathius Boilas (1059)', *DOP* 11 (1957), 263–77 (tr. at 264–72); M. Hendy, *Studies in the Byzantine Monetary Economy, c.300–1450* (Cambridge, 1985), 209–20; G. Dagron, 'Hériter de soi-même', in J. Beaucamp and G. Dagron (eds), *La Transmission du patrimoine. Byzance et l'aire méditerreanéenne* (Paris, 1998), 81–99; J.-C. Cheynet, 'Aristocracy and inheritance (11th–13th centuries)', English tr. in *TBAMF*, no. 4. See also C. Holmes, 'Political literacy', in P. Stephenson (ed.), *The Byzantine World* (London, 2010), 137–48 at 144–5.

[79] *Vyzantina engrapha tes Mones Patmou*, ed. E. L. Vranouse *et al.*, 3 vols (Athens, 1980–2016).

[80] These are in the process of full publication: *Archives de l'Athos*, ed. P. Lemerle *et al.*, 23 vols to date (Paris and Leuven, 1937–). Published to date: Chilandar I; Dionysiou; Docheiariou; Esphigménou; Iviron I–IV; Kastamonitou; Kutlumus; Lavra I–IV; Pantéléèmôn; Pantocrator; Prôtaton; Vatopédi I–II; Xénophon; Xéropotamou. Forthcoming: Chilandar II–III; Vatopédi III; Zographou. See also pp. 425–6. For a copy of a cartulary of the Monastery of St Paul on Mount Latros (Latmos) in Asia Minor, see *Das Chartular des Paulos-Klosters am Berge Latros*, ed. and German tr. C. Gastgeber and O. Kresten (Vienna, 2015).

Bachkovo in what is now Bulgaria, is still a monastery.[81] In any case, these documents itemise landed possessions and prescribe what ought to be done, rather than constituting the raw data of governance.

Even so, the Athonite documents supply evidence of lively inter-actions between government officials and landholders of widely differ-ing status. The alacrity with which houses sought confirmation of privileges after regime change signals how marks of favour from the government of the day mattered to them, if also the value new rulers put on benefiting from their prayers – and on being seen to do so.[82] One gains a sense of the state's financial problems from the ever-more-detailed exemptions that eleventh-century charters list. These show how tax-collectors might query the tax-exempt status of any produce or animals not named expressly in charters, and occasionally they declare outright the vital importance of chrysobulls.[83] And the Athonite documents bear witness to Alexios Komnenos' efforts to raise revenue and reward relatives and other intimates by confiscating lands.[84] They also attest to the interconnection between fiscal and judicial issues. For example, the governor of Thessaloniki and inspec-tors of tax-liabilities adjudicated disputes over boundaries between Athonite houses and landholders, including communities of peasants.[85] This does not mean that the peasants invariably won, and it is only the charters that survive. But it was presumably for such persons of modest means that hostels were built in Constantinople; Eustathios Romaios' *Peira* covers grassroots cases coming to the notice of the central courts. Peasants, including tenants on landed estates, seemingly had access to public courts

[81] The military judge and historian Michael Attaleiates drafted the rule for his charitable foundations at Rhaidestos (on the Sea of Marmara) and in Constantinople: P. Gautier, 'La *Diataxis* de Michel Attaliate', *REB* 39 (1981), 5–143 (text 17–130); tr. A.-M. Talbot, '*Rule* of Michael Attaleiates for his almshouse in Rhaidestos and for the Monastery of Christ *Panoiktirmon* in Constantinople', in *BMFD*, i:326–76 (text 333–76). For the charter of the general Gregory Pakourianos for his monastery at Bachkovo: P. Gautier, 'Le typikon du sébaste Grégoire Pakourianos', *REB* 42 (1984), 5–145 (text 9–133); tr. R. Jordan, '*Typikon* of Gregory Pakourianos for the Monastery of the Mother of God *Petritzonitissa* in Bačkovo', in *BMFD*, ii:507–63 (text 519–63).

[82] *MLIB*, 107–9, 140–1.

[83] See e.g. *Actes d'Iviron* no. 41, ed. J. Lefort *et al.*, 4 vols (Paris, 1985–95), ii:132–4 (text); 130–1 (summary); *MLIB*, 291 and n. 65.

[84] *MLIB*, 283–8, 294; K. Smyrlis, 'The fiscal revolution of Alexios I Komnenos: timing, scope and motives', in Cheynet and Flusin (eds), *Autour du Premier humanisme byzantin*, 593–610, esp. 595–7

[85] R. Morris, 'Dispute settlement in the Byzantine provinces in the tenth century', in W. Davies and P. Fouracre (eds), *The Settlement of Disputes in Early Medieval Europe* (Cambridge, 1986), 125–48 esp. 131–5, 141–6; R. Morris, 'The *epoptēs* Thomas at work', in E. Kermeli and O. Özel (eds), *The Ottoman Empire: Myths, Realities and 'Black Holes' – Contributions in Honour of Colin Imber* (Istanbul, 2006), 23–38 at 34–7.

right up to 1204.[86] The multiple crises confronting Alexios Komnenos led him to devolve military and administrative powers extensively, granting them to members of his family and other associates, seemingly for life.[87] However, later emperors reined these in, issuing *pronoiai* only for limited terms. Michael VIII expected military service from grantees, many of whose *pronoiai* were hereditable, albeit for a limited term or on condition that they had served well or given their lives.[88] Charters of subsequent emperors concede the right of holders to bequeath *pronoiai*. Although their occasional statements that *pronoiai* could be held 'without service' leave unclear what sort of service would otherwise be expected, they do bespeak some relaxation of imperial oversight of provincial affairs.[89] By the second half of the fourteenth century, government coffers were virtually empty. However, judging by deeds and suchlike Athonite texts, the state's capacity to challenge rights to landownership and to appropriate property was resilient. Its confiscation of ecclesiastical properties in the later fourteenth century met with bitter opposition from once-favoured houses and such advocates as Nicholas Kabasilas, with government policy tending to waver.[90] The resultant documentation illustrates both the state powers still exercisable and the value attaching to deeds which institutions and other property-holders could cite in law.[91]

Between the Lines: Political Culture

Given the meagreness of our sources, tracking the ways in which individuals in Byzantium worked the system, made alternative arrangements, or sought minimal engagement with officialdom is even harder than for our other two spheres. Evidence is fullest for highfliers seeking influence behind the throne, if not the throne itself. Thus Michael Psellos' *Chronographia* lifts the lid on the foibles and faux pas of the mid-eleventh-century emperors.

[86] D. Jacoby, 'From Byzantium to Latin Romania: continuity and change', in B. Arbel *et al.* (eds), *Latins and Greeks in the Eastern Mediterranean after 1204* (London, 1989), 1–44 at 3–5.

[87] *LPIB*, 150–2.

[88] *Actes de Docheiariou*, ed. N. Oikonomides (Paris, 1984), 124–5 (commentary); *LPIB*, 266–70, 280–2, 313–15, 417–18.

[89] *LPIB*, 415–36. See also pp. 436, 445.

[90] I. Ševčenko, 'Nicolas Cabasilas' "anti-Zealot" discourse: a reinterpretation', *DOP* 11 (1957), 79–171; repr. in his *Society and Intellectual Life in Late Byzantium* (London, 1981), no. 4; K. Smyrlis, 'The state, the land and private property: confiscating monastic and church properties in the Palaiologan period', in D. G. Angelov (ed.), *Church and Society in Late Byzantium* (Kalamazoo, MI, 2009), 58–87, esp. 69–72, 76–9.

[91] For the law as an instrument of government, but also constituting a limitation upon the ruler's free exercise of his will: pp. 169–70, 279–84, 384–6, 402–4; for the rather different balance between the ruler's wishes and law in Islam: pp. 104–5; as also for the lesser impact of the written word there: pp. 126–7.

Scenes play out mostly within the palace complex. Presenting himself as once and future trusty counsellor, Psellos has to reconcile his unflattering portraits of emperors like Constantine IX with past encomia he had delivered before them: an orator's function is to accentuate the positive.[92] Orations provided means to advancement for ambitious bureaucrats like Psellos, who would vet one another's compositions before their submission to be considered for delivery at court.[93]

Literary accomplishment was bound up with political profile, and, in the twelfth century, households of the Komnenian aristocracy vied to host performances of poems and suchlike at literary gatherings (*theatra*).[94] Seeing that letters, mostly written in Attic Greek, were often collected and circulated by their authors, one might dismiss them as too mannered to yield insights into political culture. Yet such letters were grist to the mill of office-holders seeking advantage, and they can be revealing. For example, letters flowed forth from Niketas Magistros, a former senior office-holder banished to his country estate after allegedly hatching a plot to unseat Romanos I. Obsequiousness pervades his letters to John Mystikos, who maintained close ties with court even after his own disgrace, and rehabilitation was never far from Niketas' agenda. A letter to another office-holder, Constantine Kombos, asks him to intercede at court on Niketas' behalf in the effective manner that John Mystikos had once done to clear Kombos himself of a charge.[95] Assignment to the provinces was bemoaned by letter-writing (and versifying) prelates as tantamount to exile, to the point of being a commonplace.[96] Such laments were not, however, mere stereotypes. Expulsion from Constantinople was the penalty for a variety of offences, and, for the aspirational, being debarred was a blow

---

[92] Michael Psellos, *Chronographia* VI.25–6, ed. D.-R. Reinsch, 2 vols (Berlin, 2014), i:117–18; tr. E. R. A. Sewter, *Fourteen Byzantine Rulers: The* Chronographia *of Michael Psellos*, rev. edn (Harmondsworth, 1966), 167–8.

[93] F. Lauritzen, 'Christopher of Mytilene's parody of the haughty Mauropous', *BZ* 100 (2007), 125–32, esp. 128–30.

[94] See M. Mullett, 'Aristocracy and patronage in the literary circles of Comnenian Constantinople', in *TBA*, 173–201; *EMK*, 335–56. E. Jeffreys, 'Literary trends in the Constantinopolitan courts in the 1120s and 1130s', in A. Bucossi and A. Rodriguez Suarez (eds), *John II Komnenos, Emperor of Byzantium: In the Shadow of Father and Son* (Abingdon, 2016), 110–20.

[95] Niketas Magistros, *Lettres d'un exilé (928–946)* no. 22, ed. and tr. L. G. Westerink (Paris, 1973), 108–9 and note on 106. On John Mystikos and Constantine Kombos see, respectively, entries in *PmbZ²* #22938, #23840.

[96] On the theme of 'exile' in letters, see M. Mullett, *Theophylact of Ohrid: Reading the Letters of a Byzantine Archbishop* (Birmingham, 1997), 248–67, 274–7; M. Mullett, 'Originality in the Byzantine letter: the case of exile', in A. R. Littlewood (ed.), *Originality in Byzantine Literature, Art and Music* (Oxford, 1996), 39–58; C. Livanos, 'Exile and return in John Mauropous, Poem 47', *BMGS* 32 (2008), 38–49. See also J. M. Hussey, *The Orthodox Church in the Byzantine Empire* (Oxford, 1986), 321.

to career and social status alike. In contrast, inhabiting the City brought access to the fringes of the court, at least. Losing one's post, capacity for patronage and being in the thick of it is hard to endure, a tenth-century letter-writer acknowledges. Although urging a keeper of the emperor's bedchamber to accept what God willed, he exclaims: 'What could be more delightful than to find oneself in the emperor's entourage, to participate in the imperial lifestyle, to wear magnificent costumes, to share an intimate association with the emperor?'[97]

Surviving letter-collections are skewed towards court and capital. Exceptions tend to prove the rule, as for example the letters of the archbishop of Bulgaria at the turn of the eleventh and twelfth centuries, Theophylact. Many letters address friends and former colleagues and pupils in Constantinople, complaining of the 'deathly stench' of Ohrid's streets and pining for the City, fearing that he is himself 'becoming a barbarian amidst the Bulgarians'.[98] Others deal with local issues, notably the well-being of his agrarian tenants and the villainy of Bulgaria's chief tax-collector.[99] Theophylact offers counsel to Gregory Pakourianos, newly appointed governor of Ohrid, urging him assiduously to exercise reason and show 'decency' (*chrestotes*) towards those under his command.[100] Such sentiments, like requests for officials to come and punish lawbreakers,[101] are common enough, but the invocations of norms were not commonplaces. The letters of Psellos attest unceasing communications between men of influence in the capital and the provinces, wheels within wheels. At least a fifth of the 500 or so extant letters are addressed to *kritai* – provincial judges with wide-ranging responsibilities. These were largely working letters, assembled after Psellos' death, and not stylistic party-pieces.[102]

---

[97] Theodore Daphnopates, *Correspondance* no. 38, ed. and tr. J. Darrouzès and L. G. Westerink (Paris, 1978), 216–17; H. Maguire, 'Images of the court', in *GOB*, 183–91 at 183. On the keeper of the bedchamber (*koitonites*) John, see *PmbZ*² #23095. For a similar letter, see Theodore Daphnopates, *Correspondance* no. 40, ed. and tr. Darrouzès and Westerink, 226–7; *PmbZ*² #31459.

[98] Theophylact of Ohrid, *Lettres* nos 6, 34, ed. and tr. P. Gautier (Thessaloniki, 1986), 146–7, 242–3; D. Obolensky, *Six Byzantine Portraits* (Oxford, 1988), 48, 58; Mullett, *Theophylact*, 267–71, 295, 306.

[99] Theophylact of Ohrid, *Lettres* nos 11, 88, 96, ed. and tr. Gautier, 162–5, 460–3, 482–7; Obolensky, *Six Byzantine Portraits*, 53–4; Mullett, *Theophylact*, 123–7, 297, 328, 331–2.

[100] Theophylact of Ohrid, *Lettres* no. 68, ed. and tr. Gautier, 372–5; Mullett, *Theophylact*, 319–20.

[101] See e.g. a letter of the metropolitan of Athens, Michael Choniates, to George Tessarokantapelos, asking him to encourage an energetic (and honest) tax-collector to come and set things to right in Attica: *Epistulae* no. 28, ed. F. Kolovou (Berlin, 2001), 38–9 (text); 65*–66* (summary).

[102] S. Papaioannou, '"Fragile literature": Byzantine letter-collections and the case of Michael Psellos', in P. Odorico (ed.), *La Face cachée de la littérature byzantine: le texte en tant que message immédiat* (Paris, 2012), 289–328 at 305–7, 319. Invaluable summaries of all Psellos' known letters are given in Michael Psellos, *Letters*, ed. M. Jeffreys and

Psellos often writes on behalf of protégés or friends. Invocations of 'friend-ship' (*philia*), a term with many shades of meaning, and avowals of an individual's personal ties with Psellos blend with professions of public service and appeals for clemency. Wheedling and dangling inducements, Psellos takes provincial office-holders' feathering of their nests for granted. Yet he is alert to tales circulating between court and provinces and is concerned for reputation, implying standards of a sort.[103]

That checks and balances could hold, with help from law-courts and an ethos of public service, emerges from cases reviewed in the eleventh-century *Peira* and from the Thebes tax-register. Crosschecking of claims to land-ownership with what the tax-rolls said provided a means of safeguarding smallholders who lacked title-deeds or influential connections. The *Peira* shows sympathy for peasants, even tenants (*paroikoi*) litigating against 'the powerful'.[104] Weight is attached to word-of-mouth allegations against powerful persons or institutions acquiring land from 'the poor', but oral testimony against the latter by 'the powerful' is inadmissable.[105] This chimes in with the later eleventh-century 'Counsels and Tales' of Kekaumenos, although from a different vantage point. The retired commander Kekaumenos inclines towards *private*-spiritedness. Thus he advises the reader – presumably a man of property – to visit the local dignitary (probably a judge), but not too often, and on no account to take up publicly the cause of common folk over any of his misdeeds; a discreet word with the official will do the business better.[106] For office-holding readers, Kekaumenos offers pragmatic advice. For example, a provincial judge must beware of

M. D. Lauxtermann, *The Letters of Michael Psellos: Cultural Networks and Historical Realities* (Oxford, 2017). For the letters addressed to *kritai*, see *ibid.*, 10, 435–41; Nilsson, *Aristocracy, Politics and Power*, 47–9.

[103] See e.g. Psellos' letter commending the *krites* Pothos, one of his ex-students, for filling a measure of justice as well as his own purse; others warn of the risk to one's reputation from overdoing the purse-filling: summaries in Psellos, *Letters* KD 35, 55, 90, ed. Jeffreys and Lauxtermann, 184, 196–7, 213 (see also for useful discussion 30, 423); Nilsson, *Aristocracy, Politics and Power*, 57–9, 65–6, 78–81, 107–19, 125–42; Chitwood, *Byzantine Legal Culture*, 67–9.

[104] *Peira* XV.2, XXIII.3, XXXVI.18, XL.1–4, 12, XLII.18–19, ed. Zepos and Zepos, iv:49, 85, 146–7, 165–6, 167, 177–8; G. G. Litavrin, 'Vizantiiskaia znat' (dinaty) pered vysshim konstantinopol'skim sudom (X-pervaia polovina XIv.). Iz kommentariia k "Pire" Evstafiia Romeia', *Vizantiiskii Vremennik* 69 (94) (2010), 8–31 at 18–19, 29–30; Chitwood, *Byzantine Legal Culture*, 82, 85–6.

[105] *Peira* VIII.1, IX.1, 6, XXIII.3, ed. Zepos and Zepos, iv:32, 38, 39, 85–6; Nilsson, Aristocracy, Politics and Power, 230–5; W. Danny, *Society and State in Byzantium 1025–1071* (unpublished DPhil thesis, University of Oxford, 2008). See also p. 421.

[106] Kekaumenos, 'Counsels and tales', ed. and Russian tr. G. G. Litavrin, *Sovety i rasskazy Kekavmena*, 2nd edn (St Petersburg, 2003), 214–17; tr. C. Roueché, 'Consilia et narrationes', (2013), 40.32–42.09, www.ancientwisdoms.ac.uk/library/kekaumenos-consilia-et-narrationes/ (accessed 30 January 2020); Nilsson, *Aristocracy, Politics and Power*, 285–7.

giving subordinates grounds for formally reporting against him, whilst a junior official should think twice before reporting to anyone a superior's error, lest all concerned shun him 'like a snake'.[107] A man of substance's reputation in the provinces was determined by quite a broad band of opinion, involving interaction between persons at court, state officials, *dynatoi* and provincial worthies: trading favours and working the system for personal gain went with a certain sense of public service.

Middle Byzantine society was, then, quite localised. A strong sense of regional affinity is shown in saints' *Lives*, where an individual's *patris* ('homeland') tends to be his native region. Indeed, he was often a *xenos* ('stranger, foreigner') virtually from the moment he left his home village.[108] The same picture emerges from analysis of the find-spots of lead seals. They are far more likely than not to occur in the vicinity of where they had been struck, with the exception of seals issued or found in the capital. This implies that their circulation was generally quite restricted, whether they belonged to office-holders, churchmen or local notables. Provincial districts were small worlds, where even the elites seldom travelled far afield.[109] Individuals asserted status by means of both personal seals and seals declaring their titles and offices; the line drawn between their private and public roles in the provinces was far from clear.[110] Kekaumenos assumes that local grandees will pull every string available, locally or in Constantinople, and the case has been made for quite sweeping devolution of authority in the provinces.[111] Even so, notables did not monopolise communications utterly: as seen, protests from below might get through to the capital.[112]

After 1204

These checks and balances did, however, presuppose a functioning capital. Such was no longer available for two generations after Constantinople's fall

---

[107] Kekaumenos, 'Counsels and tales', ed. and tr. Litavrin, 146–7, 142–3; tr. Roueché, 7.10–21; 5.25–8; Nilsson, *Aristocracy, Politics and Power*, 262–3, 294–5; Chitwood, *Byzantine Legal Culture*, 64–5.

[108] E. Malamut, *Sur la route des saints byzantins* (Paris, 1993), 114, 121, 280–3.

[109] J.-C. Cheynet and C. Morrisson, 'Lieux de trouvaille et circulation des sceaux', *Studies in Byzantine Sigillography* 2 (1990), 105–36; repr. in Cheynet, *La Société byzantine*, i:85–112, esp. 93–5; J.-C. Cheynet, 'Les sceaux du musée d'Iznik', *REB* 49 (1991), 377–412, esp. 390–410.

[110] J.-C. Cheynet, 'Official power and non-official power', in A. Cameron (ed.), *Fifty Years of Prosopography: The Later Roman Empire, Byzantium and Beyond* (Oxford, 2003), 137–51 at 139–41.

[111] See L. Neville, *Authority in Byzantine Provincial Society, 850–1100* (Cambridge, 2004).

[112] On the localisation of power, continued links between centre and periphery and access to paramount figures of authority in the Latin west and Islam, see pp. 142–3, 145–6, 148–50, 401–4, 407–9, 220–2, 225, 227–8, 245–6, 350–3, 359–64, 472–7.

to the Fourth Crusaders, while by any account Michael VIII's returning of empire to the City left its material resources shrunken. Not that all the lights went out in 1204. Ample sources survive to suggest social cohesiveness and administrative order in the polity Michael and his precursors had headed at Nicaea, acting in close but not unbroken harmony with churchmen there. Indeed, ecclesiastical organisation in towns like Nicaea and Ephesos proved quite self-reliant after imperial rule receded.[113] Senior churchmen seem to have played a key role in maintaining the social fabric in the rival Byzantine state in Epiros, too. Archbishop Demetrios Chomatenos issued authoritative rulings and sought to resolve disputes across a broad spectrum of civil issues, including marriage and the oversight of propertied orphans.[114] That the body of written judgements of Chomatenos is not simply the mark of an exceptionally learned and ambitious churchman's activities[115] is suggested by other hints of concern for mutual welfare and corporate cults of icons, at least among propertyholders. A text attests to what seems to have been a confraternity akin to that already noted at Thebes but functioning in Epiros during the 1220s.[116] The adaptability to straitened circumstances already shown by the Nicaean rulers is manifest in subsequent emperors' use of *pronoiai* to harness the self-interest (if not loyalties) of a broad band of provincials well into the second half of the fourteenth century.[117] The solemnity of Roman law underpinned the right of the state to revoke grants of privileges and lands, even to institutions like Athos. This helps to explain why imperial

---

[113] M. Angold, *A Byzantine Government in Exile: Government and Society under the Laskarids of Nicaea, 1204–1261* (Oxford, 1975), esp. 202–78; J. Pahlitzsch, 'The Greek orthodox communities of Nicaea and Ephesus under Turkish rule in the fourteenth century: a new reading of old sources', in A. C. S. Peacock *et al.* (eds), *Islam and Christianity in Medieval Anatolia* (Burlington, VT, 2015), 147–64.

[114] Demetrios Chomatenos, *Ponemata diaphora*, ed. G. Prinzing (Berlin, 2002), e.g. nos 84, 85 and 90 on 286–96, 307–11, 175*–9* (text), 186*–8* (commentary). On Chomatenos' wide-ranging concerns and the distinctive status of his archbishopric, see G. Prinzing, 'The autocephalous Byzantine ecclesiastical province of Bulgaria/Ohrid', *Bulgaria Medievalis* 3 (2012), 355–83 at 371–3; G. Prinzing, 'Abbot or bishop? The conflict about the spiritual obedience of the Vlach peasants in the region of Bothrotos ca. 1220: case no. 80 of the legal works of Demetrios Chomatenos reconsidered', in Angelov (ed.), *Church and Society in Late Byzantium*, 25–42; G. Prinzing, 'Konvergenz und Divergenz zwischen dem Patriarchatsregister und den Ponemata Diaphora des Demetrios Chomatenos von Achrida/Ohrid', in Gastgeber *et al.* (eds), *Register of the Patriarchate of Constantinople*, 9–32.

[115] See Angold, *Church and Society in Byzantium*, 139–57, 175–8, 197–239.

[116] G. Prinzing, 'Spuren einer religiösen Bruderschaft in Epiros um 1225? Zur Deutung der Memorialtexte im *Codex Cromwell* 11', *BZ* 101 (2008), 766–72; G. Prinzing, 'Epiros 1204–1261: historical outline – sources – prosopography', in J. Herrin and G. Saint-Guillain (eds), *Identities and Allegiances in the Eastern Mediterranean after 1204* (Farnham, 2011), 87–92 and fig. 5.1. For other instances of self-help on a collective basis: pp. 172, 485.

[117] See p. 441.

ceremonies and titles bespeaking access to the court still had some allure for aspirants to security of wealth and land-tenure, as well as status. The fact remained that material resources could now be amassed without direct service of, or reference to, the emperor. He could only raise around 30,000 (debased) gold coins from Constantinople's customs duties, whereas the Genoese pocketed 200,000 pieces in their quarter in the Pera, across the Golden Horn. Such, at least, is the estimate of the last great classicising historian.[118] Small wonder that, from around the time Nikephoros Gregoras wrote, ever more elite families and individuals were looking to other quarters for self-enrichment and personal and financial security: to Italian merchants and also the Turks.[119] Perhaps more noteworthy is the fact that political culture turned round the emperor's court for so long after he had lost most visible means of support.

---

[118] Nikephoros Gregoras, *Byzantina historia* XVII.1, ed. Schopen and Bekker, ii:841–2.
[119] See *BBOL*, 200–14; see also pp. 442–3, 447–52.

The Islamic World
Sources

Jo Van Steenbergen and Jonathan Shepard

Figure 6.1 Rare example of figural coinage: 'Standing Caliph' gold dinar showing the Umayyad caliph, Abd al-Malik, probably minted at Damascus in 697 (20mm); © Ashmolean Museum, University of Oxford

The Qur'an, the Prophet and His 'Deputies'

The Qur'an offers injunctions on virtually every aspect of behaviour and on interrelationships with other communities. It lays down rules for worship and for living by God's commandments, as revealed uniquely to the Prophet. The language is colourful, often poetic, and allusions to episodes of Muhammad's life are frequent. To this extent, Muslims had wider-ranging maxims to guide them than did the followers of Christ. However, the Qur'an's vibrancy does not make for clarity. Nor does it amount to a comprehensive code of conduct. And then comes the question of the long-term future of the *umma* ('community') Muhammad had formed: who, if anyone, could and should take his place? The need for a commander-in-chief was acute, given the conflict under way against those resisting his call to submit to the Will of God.

A series of 'deputies' (*khalifa*) emerged from Muhammad's entourage to head the *umma* in the generation following his death in 632.[1] Methods of deciding who should be caliph varied. At the same time, sayings attributed to the Prophet but not found in the Qur'an proliferated along with amplifications of statements in that text. Eventually, the sayings were gathered into collections known as *hadith*s which list the names of informants who have passed the word on. These were circulating, together with commentaries, by the eighth century. Narratives purporting to contextualise them were embedded in later historical writings. Neither the authorship of the *hadith*s nor the actuality of the stories that were told of rival caliphs' conflicts in the mid-seventh century is our prime concern.[2] But detailed narratives became integral parts of Islamic political culture, acknowledging the tensions but insisting on the cohesiveness of the *dar al-Islam*. Uncertainty as to what forms of worship and rites Muhammad's teachings entailed is apparent in texts from the seventh century.[3] One may presuppose similar pragmatic experimentation in political structures, as deals were struck and treaties made with the urban centres in the conquerors' path. Still only a small minority among the Christian, Zoroastrian and polytheist populations under their sway, the Arabic-speaking Muslims had good reason to close their ranks behind a leadership professing Muhammad's teachings.

Performative Communication: Sources for Historical Context, Ideology, Ceremonial and Prescriptive Writings

Early Islam

By 700, the Umayyad family was well-enough established to supply a series of leaders of the *umma*. The Umayyads did not sponsor historical writing or

[1] See pp. 214–15.
[2] See *SOH*, 3–17. The question of dating the canonical text of the Qur'an – traditionally ascribed to Caliph Uthman's sponsorship – has been reopened by H. Chahdi, *Le Mushaf dans les débuts de l'Islam: recherches sur sa constitution et étude comparative de manuscrits coraniques anciens et de traités de qira'at, rasm et fawasil* (unpublished PhD thesis, École Pratique des Hautes Études Paris, 2016). The scholarly state of play is also presented by A. Fedeli, 'Dating early Qur'anic manuscripts: reading the objects, their texts and the results of their material analysis', in G. Dye (ed.), *Early Islam: The Sectarian Milieu of Late Antiquity?* (Chicago, 2020); eadem, *Qur'anic Manuscripts, Their Text, and the Alphonse Mingana Papers Held in the Department of Special Collections of the University of Birmingham* (unpublished PhD thesis, University of Birmingham, 2015); F. Déroche, *La Voix et le calame: les chemins de la canonisation du Coran* (Paris, 2016); idem, *Le Coran, une histoire plurielle: essai sur la formation du texte coranique* (Paris, 2019). The broader cultural backdrop is set out by A. Neuwirth, *The Qur'an and Late Antiquity: A Shared Heritage* (New York, 2019).
[3] R. Hoyland, 'New documentary texts and the early Islamic state', *BSOAS* 69 (2006), 395–416.

literary culture at court. Nor did they favour elaborate ceremonial, preferring the themes of austerity and desert warrior values. They were, however, ready enough to proclaim piety through visual media. The Dome of the Rock was built to assert the Islamic presence in Jerusalem, setting in stone the triumph of Islam; gold mosaic inscriptions emphasise the Oneness of God in pointed contrast to the Christian concept of the Trinity, spelling out the name of the caliph responsible for the building, Abd al-Malik (685–705).[4] His son, Walid I, built the Great Mosque in Damascus on the site of a church. Construction of mosques and palaces became a standard means of expressing piety and earthly dominion, especially by those newly come to power.[5] It was Abd al-Malik who put the coinage on a firm footing by issuing what became standard types of coins: silver dirhams and gold dinars circulated throughout the caliphate. Their inscriptions cited the Qur'an or were, essentially, religious slogans. Along with the mint and date, they carried the ruler's name, a means of impressing his authority, piety and utility to commerce on anyone who could read or recognise Arabic. *Sikka*, the right to strike coins with the ruler's name on them, became a hallmark of sovereignty.[6] Unsurprisingly, would-be hegemons were apt to lay claim to such rights when caliphal authority was faltering, as in the later years of the Umayyad's successors, the Abbasids.[7] But the *sikka*'s interlacing of caliphal mystique with common economic self-interest was a stabiliser.

The later phases of Umayyad rule saw fullest expositions of the caliph's authority. The court poets make him out to be laying down the law for all as judge, citing the Qur'an (38:25), where God tells David: 'We have made you a caliph on earth'. The court poet Farazdaq calls caliphs 'imams of guidance and beaters of skulls', while his rival Jarir urged more measuredly: 'He is the caliph, so accept what he judges for you in truth'.[8] A letter addressing provincial governors expatiates on the caliph's

[4] O. Grabar, *The Dome of the Rock* (Cambridge, MA, 2006), esp. 3–10, 59–93. See, for a cogent attribution of the Dome to Abd al- Malik, J. Lassner, *Medieval Jerusalem: Forging an Islamic City in Spaces Sacred to Christians and Jews* (Ann Arbor, MI, 2017), 81–95, esp. 84–5, 92–5; A. George, 'Paradise or empire? On a paradox of Umayyad art', in A. George and A. Marsham (eds), *Power, Patronage, and Memory in Early Islam: Perspectives on Umayyad Elites* (New York, 2018), 39–67 at 40–9.

[5] George, 'Paradise or empire?', 52–9. See also Figure 9.1.

[6] C. E. Bosworth *et al.*, *EI²* s.v. 'Sikka'; see also Figure 6.1; F. Bessard, *Caliphs and Merchants: Cities and Economies of Power in the Near East (700–950)* (Oxford, 2020). Compare the *basileus*' monopoly pp. 87–8, 88–9 and see also pp. 405–6.

[7] W. L. Treadwell, *Buyid Coinage: A Die Corpus (322–445 AH)* (Oxford, 2001), xiv; *idem*, 'The numismatic evidence for the reign of Ahmad b. Tulun (254–270/868-883)', *Al-'Usur al-Wusta* 25 (2017), 7–33. On *sikka*: pp. 344, 345–6, 460.

[8] *Cal*, 72. It seems to have been the Umayyad dynasty and their allies who made the title 'God's caliph' a monarchic and imperial formula: A. Marsham, '"God's Caliph" revisited: Umayyad political thought in its late antique context', in George and Marsham (eds), *Power, Patronage, and Memory*, 3–37 at 25–8.

untrammelled right to judge, in effect making law on behalf of the One who had appointed him. The author was the caliph al-Walid II (743–4). He insisted on his entitlement to determine without consulting others all issues, notably the succession of his two sons.[9] Such claims were not sheer rhetoric. The Umayyads issued rulings on all kinds of matters: a decree of Umar II (717–20) covers the taxing of non-Muslims and converts to Islam, a complex issue touching on both administration and belief. [10] This trail of evidence, however, peters out. The Abbasids after 750 and later dynasties did not treat law-making or adjudication as integral to their rulership, beyond everyday matters of governance – violent crime, for instance. Leadership involving *shari'a* in the broader sense of lifestyle and ethical dealings with fellow Muslims was not within the caliph's remit. So when family matters, property, inheritance or commercial contracts were in question, it was for experts (*'ulama'*) to make pronouncements in light of the Traditions of the Prophet and Islamic law, while judges (*qadi*) decided cases in court and enforced them.

There are signs that the early Abbasids did aspire to responsibilities in this field. Ruling with justice and in accordance with the Will of God was prominent in the manifesto put out by their first caliph, Abu l-Abbas, justifying his ousting of the Umayyads.[11] And it was with a view to pronouncing on general matters of right and wrong that Caliph al-Ma'mun (813–33) took up the doctrine of the 'createdness' of the Qur'an. Here was a way towards arbitrating on what constituted correct belief and adjudicating points of Islamic law. Al-Ma'mun was intelligent and ruthless enough to present his vision of caliph as theologian compellingly. But opponents such as the jurist Ahmad b. Hanbal (d. 855) persisted and eventually carried the day: decisions about Islamic law and practice must only rest on the Traditions of the Prophet; the mass of materials comprising them was beyond the wit of any man to master; so their interpretation was reserved for the scholars who collected and studied them.[12] One has to look to commentaries and legal textbooks of the four main schools of law for the procedures and principles that guided judges in law-courts. The *'ulama'* and judges engaged in continual debate, opening up opportunities for dissension. Nor had they the means to prevent overheavy taxation or exactions by the caliph's officials,

---

[9] P. Crone and M. Hinds, *God's Caliph: Religious Authority in the First Centuries of Islam* (Cambridge, repr. 2003), 118–26 (tr.); *Cal*, 81–2.

[10] Crone and Hinds, *God's Caliph*, 78–9.

[11] al-Tabari, *Ta'rikh al-rusul wa-al-muluk [Annales quos scripsit Abu Djafar Mohammed ibn Djarir at-Tabari]*, ed. M. J. de Goeje *et al.*, 15 vols (Leiden, 1879–1901), iii.1:29–33; tr. J. A. Williams, *The Abbasid Revolution [= The History of al-Tabari* 27] (Albany, NY, 1985), 152–7.

[12] H. Laoust, *EI²* s.v. 'Ahmad b. Hanbal'; *Cal*, 93–4.

administrative acts kept apart from law. Nonetheless, their judgements and schools of jurisprudence provided a metronome, ticking on regardless of the political arena and excesses of individual caliphs.[13]

Not that one would gain much sense of these limitations from the displays of ceremonial, riches and pretensions to divine guidance laid on by the earlier Abbasids. The circular city of Baghdad was built to symbolise world dominance, and the scores of palaces, fountains and parks set them and their court apart from the rest of mankind.[14] So, too, did elaborate palace ceremonial, where authority symbols partly deriving from the Sasanian rulers of Iran marked them out from previous Muslim rulers, who had eschewed imperial pomp. They also began to bestow robes of office on governors and such-like office-holders who might exercise considerable discretionary powers.[15] The Abbasids reinforced their dynastic right to rule with conspicuous piety, facilitating pilgrimages to Mecca (the *hajj*) by clearing stones from the path across central Arabia.[16] At the same time, no expense was spared in seeking knowledge with the aid of texts and scholars.[17] These were showcased in palace library-complexes such as the House of Wisdom. Beside works on Sasanian court culture and principles of government translated from Pahlavi into Arabic, mathematical, scientific and medical works were translated from Syriac and Greek, including writings by Aristotle. These fostered new treatises on political economy and compositions offering advice to the ruler, often imbued with Persian traditions.[18]

It was, however, another branch of literature that expressed concepts of political order most effectively. These were the historical writings that began

[13] See M. H. Kamali, *EI*³ s.v. 'Authority, judicial'.

[14] N. M. El Cheikh, 'The institutionalisation of Abbasid ceremonial', in J. Hudson and A. Rodríguez (eds), *Diverging Paths? The Shapes of Power and Institutions in Medieval Christendom and Islam* (Leiden, 2014), 351–70 at 355–8; *Cal*, 133–7.

[15] See pp. 336–9; N. A. Stillman, *EI*² s.v. 'khil'a'; Y. K. Stillman *et al.*, *EI*² s.v. 'libas'; D. Sourdel, 'Robes of honor in Abbasid Baghdad during the eighth to eleventh century', in S. Gordon (ed.), *Robes and Honor: The Medieval World of Investiture* (New York, 2001), 137–45 at 137–9; *RIM*, 192, 197–211, 265–71; El Cheikh, 'Institutionalisation of Abbasid ceremonial', 352–5, 358–63. The bestowal of vestments denoting rank was prominent in Byzantine ceremonial: pp. 309–10, 315–16, 432.

[16] *Cal*, 110–11.

[17] On the role and esprit de corps of the *kuttab* (scribe), see M. van Berkel, 'The people of the pen: self-perceptions of status and role in the administration of empires and polities', in M. van Berkel and J. Duindam (eds), *Prince, Pen, and Sword: Eurasian Perspectives* (Leiden, 2018), 384–451 at 397–9, 415–16.

[18] C. E. Bosworth, 'The heritage of rulership in early Islamic Iran and the search for dynastic connections with the past', *Iran* 11 (1973), 51–62; D. Gutas, *Greek Thought, Arabic Culture: The Graeco-Arabic Translation Movement in Baghdad and Early 'Abbasid Society (2nd–4th/8th–10th Centuries)* (London, 1998), 2, 29–34, 53–60, 72–4, 128–41, 180–6; S. Savant, '"Persians" in early Islam', *Annales islamologiques* 42 (2008), 73–92; L. Marlow, *EI*³ s.v. 'Advice and advice literature'.

to crystallise in the mid-ninth century from a welter of earlier narratives, ranging from *Lives* of the Prophet to collections of biographies and bids at universal history.[19] They give detailed accounts of the struggles of the Prophet and his successors, putting a positive spin on events without concealing the setbacks. There is celebration of the achievements of the first century after the Hegira, as in the suggestively named 'Conquest of the Lands' (*Futuh al-buldan*) by Ahmad al-Baladhuri. The author sets out the contents of treaties alongside campaigns in remote regions like the Caucasus, showing how disparate societies were subjected to Islam and providing details of administration.[20] Al-Baladhuri (d. 892), writing at a time of turbulence in Baghdad and of regional unrest, was probably painting a neater picture of governance than had ever obtained.[21] Some accounts of current or recent caliphs' feats amounted to official history, narrating for example Caliph al-Muʿtasim's campaigns against the Byzantines.[22] And in 932 a new caliph, al-Qahir, instructed a courtier to write up the achievements of his predecessors. Reciting his text in sight of the irascible caliph's spear, he depicted them in unrelentingly positive tones, while also singing the praises of Harun al-Rashid's favourite wife, Zubayda. These works did not, however, enjoy widespread circulation. They remain only as sections incorporated in more popular works, respectively al-Tabari's 'History of Messengers and Kings' (*Ta'rikh al-rusul wa-al-muluk*) and al-Masʿudi's 'Golden Meadows' (*Muruj al-dhahab*).[23] What is striking about these histories, written independently, is not so much the forthrightness about caliphs' misdeeds as their formatting of events by caliphal reigns. Marshalling sometimes contradictory materials into a vast gallery of characters, al-Tabari's 'History' offers the fullest surviving account of the advance of Islam. He portrays individual caliphs and their year-by-year doings up to

[19] C. F. Robinson, *Islamic Historiography* (Cambridge, 2003), 30–8; C. F. Robinson, 'Islamic historical writing, eighth through the tenth centuries', in S. Foot and C. F. Robinson (eds), *The Oxford History of Historical Writing, II: 400–1400* (Oxford, 2012), 238–66 at 250–5. For the importance of narratives in formatting and propagating ideas of political order in the west and Byzantium: pp. 252, 255–9, 81–2.
[20] al-Baladhuri, *Futuh al-buldan [Liber expugnationis regionum]*, ed. M. J. de Goeje (Leiden, 1866); tr. P. K. Hitti and F. C. Murgotten, *The Origins of the Islamic State*, 2 vols (New York, 1916–24; repr. London, 2015).
[21] A. Noth, 'Futuh-history and Futuh-historiography', *Al-Qantara* 10 (1989), 453–62; Robinson, *Islamic Historiography*, 34–6, 40–3; N. Evans, *Mountains, Steppes and Empires: Approaches to the North Caucasus in the Early Middle Ages* (Oxford, forthcoming).
[22] al-Tabari, *Ta'rikh al-rusul wa-al-muluk*, ed. de Goeje et al., iii.2:1234–56; tr. C. E. Bosworth, *Storm and Stress along the Northern Frontiers of the Abbasid Caliphate* [= *The History of al-Tabari* 33] (Albany, NY, 1991), 94–121.
[23] al-Masʿudi (d. c.956), *Muruj al-dhahab*, ed. C. Pellat, *Muruj al-dhahab wa-maʿadin al-jawhar*, 7 vols (Beirut, 1966–79); French tr. C. Barbier de Maynard and A. Pavel de Courteille, rev. C. Pellat, *Les Prairies d'or*, 5 vols (Paris, 1962–97). See Robinson, *Islamic Historiography*, 32, 34–6, 78–9, 95–8, 124–5, 137.

his own present day, including the flaws which laid some low. The qualities that saw a caliph through a successful reign were, to al-Tabari's eyes, readiness to defend Muslims, wisdom, behaving with moderation and dealing justly with all men. Al-Tabari was encapsulating the norms and values held in common by the office-holders and members of urban elites across the Islamic world, not just in Baghdad, where he lived and wrote until his death in 923. Within a generation or so of his death, al-Tabari's 'History' became the go-to book for events since the Creation. Here were the coordinates for benign governance, all the more telling for being without any particular regime's bias. Al-Tabari's scrupulous citation of the sources – often oral – he was drawing upon sat comfortably within the tradition of *hadith*s, lending even greater authority to its bulk (forty volumes in English translation).[24] The expectations of what he regularly termed 'this [caliphal] authority' (*hadha l-amr*)[25] made sense to powerholders and officials across the Islamic world, beyond the reach of advice literature to rulers or the celebrations of hunting and drinking that streamed forth from court poets and panegyrists in Baghdad.[26] By the late tenth century, al-Tabari's work had been epitomised, continued and rendered into Persian.[27]

'Medieval' Islam

By the time al-Tabari and al-Mas'udi stopped writing, their vision of an *umma* united under caliphal direction was more aspirational than real. A plethora of more or less autonomous regimes prompted attempts at justifications, alongside ceremonies and building projects. The Samanids' sponsorship of the translation of al-Tabari reflected their ambition to become a power in Central Asia, showing only nominal deference to the Abbasid caliph. The cultural norms they sought were even more thoroughly imbued with Persian thought than the Abbasids', while they sought a cooperative relationship with the *'ulama'* in their cities. This is clear from, for example, the boundary-setting tract they sponsored, the *al-Sawad al-a'zam*.[28] And *c*.937–40 an author now known as Pseudo-Mawardi wrote a 'Counsel for Kings' (*Nasihat al-muluk*),

---

[24] See n. 11 above.
[25] M. Bonner, 'The waning of empire, 861–945', in *NCHI* 1, 305–59 at 307.
[26] B. Gruendler, *Medieval Arabic Praise Poetry: Ibn al-Rumi and the Patron's Redemption* (London, 2003); H. Kennedy, *The Court of the Caliphs: The Rise and Fall of Islam's Greatest Dynasty* (London, 2004), 112–29, 247–9, 251–3; P. F. Kennedy, *Abu Nuwas: A Genius of Poetry* (Oxford, 2005), 57–78, 109–17.
[27] Bosworth, 'Heritage of rulership', 58–9; Robinson, *Islamic Historiography*, 114–16, 120; Robinson, 'Islamic historical writing', 240.
[28] L. Marlow, *Counsel for Kings: Wisdom and Politics in Tenth-Century Iran: The Nasihat al-muluk of Pseudo-Mawardi*, 2 vols (Edinburgh, 2016), i:180.

advocating an austere lifestyle and religious devotions, governing in collaboration with the *ʿulama*ʾ, veneration of whom was a mark of legitimacy. The author seems to have been seeking to dissuade the emir Nasr II (914–43) from converting to Ismaʿili Shiʿism. The ruler stood, according to Pseudo-Mawardi, at the peak of an elaborate hierarchy, and the example he set would filter down the socio-political pyramid. This model of political and religious leaderships working in tandem harked back to Sasanian texts.[29] At the same time, the Samanids were enthusiasts for the Islamic tradition of jihad, rallying units led by 'fighting scholars', and this helped legitimise their rule.[30]

Far to the west, in al-Andalus, a branch of the Umayyads that had held out against the Abbasids felt, in 929, secure enough to lay claim to caliphal status. They took on much the same attributes as the Abbasids had done a century or more earlier, adopting *laqab*s highlighting a facet of rulership, for example al-Nasir ('the victorious').[31] Later in the century they enlarged the Grand Mosque in Cordoba, decorating it with mosaics and ideologically charged inscriptions of verses from the Qurʾan; they also built a magnificent palace (*Madinat al-Zahra*) overlooking Cordoba, replete with a library reportedly containing 400,000 books.[32]

Meanwhile a rival dynasty had arisen in North Africa to pose a formidable challenge to the Abbasids under the God-guided leadership of a Mahdi. Proclaiming allegiance to the 'Seventh Imam', who would return to lead the faithful to salvation, the Fatimids also claimed descent

---

[29] Marlow, *Counsel for Kings*, i:180–1, 184–5, 186–7, 189–90. Large sections of the text are presented in translation, together with exegesis and contextualisation, in *ibid.*, ii:73–252.

[30] D. G. Tor, *Violent Order: Religious Warfare, Chivalry, and the ʿAyyār Phenomenon in the Medieval Islamic World* (Würzburg, 2007), 207–8, 210–13, 216–17, 264–5; R. Frye, 'The Samanids', in R. Frye (ed.), *The Cambridge History of Iran, IV: The Period from the Arab Invasion to the Saljuqs* (Cambridge, 1975), 136–61 at 155. On jihad (and memory of past jihad), see R. Gleave and I. Kristó Nagy (eds), *Violence in Islamic Thought from the Qurʾan to the Mongols* (Edinburgh, 2016), esp. D. Urvoy, 'The question of divine help in the jihad', 27–32; A. Rippin, 'Reading the Qurʾan on jihad: two early exegetical texts', 33–48; S. B. Savant, 'Shaping memory of the conquests: the case of Tustar', 70–89; see also p. 359. Byzantine enthusiasm for warfare in God's name was more tempered, although military saints had their cults, and some emperor presented themselves as warriors: pp. 317–18. Western appetites for such warfare were generally more robust: pp. 25, 145, 379.

[31] On *laqab*s: pp. 344–5; Bonner, 'Waning of empire', 343. Five Turkish Cairo sultans adopted the regnal title 'al-Nasir', as did two Ayyubid sultans – including the dynasty's founder, Saladin – and it was also adopted by dynasts from the Almohads and Hammadids.

[32] M. Fierro, *ʿAbd al-Rahman III: The First Cordoban Caliph* (Oxford, 2005), 117–18; P. Guichard, *From the Arab Conquest to the Reconquest: The Splendour and Fragility of al-Andalus* (Granada, 2002); S. Calvo Capilla, 'The visual construction of the Umayyad caliphate in al-Andalus through the Great Mosque of Cordoba', *Arts* 7 (2018), 36, https://doi.org/10.3390/arts7030036; S. Calvo Capilla, *EI*[3] s.v. 'Cordoba, architecture'.

from Fatima, daughter of the Prophet. But their impetus sprang from a sense of the End Time. Proponents like the jurist al-Qadi al-Nuʿman (d. 975) spewed forth pamphlets and tracts broadcasting the messianism of a movement aiming to convert the world.[33] The *Sirat Jaʿfar* are the reminiscences of the Mahdi's manservant, dictated sometime after 969.[34] Full and detailed narratives of the Fatimid dynasty survive only in much later works, but the fifteenth-century histories of al-Maqrizi and the Yemeni Ismaiʿli scholar Idris Imad al-Din draw on detailed early texts. Parts are available in translation, notably their coverage of the reign of al-Muʿizz (953–75) and the conquest of Egypt down to his death.[35] The Fatimids followed up their conquest of Egypt in 969 with sermons[36] and proclamations of piety – an understandable move, given that most of their subjects were Sunnis, as well as Eastern Christians or Jews. They innovated in devising round-the-year ceremonial that bound up their rulership with their new capital, Cairo. The calendar of processions and receptions laid on in the 'ritual city' and recorded by contemporaries may owe something to the pomp and circumstance that wedded the Byzantine emperor to his City.[37] At any rate, having the caliph mentioned in the Friday prayers (*khutba*) was a primary means of legitimisation. Ensuring that this was the case in the mosque frequented by Muslim merchants in Constantinople features in a treaty made with Byzantium already in 988.[38]

For all these new dynasties' claims to legitimacy, they were essentially variations on long-standing themes. However, at the ancient centre of the caliphate, new dynamics of power came into play once the Buyids seized

---

[33] Qadi al-Nuʿman, *al-Majalis wal-musayarat* (Tunis, 1978), paras 201, 224, 467, 487; Bonner, 'Waning of empire', 341; H. Halm, *The Empire of the Mahdi: The Rise of the Fatimids*, tr. M. Bonner (Leiden, 1996), 203–6, 209–21, 338–77; M. Brett, *The Fatimid Empire* (Edinburgh, 2017), 65–8; P. E. Walker, *Exploring an Islamic Empire: Fatimid History and its Sources* (London, 2002), 137–8.

[34] *Sirat Jaʿfar*, ed. W. Iwanow, *Bulletin of the Faculty of Arts of the Egyptian University* 4 (1936), 107–33; tr. W. Ivanow, *Ismaili Tradition Concerning the Rise of the Fatimids* (London, 1942), 184–223.

[35] al-Maqrizi, tr. in S. Jiwa, *Towards a Shiʿi Mediterranean Empire: Fatimid Egypt and the Founding of Cairo* (London, 2009); Idris Imad al-Din, tr. in S. Jiwa, *The Founder of Cairo: the Fatimid Imam-Caliph Al-Muʿizz and His Era* (London, 2013).

[36] The Fatimids were already issuing *khutba*s before the conquest: the texts of thirteen sermons are translated in P. E. Walker, *Orations of the Fatimid Caliphs: Festival Sermons of the Ismaili Imams* (London, 2009), 87–150.

[37] See P. Sanders, *Ritual, Politics, and the City in Fatimid Cairo* (Albany, NY, 1994), 8–10, 44–52; J. Oesterle, *Kalifat und Königtum: Herrschaftsrepräsentation der Fatimiden, Ottonen und frühen Salier an religiösen Hochfesten* (Darmstadt, 2009), 95–128. See also M. Canard, 'Le cérémonial fatimite et le cérémonial byzantin: essai de comparaison', *Byzantion* 21 (1951), 355–420. On Byzantium: pp. 303–6.

[38] F. Dölger, *Regesten der Kaiserurkunden des oströmischen Reiches*, rev. edn P. Wirth, A. E. Müller and A. Beihammer, 3 vols to date (Munich, 1977–), i.2: no. 770.

Baghdad in 945. They sought robes of honour and *laqab*s from the caliph, only to oust him soon afterwards and replace him with another Abbasid scion. In signalling their deference to unique charisma even while treating individual honorary heads as expendable, their stance was not unlike that of, say, Otto I towards the papacy.[39] The Buyids were essentially warlords intent on exploiting the rich lands of Iraq and Iran without engaging closely in the administration of Baghdad or other Iraqi cities, so long as revenues were forthcoming to pay the full-time Turkish warriors (*mamluk*s) constituting the core of their military support.

This was still more true of the Seljuks, paramount chieftains of the clans of Turkish tribesmen that overran swathes of Central Asia, Khurasan and Iran. In 1055, under the command of Tughril Beg, they entered Baghdad at the caliph's request, and Tughril Beg declared himself sultan. As will be shown in later chapters, these newcomers brought a new rhythm to political life, a largely itinerant leadership of far-flung war-leaders, held together by family ties, impelled by rivalries and not averse to settling things by the sword. Little of this cultural shift is conveyed by contemporary encomia, poetry or other court literature,[40] although their eleventh-century coins drew attention to their origins with their bow-and-arrow symbol.[41] In fact, the Seljuks never sponsored a literature in Turkish, and it was the Qarakhanids in the steppes of Central Asia who sponsored a Turkish Mirror for Princes, the *Qutadğu Bilig*, in the mid-eleventh century.[42] Although practising collective leadership of a charismatic clan in a manner divergent from norms in the caliphate, the Qarakhanids favoured presentation of Islamic rulership in terms of Iranian kingship, accentuating royal autocracy. They stimulated other reformulations, and the eleventh century has been described as 'the age which produced the classic definition of caliphal authority'.[43]

It was, in fact, the Ghaznavids – the Seljuks' precursors and rivals for dominion over swathes of the eastern Iranian lands – who commissioned a synthesis of Persian kingship with Islamic ideals. Bayhaqi's 'History of Mas'ud' (*Tarikh-i Mas'udi*), written in Persian, highlights terror's utility in disciplining officials and courtiers.[44] The outlook of this bureaucrat is

[39] See pp. 223, 242–3, 335–6. For the uses of the papacy and the city of Rome to would-be emperors: pp. 14, 143.
[40] *GSE*, 185–6. On sources concerning the Seljuks, see also *ibid.*, 12–19.
[41] C. Cahen, 'La tuğra seljukide', *Journal Asiatique* 234 (1943–5), 167–72; K. Shimizu, 'The bow and arrow on Saljuqid coins', *Memoirs of the Toyo Bunko* 56 (1998), 85–106. See also *IHFI*, 167.
[42] Kutadgú Bilïg, tr. R. Dankoff, *Wisdom of Royal Glory: A Turko-Islamic Mirror for Princes* (Chicago, 1983).
[43] *IHFI*, 154.
[44] Abu'l-Fadl Bayhaqi, *Tarikh-i Mas'udi [Tarikh-i Bayhaqi]*, ed. A. A. Fayyad (Mashhad, 1971); tr. C. E. Bosworth and M. Ashtiany, *The History of Beyhaqi: The History of Sultan*

mirrored by another vizier, Nizam al-Mulk, addressing his employer, the Seljuk sultan Malikshah (1072–92).[45] He, too, sets store by ranking and social stability; this amounts to justice, a means to harness fortune's wheel: the sultan must enforce it unremittingly. Still more appetite for authoritarianism is shown by Abd al-Malik al-Juwayni (d. 1085) in his 'Succour of the Nations' (*Ghiyath al-umam*). He prizes martial prowess and political decisiveness and sees in the Seljuk sultan a champion of organisation who could revive *shari'a*-mindedness and embody both power and authority: his benefit to the *umma* might even qualify him to take over as caliph, lack of dynastic legitimacy notwithstanding.[46] Several other texts of the later eleventh century advocate masterful rulers, floating the image of a warrior caliph (and a non-Abbasid) who will fend off infidels and false prophets while heeding the *'ulama'* on matters of belief and law. Ideals like these accommodated Turkish military might within the world of scholars, clerks and urban elites who kept the wheels of administration turning and tax revenues flowing. In fact, the ferment of the eleventh century produced some classic formulations on the good of the *umma*. These, too, highlight the figure of the monarch, sometimes accentuating his role in setting an example. This is set out in the treatise 'Counsel for Kings' (*Nasihat al-muluk*) attributed to al-Ghazali (d. 1111): if the ruler's personal conduct is pious and sound, sage governance and all good things will follow. By these lights, the sultan should be a setter of standards, neither a war-leader nor an imam in the Fatimid style.[47]

This conceptual framework provided for a kind of cohabitation between the Seljuk sultan – invested with trappings of office and exercising force majeure – and the Abbasid caliph. It proved resilient, for all the surface-noise of conflict and, at Baghdad itself, coups. Indeed, as dominion became more subdivided between the Seljuks and their associates, the idea of a charismatic figurehead with an overarching care for believers grew ever more appealing. The Abbasids' standing rose, and they found

Mas'ud of Ghazna, 1030–1041, 3 vols (Boston and Washington, DC, 2011); *IHFI*, 137–8, 141–3, 144, 163.

[45] Nizam al-Mulk, *Siyasat-nameh*, tr. H. Darke, *The Book of Government, or Rules for Kings: The Siyar al-muluk or Siyasat-nama of Nizam al-Mulk*, 2nd edn (London, 1978). For reassessments of Nizam al-Mulk's treatise, see N. Yavari, *Advice for a Sultan: Prophetic Islam* (London, 2014), 18–23, 84–5, 109–28; *GSE*, 18, 66–7, 137–8, 157–64, 201–3.

[46] Abd al-Malik al-Juwayni, *Ghiyath al-umam fi iltiyath al-zulam*, ed. F. Abd al-Mun'im and M. Hilmi (Alexandria, 1979); W. B. Hallaq, 'Caliphs, jurists and the Saljuqs in the political thought of Juwayni', *MW* 74 (1984), 26–41; repr. in C. Kersten (ed.), *The Caliphate and Islamic Statehood*, 3 vols (Berlin, 2015), ii:210–25; *Cal*, 225–6.

[47] *Ghazali's Book of Counsel for Kings (Nasihat al-muluk)*, tr. F. R. C. Bagley (London, 1964); *IHFI*, 161, 164–5; A. K. S. Lambton, 'The theory of kingship in the *Nasihat al-muluk* of Ghazali', *Islamic Quarterly* 1 (1954), 47–55 esp. 54–5; *SGMI*, 107–31. See also pp. 348–9.

themselves on the receiving end of requests for titles and robes of honour
from al-Andalus to Delhi.[48] The Seljuks' appetite for campaigning
waned. Those in Asia Minor and northern Syria tended towards coexistence with Byzantium, whereas fresh groupings operating loosely under
Seljuk aegis or legacy made their name from jihad against the Crusaders,
notably the Ayyubids.[49] Their founder, Saladin, prompted a spate of
writings, and, according to one of his secretaries, Imad al-Din, Saladin
could not stop reading a work on jihad that he had commissioned.[50] Imad
al-Din was, admittedly, the author! For their part, the Seljuk sultans'
pretensions found expression in titles and inscriptions proclaiming vic-
toriousness and universal rule.[51] The later Seljuks also sought to mark out
their territory through elaborate construction works, palaces, mosques
and mausolea.[52]

It was, however, a development beyond their control that opened up seams
capable of yielding information to us about political culture. The eleventh
century saw the beginnings of a sea-change in historical writing. If earlier
narratives had been imbued with issues of the faith, a certain specialisation set
in, with writers about specific dynasties and local events showing less regard
for the spiritual plane. Instead, matters of dynastic legitimisation and of
governance loom large, and historians draw on a broader band of sources.
They also take closer interest in the doings of the officials and urban notables
who make up the secondary and tertiary elites across the Islamic world.[53]
This politically oriented historiography (*siyasa*) reflects the widening gap
between effective powerholders and those holding some sort of religious or
culturo-social sway. The two types of narrative and authority-figures were

[48] Ibn al-Athir, *Chronicle*, tr. D. S. Richards, 3 vols (Aldershot, 2006–8), i:208;
T. W. Arnold, *The Caliphate* (Oxford, 1924), 85–7; E. Hanne, *Putting the Caliph in his
Place: Power, Authority, and the late Abbasid Caliphate* (Madison, WI, 2007), 117–18,
134–41, 190–1, 204–10; *Cal*, 203–11; on titles, see pp. 344–5; on robes of honour
pp. 338–9.
[49] See p. 228.
[50] Robinson, *Islamic Historiography*, 122. See also P. M. Holt, 'The sultan as ideal ruler:
Ayyubid and Mamluk prototypes', in M. Kunt and C. Woodhead (eds), *Süleyman the
Magnificent and his Age: The Ottoman Empire in the Early Modern World* (London, 1995),
122–37 at 122–8.
[51] J. Sauvaget, *Quatre décrets seldjoukides* (Beirut, 1947); D. Korobeinikov, '"The king of the
east and the west": the Seljuk dynastic concept and titles in the Muslim and Christian
sources', in A. C. S. Peacock and S. N. Yıldız (eds), *The Seljuks of Anatolia: Court and
Society in the Medieval Middle East* (London, 2013), 68–90; O. Pancaroğlu, 'The House of
Mengüjek in Divriği: constructions of dynastic identity in the late twelfth century', in
ibid., 25–67 at 50–1.
[52] A. C. S. Peacock, 'The great age of the Seljuqs', in S. R. Canby *et al.* (eds), *Court and
Cosmos: The Great Age of the Seljuqs* (New Haven, CT, and London, 2016), 17–19.
[53] D. P. Little, 'Historiography of the Ayyubid and Mamluk epochs', in C. F. Petry (ed.),
The Cambridge History of Egypt, I: 640–1517 (Cambridge, 1998), 412–44 at 413;
Robinson, *Islamic Historiography*, 97–102, 110–20.

not, of course, mutually exclusive, and by the later twelfth century the Abbasids still had control of substantial parts of Iraq. But the diverging priorities gave rise to detailed accounts of the working norms of governance and their ramifications far from Abbasid or Fatimid courts. They offer information about the polities of 'Berber' origins that emerged in North Africa and al-Andalus: for example, Ibn Sahib al-Salat's dynastic chronicle gives eyewitness accounts of the Almohad ruler Abu Ya'qub Yusuf's dedication to jihad despite a penchant for discussing theology with his religious scholars.[54] But they are most revealing about the nodes of power and resources that emerged between the Oxus and the Nile valley in the second half of the thirteenth century. Given their importance for reconstructing the historical context of political culture and its workings, they will be left until the final section of this treatment of the Islamic sources.

From the eleventh century onwards there was a tendency towards dynastic histories, although some still attempted universal histories reaching back to the Creation. Works celebrating lines of rulers are inevitably biased. But their very efforts at legitimising a regime are informative about the prevailing political culture. Moreover, they can to some extent be cross-checked against other types of writings that became common at around the same time. These were focused on a particular locale, often a city, or gave potted biographies of all the persons of importance to the city. Thus an analytical account of the Buyids' takeover and earlier years behind the throne is given in the 'Universal History' (*Tajarib al-umam*) written by an official, Ibn Miskawayh.[55] Unsurprisingly, Baghdad itself prompted a biographical dictionary containing some 7,800 entries, the *Tarikh Baghdad* of al-Khatib al-Baghdadi (d. 1071), while Damascus' internal and external affairs gave rise to the *Dhayl ta'rikh Dimashq* of Ibn al-Qalanisi.[56] Some self-contained regions inspired extensive historical works. A sense of the robustness of local pride and self-sufficiency emerges from the *Tarikh-e Sistan* ('History of Sistan').[57] Writing in Persian at the time of the Seljuk invasions, its anonymous author looked back in awe and affection at the Saffarid dynasty which had, to his eyes,

[54] Ibn Sahib al-Salat, *al-Mann bi'l-imama*, ed. A. H. al-Tazi (Beirut, 1987); A. K. Bennison, *The Almoravid and Almohad Empires* (Edinburgh, 2016), 93–8. See also on the contrasting modes and values of the Almohads and Almoravids, *ibid.*, 48–54, 67–9, 80–6, 130–5.
[55] Ed. and tr. H. F. Amedroz and D. S. Margoliouth, *The Eclipse of the Abbasid Caliphate: Classical Writings of the Medieval Islamic World*, intro. H. Kennedy, 2 vols (London, 2015); repr. of Oxford 1920–1, vols 4–5). See, on the principles Ibn Miskawayh sought to distil from events, R. Mottahedeh, *Loyalty and Leadership in an Early Islamic Society*, rev. edn (London, 2001), 30–5, 77–81.
[56] Partial tr. by H. A. R. Gibb, *The Damascus Chronicle of the Crusades* (London, 1932); partial French tr. by R. Le Torneau, *Damas de 1075 à 1154* (Damascus, 1952).
[57] *Tarikh-i Sistan*, ed. M. T. Bahar (Tehran, 1935); tr. M. Gold, *The Tarikh-e Sistan* (Rome, 1976).

provided his region with order and security from the later ninth century until 1003. Although tinged with nostalgia, his portrayal shows how a line of former warlords entrenched themselves by appealing to localist sentiments in a mountainous region. What is most striking is that the rise and heyday of the Saffarids is presented in straightforwardly secular terms, not as a divinely led movement.[58] This more earth-bound perspective may, paradoxically, reflect the shift towards Islamic observance of the majority of the population under caliphal rule by the turn of the tenth and eleventh centuries, even in regions where towns were few. This did not make for unanimousness. On the contrary, different shades of religious observance and legal rulings were proliferating. This made it harder for power-seekers after the Fatimids to represent themselves in starkly messianic terms. Arrivistes from the steppes such as Sabuktagin and his son Mahmud, slave-soldiers of Turkish origin and converts to Islam, found it more politic to declare their allegiance to the observances prevalent in Baghdad and to proclaim their loyalty to the caliph. This, together with the prowess of their fellow-warriors, enabled them to found an initially potent dynasty now known after its capital city Ghazni, the Ghaznavids.

Ghazni does not seem to have spawned local histories, and the court of Sabuktagin and his successors was itinerant. Nonetheless, the dynasty received powerful advocacy in the form of the aforementioned 'History of Mas'ud'. Bayhaqi covers just one reign, from 1030 until 1041, and the 'History of Mas'ud' is only a fragment of the massive – and now lost – original work. However, Bayhaqi demonstrates the importance for legitimising a regime of protecting the *hajj* and furthering jihad, and he offers a blow-by-blow account of Mas'ud's investiture as sultan by an envoy of the Abbasid caliph in 1031, while citing the letters and sworn undertakings exchanged at this time.[59] Bayhaqi, an official of Persian stock, wove his stories and wise saws into an elaborate pattern, aiming to instruct rulers and fellow-bureaucrats in the need for deference to the sovereign along with self-sacrifice, tempered by due process and the appearance (if not the substance) of lawfulness.[60] He was drawing on the Sasanian heritage of severe yet just kingship, presenting it as an alternative to arbitrary and flagrantly self-indulgent conduct. In this way one could hope that incoming warlords might be accommodated and, even, become bulwarks of the caliphate. Bayhaqi's precepts and cautionary tales were to no avail, and the Ghaznavids succumbed to the Seljuks, surviving only as a lesser power.

[58] *IHFI*, 132; M. Hanaoka, *Authority and Identity in Medieval Islamic Historiography: Persian Histories from the Peripheries* (Cambridge, 2016), 58–61.
[59] Bayhaqi, *Tarikh-i Mas'udi*, ed. Fayyad, 380–402; tr. Bosworth and Ashtiany, *The History of Beyhaqi*, i: 401–24.
[60] *IHFI*, 144–5.

Later Islam

The execution by Mongol unbelievers of the last Abbasid caliph in 1258 might seem a death blow to the whole idea of an *umma* under a caliph's guidance. And the irruption of the Mongols and their nomadic allies as far as Palestine and the Indus brought new modes of dominance, while triggering counterforces that also hailed from the steppes. The outcome, though, was gradual stabilisation: the new regimes wrapped themselves with ceremonial rhetoric and traditional-looking institutions to reassure their supporters as well as their rivals of continuity.

Prime examples were the Ayyubid military strongmen, or emirs, in Cairo, who reconstituted a caliph in the person of an Abbasid fugitive from Baghdad, while effective power was exercised by a sultan from their ranks. Precisely because many of these 'Turkish' rulers and elites were newcomers, their first sultans Aybak, Baybars and Qalawun being slaves from the Qipchaq steppes, their entourages sought exposition in all kinds of symbolic forms of communication. These included various genres of writing and stimulated what has been called 'the veritable explosion that history writing experienced in Syria and Egypt from the [...] thirteenth century onwards'.[61] These forms of communication proved especially useful when occasional dynastic shifts had to be explained, particularly in the mid-thirteenth, the later fourteenth and the fifteenth centuries. There was a fierce competitiveness between and within the familial military households which made up the political elite, where much the same principle of survival of the fittest was observed as among Mongols, Turkmen and Turco-Mongols.[62] The ways in which radical elite reconfigurations actually took place are partly obscured by the treatises on decorum and the duties of a ruler that poured forth from writers enjoying – or seeking – court patronage, together with chronicles, collective biographies, panegyrics, lavishly illustrated manuscripts of the Qur'an and similarly intricate and bedazzling cultural artefacts.[63] Foremost among handbooks on court protocol is Ahmad al-Qalqashandi's massive 'Dawn of the Benighted Concerning the Chancery Craft' (*Subh al-a 'sha fi sina 'at*

---

[61] K. Hirschler, 'Studying Mamluk historiography: from source-criticism to the cultural turn', in S. Conermann (ed.), *Ubi Sumus? Quo Vademus? Mamluk Studies, State of the Art* (Göttingen, 2013), 159–86 at 161.

[62] See pp. 244–6.

[63] P. M. Holt, 'Literary offerings: a genre of courtly literature', in U. Haarmann and T. Philipp (eds), *The Mamluks in Egyptian Politics and Society* (Cambridge, 1998), 3–16; *KI*, 13–15; J. Van Steenbergen, 'Qalawunid discourse, elite communication and the Mamluk cultural matrix: interpreting a 14th-century panegyric', *JAL* 43 (2012), 1–28; W. Flinterman and J. Van Steenbergen, 'Al-Nasir Muhammad and the formation of the Qalawunid State', in A. S. Landau (ed.), *Pearls on a String: Artists, Patrons, and Poets at the Great Islamic Courts* (Baltimore, MD, 2015), 87–113 at 89–92, 98–100.

al-insha), whose survey tabulates the realm's elites and office-holders and highlights the merits of his own profession, of chancery secretaries.[64] Panegyrists, chroniclers and thinkers alike often sang sultans' praises in the traditional terms befitting a caliph of old.[65] Their God-sent championship of the Faith, rallying believers against the Mongols' aggression, was celebrated by the likes of Ibn Taymiyya.[66]

The first set of 'Turkish' sultans set their presence in Cairo in stone through such projects as the Mansuriyya complex, which housed a public hospital, mosque and madrasa together with a mausoleum for al-Malik al-Mansur Qalawun and his dynastic successors.[67] This looked onto what had been the route for Fatimid processions and stood opposite the mausoleum of Saladin's heir, al-Salih Ayyub: his death preparing to fight the Crusaders in 1249 inspired an inscription.[68] Thus Qalawun and his emirs and descendants, who reigned as sultans in Cairo between 1279 and the 1380s, linked their regime with their Fatimid and Ayyubid predecessors, holding investiture ceremonies in the city.[69] Their ritualisation of public spaces is described in melancholy detail by the scholarly devotee of his native Cairo, al-Maqrizi.[70] These pronouncements and symbols did not, however, dampen the competitiveness that a lack of clear-cut arrangements for seniority and the order of succession brought to Cairo's rulership. Most strikingly, parts of the route leading down from the court in Cairo's Citadel of the Mountain to the former Fatimid *Bayna al-Qasrayn* esplanade – where newly appointed emirs were invested – became lined with palaces of other leading members of the ruling elite. These attested competitive distinction in their emulating of the Qalawunid court along with its dynastic idiom of hegemony and

[64] Al-Qalqashandi, *Subh al-a'sha fi Sina'at al-insha'*, 14 vols (Cairo, 1910–20; repr. 1985); *Selections from Subh al-A'sha by al-Qalqashandi, Clerk of the Mamluk Court: Egypt: 'Seats of Government' and 'Regulations of the Kingdom', from Early Islam to the Mamluks*, ed. T. J. Abd al-Hamid and H. El-Toudy (Abingdon, 2017); M. van Berkel. 'al-Qalqashandi', in J. E. Lowry and D. J. Stewart (eds), *Essays in Arabic Literary Biography, II: 1350–1850* (Wiesbaden, 2009), 331–40; RPCMC, 228.
[65] See e.g. Ibn Jama'a, *Summary of the Rules to Govern the People of Islam [Tahrir al-ahkam fi tadbir ahl al-Islam]*, ed. F. Abd al-Mun'im (Doha, 1988); SGMI, 138–43; see p. 244.
[66] For his clearest arguments on the duty of 'the jihad of the sword', see 'The religious and moral doctrine of *Jihad*', a chapter in his book *Governance According to Allah's Law in Reforming the Ruler and His Flock*. The chapter is translated in R. Peters, *Jihad in Classical and Modern Islam: A Reader* (Princeton, 1996), 44–54. See also SGMI, 143–51.
[67] RPCMC, 234.
[68] *Thesaurus d'épigraphie islamique*, ed. L. Kalus and F. Soudan (Paris and Geneva, 2009), fiche no. 2756; RPCMC, 252; see also *ibid.*, 231, 235, 245.
[69] RPCMC, 245, 249, 256, 261–5.
[70] Ahmad b. Ali al-Maqrizi, *al-Mawa'iz wa-l-i'tibar fi Dhikr al-Khitat wa-l-athar [Admonitions and Reflections on the Story of the Quarters and Monuments]*, ed. A. F. Sayyid, 5 vols (London, 2002–4).

Islamic sovereignty.[71] When the sultan could not trump his rivals and peers with lineage, as happened in the mid-thirteenth and in the fifteenth centuries, the spotlight fell on his outstanding talents and other personal qualifications. These hark back to the confederations of the steppes and so, too, do the paeans and celebrations of martial prowess and hunting skills.[72] They are at their liveliest in the biography of Baybars written by his chief chancery clerk, Ibn Abd al-Zahir.[73] The aim of the monuments and propaganda was to reserve the throne for Baybars' descendants, but it allowed for the bloody workings of this 'military patronage state'.[74]

The Mongols, arch-fiends in the propaganda of the Cairo sultans, had their own ideas about rulership and modes of control: units of well-trained horsemen, far-flung but held together by an elaborate system of communications and awe for a charismatic ruling clan, the Jingizids, who claimed a heavenly mandate to rule the world.[75] Islam was adopted by the descendants of Jochi, whose father, Genghis (Jingiz) Khan, had given him Khwarazm and the western steppes beyond. This portion, encompassing Rus but centred on the Lower Volga, is conveniently known as the Golden Horde. Too few texts survive from the Golden Horde to warrant appraisal here of its blend of Islamic and Mongol political culture, even though their diplomacy gave rise to letters and descriptions of their rule.[76] Our sources are fuller for the branch of Jingiz's descendants known as the

[71] J. Van Steenbergen, *Order out of Chaos: Patronage, Conflict, and Mamluk Socio-Political Culture, 1341–1382* (Leiden, 2006), 94–100; RPCMC, 257–65; *KI*, 145–8.
[72] Holt, 'Sultan as ideal ruler, 129–33; RPCMC, 228–9, 253–7.
[73] Ibn Abd al-Zahir, *al-Rawd al-zahir fi sirat al-Malik al-Zahir*, ed. A. al-Huwaytir (Riyadh, 1976); Holt, 'Sultan as ideal ruler', 129–30.
[74] On the nature and origins of this setup: M. Chamberlain, 'Military patronage states and the political economy of the frontier, 1000–1250', in Y. M. Choueiri (ed.), *A Companion to the History of the Middle East* (Malden, MA, 2005), 135–53 at 141–52. See also RPCMC, 265; J. Van Steenbergen, 'The Mamluk sultanate as a military patronage state: household politics and the case of the Qalawunid bayt (1279–1382)', *JESHO* 56 (2013), 189–217.
[75] D. Morgan, *The Mongols*, 2nd edn (Oxford, 2007), 90–4; P. Jackson, *The Mongols and the Islamic World: From Conquest to Conversion* (New Haven, CT, 2017), 95–101, 113–24, 182–6, 204–9, 282–6. For the law or decrees of Jingiz, see D. Aigle, 'Le grand *jasaq* de Gengis-Khan, l'empire, la culture mongole et la *shari'a*', *JESHO* 47 (2004), 31–79.
[76] T. Allsen, *Culture and Conquest in Mongol Eurasia* (Cambridge, 2001), 22–3, 51–4; C. Halperin, *Russia and the Golden Horde: The Mongol Impact on Medieval Russian History* (Bloomington, IN, 1985); M. Favereau, 'Zolotaia Orda i eë sosedi [The Golden Horde and its neighbours]', in R. S. Khakimov and M. Favereau (eds), *Zolotaia orda v mirovoi istorii [Golden Horde in the World]* (Kazan, 2016), 334–53 at 335–6; M. Favereau Doumenjou and L. Geevers, 'The Golden Horde, the Spanish Habsburg monarchy, the construction of ruling dynasties', in van Berkel and Duindam (eds), *Prince, Pen, and Sword*, 452–512; *KI*, 20, 50–8; Jackson, *Mongols and the Islamic World*, 14, 33–4, 36–8, 44–5; M. Favereau, *La Horde d'or et le sultanat mamelouk: naissance d'une alliance* (Cairo, 2018).

Ilkhans, who took over the central lands of the former Abbasid caliphate. This abundance of writings is a mark of the cultural diversity and sophistication of their subjects in Iran, Mesopotamia, Afghanistan and the Transcaucasus. In fact, Buddhism was (after ancestral Shamanism) most in favour before the leadership's final conversion to Islam. The Ilkhans' hereditary right to rule autonomously within the Jingizid whole was not quite as clear-cut as that of the Jochids to the western lands; for some time they looked to the Great Khan for robes of honour, recognition and investiture with crowns.[77]

Precisely for this reason Ghazan, the ruler who converted to Islam during his struggle for the throne in 1295, made much of his Muslim credentials, as with the titles on his coins' Arabic inscriptions.[78] Rivalry and conflict with the Qalawunids triggered numerous pronouncements which upheld Ghazan as Guardian of Islam, enjoying divine support and uniquely fit to lead the *umma*. These criteria for rulership feature in five letters and decrees issued around the time of Ghazan's occupation of Damascus.[79] Competing formulations of Islamic leadership are no less clear in his letter to the Qalawunid sultan al-Nasir Muhammad in 1301 and in the answer penned in Muhammad's name.[80] While Qalawunid propaganda highlighted the recentness of the Ilkhans' conversion, Ghazan and his successors played on the lowly origins of the Qalawunids: they, in contrast, were Jingizids and fit to rule worldwide.[81] In doing so, the Ilkhans actually sought to synthesise Islamic and Mongol concepts, flagging up their genealogy and the Great Khan's assignment of lands to them, while imposing on foreign ambassadors rites of purification that entailed walking between two fires.[82] The power of this synthesis owes something to Rashid al-Din, 'arguably the first truly universal historiographer' in any of our three spheres.[83] His 'Compendium of Chronicles' (*Jami' al-tawarikh*) bears out the claim to worldwide dominion of his Ilkhan lords, marshalling information from

---

[77] Allsen, *Culture and Conquest*, 25–6, 29.

[78] Allsen, *Culture and Conquest*, 31–2; Jackson, *Mongols and the Islamic World*, 341, 344, 362–9. For coins, see e.g. M. A. Seifeddini, *Monetnoe delo i denezhnoe obrashchenie v Azerbaidzhane XII–XV vv.*, 2 vols (Baku, 1978–81), i:227–9. See also, for rare literary attestation of the significance of coin inscriptions, *Das mongolische Weltreich. Al-'Umari's Darstellung der mongolischen Reiche in seinem Werk Masalik al-absar fi mamalik al-amsar*, ed. and comm. K. Lech (Wiesbaden, 1968), 103.

[79] The texts are scattered in different publications, and only some are available in translation. For summary and exegesis, see *KI*, 74–80.

[80] For French translations of these letters, see Baron C. d'Ohsson, *Histoire des Mongols, depuis Tchinguiz-khan jusqu'à Timour bey ou Tamerlan*, 4 vols (Amsterdam, 1852), iv:288–93, 295–309. See *KI*, 80–5.

[81] *KI*, 94–5, 100–01, 107.   [82] *KI*, 24; Jackson, *Mongols and the Islamic World*, 363–6.

[83] A. Marsham, 'Universal histories in Christendom and the Islamic world, *c.* 700–*c.* 1400', in Foot and Robinson (eds), *Oxford History of Historical Writing*, 431–56 at 452.

every culture about other peoples.[84] Writing as chief minister of Ghazan, Rashid al-Din set about concocting an ideology, adding the Jingizids' track record of worldwide mission to Islamic ideas of championship of the monotheistic Faith. He presents his ideas in the decrees he drafted, and these are incorporated into his history. Rashid al-Din was the mind behind the factual data and propaganda issuing forth from the Ilkhanid court at the turn of the thirteenth century and during the fourteenth.[85]

No other Muslim power of the later middle ages can boast quite such ideas and openness to innovations as the Ilkhans, including (from the Chinese) the printing of paper money.[86] Their achievements were vibrant enough two generations after their collapse in the later 1330s for the Central-Asian Turco-Mongol ruler Timur to draw upon their ideology. Timur's exchanges with the Cairo sultan echo their line on, for example, the ignominy of servile origins; one of his letters even copies the demand for Egypt's submission that Hülegü had sent in 1259/60.[87] By 1402–3 Timur was exacting formal subordination from the sultan, to the point of offering to act as father for Sultan Faraj. Timur's propaganda blended triumphalism, ancestry and piety.[88]

Timur had other reasons for paying close attention to the past, beside the utility of all materials belittling the 'slave' regime in Cairo. In trying to replicate the actions of the Jingizids and citing their documents, he represented himself as their true successor. Striking out, like them, in almost every direction, and on the point of invading China at the time of his death, Timur's campaigns had the air of a mission performed at God's behest with, of course, the victories bolstering the legitimacy of his rule. He finessed on Genghis Khan's claim to a divine mandate by styling himself the new world-conqueror and Lord of the Auspicious Conjunction; the latter title had already been sported by Sultan Baybars

---

[84] Rashid al-Din, *Rashiduddin Fazlullah's Jami'u't-tawarikh [Compendium of Chronicles: A History of the Mongols]*, tr. W. M. Thackston, 3 vols (Cambridge, MA, 1998–9); Jackson, *Mongols and the Islamic World*, 26, 230.

[85] See J. Pfeiffer, 'The canonization of cultural memory: Ghazan Khan, Rashid al-Din, and the construction of the Mongol past', in A. Akasoy *et al.* (eds), *Rashid al-Din: Agent and Mediator of Cultural Exchanges in Ilkhanid Iran* (London, 2013), 57–70; R. Amitai, 'Rashid al-Din as historian of the Mamluks', in *ibid.*, 71–88; Morgan, *Mongols*, 17–20, 165–70; Jackson, *Mongols and the Islamic World*, 327, 363, 372–6.

[86] Allsen, *Culture and Conquest*, 184–5.

[87] W. Brinner, 'Some Ayyubid and Mamluk documents from non-archival sources', *Israel Oriental Studies* 2 (1972), 117–43 at 120, 122; *KI*, 181. See also J. E. Woods, 'Timur's genealogy', in M. M. Mazzaoui and V. B. Moreen (eds), *Intellectual Studies on Islam: Essays Written in Honor of Martin B. Dickson* (Salt Lake City, UT, 1990), 85–125 at 103–9.

[88] B. F. Manz, 'Family and ruler in Timurid historiography', in D. A. DeWeese (ed.), *Studies on Central Asian History in Honor of Yuri Bregel* (Bloomington, IN, 2001), 57–78 at 57–9, 63–5, 78; *KI*, 194.

as well as by Mongol and Ilkhanid rulers.[89] At the same time he was avowedly conducting warfare sanctioned by Islam and sought holy men's blessings for his ventures.[90] Such a dual approach helped to compensate for his lack of actual Jingizid blood. So, too, did the puppet khans he fielded from 'the golden family', while a string of Jingizid wives served to justify his title of Imperial Son-in-Law.[91] Besides rewriting Mongol history to make room for himself,[92] Timur wished to have his own deeds recorded for eternity. Secretaries took down his every word and action, memoranda often read aloud to him for approval before being written up for more polished works in Persian and Turkish. In this vein, he gave interviews to the scholarly statesman Ibn Khaldun.[93] Indeed, 'The Book of Conquest' (*Zafarnama*) was commissioned by Timur, according to its author Nizam al-Din Shami. This, the sole extant history written in his lifetime, conveys his sense of destiny and desire to be seen as model ruler, combining benevolence and mercy with military might and capacity for revenge.[94]

Timur's exploits and attainments themselves provided role-models after his unexpected death in 1405, with potentates vying to associate themselves with him as well as with the Jingizids. Timur had taken an interest in multiple branches of knowledge, besides instigating majestic architectural complexes, reminiscent of early Islamic rulers' works.[95] Timur passed his scientific curiosity on to his progeny, as witness the observatory of his grandson Ulugh Beg at Samarqand:[96] knowledge of the heavens and their workings held the key to universal – and rightful – mastery. Ulugh Beg's father, Shah Rukh, commissioned many works of scholarship, including the *Shams al-Husn*, a continuation of 'The Book of

[89] Manz, 'Family and ruler', 63-4; *KI*, 170, 178–9; see pp. 353–5.
[90] B. F. Manz, 'Temür and the problem of a conqueror's legacy', *JRAS* 3rd series 1 (1998), 21–41 at 25–6.
[91] Woods, 'Timur's genealogy', 100–3; *KI*, 168.
[92] B. F. Manz, 'Mongol history rewritten and relived', *REMMM* 89–90 (2000), 129–49.
[93] J. E. Woods, 'The rise of Timurid historiography', *JNES* 46 (1987), 81–108 at 82.
[94] Nizam al-Din Shami, *Zafarnama*, ed. F. Tauer, 2 vols (Prague, 1937–56); Woods, 'Rise of Timurid historiography', 83, 85–7; C. Melville, 'The Mongol and Timurid periods', in C. Melville (ed.), *Persian Historiography* (London, 2012), 155–208 at 160–1; *INTI*, 166–8.
[95] See e.g. K. Z. Ashrafyan, 'Central Asia under Timur from 1370 to the early fifteenth century', in M. S. Asimov and C. E. Bosworth (eds), *History of Civilizations of Central Asia, IV* (Paris, 1998), pp. 319–45 at 338–40; R. G. Mukminova, 'The role of Islam in education in Central Asia in the 15th–17th centuries', *Oriente Moderno* n.s. 87 [*Studies on Central Asia*] (2007), 155–161; S. Rahmatullaeva, 'Samarqand's Rigestan and its architectural meaning', *Journal of Persianate Studies* 3 (2010), 156–91 at 161–3. On earlier Islamic rulers' building works: pp. 103, 105.
[96] Rahmatullaeva, 'Samarqand's Rigestan', 163–4; I. Ridpath, 'Ulugh Beg', in *A Dictionary of Astronomy*, 2nd rev. edn (Oxford, 2012).

Conquest'.[97] Shah Rukh was, at the time (1410), striving to oust or subdue his rivals, and most of the Timurid chronicles were written for him or his descendants. But his opponents sponsored literary works, too, notably the offspring of his half-brother, Umar-Shaykh. Works attributable to Mu'in al-Din Natanzi, written by turns for his nephew, Iskandar b. Umar-Shaykh, and for Shah Rukh himself, constitute 'a perfect laboratory to discuss the formation of princely political discourse [...] in a Timurid princely apanage'.[98] Natanzi initially dedicated his universal chronicle to Iskandar. But within a year of Iskandar's defeat and capture by Shah Rukh, Natanzi revised and rededicated it – to Shah Rukh, on 7 October 1414! He also wrote a 'Synoptic Account' of the Timurid dynasty.[99] The first version of the chronicle, which survives, expresses Iskandar's own attempt to redefine the Timurid imperial project, dubbing him the Messiah of the Last Days, and eschatological ideas seem to have flourished around his powerbase at Fars.[100] Rather than merely signalling opportunism on Natanzi's part, the episode suggests how succession-disputes could stimulate not only historical narratives but also original thinking about religious authority and sacral kingship.[101] Indeed, Timur's regimen followed by the sparring between his descendants prompted an outpouring of texts, the work of intellectuals given to experiment as much as to career enhancement. Diverse notions of authority deriving from the steppes fused with classical Persian precepts on a ruler's duties. The networks of thinkers and writers spanned the urban centres between the Oxus and the Persian Gulf, in a kind of ongoing debate through the first fifty years or so of the fifteenth century.[102] Meanwhile in mountainous regions less touched by Timurids, local dynasties such as the White Sheep (Aq Qoyunlu) Turkmen in Azerbaijan developed their own political cultures, aligning with the popular preachers of the Sufi orders.[103]

It was, however, another group of dynasts hailing ultimately from the steppes who created the most enduring mixture of ideology and practices of rulership. The Ottomans have left few early texts in their own, Turkish,

[97] Taj al-Din Salmani, *Sams al-Husn: Eine Chronik vom Tode Timurs bis zum Jahre 1409*, ed. (facsimile of MS) and German tr. H. R. Roemer (Wiesbaden, 1956); Woods, 'Rise of Timurid historiography', 88–9.
[98] *INTI*, 185. On the close ties between historical writers and the courts (not least the grand viziers), see Melville, 'Mongol and Timurid periods', 198–206.
[99] *Synoptic Account of the Timurid House*, ed. and tr. W. M. Thackston, in *Album Prefaces and Other Documents on the History of Calligraphers and Painters* (Leiden, 2001), 88–98; *INTI*, 187.
[100] *INTI*, 196. See also Melville, 'Mongol and Timurid periods', 189.
[101] See n. 105; see also pp. 322–7, 244–5.   [102] *INTI*, 251–78, 284–6.
[103] J. E. Woods, *The Aqquyunlu: Clan, Confederation, Empire* (Salt Lake City, UT, 1999), 9, 18, 83–5, 89, 106–7, 138, 156; *INTI*, 291; see p. 230.

language. But they put to new purposes the discipline and sense of mission leading to universal dominion that had carried other Turkish and Mongol war-bands so far, while ensuring that their realm avoided the fragmentation befalling so many other polities, by virtue of decisively fratricidal struggles for sole rulership.[104] The question of what role ideas of jihad and messianism played in their advance across the Balkans is controversial. This is partly because we have so few texts emanating directly from the leadership before the mid-fifteenth century.[105] But it also reflects the Ottomans' talent for tailoring ideological stance to their constituencies. This manifested itself upon the fall of Constantinople in 1453. Without foregoing claims to 'proof' of superiority through charismatic genealogy and the divine favour inherent in their victory, Mehmed II Fatih ('the Conqueror') and his advisors moved fast to exploit the aura of legitimacy that mastery of 'the City' generated.[106] Mehmed is credited with a many-faceted personality, and his multiple titles and ideological symbols struck a chord among the interest groups with which he had to deal. These ranged from Genoese merchants ensconced across the Golden Horn – who had the sultan confirm their privileges in Galata only days after the fall – to the orthodox patriarch, who soon came to be housed again in Constantinople, then as now.[107] Styling himself *basileus* and *autokrator*, among other titles, and adapting elements of Byzantine

[104] D. Kastritsis, 'Conquest and political legitimation in the early Ottoman empire', in J. Harris *et al.* (eds), *Byzantines, Latins, and Turks in the Eastern Mediterranean World after 1150* (Oxford, 2012), 222–45 at 229–30.

[105] C. Imber, 'Ideals and legitimation in early Ottoman history', in Kunt and Woodhead (eds), *Süleyman the Magnificent*, 138–53 at 139–49, 149; C. Imber, *The Ottoman Empire, 1300–1650: The Structure of Power*, 3rd edn (Basingstoke, 2019), 92–4; R. Lindner, 'Anatolia, 1300–1451', in K. Fleet (ed.), *The Cambridge History of Turkey, I: Byzantium to Turkey 1071–1453* (Cambridge, 2009), 102–37 at 103–6, 134–5; Kastritsis, 'Conquest and political legitimation', 223–34. However, the compilation of 1484 known as the 'Oxford Anonymous Chronicle' (see p. 125) drew heavily on an early fifteenth-century narrative. This narrative was one of several accounts of the Ottoman civil war of 1402–13, written during the conflict or shortly afterwards: ed. and tr. D. Kastritsis, *The Tales of Sultan Mehmed, Son of Beyezid Khan (Ahval-i Mehmmed bin Bayezid Han)* (Cambridge, MA, 2007); see also D. J. Kastritsis, *The Sons of Bayezid: Empire Building and Representation in the Ottoman Civil War of 1402–1413* (Leiden, 2007), 195–220; D. J. Kastritsis, 'Historical epic Ahvāl-i Sultān Mehemmed (The Tales of Sultan Mehmed) in the context of early Ottoman historiography', in H. Erdem Çıpa and E. Fetvacı (eds), *Writing History at the Ottoman Court: Editing the Past, Fashioning the Future* (Bloomington, IN, 2013), 1–22.

[106] On Constantinople: pp. 303–9; for Rome and the aspirants to emperorship in the west: pp. 14, 143.

[107] See A. Bryer, 'The Roman orthodox world (1393–1492)', in *CHBE*, 852–80 at 865–6 and fig. 65 on 867; K. Fleet, *European and Islamic Trade in the Early Ottoman State: The Merchants of Genoa and Turkey* (Cambridge, 1999), 128–9; E. A. Zachariadou, 'The Great Church in captivity 1453–1586', *CHC* 5, 169–86 at 169–77. On the patriarchate, see S. Runciman, *The Great Church in Captivity* (Cambridge, 1968), 165–89.

ceremonial, Mehmed conjoined imperial attributes with riches and monumental constructions unseen in the City for many centuries.[108] These manifestations of overarching authority were followed up by a series of decrees and pronouncements on matters not covered by sacred law, distinguishing sharply between taxpayers and the sultan's servants, non-taxpayers who became known as the military class. The Criminal Code issued at Bayezid II's command in 1499 defined membership of the military class. The Code was augmented, some sections applying to particular groups (like the Balkan Vlachs). It reached final form and a fair degree of implementation under Suleiman I the Magnificent (1520–66).[109] What was new was that the ruler and his officials had a greater role in regulating commercial affairs and in the dispensing of justice and distribution of property than had been the case before. Their decrees (*fermans*) and sultanic law (*kanun*) applied to all subjects – unlike *shari'a* (*şeriat*) – and part of their provincial administrators' revenues came from fines collected for various crimes and transgressions. The Topkapı palace, built by Mehmed and modified by Suleiman, had at its highest point a Tower of Justice, from which the sultan could literally oversee his viziers hearing petitions and transacting suchlike affairs of state.[110]

There was, however, a precedent for a pious and victorious ruler leading the world of Islam and yet presiding over sizable populations of Peoples of the Book. This was the early caliphate. Selim I (1512–20) forbore from formally assuming the title of caliph when he took control of Cairo in 1517 and seized the puppet Abbasid caliph and his regalia. Instead, Selim styled himself *Khadim al-haramayn al-sharifayn* (Servant of the Two Noble

---

[108] See pp. 231–2, 306, 329, 452–3; Kastritsis, 'Conquest and political legitimation', 237–40; H. Inalcik, 'The policy of Mehmed II toward the Greek population of Istanbul and the Byzantine buildings of the city', *DOP* 23–4 (1969–70), 229–49; Ç. Kafescioğlu, *Constantinopolis/Istanbul: Cultural Encounter, Imperial Vision, and the Construction of the Ottoman Capital* (University Park, PA, 2009), esp. 53–109, 170–7; G. Necipoğlu, 'From Byzantine Constantinople to Ottoman Kostantiniyye: creation of a cosmopolitan capital and visual culture under Sultan Mehmed II', in *Byzantion to Istanbul: 8000 Years of a Capital* (Istanbul, 2010) 262–77 at 264–9; S. Malmberg, 'The new palace of Mehmed Fatih and its Byzantine legacy', in A. Ödekan *et al.* (eds), *The Byzantine Court: Source of Power and Culture* (Istanbul, 2013), 49–52.

[109] The Turkish text of Suleiman's Code, followed by an English translation, may be found in U. Heyd, *Studies in Old Ottoman Criminal Law*, ed. V. L. Ménage (Oxford, 1973), 54–131. See also *ibid.*, 11–32, 171–83, 237–57; Imber, *Ottoman Empire*, 155–69, 186–7, 227–35.

[110] M. Kunt, *The Sultan's Servants: The Transformation of Ottoman Provincial Government, 1550–1650* (New York, 1983), 9, 12–15, 21–5; M. Kunt, 'State and sultan up to the age of Süleyman: frontier principality to world empire', in Kunt and Woodhead (eds), *Süleyman the Magnificent*, 3–33 at 25–6, 27–8; C. Woodhead, 'Perspectives on Süleyman', in *ibid.*, 164–90 at 187; Kastritsis, 'Conquest and political legitimation', 236–7.

Sanctuaries).[111] But in associating his rule closely with Medina and Mecca and spending vast sums on furthering the *hajj*, Selim and his son Suleiman the Magnificent were following in the steps of caliphs like Abd al-Malik and Harun al-Rashid. Even without flaunting or making much regular use of the title, the Ottomans had earned the moral stature of a caliph: the vizier Lütfi Pasha argues in a pamphlet of around 1553 that the caliphate belongs to whoever effectively protects the Muslim people, irrespective of whether he was a member of the Prophet's tribe of Quraysh.[112] Lütfi Pasha himself seems to have commissioned a new criminal code. Indeed, through taking on justice and everyday matters of law and order while maintaining an elaborate system of tax-assessment and collection, the Ottoman sultan was following in the footsteps of the Byzantine *basileus*. Mehmed's sporting of that title was not vainglorious. Tax registers of his and subsequent reigns survive to prove it.[113] And so, in their way, do the court records they introduced into all the Arab provinces of their empire. These registers kept track of all legally significant actions undertaken at the *qadi*'s court, including the stages in a case or process preceding the *qadi*'s final judgement.[114]

More or less in step with their approach to governance, the Ottomans set about constructing a grand narrative of their pathway to predominance. This was, until the late fifteenth century, largely a matter of patching together the tales known as *gazavat-name* ('Book of Exploits'), recounting feats in the borderlands, along with those from the *menakib-name* ('Book of Glorious Deeds'). The latter genre focuses on holy men, but some were valiant warriors, too. The life story of one such, Osman, gives us the earliest known narrative of the origins of the Ottoman ruling house. This text was incorporated into the chronicle compiled in the late fifteenth century by the pious Sufi war-veteran Aşıkpaşazade.[115] In his eyes, the Turks had a past in common with their fellow nomads, the Mongols, with Osman gaining

[111] Imber, 'Ideals and legitimation', 149; *Cal*, 342–5. Selim did, according to Lüfti Pasha, officially proclaim that he alone had the right to be called caliph: M. Hassan, *Longing for the Lost Caliphate: A Transregional History* (Princeton, 2016), 9–10 and n. 55 on 268.

[112] *Lütfi Paşa: Asafname*, ed. A. Uğur (Istanbul, 2017); Imber, 'Ideals and legitimation', 149–50.

[113] On the registers – *tahrir defter*s – see A. Bryer and H. W. Lowry, 'Introduction', in A. Bryer and H. W. Lowry (eds), *Continuity and Change in Late Byzantine and Early Ottoman Society* (Washington, DC, 1986), 1–7; H. W. Lowry, 'Privilege and property in Ottoman Maçuka in the opening decades of the *Tourkokratia*: 1461–1553', in *ibid.*, 97–128 at 97–110; H. W. Lowry, 'The island of Limnos: a case study in the continuity of Byzantine forms under Ottoman rule', in *ibid.*, 235–59 at 235–9, 249–56. See also p. 454.

[114] C. Müller, 'The power of the pen: *cadis* and their archives', in A. Bausi *et al.* (eds), *Manuscripts and Archives: Comparative Views on Record-Keeping* (Berlin and Boston, 2018), 361–86 at 378–80.

[115] Aşıkpaşazade, 'Tevârîh-i Âl-i ʿOsman', ed. N. Atsız Çiftçioğlu, in *Osmanlı Tarihleri* (Istanbul, 1949), 77–319; B. Tezcan, 'Ottoman historical writing', in J. Rabasa *et al.* (eds), *The Oxford History of Historical Writing, III: 1400–1800* (Oxford, 2012), 192–211 at 195.

credentials for rulership through a hard life in the saddle while tapping into the Jingizids' legitimacy. In highlighting the Mongols, who had been the overlords of Turkish chieftains like Osman in the thirteenth and fourteenth centuries, and by writing in Turkish, Aşıkpaşazade was holding out against his contemporaries.[116] They were mostly looking to Persian models of rulership and historical writing, and their works were in Persian or Arabic.

During the reign of Bayezid II, a royal tradition of narrative began to develop. Thus the author of the 'Oxford Anonymous Chronicle' states that Bayezid had commissioned him to write a history of the dynasty in the Turkish language.[117] Tracing the Ottomans' ancestry back to Esau, son of Isaac, he portrays their leaders as *ghazis*, winning these lands for Islam. The anonymous author recounts Mehmed's capture of Constantinople,[118] taking the story up to the time of writing, 1484. Yet he also gives ample coverage of succession disputes, notably those between the sons of Bayezid I after his defeat at the hands of Timur in 1402. It is probably no accident that his patron had a potential rival in the form of his brother Cem, living as a captive in western Europe.[119] Such dynastic works burgeoned into a full-blown 'universal history', placing the sultan at the centre of the world. It was Suleiman the Magnificent who commissioned the 'Quintessence of Histories' (*Zübdetü't-tevarih*). The court historian responsible, Arifi, after listing the genealogies of all previous Muslim dynasties, depicts them as reaching the end of the line, leaving Suleiman the ultimate world ruler.[120] His monumental work, written on the 'Imperial Scroll', depicts Suleiman as paralleling the work of God, 'the Creator of the Worlds'; now Suleiman is creating a new world, and the rest of mankind – including its rulers – must duly submit to him, 'defender of the faith'.[121] This presentation of history since the Creation gave Suleiman's absolutism teleological significance, and its ideology was backed up firmly by the Criminal Code that he was finalising.

Documents and Archives

Evidence concerning the regular administrative procedures of rulership is scanty, whilst memos and other such chance survivals are scarce, too.

---

[116] B. Tezcan, 'The memory of the Mongols in early Ottoman historiography', in Erdem Çıpa and Fetvacı (eds), *Writing History*, 23–38 at 33.

[117] *An Early Ottoman History: The Oxford Anonymous Chronicle (Bodleian Library, Ms Marsh 313)*, tr. and comm. D. J. Kastritsis (Liverpool, 2017), 50.

[118] *Early Ottoman History*, tr. and comm. Kastritsis, 177–80.

[119] *Early Ottoman History*, tr. and comm. Kastritsis, 117–51 (text); 1–3, 7, 14–15 (introduction). See n. 105 for a modern translation of the originally separate text recounting the succession disputes.

[120] Tezcan, 'Ottoman historical writing', 206, 208–9.

[121] Tezcan, 'Ottoman historical writing', 207–8.

This reflects the paucity of archival documents or detailed records of administration at the nodal points bearing on our survey. Such dearth is surprising: members of many elites and their officials resorted readily to the written word. Indeed ninth-century Baghdad may have been one of the first human societies, if not the first, 'in which a man or a woman could make a living as an author'.[122] And the Fatimid emir al-Musabbihi kept a kind of diary, basing on it his historical work, 'Reports of Egypt' (*Akhbar Misr*).[123] Unfortunately, the diary does not survive. The same goes for archival collections of administrative documents, and our few assortments are fragmentary.[124] A set of privileges mostly granted to the monastery of St Catherine's on Sinai shows what is recoverable from monastic archives, but also the limitations on our knowledge.[125]

To some extent, regime change and trashing of the records of previous dynasties are to blame. However, climates such as Egypt's preserve documents, and most of our surviving materials come from there. Papyri in Greek, Coptic and Arabic attest high levels of literacy and deftness on the part of the Arab overlords, even from the opening years of their occupation. A corpus of letters written to a Muslim administrator at Fayyum reveals their light touch, with Arabs becoming closely involved with local government only around 700 and being joined in this by non-Arab Muslims towards mid-century.[126] An immense amount of writings will have been generated by these activities, with copies kept of texts of consequence to individuals or institutions. If, despite this, few public collections were made, this reflects the status of the written word: documents do not, in Islamic jurisprudence, constitute legal proof. An act, however phrased, was not the last word of authority, which rested with the *qadi*'s right of adjudication exercised with the aid of accredited witnesses and consultation of his archive of documents.[127] What mattered most was a kind of institutionalised memory, with the judge applying sacred law reaching back to the

[122] *Cal*, 148.   [123] Walker, *Exploring an Islamic Empire*, 142.
[124] *IHFI*, 40; A. Meier, *EI³* s.v. 'Archives and chanceries: Arab world'.
[125] S. Stern, *Fatimid Decrees: Original Documents from the Fatimid Chancery* (London, 1964), 15–84 (ed. and tr.); M. van Berkel, *EI³* s.v. 'Archives and chanceries: pre-1500, in Arabic'.
[126] P. M. Sijpesteijn, *Shaping a Muslim State: The World of a Mid-Eighth Century Egyptian Official* (Oxford, 2013), 261–2. Several other administrative documents from Egypt's early Islamic period are published and elucidated in contributions to A. Kaplony et al. (eds), *From Bawit to Marw: Documents from the Medieval Muslim World* (Leiden, 2015).
[127] Sijpesteijn, *Shaping a Muslim State*, 238; C. Müller, *Der Kadi und seine Zeugen: Studie der mamlukischen Haram-Dokumente aus Jerusalem* (Wiesbaden, 2013), 33, 37, 349–53. See Müller, 'Power of the pen', esp. 361–71, 380–2; J. Paul, 'Archival practices in the Muslim world prior to 1500', in Bausi et al. (eds), *Manuscripts and Archives*, 339–60.

Prophet to earthly situations in collaboration with reputable members of the *umma*, past and present. In much the same vein, one finds in historical writings the chain of names of persons who have relayed, supposedly orally rather than just in writing, a story or items of information. These chains are termed *isnad* and, as noted already, the *hadiths'* claim to authenticity stems from listing all the persons to have passed on the Word from the Prophet himself. This made preservation of acts, privileges and suchlike texts issued by governmental authority less essential to property-holders. So although ordinary Egyptians prized written words above spoken ones and made private collections, as secretaries or landholders, neither they nor Muslims elsewhere gave topmost priority to storing decrees or other emanations of institutional authority.[128] In that sense, the monks of St Catherine's turn out to be the exception proving the rule, behaving more like their brethren within the Byzantine empire[129] or, indeed, property-holders in the early centuries of Islam, when the concept of full and unimpugnable ownership underwritten by title deeds was still in play, continuing the jurisprudence of previous empires.[130] To that extent, the political leadership was not so implicated in the fabric of society – Harold Lasswell's 'who gets what, when, and how' (see p. 17) – as in Byzantium or some polities of the Latin west. Issues of property, family bequests and commercial contracts were no less pressing, but they were not bound up so organically with deeds conferring unique rights and responsibilities.

This did not diminish a leadership's reliance on written records and procedures for tax-collecting and other administrative means of sustaining itself. We have an overview from works composed under the auspices of the Ayyubids and their successors in Cairo. Although the original documents are lost, digests and encyclopaedias abound for every aspect of administration. For example, in the early fifteenth century al-Maqrizi wrote (besides much else) his historical geography of Egypt, focused on Cairo and Fustat, and drawing on administrative

---

[128] Paul, 'Archival practices', 347–50, 356–7. See also p. 465.

[129] On the petitions and record-keeping of the monks of St Catherine's, see Stern, *Fatimid Decrees*, 4–5, 91–2, 98–102. For those of the Georgian house of the Holy Cross at Jerusalem, see J. Pahlitzsch, 'Documents on intercultural communication in Mamluk Jerusalem: the Georgians under Sultan An-Nasir Hasan in 759 (1358)', in A. D. Beihammer *et al.* (eds), *Diplomatics in the Eastern Mediterranean, 1000–1500* (Leiden, 2008), 373–94 at 379.

[130] H. Kennedy, 'Landholding and law in the early Islamic states', in Hudson and Rodríguez (eds), *Diverging Paths?*, 159–81 at 162, 164, 173–4, 177–81. For the importance of written deeds to the ownership of property in the other two spheres, see pp. 32, 92–3, 455, 46–7, 381, 403–4.

texts.[131] If the contents of such encyclopaedic works are often obscure, this reflects upon our lack of contextualisation. But the distinction between the prerogatives of rulers and the rights of landowners and institutions was neither clear-cut nor particularly meaningful. Disputes between powerful interest-groups did not hinge on the status or wording of documents scrutinised before courts of law. Consequently, the materials capable of throwing light on powerholders' engagement with legal processes are wanting. This probably reflects upon the central government's retreat from law-making and intensive or systematic arbitration in the ninth century. One should, in fact, beware of supposing that household govern-ance in the Cairo Sultanate marked a drastic departure from the modus operandi of earlier centuries. The interest groups and teeming personal nexuses strung across the administration of late medieval Egypt are far better documented than goings-on in ninth-century Baghdad. The Abbasids likewise relied on cohorts of clerks and highly numerate agents for fiscal and other purposes; and basic commitment to the *umma* overrode even sectarian differences across what was still, in most of their dominions, a minority religion. Yet bitter rivalries and infighting at court can still be seen from our narrative sources.[132] One may suspect that there, too, the wheels of administration were ever at the mercy of cronyism and factions. Seen from this perspective, the dearth of extant administrative documents and deeds issued by the court is not wholly misleading: the machinery of government's workings did not interlock tightly with everyday matters of law, property and inheritance.

This is not to deny either the impact of governmental agents, especially tax-assessors and -collectors, on broad bands of society or the repercussions of their activities upon political culture. Documents issued by central or regional authorities were thought well worth keeping, especially by institu-tions such as *waqf*s intent on safeguarding their endowments.[133] Beside the assortments already mentioned, one should note the texts concerning the involvement of Jewish individuals with Fatimid officials and with Islamic law-courts that ended up in Cairo's Geniza, along with countless other

[131] al-Maqrizi, *Khitat*, tr. U. Bouriant and P. Casanova, *Description topographique et histor-ique de l'Egypte*, 4 pts in 3 vols (Paris, 1895–1900) [= *Mémoires de la Mission Archéologique Française au Caire* 17 / *Mémoires publiés par les membres de l'Institut Français d'Archéologie Orientale* 3–4]; important excerpt in A. Raymond and G. Wiet, *Les marchés du Caire: traduction annotée de Maqrizi* (Cairo, 1979), 85–216. See *IHFI*, 170, 173, 175–6; Walker, *Exploring an Islamic Empire*, 12, 164–9; A. Raymond, 'Al-Maqrizi's *Khitat* and the urban structure of Mamluk Cairo', *MSR* 7 (2003), 145–67.
[132] Kennedy, *Court of the Caliphs*, 38–44, 67–9, 227–36, 261–3, 267–8; *RIM*.
[133] Paul, 'Archival practices', 346–7, 353–4. For more on the *waqf*, see pp. 484–5; and for comparisons with pious and charitable foundations in Byzantium and the west, see p. 501.

documents.[134] Other acts and marks of governmental direction have survived in assemblages strung across a vast area, from Central Asia and eastern Iran to al-Andalus.[135] Documents found to the west of Khotan include legal judgements and land-sale contracts drafted under Qarakhanid auspices.[136] And a sizable array of wills, deeds of sale and suchlike property transactions guaranteed by notaries and other authorities in Granada found their way into the Crown of Aragon's and ecclesiastical archives by way of small private collections.[137] The materials for Muslim Sicily shed light on structures there, too.[138] It is, however, probably no coincidence that materials survive thanks to collections made after the Normans' conquest of the island and to their employment of Muslim officials and administrative methods throughout the twelfth century.[139] On the whole, it was non-Muslim communities like the Jews, or societies on the fringes of the Islamic world and beyond, which saw sense in taking the political masters of the day at their written word.

[134] G. Khan, *Arabic Legal and Administrative Documents in the Cambridge Genizah Collections* (Cambridge, 1993). See also S. D. Goitein, *A Mediterranean Society: The Jewish Communities of the Arab World as Portrayed in the Documents of the Cairo Geniza*, 6 vols (Berkeley, 1967–93), esp. i:52–70; ii:395–407; Paul, 'Archival practices', 342–3; J. Goldberg, *Trade and Institutions in the Medieval Mediterranean: The Geniza Merchants and Their Business World* (Cambridge, 2012), esp. 133–5, 144–5, 150–8, 164–79. See also M. Rustow, *The Lost Archive: Traces of a Caliphate in a Cairo Synagogue* (Princeton, 2020).

[135] Paul, 'Archival practices', 344–6.

[136] V. Hansen, *The Silk Road: A New History* (Oxford, 2012), 228.

[137] M. A. Alarcón y Santón and R. G. de Linares, *Los documentos arabes diplomaticos del archivio de la Corona de Aragon* (Madrid, 1940); C. Barceló and A. Labarta, 'Los documentos árabes del reino de Granada. Bibliografía y perspectivas', *Cuadernos de la Alhambra* 26 (1990), 113–19; E. Molina López and M. del Carmen Jiménez Mata, 'From Muslim to Christian hands: the documents from the Municipal Archive of Granada', in P. Sijpesteijn (ed.), *From Al-Andalus to Khurasan: Documents from the Medieval Muslim World* (Leiden, 2007), 23–39; A. Zomeño, 'Notaries and their formulas: the legacies from the University Library of Granada', in *ibid.*, 59–77; A. Zomeño, 'From private collections to archives: how Christians kept Arabic legal documents in Granada', *Al-Qantara* 32 (2011), 461–79; C. Álvarez de Morales, 'La geografía documental arábigogranadina', in N. Martínez de Castilla (ed.), *Documentos y manuscritos árabes del Occidente musulmán medieval* (Madrid, 2010), 205–23; Bennison, *The Almoravid and Almohad Empires*, 210–15; *IHFI*, 46.

[138] M. Amari, *I diplomi arabi del R. Archivio Fiorentino*, 2 vols (Florence, 1863–7); S. Cusa, *I diploma greci ed arabi di Sicilia*, 2 vols (1868–82).

[139] For the questions which these documents can – and cannot – begin to answer, see, e.g., A. Metcalfe, 'Orientation in three spheres: medieval Mediterranean boundary clauses in Latin, Greek and Arabic', *TRHS* 6th series 22 (2012), 37–55; J. Johns, *Arabic Administration in Norman Sicily: The Royal Diwan* (Cambridge, 2002), 301–14 (catalogue of *diwani* documents). See also J. Johns and N. Jamil, 'A new Latin-Arabic document from Norman Sicily (November 595H/1198CE)', in M. A. Pomerantz and A. A. Shahin (eds), *The Heritage of Arabo-Islamic Learning: Studies Presented to Wadad Kadi* (Leiden, 2016), 111–66 at 144–9 (Arabic and Latin texts and translations).

Part II

Historical Contexts

7   The Latin West

Pluralism in the Shadow of the Past

Len Scales

Figure 7.1 The cathedral at Mainz, inaugurated under Archbshiop Willigis (975–1011), predecessor of Archbishop Aribo who presided over the coronation of Conrad II; photo Nicola Sigsworth

Concepts, Dates, Landscapes

To set bounds to the regions comprising the west is peculiarly difficult. The sphere as a whole is characterised by an absence of hegemonic systems – political, institutional, or even doctrinal – with overriding force throughout the medieval period. It corresponded to no overarching polity, like Byzantium, and neither did religion, for all its importance, infuse its political life in the manner of Islam. Because it was no single entity, this western sphere lacks sharp chronological limits. It neither 'rose' in the manner of Islam nor 'fell' like the Byzantine empire.[1] Added to this, the group of territories which it makes sense to draw within it changed shape radically and roughly doubled in overall size, while many of the component elements attained a markedly different character, over the course of the middle ages. A degree of uncertainty, even of inner contradiction, is therefore integral to this chapter. Clear unities are not on offer, and to seek them is to chase shadows. There are indeed meaningful formations and contemporary terms and concepts, as well as useful later coinages, which can be applied to the sphere as a whole and which correspond to one another at least approximately. Nevertheless, they do not fully coincide, and their respective contents and foci are different. Taken together, they describe a reality that was itself plural. So a plurality of terms and concepts can justifiably be deployed here, and their overlaps and disjunctions highlighted rather than elided.

To begin with Europe.[2] On the tripartite world maps which were widely disseminated in the medieval west, Europe took its place with the other known continents, Africa and Asia, from which it was conventionally shown as divided by the Mediterranean and the rivers Nile and Don.[3] In these depictions, Europe was often ascribed a significance which went beyond the merely geographic, as the habitation of the descendants of Noah's son Japheth (with his other two sons, Sem and the accursed

[1] For the medieval west in relation to Byzantium and Islam: M. Borgolte, *Christen, Juden, Muselmanen: die Erben der Antike und der Aufstieg des Abendlandes 300 bis 1400 n. Chr.* (Munich, 2006); W. Pohl et al. (eds), *Visions of Community in the Post-Roman World: The West, Byzantium and the Islamic World, 300–1100* (Farnham, 2012).

[2] The fullest account of the medieval idea of Europe is K. Oschema, *Bilder von Europa im Mittelalter* (Ostfildern, 2013). See also D. Hay, *Europe: The Emergence of an Idea*, 2nd edn (Edinburgh, 1968); K. J. Leyser, 'Concepts of Europe in the early and high middle ages', *P&P* 137 (1992), 25–47; T. Reuter, 'Medieval ideas of Europe and their modern historians', *History Workshop* 33 (1992), 162–75; R. Balzaretti, 'The creation of Europe', *History Workshop* 33 (1992), 176–80; M. Rubin, 'The culture of Europe in the later middle ages', *History Workshop* 33 (1992), 181–96; P. den Boer, 'Europe to 1914: the making of an idea', in K. Wilson and J. van der Dussen (eds), *The History of the Idea of Europe* (London and New York, 1993), 13–38; (for the close of the middle ages) J. Hale, *The Civilization of Europe in the Renaissance* (London, 1993), 3–50.

[3] Den Boer, 'Europe to 1914', 22–9.

Ham, located in Asia and Africa respectively).[4] The more detailed *mappae mundi* show Europe as densely packed with towns and, by contrast, largely devoid of the monstrous beings which were believed to crowd particularly into Africa beyond the Nile.[5] Medieval western scholars, following and adapting the geographers and ethnographers of antiquity, sometimes perceived in Europe a kind of golden mean: an ideal environment for human habitation.[6] It seemed to them far from a 'miserable backwater'.[7]

Yet the Europe of medieval imagination is both too large and too limited single-handedly to serve our ends. It in no way constituted a coherent zone of politics. Only fleetingly, and with much myopia and wishful thinking, did it sometimes seem possible to discern pan-European political formations: the empire of Charlemagne was sometimes described by his flatterers in this way.[8] Medieval Europe itself could not claim even the cultural and historical unities which might have supplied raw materials for a common political culture.[9] Europe's pasts were not just several but divergent. Our sphere encompasses historic landscapes around the Mediterranean which had already been part of advanced, urban civilisations for thousands of years; but also regions which in the earlier middle ages were still entirely without towns and, over vast areas, largely without people: regions within which human life as urbane southerners knew it scarcely seemed liveable at all. While such regional disparities became less over the course of the middle ages, they were rarely obliterated altogether.[10] In 1500, many of the largest cities still lay close to the Mediterranean. The tide-line of antique culture remained visible, among other things, in the divide between a Europe which spoke languages derived from Latin – with correspondingly more direct access to Latinate culture itself – and another which did not.

---

[4] See generally B. Braude, 'The sons of Noah and the construction of ethnic and geographical identities in the medieval and early modern periods', *William and Mary Quarterly* 54 (1997), 103–41.

[5] J. B. Friedman, *The Monstrous Races in Medieval Art and Thought* (Cambridge, MA, 1981); P. D. A. Harvey, *Medieval Maps* (London, 1991).

[6] Den Boer, 'Europe to 1914', 18–19.

[7] N. Ferguson, *Civilization: The West and the Rest* (London, 2011), 4.

[8] Leyser, 'Concepts of Europe', 32–4.

[9] For a different view, seeking such unities: T. Kaufmann, 'Die Einheit Europas zwischen Vormoderne und Moderne', in C. Jaser *et al.* (eds), *Alteuropa – Vormoderne – Neue Zeit: Epochen und Dynamiken der europäischen Geschichte (1200–1800)* (Berlin, 2012), 59–77.

[10] P. Moraw, 'Über Entwicklungsunterschiede im deutschen und europäischen Mittelalter: ein Versuch', in U. Bestmann *et al.* (eds), *Hochfinanz, Wirtschaftsräume, Innovation: Festschrift für Wolfgang von Stromer*, 2 vols (Trier, 1987), ii:583–622. On shared literary and cultural parameters, see nonetheless pp. 38–9, 65–7, 254, 274. For disparities in the vast Islamic sphere, see e.g. pp. 472–7.

Europe's diversities were more numerous and less bipolar than that, however. The continent was a cocktail of language groups, languages and dialects. While medieval Europeans often proved remarkably adept at communicating with one another, the effort required should not be underestimated.[11] Even at the end of the middle ages, and among the more urbane type of traveller, to journey across the continent was to confront the unknown and the startlingly strange. We may discern the influence of classical topoi behind the humanist pope Pius II's images of a fifteenth-century Northumbria harsh and exotic enough to rival the steppes of Central Asia.[12] However, the culture shock which the entourage of a contemporary Bohemian nobleman both experienced and induced as they made their way through the regions of western Europe seems to have been spontaneous enough.[13]

In many ways preferable is to speak, as medieval Europeans did, of Christendom.[14] Insofar as we can observe efforts to impose a common culture throughout our sphere, the intent and (to a very imperfect degree) achievement were those of the Catholic church.[15] The geographical extension, over the millennium down to the fifteenth century, of the church's ambit mapped – and to a substantial degree impelled and legitimised – the growth and stabilisation of the political communities which our sphere came to comprise. Where new realms were established in the wake of crusade and Holy War, the church's part in their making was direct and inescapable. Catholic Christendom was a community of obligation for all baptised Christians living within its bounds.[16] It was a community resting on law and coercion, whose hierarchy could authorise the most drastic punishments. Its extent has a sharpness and substance unique among very large pre-modern communities: the church's capacity for setting boundaries, material and conceptual, was unrivalled. Its identity-forming potential was inseparable from the readiness with which it

[11] P. Wolff, *Les Origines linguistiques de l'Europe occidentale* (Paris, 1970).
[12] Pius II, *Commentaries*, ed. M. Meserve and M. Simonetta, 3 vols (Cambridge, MA, 2004–18), i:24–5.
[13] *The Travels of Leo of Rozmital through Germany, Flanders, England, France, Spain, Portugal and Italy, 1465–1467*, ed. and tr. M. Letts (Cambridge, 1957); W. Paravicini, 'Leo von Rožmitál unterwegs zu den Höfen Europas (1465–66)', *Archiv für Kulturgeschichte* 92 (2010), 253–307.
[14] N. Berend, 'The concept of Christendom: a rhetoric of integration or disintegration?', in M. Borgolte and B. Schneidmüller (eds), *Hybride Kulturen im mittelalterlichen Europa* (Berlin, 2009), 51–62.
[15] For introductions to the medieval western church: J. H. Lynch and P. C. Adamo, *The Medieval Church: A Brief History*, 2nd edn (London, 2014); B. Hamilton, 'The western church', in his *Religion in the Medieval West* (London, 1986), 5–84.
[16] J. van Engen, 'The Christian middle ages as a historiographical problem', *American Historical Review* 91 (1986), 519–52 at 540–1.

identified and branded 'the other': the church gathered in as it shut out.[17] For most of the middle ages, systematic thought and writing, including political writing, were a near-monopoly of clerics, whose medium, Latin, was the universal language of the educated. To speak of Latin Christendom (or Latin Europe, or the Latin west) is therefore to invoke the main sources both of the unity and of the cultural distinctiveness of our sphere. In the political arena, the Catholic church almost everywhere became indispensable to the making, and on occasion un-making, of rulers and regimes. The supernatural authority to which it controlled access secured the oaths which at all points bound together the component elements of political society. Once tied, those bonds could be loosened only by the church.

The political map of Latin Europe as it developed over the course of the middle ages was profoundly shaped by the church and its heads, the bishops of Rome. The making of western peoples in the post-Roman period is inseparable from the emergence of an independent papacy with the power to confer legitimacy and identity on those peoples.[18] By instigating the conversion of the Germanic settlers in Britain, Pope Gregory I (590–604) bound the Anglo-Saxons and their rulers into a larger European political sphere, under papal headship.[19] The Visigothic kings in Spain, by abandoning their Arianism for Catholicism in 589, opted to join this growing community – and were duly rewarded with anointing as a badge of membership.[20] In the centuries before 1000, Rome – the city of the Apostles – itself became a common religious focus for the barbarians, to which remote northern kings made their way as pilgrims.[21] The recurrent and intensifying estrangements of the Latin church and its heads from Byzantium were a further factor in sharpening the contours of a distinct western Christendom. At the close of the middle ages, after the loss of the Crusader principalities in the Levant and after the downfall of Eastern Christian Byzantium itself, Catholic Christendom would briefly (before its extension into the New World) match with some precision a 'Latin' Europe.

---

[17] R. I. Moore, 'Medieval Europe in world history', in C. Lansing and E. D. English (eds), *A Companion to the Medieval World* (Chichester, 2009), 563–80 at 576–7.

[18] R. Fletcher, *The Conversion of Europe: From Paganism to Christianity, 371–1386 AD* (London, 1997), 97–129; C. Wickham, *The Inheritance of Rome: A History of Europe from 400 to 1000* (London, 2009), 170–202.

[19] C. Leyser, 'The memory of Gregory the Great and the making of Latin Europe, 600–1000', in K. Cooper and C. Leyser (eds), *Making Early Medieval Societies* (Cambridge, 2016), 181–201.

[20] R. Collins, *Early Medieval Spain: Unity in Diversity, 400–1000*, 2nd edn (London, 1995), 32–57.

[21] J. M. H. Smith, *Europe after Rome: A New Cultural History, 500–1000* (Oxford, 2005), 253–92.

Latin Christendom was repeatedly shaped by the papacy's own political choices – most momentously, in abandoning its old-established relationship with the *basileus* for a new one with the Carolingian Franks in the eighth century. Latin Christian mission advanced in step with, and underpinned, the territorial expansion of western realms and the accession of new convert-kings to the community.[22] The sphere of adherence to the church of Rome continued to grow during the central medieval period, impelled by a complex amalgam of dynamic factors. At each stage it was the church itself that set down the most visible markers of that growth and created the durable frameworks within which consolidation could proceed. As late as 1209, Pope Innocent III established the first Catholic bishopric in Finland.[23] This chapter therefore takes as its bounds the expanding community of realms and regions whose elites professed loyalty to some form of Catholic Christianity. There is a practical reason for this, too: however much the northern convert peoples may have owed to their pre-Christian pasts, it is only after their conversion that written sources survive which render them susceptible to historical, as against purely archaeological, study.

Yet to speak only of Christendom brings its own problems. Some realms in our sphere were more Latin-Christian than others. Particularly towards the geographical margins, a more complex picture prevailed. Medieval Hungary, for example, was home to pagans, Muslims and Jews and to orthodox as well as Catholic Christians.[24] Nor did rulers employ only adherents of the Latin church as their servants. The twelfth-century kings of Sicily appointed orthodox Christians and Muslims to significant positions in their government.[25] Jews were widely employed by the Iberian monarchs.[26] In frontier regions, Catholic Christians themselves did not always wholly appear as such to disapproving co-religionists. To the twelfth-century English chronicler William of Newburgh, the Latin settlers in the Holy Land were 'a kind of neutral being between the Christian and the Saracen population'.[27] As late as the fifteenth century, visitors from central Europe were shocked to be received by King Henry IV of Castile and his queen sitting on the floor in the Moorish fashion. The king, noted

[22] Fletcher, *Conversion of Europe*, 417–50.   [23] Fletcher, *Conversion of Europe*, 500.
[24] N. Berend, *At the Gate of Christendom: Jews, Muslims and 'Pagans' in Medieval Hungary, c.1000–c.1301* (Cambridge, 2001).
[25] D. Matthew, *The Norman Kingdom of Sicily* (Cambridge, 1992), 209–28. See also J. Johns, *Arab Administration in Norman Sicily: The Royal Diwan* (Cambridge, 2002); A. Metcalfe, *The Muslims of Medieval Sicily* (Edinburgh, 2009).
[26] J. F. O'Callaghan, *A History of Medieval Spain* (Ithaca, NY, 1975), 283–6, 464–6.
[27] William of Newburgh, 'Historia Rerum Anglicarum' III.15, in *Chronicles of the Reigns of Stephen, Henry II and Richard I*, ed. R. Howlett, 4 vols, *Rolls Series* 82 (London, 1884–9), i:254.

the scandalised reporter, ate, dressed and even worshipped like a Muslim.[28] In isolated cases, a prince might reject the doctrines of the church outright: in the early thirteenth century, the Cathar heretics of Languedoc were thought to enjoy the protection of the main regional power, the count of Toulouse.[29] Catholicism itself was in any case far from unified. There was never only one way of conceiving of the church as a system of Christian governance; and in the late middle ages there were radically different models on offer.[30]

A final objection is methodological. Particularly for a study of political culture, Christendom carries the suggestion that the culture that counted emanated from the minds and pens of clerics. There is no doubt that the church did much to shape medieval thought and assumptions about politics, as well as instigating and staging some of the most powerful rituals through which these found expression. Nevertheless, it would be a mistake to suppose either that clerks and monks were the only people who thought seriously about politics or that when others did so they invariably followed and agreed with the clergy. Such a view overlooks several things. It fails to acknowledge the substantial accommodations with pre-existing modes of thought and action that the western church had been forced to make in order to establish itself among the barbarian peoples at all.[31] It neglects the obvious fact that even the most cloistered thinkers had contacts with laypeople, among whom they had usually spent formative early years. They therefore inevitably shared many of the commonplace political assumptions of their kin, lords and neigh-bours, often representing them in their writings in more abstract forms. And it treats the comparative scarcity of medieval evidence for the polit-ical ideas of laypeople as indicating the relative absence of the ideas themselves. Such an assumption is unwarranted: where we do have materials for a distinctively (though not exclusively) lay culture – as in the literature of courtly chivalry – they reveal values partly independent of, and sometimes at odds with, those of pulpit and scriptorium.[32]

Names are therefore a problem. Even that enduring favourite, the west, despite the merit of vagueness, is undermined by significant Muslim polities occupying that most westerly of regions, Iberia, for much of the period under consideration. Pragmatism is called for, and recognition of

---

[28] *Travels of Leo of Rozmital*, ed. and tr. Letts, 91–2.
[29] M. Lambert, *The Cathars* (Oxford, 1998), 63, 99–105.
[30] B. Tierney, *Foundations of the Conciliar Theory: The Contribution of the Medieval Canonists from Gratian to the Great Schism* (Cambridge, 1955).
[31] W. A. Chaney, *The Cult of Kingship in Anglo-Saxon England: The Transition from Paganism to Christianity* (Berkeley and Los Angeles, 1970).
[32] M. Keen, *Chivalry* (New Haven, CT, 1984), 18–43. See also pp. 56, 267–8.

the limited load-bearing capacity of single terms. A similarly flexible approach must be applied to dates – since, once again, we are dating not one phenomenon but several. There is much to be said for a study of western political culture beginning with Pirenne's axial eighth century.[33] Not only did the papacy then make its decisive westward turn; it is also from this point that explicitly Christian models of rulership grew increasingly influential in western Europe. It is no coincidence that from around this time the political map gradually gains firmer contours: in the centuries that follow, the outlines of distinct and enduring realms become discernible. Henceforth, too, perceptions of what divided the west both from Byzantium and from the Islamic world became sharper. Yet it will be necessary to examine one of the most salient features of this sphere, namely its political plurality; and the preconditions for *that* were to a large degree set already between the fourth and sixth centuries, with the establishment of multiple 'peoples', political groupings and regimes on the soil of the Roman empire in the west.[34] Moreover, if it is accepted that one key to medieval western political culture lies in the particular relationships which developed between religion and (temporal) rulership, it becomes necessary also to retain a remoter vision: of the conversion of Constantine and the establishment of Christianity as a basis for political legitimacy in the Roman empire.[35] Occasional backward glances from the Carolingian and post-Carolingian to the late Roman world are therefore necessary. Establishing a terminal point is more straightforward.[36] For this, the later fifteenth century – by which time the political forms and institutions that would endure until modernity were embedded in the west but had yet to be exported to the New World – will serve as well as any.

The western sphere can also, finally, be understood as a series of distinct, interconnecting, physical environments, within which political

---

[33] A. F. Havighurst (ed.), *The Pirenne Thesis: Analysis, Criticism, and Revision*, rev. edn (Lexington, MA, 1969). See also M. McCormick, *Origins of the European Economy: Communications and Commerce* (Cambridge, 2001); M. Ančić et al. (eds), *Imperial Spheres and the Adriatic: Byzantium, the Carolingians and the Treaty of Aachen (812)* (Abingdon, 2018), esp. N. Budak, 'One more Renaissance? Dalmatia and the revival of the European economy' (174–91) and S. Gelichi, 'Aachen, Venice and archaeology' (111–20).

[34] G. Halsall, *Barbarian Migrations and the Roman West, 376–568* (Cambridge, 2007).

[35] For Constantine's exemplary role in the conversion of early medieval kings: P. Sarris, *Empires of Faith: The Fall of Rome to the Rise of Islam, 500–700* (Oxford, 2011), 205–25.

[36] Although not wholly without problems; for the difficulty of establishing when the middle ages can be said to end: C. Jaser et al., 'Alteuropa – Vormoderne – Neue Zeit: Leistungen und Grenzen alternativer Periodisierungskonzepte für die europäische Geschichte', in Jaser et al. (eds), *Alteuropa – Vormoderne – Neue Zeit*, 9–24; G. Schwerhoff, 'Alteuropa: ein unverzichtbarer Anachronismus', in *ibid.*, 27–45.

activity took place and which helped to shape its character.[37] If western history and culture fostered division, European geography tended to favour interconnection and exchange. While medieval Europeans seldom travelled fast, the barriers which the landscape itself set in their way were relatively low. No major deserts separated populations, and the forests that had covered much of early medieval Europe north of the Alps retreated over the course of the period with the advance of settlement. European rivers were highways rather than hurdles, as witnessed by the fact that most major towns lay on navigable waterways. Mountains channelled rather than stifled movement. Most European ranges were, globally speaking, fairly low; and even the Alps, for all their fabled terrors, bore a heavy human traffic over their passes. Godfrey of Viterbo, courtier and chronicler under the twelfth-century emperor Frederick Barbarossa, claimed to have made the journey from Germany to Rome no fewer than forty times.[38] Europe was well shaped for communications.[39] Peninsulas and islands made up, compared to other continents, an unusually high proportion of the land area.[40] The sea, relatively speaking seldom far away, was the broadest highway of all: medieval Europe's most extensive hegemonies were mainly seaborne.[41]

Of course, the lie of the land does help to explain a multi-speed, multi-track medieval Christendom.[42] Political formations and practices that would have looked archaic, indeed barbarous, to an English or Scots lowlander were able long to survive in the uplands of native Wales and Ireland. The high-medieval urban commune held out more tenaciously in the Tuscan hill country than on the Lombard plain. Marginal landscapes – Swiss Alpine pasture, Icelandic lava fields, the coastal marshes of Frisia – fostered distinct political arrangements, resistant to classic pyramidal lordship, inconceivable in the champion country of northern France.[43] Post-Roman decline added its part, with

---

[37] N. Davies, *Europe: A History* (Oxford, 1996), 47–65.

[38] G. Baaken, 'Zur Beurteilung Gottfrieds von Viterbo', in K. Hauck and H. Mordek (eds), *Geschichtsschreibung und geistiges Leben im Mittelalter: Festschrift für Heinz Löwe zum 65. Geburtstag* (Cologne and Vienna, 1978), 373–96 at 373. See also pp. 369–71.

[39] For the importance of movement in 'making' medieval Europe: W. C. Jordan, '"Europe" in the middle ages', in A. Pagden (ed.), *The Idea of Europe from Antiquity to the European Union* (Cambridge, 2002), 72–90 at 73.

[40] N. Ohler, *The Medieval Traveller*, tr. C. Hillier (Woodbridge, 1989), 3.

[41] J. R. S. Phillips, *The Medieval Expansion of Europe*, 2nd edn (Oxford, 1998); F. Fernandez-Armesto, *Before Columbus: Exploration and Colonisation from the Mediterranean to the Atlantic, 1229–1492* (Philadelphia, 1987).

[42] For political fragmentation as topographically determined: J. Diamond, 'How to get rich: a talk by Jared Diamond [6.6.99]', *Edge* 56 (1999), www.edge.org/conversation/jared_diamond-how-to-get-rich (accessed 31 January 2020); Ferguson, *Civilization*, 11–12.

[43] For the independent and quasi-independent peasant polities of such regions: P. Freedman, *Images of the Medieval Peasant* (Stanford, CA, 1999), 177–203.

the decay of the road system, local efforts notwithstanding, in former imperial territories.[44] Yet there was never a time when medieval westerners did not feel impelled to wrestle with the limits of landscape, to build connections. Sometimes the inspiration was directly Roman, as with the bridge that Charlemagne threw across the Rhine at Mainz. More important were innumerable local and regional efforts at making and mending roads, bridges and waterways and keeping them open and safe. After the eleventh century, these efforts seem to quicken: soon the Alps themselves were breached by new routes.[45] The 'optimal fragmentation' which one commentator has discerned in the pre-modern west could just as well be termed 'optimal connectivity'.[46] It was a flexible connectivity, however, impelled by shifting patterns of perceived common interest among a colourful array of participants, not by hegemonic systems or visions of ideal unity.

The Shape of Political Development

Although western history across the middle ages displays clear elements of shape and pattern, it permits no grand narrative such as can justifiably be offered for Byzantium or, with more qualification, the Islamic world. Instead, there are multiple parallel and interwoven strands, precluding brief summary.[47] That too illuminates the distinctiveness of the western sphere. The course of political events begins with imperial break-up: the fragmentation of Rome's western provinces. While empire, both formal and less formal, was henceforth a recurrent factor in medieval western history, Latin Europe was never defined by imperial rule, in the manner of Byzantium, or even by large quasi-imperial hegemonies, like those recurrently found in the Islamic sphere. Political pluralism was the keynote from the start. During the fifth and sixth centuries Germanic military elites – Goths, Franks, Burgundians, Lombards, Angles, Saxons and others – established loosely framed kingdoms within the western territories of the Roman empire. With the important exception of Spain, where

[44] B. Ward-Perkins, *The Fall of Rome and the End of Civilization* (Oxford, 2005).
[45] P. Spufford, *Power and Profit: The Merchant in Medieval Europe* (London, 2002), 187–92.
[46] For 'optimal fragmentation': Diamond, 'How to get rich'.
[47] For good introductions to the history of the medieval west: C. Wickham, *Medieval Europe* (New Haven, CT, 2016); B. H. Rosenwein, *A Short History of the Middle Ages* (Peterborough, ON, 2004); for more detail, see the volumes of the *New Cambridge Medieval History*; for an excellent historical atlas: *Großer historischer Weltatlas, II: Mittelalter*, ed. J. Engel (Munich, 1979); for introductions to medieval western political culture: R. McKitterick, 'Politics', in R. McKitterick (ed.), *The Early Middle Ages: Europe 400–1000* (Oxford, 2001), 21–56; B. Weiler, 'Politics', in D. Power (ed.), *The Central Middle Ages: Europe 950–1320* (Oxford, 2006), 91–120; J. Watts, *The Making of Polities: Europe, 1300–1500* (Cambridge, 2009), 129–57.

Visigothic rule was extinguished in 711, the western sphere, unlike Byzantium, was affected only fairly peripherally by the rise of Islam. It is true that access to the Mediterranean, with its connections to worlds beyond, was significantly – though never completely – impeded for a time.[48] But more momentous for the longer term was the growing acceptance among the new western rulers – some of them previously pagan, many Arian Christians – of Catholic Christianity under the spiritual headship of the bishop of Rome.

A significant new phase was entered with the accession of the Carolingian dynasty to power in Francia in 751, supplanting the Merovingian kings. The Carolingians, whose accession enjoyed papal support, went on to extend substantially both their own sphere of rule and the bounds of Catholic Christianity, particularly east of the Rhine. The revival of the Roman imperial title, through Charlemagne's coronation at Rome on Christmas Day 800, was one reflection of a newly ambitious conception of militant Christian mission under the monarch.[49] This proved to be transferable to the neighbouring polities and peoples with which the Carolingians had dealings and which adopted elements of their style, practices and doctrines of rule. In England, where multiple regional kings held sway, the ninth century brought an expansion of the south-western kingdom of Wessex, to form the core of what over time would become a single English realm.[50]

The fragmentation of the Carolingian hegemony was followed in the tenth century by the emergence of a new power in eastern Francia, the Ottonian dynasty of Saxon kings.[51] The coronation of Otto I at Rome in 962 revived again the western imperial title, which henceforth endured unbroken, in the hands of monarchs based in German-speaking Europe, to the end of the middle ages and far beyond.[52] In western Francia the Carolingians were succeeded in 987 by the Capetian dynasty, ruling over what later medieval centuries would come to call the kingdom of France.[53] The continuation by the Ottonians of the Carolingian traditions of missionary warfare and diplomacy on their frontiers, meanwhile, underlay further territorial extensions of the Latin-Christian sphere in the

[48] For changes in the Mediterranean and beyond: J. Shepard, 'Europe and the wider world', in McKitterick (ed.), *Early Middle Ages*, 201–42.
[49] J. L. Nelson, 'Kingship and empire', in *CHMPT*, 211–51; W. Ullmann, *The Carolingian Renaissance and the Idea of Kingship* (London, 1969).
[50] J. Campbell, *The Anglo-Saxon State* (London, 2000).
[51] For fragmentation in this era in the Islamic world: pp. 220–2. Byzantium, in contrast, saw territorial and economic expansion: pp. 183–5.
[52] P. H. Wilson, *The Holy Roman Empire: A Thousand Years of Europe's History* (London, 2016).
[53] E. M. Hallam and J. Everard, *Capetian France, 987–1328* (Harlow, 2001).

tenth and early eleventh centuries. New Christian realms came into being in the east, in Poland, Bohemia and Hungary.[54] During the same period, a broadly comparable mix of religious conversion and political consolidation under monarchs resulted in the emergence of more settled kingdoms to the Empire's north, in Denmark and Norway (and somewhat later in Sweden). On the coast of western Francia, the Scandinavian convert community settled there under the later Carolingians solidified by the eleventh century as the duchy of Normandy.[55]

In Italy, the fading of Byzantine power, military interventions by the Carolingians and their imperial successors, and the activities of Muslim raiders and colonists in the Mediterranean all combined to produce a fragmented landscape.[56] The establishment of the papacy as a dominant territorial power in the centre of the peninsula would form a basis for the popes' increasingly comprehensive claims to the spiritual direction of western society after the eleventh century. As early as the ninth, Venice, though notionally a Byzantine dependency, had begun to emerge as an independent power in the north-east. Other urban centres developed with their own regional and wider importance, in a context of economic vitality, with Milan gaining early dominance in the Lombard plain. South of Rome, bands of Norman adventurers advanced during the eleventh century, with papal support, to establish new lordships at the expense of local powers and of Byzantium and Islam.

Between the tenth and fourteenth centuries, although to varying degrees and following different chronologies in different regions, the lands of Latin Europe underwent far-reaching processes of social and economic change.[57] These in turn opened the way to new developments in political life.[58] Underpinning all was a sustained, long-term growth in population, particularly in the core lands of the Latin west – in France, the Low Countries, western Germany, Italy and lowland Britain. The countryside and its inhabitants were subjected to more intensive and rigorous forms of exploitation.[59] Towns multiplied, even in regions which had hitherto known little of urban life: if cities are equated with civilisation,

[54] P. Heather, *Empires and Barbarians* (London, 2009).
[55] D. Bates, *Normandy before 1066* (London, 1982).
[56] C. Wickham, *Early Medieval Italy: Central Power and Local Society, 400–1000* (London, 1981), esp. 168–93; D. Abulafia (ed.), *Italy in the Central Middle Ages 1000–1300* (Oxford, 2004). For the impact on landholding: p. 370.
[57] N. J. G. Pounds, *An Economic History of Medieval Europe*, 2nd edn (London, 1994).
[58] For the difficulty of periodising expansion, however: C. Wickham, 'Making Europes', *New Left Review* I/208 (November/December 1994), 133–43.
[59] Pounds, *Economic History*, 30–55. For developments in the Low Countries, highlighting regional variations and socio-institutional as well as economic and geographical reasons: B. Van Bavel, *Manors and Markets: Economy and Society in the Low Countries, 500–1600* (Oxford, 2010).

then Europe was a far more civilised place in 1350 than in 950.[60] Trade and industry flourished, and the use of money became commonplace among all sections of the populace, paving the way for the development of taxation by secular regimes. The combined effect of these transform- ations was to multiply political formations and to stimulate diverse forms of political life and more pronounced regional political cultures.

The fragmentation of Muslim power in Spain following the end of the caliphate of Cordoba in 1031 encouraged the consolidation and expan- sion of the northern Latin-Christian kingdoms of León, Castile and Aragon, with the old Visigothic capital of Toledo falling to the Castilian king Alfonso VI in 1085.[61] The same aggressive dynamism – though temporarily checked by the interventions of Muslim invaders from North Africa – was reflected in the emergence in the twelfth century of a new kingdom, Portugal, and in a progressive southward shift of the Christian frontier. Doctrines of Christian Holy War, which played a part in expansion against the Muslim powers in twelfth-century Iberia, had a much more fundamental role in the establishment of new western settler-communities in the south-eastern Mediterranean, in Syria and Palestine, in the wake of the First Crusade (1095–9).[62] The last of these Latin enclaves, which included a kingdom of Jerusalem, were only extinguished by their Muslim neighbours at the end of the thirteenth century.

The twelfth and thirteenth centuries witnessed, by and large, the further expansion, institutional growth and sharper definition of west- ern polities.[63] In the British Isles, the French-speaking ruling elite that had seized the English kingdom in 1066 extended its control over much of southern and eastern Ireland in the following century.[64] From 1130 Sicily, another Norman acquisition, became a kingdom.[65] In the late thirteenth century, the English king Edward I conquered neighbouring Wales and incorporated it into his realm, while to the north the kingdom of Scotland was reinforced in its independence

---

[60] For cities as the measure of civilisation: Ferguson, *Civilization*, 5; Moore, 'Medieval Europe', 568. As Moore emphasises, it was not only in Latin Europe that this period saw major urbanisation.

[61] O'Callaghan, *History of Medieval Spain*; A. McKay, *Spain in the Middle Ages: From Frontier to Empire, 1000–1500* (Basingstoke, 1977). See Map 5 (inset).

[62] M. Barber, *The Crusader States* (New Haven, CT, 2012). See Map 8c.

[63] For the political 'regionalisation' of Europe in the central and later middle ages: Borgolte, *Christen, Juden, Muselmanen*, 473–516.

[64] For English imperialism in the British Isles: R. Frame, *The Political Development of the British Isles, 1100–1400* (Oxford, 1995).

[65] Matthew, *Norman Kingdom of Sicily*, 33–68. See also G. Loud and A. Metcalfe (eds), *The Society of Norman Italy* (Leiden, 2002); A. Metcalfe, *Muslims and Christians in Norman Sicily: Arabic-Speakers and the End of Islam* (London, 2003).

through the process of resisting English aggression. The kingdom of France now attained an extent much closer to its modern frontiers, partly through conquest from the French king's Plantagenet neighbours, partly under the mantle of crusade against heresy in the south. The capture of Constantinople in 1204 by western crusading forces benefited particularly the republic of Venice, which made major territorial gains in the eastern Mediterranean.[66] Also in this period, Iceland, self-governing and kingless since its settlement in the ninth and tenth centuries, submitted to the kings of Norway.

Different patterns are evident in the central European and Italian lands subject to the western emperors. Of crucial importance was the special relationship that existed between the German successors to the Carolingians in the empire and the bishops of Rome. In the late eleventh century that relationship turned sour, in a clash between the Salian emperor Henry IV and a newly assertive papacy in the person of Gregory VII. Ostensibly centred on control of appointments to the church, the dispute (known as the Investiture Contest) also reflected the collision of imperial and papal spheres of interest in Italy. The following 150 years were marked by recurrent crises between popes and emperors (only two of whom avoided excommunication) and recurrent, burdensome and disruptive, imperial military campaigns in Italy.[67]

One result was to reinforce the regional and local powers already important in the empire both north and south of the Alps. Increasingly the empire took on the character of a loose (though surprisingly stable) federation under its monarchical heads, with day-to-day government lying mainly in the hands of variable combinations of secular and ecclesiastical princes, lesser nobles and urban communities. Between the thirteenth and the sixteenth centuries in the empire's Alpine lands, the Swiss Confederation – a league of towns and peasant communes – attained an increasingly independent constitutional life. During broadly the same period the Hansa, a far-flung alliance of mainly German trading towns along the Baltic and North Sea coasts and in their hinterlands, became a major independent actor in regional politics as well as economic

---

[66] F. C. Lane, *Venice: A Maritime Republic* (Baltimore, MD, 1973), 30–43. See also the studies of David Jacoby in his *Trade, Commodities and Shipping in the Medieval Mediterranean* (Aldershot, 1997); *Byzantium, Latin Romania and the Mediterranean* (Aldershot, 2001); and 'The Venetian government and administration in Latin Constantinople, 1204–1261: a state within a state', in G. Ortalli *et al.* (eds), *Quarta crociata: Venezia, Bisanzio, Impero latino* (Venice, 2006), i:17–79; and S. McKee, *Uncommon Dominion: Venetian Crete and the Myth of Ethnic Purity* (Philadelphia, 2000).

[67] S. Weinfurter, *Das Reich im Mittelalter: Kleine deutsche Geschichte von 500 bis 1500* (Munich, 2008), 82–180.

affairs.[68] Traditional centres of political gravity shifted in the fourteenth century: the papacy northwards and westwards, to Avignon, the imperial monarchy eastwards, first to Bavaria, then Bohemia.[69]

In western continental Europe and the British Isles in the last two medieval centuries, the greater resources that regnal governments were now able to mobilise were applied in a series of protracted, interconnected wars. The largest of these was the misnamed Hundred Years War (1337–1453), in which the main, although by no means sole, protagonists were the kings of France and England.[70] Its source lay in the intractable rival claims of the two dynasties to lands and titles in France (including the French crown itself), exacerbated by social and economic crisis following the dramatic population falls resulting from the Black Death. A further factor was the protracted ('Great') schism in the papacy, which lasted from 1378 to 1417. During this period there were always at least two, and for a while three, rival popes competing for the allegiance of western princes and their subjects. These pressures and divisions contributed particularly to the fragmenting of the French kingdom, where a major new political actor, the Valois duchy of Burgundy, was able to emerge, ruled by a junior line of French royal princes. The strength of Burgundy (until the death of the last Valois duke in 1477) lay particularly in the rich revenues that its rulers drew from their dynamic and urbanised, though also turbulent, northern territories centred on Flanders.[71]

On the cultural frontiers of late medieval Europe, nativist movements pushed back, sometimes successfully, against the colonising practices of more powerful neighbours. English expansion in Ireland was checked and partially reversed. In Bohemia, where tensions between Czech-speakers and German settlers were exacerbated by religious controversy, in the Hussite movement, an entire kingdom seceded for a time from the

[68] T. A. Brady, *Turning Swiss: Cities and Empire, 1450–1550* (Cambridge, 1985); P. Dollinger, *The German Hansa*, tr. and ed. D. S. Ault and S. H. Steinberg (London, 1970). See also R. Hammel-Kiesow, *Die Hanse*, 2nd edn (Munich, 2002); S. Selzer, *Die mittelalterliche Hanse* (Darmstadt, 2010); D. J. Harreld (ed.), *A Companion to the Hanseatic League* (Leiden and Boston, 2015); C. Jahnke, *Die Hanse* (Stuttgart, 2014); U. Ewert and S. Selzer, *Institutions of Hanseatic Trade: Studies on the Political Economy of a Medieval Network Organisation* (Frankfurt am Main, 2016). See Map 8d.
[69] G. Mollat, *The Popes at Avignon, 1305–1378* (London, 1963); J. K. Hoensch, *Die Luxemburger: eine spätmittelalterliche Dynastie gesamteuropäischer Bedeutung 1308–1437* (Stuttgart, 2000), 51–192.
[70] A. Curry, *The Hundred Years War* (Basingstoke, 2003). See also J. Sumption, *The Hundred Years War*, 4 vols (London, 1990–2015); M. Prestwich, *A Short History of the Hundred Years War* (London, 2017); A. Curry (ed.), *The Hundred Years War Revisited* (London, 2019).
[71] R. Vaughan, *Valois Burgundy* (London, 1975); R. Stein, *Magnanimous Dukes and Rising States: The Unification of the Burgundian Netherlands, 1380–1480* (Oxford, 2017). See Map 4 (inset).

Catholic church in the fifteenth century.[72] On the whole, however, the trend at the close of the middle ages was towards the stabilising and in some cases further growth of established realms and regimes. By the late fifteenth century the French kingdom was again strong and expanding, the English having been expelled from French soil with the sole exception of Calais.[73] After 1420 the popes were re-established in Rome, where their rule came increasingly to resemble that of other Italian princes.[74] At the margins of Christendom expansion might still be accompanied by the territorial extension of the Catholic faith. Marriage with neighbouring Poland in 1386 brought Lithuania, Europe's last major pagan polity, into the Latin-Christian fold, while in 1492 Granada, the final Muslim enclave in Iberia, fell to the forces of the 'Catholic monarchs' of recently united Castile and Aragon.[75] A picture of complex, sometimes intricate but relatively settled regnal pluralism prevailed across a now much-extended western sphere.

Political Formations

Characterising the political formations of Latin Europe across the span of the middle ages is not simple. Not only were they many and varied: their character, mix and variety also changed considerably over time, as the societies and economies which sustained them were transformed. The Germanic kingdoms which succeeded to portions of the Roman empire were amorphous: warbands under dynastic heads, whose coherence was reaffirmed at annual military gatherings. These were not stable or enduring territorial entities, despite their rulers being able in varying degrees to draw upon Roman institutions, ideas and practices.[76] Public life in the Roman manner broke down after the empire's disintegration in the west, despite the efforts made particularly by bishops, with their seats in the decaying towns, to maintain the vestiges of civic infrastructure and amenities. In one respect, however, the Roman legacy was important: in the legitimacy which it bestowed upon the barbarian kingdoms as separate and multiple political formations. This was conveyed particularly through the written laws which their kings caused to have set down, generally in Latin, and through the Latin origin-stories, which furnished their

[72] F. Šmahel, *Die Hussitische Revolution*, tr. T. Krzenc, 3 vols (Hanover, 2002).
[73] D. Potter, *A History of France, 1460–1560* (Basingstoke, 1995), 251–83.
[74] D. Hay, *The Church in Italy in the Fifteenth Century* (Cambridge, 1977).
[75] J. W. Sedlar, *East Central Europe in the Middle Ages, 1000–1500* (Seattle, 1994), 362–400; J. H. Elliott, *Imperial Spain, 1469–1716* (London, 1963), 45–76.
[76] P. D. King, 'The barbarian kingdoms', in *CHMPT*, 123–53; for the Roman legacy generally: Y. Hen, *Roman Barbarians: The Royal Court and Culture in the Early Medieval West* (Basingstoke, 2007). On political formations, see also pp. 373–4, 402–4.

composite warrior elites with myths of common blood and endeavour: for each its own *Aeneid*.[77] Henceforward in western history *Romanitas*, with its promise of political unity, became a dream – albeit a powerful, long-lasting and highly adaptable one: it was no longer a workable system.

Changes with great long-term importance occurred in the eighth and ninth centuries, following the accession of the Carolingians in Francia. Their rule was a new departure in two related fields: in their exalted view of monarchy, as a divine trust, its exercise an all-embracing Christian project; and in the high ambition which they brought to the material business of government.[78] Textual didacticism, accountability and written records stood at the heart of the Carolingian venture.[79] Even if Carolingian government inevitably often delivered less than it promised, the template was highly influential. It helped to shape the theory and practice of kingship in neighbouring realms like Anglo-Saxon England and, eventually, the understanding of monarchy across Christendom generally.[80] The central role in government that the Carolingian model allotted to churchmen was also destined for a large future. This is evident under their successors in eastern Francia, the Ottonians, who entrusted bishops and abbots with principalities to govern on the king-emperor's behalf.[81] Particularly in the lands of the empire, a pattern of quasi-independent territorial niches developed, in the hands of great prelates, protected by privileges of immunity and largely sealed off from outside interference.[82] Western society was becoming honeycombed with enclaves, down to the most local levels.

The late ninth and early tenth centuries saw western realms placed under strain by outside attacks from Latin Europe's non-Christian neighbours: pagan Norsemen along the coasts of continental Europe and the British Isles and Magyars in central Europe, as well as Muslims in the Mediterranean sphere. But while these incursions helped speed the break-up of the Carolingian patrimony, their effect was not only destructive. In those kingdoms which endured, or emerged from the ruins, defensive measures under the ruler – such as the proto-urban foundations

---

[77] Smith, *Europe after Rome*, 253–92; Sarris, *Empires of Faith*, 275–306; P. J. Geary, *The Myth of Nations: The Medieval Origins of Europe* (Princeton, 2002). See also A. Plassmann, *Origo gentis: Identitäts- und Legitimitätsstiftung in früh- und hochmittelalterlichen Herkunftserzählungen* (Berlin 2006).

[78] M. Innes, 'Charlemagne's government', in J. Storey (ed.), *Charlemagne: Empire and Society* (Manchester, 2010), 71–89.

[79] R. McKitterick (ed.), *Carolingian Culture: Emulation and Innovation* (Cambridge, 1994).

[80] For its influence on neighbours: McKitterick, 'Politics', esp. 22–3.

[81] T. Reuter, *Germany in the Early Middle Ages, 800–1056* (London, 1991), 236–46.

[82] J. Eldevik, *Episcopal Power and Ecclesiastical Reform in the German Empire: Tithes, Lordship and Community, 950–1150* (Cambridge, 2012).

(*burhs*) established in Wessex under Alfred the Great (871–99) and perhaps roughly comparable innovations in the Saxony of Henry I (919–36) – encouraged consolidation.[83] In England, the earliest general taxation was a response to the Scandinavian incursions.

With the breakdown of the Roman fiscal state in the early medieval west, land became the main basis of power.[84] The naturally centrifugal quality of this change was amplified by the fragmentation of the Carolingian empire and its aftermath.[85] Boundaries between different spheres of rule and administration were now increasingly sharply articulated.[86] Between the tenth and twelfth centuries, parishes became established throughout Christendom as basic units of ecclesiastical government – often corresponding to village communities, which also now took on firmer contours. The house of the military lord was increasingly visibly distinct from the dwellings of those whose labours fed and armed him.[87] The process of laying closer hold upon the land was far from being one of straightforward state-making, and where the power of kings and princes was weak its result was an intense fragmentation of the landscape. This was the case in much of France in the tenth and eleventh centuries, where local warlords were able to employ powerful new technologies of domination, notably castles in conjunction with bands of armoured, mounted warriors, to carve up the land into a myriad of tiny, defensible parcels.[88]

The new kingdoms and principalities that were established at Christendom's margins between the tenth and the thirteenth centuries drew their populations partly from the swelling human reservoirs of western continental Europe.[89] Ruling dynasties came especially from a mainly French-speaking western core. The balance of power between the new regimes and their subject populations varied markedly. In Sicily, where the Norman monarchy drew upon existing traditions of bureaucratic authoritarianism, the king's hand weighed heavily upon the people. In the lands of the crown of Aragon, by contrast, or in the Latin kingdom

[83] F. M. Stenton, *Anglo-Saxon England,* 3rd edn (Oxford, 1971), 525–37; Reuter, *Germany,* 142–4.

[84] Wickham, *Inheritance of Rome,* 76–108.

[85] The classic account remains M. Bloch, *Feudal Society,* tr. L. A. Manyon, 2 vols (London, 1961).

[86] Moore, 'Medieval Europe', 576–7.

[87] M. Innes, *Introduction to Early Medieval Western Europe, 300–900: The Sword, the Plough and the Book* (London, 2007), 446–7.

[88] For the scholarly literature: C. Wickham, 'The "feudal revolution"', *P&P* 155 (1997), 196–208; C. West, *Reframing the Feudal Revolution: Political and Social Transformation between Marne and Moselle, c. 800–c. 1100* (Cambridge, 2013).

[89] R. Bartlett, *The Making of Europe: Conquest, Colonization, and Cultural Change, 950–1350* (Harmondsworth, 1993), 5–23.

of Jerusalem, powerful military aristocracies gained a growing ascendancy over the monarch. Inter-ethnic relations in these colonial kingdoms showed no single course of development. In post-Conquest England, the Norman elite reinvented itself as English within a fairly short span of generations, despite the long persistence of linguistic and other divisions from the native populace.[90] In Sicily, by contrast, Normans (and after them Swabians, Angevins and Aragonese) domineered over populations of Greeks, Muslims and Lombards, with whom they cultivated only superficial and utilitarian affinities.[91] In Ireland, Anglo-Norman behaviour followed the Sicilian pattern.[92]

The proliferation of towns within Latin Europe brought new modes of political life to the fore.[93] While the principles of common responsibility and identification in which they were rooted are less novel than is sometimes thought, the position of towns within a world of feudal military hierarchies nevertheless led to conflicts and appeared to some as anomalous. The role of towns in their society varied from place to place and between towns, and often also changed over the course of time. In some regions, such as England or Sicily, townspeople had only fairly limited self-government and were firmly subjected to royal law and oversight by royal officials. Elsewhere, towns enjoyed considerable autonomy, made their own laws and were able with time to purchase privileges from their lords or exact them through political and military pressure. Where urbanisation was heaviest and lordship most contested – in the Low Countries, in parts of southern and western Germany, and above all in Italy north of Rome – fully formed city states emerged. Such communities were independent political actors, conducting their own external relations with urban and princely neighbours and in some cases extending their domination over other towns and far-flung rural hinterlands.[94] To outside eyes, this urban political landscape appeared strange and remarkable. The

---

[90] H. M. Thomas, *The English and the Normans: Ethnic Hostility, Assimilation, and Identity, 1066–c.1220* (Oxford, 2003).

[91] D. Abulafia, 'The Italian other: Greeks, Muslims, and Jews', in Abulafia (ed.), *Italy in the Central Middle Ages*, 215–36.

[92] J. Gillingham, 'The beginnings of English imperialism', *Journal of Historical Sociology* 5 (1992), 392–409; repr. in his *The English in the Twelfth Century: Imperialism, National Identity and Political Values* (Woodbridge, 2000), 3–18. See also S. Burkhardt and T. Foerster (eds), *Norman Tradition and Transcultural Heritage: Exchange of Cultures in the 'Norman' Peripheries of Medieval Europe* (Farnham, 2013).

[93] D. Nicholas, *The Growth of the Medieval City: From Late Antiquity to the Early Fourteenth Century* (London, 1997), 141–68.

[94] P. Jones, *The Italian City-State: From Commune to Signoria* (Oxford, 1997); D. Waley, *The Italian City-Republics*, 3rd edn (London, 1988); C. Dartmann, *Politische Interaktion in der italienischen Stadtkommune (11.–14. Jahrhundert)* (Ostfildern, 2012). See also C. Wickham, *Sleepwalking towards a New World: The Emergence of Italian City Communes in the Twelfth Century* (Princeton, 2017).

twelfth-century Jewish traveller Benjamin of Tudela remarked of the inhabitants of Pisa ('a very great city, with about 10,000 turreted houses') that 'they possess neither king nor prince to govern them, but only the judges appointed by themselves'.[95] In Italy, subdivision into ever-smaller units did not pause even at the town gates. In a climate of intense competition between urban clans and factions, exacerbated in the thirteenth century by mounting social tensions, overlapping and competing organs of government sought to assert themselves within individual communes.

The church developed its own distinctive forms of rule. In this it was able, particularly after the eleventh century, to benefit from the relative invulnerability of its properties to the dynastic divisions, alienations and failures of heirs which constantly threatened the material foundations of temporal lordship. The advanced literate and organisational skills which their members commanded made religious institutions particularly sharp-eyed governors of territory. It is little wonder, therefore, that churchmen also attained central importance in the government of secular rulers.[96] It was not, however, only in government that the church showed innovation but in the forms of political life more generally. It was through the acts of churchmen that there came into being in the wake of the First Crusade a quite new political, as well as religious, formation: the order of fighting (and ruling) monks.[97] The military orders established a presence on more than one crusading frontier. However, their political importance was particularly great in the eastern Baltic, where the Teutonic Order, one of the later foundations, established its *Ordensstaat*: a closely governed sphere of independent corporate rule, vast in size but sharply defined and voraciously extended by military and diplomatic action.[98]

While across much of Europe the population was subjected to forms of military-aristocratic lordship founded on the exploitation of arable land, the political superstructures built upon this agrarian base took various forms. Although constitutionally most territories were under a king, or a quasi-king such as the emperor or pope, the rule experienced by their populations was often that of a prince or magnate without royal title – generally exercising power via some form of investiture from above but in practice largely independent. Kingship and royal government were by no

---

[95] *The Itinerary of Benjamin of Tudela*, ed. and tr. M. N. Adler (London, 1907; repr. New York, n.d.), 5.

[96] Two specific examples: J. Mötsch and F.-J. Heyen (eds), *Balduin von Luxemburg, Erzbischof von Trier – Kurfürst des Reiches: Festschrift aus Anlaß des 700. Geburtsjahres* (Mainz, 1985); C. R. Cheney, *Hubert Walter* (London, 1967).

[97] A. Forey, *The Military Orders: From the Twelfth to the Early Fourteenth Centuries* (Basingstoke, 1992).

[98] K. Militzer, *Die Geschichte des Deutschen Ordens* (Stuttgart, 2005), 95–142.

means always close at hand. Throughout the medieval period, rulers often exercised loose hegemonies over agglomerations of realms and lordships, held under all manner of titles. Such composite patrimonies possessed very varied levels of stability. Where the unity was merely personal, as in the rule exercised by Cnut (d. 1035) over England, Denmark, and parts of Norway and Sweden, it could prove fleeting indeed.[99] Given more substantial infrastructures of rule, fragmentation might be less abrupt and the memory of titles more durable.[100] When kingdoms were bound into a larger hegemony by ties of law, public ritual and political identity, as were the component realms of the western empire (Germany, Italy and Burgundy), the assemblage, despite all elements of weakness, might survive for centuries.

European kingdoms developed in different ways, reflecting their varied histories and circumstances. Some, like post-Conquest England or Norman Sicily, inherited pre-existing traditions of literate, centralised government upon which they built. Others, such as Capetian France, acquired these elements over time. Each realm had its own chronological patterns. Poland, established as a duchy in the tenth century and ruled by kings in the eleventh, had fragmented into multiple principalities in the twelfth, only to be re-established as a single kingdom early in the fourteenth.[101] It was the differences even between close neighbours that sometimes struck contemporaries. To the French lawyer Pierre Dubois the elective crown, in the gift of seven great princes, which had developed in the German lands of the empire in the thirteenth century, contrasted sharply with his own dynastic realm.[102] It produced and reflected quite different – in his view less orderly – social relations than a kingdom transmitted by heredity.

The last two centuries of the middle ages were marked by acute political instability across much of Europe.[103] One general consequence was to stimulate the emergence of political formations which, if not altogether new, represented significant developments of, or deviations from, what had gone before. Rulership in various parts of Europe was afflicted by

[99] Stenton, *Anglo-Saxon England*, 401–11. See also M. K. Lawson, *Cnut, England's Viking King, 1016–35*, 2nd edn (Stroud, 2011); B. Hudson, *Viking Pirates and Christian Princes: Dynasty, Religion, and Empire in the North Atlantic* (New York and Oxford, 2005); T. Bolton, *The Empire of Cnut the Great: Conquest and the Consolidation of Power in the Early Eleventh Century* (Leiden, 2009).

[100] Thus e.g. M. Aurell, *The Plantagenet Empire, 1154–1224*, tr. D. Crouch (Harlow, 2007).

[101] A. Gieysztor, 'Medieval Poland', in A. Gieysztor *et al.*, *History of Poland*, tr. K. Cękalska, 2nd edn (Warsaw, 1979), esp. 47–137.

[102] *De recuperatione terre sancte: traité de politique générale par Pierre Dubois* ch. 13, ed. C.-V. Langlois (Paris, 1891), 12.

[103] See generally Watts, *Making of Polities*.

crises of legitimacy, which found expression in the ousting of reigning monarchs by various combinations of force and constitutional process and the installation of new figures in their place. In the towns across much of northern Italy, the change of rule took a particular form, as the communal governments of the central middle ages gave way to one-man regimes – sometimes of violent and unstable character, and usually of constitutionally debatable origins. While both the oppressiveness of the *signori* and their lack of traditional legitimacy have been exaggerated, their style of rule and its ideological underpinnings remain in some ways distinctive.[104]

One effect of the demographic, economic and political crises of the late middle ages was to increase the scope for new individuals and social groups to engage in politics. Their engagement was facilitated by the development of parliaments and estates, which now came to exercise a significant voice in the affairs of some realms and regions. In a less formalised development, new participants also forced a way into the political process, albeit often only fleetingly, via the numerous tumults and revolts, mostly highly localised but some more extensive, which mark the period.[105] Many of these late medieval extensions of the political community were to be undermined with the strengthening of regimes and the reassertion of hierarchies across much of Europe at the end of the middle ages. However, some changes – such as the growth of the English Parliament – left a more tenacious political legacy.[106]

Leagues, alliances and associations of various character and varying degrees of formality and durability are to be found at all levels of European society and in all regions – though most densely where political authority was most contested.[107] Their formation was favoured particularly in the later middle ages by processes of advancing social and cultural integration and the development of inter-regional ties.[108] Towns joined

---

[104] Famously by J. Burckhardt, *Die Cultur der Renaissance in Italien: ein Versuch* (Basel, 1860); tr. S. G. C. Middlemore, intro. P. Burke, *The Civilization of the Renaissance in Italy* (Harmondsworth, 1990). See J. Law, *The Lords of Renaissance Italy: The Signori, 1250–1500* (London, 1980); T. Dean, 'The rise of the *signori*', in Abulafia (ed.), *Italy in the Central Middle Ages*, 104–24.

[105] S. K. Cohn, *Lust for Liberty: The Politics of Social Revolt in Medieval Europe, 1200–1425* (Cambridge, MA, 2006).

[106] J. R. Maddicott, *The Origins of the English Parliament, 924–1327* (Oxford, 2010).

[107] For the associative principle in peace-keeping in the late medieval empire: D. Hardy, 'Between regional alliances and imperial assemblies: *Landfrieden* as a political concept and discursive strategy in the Holy Roman Empire *c*.1350–1520', in H. Baumbach and H. Carl (eds), *Landfrieden – epochenübergreifend: Neue Perspektiven der Landfriedensforschung auf Verfassung, Recht, Konflikt* (Berlin, 2018), 85–120. See also D. Hardy, *Associative Political Culture in the Holy Roman Empire* (Oxford, 2018).

[108] P. Moraw, *Von offener Verfassung zu gestalteter Verdichtung: das Reich im späten Mittelalter 1250 bis 1490* (Berlin, 1985).

with other towns against regional princes and nobles, or with nobles against their neighbours, or engaged in a host of other forms of political association. Princes and nobles allied against towns, against their monarchs or against other nobles. The Hansa and the Swiss Confederation are merely especially large, institutionalised, and long-lasting manifestations of a more general phenomenon.[109] Latin Europe's political formations and actors were naturally well suited to coming together in fleeting or longer-term marriages of convenience. Such conjunctions, often functioning at a local level and easily overlooked (since they are too numerous, protean and insubstantial to be depicted in historical atlases), are characteristic of Europe in the central and later middle ages.

Above this complex and shifting array of polities stood universal institutions asserting claims to rule throughout, and on some views far beyond, Latin Christendom: the papacy and the western empire. However, neither the papal nor the imperial monarchy was, in political affairs, as truly universal as might appear. Of the two, the papacy has the more substantial claim. During a fairly brief heyday, between the late eleventh and the early fourteenth centuries, popes asserted, and occasionally exercised, a power to discipline and even depose rulers judged to have deviated from their duty as Christian princes.[110] Yet already at the end of the thirteenth century, the open and successful defiance offered to Boniface VIII (d. 1303) by the kings of France and England made clear how blunt was the edge of papal coercion when faced with resistance from powerful monarchs.[111] Universal claims were in any case only one side of the papacy's historic dealings with the peoples and realms of western Europe. Far from being the enemy of political multiplicity, the papacy had from the earliest times had a central part in fostering and affirming a world of many polities. A fragmented map suited the territorially vulnerable popes: it ensured there was always somewhere else to turn. It seemed, indeed, to reflect the hand of God: as Clement V declared, early in the fourteenth century, 'the king of glory formed different kingdoms for diverse peoples according to differences in language and race'.[112] Papal

[109] A salient earlier example is the Lombard League, an alliance of north Italian towns which resisted the Hohenstaufen emperors in the twelfth and early thirteenth centuries: G. Raccagni, *The Lombard League,1167–1225* (Oxford, 2010). On the impact of communal government, see also pp. 65, 268–9, 273.
[110] C. Morris, *The Papal Monarchy: The Western Church from 1050 to 1250* (Oxford, 1989), 109–33, 182–204, 505–26.
[111] T. S. R. Boase, *Boniface VIII* (London, 1933).
[112] Quoted in J. R. Strayer, 'France: the Holy Land, the Chosen People, and the Most Christian King', in T. K. Rabb and J. E. Seigel (eds), *Action and Conviction in Early Modern Europe: Essays in Memory of E. H. Harbison* (Princeton, 1969), 3–16 at 15.

decretals were cited in defence of the sovereign independence of the late-medieval realm.[113]

The universalism of the empire, although loudly enunciated by its learned champions and embraced as an ideal by at least some of its rulers, had an importance that was mainly symbolic and discursive.[114] It never received more than fitful and formal acknowledgement outside the empire's territorial bounds. Even in western emperorship's twelfth-century heyday it was denied and openly derided by some opponents.[115] The imperial theme and the political legacy of Rome were also pressed into service by regimes far from universal in their horizons – such as the late medieval king of France, 'emperor in his own kingdom'.[116] Even as aspiration, imperial universalism acknowledged a politically plural world.[117] Those who wrote in the emperor's defence commonly affirmed his duty to govern different peoples according to their own laws and customs, recognised the reality of multiple realms and noted the historic independence of some from imperial jurisdiction.[118] By the late thirteenth century, moreover, regnal pluralism had its own learned champions, ready to argue against the imperial theme and, particularly under Aristotelian influence, to champion on principle a world of many and separate polities.[119] Towards the close of the middle ages, the empire came to be perceived increasingly as a German realm.[120] In the same way, the papacy, to some eyes a French institution for much of the fourteenth century, appeared as an Italian one in the fifteenth.

Participants

The range of social groups participating in political life in Latin Europe increased considerably over the course of our long medieval

[113] S. Tebbit, 'Papal pronouncements on legitimate lordship and the formulation of nationhood in early fourteenth-century Scotland', *Journal of Medieval History* 40 (2014), 44–62.

[114] For the qualities of the western imperial idea: B. Schneidmüller, 'Kaiser sein im spätmittelalterlichen Europa: Spielregeln zwischen Weltherrschaft und Gewöhnlichkeit', in C. Garnier and H. Kamp (eds), *Spielregeln der Mächtigen: Mittelalterliche Politik zwischen Gewohnheit und Konvention* (Darmstadt, 2010), 265–90.

[115] T. Reuter, 'John of Salisbury and the Germans', in M. Wilks (ed.), *The World of John of Salisbury* (Oxford, 1984), 415–25.

[116] For France and the imperial tradition: J. Krynen, *L'Empire du roi: idées et croyances politiques en France XIIIe–XVe siècles* (Paris, 1993); C. Jones, *Eclipse of Empire? Perceptions of the Western Empire and its Rulers in Late-Medieval France* (Turnhout, 2007).

[117] M. Fuhrmann, *Alexander von Roes: ein Wegbereiter des Europagedankens?* (Heidelberg, 1994), 34.

[118] L. E. Scales, 'France and the Empire: the viewpoint of Alexander of Roes', *French History* 9 (1995), 394–416.

[119] Schneidmüller, 'Kaiser sein', 275–80.

[120] U. Nonn, 'Heiliges Römisches Reich Deutscher Nation: zum Nationen-Begriff im 15. Jahrhundert', *Zeitschrift für historische Forschung* 9 (1982), 129–42.

period.[121] The proportion of the total population involved in politics probably also grew. These statements require a number of qualifications, however. First, such growth was neither linear nor inexorable, did not everywhere follow the same pattern or attain the same extent, and in many parts of Europe had been reversed by the end of the period. Second, the impression of wider involvement over time may be partly an illusion produced by the nature and distribution of the sources, which permit a closer view of the workings of politics in the later rather than the earlier medieval centuries. Thirdly, our vision may be distorted by our own assumptions about what constitutes 'politics': for a number of reasons, a distinct political sphere becomes easier to define in the later middle ages. Finally, our conclusions will depend in part upon what we mean by 'participation'.

A number of general statements can be made about access to political power, valid for most regions and social formations in Latin Europe between the eighth and the fifteenth centuries. Political activity was strongly marked by the idea and reality of hierarchy: power was very unequally distributed, with many people having effectively none and decisive power nearly always lying in relatively few hands. The principle of hierarchical organisation was almost universally accepted, even while the actual distribution of power between individuals and groups was frequently contested. What distinguished many of those towards the top of local or larger power-hierarchies was enjoyment of the right, the means and the readiness to bear arms (or at least, the ability plausibly to associate themselves with arms-bearing). Martial activity became linked from an early date with the idea of birth into a power-worthy kin-group, with enjoyment of substantial (particularly landed) property and with adherence to legitimising norms of elite group behaviour. It almost invariably assumed maleness.

The group of politically eligible arms-bearers was therefore always limited in size. With time, however, a further restriction developed: the form of military activity granting access to power came to be defined as that of the specialist mounted warrior. Already under the Carolingians, the secular magnates who shared power with the monarch went to war as armoured cavalrymen.[122] As the technologies of violence advanced in the centuries that followed, so too did both their cost and their capacity to concentrate power in the hands of those who wielded them or commanded their use. During the central middle ages, across much of

---

[121] See also pp. 277–80, 283–4, 390–1, 401–2; for Byzantium: pp. 326–7, 437, 440–1, 447–9; for Islam: pp. 234–47, 477–9.

[122] F. L. Ganshof, 'Charlemagne's army', in his *Frankish Institutions under Charlemagne*, tr. B. and M. Lyon (Providence, RI, 1968), 57–68.

Europe the qualities of such expensively equipped warriors were crystallised in the title of knight.[123] This title eventually became hereditary, became linked to a distinctive ('chivalric') culture and style of life, and over time became synonymous with nobility.[124] Only at Latin Europe's colonial margins, where military manpower was at a premium and land for its support relatively abundant, did the rise of the armoured fighting man sometimes serve to facilitate upward social mobility and thus the enlargement of the political stratum. This was the case in Iberia between the eleventh and the thirteenth centuries, where even relatively poor men were able (as *caballeros villanos*) to enter the arms-bearing elite.[125]

By and large, however, as the cult of the chivalrous knight rose, so too did the social and political barriers. By the late middle ages, knighthood had grown too costly even for many members of the elite to bear, so that formal knighting increasingly gave way to a more loosely framed model of high-status equestrian arms-bearing: the man-at-arms.[126] Nevertheless, the conceptual links between mounted warfare and political participation, forged during knighthood's medieval high summer, lived on – explicitly in the knights of the shire, petty noblemen who represented their county communities in the English Parliament.[127] In Valois Burgundy at the close of the middle ages, ducal chancellors were still knighted as a matter of course on taking up office.[128]

The character of social life in the west favoured the domination of politics by warrior-aristocrats. It was a hegemony built upon firm material foundations, which over time also acquired strong cultural and doctrinal underpinnings. Across much of Europe, to the end of the middle ages and beyond, a broad, middling agrarian nobility formed the bedrock of local and regional government (as well as, where government was weak, the main force for its further disruption).[129] Credible claims to power came to depend upon appropriating the material advantages and imitating the style of the landed elite. Wealthy urban families built fortified stone

---

[123] J. Flori, *L'Essor de la chevalerie: XIe–XIIe siècles* (Geneva, 1986).
[124] D. Crouch, *The Birth of Nobility: Constructing Aristocracy in England and France, 900–1300* (Harlow, 2005); D. Barthélemy, *La Chevalerie: de la Germanie antique à la France du XIIe siècle*, rev. edn (Paris, 2012). On knighthood and chivalry, see also p. 390.
[125] MacKay, *Spain in the Middle Ages*, 36–57.
[126] P. Contamine, *War in the Middle Ages*, tr. M. Jones (Oxford, 1984), 119–72.
[127] G. Harriss, *Shaping the Nation: England 1360–1461* (Oxford, 2005), 66–74. Despite this term, not all county representatives were knights.
[128] W. Blockmans and E. Donckers, 'Self-representation of court and city in Flanders and Brabant in the fifteenth and early sixteenth centuries', in W. Blockmans and A. Janse (eds), *Showing Status: Representations of Social Positions in the Late Middle Ages* (Turnhout, 1999), 81–111 at 85.
[129] J. Morsel, *L'Aristocratie médiévale Ve–XVe siècle* (Paris, 2004).

houses, both to symbolise and to make real the power which they exercised or claimed within their communities.[130] They assumed armorials, cultivated horsemanship, tourneyed and copied the dress, lifestyle and cultural patronage of the military aristocracy. Some intermarried with nobles. Those challenging for power from below behaved similarly. Guildsmen adopted quasi-military liveries and paraded behind banners, just as their archery and crossbow confraternities cultivated skill in arms, honed and displayed in inter-town competitions, and encouraged pride in martial attainment.[131]

Admittedly, not everyone who claimed or exercised power actually fought, and armed force was never the only justification for power. Kings often took up arms, and military symbols and imagery were central to their rule. But the royal office itself was in most places and at most times something different from, or more than, that of merely supreme warlord.[132] Some kings chose to take little or no personal part in military activity, resting their claim to rule instead upon quasi-religious attributes.[133] Those whom the king called to exercise power in his name might also remain outside the military hierarchy. For most of the middle ages, the men appointed to senior administrative posts were experienced and often high-ranking clerics. Only in the fourteenth and fifteenth centuries do we start to find laymen – commonly of bourgeois background and university education – appointed to major governmental offices, such as that of chancellor.[134] Such figures, like the lay financiers and lawyers who also become increasingly prominent as royal counsellors in the later middle ages, derived their power from their offices and from the wealth and expertise which had secured their appointment: they had no obvious need to appear in arms. Yet even among royal servants and among those of clerical rank, the allure of an equestrian image might prove hard to

---

[130] E.g. W. De Clercq et al., '"Vivre noblemen": material culture and elite identity in late medieval Flanders', Journal of Interdisciplinary History 38 (2007), 1–31.

[131] P. Arnade, Realms of Ritual: Burgundian Ceremony and Civic Life in Late Medieval Ghent (Ithaca, NY, 1996), 65–94. See also pp. 377–8. For arms-bearing and the role of warfare in the political culture of the other two spheres: pp. 25–6, 298–9, 307–8, 317–18, 108, 213–15, 217–18, 221–3, 225, 245–6, 473.

[132] For varieties of kingship: A. J. Duggan (ed.), Kings and Kingship in Medieval Europe (London, 1993). On the appropriation of norms to challenges elites, and on the competition for participation, see also pp. 280–1.

[133] M. Bloch, The Royal Touch: Sacred Monarchy and Scrofula in England and France, tr. J. E. Anderson (London, 1973). See, however, the warning remarks by J. I. Engels, 'Das "Wesen" der Monarchie? Kritische Anmerkungen zum "Sakralkönigtum" in der Geschichtswissenschaft', Majestas 7 (1999), 3–39.

[134] Two examples: J. Heers, Jacques Coeur 1400–1456 (Paris, 1997); H. Heimpel, Die Vener von Gmünd und Straßburg 1162–1447: Studien und Texte zur Geschichte einer Familie sowie des gelehrten Beamtentums in der Zeit der abendländischen Kirchenspaltung und der Konzilien von Pisa, Konstanz und Basel, 3 vols (Göttingen, 1982).

resist. Thomas Hatfield, bishop of Durham (1345–81), a valued administrator under Edward III of England, appears on his chancery seal armed and armoured, astride a charging warhorse.[135]

By the eleventh century, the church's own teaching on the proper order of society appeared to affirm the place of a compact, self-conscious warrior elite at its head: there were those who worked, those who prayed and those who fought (the Three Orders).[136] At no time in the middle ages was fighting easily distinguishable from ruling. Viewed in this way, the circle of those with a legitimate part in medieval politics appears small. Such thinking was combined, moreover, with highly negative judgements on the political capacities of those outside this circle. Lower-class rebels were portrayed as unreasoning brute beasts.[137] 'The madness of crowds' was a watchword among the educated and powerful.[138] The political aspirations of most people were held to count for nothing at all.

Yet whatever elite figures may have professed to think, the reality of medieval politics was always less rigidly exclusive: even in principle, hierarchy and subordination were elements in a more complex picture. Rulers did not rule alone. Consultation was an obligation of power at all levels: kings and princes were expected to consult with their magnates and great churchmen, nobles with their military retainers, before taking decisions which would affect others. For all the prominence which chroniclers gave to the deeds of outstanding individuals, medieval assumptions about political activity were in an important sense collectivist.[139]

Medieval Europeans derived their sense of selfhood from membership of communities which were held to have compelling reality. 'I am Pia; Siena made me', says a character in Dante's *Divine Comedy*.[140] Collective groups, from the local to the regnal, were imagined as units of common history and even descent.[141] Everyone was included, at least in imagination: medieval origin myths, unlike some from later times, did not

---

[135] Illustrated in M. Prestwich, *Armies and Warfare in the Middle Ages: The English Experience* (New Haven, CT, 1996), 170. Hatfield had exercised military command on Edward's expedition to Normandy in 1346.

[136] Georges Duby, *The Three Orders: Feudal Society Imagined*, tr. A. Goldhammer (Chicago, 1980).

[137] J. Dumolyn, '"Criers and shouters": the discourse on radical urban rebels in late medieval Flanders', *Journal of Social History* 42 (2008), 111–35.

[138] Pius II, *Commentaries*, ed. Meserve and Simonetta, i:92–3.

[139] J. Quillet, 'Community, counsel and representation' in *CHMPT*, 520–72; also B. Schneidmüller, 'Rule by consensus: forms and concepts of political order in the European middle ages', *Medieval History Journal* 16 (2013), 449–71; p. 273.

[140] *The Divine Comedy of Dante Alighieri: II Purgatorio*, tr. J. D. Sinclair (London, 1971), canto 5, ll. 133–4. I follow the translation of J. M. Najemy, 'Introduction', in J. M. Najemy (ed.), *Italy in the Age of the Renaissance* (Oxford, 2004), 1–17 at 4.

[141] S. Reynolds, *Kingdoms and Communities in Western Europe, 900–1300*, 2nd edn (Oxford, 1997).

ascribe different and inferior roots to those of lower social status.[142] Communities were understood as units of common political endeavour. Perception was affirmed by everyday experience, since medieval people did indeed participate regularly in their own governance – albeit in vertically ordered, highly unequal ways – at many levels.

This is observable in the most intimate, face-to-face forms of organisation. The village communities which proliferated between the tenth and twelfth centuries generally took collective responsibility, under the leadership of their wealthier, more senior or more commanding members, for their own affairs.[143] Village assemblies formulated and enforced local bye-laws. Assemblies, indeed, were fundamental to political activity at all levels from the earliest times: some of the first evidence to survive for organised political life in Europe concerns meeting sites.[144] When the first regnal and provincial parliaments and estates took shape in the late twelfth and thirteenth centuries, with formalised proceedings and membership, this marked no new principle in European politics but an extension of ancient ones.[145]

The character of assemblies varied greatly, both over time and between different places at the same time.[146] While the Icelandic *Althing*, as a gathering of free landowners, met without a monarch as head (though not without hierarchies), other meetings – exemplified by the French Estates General of 1302, summoned by Philip IV at the height of his clash with the pope – served mainly as mouthpieces for rulers.[147] Nevertheless, it is the social breadth of the groups that by the late middle ages had attained at least a limited and formal voice in political affairs that

---

[142] S. Reynolds, 'Medieval *origines gentium* and the community of the realm', *History* 68 (1983), 375–90.

[143] P. Blickle (ed.), *Resistance, Representation and Community* (Oxford, 1997)

[144] A. Pantos and S. Semple (eds), *Assembly Places and Practices in Medieval Europe* (Dublin, 2004).

[145] That is not to propose continuity in the character of the assemblies themselves between pre-history and the middle ages. For the early medieval period: P. S. Barnwell, 'Political assemblies: introduction', in P. S. Barnwell and M. Mostert (eds), *Political Assemblies in the Earlier Middle Ages* (Turnhout, 2003), 1–10. For the difficulty of assessing the diverse functions and the composition of e.g. the *cortes* of Castile-León: J. F. O'Callaghan, *The Cortes of Castile-León, 1188–1350* (Philadelphia, 1989).

[146] A. R. Myers, *Parliaments and Estates in Europe to 1789* (London, 1975); W. Blockmans, 'A typology of representative institutions in late medieval Europe', *Journal of Medieval History* 4 (1978), 189–215; W. Blockmans, 'Representation', in *NCMH* 7, 29–64; B. Guenée, *States and Rulers in Later Medieval Europe*, tr. J. Vale (Oxford, 1985), 171–87.

[147] J. Byock, 'The Icelandic *Althing*: dawn of parliamentary democracy', in J. M. Fladmark and T. Heyerdahl (eds), *Heritage and Identity: Shaping the Nations of the North* (London, 2002), 1–18; A. Sanmark, *Viking Law and Order: Places and Rituals of Assembly in the Medieval North* (Edinburgh, 2017); for the French estates-general: J. R. Strayer, *The Reign of Philip the Fair* (Princeton, 1980), 271–5.

deserves emphasis. In the estates of the Tirol, by the fourteenth century the peasantry too enjoyed legal representation, alongside nobles and clergy.[148] Lordship and inequality were fused, in medieval thought and life, with assumptions of mutuality.

These tended to legitimise political participation. The military-vassalic tie, which bound the vassal only so long as his lord gave him the benefits of good lordship, provided a template for the relations of other free men and groups with their superiors. Urban communities came to petition kings and princes for the guarantee and extension of their privileges in return for fealty and the promise of service.[149] Mutuality was implicit in the idea of the Three Orders itself, raising the possibility that when the noble 'protector' order failed in its obligations, others might act – and act *politically* – to exact them by force. Precisely this was alleged at the time to have motivated the peasant instigators of the violent revolt known as the Jacquerie, which flared briefly in the Paris Basin in 1358, in the aftermath of French military disaster.[150] The rebels, it was said, had turned against lords who, through failure on the battlefield, had shown themselves no more mindful of their protective duties, and therefore no more deserving of loyalty, than the invading English.

In the late middle ages the complex, seemingly contradictory pattern of collective activity and extended participation combined with enduring elite domination is observable especially in the towns. The constitution of fourteenth-century Florence granted access to civic power through the guilds, whose members had to be over the age of thirty and free of debt in order to qualify for office.[151] This still left an estimated one in five of the male population of the city eligible to take part in some form of political activity.[152] Yet real power always lay with a much smaller group, the wealthy members of the greater guilds (*arti maggiori*), who were guaranteed disproportionate representation on the main governing council, the *Signoria*.

Constitutional structures, once established, could be extended to encompass new, previously unrepresented groups, and the economic and political crises of the late middle ages generated pressure for such

---

[148] W. Köfler, *Land, Landschaft, Landtag: Geschichte der Tiroler Landtage von den Anfängen bis zur Aufhebung der landständischen Verfassung 1808* (Innsbruck, 1985).

[149] Blockmans and Donckers, 'Self-representation', 85.

[150] In the chronicle attributed to Jean de Venette; for the relevant passage: *Popular Protest in Late Medieval Europe: Italy, France and Flanders*, ed., tr. and comm. S. K. Cohn (Manchester, 2004), 170–2 at 171; and see J. Firnhaber-Baker, 'The eponymous Jacquerie: making revolt mean some things', in J. Firnhaber-Baker and D. Schoenaers (eds), *The Routledge History Handbook of Medieval Revolt* (Abingdon, 2017), 55–75.

[151] J. M. Najemy, *A History of Florence, 1200–1575* (Oxford, 2006), 124–55.

[152] J. Larner, *Italy in the Age of Dante and Petrarch, 1216–1380* (London, 1980), 122.

extensions. Both the extent and the limits of what might be achieved are again well illustrated in Florence, where in 1378, in the *Ciompi* uprising, hitherto-unrepresented textile workers forced the creation of new guilds, thereby securing at least a nominal voice in government.[153] However, the power of the elite remained fundamentally unshaken, and within just a few years the city's richest families had acted not only to recoup but to entrench and extend the power in their own hands.

Nevertheless, the evidence from this same period of established regimes yielding to pressure from those previously outside the political sphere remains too substantial to ignore. It has a number of explanations. As rulers extended the burdens upon their subjects in an age of war, they found it necessary to secure both more regular and more broadly based assent to their demands.[154] As government and its needs grew, those whose skills and resources served the prince's (or republic's) rule and wars – merchant-financiers, lawyers and a new breed of military commander – made their presence felt at the centres of power. Allowing the voices of new groups to be heard seemed in any case a matter of prudence in an age which saw plebeian infantry armies on several occasions inflict savage defeats on aristocratic cavalry forces.[155] By the fourteenth century, the armoured, mounted noble-man no longer sat quite so firmly in his saddle – or on his seat of rule.

Regimes learned both to fear the power of public opinion and to exploit it, at a time when the channels of political communication were growing more varied and pervasive. The late middle ages saw the birth of a new vernacular politics, as princes felt themselves impelled to adopt the lan-guage of key groups of their subjects, even when it was not their own.[156] At the close of the middle ages, the social limits of those with at least an indirect role in shaping political decisions cease to be clearly definable. This is true particularly in the urban sphere, where public gatherings, processions and cries but also anonymous bills and libels, graffiti and calculated acts of nocturnal vandalism might all help to set the mood in which councils and princes sat down to take decisions.[157]

---

[153] Najemy, *History of Florence*, 156–87.

[154] For the pressures of late medieval war on government: R. W. Kaeuper, *War, Justice, and Public Order: England and France in the Later Middle Ages* (Oxford, 1988).

[155] K. DeVries, *Infantry Warfare in the Early Fourteenth Century: Discipline, Tactics, and Technology* (Woodbridge, 1996).

[156] For England: C. Allmand, *Henry V* (London, 1992), 419–25; for Burgundy: C. A. J. Armstrong, 'The language question in the Low Countries: the use of French and Dutch by the dukes of Burgundy and their administration', repr. in his *England, France and Burgundy in the Fifteenth Century* (London, 1983), 189–212; more generally: C. Fletcher *et al.* (eds), *Government and Political Life in England and France, c.1300–c.1500* (Cambridge, 2015).

[157] D. Hay and J. Law, *Italy in the Age of the Renaissance, 1380–1530* (London, 1989), 77–81; V. Groebner, *Defaced: The Visual Culture of Violence in the Late Middle Ages*, tr.

If low-status men found a political voice through collective action, women mostly feature in medieval politics as lone actors. This points to the scarcity of formal channels open to them: when they acted, it was usually because established structures had broken down or within the unstructured spaces of life. Opportunity, and the ability and will to seize it, were all. Throughout the long medieval period, queens and queen-mothers came to the fore when the male heir was a minor, absent or incapacitated.[158] The court offered them opportunities to exercise informal power, but the route was high risk, as is signalled by the interlinked charges of plotting, sexual impropriety and even black magic to which powerful royal women were vulnerable. The figure of Joan of Arc (d. 1431) offers a unique example of the unexpected access to power that radical political failure could afford a charismatic woman – but also her extreme vulnerability once the tide turned.[159] The career of St Catherine of Siena (d. 1380), an artisan's daughter whose political advice was heeded by the pope, highlights new routes open to an exceptional woman in the relatively fluid world of the late-medieval town.[160]

For a sphere which, throughout the middle ages (although less completely towards their close), remained dominated by agrarian-military elites, Latin Europe displays considerable social breadth of participation in politics – albeit in varied ways and to very different degrees. This reflected a range of factors. Deep-rooted assumptions and social and legal practices long favoured certain kinds of involvement, while social, economic and political change drew in new groups over the course of time. The church had a special role in political mobilisation. In particular, the fragmented and contested nature of the political landscape ensured a vibrant market for allies, supporters and factions, for material and ideological manpower.

Trans-European patterns of political participation should not, however, be drawn too boldly, since differences between broad regions and types of society are also evident, which were not superficial but deep-rooted and enduring. At the margins of the Latin west regimes were established, especially during the growth period of the central middle ages, which in varying degrees limited legitimate political activity to settler-elites from the European core. Arguments from religion, perceived level of development and even purportedly inherent racial characteristics

---

P. Selwyn (New York, 2004), 37–65; W. Scase, '"Strange and wonderful bills": bill-casting in late medieval England', in R. Copeland *et al.* (eds), *New Medieval Literatures* (Oxford, 1997), 225–47.

[158] T. Earenfight, *Queenship in Medieval Europe* (Basingstoke, 2013); A. J. Duggan (ed.), *Queens and Queenship in Medieval Europe* (Woodbridge, 1997).

[159] H. Castor, *Joan of Arc: A History* (London, 2014); A. Fößel, *Die Königin im mittelalterlichen Reich* (Stuttgart, 2000).

[160] F. T. Luongo, *The Saintly Politics of Catherine of Siena* (Ithaca, NY, 2006).

were drawn upon to justify substantially or completely excluding some native populations from power.[161] In the Latin kingdom of Jerusalem, formal participation in government lay exclusively with the immigrant 'Franks'.[162]

Other inter-regional contrasts were of more ancient origin and less deliberately contrived. In some realms, particularly in the western European heartlands, public political discourse was conducted via well-understood and highly formalised vocabularies of ritual, which served particularly to highlight hierarchical structures and relationships.[163] Elsewhere, however, in Scandinavia and in parts of east-central Europe and the British Isles (though less so in England), the articulation of hierarchies took different forms, or was less pronounced. It is tempting to draw a broad distinction between regions that had lain within and those that remained outside the Roman and Carolingian empires and their immediate spheres of influence. There are some indications that in these latter zones monarchy was, on the whole, less exalted and the persons of monarchs less elaborately respected. Not everywhere quickly embraced the Frankish-clerical vision of the king as the Lord's anointed.[164] There are signs that, beyond Roman and Carolingian Europe, speech acts in the presence of the powerful may have been less constrained (or differently constrained) by ritual. This in turn was probably linked to the persistence in some areas of ancient cultures of public assembly, less susceptible than the Frankish heartlands to monarchical stage-management.[165]

Tensions and Paradoxes

It is not only the rich inner diversity of Latin Europe that often frustrates general statements about its political culture(s). The self-professed ideals of medieval Europeans sometimes appear at odds with their habitual and

---

[161] Bartlett, *Making of Europe*, 197–242; L. Scales, *The Shaping of German Identity: Authority and Crisis, 1245–1414* (Cambridge, 2012), 383–446.

[162] H. E. Mayer, 'Latins, Muslims and Greeks in the Latin Kingdom of Jerusalem', *History* 63 (1978), 175–92.

[163] G. Althoff, *Die Macht der Rituale: Symbolik und Herrschaft im Mittelalter* (Darmstadt, 2003).

[164] For some evidence: E. Christiansen, *The Northern Crusades: The Baltic and the Catholic Frontier, 1100–1525* (London, 1980), 6–47.

[165] S. Brink, 'Legal assemblies and judicial structure in early Scandinavia', in Barnwell and Mostert (eds), *Political Assemblies*, 61–72; J. M. Bak with P. Lukin, 'Consensus and assemblies in early medieval central and eastern Europe', in *ibid.*, 95–113. Although the evidence for early assemblies is less strong for east-central Europe, medieval historiographers – notably Cosmas of Prague – looked back to idealised pasts in which rule derived from popular consensus rather than the will of a monarch. See also B. Weiler, 'Tales of first kings and the culture of kingship in the west, *c.*1050–1200', *Viator* 46 (2015), 101–28 at 107–9.

characteristic practices. The ends which they claimed to seek were often rather different from their attainments. The political landscape which they affected to see bore in important respects little relation to what was actually there – although what was there might itself change over time to reflect imagination. The elements of vitality in western political culture, moreover, are often most discernible where crises and conflicts also appear greatest: where fragmentation and contestation are most endemic. It is in the niches and uncertain spots which endured between and within seemingly orderly political structures that significant developments and sophisticated forms of life are found.

Medieval Europeans championed peace and harmony as supreme political goods; yet they evolved forms of political action and discourse that were notably contentious. Peace-keeping, as we have seen, lay predominantly in the hands of elites for whom violence was no mere profession but a source of identity. Not only to embrace bloodshed but actively to seek out opportunities to practise it was a virtue emphasised by those who, to the end of the middle ages, wrote to guide the development of young noblemen.[166] That feuding, despite the proliferation of judicial institutions, so long retained its prominence as a mode of dispute-settlement among the powerful is scarcely cause for wonder.[167]

However, western Europeans also proved capable of imagining harmony, while simultaneously contriving bitter and pervasive contention, on a more cosmic scale. An illustration in a manuscript of the thirteenth-century German law-code known as the *Sachsenspiegel* ('Mirror of the Saxons') shows a prelate and a king (or emperor) with the symbols of their rule.[168] They sit together on a single throne, embracing in a gesture of concord. The accompanying text concerns the collaboration owed by spiritual and secular powers. The image gives graphic form to a widely repeated and universally acknowledged principle of medieval political theology.

Yet it was notably elusive in practice. Conflicts over the proper limits of spiritual and secular power – and over the terms on which princes and prelates should work together – were among the most prominent and intractable of the middle ages. The most celebrated, longest-running and catastrophically disruptive of these contentions were those between the papacy and the rulers of the western empire.[169] During the most

---

[166] Keen, *Chivalry*, 179–99; R. W. Kaeuper, *Chivalry and Violence in Medieval Europe* (Oxford, 1999).

[167] H. Kaminsky, 'The noble feud in the late middle ages', *P&P* 177 (2002), 55–83.

[168] Cod. Pal. germ. 164, Eike [von Repgow], *Heidelberger Sachsenspiegel*, http://digi.ub.uni-heidelberg.de/diglit/cpg164/0057 (accessed 6 May 2019).

[169] H. J. Mierau, *Kaiser und Papst im Mittelalter* (Cologne, Weimar and Vienna, 2010); U.-R. Blumenthal, *The Investiture Controversy: Church and Monarchy from the Ninth to the Twelfth Century* (Philadelphia, 1988).

intense phase, in the reign of the last Hohenstaufen emperor, Frederick II (1212–50), papal and imperial partisans scaled new rhetorical heights, with each party discerning in the leader of the other the apocalyptic Antichrist.[170] The contests of Christendom's self-proclaimed temporal and spiritual heads proved highly divisive, particularly within the territories of the empire itself. Communities and even families were split apart, and the excommunications and interdicts, imposed as instruments of political coercion and not always quickly lifted when conflict died down, left a bitter legacy. In Italy, the papal and imperial factions in the towns, Guelfs and Ghibellines, hardened into institutionalised blocs which endured, as a further element of division in an acutely divided landscape, well into the late middle ages.[171]

The two elements in the political firmament which were claimed to stand pre-eminently for unity and harmony therefore presented medieval Europeans with a lurid spectacle of contention. The entrenched disunity of the supreme spiritual and secular heads of Christian society is a distinctive feature of Latin Europe as a sphere of political culture. Division was symbolised, as it is partially explained, by physical location. Whereas in Byzantium, the imperial and patriarchal seats were located side by side in the capital, for the western emperor to visit the pope, or vice versa, meant a long and often punishing journey. From an early date, moreover, the rival claims of papal and imperial partisans came to be encased in Latin treatises, which sought justification in the Bible and other fundamental authorities. Learned polemic became a habit.[172] Medieval Europeans were provided with a stark demonstration that, whatever the theorists might pretend, the rightful political order was not self-evident but a matter for debate. There was no single answer – and, indeed, no universally acknowledged order. Latin Christendom was, in its political aspect, an ongoing argument.[173]

'Rule by strangers is the worst evil', wrote the chronicler Thietmar of Merseburg in the eleventh century.[174] In this he was voicing a commonplace

---

[170] W. Stürner, *Friedrich II. 1194–1250* (Darmstadt, 2009), 458–592; B. McGinn, *Visions of the End: Apocalyptic Traditions in the Middle Ages* (New York, 1979), 168–79.

[171] J. K. Hyde, *Society and Politics in Medieval Italy: The Evolution of the Civil Life, 1000–1350* (London, 1973), 132–41.

[172] L. Melve, *Inventing the Public Sphere: The Public Debate during the Investiture Contest*, 2 vols (Leiden, 2007).

[173] Byzantium was, until 1204, more successful in keeping up appearances of internal unity in harmony with the universe: pp. 80–1, 85–7, 291–3, 302–7, 418–25. The Islamic sphere, however, accommodated a fair amount of debate over issues like law and diversity in religious observance, despite the court hierarchies and favoured narratives: pp. 104–7, 109, 110–14, 120–1, 220–7, 236–40, 242–3, 246–7, 334–9, 340–3, 347–9, 353–8.

[174] Thietmar of Merseburg, *Chronicon* I.19, ed. R. Holtzmann, rev. and German tr. W. Trillmich (Darmstadt, 2002), 22–3.

of medieval political assumption: that political communities were naturally coherent and organic, manifestations of common history and descent.[175] Foreign lordship was unnatural: an aberration. Here is a mode of thinking which, in Latin Europe, is traceable back to Roman ethnographers of late antiquity, who portrayed the barbarian peoples within the empire as distinct communities of blood and law.[176] Such ideas were transmitted to later centuries via widely consulted encyclopaedic works synthesising late-Roman learning, notably the *Etymologies* of Isidore of Seville, as well as by the writings of Roman-influenced historians. Latin Europeans came to imagine their world as composed of separate, natural political units, each different from its neighbours but organically one in itself.

Such a vision was always illusory. Royal and aristocratic kindreds intermarried across frontiers in ways that made a nonsense of any idea of discrete ethno-territorial blocs. After the eleventh century, as the population expanded, kingdoms grew in size and new regimes came to power both within Latin Europe and at its margins, it was falsified by the briefest view of the political landscape. Far from being anomalous, the rule of alien princes was closer to a norm, in a world in which the foreign in any case seldom began far from home. Yet it did not as a result come to seem less unnatural or objectionable. In 1070, as the Normans advanced, ravaging, through the north of England, Bishop Aethelwine of Durham took flight to the court of Malcolm III, king of Scots, 'fearing the severe lordship of a foreign people whose language and customs he did not know'.[177] It was a time when, throughout Europe, large numbers of people who lacked a bishop's freedom of movement were reconciling themselves to the rule of newcomers. This in any case doubtless looked rather different, and less obviously distinct from what had gone before, when viewed from the villages and common fields rather than the court of a literate and politically engaged prelate. Nevertheless, those who left a record might still write dynastic change as ethnic oppression: the image of the English people's subjugation to a vexatious alien yoke in 1066 is of medieval manufacture.[178]

The rhetoric of 'us'-ness, however delusional and self-serving, ran deep and possessed considerable mobilising power. Rulers throughout the middle ages maintained cosmopolitan courts as a source of prestige; but, as kingdoms grew in inner coherence, some came under pressure

---

[175] Reynolds, *Kingdoms and Communities*, 250.   [176] Geary, *Myth of Nations*, 41–92.

[177] Simeon of Durham, 'Historia Regum' ch. 155, in *Symeonis monachi opera omnia*, ed. T. Arnold, 2 vols, *Rolls Series* 75 (London, 1882–5), ii:190. On trans-regnal dynasticism: R. Bartlett, *Blood Royal* (Cambridge, 2020).

[178] C. Given-Wilson, *Chronicles: The Writing of History in Medieval England* (London, 2004), 153–214.

to banish outsiders from their presence and to appoint 'true-born' natives in their place.[179] Over time, there was a tendency for European realms to be forcibly re-made to resemble more closely the enduring fiction of the organically coherent polity. Particularly at Latin Europe's polyethnic margins, in the later middle ages steps were taken to enforce a new homogeneity. In the kingdom of Sicily, the island's Muslim population was banished to a mainland colony in the thirteenth century, and from there it was sold into slavery and eliminated altogether at the century's close.[180] But comparable impulses found expression in Europe's heartlands too. In France, where the common identity promoted by the kings made much of the Christian faith which they shared with their subjects, pursuit of an ideal imagined oneness opened the way to (even if it does not wholly explain) the expulsion of the kingdom's Jews early in the fourteenth century.[181]

By the close of the middle ages, princes commanded the means to fabricate seemingly cohesive political bodies out of the most varied and multi-coloured materials. Such a goal was most readily attained (and most urgent) among the circle of elite figures who met face-to-face in the ruler's presence and to whose integration the wealthiest princes could now devote a dazzling array of resources. The Valois dukes of Burgundy, whose patchwork patrimony straddled the Franco-imperial border, employed their rich court to this end. The chivalric Order of the Golden Fleece, founded in 1430, brought together nobles from across the ducal domains, in a glittering and myth-laden common life, whose central theme was the unity established by shared loyalty to the duke.[182] By an assortment of means and down diverse routes, the mirage of common identity was conjured into being within realms across much of Europe.

Even while medieval Europeans were convincing themselves of their difference from neighbours beyond the frontier, the political communities which they inhabited, seen objectively, tended in the long term to grow broadly more alike. By the close of the middle ages the general trend is unmistakable. Rulers and regimes took over principles and techniques of rule (and, particularly in the late middle ages, specialised personnel) from one another. Important differences naturally remained, and in some ways became more entrenched; but they did so within an increasingly interconnected world of European powers, where comparisons were

---

[179] For some extreme examples: L. Scales, 'Bread, cheese and genocide: imagining the destruction of peoples in medieval western Europe', *History* 92 (2007), 284–300.

[180] J. A. Taylor, 'Lucera Sarracenorum: a Muslim colony in medieval Christian Europe', *Nottingham Medieval Studies* 43 (1999), 110–25.

[181] W. C. Jordan, *The French Monarchy and the Jews: From Philip Augustus to the Last Capetians* (Philadelphia, 1989).

[182] D. J. D. Boulton, *The Knights of the Crown: The Monarchical Orders of Knighthood in Later Medieval Europe 1325–1520* (Woodbridge, 1987), 356–96.

readily drawn and methods shared. Even in shape and size, European polities tended to become more similar. In Italy, the high medieval picture of hundreds of contending urban micro-states had simplified by the fifteenth century to just five regional powers – Milan, Venice, Florence, the papacy and Naples – and their satellites. Across much of Europe, both very small political formations and very large and loose hegemonies were becoming increasingly unsustainable.[183]

Yet the familiar story of the rise of the sovereign state leaves too much out of account. Modern scholarship on the middle ages grew to maturity in the shadow of the modern nation state and was fed by its resources. It is understandable that it has always made much of the medieval growth of proto-modern forms of government. At the time, however, such growth was rarely welcomed by its putative beneficiaries. Princely projects to codify the customary laws of their subjects sometimes had to be abandoned and the offending texts destroyed.[184] The proliferation of university-trained lawyers in the service of rulers was perceived on occasion as oppression severe enough to warrant outright revolt.[185] Nor is it clear that the opponents of princely state-building were altogether wrong in their judgements. It is striking that the regions which, particularly in their towns, developed the most sophisticated political and economic practices and boasted the most impressive cultural attainments tended to be found where territorial rule was most fragmented or contested. Its growth, by contrast, could curtail the development of more local spheres. In Brandenburg in north-eastern Germany, vigorous urban communities developed in the fourteenth century in a climate of acute political division, only to find their liberties suppressed in the fifteenth under the ambitious Hohenzollern margraves.[186] Nothing sucked the vitality from civic life like the firm rule of princes and bishops.

Latin Europe was a world of enclaves, into which the controlling hand of higher secular or spiritual power intruded itself hesitantly and with difficulty. Even during those high-medieval centuries in which western Christendom was ostensibly most united, the local proliferation of heretical sects offers an instructive contrast with the Eastern Christian sphere

---

[183] The world of Islam saw a certain tendency towards stabilisation in this period: pp. 228–30, 231–4, 245–6, 477–82. In its way, the demise of Byzantium makes the same point.
[184] As an example of such a codification: *Maiestas Carolina: Der Kodifikationsentwurf Karls IV. für das Königreich Böhmen von 1355*, ed. B.-U. Hergemöller (Munich, 1995).
[185] Thus in the 'Poor Conrad' revolt in Wurtemberg (1514): *Manifestations of Discontent in Germany on the Eve of the Reformation*, ed. and tr. G. Strauss (Bloomington, IN, 1971), 150–3.
[186] F. L. Carsten, 'Medieval democracy in the Brandenburg towns and its defeat in the fifteenth century', *TRHS* 4th series 25 (1943), 73–91.

of Byzantium.[187] At the end of the middle ages, the bolt-holes from overarching power remained many and sometimes surprisingly secure. Even when a group or movement was forced out of public life it might still prove able, as did the English Lollards, to find niches within which to continue an underground existence.[188] Not least among Europe's semi-autonomous spaces were universities: it is no coincidence that the major heretical movements of the later middle ages centred on the teachings of professional academics.[189]

Not everywhere adhered to a broad pattern of consolidation. Northern Europe's vast, mainly German-speaking, centre became over time more, not less, politically fragmented, despite the intensification of territorial government in many regions where princely dynasties held sway. The picture at the close of the fifteenth century is of bewildering complexity. Here was a landscape behind whose many frontiers subversive ideas and their authors might shelter, particularly when they enjoyed the protection of regional men of power – as the church's most formidable doctrinal adversary, Dr Martin Luther, was to show to startling effect.[190] Yet, as the case of Luther also shows, those same frontiers were not so formidable as to inhibit the rapid dissemination of dangerous new ideas within a Europe of many encounters and exchanges.[191]

Religion and Church

No institution did as much as the Catholic church to shape the landscape and influence the style of politics in the west. If political life in Europe is distinguished by multi-polarity, comparative social breadth and endemic contentiousness, for each of these qualities it owed much to the church's involvement. Catholic Christianity, as a religion of place, was readily supportive of a politics of place. Both in northern and southern Europe it had followed pre-existing pagan cults in investing supernatural power in locality by means of holy sites and objects. These served as reservoirs of sacred legitimacy which might be tapped for political ends. Saints

---

[187] For the durability of western heresy: A. P. Roach, *The Devil's World: Heresy and Society, 1100–1300* (Harlow, 2005). The Byzantine emperor was duty-bound to uphold true religion, but ideas as to what constituted 'orthodoxy' varied over time, and Jewish, Muslim and even dualist communities existed: pp. 291, 300–2, 328, 413. See also, on the Islamic sphere: pp. 224, 242–3, 331–2, 334–5, 347–8.

[188] J. A. F. Thomson, *The Later Lollards, 1414–1520* (London, 1965). Some sects, it is true, were extirpated remarkably completely – the Cathars being a notable example.

[189] Drs John Wyclif, Jan Hus and Martin Luther.

[190] B. Scribner, 'Germany', in B. Scribner *et al.* (eds), *The Reformation in National Context* (Cambridge, 1994), 4–29.

[191] For the power of cultural exchange: Rubin, 'Culture of Europe', 167.

guarded territories and provided a rallying point for their defence. The shrine of St Aethelthryth at Ely seemingly acted as a focus for native resistance to the Normans in England after 1066.[192] Holy objects set a seal on political boundaries. Processed annually round the walls of a jealously independent town, like the Holy Blood of Bruges, relics offered talismanic guarantees of security.[193] The great pan-European cults of the later middle ages were no less capable of bestowing their protection on particular places than were more obviously local saints and relics. The 'universal mother' Mary was thus able to become the special defender of, for example, the liberties of the commune of Siena.[194] The unity and integrity of many lesser urban communities were enacted each summer as the mayor took up his place beside the Host in the Corpus Christi procession.[195]

The church, as has been noted already, possessed an unequalled capacity for establishing boundaries: for translating multiplicity into difference and division. This potential was as readily unlocked on a regnal as a local stage. A number of Latin writers, invariably clerics, working particularly between the eleventh and the thirteenth centuries, produced influential chronicles purporting to give account of the distinct origins and histories of various European peoples.[196] By the late middle ages the crosses of martyrs and holy warriors were adorning the banners and surcoats of royal armies: from the sacred stuff of Christendom was sewn the national flag.[197] Rulership and the sacred were linked directly in the

---

[192] S. J. Ridyard, '*Condigna veneratio*: post-Conquest attitudes to the saints of the Anglo-Saxons', *Anglo Norman Studies* 9 (1986), 179–206 at 181–2.

[193] A. Brown, *Civic Ceremony and Religion in Medieval Bruges, c.1300–1520* (Cambridge, 2011), 37–72.

[194] K. Schreiner, '*Maria patrona*: la sainte vierge comme figure symbolique des villes, territoires et nations à la fin du Moyen Âge et au début des temps modernes', in R. Babel and J.-M. Moeglin (eds), *Identité régionale et conscience nationale en France et en Allemagne du Moyen Âge à l'epoque moderne* (Sigmaringen, 1997), 133–53; D. Norman, *Siena and the Virgin: Art and Politics in a Late Medieval City State* (New Haven, CT, 1999).

[195] C. Phythian-Adams, 'Ceremony and the citizen: the communal year at Coventry 1450–1550', in P. Clark and P. Slack (eds), *Crisis and Order in English Towns, 1500–1700* (London, 1972), 57–85; and generally: M. Rubin, *Corpus Christi: The Eucharist in Late Medieval Culture* (Cambridge, 1991).

[196] N. Kersken, *Geschichtsschreibung im Europa der 'nationes': nationalgeschichtliche Gesamtdarstellungen im Mittelalter* (Cologne, Weimar and Vienna, 1995). See also pp. 268–70.

[197] S. Riches, *St George: Hero, Myth and Martyr* (Stroud, 2000), 101–39; D. J. D. Boulton, 'The Order of the Golden Fleece and the creation of Burgundian national identity', in D. J. D. Boulton and J. R. Veenstra (eds), *The Ideology of Burgundy: The Promotion of National Consciousness, 1364–1565* (Leiden and Boston, 2006), 68–71. For the proliferation of the cross device in late medieval armies: C. Sieber-Lehmann, *Spätmittelalterlicher Nationalismus: die Burgunderkriege am Oberrhein und in der Eidgenossenschaft* (Göttingen, 1995), 131–6. See also Plassmann, *Origo*.

cults of holy monarchs which the church instituted.[198] Here is a striking instance of the divine sanction which the church could bestow upon a politically plural world: just as there were many separate realms, so there were many saint-kings. Living and reigning monarchs were strengthened by the honour thus granted to their forebears: the claims of the kings of France, including their claims over the church within their realm, drew strength from the canonisation of Louis IX (1226–70), within three decades of his death.[199] The memory of holy kings and its ideological potential were kept alive at sometimes (like that of St Louis) much-visited pilgrimage shrines.

The church not only made kings and marked them out at coronation as exalted and worthy of obedience; it also continued to glorify them throughout their reigns. Church bells rang to mark the ruler's victories and his passing. Not only did the church bless the standards that he bore into battle; it might send forth its own in his aid: the banner of St Cuthbert, for example, went north from Durham with English forces against the Scots.[200] If the king returned triumphant, the church choreographed his homecoming.[201] The papacy, whose historic rise coincided with and was inseparable from the emergence of a Europe of diverse realms and peoples, repeatedly acted to affirm a multi-regnal world.

Churchmen had been at the heart of government since the time of Constantine and, in the northern lands, the earliest convert-kings – though their ideological and administrative roles were much expanded under the Carolingians and their successors. Little wonder, then, that, when called on to choose between loyalty to ecclesiastical and royal masters, it was often the latter that prevailed. As a French treatise-writer from the time of Philip IV put it, kings were there first.[202] Rulers therefore felt able at times to handle the church in their realms fairly roughly. In times of crisis in the later middle ages, the demands that clerical wealth and property be placed at the king's disposal became louder and more radical. Kings began to claim generous powers to intervene in the ecclesiastical affairs of their kingdoms. The papacy's own

---

[198] G. Klaniczay, *Holy Rulers and Blessed Princesses: Dynastic Cults in Medieval Central Europe* (Cambridge, 2002).

[199] For his post-mortem importance: A. Rathmann-Lutz, *'Images' Ludwigs des Heiligen im Kontext dynastischer Konflikte des 14. und 15. Jahrhunderts* (Berlin, 2010).

[200] A. C. King and A. J. Pollard, '"Northumbria" in the later middle ages', in R. Colls (ed.), *Northumbria: History and Identity, 547–2000* (Chichester, 2007), 68–87 at 72.

[201] For some English examples: A. K. McHardy, 'Religion, court culture and propaganda: the chapel royal in the reign of Henry V', in G. Dodd (ed.), *Henry V: New Interpretations* (Woodbridge, 2013), 131–56.

[202] *Three Royalist Tracts 1296–1302: Antequam essent clerici; Disputatio inter clericum et militem; Quaestio in utramque partem*, ed. and tr. R. W. Dyson (Bristol, 1999).

inner rifts, above all the protracted late-medieval schism (1378–1417), reinforced rulers in control of 'their' clergy, as well as entrenching divisions between realms.[203]

Yet the church always insisted that its message was for all, not for rulers alone: kings were not the only political actors who laid claim to the supernatural favour which it mediated. Rebellious peasants placed the Virgin Mary and the saints on their banners; English rebels in 1381 mustered like a royal army behind the standard of St George.[204] When their cause prevailed, plebeian forces too might turn to the religious sphere to offer thanks and gain affirmation. It was in the church of Notre Dame in Courtrai that the artisans of Bruges hung up the gilt spurs struck from the heels of the French noblemen whom they slaughtered in battle there in 1302.[205] Yet the church did not only supply a framework for making sense of conflict but also promoted peaceful interactions and integration – notably, through religious confraternities, particularly in the towns, cementing communities of rich and poor which also had a political aspect.[206]

The church played a central part in bringing politics to a socially broader public and encouraging and legitimising wider participation. The church was the great communicator of the western middle ages. Because Catholic Christianity was a proselytising salvation religion with universal claims, the church at times felt itself not merely empowered but impelled to harness all means to get its message across. Showmanship was a Christian duty, an act of charity: to do less was to endanger souls. The church could deliver a political message directly to non-elite audiences. The Mendicant orders in particular, after their establishment in the thirteenth century, drew on examples from both history and contemporary affairs in their sermons, which reached a broad public, especially in the towns.[207] Here were lessons in ideological self-presentation from which secular regimes too could profit.

---

[203] J. A. F. Thomson, *Popes and Princes 1417–1517: Politics and Polity in the Late Medieval Church* (London, 1980).

[204] T. Scott, *Freiburg and the Breisgau: Town-Country Relations in the Age of Reformation and Peasants' War* (Oxford, 1986), 179; *The St Albans Chronicle: The Chronica Maiora of Thomas Walsingham*, ed. and tr. J. Taylor *et al.*, 2 vols (Oxford, 2003–11), i:452–3.

[205] J. F. Verbruggen, *The Battle of the Golden Spurs (Courtrai, 11 July 1302): A Contribution to the History of Flanders' War of Liberation, 1297–1305*, ed. K. DeVries, tr. D. R. Ferguson (Woodbridge, 2002), 242. The spurs, along with many banners and pennons, were still there in 1382.

[206] A. Brown, 'Bruges and the "Burgundian theatre state": Charles the Bold and Our Lady of the Snows', *History* 84 (1999), 573–89; more generally: K. Eisenbichler (ed.), *A Companion to Medieval and Early Modern Confraternities* (Leiden, 2019).

[207] M. Menzel, *Predigt und Geschichte: historische Exempel in der geistlichen Rhetorik des Mittelalters* (Cologne, Weimar and Vienna, 1998).

Perhaps even more significant was the church's role in empowering a wide spectrum of people to think about fundamental issues of public authority for themselves and to act on their convictions under the church's guidance. The Peace movement of the late tenth and eleventh centuries had drawn participation from outside the established political strata.[208] In urging people to boycott the masses of married priests, some of the more radical eleventh-century church reformers highlighted the agency of a mass movement to effect radical change.[209] The same period saw such a movement not only arise but take up arms and march against the infidel. The call to crusade in 1095, which drew a response of far greater social breadth than the pope can have anticipated, gave graphic illustration of popular receptivity.[210] Mobilisation of diverse groups took an especially pronounced political slant in the papacy's preaching campaigns north and south of the Alps against its rivals in the Empire – which naturally encouraged supporters of the emperors to cast their own net wide.[211]

In these ways the church encouraged significant numbers of people not only to act politically but to argue and take sides. There was little that was reasonable about the process, accompanied as it was by spiritual sanctions and threats of damnation. It was significant nonetheless. Literate western Europeans (nearly always clerics), meanwhile, learned in the course of the same disputes to argue on a more complex level. Their contending texts can be viewed – albeit with some qualification, in view of their almost invariable composition in demanding Latin – as constituting Europe's earliest political propaganda campaigns.[212] More generally, the church provided Latin Europe with a more sophisticated conceptual vocabulary with which to analyse political acts, institutions and personalities – and with ethical and even eschatological frameworks within which to judge them.

Ultimately of great significance is that, despite many points of contact and despite its own exercise of temporal rule, church and clergy remained distinct from secular hierarchies. To speak of two powers, spiritual and secular spheres, or even, at least by the later middle ages, church and

---

[208] T. Head and R. Landes (eds), *The Peace of God: Social Violence and Religious Response around the Year 1000* (Ithaca, NY, 1992).

[209] For both the opportunities for lay action and its limits: S. Hamilton, *Church and People in the Medieval West, 900–1200* (Harlow, 2013), 78–83. On Peace Movements: pp. 379–80.

[210] C. Tyerman, *God's War: A New History of the Crusades* (London, 2006), 58–89.

[211] J. B. Freed, *The Friars and German Society in the Thirteenth Century* (Cambridge, MA, 1977), 135–67.

[212] M. Suchan, 'Publizistik im Zeitalter Heinrichs IV. – Anfänge päpstlicher und kaiserlicher Propaganda im "Investiturstreit"?', in K. Hruza (ed.), *Propaganda, Kommunikation und Öffentlichkeit (11.–16. Jahrhundert)* (Vienna, 2002), 29–45.

state, can by justified in the west as it cannot for the Byzantine or Islamic worlds. Among Latin Europe's many borders, topographical and conceptual, this was perhaps the most historically important of all. With time the idea, already foreshadowed in the fourteenth century in the thought of Marsilius of Padua, would gain ground that politics was enacted within a distinct secular space, with its own ends and justifications, free from clerical sanction.[213]

Conclusions

Such resilience as the western sphere possessed was at least as much a product of its many and manifest weaknesses as of any putative inner strengths. Weaknesses stand out to the hastiest comparative view. The list of things that, even by pre-industrial standards, medieval Europeans did not do especially well is strikingly long. Their rulers, viewed on a world stage, were neither particularly mighty nor notably learned. Their systems of government were fairly limited: the student of pre-modern bureaucracies must look elsewhere for the most sophisticated and potent examples of the administrator's art.[214] The world's greatest cities also lay elsewhere. In a host of capabilities fundamental to sustaining a sophisticated common life – science, technology, commerce, communications – medieval Europeans were learners, not leaders. Even when set beside the achievements of their own ancient pasts, their capabilities appear small: developments often seem to run in reverse.

It was in negotiating the limitations of their world that the inhabitants of Latin Europe stumbled upon what were to become characteristic elements of their political sphere. Limited forms of government, subject to a range of checks from below, reflected weakness, not design: where rulers could domineer and oppress, they commonly did. The coercive powers of monarchs varied widely between times and places; but mostly their resources were too small and their rivals too many to permit sustained or thoroughgoing tyranny. Western rulers governed by consent, and built consensus, when they had few other options. Into the vacuum of organisation left by the withdrawal of late-antique imperial government, and within the extended western zones where it had never penetrated, there intruded over time the lineaments of an unplanned and ad hoc 'civil society'. Its elements were untidily various: local churches, village communities, guilds, confraternities, leagues, and an array of other bodies suited to discharging tasks of everyday governance and organisation.

---

[213] Marsilius of Padua, *The Defender of the Peace*, ed. and tr. A. Brett (Cambridge, 2005).
[214] For a comparison: E. Kamenka, *Bureaucracy* (Oxford, 1989).

Overarching systems of rule, as these developed, often chose to work with, co-opt, or simply ignore these many and diverse local arrangements rather than repress them in the name of uniformity. Frontiers were numerous but seldom formidable, and, because they were so many, westerners gained rich experience of their negotiation and transgression.

Medieval Europeans were less aware of the limitations of their world than is the modern observer – or indeed, than were their neighbours in Byzantium and the lands of Islam. Nevertheless, their modes of life in practice paid realistic regard to them. On the whole, westerners proved receptive to the ideas and methods which seeped across their porous and ill-defined and -defended frontiers from wider worlds beyond. The systems which they put in place to transcend the endemic fragmentation of their political life and allay its no less endemic contentiousness and violence were characteristically limited, flexible and pragmatic. Grand ideological visions shaped the political dream-world of medieval Europeans more than their daily experience. The landscape remained irremediably plural.

While the distinctiveness of the west in this regard can doubtless be overstated, the foundations of political diversity in Europe were deeper and more substantial than is sometimes thought.[215] They were laid with the disintegration of Rome's western territories and reinforced by the collapse in the west – in contrast to Byzantium and the Islamic sphere – of the antique fiscal state and its replacement by a politics of land. In the centuries that followed, we can trace a dialectical relationship between elements of unity – the Latin-Christian church and faith, the Carolingian template of government, Latinate learning, the natural connectivity of a temperate and relatively compact zone of life – and the gravitational pulls of many different centres.[216] In political life, plurality won out. The Carolingian model proved well suited to miniaturisation and replication, while the church fitted itself to, and lent its endorsement to, many and diverse modes of common life. The claim to Chosen-Peoplehood, it soon became clear, was no Frankish monopoly: by the later middle ages, building 'heaven in one country' seemed an attractive project to some western princes and their advisors. To present the big picture of medieval western political culture means capturing the shifting, multiform, multi-coloured patterns of a kaleidoscope.

---

[215] For a recent account of this multiplicity entirely disregarding its medieval roots: Ferguson, *Civilization*.

[216] Some of the tensions between centrifugal and centripetal elements in medieval European history are explored in M. Borgolte, *Europa entdeckt seine Vielfalt 1050–1250* (Stuttgart, 2002), esp. 356–92.

8   Byzantium
One or Many?

*Catherine Holmes**

Figure 8.1 The church of St Sophia, Constantinople (Istanbul), rebuilt by the emperor Justinian (527–65) following the Nika riots; photo Dr Barlas Özden Çağlayan

Defining the Byzantine sphere can be a difficult task given the rather loose set of meanings contained within the term 'Byzantium'. That is to say, when 'Byzantium' is invoked it is not always clear whether what we mean is a unitary political state under the control of a single emperor or whether we are referring to a much more fluid and plural set of political and

I am grateful to Jonathan Shepard and Rosemary Morris for ideas and materials which they have contributed to this chapter.

178

cultural practices and traditions shared by a series of polities and peoples within what has sometimes been called the Byzantine Commonwealth.[1] The haziness surrounding the term 'Byzantium' has important ramifications for the way in which the historical context to Byzantine political culture is presented. Much of this chapter will be concerned with the most straightforward of possible presentations, in which Byzantium is taken to be a unitary state governed by a single emperor (sometimes with the support of one or more junior emperors, occasionally governed by a sole empress). A relatively clear picture of the geographical and chronological contours of that Byzantine imperial space can be sketched out, albeit a picture that was subject to considerable fluctuation over time. The chapter also offers an introduction to the political formations and social groups that were integral to Byzantine political culture between the late seventh and mid-fifteenth centuries, emphasising the overlaps and tensions between the kinds of ideal and formal powers discussed in greater depth in Chapter 11, and the more informal political practices elaborated in Chapter 14. But while the focus in this chapter will be primarily on the Byzantine empire, it will also become clear that to understand Byzantine political culture more fully we also need to be aware of the far more multiple, complex and contested connections and formations which existed within Byzantium itself, as well as those which brought the empire into communication with peoples and polities beyond its own frontiers. Perhaps just as important, a fuller appreciation of Byzantine political culture also demands an awareness of when, how and why those connections and formations could be rather more illusory than real.

Geographical Scope

Throughout most of the period under consideration in this volume, Byzantium's imperial capital was firmly located in Constantinople, with the only exception being the fifty-seven-year period (1204–61) that followed the fall of the city to the armies of the Fourth Crusade. With its long-term centre located on the Bosphoros, Byzantium's principal orientations lay towards the Balkans in the west and Anatolia in the east. The sheer size of the medieval empire, stretching at its greatest extent c.1045 from the Caucasus and Syria in the east to southern Italy in the west and from the outpost of Cherson in the Crimea in the north to Cyprus in the south, meant that there were always potentially centrifugal tendencies. They deserve attention because they are so easily eclipsed by the panoply of writings, past and present, focused on the imperial centre, and the

---

[1] On the looseness and elasticity of the Byzantine sphere: pp. 77–8.

institutions and culture sustaining it.[2] Frontier zones, with their particular geopolitical imperatives of 'protect and survive', evolved their own kind of elites, often of an interethnic variety, concerned not only to defend themselves from attack when necessary but also to create a modus vivendi with both their 'non-Byzantine' neighbours and the representatives of the distant government in Constantinople. The Byzantine provinces in southern Italy, in the Balkans, and on the eastern frontier all provide useful examples to illustrate these tendencies.[3]

Geographical features could even allow space for separatism. The Balkans, where generally narrow coastal strips are separated from the mountainous interior by the high mountain ranges of the Dinaric Alps and the Pindos and Balkan mountains, is a case in point. The isolation and fragmentation of the coastland of the Adriatic, for example, facilitated the emergence of local, often Slavonic, elites whose loyalty to their nominal overlords in Constantinople was often questionable.[4] In the eastern Balkans, the plains of Thrace and Thessaly and the lands south of the Danube provided areas of major agrarian exploitation, but they are uncharacteristic of the Balkans as a whole. The Balkans was 'a fragmented world'.[5] In Anatolia, too, the Pontic Alps and Taurus ranges create northern and southern-eastern barriers to easy access from the

[2] See pp. 80, 81–2, 86–7, 91, 95–6, 291–3, 296, 298–311 and Maps 9a–f.
[3] On the nature of medieval frontiers: F. Curta (ed.), *Borders, Barriers and Ethnogenesis: Frontiers in Late Antiquity and the Middle Ages* (Turnhout, 2005), esp. F. Curta, 'Introduction' (1–9); W. Pohl, 'Frontiers and ethnic identities; some final considerations' (255–65); and, in the Byzantine context, R.-J. Lilie, 'The Byzantine-Arab borderland from the seventh to the ninth century' (13–21); also M. Naum, 'Re-emerging frontiers: postcolonial theory and historical archaeology of the borderlands', *Journal of Archaeological Method and Theory* 17 (2010), 101–31; A. Janeczek, 'Frontiers and borderlands in medieval Europe: introductory remarks', *Quaestiones Medii Aevi Novae* (2011), 5–14; on the Balkans: P. Stephenson, *Byzantium's Balkan Frontier: A Political Study of the Northern Balkans, 900–1204* (Cambridge, 2000); M. Ančić et al. (eds), *Imperial Spheres and the Adriatic: Byzantium, the Carolingians and the Treaty of Aachen (812)* (Abingdon, 2018); on Italy: V. von Falkenhausen, 'A provincial aristocracy: the Byzantine provinces in southern Italy' in *TBA*, 211–35; eadem, 'Between two empires: southern Italy in the reign of Basil II', in P. Magdalino (ed.), *Byzantium in the Year 1000* (Leiden, 2003), 135–59; on the eastern frontier: C. Holmes, 'Byzantium's eastern frontier in the tenth and eleventh centuries', in D. Abulafia and N. Berend (eds), *Medieval Frontiers: Concepts and Practices* (Aldershot, 2002), 82–104; A. Asa Eger (ed.), *The Archaeology of Medieval Islamic Frontiers from the Mediterranean to the Caspian Sea* (Louiseville, CO, 2019).
[4] For a detailed narrative: J. V. A. Fine, Jr., *The Early Medieval Balkans: A Critical Survey from the Sixth to the Late Twelfth Century* (Ann Arbor, MI, 1991); idem, *The Late Medieval Balkans: A Critical Survey from the Late Twelfth Century to the Ottoman Conquest* (Ann Arbor, MI, 2009); also Stephenson, *Byzantium's Balkan Frontier*.
[5] M. Whittow, 'Geographical survey', in *OHBS*, 220–31 at 222; also D. Obolensky, 'The geographical setting', in his *The Byzantine Commonwealth: Eastern Europe, 500–1453* (London, 1971), 5–41; M. F. Hendy, *Studies in the Byzantine Monetary Economy, c.300–c.1450* (Cambridge, 1985), 21–68.

coastlands to the central plateau, whilst, as Mark Whittow pointed out, the 'grain of the landscape runs west to east', making access to the interior much easier either from the western river valleys or from the eastern plains of Armenia and Mesopotamia than from the north or south.[6] The Anatolian plateau, too cold in winter for the growing of many crops, including olives, marked a zone particularly suited to a pastoral economy, whereas coastal zones such as the plains of Cilicia, the northern coastal strip around Trebizond and the western coasts facing the Sea of Marmara and the Aegean provided both fertile soil for agrarian production and the location for a series of prosperous ports connecting Byzantium to the Mediterranean world and to the steppe corridor to the north of the Black Sea. It is worth remembering, too, that, besides being an empire of landscapes, Byzantium was also an empire of seascapes. True, the islands of the Aegean provided stepping stones of communication for shipping in an age of cautious navigation, but each, by its very nature, remained isolated from the landmasses to a greater or lesser extent; under certain circumstances, the larger of them – Cyprus and Crete in particular – could harbour groups with separatist tendencies or provide a secure base for external rivals.[7]

In an age of modern communications, such geographical constraints matter less than they did in the medieval world. But travelling to and otherwise communicating with such a geographically diverse state was always a challenge for any administration with pretensions to wide, if not universal, rule.[8] In this regard, Byzantium held an advantage over many medieval western states, in that its network of Roman roads was known and, to a degree, kept up and used, at least in part, throughout the medieval period and beyond. The *demosios dromos* (public road), the imperially run transport and intelligence-gathering system, continued to

[6] Whittow, 'Geographical survey', 223–7.
[7] E. Malamut, *Les Îles de l'Empire byzantin, VIIIe–XIIe siècles*, 2 vols (Paris, 1988). For more on the chronology of the rise and diversification of elites: pp. 416–18, 432–3, 445–8. For Crete as the centre of an entrepreneurial maritime emirate (824–961): V. Christides, *The Conquest of Crete by the Arabs (ca. 824): A Turning Point in the Struggle between Byzantium and the Arabs* (Athens, 1984); and, after 1211, as the centre of Venetian power in the Aegean: S. McKee, *Uncommon Dominion: Venetian Crete and the Myth of Ethnic Purity* (Philadelphia, 2000). For Cyprus as a shared space between Arabs and Byzantines in the earlier centuries: R. J. H. Jenkins, 'Cyprus between Byzantines and Islam: AD 688–965', in G. E. Mylonas (ed.), *Studies Presented to David Moore Robinson*, 2 vols (St Louis, MO, 1951–3), ii:1006–14; and for its secession from Constantinople in 1184 and subsequent conquest by Richard I in 1191: P. Edbury, *The Kingdom of Cyprus and the Crusades 1191–1374* (Cambridge, 1991), 1–12.
[8] An observation attributed indeed to a long-lived emperor, Basil II (976–1025): Michael Psellos, *Chronographia* I.22, ed. D. R. Reinsch, 2 vols (Berlin, 2014), i:13; tr. E. R. A. Sewter, *Fourteen Byzantine Rulers: The Chronographia of Michael Psellus* (London, 1966), 39.

function along these roads and be serviced by publicly funded repairs to roads and bridges and the provision of hostels right up to the fall of the empire. Contact was also maintained by sea, so that in many cases, though commands and information were often long in coming, subject to delay or simply lost, it remained possible for the central administrative organs of the state – wherever they were located – to keep some sort of contact with outlying regions.[9] Byzantium also inherited from Rome various mechanisms for diplomatic exchanges, which relied on long-distance connections by land and sea.[10] But it is still important to remember that geography always mattered, even for a medieval state characterised by a relatively sophisticated administration with the capacity to harness the power of the written word in its bureaucratic and diplomatic practices, and which is usually regarded, at least until the latter centuries of its existence, as remarkably centralised in its formal articulation of power. Geography shaped who or what could be reached within Byzantium itself and beyond. Sheer distance and difficult terrain, whether mountainous, desert or forest, could always provide a challenge to the imperial writ, an opportunity for localism and the potential for subversion or reinterpretation of that which was officially sanctioned.[11]

---

[9] R. Macrides (ed.), *Travel in the Byzantine World* (Aldershot, 2002); K. Belke, 'Communications: roads and bridges', in *OHBS*, 295–308; J. Pryor, 'Shipping and seafaring', in *OHBS*, 482–91 at 483–4. The find spots of lead seals struck by imperial officials can be exploited to reach conclusions about communication across the empire: J.-C. Cheynet and C. Morrisson, 'Lieux de trouvaille et circulation des sceaux', *Studies in Byzantine Sigillography* 2 (1990), 105–31; P. Frankopan, 'The workings of the Byzantine provincial administration in the 10th–12th centuries: the example of Preslav', *Byzantion* 71 (2001), 73–97.

[10] J. Shepard and S. Franklin (eds), *Byzantine Diplomacy* (Cambridge, 1992); D. Nerlich, *Diplomatische Gesandtschaften zwischen Ost- und Westkaisern 756–1002* (Bern, 1999); for early envoys travelling to Constantinople: M. McCormick, *Origins of the European Economy: Communications and Commerce* (Cambridge, 2001), 138–47; for envoys travelling to and from Byzantium by sea: P. Squatriti, *The Complete Works of Liudprand of Cremona* (Washington, DC, 2007), 196, 280–2; A. C. Hero (tr.), '*Life* of St Theoktiste of Lesbos', in A.-M. Talbot, *Holy Women of Byzantium: Ten Saints' Lives in English Translation* (Washington, DC, 1996), 101–16; S. M. Stern, 'An embassy of the Byzantine emperor to the Fatimid caliph al-Muʿizz', *Byzantion* 20 (1950), 239–58; for land-based embassies between late-tenth-century Baghdad and Byzantium: A. Beihammer, 'Der harte Sturz des Bardas Skleros. Eine Fallstudie zu zwischenstaatlicher Kommunikation und Konfliktführung in der byzantinisch-arabischen Diplomatie des 10. Jahrhunderts', *Römische Historische Mitteilungen* 45 (2003), 21–57; see also M. Canard 'Les relations politiques et sociales entre Byzance et les Arabes', *DOP* 18 (1964), 35–56; Ibn al-Farra, *Kitab Rusul al-Muluk*, ed. and tr. A. Vaiou, *Diplomacy in the Early Islamic World: A Tenth-Century Treatise on Arab-Byzantine Relations: The Book of Messengers of Kings* (London, 2015); N. Drocourt, *Diplomatie sur le Bosphore: les ambassadeurs étrangers dans l'Empire byzantin des années 640 à 1204*, 2 vols (Louvain, 2015).

[11] On the obstacles to the exercise of monarchical power posed by physical barriers and distance in the other two spheres: pp. 140–2, 219, 239.

Chronological Context

Within Byzantium

In the early eighth century the Byzantine empire comprised a state centred on Constantinople with substantial territories in western and central Asia Minor; to these were appended a few outposts on the islands and coasts of the Aegean, the Black Sea and the Adriatic. This was a substantially smaller entity than the Byzantium of late antiquity when, between the fourth and early seventh centuries, territories under imperial management had usually included (albeit intermittently in some cases) all of the Balkans as far north as the Danube, much of North Africa (including Egypt), Syria, Palestine, large areas of Italy and parts of coastal Spain. In that late antique empire, there had also been several important civic centres; not just Constantinople but also Alexandria, Antioch and Rome.[12] Invasions and permanent conquests by a variety of new political formations in the seventh century – including the Muslim Arabs from the south, the Avars and later the Bulgars from the north, and the Lombards in Italy – as well as the development of settlements populated by Slavonic speakers in the Balkans changed the territorial complexion of the late antique Byzantine space very considerably.[13] But it is important to remember that the frontiers of the more limited territories that remained to Byzantium after the seventh century were themselves not static. This unitary state still managed to wax as well as wane. Thus, after a period of substantial administrative, military and ideological consolidation in the eighth and early ninth centuries, particularly during the reigns of the iconoclast emperors Leo III and Constantine V, the period after c.850 was one of gradual territorial expansion achieved through military conquest and diplomacy.[14] In the east, a series of campaigns saw Byzantine armies move beyond the Taurus and Anti-Taurus mountains and (re)capture important cities such as Melitene (934), Tarsus (965) and

[12] J. Herrin, *The Formation of Christendom* (Princeton, 1987), 20–127, esp. 90–127; A. Cameron, *The Mediterranean World in Late Antiquity* (London, 1993).
[13] Herrin, *Formation of Christendom*, 129–290; J. Haldon, *Byzantium in the Seventh Century: The Transformation of a Culture* (Cambridge, 1990; rev. edn 1997); *MOB*, 59–95; J. Howard-Johnston, *Witnesses to a World Crisis: Historians and Histories of the Middle East in the Seventh Century* (Oxford, 2010), 436–530; F. Curta, *The Making of the Slavs: History and Archaeology of the Lower Danube Region, ca. 500–700* (Cambridge, 2001); P. Sarris, *Empires of Faith: The Fall of Rome to the Rise of Islam, 500–700* (Oxford, 2011), 226–306.
[14] On consolidation: *MOB*, 96–133, 165–309; M. G. T. Humphreys, *Law, Power, and Imperial Ideology in the Iconoclast Era, c.680–850* (Oxford, 2015); SOE, 251–91; J. Shepard, 'Equilibrium to expansion (886–1025)', in *CHBE*, 493–536 at 493–503.

Antioch (969) from the caliphate. At the same time a mixture of force and diplomacy also enabled the Byzantines to annex or to draw within their zone of influence territories in the Anti-Taurus and beyond which were controlled by Armenian and Georgian political elites. At sea, consolidation and expansion came with the (re)conquest of Crete (961) and the annexation of Cyprus (965). In the early eleventh century, Byzantium absorbed both the territories and the political elite of its long-standing rival in the Balkans, the 'First Bulgarian Empire'. Shortly afterwards, there were attempts to extend Byzantine power deeper into the hinterland of southern Italy and, less successfully, to conquer Muslim Sicily.[15]

Nor was Byzantine expansion in this ninth- to mid-eleventh-century period limited to territorial acquisition. Literary and material evidence points towards sustained economic growth in both urban and rural contexts.[16] There was also a boom in the foundation and decoration of churches and monasteries.[17] This expansion was driven partly by economic expansion but may also have been precipitated by the end of a long struggle within the empire over icon veneration. As will be described in

[15] For the basic narrative of territorial expansion: Shepard, 'Equilibrium to expansion', 509–11, 516–22, 526–36; *MOB*, esp. 310–90. For more detailed regional narratives on eastern expansion: A. A. Vasiliev, *Byzance et les Arabes*, 3 vols (Brussels, 1950–68), ii.1: 261–307, 341–65; E. Honigmann, *Die Ostgrenze des byzantinischen Reiches von 363 bis 1071, nach griechischen, arabischen, syrischen und armenischen Quellen* (Brussels, 1935), 77–102; W. Felix, *Byzanz und die islamische Welt im früheren 11. Jahrhundert* (Vienna, 1981); T. W. Greenwood, 'Armenian neighbours (600–1045)', in *CHBE*, 333–64, esp. 349–64; *idem*, 'Patterns of contact and communication: Constantinople and Armenia 860–976', in R. Hovannisian and S. Payaslian (eds), *Armenian Constantinople* (Costa Meza, CA, 2010), 73–100; J. Shepard, 'Constantine VII, Caucasian openings and the road to Aleppo', in A. Eastmond (ed.), *Eastern Approaches to Byzantium* (Aldershot, 2001), 19–40; on the Balkans: S. Runciman, *A History of the First Bulgarian Empire* (London, 1930); Stephenson, *Byzantium's Balkan Frontier*, 1–80; on southern Italy and Sicily: J. Gay, *L'Italie méridionale et l'Empire byzantin depuis l'avènement de Basil Ier jusqu'à la prise de Bari par les Normands (867–1071)* (Paris, 1904); Shepard, 'Western approaches (900–1025)', in *CHBE*, 537–59.

[16] A. Harvey, *Economic Expansion in the Byzantine Empire 900–1200* (Cambridge, 1989); M. F. Hendy, *Studies in the Byzantine Monetary Economy, c. 300–1450* (Cambridge, 1985); M. Whittow, 'The Middle Byzantine economy (600–1204)', in *CHBE*, 465–92; J. Lefort, 'The rural economy, seventh-twelfth centuries', in *EHB*, i:231–310, esp. 266–75; G. Dagron, 'The urban economy, seventh-twelfth centuries', in *EHB*, ii:393–461, esp. 401–3; R. Ousterhout, *A Byzantine Settlement in Cappadocia* (Washington, DC, 2005); E. J. Cooper and M. Decker, *Life and Society in Byzantine Cappadocia* (Basingstoke, 2012).

[17] See *MLIB*; expansion of monasteries is also suggested by the increased number of extant *typika* (foundation documents) from this period (see *BMFD*). For the material record of church art and architecture: M. Restle, *Byzantine Wall Painting in Asia Minor*, tr. I. Gibbons, 3 vols (Recklinghausen, 1967), esp. i:17–74 (analysis), and vols 2–3 for relevant plates; C. Mango, *Byzantine Architecture* (Milan, 1978), 108–40; A. J. Wharton, *Art of Empire: Painting and Architecture of the Byzantine Periphery: A Comparative Study of Four Provinces* (University Park, PA, 1988); L. Rodley, *Byzantine Art and Architecture: An Introduction* (Cambridge, 1994), 133–262.

greater detail (see pp. 301–2), this was a conflict which had originally arisen in the early eighth century when, in the context of the territorial and ideological challenge posed by the expansion of the Arab Muslim caliphate, Emperor Leo III (716–40) had inaugurated a purge of figural representations of Christ and the saints. This iconoclast position was certainly contested, and its impact on artistic production may have been exaggerated. Nonetheless, for more than a century official political and ecclesiastical policy see-sawed between the sanctioning and outlawing of the veneration of icons, with an official pro-icon position only taking permanent root as late as 843.[18]

The growth of the Byzantine church from the mid-ninth century onwards was dynamic outside as well as within the empire. There is lively debate about whether the conversion of neighbouring powers was fostered directly by the imperial authorities in Constantinople or whether the process was driven by non-Constantinopolitan agents, such as Byzantine provincial bishops and monasteries, or by the aspirations and expectations of the 'receiving' cultures.[19] But, whatever the means of dissemination, it is undoubtedly the case that Christian institutions and practices based upon Byzantine models were widely adopted and adapted during the ninth and tenth centuries by a variety of central and eastern European polities, including Bulgaria and Rus. In this context the dates of c.864 and c.988 take on particular significance as the dates when the rulers of Bulgaria and Rus respectively are traditionally held to have converted to orthodox Christianity.[20]

Economic and religious expansion continued unabated during the eleventh century, but the same was not so true at a territorial level. By the 1050s, the Byzantines were beginning to face pressure on three frontiers from a series of new, aggressive adversaries: a variety of Norman lords in southern Italy (especially the family of de Hauteville, which by 1130 had established a royal dynasty in Sicily and southern Italy); Turks in Anatolia, including minor branches of the Great Seljuk dynasty; and several nomad confederations north of the Danube, such as the Pechenegs and Cumans.[21] The year 1071 proved especially bleak as

---

[18] L. Brubaker and J. Haldon, *Byzantium in the Iconoclast Era, c.680–850: A History* (Cambridge, 2011).

[19] Obolensky, *Byzantine Commonwealth*; J. Shepard, 'Spreading the word: Byzantine missions', in C. Mango (ed.), *The Oxford History of Byzantium* (Oxford, 2002), 230–47; S. A. Ivanov, *'Pearls before Swine': Missionary Work in Byzantium*, tr. D. Hoffman (Paris, 2015).

[20] N. Berend (ed.), *Christianization and the Rise of Christian Monarchy: Scandinavia, Central Europe and Rus', c.900–1200* (Cambridge, 2007).

[21] M. Angold, *The Byzantine Empire, 1025–1204: A Political History*, 2nd edn (Harlow, 1997), 56–98; *idem*, 'Belle époque or crisis (1025–1118)', in *CHBE*, 583–37;

Bari, Byzantium's key command centre in southern Italy, was lost to the Normans; meanwhile, in the east, the Turks defeated a large imperial army at the Battle of Manzikert near Lake Van and took the then-emperor, Romanos IV Diogenes, captive.[22] Not only did this facilitate Turkish expansion into Anatolia; it also provided the catalyst to a ten-year period of political warfare and infighting inside Byzantium itself.[23]

To some extent the retractions and convulsions of the third quarter of the eleventh century were arrested by a period of territorial and political consolidation during the subsequent century when Byzantium was governed by three long-lived male emperors, Alexios, John and Manuel, all members of the Komnenos family. During this period (1081–1180), direct control was re-imposed and in some ways strengthened over the Balkans and the western and northern coasts of Anatolia.[24] Other former Byzantine areas remained outside formal imperial control and were governed by the empire's rivals. Such twelfth-century competitors included the Norman kingdom of Sicily and the sultanate of Rum, the latter based at Konya in western Asia Minor.[25] That said, the Komnenoi, especially Manuel Komnenos (1143–80), built up an impressive array of client states on the Byzantine frontiers, particularly in the Balkans and among the Armenian and Latin principalities established in southern Asia Minor, Syria and Palestine after the First Crusade. The management of these buffer states enabled Byzantine military, political and cultural influence to extend rather further than those territories under its direct governance.[26] At home, Constantinople, the empire's capital city, boomed, in part at least because of the increase in trade between

G. A. Loud, *The Age of Robert Guiscard: Southern Italy and the Norman Conquest* (Harlow, 2000), esp. 209–23; C. Cahen, *The Formation of Turkey: The Seljukid Sultanate of Rum: Eleventh to Fourteenth Century*, tr. P. M. Holt (Harlow, 2001), 7–14; A. C. S. Peacock, *Early Seljuq History: A New Interpretation* (London, 2010), 128–64; A. Beihammer, *Byzantium and the Emergence of Muslim-Turkish Anatolia, ca. 1040–1130* (Abingdon, 2017); *GSE*.

[22] J.-C. Cheynet, 'Mantzikert: un désastre militaire?', *Byzantion* 50 (1980), 410–38.

[23] J.-C. Cheynet, *Pouvoir et contestations à Byzance (963–1210)* (Paris, 1990), 75–90, 345–58; for a reassessment of the eleventh century: M. Lauxtermann and M. Whittow (eds), *Byzantium in the Eleventh Century: Being in Between* (Abingdon, 2017). Arms-bearing and centres of power were too diffuse in the west for meaningful comparison. However, contention between army commanders was a feature of the Islamic world, especially in certain periods; see e.g. the rise of Buyids and Seljuks: pp. 221, 222–6.

[24] Angold, *Byzantine Empire*, 173–293; P. Magdalino, 'The empire of the Komnenoi', in *CHBE*, 627–46; *EMK*; A. Bucossi and A. Rodriguez Suarez (eds), *John II Komnenos, Emperor of Byzantium: In the Shadow of Father and Son* (Abingdon, 2016).

[25] H. Houben, *Roger II of Sicily: A Ruler between East and West*, tr. G. A. Loud and D. Milburn (Cambridge, 2002); Cahen, *Formation of Turkey*, 7–74; *GSE*.

[26] Angold, *Byzantine Empire*, 191–225; M. Lau, *The Reign of John II Komnenos, 1087–1143: The Transformation of the Old Order* (Oxford, forthcoming); *EMK*, 68–108; J. Harris, *Byzantium and the Crusades*, 2nd edn (London, 2014), 99–136; M. Barber, *The*

Byzantium and a variety of Italian maritime powers, including Venice, Genoa and Pisa.[27] Although the status of the empire's economy outside the capital is more difficult to judge, the kinds of evidence for prosperity in the eleventh century, especially from coin finds and building works, continue to be plentiful for the twelfth century too.[28]

At a political and territorial level, the stability of the Komnenian era was shattered in the years after the emperor Manuel died.[29] The centripetal power of Constantinople started to wane, and several provinces began to detach from imperial rule, sequestered by internal rebels or by external predators. By 1200, much of the northern Balkans had been remoulded into a new Bulgarian polity, often called the 'Second Bulgarian Empire' by historians; Cyprus was in the hands of Latin overlords; and even the empire's second city, Thessaloniki, had been briefly occupied by a Norman army from Sicily in 1185.[30] These decades were also punctuated by incidents of extreme political upheaval and violence in the heart of government.[31] Immense geopolitical flux and confusion were the circumstances within which the armies of a joint Crusader-Venetian expedition arrived at Constantinople in 1203. Whether this army ever intended to sack Constantinople a year later is a much debated issue. But in some senses the motive for the conquest of 1204 is immaterial; the outcome was more important.[32] A Latin-controlled state was established in the empire's capital city which lasted for fifty-seven years; more significant in the longer term was the dismemberment of what was left of the

Crusader States (New Haven, CT, 2012); C. MacEvitt, *The Crusades and the Christian World of the East: Rough Tolerance* (Philadelphia, 2008), esp. 157–67.

[27] *EMK*, 109–23; A. E. Laiou, 'Exchange and trade, seventh-twelfth centuries', in *EHB*, ii:697–770, esp. 736–8.

[28] *EMK*, 142–71; for the Peloponnese: T. Shawcross, *The Chronicle of Morea: Historiography in Crusader Greece* (Oxford, 2009), 13–17; also P. Armstrong, 'The survey area in the Byzantine and Ottoman periods', in W. Cavanagh et al. (eds), *The Laconia Survey: Continuity and Change in a Greek Rural Landscape*, 2 vols (London, 1996–2002), ii:361–8; a slightly more sceptical line about the twelfth century is taken by Whittow, 'Middle Byzantine economy', 490–1.

[29] For the tensions inherent in large-scale polities, and the centrifugal tendencies discernible in even the tightest-knit structure: pp. 141–3, 149–50, 218–19.

[30] For Bulgaria: Fine, *Late Medieval Balkans*; A. Madgearu, *The Asanids: The Political and Military History of the Second Bulgarian Empire (1185–1280)* (Leiden, 2017); for Cyprus: Edbury, *Kingdom of Cyprus*; A. Nicolaou-Konnari and C. Schabel (eds), *Cyprus: Society and Culture 1191–1374* (Leiden, 2005). For a detailed narrative of the Norman raid on Thessaloniki by the city's archbishop: Eustathios of Thessaloniki, *The Capture of Thessaloniki*, tr. J. R. Melville Jones (Canberra, 1988).

[31] Angold, *Byzantine Empire*, 295–328. For a more positive assessment of Byzantium's prospects in the late twelfth century: A. Simpson (ed.), *Byzantium, 1180–1204: 'The Sad Quarter of a Century'?* (Athens, 2015).

[32] M. Angold, *The Fourth Crusade* (Harlow, 2003), esp. 1–108.

Byzantine empire's provinces in the years immediately after 1204.[33] This splintering resulted in three territorial power-blocks based in the provinces, which Byzantine historians often regard as the continuation of the Byzantine empire in exile: the empire of Nicaea; the despotate of Epiros in the western Balkans; and the empire of the Grand Komnenoi centred on Trebizond on the south-east coast of the Black Sea.[34] But in addition to these Byzantine successor states, other former Byzantine territories in Greece, the Peloponnese and the Aegean, including the island of Crete, were now in the hands of a kaleidoscope of Latin rulers, some with links to Italy, particularly to Venice, and others from northern Europe.[35]

The date of 1204 is usually seen as pivotal in the history of Byzantium in as much as it signalled the end of a unitary Byzantine state. For, while it is true that there was some reconsolidation, particularly in 1261, when the Latins were forced out of Constantinople by the Palaiologan rulers of Nicaea, a single Byzantine empire with extensive reach across the Balkans and Asia Minor was never re-established. Instead, throughout the thirteenth to fifteenth centuries, Byzantium found itself in competition with a variety of regional neighbours, including not only the Byzantine 'successors' of Epiros and Trebizond but also Bulgarian, Serb, Venetian, Genoese and Frankish rulers, as well as a variety of Turkish regimes in western and northern Asia Minor.[36] This is not to suggest that the Byzantines of Constantinople should be seen as weak and in inevitable

---

[33] For the Latin Empire: R. L. Wolff, 'The Latin Empire of Constantinople, 1204–1261', in K. Setton (ed.), *A History of the Crusades*, 6 vols (Madison, WI, 1969–89), ii:187–233; *idem, Studies in the Latin Empire of Constantinople* (London, 1976); F. van Tricht, *The Latin Renovatio of Byzantium: The Empire of Constantinople (1204–1228)* (Leiden, 2011).

[34] H. Ahrweiler, 'L'histoire et la géographie de la région de Smyrne entre les deux occupations turques (1018–1307) particulièrement au XIIIe siècle', *TM* 1 (1965), 1–204; M. Angold, *A Byzantine Government in Exile: Government and Society under the Lascarids of Nicaea 1204–61* (Oxford, 1975); *idem*, 'The Greek rump states and the recovery of Byzantium', in *CHBE*, 731–58; D. Nicol, *The Despotate of Epiros* (Oxford, 1957); *idem, The Despotate of Epiros, 1267–1479: A Contribution to the History of Greece in the Middle Ages* (Cambridge, 1984); A. Bryer, *The Empire of Trebizond and the Pontos* (London, 1980); A. Savvides, *The History of the Empire of Trebizond* (St Petersburg, 2007); P. Magdalino, *The History of Thessaly, 1266–1393* (unpublished DPhil thesis, University of Oxford, 1976). For the degree to which this tripartite interpretation misrepresents a much more confused early-to-mid-thirteenth-century political reality: M. Kinloch, *Rethinking Thirteenth-Century Byzantine Historiography: A Post-Modern, Narrativist and Narratalogical Approach* (unpublished DPhil thesis, University of Oxford, 2018); the neatness of the tripartite scheme owes much to George Akropolites, writing as a Palaiologan propagandist and apologist after the 'restoration' of Byzantine power in Constantinople; see also R. Macrides, *George Akropolites: The History* (Oxford, 2007), 3–101 (introduction).

[35] D. Jacoby, 'The Latin Empire of Constantinople and the Frankish states', in *CHBE*, 759–802; McKee, *Uncommon Dominion*; Shawcross, *Chronicle of Morea*.

[36] D. Nicol, *The Last Centuries of Byzantium, 1261–1453*, 2nd edn (Cambridge, 1993); S. W. Reinert, 'Fragmentation (1204–1453)', in Mango (ed.), *Oxford History of*

decline throughout this period. Judged by contemporary eastern Mediterranean standards, the Palaiologan regime retained many strengths until deep into the fourteenth century. The reign of Michael VIII witnessed territorial expansion in the Balkans as well as the retaking of Constantinople in 1261.[37] Even after 1300 the Byzantines were able to use their financial muscle, especially their gold coinage, to raise armies against their adversaries.[38] However, whereas once the Byzantines had dominated the Balkans, the Aegean region and most of Asia Minor, now they were engaged in an ongoing competition with other powers for resources. It was a rivalry which became increasingly difficult to dominate, especially after the Byzantine civil wars which characterised the mid-fourteenth century, conflicts that were themselves shaped by competing views within the empire about how relations with Byzantium's neighbours should be handled.[39] By the late fourteenth century, the most potent competitors in a highly fluid region of territorial acquisition and military alliances were the Ottoman Turks. Having subordinated the kings of Bulgaria and Serbia, as well as the Byzantine emperors themselves, into temporary vassal relationships in the last decades of the fourteenth century, the Ottomans went on, in the fifteenth, to create a land and maritime empire, seizing Constantinople itself in 1453 after a long siege. Within six years they had captured other leading Byzantine political and cultural centres, including Mistra in the Peloponnese and Trebizond.[40]

Byzantium, 248–83; A. E. Laiou, 'The Palaiologoi and the world around them (1261–1400)', in *CHBE*, 803–34; A. Ducellier, 'Balkan powers: Albania, Serbia and Bulgaria (1200–1300), in *CHBE*, 779–802; M. Balard, 'Latins in the Aegean and the Balkans (1300–1400), in *CHBE*, 834–51; D. Korobeinikov, *Byzantium and the Turks in the Thirteenth Century* (Oxford, 2014).

[37] D. Geanakoplos, *Emperor Michael Palaeologus and the West, 1258–1282: A Study in Byzantine-Latin Relations* (Cambridge, MA, 1959); M. Bartusis, *The Late Byzantine Army: Arms and Society, 1204–1453* (Philadelphia, 1992), 43–66; A.-M. Talbot, 'The restoration of Constantinople under Michael VIII', *DOP* 47 (1993), 243–61.

[38] A. E. Laiou, *Constantinople and the Latins: The Foreign Policy of Andronicus II, 1282–1328* (Cambridge, MA, 1972); Bartusis, *Late Byzantine Army*, 67–84. The rather bleak picture offered of the achievement of the Byzantine military in this period is unduly influenced by the problems which the so-called Catalan Company of mercenaries caused for Emperor Andronikos II in the first decade of the fourteenth century. A more general overview of recruitment, manpower and resources suggests that decay should not be dated too early; for more optimistic data: Bartusis, *Late Byzantine Army*, 191–212.

[39] D. Nicol, *The Reluctant Emperor: A Biography of John Cantacuzene, Byzantine Emperor and Monk, c.1295–1383* (Cambridge, 1996); see also pp. 85, 325–7, 443–4; J. Ryder, *The Career and Writings of Demetrius Kydones: A Study of Fourteenth-Century Byzantine Politics, Religion and Society* (Leiden, 2014).

[40] *BBOL*; J. Harris, *The End of Byzantium* (New Haven, CT, 2010); C. Kafadar, *Between Two Worlds: The Construction of the Ottoman State* (Berkeley, 1995); H. Lowry, *The Nature of the Early Ottoman State* (Albany, NY, 2003); K. Barkey, *Empire of Difference: The Ottomans in Comparative Context* (Cambridge, 2008), 3–66.

Beyond Byzantium

The proliferation of different Byzantiums in the post-1204 eastern
Mediterranean world raises some doubts about the unitary nature of
the Byzantine sphere.[41] These doubts are clearly most pertinent to
these late centuries when the Byzantine grip on the empire's capital,
Constantinople, was under greatest strain and when both the written
and the material record point to a variety of other nodes of Byzantine
government and culture, including Trebizond, Thessaloniki, Arta and
Mistra.[42] However, one could argue that even in the period *before*
1204, interpreting Byzantium in terms of the linear chronology of
a single state with clearly demarked territorial frontiers is only one
way of apprehending the nature and extent of the Byzantine sphere.
Instead, rather than emphasising a fixed and singular empire, we
could focus throughout the period under consideration in this volume
on a much more fluid and plural Byzantine zone, a region consisting
not only of the empire itself but also of those peoples and polities
which came into contact with and borrowed from Byzantium's political, material and religious culture. In such circumstances the
Byzantine canvas would expand, at the most obvious level to include
the Rus, the Bulgarians and the Serbs, those peoples who – by virtue
of their mobilisation of Byzantine religious culture, political traditions
and law – were famously included by Dimitri Obolensky within
a Byzantine Commonwealth.[43] But there could be other candidates
too for inclusion if we adopt a more elastic sense of Byzantine. To the
group of orthodox cultures which were in doctrinal accord with the
orthodox church in Byzantium should be added the Georgians, who
have received relatively little coverage as members of Byzantium's

---

[41] For instances of the proliferation of power-centres in the other spheres: pp. 142–5, 220–2,
227–31.
[42] Reinert, 'Fragmentation'; Savvides, *History of the Empire of Trebizond*; A. Eastmond, *Art
and Identity in Thirteenth-Century Byzantium: Hagia Sophia and the Empire of Trebizond*
(Aldershot, 2004); A.-M. Talbot and J. Spieser (eds), *Symposium on Late Byzantine
Thessalonike* [= *DOP* 57] (Washington, DC, 2003); C. Holmes, 'De-centring twelfth-
century Constantinople: Archbishop Eustathios and the Norman conquest of
Thessalonica revisited', in N. Chrissis *et al.* (eds), *Byzantium and the West: Perception
and Reality (11th–15th c.)* (Abingdon, 2019), 141–55; S. Runciman, *Mistra: The
Byzantine Capital of the Peloponnese* (London, 1980).
[43] Obolensky, *Byzantine Commonwealth*; J. Shepard, 'Byzantium's overlapping circles', in
E. Jeffreys (ed.), *Proceedings of the 21st International Congress of Byzantine Studies, London,
21–26 August 2006, I: Plenary Papers* (Aldershot, 2006), 15–55; *idem*, 'The Byzantine
commonwealth, 1000–1500', in *CHC* 5, 3–52; for visual evidence: O. Z. Pevny, 'Kievan
Rus'', in *GOB*, 280–319; J. D. Alchermes, 'The Bulgarians', in *GOB*, 320–35.
Obolensky's Commonwealth continues to be revisited: J. Shepard *et al.* (eds),
Byzantine Spheres: The Byzantine Commonwealth Re-evaluated (Oxford, forthcoming).

commonwealth, and the Melkites – Arab-speaking Christians – usually living under Islamic rule.[44] Among these additional members could also be numbered those geographical neighbours who, despite their differences in doctrinal beliefs and liturgical practices, nonetheless borrowed images and ideas extensively from Byzantium's political lexicon: for example, Armenian princes in the Caucasus, eastern Anatolia and, after the 1080s, southern Asia Minor; the twelfth-century Norman rulers of Sicily; the Venetians; and even the twelfth- and thirteenth-century Latin kings of Jerusalem, princes of Antioch, and counts of Tripoli and (before 1144) Edessa.[45] And, at a step beyond that, we might even want to bring within the Byzantine sphere those more geographically and/or ideologically remote powers in the east and the west which invested in objects of awe or practices that had either been created or inspired by Byzantium, whether in the shape of material culture (crowns, silks, coinage, tombs, monumental architecture), ceremonial (especially processions), sacred capital (relics/body parts) or even people (brides).[46]

---

[44] Eastmond (ed.), *Eastern Approaches*; J. Pahlitsch, 'Networks of Greek orthodox monks and clerics between Byzantium and Mamluk Egypt and Syria', in S. Connerman (ed.), *Everything is on the Move: The Mamluk Empire as a Node in (Trans)Regional Networks* (Bonn, 2014), 127–44.

[45] *GOB*, esp. S. P. Cowe, 'The Georgians' (336–49), H. C. Evans, 'The Armenians' (350–63), T. K. Thomas, 'Christians in the Islamic east' (364–87), J. Folda 'Crusader Art' (388–401) and W. D. Wixom, 'Byzantine art and the Latin west' (434–509); T. K. Thomas, 'The arts of Christian communities in the medieval Middle East', in H. C. Evans (ed.), *Byzantium: Faith and Power (1261–1557)* (New York, 2004), 415–48; A. Derbes and A. Neff, 'Italy, the mendicant orders, and the Byzantine sphere', in *ibid.*, 449–61; M. Georgopoulou, 'Venice and the Byzantine sphere', in *ibid.*, 449–514. The literature on the relationship of Byzantium to Venice and Norman Sicily is vast, particularly for material culture. On Norman use of Byzantine imagery in a political context: Houben, *Roger II of Sicily*, esp. 113–35; also E. Borsook, *Messages in Mosaic: The Royal Programmes of the Norman King of Sicily* (Oxford, 1990); on Venetian use of Byzantine material culture after the sack of Constantinople in 1204: M. Jacoff, *The Horses of San Marco and the Quadriga of the Lord* (Princeton, 1993); for engagement by the Latins of the east with Byzantine political traditions and formations: MacEvitt, *Crusades and the Christian World*.

[46] On inclusion of the more geographically distant Latins within a Byzantine cultural sphere of influence: Shepard, 'Byzantium's overlapping circles', 40–53; Wixom, 'Byzantine art and the Latin west'; R. S. Nelson, 'Byzantium and the rebirth of art and learning in Italy and France', in Evans (ed.), *Byzantium: Faith and Power*, 515–44; M. W. Ainsworth, '"À la façon grèce": the encounter of northern Renaissance artists with Byzantine icons', in *ibid.*, 545–93. Many edited collections have focused on Byzantine-western relations, e.g. I. Hütter (ed.), *Byzanz und der Westen* (Vienna, 1984); J. D. Howard-Johnston (ed.), *Byzantium and the West* (Amsterdam, 1988). On political and cultural interactions with the Ottonians: A. Davids (ed.), *The Empress Theophano: Byzantium and the West at the Turn of the First Millennium* (Cambridge, 1995). On the dispatch of crowns: J. Shepard, 'Crowns from the *basileus*, crowns from heaven', in M. Kaimakamova *et al.* (eds), *Byzantium, New Peoples, New Powers: The Byzantino-Slav Contact Zone, from the Ninth to the Fifteenth Century* (Cracow, 2007), 139–59.

In the Latin west, such an expansive view of Byzantium could mean paying some attention to the Carolingian, Ottonian and Salian emperors, as well as over the course of several centuries the kings of France, Italy and Hungary, all at some point in the period covered by this volume active in negotiating, and in some cases transacting, marriage agreements with the empire, deals which could entail the transfer of large amounts of material culture.[47] It could also mean taking account of a variety of other secular and ecclesiastical powers, whether laymen or clerics, who were, as Alexios Komnenos was to prove in the late eleventh century during his negotiations with western powers for martial aid to combat the Seljuk Turks, eager recipients of imperially curated relics.[48] And, perhaps most surprising of all, given the doctrinal and jurisdictional disputes which shaped relations between the Byzantine and Latin churches over the entirety of this period, we might also wish to place within the Byzantine sphere the papacy.[49] Exploring this orientation, we might consider the translation of the relics of Clement to Rome from the Crimea by the Byzantine missionary saints Cyril and Methodios in the ninth century;[50] the movement of a porphyry tomb into the Lateran Palace during the pontificate of Innocent II for his own occupancy in 1143 – in line with his increased use of a papal tiara for processions and ceremonial *adventus* into Rome – and the allusions to Byzantine iconography in the mosaics and marble of the Church of Maria the Blessed Mother of God in Trastevere;[51] and the

---

[47] J. Shepard, 'Marriages towards the millennium', in Magdalino (ed.), *Byzantium in the Year 1000*, 1–34; A. Davids, 'Marriage negotiations between Byzantium and the west and the name of Theophano in Byzantium (eighth to tenth centuries)', in Davids (ed.), *Empress Theophano*, 99–120.

[48] J. Shepard, 'Cross-purposes: Alexius Comnenus and the First Crusade', in J. Phillips (ed.), *The First Crusade: Origins and Impact* (Manchester, 1997), 107–29; *idem*, 'The "muddy road" of Odo Arpin from Bourges to La Charité-sur-Loire', in P. Edbury and J. Phillips (eds), *The Experience of Crusading, II: Defining the Crusader Kingdom* (Cambridge, 2003), 11–28.

[49] On the tensions, real or supposed, between the papacy and Byzantium: S. Runciman, *The Eastern Schism: A Study of the Papacy and the Eastern Churches during the XI and XIIth Centuries* (Oxford, 1955); for the ninth century: T. M. Kolbaba, *Inventing Latin Heretics: Byzantines and the Filioque in the Ninth Century* (Kalamazoo, MI, 2008); for the schism of 1054: J. Ryder, 'Changing perspectives on 1054', *BMGS* 35 (2011), 20–37; for relations post-1204: N. Chrissis, *Crusading in Frankish Greece: A Study of Byzantine-Western Relations and Attitudes, 1204–1282* (Turnhout, 2012); Chrissis *et al.* (eds), *Byzantium and the West*; E. Chrysos, 'Rome and Constantinople in confrontation: the quarrel over the validity of Photius's ordination', in D. Slootjes and M, Verhoeven (eds), *Byzantium in Dialogue with the Mediterranean: History and Heritage* (Leiden, 2019), 24–46.

[50] *Life of Cyril* ch. 17, ed. B. S. Angelov and K. Kodov, in *Kliment Okhridski, S'brani s'chineniia III* (Sofia, 1973), 107–8; tr. M. Kantor, *Medieval Slavic Lives of Saints and Princes* (Ann Arbor, MI, 1983), 76; F. Dvornik, *Byzantine Missions among the Slavs: SS. Constantine-Cyril and Methodius* (New Brunswick, 1970), 135, 137, 140.

[51] J. Deér, *The Dynastic Porphyry Tombs of the Norman Period in Sicily*, tr. G. A. Gillhoff (Cambridge, MA, 1959), 146–54; M. Stroll, *Symbols as Power: The Papacy Following the*

gifting of an orthodox icon by Helena of Anjou, queen of Serbia and patron of the Monastery of Gradac, to Pope Nicholas IV in the late thirteenth century.[52] Moving beyond the west and north and adopting an inclusive approach to the south and east of Byzantium would involve finding space in a Byzantine sphere for neighbouring political regimes that were Islamic (or in some cases pagan), including the Fatimids of Egypt and the Umayyads of al-Andalus in the tenth century, a variety of Turkish polities in the twelfth to fourteenth centuries, the Mongols in the later thirteenth and early fourteenth, and the Ottomans in the fifteenth and sixteenth, all regimes which borrowed to some degree from Byzantium's visual and performative repertoire of power and, in some cases, also received Byzantine brides.[53]

In this context of a more capacious Byzantium, it is worth registering that references in contemporary written accounts, surviving objects and a wealth of scholarly research all make it clear that Byzantine written and material culture, including the artefacts and practices specifically associated with imperial rule, were disseminated very widely among the

Investiture Contest (Leiden, 1991), 162–3, 168, 170, 174–5, 181–2; S. Twyman, *Papal Ceremonial in Rome in the Twelfth Century* (London, 2002), 25–7, 102–4, 172–4; J. Croisier, 'I mosaici dell'abside e dell'arco trionfale di Santa Maria in Trastevere', in M. Andaloro and S. Romano (eds), *La pittura medievale a Roma 312–1431, IV: Riforma e tradizione 1050–1198* (Milan, 2006), 305–311 at 307; J. F. Romano, 'Innocent II and the liturgy', in J. Doran and D. J. Smith (eds), *Pope Innocent II (1130–1143): The World vs the City* (Abingdon, 2016), 326–351. For scepticism as to any 'imperialising programme' in Innocent II's monumental works and visual imagery: D. Kinney, 'Patronage of art and architecture', in *ibid.*, 352–388 at 374–6, 384–8.

[52] Evans (ed.), *Byzantium: Faith and Power*, no. 23 on 50.

[53] Shepard, 'Byzantium's overlapping circles', 28–40; S. Redford, 'Byzantium and the Islamic world, 1261–1557', in Evans (ed.), *Byzantium: Faith and Power*, 389–414; on parallels between Fatimid and Byzantine ceremonial: M. Canard, 'Le cérémonial fatimite et le cérmoniale byzantine: essai de comparison', *Byzantion* 21 (1951), 355–420; J. Oesterle, *Kalifat und Königtum: Herrschaftsrepräsentation der Fatimiden, Ottonen und frühen Salier an religiösen Hochfesten* (Darmstadt, 2009), esp. 15–22, 79–95; for the reception of Byzantine material culture by the Umayyad caliphs of Cordoba in the mid-tenth century: see P. Soucek, 'Byzantium and the Islamic east', in *GOB*, 408–10; for similarities in iconography on coins and other material culture between Byzantium and the primarily Turkish elites of the Middle East in the twelfth to sixteenth centuries: D. Kastritsis, 'Conquest and political legitimation in the early Ottoman empire', in J. Harris *et al.* (eds), *Byzantines, Latins, and Turks in the Late Medieval Eastern Mediterranean World* (Oxford, 2012), 221–46; E. Georganteli, 'Transposed images: currencies and legitimacy in the late medieval eastern Mediterranean', in *ibid.*, 141–80; for Byzantine brides in Seljuk contexts: R. Shukurov, 'Harem Christianity: the Byzantine identity of Seljuk princes', in A. C. S. Peacock and S. N. Yıldız (eds), *The Seljuks of Anatolia: Court and Society in the Muslim Middle East* (London, 2012), 115–50; on Ottoman appropriation of Byzantine political sites and culture: G. Necipoğlu, *Architecture, Ceremonial, and Power: The Topkapı Palace in the Fifteenth and Sixteenth Centuries* (Cambridge MA, 1991); on Byzantine imperial brides and the Mongols: C. Connor, *Women of Byzantium* (New Haven, CT, 2004), 309–16.

empire's neighbours throughout the eighth to fifteenth centuries. This diffusion of Byzantine culture was partly the result of a striking readiness on the part of successive imperial governments to deploy material culture as a diplomatic tool, a principle which is espoused explicitly in the instructions provided by Constantine VII Porphyrogennetos in the *De administrando imperio* ('On Governing the Empire') for the distribution of precious gifts to northern nomads, as well as in the list of silks detailed for disbursement to Byzantine allies in Italy in the roughly contemporaneous *De cerimoniis* ('Book of Ceremonies').[54] But it is also important to remember that the diffusion of Byzantine material and sacred culture, and even the transmission of living people from the empire, was also driven by the desire on the part of many neighbouring regimes, particularly those which were of recent formation, to legitimise their own authority and to reward their families and political supporters with highly prized Byzantine resources.[55] This imperative is particularly evident when we consider the uses to which the precious material goods such as ivories, silks and enamels as well as plentiful gold coinage that accompanied Byzantine imperial brides were put. Indeed, it has been argued that this pattern of new regimes harnessing the charisma of the venerated allows us to fit Byzantium's relations with many neighbouring polities into the model for cultural exchange developed by the anthropologist Mary Helms whereby peripheral states draw for legitimacy and resources on a superordinate centre.[56] The evidence supporting this more diffusionist approach to Byzantium – and to the societies and polities with which it was in contact – should caution us against assuming that the Byzantine sphere was ever entirely coterminous with the political and territorial state of Byzantium itself.

Political Formations, Social Groups, Endemic Tensions: Competing Models and Change over Time

Beyond Byzantium

The lack of perfect fit between the wider Byzantine sphere and the narrower Byzantine unitary state has important implications for interpretations of the

---

[54] *DAI* chs 4, 6, 50–3; *DC* II.44, ii:661–2; Shepard and Franklin (eds), *Byzantine Diplomacy*.

[55] For the role of royal women in cementing alliances, fomenting peace and, on occasion, diffusing culture in the other two spheres: pp. 55, 164, 397–8, 407, 23–4.

[56] Shepard, 'Marriages towards the millennium'; on applying Helms' ideas about super-ordinate centres (and ultimately those of Clifford Geertz) to Byzantium: *idem*, 'Byzantine commonwealth', 12–14.

component parts of Byzantine political culture. Thus, in the case of political formations, social groups and endemic tensions in Byzantine politics, the plurality of the Byzantine sphere suggests that any full account of Byzantine political culture should include not just the groups and structures of power which surrounded (and sometimes challenged) the emperors in Constantinople: it should also include those which clustered around other rulers – especially those within the orthodox commonwealth, such as the kings of Bulgaria and Serbia and the princes of Rus – and around other elites who were exposed to Byzantine culture.[57] An inclusive approach to the Byzantine sphere also provokes a series of important questions about political processes. How did rulers in other polities use the religious beliefs and practices and the motifs of hegemony which they borrowed from Byzantium to shape the political societies they governed? How far were processes of borrowing the responsibility of a ruler alone, and how far was such translation more widely practised within his or her governing elite? How far did indigenous or alternative social and political structures condition and shape the borrowing process? Such a broad apprehension of the Byzantine sphere has the potential to offer a tremendously rich picture of Byzantine political formations, albeit one complicated and destabilised by a large number of localised contexts.[58]

Yet, while acknowledging that a full account of Byzantine political culture should take account of the full panoply of polities which received and made use of elements of Byzantium's political and religious traditions, in the remaining phases of this chapter I will look in most detail at the political formations of Byzantium the unitary state rather than casting the net more widely. There are a number of reasons for this approach. At one level, to focus on Byzantium the unitary state most easily facilitates the main objective of this volume, which is to catalyse the process of making comparisons between three spheres: Latin western, Byzantine and Islamic. But, in a more nuanced sense, to focus on the Byzantine empire itself is also a necessary first step for calibrating sensitively and responsibly the precise resonances of Byzantine political culture in receiving polities. To put it in a different way, and perhaps more negatively,

---

[57] On political formations in Serbia and Bulgaria: Fine, *Early Medieval Balkans*; idem, *Late Medieval Balkans*; on Rus: S. Franklin and J. Shepard, *The Emergence of Rus, 750–1200* (London, 1996); N. S. Kollman, *Kinship and Politics: The Making of the Muscovite Political System, 1345–1547* (Stanford, CA, 1987).

[58] This, of course, is not to argue against complexity and destabilisation; indeed, one of the criticisms of the study of political culture is that it can be too schematic, failing to take account of nuance and change in time and space: G. Gendzel, 'Political culture: genealogy of a concept', *Journal of Interdisciplinary History* 28 (1997), 225–50; R. P. Formisano, 'The concept of political culture', *Journal of International History* 31 (2001), 393–426.

while the Byzantine sphere may be bigger than the Byzantine empire alone, it may not always be productive to apply the label 'Byzantine' to neighbouring societies without careful consideration. Simply because other neighbours appear to have borrowed images, ideas and languages of power from the Byzantines does not necessarily make them Byzantine.

In this more ambiguous context, it is important to remember that the process of 'borrowing' from Byzantium was not always first-hand. For instance, the Rus took most of the linguistic and textual infrastructure of orthodox Christianity from the Bulgarians rather than from Byzantium directly.[59] Moreover, borrowing was not always about emulation as much as about subversion, competition or even subjugation. The copying and illustrating of John Skylitzes' eleventh-century history in twelfth-century Norman Sicily and the rather similar treatment of Constantine Manasses' twelfth-century chronicle in fourteenth-century Bulgaria have been interpreted as challenges to Byzantine political authority by the kings of Sicily and Bulgaria, rather than as the quiescent acknowledgement of imperial superiority by second-class neighbouring powers.[60] In a similar way the transfer of *spolia* from Constantinople to the façades of San Marco in Venice after the Latin invasion of Byzantium in 1204 can be read as signs of a decayed empire conquered rather than of an authoritative culture held in deep respect. Just as important, the Byzantine origins to such borrowings were often quite quickly and easily forgotten: the Pilastri Acritani, *spolia* brought from the church of St Polyeuctos in Constantinople after the Fourth Crusade, were regarded by Venetians in the fourteenth century as trophies of war that had been seized from Acre during conflict with the Genoese; thus, by 1300 they had entirely lost their Byzantine moorings.[61] And in a related sense, the meaning invested in Byzantine products and practices could change radically in the process of importation, as translated artefacts and processes were fused and juxtaposed with other traditions on the part of the importing culture – or were simply ignored.[62]

Finally, even among those societies and polities most intimately associated with Byzantine traditions, such as Bulgaria, Serbia and Rus, it would be a mistake to assume that Byzantium was the only important

---

[59] S. Franklin, 'Byzantium and the origins of written culture in Rus', in C. Holmes and J. Waring (eds), *Literacy, Education and Manuscript Transmission in Byzantium and Beyond* (Leiden, 2002), 187–97; *idem*, *Writing, Society and Culture in Early Rus, c. 950–1300* (Cambridge, 2002), esp. 187–228.

[60] E. N. Boeck, *Reimagining the Byzantine Past: The Perception of History in the Illustrated Manuscripts of Skylitzes and Manasses* (Cambridge, 2015).

[61] R. S. Nelson, 'The history of legends and the legends of history: the Pilastri Acritani in Venice', in R. S. Nelson and H. Maguire (eds), *San Marco, Byzantium and the Myths of Venice* (Washington, DC, 2010), 63–90.

[62] Franklin, *Writing, Society and Culture*, 129–86.

reference point in their own complex and evolving political cultures. Nowhere is this clearer than in the example of the power most usually regarded as 'heir' to Byzantium in the late medieval and early modern worlds, the principalities of Rus. Here, north of the Black Sea, it was certainly true that some connections with the wider Byzantine world in the thirteenth to sixteenth centuries continued to prosper and even to thicken, especially if we focus on pilgrim journeys from Rus to the monasteries on Mount Athos, near Thessaloniki; on the reuse of monastic foundation documents; and on the increasingly intensifying and diversifying landscape of Eastern Christian book culture.[63] But at the same time, the political culture of the Rus principalities of this late Byzantine period was to be shaped as much, if not more, by the practical demands and governing models of their near neighbours, the Jagiellonian kings of Poland-Lithuania and, to an even greater extent, the Golden Horde, that fraction of the Mongol empire which had emerged as the dominant power on the western Eurasian steppe in the middle of the thirteenth century and to which the late medieval Rus were tribute payers.[64] Of course, one of the paradoxes of the Byzantine sphere, particularly in the later medieval period, is that the principalities of Rus were far from the only polities within the Byzantine Commonwealth shaped quite profoundly by political cultures other than the Byzantine. The same was true of Bulgaria and Serbia and even, given Byzantium's own multiple political, social and commercial relations with external powers (whether Seljuk, Mongol, Ottoman or Latin) of the Byzantine empire itself.

The reservations expressed above suggest that an exhaustive account of political culture in the Byzantine sphere from the eighth to the fifteenth centuries requires the very careful calibration of the ways in which a variety of traditions, structures and processes, not all of them Byzantine in origin, intersected in particular situational contexts. But in taking what are initial steps in the adumbration of Byzantine political culture, and in turning now to consider political formations, relevant social groups and endemic tensions, I will be most concerned with Byzantium the unitary state until 1204 and, for the period after the Fourth Crusade, with those polities which arose in the territories of the erstwhile Byzantine empire and which continued to refer most actively to Byzantine political traditions. Nonetheless, it should not be assumed that limiting the focus in this way will produce an entirely uncontested picture.

[63] Obolensky, *Byzantine Commonwealth*, 237–361; G. P. Majeska, *Russian Travelers to Constantinople in the Fourteenth and Fifteenth Centuries* (Washington, DC, 1984).
[64] D. Ostrowski, *Muscovy and the Mongols: Cross-Cultural Influences on the Steppe Frontier, 1304–1589* (Cambridge, 1998); S. Rowell, *Lithuania Ascending: A Pagan Empire within East-Central Europe, 1295–1345* (Cambridge, 1994).

Instead navigation between several competing and overlapping interpretations is required.

Within Byzantium

One possible interpretation of the formations, groups and tensions in Byzantium[65] is to regard the empire as a clearly defined and highly centralised bureaucratic state which was governed by the written word, efficient (by medieval standards) in the collection of taxes, and reliant on imperially sanctioned legal codes and officials.[66] This was a state built around an emperor resident in a single large palace complex which was itself the hub of a bureaucracy that was located at the centre of a wealthy capital city, Constantinople. With this picture uppermost, the most relevant political formations can be identified in terms of institutions: the offices of emperor and of empress;[67] the Constantinopolitan court as a centre of carefully regulated imperial ceremonial;[68] the bureaucracy (both central and provincial); the salaried army; the state-controlled church.[69] On the other hand, reading the testimonies of many of the medieval historians of Byzantium such as Leo the Deacon, Michael Psellos, Anna Komnene, Niketas Choniates, George Akropolites and Nikephoros Gregoras can make institutions seem far less relevant. Such histories tend to focus on political machinations within the imperial court, the building of factions and the efforts of military commanders to raise their armies in coups against the incumbent emperor.[70] In this context, rather than institutions, the relevant political formations can appear to be

---

[65] For the means whereby power was concentrated, devolved or shared in other spheres: pp. 148–54, 156–63, 373–8, 389–91, 401–4, 406–9, 234–8, 241–3, 245–7, 341–5, 350–3, 458–64, 468–9, 474–7.

[66] For fuller consideration of the themes raised here: pp. 91, 92–3, 295–7, 321, 433–5. The Abbasid empire in its heyday bears comparison with Byzantium: pp. 460–4.

[67] G. Dagron, *Emperor and Priest: The Imperial Office in Byzantium*, tr. J. Birrell (Cambridge, 2003); L. Garland, *Byzantine Empresses: Women and Power in Byzantium, AD 527–1204* (London, 1999); J. Herrin, *Women in Purple: Rulers of Medieval Byzantium* (London, 2001).

[68] *BCC.*

[69] For the general contours: *MOB*, 96–133, 165–93; J.-C. Cheynet (ed.), *Le Monde byzantin, II: L'Empire byzantin (641–1204)* (Paris, 2006), 69–174; for development over the ninth to eleventh centuries: N. Oikonomides, *Les Listes de préséance byzantines des IXe et Xe siècles* (Paris, 1972); idem, 'L'évolution de l'organisation administrative de l'Empire byzantin au XIe siècle', *TM* 6 (1976), 125–52.

[70] It is this historiographical evidence which lies at the heart of the most far-reaching analysis of the political culture of Byzantine rebellion: Cheynet, *Pouvoir et contestations*. Two accessible narratives of this variety from the eleventh century are Michael Psellos, *Chronographia*, ed. Reinsch; tr. Sewter; John Skylitzes, *Synopsis historiarum*, ed. H. Thurn, *CFHB* 5 (Berlin, 1973); tr. J. Wortley, *John Skylitzes: A Synopsis of Byzantine History, 811–1057* (Cambridge, 2010). On the court-centred nature of Byzantine narratives: pp. 80–2, 95.

imperial dynasties, family structures and extended patronage networks. And even within this more informal and agonistic paradigm, there is variety. At some points imperial dynasties characterised by considerable continuity can be identified, such as the Macedonians and Lekapenoi in the tenth century; the Komnenoi in the twelfth; and the Palaiologoi from the mid-thirteenth to the fifteenth. In other periods, for instance the eleventh century, much less imperial dynastic continuity is evident. Instead, at such times competition between various powerful families for imperial authority seems more important.[71]

How we identify and interpret the social groups and individuals at the centre of Byzantine politics then depends to a large extent on whether we choose to emphasise an institutional and formal or a more personal and informal reading of the structure of power in the empire. That is to say, close focus on a centralised, salaried, fiscally efficient model can suggest that Byzantine politics was essentially about individuals whose prominence was achieved through specialist service to the state. Relevant groups within this meritocratic interpretation include the salaried military; civil bureaucrats in the capital and in the provinces, some dealing with tax, others with justice and still others who dealt with both; and members of the organised clergy, especially the episcopacy and the abbots (*hegoumenoi*) of important monasteries: in short, those who appear in the administrative records of Byzantium and whose lead seals that were used to authenticate official documents still survive in large numbers.[72] On the other hand, if one thinks less about a formal bureaucratic model and more about an informal politics based around dynastic competition, then other social groups and processes seem relevant, above all the empire's most significant families (increasingly identifiable from the eighth to ninth centuries onwards through the use of family names) and the networks of clients which surrounded those families.[73] In this context, one of the

---

[71] Cheynet, *Pouvoir et contestations*, 337–58.

[72] In a *novella* issued in 934, Emperor Romanos I Lekapenos listed those office and title holders he considered to be the most powerful officials within the Byzantine empire: J. Zepos and P. Zepos (eds), *Jus Graecoromanum*, 8 vols (Athens, 1931), i:209, 213; tr. E. McGeer, *The Land Legislation of the Macedonian Emperors* (Toronto, 2000), 54–5, 59. For further analysis of the sigillographical record: pp. 89, 98, 418; for the lists of precedence produced in the imperial court milieu which are used to reconstruct administrative hierarchies and solidarities: pp. 86, 310.

[73] There is an extensive literature on the most significant of the Byzantine aristocratic families, their origins and their adoption of family names. In addition to prosopographical studies of individual families (many of which make substantial use of sigillographical as well as textual evidence) see more general works such as *TBA*; M. Kaplan, *Les Hommes et la terre à Byzance du VIe au XIe siècle* (Paris, 1992); Cheynet, *Pouvoir et contestations*; *TBAMF*.

crucial Byzantine political structures, especially at the levels of provincial, non-imperial, and grassroots power, was the *oikos*, or household.[74]

It is often assumed that the Byzantine countryside was the arena where the political influences and actions of great families and their affinities were at their most visible. This assumption is based on the anxiety evident in tenth-century imperial legislation about the illegal acquisition of property in tax-paying villages by those whom the emperors called 'the powerful' (*dynatoi*). But however extensive the provincial estates of powerful clans and other institutions, especially monasteries, within the Byzantine countryside, the most powerful *oikoi* customarily also included an important urban base, usually in Constantinople. Thus, one of the most powerful of ninth- and tenth-century families, the Phokas, have been identified through textual and material evidence with the theme of Cappadocia; yet we know that they also possessed an important mansion in the empire's capital city too. The same was true of the Lekapenoi, a dynasty from the Armeniakon theme in north-eastern Anatolia, who also built a palace in the City, whose chapel is still extant in Istanbul. Strikingly, there is evidence to suggest that the sorts of influential and pervasive political networks which urban aristocratic hubs generated in Mamluk Cairo had analogies in Constantinople too.[75] Young provincial hopefuls coming to Constantinople to find fame and fortune were frequently attached to the households of great patrons, or at the very least sought the intervention of such sponsors as they made their way up the greasy political pole in the capital. The scale of such urban networks probably varied considerably, but evidence from the year 963, when supporters of the court eunuch Basil Lekapenos came out in support of the martial coup attempt of the general (and soon-to-be emperor) Nikephoros Phokas, suggests that some affinities were very large indeed.[76] Meanwhile, it is quite possible that such connections were, as Stephen Humphreys suggests for Cairo,

---

[74] The seminal study of the *oikos* is P. Magdalino, 'The Byzantine aristocratic *oikos*', in *TBA*, 92–111; see also L. Neville, *Authority in Byzantine Provincial Society, 950–1100* (Cambridge, 2004), 66–118.

[75] On the Phokas family: G. Dagron, and H. Mihăescu, *Le Traité sur la guérilla (De velitatione) de l'empereur Nicéphore Phocas* (Paris, 1986); for evidence of their connections to Cappadocia: A. J. Wharton Epstein, *Tokalı Kilise: Tenth-Century Metropolitan Art in Byzantine Cappadocia* (Washington, DC, 1986); L. Rodley, 'The Pigeon House Church, Çavuşin', *JÖB* 33 (1983), 301–39; references to a Phokas house in Constantinople surface during the assassination of Emperor Nikephoros II Phokas in 969 (Skylitzes, *Synopsis*, ed. Thurn, 281; tr. Wortley, 269); on the Myrelaion palace and chapel of the Lekapenoi: Rodley, *Byzantine Art and Architecture*, 135–6. On Mamluk Cairo: pp. 116–17, 363, 480–2.

[76] Leo the Deacon, *Historiae libri decem*, ed. C. B. Hase, *CSHB* (Bonn, 1828), 47; tr. A.-M. Talbot and D. F. Sullivan, *The History of Leo the Deacon: Byzantine Military Expansion in the Tenth Century* III.7 (Washington, DC, 2005), 97. More light is shed on Constantinopolitan great households in the mid-tenth century by the (probably fictional) *Life* of St Basil the

conduits through which the power and political influence of women could be wielded.[77] This may have been particularly true of the late eleventh and twelfth centuries during the supremacy of the Komnenoi, when a variety of women, particularly those linked to the imperial family by birth or by marriage, including those whose origins may lie outside Byzantium itself, appear to have been active cultural patrons within the imperial court and across Constantinople.[78]

Yet for all the significance of the *oikos* in the politics of town and countryside, it is important not to overstate the importance of any one great family or network within the political culture of Byzantium. Instead, there is considerable evidence to suggest that control of private resources alone was never enough to threaten the institutional apparatus which supported imperial authority; instead threats could only come when a would-be rebel controlled one of the key components of that apparatus, by holding high office in the imperial court or the army, for example.[79] It is also clear that, until the later Byzantine centuries, liquid resources such as coins, precious fabrics or luxury goods, many acquired as imperial salaries, outstripped non-movables (in the shape of land) in the asset portfolios of almost all Byzantine aristocratic families.[80] Research has also suggested that, even when one particular family held the reins of imperial power, dynastic connections were never the sole guarantors of authority; indeed, family relationships were just as likely to undermine as to shore up the emperor's position.[81]

As will already be clear, dealing with Byzantine politics requires constant navigation between two apparently conflicting models: the one institutional, hierarchical and centralised; the other informal, competitive

---

Younger: *The Life of St Basil the Younger: Critical Edition and Annotated Translation of the Moscow Version*, ed. and tr. D. F. Sullivan *et al.* (Washington, DC, 2014).

[77] See p. 24. Women's capacity to set the tone of courts and influence policy and successions is apparent in other cultures, too: pp. 21, 55, 407, 232, 471, 502.

[78] B. Hill, *Imperial Women in Byzantium, 1025–1204: Power, Patronage, and Ideology* (Harlow, 1999), esp. 153–80; the patronage offered to the Pantepoptes monastery in Constantinople by Anna Dalassene, the powerful mother of Emperor Alexios I, is a particularly interesting case in this respect (*ibid.*, 165). Note also the cultural patronage of the *sebastokratorissa* Eirene Komnene, who has been identified as having a Norman background: E. Jeffreys, 'The sevastokratorissa Eirene as literary patroness: the monk Iakovos', *JÖB* 32 (1982), 63–71; see now, however, *eadem*, 'Literary trends in the Constantinopolitan courts in the 1120 and 1130s', in A. Bucossi and A. Rodriguez Suarez (eds), *John II Komnenos, Emperor of Byzantium: In the Shadow of Father and Son* (Abingdon, 2016), 110–20.

[79] C. Holmes, *Basil II and the Governance of Empire* (Oxford, 2005), 461–8.

[80] J.-C. Cheynet, 'Fortune et puisssance de l'aristocratie', in V. Kravari *et al.* (eds), *Hommes et richesses dans l'Empire byzantin*, 2 vols (Paris, 1989–91), ii:199–213; see also pp. 420–2.

[81] P. Frankopan, 'Kinship and the distribution of power in Komnenian Byzantium', *EHR* 121 (2007), 1–34.

and tangled. The question which then arises is how to reconcile the obvious overlaps and tensions between these two interpretations. One answer is chronological and suggests that there was a subtle change from one model to another over time: in other words, that there was an early medieval period in which Byzantium was typified by a meritocracy of individuals chosen for their specialist talents, dedicated to state service and duly rewarded; but that this situation gradually gave way to a political society in which family interest and pedigree were of greater importance. This change, one could argue, was accompanied by the gradual erosion of the public by the private and by the change from a centripetally organised state to one which had to take more account of centrifugal processes, including political formations in the provinces.[82] Nonetheless, even if we think such trajectories can be detected, dating these changes is difficult. Was a shift from public to private already visible in the tenth century, when emperors expressed concern about the growing resources of the *dynatoi* particularly in their legislation?[83] Did it occur in the twelfth century with the more conspicuous and regular use of the *pronoia*, a device the workings of which are difficult to fathom but which is generally assumed to have involved the temporary transfer of fiscal revenues to public servants and private individuals and institutions?[84] Or was the dispersal and permanent alienation of state resources, such as taxation, jurisdiction and land, only more widespread in the post-1204 centuries?[85] Or was it a hallmark of Byzantine politics that the state exercised strong control over the allocation of property even beyond 1204, a trait which ensured that Byzantine politics retained an essentially centripetal character even in the later medieval period?[86]

The likelihood is that Byzantium was never entirely meritocratic, centralised, public and formal; nor was it ever completely familial,

[82] *MOB*, 310–57; A. P. Kazhdan and A. J. Wharton Epstein, *Change in Byzantine Culture in the Eleventh and Twelfth Centuries* (Berkeley, 1985), 63–70. On such tendencies in other spheres: pp. 149–52, 156, 165–6, 375, 400–2, 408, 219–21, 227–9, 473–5.

[83] Zepos and Zepos, *Jus Graecoromanum*, 198–273; McGeer, *Land Legislation*; J. D. Howard-Johnston, 'Crown lands and the defence of imperial authority in the tenth and eleventh centuries', *Byzantinische Forschungen* 21 (1995), 76–99.

[84] P. Lemerle, *The Agrarian History of Byzantium from the Origins to the Twelfth Century: The Sources and Problems* (Galway, 1979), 222–41 (especially in the context of military recruitment and service); however, see now *LPIB*; p. 436; see also p. 94.

[85] Angold, *Byzantine Government in Exile*, 121–43; for the use of *pronoia* in army funding in the later period: Bartusis, *Late Byzantine Army*, 157–90; pp. 445–6. On comparable transfers of rights, notably the *iqta'*, in the Islamic sphere: pp. 472, 484. Grants of land were rather less nuanced and were not just the prerogative of the ruler in the Latin west: pp. 32, 74–5, 377.

[86] K. Smyrlis, 'The state, the land, and private property: confiscating monastic and church properties in the Palaiologan period', in D. Angelov (ed.), *Church and Society in Late Byzantium* (Kalamazoo, MI, 2009), 58–87.

decentralised, private and informal.[87] Across many centuries, entry into imperial service was difficult without personal connections and private wealth; and yet, without the rewards and status which came from imperial service, personal resources and social contacts were impossible to accumulate and sustain. To put it crudely, institutions powered connections and connections powered institutions. This is the two-way conversation which shaped Byzantine politics on an ongoing basis.[88] It was a conversation with important implications for how we interpret the actions, assumptions and expectations of the most powerful male protagonists of the medieval histories (from which we glean much of our knowledge about Byzantine politics),[89] as well as for our understanding of the political activities and interest of other parties, including aristocratic and non-aristocratic women, eunuchs, provincial worthies and leading townsmen (sometimes identified as *archontes* in our sources), and peasant communities. For although they are often overlooked in medieval narratives (or at least not highlighted in modern interpretations of those narratives), it would be dangerous to assume that such groups lacked political agency either as collectives or as individuals – or to argue that such political actors only exercised informal influence rather than formal power. Instead, just as functioning on the boundaries of the formal and the informal was the modus operandi for the most prominent of Byzantine male political figures, so was this true for other apparently more marginal figures too.[90]

In the case of imperial and aristocratic women, for instance, it was not just as mothers, sisters, wives, private educators and patrons that they

---

[87] For discussion of the problematic use of binary interpretations (public versus private, institutional versus informal) in the study of early medieval western politics: M. Innes, *State and Society in the Early Middle Ages: The Middle Rhine Valley, 400–1000* (Cambridge, 2000). Innes' criticism is relevant for the Byzantine context too; however, the survival of more robust imperial administrative structures in post-Roman Byzantium suggests that it may be premature to discard entirely the notions of the 'state' or the 'public' in the way that Innes proposes for the Carolingian west.

[88] For a development of this argument in relation to the eleventh century: J. Nilsson, 'Strengthening justice through friendship and friendship through justice: Michael Psellos and the provincial judges', in N. Matheou *et al.* (eds), *From Constantinople to the Cities: The City and the Cities* (Leiden, 2016), 98–108; further elaborated in *idem*, *Aristocracy, Politics and Power in Byzantium (1025–1081)* (unpublished DPhil thesis, University of Oxford, 2017).

[89] For the predominantly, but not exclusively, patriarchal stance of our sources: pp. 41–5, 55, 72, 136–7, 163, 172, 251–68, 380, 80–2, 95–8, 106–7, 126–7.

[90] For the exercise of marginal power by apparently marginal figures such as village headmen, leading townsmen and women in Byzantium: pp. 417–18, 426–7, 429; for the west: pp. 160–3, 375, 379, 391–2, 402–4, 407; for the Islamic world: pp. 113–14, 121, 238, 246–7, 466, 471, 475–7.

could exercise behind-the-scenes political influence.[91] Instead, women also had visible public roles and even audible voices in the conduct of political life. This visibility and audibility could take many forms: on occasion, women could be empresses in their own right, as in the cases of Eirene (790, 797–802) and Zoe and Theodora (1042, and Theodora alone 1055–6);[92] more frequently they were regents, as in the case of Theodora, mother of the young Michael III, under whose auspices the final restoration of icons was achieved in 843;[93] many others were regular, prescribed and authorised participants in imperial ceremonial (a phenomenon still far from understood and relatively under-explored); even more were the possessors of official titles; some were critics of the incumbent imperial regime, as we see most explicitly in the case of Anna Komnene's use of the biography of her father, Alexios I, to chastise her nephew, Manuel I.[94] What holds true for imperial and aristocratic women can also be extended to eunuchs, who were an integral part of Byzantine political culture until at least the late eleventh century, primarily through the administrative and ceremonial roles which they performed in the imperial court but also on occasions as army commanders too.[95]

Evidence from saints' *Lives* and those rare extant archival documents from deposits such as the monasteries on Mount Athos also suggests that we should not just add elite women and eunuchs to the dramatis personae of Byzantine political culture. City-dwellers both inside and beyond the political hothouse of Constantinople as well as peasant communities were often well aware of the workings of the imperial administration both in the centre and the provinces, and they were fully prepared to grease the wheels which made those workings turn in their favour.[96] Indeed, we may be able

[91] A. Kaldellis, *Mothers and Sons, Fathers and Daughters: The Byzantine Family of Michael Psellos* (Notre Dame, IN, 2006). See also, on women's political touch: pp. 301–2, 307, 311. Although extensive data has yet to be marshalled from the Islamic world pp. 23, 471, strong hints can be found in the Latin west: pp. 164, 407.

[92] J. Herrin, 'The imperial feminine in Byzantium', *P&P* 169 (2000), 3–35; for Eirene: J. Herrin, *Women in Purple* (London, 2001), 51–130; R.-J. Lilie, *Byzanz unter Eirene und Konstantin VI. (780–802)* (Frankfurt am Main, 1996); for Zoe and Theodora: Connor, *Women of Byzantium*, 207–37; Hill, *Imperial Women*, 36–58.

[93] Herrin, *Women in Purple*, 185–239.

[94] For a reassessment of women's roles in public ceremonial contexts: J.-C. Cheynet, 'La patricienne à ceinture: une femme de qualité', in P. Henriet and A. Legras (eds), *Au Cloître et dans le monde: femmes, hommes et sociétés (IXe–XVe siècle)* (Paris, 2000), 179–87; on Anna as critic: P. Magdalino, 'The pen of the aunt: echoes of the mid-twelfth century in the *Alexiad*', in T. Gouma-Peterson (ed.), *Anna Komnene and her Times* (New York, 2000), 15–43; for a revisionist and less politicised view of Anna: L. Neville, *Anna Komnene: The Life and Work of a Medieval Historian* (Oxford, 2016).

[95] K. Ringrose, *The Perfect Servant: Eunuchs and the Social Construction of Gender in Byzantium* (Oxford, 2003); S. Tougher, *The Eunuch in Byzantine History and Society* (London, 2008).

[96] See pp. 421–2, 428–9.

to go further and suggest that non-elite and non-Constantinopolitan individuals and communities did not simply react to a political culture orches-
trated by leading actors within the imperial hierarchy and that of the
patriarchate; instead, their activities, interests, ideas and political traditions
may have actively shaped the practices, assumptions and expectations
which underpinned political society in Byzantium more broadly.
Research into the continuity of a republican tradition in Byzantine political
thought has emphasised a dynamic politics underpinned by a profoundly
bottom-up logic which drew on ideas of popular sovereignty. The implication is that those in power were expected to be held to account by a wide
range of political actors, including those outside the narrow circles of the
imperial court and church.[97] Given the palace-centric nature of many of
our sources, it may be difficult to prove conclusively that the strong interest
in republican ideas evident among Byzantine intellectuals and courtiers in
certain periods was ubiquitous or powerful enough to mobilise popular
political action on the ground. Nonetheless, even if the evidence for a living
tradition of republican sentiment in the political lives of non-elite actors
may be hard to find, we should not underestimate the ways in which those
outside elite circles or indeed those beyond the empire's frontiers could
shape both the formal and informal behaviours of Byzantine political life.

The bottom-up and outside-in dynamics to Byzantine political culture
become particularly evident if we think about the degree to which the
tangible manifestations of that culture were produced as much by the
expectations and demands of those who engaged with the political elite as
by the top-down mechanics and theatrics of government. We see glimmerings of this in the roles that petitioning by those across the domestic
and international order played in the exercise of power in Byzantium.
Whether it was representatives of village communities presenting requests
for protection or redress to imperial officials in the localities and journey-
ing to Constantinople itself to gain a hearing, or whether it was foreign
envoys seeking alliances, payments, peoples and objects that might
enhance and serve the strategic and legitimising purposes of those regimes
they served, all had a role in the processes and productions associated
with Byzantine political cultures; all sought formal responses to their
requests; all required knowledge of how to navigate the informal politics
of access which surrounded the emperor and his or her court. The tenth-
century western envoy Liudprand of Cremona offers us an unparalleled

---

[97] A. Kaldellis, *The Byzantine Republic: People and Power in the New Rome* (Cambridge, MA,
2015); D. Krallis, '"Democratic" action in eleventh-century Byzantium: Michael
Attaleiates's "republicanism" in context', *Viator* 40 (2009), 35–53; see also p. 327.
Assemblies and debaters in some later medieval western polities did show signs of holding
the ruler to account: pp. 63, 66–70, 161, 163, 270, 280, 288–9, 382, 402.

in-depth account of the opportunities and frustrations which those looking to approach imperial authority for favour could encounter in the Byzantine centre, as well as of the way in which the demands of the outside world could fuel the operation of Byzantine politics there. But while they are atypical in their level of detail, Liudprand's testimonies are an entirely reliable witness to the web of both the formal and the informal communicative processes that were integral to the day-to-day operation of Byzantine political culture. More concrete and formal manifestations of the essential reciprocity of Byzantine political culture are the resources, gifts and protections that both humble and lofty petitioners received from the imperial authorities and which were usually confirmed by a document bearing an imperial seal, whether in the shape of the quotidian imperial letters (*basilika grammata*) that saints' *Lives* tell us village worthies sought to extract from the emperors and their officials, or the highly elaborate gold-lettered missives on purple parchment authenticated with a gold seal and encased in ivory caskets, which were received by distant potentates such as the Umayyad caliphs of Cordoba and the Ottonians.[98]

Finally the creative tension between formality and informality may also be a fruitful way of approaching the religious coordinates within Byzantine political culture. Thus, from a formal perspective, it is impossible to understand Byzantine political life without an awareness of the empire's long-standing religious practices, beliefs and structures, many of them most strongly expressed, authorised and re-authorised over many generations by political elites in the empire's capital city. These deeply rooted formal elements included, perhaps most obviously, the physical infrastructure of churches and monasteries, some of which had been stamped upon the built environment in late antiquity and continued to be used – most famously, in Constantinople itself, the Church of Holy Wisdom (St Sophia) and the Church of the Holy Apostles, the burial place of emperors.[99] Some, of course, were newly built in the post-700 centuries. Other foundational religious coordinates to Byzantine political culture were the general church councils of the fourth to seventh centuries, especially the legal authority of the canons produced by those

---

[98] *The Life and Miracles of St Luke of Steiris*, ed. and tr. C. L. Connor and W. R. Connor (Brookline, MA, 1994), 6–8; Soucek, 'Byzantium and the Islamic east', 408–9; C. Holmes, 'Political literacy', in P. Stephenson (ed.), *The Byzantine World* (London, 2010), 137–48 at 145–6; the culture of petitioning in the eleventh century has been explored in some depth by Nilsson, *Aristocracy, Politics and Power*; see also pp. 34–5. For the uses of literacy and petitioning in other political cultures: pp. 47–50, 61–5, 68–70, 162–3, 256, 274–83, 388, 403–4, 113–16, 118–19, 127, 360–2, 464–6.

[99] P. Grierson, 'The tombs and obits of Byzantine emperors', *DOP* 16 (1962), 1–62; see also p. 304.

meetings, as well as the still widely read patristic writings from late antiquity, particularly those of the fourth-century Cappadocian fathers Basil of Caesarea and Gregory Nazianzus as well as John Chrysostom, the patriarch of Constantinople. Also of seminal importance was the central role accorded to the emperor for the defence, expansion and regulation of faith from the moment of Emperor Constantine I's conversion to Christianity in 312. All emperors in this sense were regarded both as a new Constantine and as the thirteenth apostle. These were powerful models which not only authorised the imperial office itself but could be mobilised to legitimise the tenure of that office by individual incumbents and their families. Equally they were models with the potential to provide ideological ballast in efforts to undermine the credentials of displaced imperial predecessors or critique sitting emperors with the wrong priorities or policies.[100] And, of course, among those expected to support the formal apparatus of empire but also, in difficult circumstances, to restrain imperial excess were the senior personnel of the church, especially patriarchs, metropolitans and bishops. Such figures were simultaneously imperial officials but also moral authorities with the power to counsel and chastise, a dynamic which played out with particular drama during the crisis years of the early reign of Alexios Komnenos, when the emperor and his family found themselves publicly criticised by John the Oxite, the patriarch of Antioch, for personal excess during a time of political and military crisis.[101]

However, just as the church, its law, its teachings and its senior staff members should be regarded as integral to the formal operation of Byzantine political society, it is also important to include within Byzantium's key religious coordinates, individuals, groups and practices which can initially seem more informal or even subversive. These included the holy man, who was a ubiquitous figure in town and countryside, not just in Byzantium itself but in many orthodox societies; a figure with the

---

[100] P. Magdalino (ed.), *New Constantines: The Rhythm of Imperial Renewal in Byzantium, 4th–13th Centuries* (Aldershot, 1994), e.g. P. Magdalino, 'Introduction' (1–9), A. Markopoulos, 'Constantine the Great in Macedonian historiography: models and approaches' (159–70) and R. Macrides, 'From the Komnenoi to the Palaiologoi: imperial models in decline and exile' (269–82); Dagron, *Emperor and Priest*; Humphreys, *Law, Power, and Imperial Ideology*, 105–13, 128–9 (arguing for an Old Testament turn by the iconoclast emperors); see also F. H. Tinnefeld, *Kategorien der Kaiserkritik in der byzantinischen Historiographie: von Prokop bis Niketas Choniates* (Munich, 1971); pp. 302, 304.
[101] J. Hussey, *The Orthodox Church in the Byzantine Empire*, rev. edn A. Louth (Oxford, 2010), 304–10, 312–14; P. Frankopan, 'Where advice meets criticism in eleventh century Byzantium: Theophylact of Ohrid, John the Oxite and their (re)presentations to the emperor', *Al-Masaq* 20 (2008), 71–88. For a new interpretation of John's oration: J. Ryder, 'The role of the speeches of John the Oxite in Komnenian court politics', in T. Shawcross and I. Toth (eds), *Reading in the Byzantine Empire and Beyond* (Cambridge, 2018), 93–115.

potential to stand in for established authorities where such authorities were absent or distrusted; someone who could also act as a broker between local individuals and communities and imperial office-holders; and someone who might under certain circumstances operate as a spiritual and informal political inspiration to the powerful themselves, including the emperor.[102] Less explored but worthy of more attention in Byzantine studies is the political significance of holy women, including imperial or royal figures with a visible impact on the public face of religion such as Theodora, mother of Michael III, in the mid-ninth century, or Anna, sister of Basil II and bride of Vladimir of Kiev in 988, who is credited with the foundation of many churches in the newly converted lands of her husband. Whether holy women outside imperial and royal families could exercise power is a topic which awaits further discussion.[103]

Often home to holy men and women, and equally prominent as informal political actors and brokers, were monastic communities. Such communities had both the potential to act as supporters of regimes and grateful recipients of official patronage at the political centre and in localities but also to be the incubators of protest or preservers of de-authorised traditions, as is evident among those monasteries which sought to overturn iconoclasm in the eighth and ninth centuries.[104] Striking in this regard were monasteries acting as centres of mystical traditions, practices and institutions around which other political conflicts and debates turned. Thus, we might contrast the efforts of tenth-

---

[102] On the holy man's social and political significance: P. Brown, 'The rise and function of the holy man in late antiquity', *Journal of Roman Studies* 61 (1971), 80–101. Many of the contributions to S. Hackel (ed.), *The Byzantine Saint* (London, 1981) explore the holy man's roles in later Byzantine centuries, although note the scepticism expressed by Paul Magdalino about the political centrality of the holy man by the twelfth century: 'The Byzantine holy man in the twelfth century', in *ibid.*, 51–66. See also contributions on holy men in Byzantium and Rus in J. Howard-Johnston and P. Hayward (eds), *The Cult of Saints in Late Antiquity and the Early Middle Ages* (Oxford, 1999); S. A. Ivanov, *Holy Fools in Byzantium and Beyond*, tr. S. Franklin (Oxford, 2006).

[103] For representations, visual and verbal, of Theodora during her lifetime and in the *Life* written decades after her death: K. Kotsis, 'Empress Theodora: a holy mother', in C. Fleiner and E. Woodacre (eds), *Virtuous or Villainess? The Image of the Royal Mother from the Early Medieval to the Early Modern Era* (New York, 2016), 11–36; see also pp. 312–13. Relatively plentiful information about women's piety, donation and founding of monasteries comes from Athos: A.-M. Talbot, 'Searching for women on Mt Athos: insights from the archives of the Holy Mountain', *Speculum* 87 (2012), 995–1014. On Anna: Shepard, 'Marriages towards the millennium', 25–8. Holy women – or those conveying divine revelations – have an impact in the late medieval west, albeit precariously or vicariously: p. 164. In the Islamic world they seem to feature mainly as patrons of pious institutions, rather than as holy persons: p. 501.

[104] For the iconophile monk and precocious letter writer Theodore the Studite: Brubaker and Haldon, *Byzantium in the Iconoclast Era*, 378–81; as they point out, not all monks or monastic communities adopted Theodore's trenchant opposition to iconoclasm; see also p. 315.

and eleventh-century governments to curb Symeon the New Theologian, a monastic founder whose mystical practices and beliefs attracted official suspicion, with the much greater influence that hesychasm, a rather similar devotional culture associated with many monasteries on Mount Athos, enjoyed among leading politicians in Byzantium itself and further afield in the fourteenth century.[105] Significantly, it was also possible for monastic foundations to support, be supported and subvert, all at the same time. Noteworthy in this context are monasteries in provinces which were detached from Byzantine direct rule in the later period. Sometimes such foundations enjoyed close relationships with new regional rulers and even their direct patronage, including with non-orthodox Christian potentates; at the same time they generated propaganda which undermined the legitimacy of those incomers' beliefs and practices and sought to retain contacts with co-confessionalists elsewhere in the former Byzantine space. A remarkable instance of such double-play was Neophytos the Recluse, the founder of the Enkleistra monastery that survived the 1191 takeover of Cyprus by the Latins and prospered under the rule of the new Lusignan dynasty, but who nonetheless deplored the cacodoxy of his new benefactors.[106]

Nor were monasteries the only hub of alternative political affiliations and ideas structured around religious belief and practice. In Constantinople itself, but also in regional and urban centres outside the City, among the religious coordinates which bridged the formal and informal divide were confraternities and the organisations integral to the celebration of saints' cults. Such groupings could be intimately involved in the generation and sustenance of local political hierarchies and affiliations as well as in the formation of wider socio-political loyalties, some of which transcended the political frontiers of Byzantium.[107] And below

---

[105] Niketas Stethatos, *The Life of Saint Symeon the New Theologian*, ed. in and tr. R. P. H. Greenfield (Washington, DC, 2013); B. Krivocheine, *Symeon the New Theologian (949–1022)* (New York, 1986); J. McGuckin, 'St Symeon the New Theologian and Byzantine monasticism', in A. Bryer and M. Cunningham (eds), *Mount Athos and Byzantine Monasticism* (Aldershot, 1996), 17–35. For the political importance of hesychasm: Hussey, *Orthodox Church*, 257–60, 287–90; J. Meyendorff, *Byzantine Hesychasm* (London, 1974); M. Angold, 'Byzantium and the west, 1204–1453', in *CHC* 5, 53–78 at 61–66; D. Krausmüller, 'The rise of hesychasm', in *ibid.*, 101–26.

[106] C. Holmes, '"Shared worlds"? Religious identities – a question of evidence', in Harris *et al.* (eds), *Byzantines, Latins, and Turks*, 31–60 at 40–3. For the pragmatic readiness of monasteries to cater for corsairs' needs: M. Gerolymatou, 'Vivre avec les pirates aux XIIe–XIIIe siècles: l'exemple de Patmos', in B. Caseau *et al.* (eds), *Mélanges Jean-Claude Cheynet* [= *TM* 21/1] (Paris, 2017), 256–65; and to come to terms with Ottoman conquerors: p. 442.

[107] J. Baun, *Tales from Another Byzantium: Celestial Journey and Local Community in the Medieval Greek Apocrypha* (Cambridge, 2007), 319–85, esp. 371–85 for confraternities.

such loose webs of cult-based affiliation, at a more atomic but no less influential level lay the highly personalised bonds of artificial family, such as godparenthood, brotherhood and adoption, which, with church blessing, individuals could use to develop social arrangements. Such bonds not only helped give ecclesiastical sanction to the many complex social connections that were the warp and weft of Byzantine political culture in action; they were also the means by which those within Byzantium, whatever we choose to mean by that term, might connect with those outside. As research into the rituals of brother-making (*adelphopoesis*) has suggested, such were the ways in which those in Byzantium and beyond during the medieval centuries and afterwards could create linkages between families, classes, ethnic and religious identities, and even genders.[108]

The historical context to the Byzantine sphere varies according to where and when we choose to look – and to the meaning we attribute to the beguiling yet highly mutable term 'Byzantium'. As we have seen, the territorial empire, the frontier regions and the neighbouring powers are all relevant to the Byzantine context but in rather different ways; these different 'wheres' were never coterminous. The same is true of the 'when': Byzantium was a very different territorial power in the mid-eighth century, the mid-eleventh and the mid-fifteenth. The empire's relationships with outsiders, whether near neighbours or more distant societies, were also subject to considerable flux over time: we might think of the Byzantines responding to the requests of others for help in the earlier centuries, as when Slavic princes sought Christian missionaries; but in later periods it was the Byzantines who went begging at the courts of western Europe for help against the Ottomans. Nevertheless, for all the variations in space and time in the Byzantine sphere, certain continuities are striking. On the one hand, particularly when regarded as a territorial state, the Byzantine sphere was almost always typified by a palace-based emperor (and occasionally an empress) whose charismatic authority and bureaucratic infrastructure drew those within and outside Byzantium to

---

On the socio-political importance of local cults: S. Vryonis, 'The panegyris of the Byzantine saint', in Hackel (ed.), *Byzantine Saint*, 196–228. Thessaloniki is an interesting city to explore in this context: R. Cormack, 'The making of a patron saint: the powers of art and ritual in Byzantine Thessalonike', in I. Lavin (ed.), *World Art: Themes of Unity in Diversity* (State College, PA, 1989), 547–54; for Thessalonian connections with the twelfth-century central Mediterranean: Holmes, 'De-centring twelfth-century Constantinople'. For cults, monastic networks and religious foundations and movements spanning political boundaries, see e.g. pp. 79, 99, 441–2, 453, 170–5, 379–80, 19–21, 108–9, 121, 247, 335, 355, 484–6.

[108] R. Macrides, 'The Byzantine godfather', *BMGS* 11 (1987), 139–62; C. Rapp, *Brother-Making in Late Antiquity and Byzantium: Monks, Laymen and Christian Ritual* (Oxford, 2016).

the imperial centre in Constantinople. On the other hand, there are also marked continuities of fragmentation and of a politics which was often greater in the illusion than in the reality: the physical geography of the Byzantine sphere could act as constraint as well as enabler; outsider regimes could be disdainful, dismissive or simply uninterested in the self-proclaimed grandeur of the empire; frontier elites could be as attracted to neighbouring powers as to Byzantium; the inner politics of the Byzantine court were consistently predicated on intense, and sometimes destructive, competition, whether between families or between functionaries (or both simultaneously). The historical context to the Byzantine sphere was consistently stable *and* unstable. The political culture of this sphere amounted to the real-time interplay of these two dynamics. Winners in this culture were those who could exploit best the tensions between what was fixed and fluid, singular and plural, real and illusory.

9 The Islamic World
Conquest, Migration and Accommodating Diversity

Andrew Marsham, Eric Hanne and Jo Van Steenbergen

Figure 9.1 The Dome of the Rock, commissioned by Abd al-Malik (685–705) to assert the Islamic presence in Jerusalem; photo Nicola Sigsworth

Introduction

For almost a millennium, Islam was the pre-eminent cultural, political and religious force across most of western Eurasia and northern Africa. By the mid-630s, many of the nomadic and settled peoples of the Arabian peninsula had been brought together under the monotheist leadership of settled tribesmen from central western Arabia. Almost immediately, they had begun to raid and then campaign beyond the peninsula. During the seventh and eighth centuries these Arabian conquerors had connected the southern ports of the Mediterranean Sea, the Silk Roads of the Iranian plateau and the maritime trade routes of the Gulf and the Indian Ocean. Throughout these regions and beyond, Arabic (and to a lesser extent, Persian) quickly became a lingua franca, and laws and customs deriving their authority from the Qur'an or from the actions of Islam's Prophet and Companions proved a highly adaptable and effective framework for politics, commerce and social interaction, both among Muslims and also between Muslims and the many non-Muslim populations of the Islamic world.

This chapter provides a very brief overview of the political history of that world, from the seventh-century Arabian conquests until the formation, during the fifteenth and sixteenth centuries, of the three great early modern Muslim empires: the Ottomans in Asia Minor, the Safavids in Iran and the Mughals in India. The chapter's structure reflects the major political formations and transformations of this period: firstly, the Arabian 'conquest polity' which replaced the late antique balance between Rome and Iran;[1] then, after the demise of that empire in the mid-tenth century, the tumultuous era of Berber, Daylami and Turkic leadership; and finally, following the cataclysmic Mongol conquest of the eastern Islamic lands in 1258, the assimilation of these Turco-Mongol conquerors in the east and the political achievements of military strongmen and entrepreneurs in Syria, Egypt, Yemen and Anatolia. We shall then look at the elites and political structures that shaped and underlay this history, noting their interaction with Islam. Having developed from a somewhat volatile variant of Judaeo-Christian monotheism in the early centuries to become a more fully articulated and stable ideological system, much of Islam's continued success lay in the capacity of new elites to adopt it and to adapt it to their needs.[2]

---

[1] An adaptation of the term 'conquest society', used by Patricia Crone in *SOH*, 29.
[2] For the survival of old elites and emergence of new ones in Byzantium, as also for broader considerations about what constitutes an elite: pp. 416–21, 428–30.

Historical Overview

Conquest and Consolidation (c. 650 to c. 950)

Muhammad established his religio-political community in 622, at the small oasis town of Yathrib (later Medina) in the region of central western Arabia known as the Hijaz.[3] He founded this monotheist polity in a politically fragmented world, beyond the direct influence of the great empires of Rome and Iran to the north and also outside the direct control of the weakening regional settled powers of Aksum in East Africa and Himyar in southern Arabia. Muhammad's hometown of Mecca, about 350 kilometres to the south of Medina, was incorporated into his dominions in 630, less than two years before his death. In the subsequent decades, a series of his closest former associates presided over the unification and conquest of the Arabian peninsula, proceeding to subjugate Roman North Africa, Egypt and Greater Syria, and the Sasanian empire of Iraq and Iran. Victories in the mid-630s and the early 640s brought Syria, Egypt and southern Iraq under Arabian control; between the 650s and the 670s, campaigns targeted modern Libya and Tunisia, as well as the lands of eastern Iran and western Afghanistan.

These seventh-century phases of conquest and expansion were punctuated by two major periods of political crisis and violent internal conflict, driven by tensions within the fast-expanding empire. Elements in the conquering Arabian armies looked to various members of the Prophet's tribe of Quraysh for leadership that would favour their interests. In these contests, the Qurayshi clan descended from Umayya b. Abd Shams (the Umayyads), and the armies of the frontier province of Greater Syria (*Bilad al-Sham*) were repeatedly successful. After two fathers-in-law of Muhammad, Abu Bakr (632–4) and Umar (634–44), had presided over the initial burst of consolidation and expansion, a son-in-law of Muhammad from the Umayyad clan, Uthman b. Affan (644–56), took power. Uthman's reliance on relatives by blood and marriage from the clan of Abd Shams provoked his killing by resentful members of the conquering armies in 656. Five years of conflict followed before the Syrian commander and second cousin of Uthman, Mu'awiya b. Abi Sufyan, took control of the nascent empire in 661. Mu'awiya's death in 680 triggered twelve years of further violent conflict from which the

---

[3] See H. Kennedy, *The Prophet and the Age of the Caliphates: The Islamic Near East from the Sixth to the Eleventh Centuries*, 3rd edn (Abingdon and New York, 2016); *NCHI* 1, esp. C. F. Robinson, 'The rise of Islam, 600–705', 173–225; P. M. Cobb, 'The empire in Syria, 705–763', 226–68; T. El-Hibri, 'The empire in Iraq, 963–861', 269–304; and M. Bonner, 'The waning of empire, 861–945', 305–59.

Syrians again emerged victorious, this time under the leadership of Abd al-Malik, from a third branch of the Umayyad clan, the Marwanids.

However, these civil wars (*fitna*s) of 656–61 and 680–92 caused only temporary setbacks in the expansion of the new polity. By around 700, armies of *mu'minin* (the Arabian 'faithful') and their allies were raiding Visigothic Spain in the west and Sind (modern southwestern Pakistan) in the east: two frontiers some 8,000 kilometres apart. In the north, they were marching through the valleys of the Transcaucasus (modern Turkey, Georgia, Armenia and Azerbaijan) and encountering the armies of Nubia (modern Sudan) in the south. The Arabian monotheists were already a significant naval power: in the Mediterranean they had attacked all the major islands and even Constantinople itself, and Arabian merchants were doing business on the East African coast, the Persian Gulf and the Indian Ocean. In this period of conquest, the revelations that Muhammad had received from God had been codified in the Qur'an, and the memory of his words and deeds began to form part of the basis of a distinct Islamic religious practice.

These developments reshaped the identities of both conquerors and conquered. By the first decades of the eighth century, the term *muslim* (Muslim) begins to replace *mu'min* (faithful) and *muhajir* (emigrant) in the sources, and a stronger sense of *al-'arab* (the Arabs) begins to supplant older tribal and group identities from the Arabian peninsula.[4] Thus, the speed with which the religio-political landscapes of the southern Mediterranean and the Middle East were reshaped during the seventh and eighth centuries marks out the Islamic world from this volume's other two spheres. The development of a clearly articulated and distinctive Islamic religious identity, expressed primarily in Arabic and central to the political practice of almost all the region, was a direct product of the mission of the Prophet and the actions of his immediate successors.[5] As one historian put it, 'Islamic civilization is the only one in the world to begin in the mind of a single man'.[6]

Perhaps it is true that without Muhammad there would have been no Islam. However, from another perspective, the rapid expansion of Islamic

---

[4] I. Lindstedt, 'Muhajirun as a name for the first/seventh century Muslims', *JNES* 74 (2015), 67–73; P. Webb, *Imagining the Arabs: Arab Identity and the Rise of Islam* (Edinburgh, 2016). For an influential proposal about the evolution of Islam itself in the first century of the conquests: F. M. Donner, *Muhammad and the Believers at the Origins of Islam* (Cambridge, MA, 2010).

[5] Surveys of the 'formative' centuries of Islamic civilisation include: M. G. S. Hodgson, *The Venture of Islam: Conscience and History in a World Civilization*, 3 vols (Chicago, 1974), I: *The Classical Age of Islam*; J. Berkey, *The Formation of Islam: Religion and Society in the Near East 600–1800* (Cambridge, 2003); Kennedy, *Prophet*.

[6] *SOH*, 25.

religio-political culture can be seen as a function of much longer-term developments within the Roman empire and on its frontiers.[7] From the third century on, the structures of the whole Roman empire had been transformed both by the success of Christianity and the pressures of maintaining security and stability over a vast geographical expanse. In the Latin west, new political elites emerged among the former barbarian federates and neighbours of Rome. Their rulers looked to Latin Christianities as the basis of their legitimacy – at first in their Arian and then in Catholic forms. These processes of ethnogenesis, whereby the new Germanic 'peoples' articulated distinctive social and political identities, have been the subject of extensive scholarship.[8] Parallel developments took place on the frontiers of the eastern empire and beyond, as well as on the Iranian frontiers.[9]

In the east as in the west, a crucially important development was the spread of monotheism. In the east, this was usually in the form of a non-Chalcedonian Christianity, alongside Rabbinic and other forms of Judaism. Whereas the Gothic Arian Bible and the Venerable Bede's forays into translating the Gospels into Anglo-Saxon were exceptional in the Germanic world, vernacular Christianity was typical of the east. By the sixth century, the churches of Armenia and Ethiopia were over 300 years old. Both had scriptures and liturgies in the local languages (Armenian and Ge'ez respectively); the Christianisation of Iberia in the Caucasus had also led to a Georgian Bible. Populations of Christians who used Syriac as their scriptural and liturgical language were found across

---

[7] This idea was set out – with respect to religious developments in particular – by Peter Brown in *The World of Late Antiquity: From Marcus Aurelius to Muhammad* (London, 1971). Developed by Garth Fowden in *Empire to Commonwealth: Consequences of Monotheism in Late Antiquity* (Princeton, 1993), it is now quite widely accepted: see e.g. Islam's inclusion in P. Rousseau (ed.), *A Companion to Late Antiquity* (Chichester, 2009). For comparisons with social, political and economic developments in the late antique west, see e.g. W. Ball, *Rome in the East: The Transformation of the Roman East* (London and New York, 2000), 101–5; G. Fisher, 'A new perspective on Rome's desert frontier', *JAOS* 336 (2004), 49–60; G. Fisher, 'The political development of the Ghassan between Rome and Iran', *Journal of Late Antiquity* 1 (2008), 310–34.

[8] See e.g. W. Pohl and H. Reimitz (eds), *Strategies of Distinction: The Construction of Ethnic Communities, 300–800* (Leiden, 1998); P. Geary, *The Myth of Nations: The Medieval Origins of Europe* (Princeton, 2002); W. Goffart, *Barbarian Tides: The Migration Age and the Late Roman Empire* (Philadelphia, 2006); I. H. Garipzanov et al. (eds), *Franks, Northmen and Slavs: Identities and State Formation in Early Medieval Europe* (Turnhout, 2008).

[9] But see pp. 190–1, and G. Fisher (ed.), *Arabs and Empires before Islam* (Oxford, 2015). For two quite different pictures of the situation in Iran: J. Howard-Johnston, 'The two great powers of late antiquity: a comparison', in A. Cameron (ed.), *The Byzantine and Islamic Near East, III: States, Resources and Armies* (Princeton, 1995), 157–226; P. Pourshariati, *Decline and Fall of the Sasanian Empire: The Sasanian-Parthian Confederacy and the Arab Conquest of Iran* (London and New York, 2008).

the Fertile Crescent between Rome and Iran, as well as far into the Iranian plateau and beyond. In Egypt, Coptic Christianity was the dominant form of the religion. Both Judaism and Christianity had also made inroads into the Arabian peninsula. For example, non-Chalcedonian bishops from the eastern Arabian coasts attended church councils at Ctesiphon with the patronage of the Sasanian King of Kings (*shahanshah*). And in the kingdom of Himyar, which had dominated southern Arabia in the fourth and fifth centuries, the ruling elite adopted first Judaic monotheism and then a form of Christianity.[10]

The Romans had similar policies of client management and federation in the east as in the west. On the Arabian frontier, the federations of Tanukh, Salih and then Ghassan made alliances with the empire, in the fourth, fifth and sixth centuries respectively. Had the eastern imperial centre collapsed as that of the west did, these groups might perhaps have formed independent post-Roman realms in the former territories of the Roman world. However, the political structures of the east were sturdier than those of the west, and Constantinople was far better fortified than Rome. As a result it took a catastrophic war with Sasanian Iran in the first decades of the seventh century to expose Rome's eastern provinces – and all Iran – to fresh conquest.[11] This conquest was led not by Christian former allies and neighbours but by a group from the distant margins of the Roman and Iranian world who brought with them their own vernacular scripture, rooted in Judaeo-Christian traditions but sufficiently distinct from them to secure and develop their separate identity in the conquered territories. Nor did these conquests contribute, as they did in the west, to the disintegration of empire. Rather they led to the formation of a new one of unprecedented scale: the eighth-century Islamic empire was the largest in terms of land area in world history until the thirteenth-century, when it was surpassed by the Mongol empire.[12]

---

[10] On Armenia: R. Thomson, 'Mission, conversion and Christianization: the Armenian example', *Harvard Ukrainian Studies* 12 (1988), 28–45. For comparison of Iberia and Aksum: C. Haas, 'Mountain Constantines: the Christianization of Aksum and Iberia', *Journal of Late Antiquity* 1 (2008), 101–26. On Syriac Christianity: D. Taylor, 'The coming of Christianity to Mesopotamia', in D. King (ed.), *The Syriac World* (London and New York, 2019), 68–87; N. Andrade, 'Syria and Syrians in the later Roman empire: questions of identity', in *ibid.*, 157–74. On southern Arabia: C. Robin, 'Himyar, Aksum, and *Arabia Deserta* in late antiquity: the epigraphic evidence', in G. Fisher (ed.), *Arabs and Empires before Islam* (Oxford, 2015), 127–72.

[11] J. Howard-Johnston, *Witnesses to a World Crisis: Historians and Histories of the Middle East in the Seventh Century* (Oxford, 2010).

[12] On the size of empires: J. Myrdal, 'Empire: the comparative study of imperialism', in A. Hornborg et al. (eds), *Ecology and Power: Struggles over Land and Material Resources in the Past, Present, and Future* (London, 2012), 37–51; R. Taagepera, 'Size and duration of empires: systematics of size', *Social Science Research* 7 (1978), 108–27.

A monarchical institution for the leadership of this new Arabian empire quickly emerged in the form of the caliphate (*khilafa*) – 'vicegerency' (of God), or 'succession' (to Muhammad).[13] Leadership was always monopolised by leaders of Meccan heritage: first by close associates and contemporaries of the Prophet himself (from his death in 632 until 644); then predominantly by descendants of the Umayyad branch of the Prophet's tribe of Quraysh (644–750); and finally – for over half a millennium – by the Abbasid branch of the same tribe (750–1258). However, a single, notionally united, empire survived only until the 750s, and even then it was in constant turmoil. The Marwanid branch of the Umayyads (692–750) and their Syrian armies faced repeated rebellions against their rule in the first half of the eighth century, culminating in the Abbasid Revolution of 750, which saw disaffected groups from the eastern frontier province of Khurasan take advantage of internal crisis in the Umayyad elite and to overthrow them and install members of the Abbasid clan in their place.

The revolts of the 740s, including the Abbasid Revolution itself, mark a watershed in Islamic political culture because, for the first time, large numbers of people of non-Arabian heritage expressed their political aspirations in Islamic terms: Islam was becoming an ideology that could be adopted by non-Arabian peoples. The major upheavals were on the western and eastern frontiers. In the Maghreb ('the west' – modern Algeria and Morocco), groups among the Berber populations rebelled in 739–40 in the name of Kharijite Islam. In the east, elements of the post-Sasanian indigenous population of Khurasan (modern north-east Iran and Turkmenistan) joined forces with groups of Arabian heritage to bring about the Abbasid Revolution.

In what might be termed the long ninth century (*c*.743–*c*.945) the structures of power were repeatedly reconfigured. Caliphal succession politics within the Abbasid dynasty were driven by factional competition within the military elite of the empire. The foundation of the new imperial capital at Baghdad, in Iraq, in 762 contributed to a dynamic of sometimes violent competition between provinces. This culminated in a civil war over the caliphate in 809–13, with provincial unrest lasting into the 820s. The victor in this war, al-Ma'mun (810–33), installed a new army and

---

[13] When precisely the epithet *khalifa* ('caliph') became widely used is not clear; it is well attested after *c*.690. The formal title of the Islamic leader was *amir al-mu'minin* ('Commander of the Faithful'), attested in documentary evidence from 661: A. Marsham, *EI*³, s.v. 'Commander of the Faithful'; *idem*, '"God's Caliph" revisited: Umayyad political thought in its late antique context', in A. George and A. Marsham (eds), *Power, Patronage and Memory in Early Islam: Perspectives on Umayyad Elites* (Oxford, 2018), 3–37.

administration from Khurasan and Transoxiana (Turkmenistan, Uzbekistan and points east) in Iraq, and his successor, al-Muʿtasim (833–42), in turn gained power with a new army recruited from Transoxiana and Central Asia. These new troops, known in the sources as 'the Turks', were garrisoned at a new capital at Samarra, about 100 kilometres north of Baghdad. Factions in this new army gained control over the caliphal succession and brought about a second decade of civil war in 861–70, which left the military and fiscal reach of the Abbasid empire significantly diminished. A further crisis in the 920s led to the collapse of Abbasid power; by 945 the caliph could not act as a fully independent monarch in his own capital Baghdad.[14]

During the first half of the long ninth century, as the Abbasids and their allies sought to consolidate their hold over the empire, further internal frontiers opened up. The Abbasids never sought to restore western North Africa (the Maghreb) and the Iberian peninsula (al-Andalus) to central-ised control, and independent emirates developed in these regions that did not recognise Abbasid authority. In the Nile Delta there were rebel-lions about every fifteen years, triggered by the fiscal demands of the rulers and environmental pressures at least in part caused by low Nile flood levels.[15] On the Iranian plateau and in Khurasan, disappointments with the outcomes of the Abbasid Revolution saw a series of 'nativist' revolts with a syncretic religious character. Remote regions such as Sistan and Azerbaijan witnessed extended violent unrest, as local actors con-tended for power; in Azerbaijan, the Abbasid centre intervened, with a protracted campaign by the Abbasid army against a non-Muslim ruler, Babak.[16]

As Abbasid power faltered in the mid-ninth century, rebellions and insurrections became more prolonged, and there were significant threats to the caliphal centre.[17] There were various lengthy insurrections against centralised authority and violent bids for control over the resources of the empire itself – some very successful, others less so. The slave revolt of the Zanj, in southern Iraq, lasted from 868 until 883. The success of the Saffarid warlords of Sistan (western Afghanistan) after 854 ended only with the rise of the Samanids, who went on to rule with de facto inde-pendence in Khurasan from 902. In Egypt first the Tulunids (868–905)

---

[14] For this process of collapse and its consequences: H. Kennedy, 'The decline and fall of the Abbasid caliphate', *Der Islam* 81 (2004), 3–30.

[15] On these rebellions: M. C. Dunn, *The Struggle for Abbasid Egypt* (unpublished PhD thesis, Georgetown University, 1975); P. Booth and A. Marsham, 'Environment, empire, and rebellion in early Islamic Egypt' (forthcoming).

[16] On these revolts in what had been Sasanian territories: P. Crone, *The Nativist Prophets of Early Islamic Iran* (Cambridge, 2012).

[17] Kennedy, 'Decline and fall'.

and then the Ikhshidids (after 935) acted independently of Abbasid control, although they continued to recognise notional Abbasid authority. In the Syrian desert, the Shiʿi Carmathian movement (*Qaramita*) was a serious and persistent threat to Abbasid power in the ninth and early tenth centuries. Ifriqiya (modern Tunisia), which had been held by the Aghlabid dynasty, who were notionally loyal to the Abbasids, fell to a messianic Berber movement in the early tenth century, and a new Fatimid caliphate was declared in Ifriqiya in 909.

Accommodating Newcomers, Disruption and Fragmentation (c.950 to c.1250)

Political culture in the Muslim world in the three centuries following the disintegration of the Abbasid empire in 945 can best be described as growing ever more complex. Traditional, centripetal institutions and ideas of Islamic rule somehow remained intact – at least as symbolic devices of legitimacy and order – despite the centrifugal forces which threatened anarchy from within and vulnerability to invasion from without.[18] Between the mid-tenth-century rise of the Buyid emirate in the central Islamic lands and the Mongol onslaught in the thirteenth, the political borders of the Islamic world changed drastically. Beyond the confines of Abbasid Baghdad, a vast array of rulers struggled to create stable power bases, and a 'commonwealth' of new Islamic political entities supplanted the unified empire.[19] The collapse of Abbasid power in the east even allowed major new, rival caliphates to be proclaimed in the west: in 909 by the Shiʿi Fatimids in North Africa and twenty years later by the Umayyads in al-Andalus. By the early tenth century, the Fatimid caliphs were the rising imperial power in the western and central Islamic world, having conquered Egypt and then Syria from their core lands in Ifriqiya. In 969 they founded Cairo as their imperial capital, and it quickly eclipsed Baghdad as the centre of an extremely ambitious and initially highly successful eastern Mediterranean polity. However, within

---

[18] According to Marshall Hodgson, 'After 945 CE, the most characteristic traits of the classical ʿAbbâsî world, with its magnificent caliphal empire and its Arabic-language culture, were gradually altered so greatly that we must set off a new major era': Hodgson, 'Prologue to Book Three: The establishment of an international civilization', *Venture of Islam, II: The Expansion of Islam in the Middle Periods*, 3.

[19] The term is Fowden's, borrowing from Dimitri Obolensky, *The Byzantine Commonwealth: Eastern Europe 500–1453* (New York, 1971); Fowden, *Empire to Commonwealth*. For the culturo-religious expansion and political rivalries beyond the imperial core lands, amounting to a commonwealth: pp. 78–80. The Latin west's fissures were even more spectacular, yet formed recurrent patterns: pp. 165–74, 271–3, 287–9, 372–5.

a century the last of the region's late antique empires, with their universalist ambitions,[20] was confronted with the same realities as the Abbasids of Baghdad and the Umayyads of Cordoba. A new era was breaking, bringing new elites, new power structures and new ideas of rulership. Yet this new political culture emerged wearing the old robes of Islamic rule and community of the Islamic commonwealth east and west.

So where did the dismemberment of the Abbasid empire leave the Islamic world? The Buyids (945–1055), a dynasty of Daylami origin, controlled much of the geographic centre of the Muslim world – Iraq and Iran – including central Iraq, Fars, Rayy, Isfahan and Jibal.[21] To the east, the Samanids (819–999) ruled Khurasan and Transoxiana, having wrested control of these lands from the Saffarids of Sistan (861–1003). The Hamdanids (905–1004) controlled northern Iraq, while the Daylamis were based in the south-western Caspian region. To the west, the Fatimids (969–1171), who had controlled the Maghreb and Ifriqiya since 909, took over Egypt, Palestine and parts of Greater Syria from the short-lived dynasty of the Ikhshidids in 969. The areas now constituting Algeria and Morocco were divided up for short periods between local powers such as the Hammadids (1015–1152). The Umayyads ruled al-Andalus until 1031, a power sometimes known as the western caliphate, but they fell victim to the same problems as their eastern counterparts: over the next sixty years, the Iberian peninsula was broken up into smaller *taifa* states, ruled by the *muluk al-tawa'if*.

Without being exhaustive, this survey gives a sense of just how many successor polities filled the void of caliphal authority. Over the next three centuries, new powers would emerge from the fringes of the Islamic world, notably the Turkic dynasties of the Ghaznavids (975–1187) and the Seljuks (1055–1194) in the east and the Berber dynasties of the Almoravids (1056–1147) and the Almohads (1130–1269) in the west. Competition for regional pre-eminence between these many dynasties, their local offshoots and opponents was constant, and the multiple frontier zones between them were extremely fluid. Powers of varying size and longevity rose and fell, including the Crusader polities of the Levant (*c.*1099–1291); the Ayyubids in Egypt (*c.*1171–1250) and the Hafsids in Ifriqiya (1229–1574); the Qarakhanids (*c.*840–1211) and the Khwarazmshahs (*c.*1077–1231) in Central Asia; and the Eldiguzids who flourished in north-western Iran and the eastern Transcaucasus during the twelfth century; alongside a myriad of smaller entities such as the Uqaylids of Jazira and Syria (*c.*990–1169), the

---

[20] M. Brett, *The Rise of the Fatimids: The World of the Mediterranean and the Middle East in the Tenth Century CE* (Leiden, 2001).
[21] The following draws heavily on J. Kraemer, *Humanism in the Renaissance of Islam: The Cultural Revival during the Buyid Age* (Leiden, 1993), 31–7.

Mazyadids of central Iraq (*c*.961–*c*.1163) and the Mirdasids in Morocco (823–977). The Mongols proved to be the great equaliser in the thirteenth century: they swept from northern China through Central Asia and into the central Islamic lands, subduing the remnants of these successor polities and establishing the Ilkhanate (1256–1335).

The lexicon of political culture had also expanded by the time the Mongols appeared on the scene. We find many new terms for the rulers of these post-Abbasid successor polities. Although we should bear in mind that a nominal caliphate remained in existence, it now shared the political stage with chief emirs (*amir al-umara'*), sultans, *atabeg*s, maliks and khans. Many of these new power-holders and dynasties started out as governors, slave-soldiers or military commanders in the pay of the caliphate or later successor polities. They represented ethnicities and cultures that, while being part of the larger mosaic of medieval Islamic civilisation, had not initially belonged to the Muslim ruling elite; examples include the Daylamis, Kurds and Turkic peoples. Although culturally diverse, all bar the Mongols adhered to the Muslim faith to some degree; the ethnic and cultural diversity they brought was, at times, paralleled by their sectarian diversity, whether Sunni, Imami Shi'i, Isma'ili Shi'i or Zaydi Shi'i. Besides adding cultural and religious diversity, these new powers also brought with them new ways of organising their rule, founded on a heritage of familial ties and tribal customs, such as family confederations (sometimes known as apanage states) and the *atabeg* system. Taking on new titles as they established their own dynasties, these new players added much to the political culture of their day.

To focus this overview, we shall consider what two of the dominant powers of the era – the Buyids and the Seljuks – brought to the political arena, as well as the problems they faced in establishing and maintaining their presence in the region. Neither was able to establish complete hegemony over the central Islamic lands, let alone an empire along the lines of the Umayyads or early Abbasids.[22] This did not stem from any individual ruler's weakness. Rather, it reflects the increasingly porous nature of the political arena: smaller powers regularly came and went, adding to the region's overall sense of volatility. Another key factor affecting Buyid and Seljuk control was the family-based nature of their ruling institutions: the Buyids ruled as a loose family confederation, while Seljuk household politics played out on a regional level. Both called for

---

[22] The Byzantine emperor, in contrast, retained a considerable degree of control at grass-roots until 1204: pp. 96–8, 200–2, 417–25, 435–8. In the Latin west, the interplay between local and royal powers varied greatly, in line with the latter's effectiveness: pp. 62–73, 148–56, 176–7, 376–80, 384–6, 400–4, 408–9.

the extensive and frequent use of marriage alliances, and this opened up to elite women within the respective kin-groups and networks further pathways to influence and power.[23]

In 945, the Shiʻi emir Ahmad b. Buya entered the Abbasid capital Baghdad and forcibly removed the caliph, al-Mustakfi (944–6), from the throne, replacing him with an Abbasid kinsman, al-Muti. The Abbasid caliphs would remain in Baghdad until its destruction by the Mongols in 1258, but they struggled to regain any control or autonomy. Actual power now lay with the Buyids, who set about governing much of Iraq and Iran.[24] The dynasty was named after Ahmad's father, and its heyday lasted until the early eleventh century.[25] Ahmad and his brothers, Ali and Hasan, came from the mountainous region of Daylam and began to make a name for themselves in Iraq and Iran in the mid-tenth century. Of 'Persian' background, they were able to gain the support of Daylami foot soldiers and Turkish mounted warriors and set themselves apart from the more established powers around them, such as the Ziyarids, the Hamdanids and the Samanids. By 945, Ahmad had gained military control over many of the caliphal lands and proceeded to request *laqab*s (honorific titles) and robes of honour (*khilʻa*) for himself and his brothers from Caliph al-Mustakfi. These were duly granted: Ahmad became Muʻizz al-Dawla (literally 'strengthener of the state'), while Ali was granted the *laqab* of Imad al-Dawla and Hasan that of Rukn al-Dawla (respectively 'support' and 'pillar' of 'the state'). Despite this, Muʻizz al-Dawla soon returned to oust al-Mustakfi. Around a century later, when the Abbasid caliph al-Qaʾim officially recognised al-Malik al-Rahim as chief emir of the Buyids in 1048, both men must have known that the latter's dynasty was on its last legs. The Buyid style of family regime proved to be too much of a burden on an already unstable polity at a time when formidable new powers were entering the region.

---

[23] For versions of family confederations in the Islamic and other spheres, see pp. 241–2; and for the household in their respective political cultures, pp. 240–1. See also pp. 502–4 on patriarchy and the role of women in the three spheres.

[24] Major works on the Buyids include A. Mez, *The Renaissance of Islam*, tr. S. K. Bukhsh and D. S. Margoliouth (London, 1937) [tr. of *Renaissance des Islams* (Heidelberg, 1922)]; A. H. Siddiqi, 'Caliphate and kingship in medieval Persia', *Islamic Culture Hyderabad* 9 (1935), 560–79; 10 (1936), 97–126, 260–80; 11 (1937), 37–59; M. Kabir, *The Buwayhid Dynasty of Baghdad, 334/946–447/1055* (Calcutta, 1964); H. Busse, *Chalif and Grosskonig: die Buyiden im Iraq (945–1055)* (Beirut, 1969); R. P. Mottahedeh, *Loyalty and Leadership in an Early Islamic Society* (London, 2001); *BDI*; C. Cahen, *EI*[2] s.v. 'Buyids/Buwayhids'.

[25] The Buyid age was divided into the early years (945–77); the heyday of empire (977–1012); and the period of decline (1012–55) by Busse, *Chalif und Grosskönig*; see also Kraemer, *Humanism*, 37.

At the beginning of the eleventh century the Turkish Ghaznavids had appeared under the forceful leadership of Mahmud of Ghazna (d. 1030). Initially slave-soldiers attached to the Samanid dynasty in Khurasan, they broke free from their masters, taking much of the former Samanid territory and moving further south towards the Indian sub-continent.[26] The Ghaznavids, although staunch Sunnis, were more focused on the acquisition and control of the eastern borderlands of the Islamic world than in fighting with the Buyids for sectarian reasons. In the 1030s, Mahmud's successors faced a threat to their regional pre-eminence in the form of a new group of Sunni Turkish warriors – the Seljuks. At the beginning of the 1040s, the Seljuks decisively defeated the Ghaznavids, expanding their control of the territory westwards toward Iraq.

The Seljuks' homeland lay to the north-east of the Aral Sea in Central Asia. They were part of a larger confederation of Turkish tribesmen, known collectively as the Oghuz, who had been moving from these lands in the previous centuries.[27] Their name, Seljuk, comes from the eponymous founder of the dynasty, Saljuq b. Duqaq, who converted to Sunni Islam in the early eleventh century and whose descendants would change the face of the central Islamic lands. Saljuq's sons entered the political arena as retainers to the Ghaznavids. Two of his grandsons, Tughril Beg and Chaghri Beg, established themselves by defeating the Ghaznavids at the Battle of Dandanqan in 1040, which opened up to them the region around Khurasan. Making the most of the opportunity, the Seljuks took control of a number of key cities and regions including Khwarazm, Burujird and Hamadhan (1042); Qirmisin (1045); and Isfahan (1046). Although still under the Buyids' thumb, the Abbasids opened lines of communication with the Seljuks without formally recognising them at first. However, in 1055 Tughril Beg entered Baghdad at the request of al-Qa'im: the Seljuk sultanate that he established would last until 1194.[28]

The term 'sultan' was not coined by the Seljuks: Mahmud of Ghazna had already proclaimed himself as such earlier that century. But much as the Buyids had put their own stamp on the position of chief emir, the Seljuks developed the institution of the sultanate. They adopted and adapted the Buyid system of governing their lands by way of family ties,

[26] See C. E. Bosworth, 'The imperial policy of the early Ghaznavids', *Islamic Studies* 1 (1962), 49–82.
[27] On the Seljuks see e.g. D. Durand-Guédy, *Iranian Elites and Turkish Rulers: A History of Isfahan in the Saljuq Period* (London, 2010); *GSE*; C. Lange and S. Mecit (eds), *The Seljuqs: Politics, Society and Culture* (Edinburgh, 2011).
[28] We are referring here to the 'Great Seljuks' (1055–1194) and not various offshoots such as the Seljuks of Rum, Kirman or Iraq, whose dates vary. See *GSE;* Lange and Mecit, *Seljuqs.*

and collectively the early Seljuk set-up has been aptly characterised as 'a loose confederation of semi-independent kingdoms over which the sultan exercised nominal authority [. . .] Only for a brief period towards the end of Malikshah's reign was any degree of unity achieved'.[29] Members of the extended Seljuk family were assigned various regions to govern, although to start with the system was quite centralised.[30] Ruling with the support of their fellow Turkmen warriors and a cadre of extremely capable Persian viziers such as al-Kunduri and Nizam al-Mulk, the Great Seljuks built upon existing institutions and developed a new relationship with the Abbasid caliphate.

The Seljuks have been depicted as the 'saviours of the caliphate', vanquishers of the threat posed by the tenth-century 'Shi'i intermezzo',[31] and their rule has been described as 'the consolidation of Sunni authority as the dominant ethos of rule in the central Islamic lands'.[32] Others have argued that the eleventh-century Sunni revival had its roots in the previous century and that the Seljuk leadership under such figures as Tughril Beg and Nizam al-Mulk adopted a more pragmatic approach to intellectual debates, eschewing the staunch backing of orthodox traditionalists.[33] Either way, the sultans' main focus was to maintain control over the lands they had overrun by means of effective ties with local elites, while also seizing the opportunity to expand their lands whenever possible. Tughril Beg began building works in Baghdad, but neither he nor his successors ever succeeded in making it their capital city; instead they installed an official liaison (*shihna*) to oversee the city on their behalf.[34]

When Tughril Beg died in 1063, his nephew Alp Arslan (1063–72) succeeded him, spending most of his reign on campaign against the

---

[29] A. K. S. Lambton, 'The internal structure of the Saljuq empire', in *CHI* 5, 203–82 at 218.

[30] Modern scholars have tended to distinguish the Great Seljuk empire, which encompasses the reigns of Tughril Beg (1055–63) to Sanjar (1118–53), from the lesser branches of the family. These include the Seljuks of Iraq (1118–94), of Kirman (1041–1187) and of Rum (1077–1243), whose more geographically limited polities were ancillary to, and in some cases continued after, the Great Seljuk empire.

[31] Also known as the 'Iranian intermezzo': the century or so between the decline of Abbasid power and the emergence of the Seljuks which saw various Muslim dynasties from Iran rise to power, including the Tahirids, Sajids, Saffarids, Samanids, Ziyarids, Buyids and Sallarids.

[32] C. E. Bosworth, *EI*² s.v. 'Saldjukids'. For sources on the Seljuks: *Annals of the Saljuq Turks: Selections from al-Kamil fi'l-Ta'rikh of Izz al-Din Ibn al-Athir*, tr. and comm. D. S. Richards (New York, 2002) (for the years 420–90/1029–96/7); D. S. Richards, *The Chronicle of Ibn al-Athir*, 3 vols (London, 2010) (for the years 491–629/1097–1231). On the Persian sources: J. S. Meisami, *Persian Historiography to the End of the Twelfth Century* (Edinburgh, 1999).

[33] For discussion of the socio-political aspects of the Sunni revival: G. Makdisi, 'Sunni revival', in D. H. Richards (ed.), *Islamic Civilization, 950–1150* (Oxford, 1973), 155–68. See also *GSE*, 247 n. 7, 249–51.

[34] A. K. S. Lambton, *EI*², s.v. 'Shihna'.

Fatimids and the Byzantines. Soon after his victory against the latter at the battle of Manzikert in 1071, Alp Arslan was murdered by a prisoner, and his nineteen-year-old son Malikshah (1072–92) succeeded him. For the next twenty years Malikshah fought to secure the Seljuk lands under his rule. In some cases, rivals came from his extended family, underscoring the perennial problem of lacking firm conventions for the transmission of paramount authority. The task of administration fell to a corps of mainly Persian viziers, the most famous of whom, Nizam al-Mulk, ran the Seljuk sultanate almost single-handedly for the duration of Malikshah's reign. Just before his death, Malikshah turned his attention to Baghdad with the hope of establishing a more permanent and personal presence in the city. However, his machinations were unsuccessful, and he died in 1092 without a designated heir. Nizam al-Mulk had died a couple of weeks beforehand, leaving a political vacuum. Their deaths were followed shortly by that of the caliph, al-Muqtadi, and led to a chaotic period of political intrigue.[35]

In the generations following the death of Malikshah, the central Islamic lands were plagued by civil war, invasion and occupation, notably by the Crusaders. The centrifugal forces that had been in abeyance during Malikshah's reign 'now had free play'.[36] Although Sanjar (1118–53) and his supporters considered him the last of the Great Seljuks, the historical record shows that respect for Sanjar ebbed and flowed just as much as his ability to maintain control over the Seljuk lands. Confined in large part to the eastern regions of the sultanate, Sanjar attempted to rule by proxy through his younger kinsmen in Iraq,[37] although the Seljuks of Iraq were more interested in gaining autonomy from their fellow Seljuks and the Abbasid caliphs. And Sanjar had more serious threats on his eastern flank in the form of the Qarakhitay, nomads from the north-eastern approaches of China who had moved into Central Asia around 1125, and from Oghuz tribesmen. In 1153, rebel tribesmen captured and imprisoned Sanjar; although managing to escape in 1156, he died the following year, a broken man. The last of the Seljuks of Iraq, Tughril III b. Arslan, died at the hands of the newly ascendant Khwarazmshahs in 1194. Before we move into the thirteenth century and the arrival of the Mongols, we should note Clifford Bosworth's assessment of relations between caliph and sultan:

[35] C. Hillenbrand, '1092: a murderous year', *Arabist* 15–16 (1995), 281–96.
[36] C. E. Bosworth, 'The political and dynastic history of the Iranian world (AD 1000–1217)', in *CHI* 5, 1–202 at 119.
[37] On the period of Seljuk decline: M. F. Sanaullah, *The Decline of the Saljuqid Empire* (Calcutta, 1938); K. A. Luther, *The Political Transformation of the Saljuq Sultanate of Iraq and Western Iran, 1152–1187* (unpublished PhD thesis, Princeton University, 1964); and, importantly, *GSE*.

Yet through the co-existence for something like one hundred and thirty years of the two dynasties, the conditions were created for the development within Islam, even if dictated by practical necessity, of the concept of the caliph-imam as spiritual and moral leader and the sultan, in this case the Saldjuk one, as secular, executive leader of a larger proportion of the Muslims [...].[38]

On the surface this looks like a simple division of labour between the two powers. It is only when we begin to delve deeper and address the methods by which the myriad powers sought legitimacy, established themselves and maintained control over their lands that a much more complex system emerges.[39]

Accommodating Newcomers, Disruption – and Tendencies towards Stabilisation (c. 1250 to c. 1500)

Despite considerable instability, the later 'medieval' period saw continued expansion, and the Islamic world now reached into Sub-Saharan Africa and South-East Asia. Its political geography gradually stabilised, culminating in the rise of its great early modern empires,[40] formidable powers which put an end to centuries of political fragmentation. Three regions dominated its political history, each with its own regional dynamics: al-Andalus and North Africa; the eastern Mediterranean from the Nile to the Euphrates; and the West Asian landmass beyond the Euphrates, stretching into Transoxiana and Anatolia. Without denying the significance of al-Andalus and its neighbours, we will focus primarily on the latter two regions, termed the Nile-to-Oxus region when taken together.

For much of the Islamic world, 1258 was a symbolic ground zero: it was then that the Mongol leader Hülegü – grandson of the formidable Genghis (Jingiz, Chingiz) Khan (1206–27) – and his armies raided the ancient capital of Baghdad and ended half a millennium of Islamic leadership by executing the last Abbasid caliph and his family. Left without a supreme guide and therefore without divine sanction and the prospect of salvation, the *umma* (community of believers) was forced to come to terms with this new challenging reality and would continue to do so in highly creative ways.

The Abbasid caliphate was soon reinvented in one of the new centres of the Islamic world, Cairo. This was the capital of the 'Turkish' (or Mamluk)

---

[38] Bosworth, *EI²* s.v. 'Saldjukids'.
[39] As now argued by *GSE*, 135–45, 151–5. For the proliferation of claimants to imperial authority in Byzantium after 1204: pp. 187–9, 321–4; and for the various means of legitimising royal rule in the west: pp. 56–8, 62–3, 255–9, 266–71.
[40] Especially the Ottomans in the west, the Safavids in Iran and the Mughals in India.

sultanate of Egypt and Syria (1250–1517),[41] newly emerging around the only military leadership to have resisted Hülegü and his armies. While the Mongols and their Turco-Mongol successors set up various unstable khanates to the east and north, the sultanate became one of the more stable areas of the Islamic world. And while most of the Mongol elites adapted only very gradually to the predominantly Islamic identities of their new territories in the eastern Mediterranean, sovereignty, culture and religion were – at least theoretically – safeguarded in an uninterrupted continuity with the past and offered a safe haven for the community's future. The Cairo Sultanate rested heavily on the achievements of Saladin (Salah ad-Din Yusuf b. Ayyub) and his heirs of the Ayyubid dynasty (c.1171–1250). Of Kurdish origin, Saladin had been sent to Shiʻi-ruled Fatimid Egypt by his post-Seljuk Zengid lord, Nur ad-Din. Military successes against the Crusaders led to his appointment as Fatimid vizier in 1169, despite his Zengid allegiance. On the death of the last Fatimid caliph, Saladin abolished the Fatimid caliphate and restored Egypt's nominal integration in the Abbasid caliphal order, at that time still centred in Baghdad; shortly afterwards he was proclaimed an autonomous ruler in Egypt. A decade of conquests followed, including most of the Crusader principalities, and soon the Ayyubids were ruling over Egypt, Syria, most of Yemen, the Hijaz and northern Mesopotamia. The different sets of dynastic and non-dynastic 'Turkish' rulers who succeeded them from the 1250s onwards formed a relatively stable, centralised leadership over most of these lands, referred to as the sultanate of Egypt and Syria, or the Cairo Sultanate. In the course of the fourteenth century the sultan of Cairo even managed to extend his political authority and symbolic influence over some of the former Mongol territories beyond the Euphrates and the Taurus mountains, as well as over coastal zones of the Red and, to some extent even, Arabian Seas which were becoming increasingly important commercially. In North Africa and al-Andalus, four local dynasties of Berber origin, with their political centres at Granada, Fez, Tlemcen and Tunis, emerged as local successors to the former Berber empires of the Almohads and Almoravids.[42] Much like the sultans in Cairo, they upheld and adapted the political cultures of their predecessors in ways that made for unprecedented stability.[43]

---

[41] For a discussion of the sultanate's name: pp. 233–4.

[42] On the Berber – or Imazighen (s. Amazigh) – empires: A. K. Bennison, *The Almoravid and Almohad Empires* (Edinburgh, 2016). The local dynasties were the Nasrids at Granada (1232–1492), the Marinids at Fez (1217–1465), the Zayyanids at Tlemcen (1236–1555) and the Hafsids at Tunis (1229–1574). See F. Rodríguez Mediano, 'The post-Almohad dynasties in al-Andalus and the Maghrib (seventh–ninth/thirteenth–fifteenth centuries)', in *NCHI* 2, 106–43.

[43] This period tends to be cursorily treated and from the perspective of the rise of pre-modern Muslim empires, although useful overviews include: P. M. Holt, *The Age of the*

Mongol expansion into most of Eurasia resulted in a rash of new polities springing up. Originally apanages of leading members of the Jingizid family, they soon went their separate ways. The Pontic-Caspian steppes to the north of the Black Sea saw the rise of the Golden Horde (1223–1502), which took on a Muslim guise unusually early. In eastern Anatolia, Azerbaijan, Mesopotamia and Iran, Hülegü's descendants established a regional Mongol power, the Ilkhanate (1256–1335; 'il-khan' stands for – depending on the interpretation – either 'subordinate khan' or 'sovereign khan'). This Hülegüid dynasty experimented with various creeds before rather grudgingly turning to Sunni Islam, followed by the majority of its Mongol elites. Further east, in the region of Transoxiana, similar Jingizid dynastic polities sprang up in the early to mid-thirteenth century, organised around the khans of Chaghadai (1227–1363), named after Genghis Khan's second son. All drew on their experience from the steppes of Central Asia to remould age-old local traditions of political, social, cultural and economic organisation. Their elites engaged in fierce competition for resources, with internecine warfare constantly threatening to break up their polities. Most of these Islamising Jingizid polities did just that during the fourteenth century, opening up control of politics and resources to others. Local tribal chiefs and Turco-Mongol military leaders soon filled the vacuum, manoeuvring themselves into the Jingizid legacy and carving out new realms for them and their followers. They used Jingizid-style ideologies of tribal genealogy and divine sanction to explain their rise to power. The emergence of these new, post-Mongol dynasties, elites and ideologies during the fourteenth century fundamentally redefined the political landscape of the entire Nile-to-Oxus region for centuries to come.[44]

The best-known, and by far the most characteristic, exponent of this process is the illustrious Timur (Temür, Tamberlaine) in distant Samarqand. Beginning as a military commander and tribal leader in the Chaghadai Mongol domains of Transoxiana, he married into the Chaghadai Jingizid dynasty and embarked upon a career of more than three decades of military conquest and raiding in east and west. He died

Crusades: The Near East from the Eleventh Century to 1517 (London, 1986); D. Morgan, *Medieval Persia, 1040–1797* (New York, 1988); Hodgson, 'Book Four: Crisis and renewal: the age of Mongol prestige', *Venture of Islam, II*, 369–574.

[44] See B. Spuler, *Die Mongolen in Iran: Politik, Verwaltung und Kultur der Ilchanenzeit 1220–1350* (Berlin, 1963); idem, *Die Goldene Horde: Die Mongolen in Russland, 1223–1502* (Wiesbaden, 1962); C. Cahen, *The Formation of Turkey: The Seljukid Sultanate of Rum, Eleventh to Fourteenth Century* (New York, repr. 2001); D. Morgan, *The Mongols* (Oxford, 1986); Morgan, *Medieval Persia*; D. Aigle, *Le Fars sous la domination Mongole: politique et fiscalite (XIIIe—XIVe s.)* (Paris, 2005); P. Jackson, *The Mongols and the Islamic World: From Conquest to Conversion* (New Haven, CT, 2017).

suddenly in 1405 en route to invade Ming China, leaving his realm in Iran, Khurasan and Transoxiana to the rivalry of his sons, grandsons and generals. The Timurid polity eventually re-emerged in these regions under Timur's son Shah Rukh (1409–47). The cultural patronage and efflorescence generally associated with Shah Rukh and his Timurid competitors and successors was bedazzling, but it could barely mask the realm's fragility. After Shah Rukh's death, the Timurid lands were split between different members of the dynasty and Turkmen outsiders, only to succumb to internal and external pressures in the early sixteenth century. One Timurid adventurer, Babur (1483–1530), ended up in Delhi, where he managed to initiate the continuation of Timur's legacy in the form of the long-standing Mughal empire (1526–1858).[45]

The empowerment of Turkmen outsiders was another legacy of both Mongol conquests and Timurid raids. The vacuums left by the Jingizids and the Timurids in, respectively, Asia Minor in the fourteenth century and Azerbaijan in the early fifteenth were filled by local Oghuz Turkish leaderships and their pastoral nomadic followers who had roamed the area since migrating there in the late eleventh century. In Azerbaijan, rival transhumant Turkmen confederations – the Black Sheep (Qara Qoyunlu) and White Sheep (Aq Qoyunlu) – appeared under dynamic tribal leaders such as the former's Qara Yusuf (1389–1400, 1406–20) and Jahan Shah (1438–67) and the latter's Qara Uthman (1378–1435) and Uzun Hasan (1466–78). Jahan Shah and Uzun Hasan in particular managed to transform their polities into ambitious regional empires of conquest, reaching from eastern Anatolia to the Persian Gulf and Khurasan, in constant competition with the Timurids in the east and with other Turkmen principalities in the west. These Oghuz Turkmen empires would eventually consolidate with the help of a religious overlay: in the early sixteenth century, the charismatic leader of an immensely popular Sufi movement, Ismaʿil, assumed its leadership and welded together messianic ideology and Turkmen tribal muscle into the formidable new Safavid empire (1501–1722).[46]

That the Safavids eventually adopted a Turco-Persianate rather than a Turkic culture had everything to do with that other great 'gunpowder empire' of the Islamic world: the Ottomans. In 1514, the Ottoman sultan

[45] On Timur: B. F. Manz, *The Rise and Rule of Tamerlane* (Cambridge, 1989); for the Timurids: *idem, Power, Politics, and Religion in Timurid Iran* (Cambridge, 2007); *TIT*; for Timurid literary culture, trans-regional intellectual networks, and political patronage: *INTI*.

[46] On these Turkish imperial enterprises: J. Woods, *The Aqquyunlu: Clan, Confederation, Empire*, rev. edn (Salt Lake City, UT, 1976; repr. 1999); for the Safavids' beginnings: A. J. Newmann, *Safavid Iran: Rebirth of a Persian Empire; Persia between the Medieval and the Modern* (London, 2006).

Selim (1512–20) won a decisive battle against Isma'il and his Turkmen supporters at Chaldiran in Azerbaijan. This victory enabled Selim to prevail in the local scramble for influence among the tribes of eastern Anatolia and to drive the Safavids eastwards. Like the Safavids', the Ottomans' complex history was rooted in the Oghuz Turkish leaderships which had filled the vacuum left by the Jingizid disintegration in Asia Minor. Here, too, the fourteenth century saw the empowerment of Oghuz Turkish tribes that had been migrating westwards into former Byzantine provinces over the preceding two centuries. Under the leadership of local lords, tribal chiefs and successful military commanders, dozens of principalities (*beyliks*) emerged throughout Anatolia: a volatile constellation of territorial rivals, all 'strongly Turkish and tentatively Islamic'.[47]

One successful *beylik* was that of the Karamanids (1256–1483) in central Anatolia, with its political centre in the former Seljuk city of Konya. Another emerged in the newly occupied Byzantine territories of western Anatolia. It coalesced around the energetic leadership, successful raiding and territorial expansion of the semi-mythical Osman (d. 1324) and, in particular, of his son Orkhan (*c*.1324–62) and would go on to become the Osmanli (Ottoman) sultanate. Orkhan and his immediate successors were as capable in battle and as adept at expanding their territories as other Anatolian Turkish leaders. What set them apart was their pragmatic integration of both local Greek and Turkish power elites and their successful leadership of the Oghuz Turkish tribes' ongoing migration westwards, across the Dardanelles and into the Christian realms of the Byzantines, Bulgarians and Serbians in Thrace and the Balkans. Thus, by the second half of the fourteenth century, the Ottomans were uniquely equipped to impose their overlordship on most of Anatolia's *beyliks*, as well as over large parts of the Balkans. Timurid and Ottoman waves of expansionism were bound to clash. However, Timur's defeat of the Ottoman army and capture of its sultan near Ankara in 1402, and his restoration of local Turkmen *beyliks* and tribal leaderships, proved only a temporary setback.[48]

When Byzantine Constantinople fell to the Ottoman sultan Mehmed II (1451–81) on 29 May 1453, the prestige it gave him enabled him to transform his polity into a sultanate of imperial, 'Roman' standing. The key to this transformation remained military violence and expansion both

---

[47] C. Imber, *The Ottoman Empire, 1300–1650: The Structure of Power*, 3rd edn (London, 2019), 6.
[48] See esp. C. Kafadar, *Between Two Worlds: The Construction of the Ottoman State* (Berkeley, 1995); H. Lowry, *The Nature of the Early Ottoman State* (Albany, NY, 2003); D. Kastritis, *The Sons of Bayezid: Empire Building and Representation in the Ottoman Civil War of 1402–1413* (Leiden, 2007).

east and west. Competition with the White Sheep Turkmen and the Safavids to the east culminated in 1514 with the battle of Chaldiran. Further west, in Asia Minor, Mehmed's successors managed to subdue and integrate the last remaining Anatolian *beylik*s. In the autumn and winter of 1516–17 they completed their scramble for regional pre-eminence, adding Syria, Egypt and the Hijaz to their domains. Thus, by the sixteenth century, Ottoman military successes had been transformed into a more complex, grander and coherent political organisation under the direct control of members of Osman's Sunni dynasty and its many military and administrative representatives. Another early modern empire was emerging.[49]

Most severely affected by the Ottomans' rise and expansion was the 'Turkish' sultanate of Egypt and Syria (1250–1517).[50] Despite its claim to be the only Muslim polity in western Asia that had managed to stem the tide of Mongol infidels in the mid-thirteenth century, it was as much the product of contingent change and transformation around this time as any other polity. Ayyubid dynastic power in Egypt and Syria faced existential threats in the form of the crusading Latins – in particular Louis IX of France and the Seventh Crusade from 1248 to 1250 – and warmongering Mongols. These threats had generated ambivalent and contradictory responses: violent competition for Saladin's legacy, leading to fragmenta-tion and even its dissolution; and at the same time a closing of ranks behind the powerful military commanders of Egypt's last Ayyubid ruler, al-Malik al-Salih (1240–9), first in Egypt and then, by 1260, in Syria, too.[51]

The power that emerged is mostly referred to in modern studies as the Mamluk sultanate, in token of the common social status of the first gener-ation of its new political leaders, almost all of whom entered Egypt and Syria as military slaves (*mamluk*s). In contemporary sources they were known as the Dynasty of the Turks (*dawlat al-atrak*), commemorating

---

[49] S. Har-El, *Struggle for Domination in the Middle East: The Ottoman-Mamluk War, 1485–91* (Leiden, 1995); A. Allouche, *The Origins and Development of the Ottoman-Safavid Conflict (906–962/1500–1555)* (Berlin, 1983).

[50] We lack an English-language survey. For the period to 1382: R. Irwin, *The Middle East in the Middle Ages: The Early Mamluk Sultanate, 1250–1382* (London, 1986); focusing on military society: J. Loiseau, *Les Mamelouks: XIIIe–XVIe siècle: une expérience du pouvoir dans l'Islam médiéval* (Paris, 2014).

[51] On Ayyubid-Mamluk continuities: R. S. Humphreys, 'The emergence of the Mamluk army', *Studia Islamica* 45 (1977), 67–99; *Studia Islamica* 46 (1977), 147–82; D. Ayalon, 'From Ayyubids to Mamluks', *Revue d'études islamiques* 49 (1981), 43–57. One reason for the intense scholarly attention paid to the transition is the remarkable, but very short-lived, reign as female sultan of Shajar al-Durr, widow of al-Malik al-Salih: G. Schregle, *Die Sultanin von Ägypten: Šağarat al-Durr in der arabischen Geschichtsschreibung und Literatur* (Wiesbaden, 1971); A. Levanoni, 'Šağar ad-Durr: a case of female sultanate in medieval Islam', in U. Vermeulen and J. Van Steenbergen (eds), *Egypt and Syria in the Fatimid, Ayyubid and Mamluk Eras III* (Leuven, 2001), 209–18.

the Qipchaq Turkish origins of most of their triumphant commanders. Throughout the second half of the thirteenth century and the first decade of the fourteenth, warbands and their *mamluk* commanders – including the sultan as *primus inter pares* – proved more than capable of continuing to defend and dominate from Egypt the giant frontier zone that the Syrian regions became, under constant threat from Mongol II-Khans and Latin Crusaders alike.[52]

In the course of the lengthy third reign of Sultan al-Nasir Muhammad b. Qalawun (1293–4, 1299–1309, 1310–41), the renewed sultanate emerged victorious, driving all Crusaders and other Latins from the Syrian littoral. It also imposed peace upon the Ilkhanate, which had rapidly fragmented into several successor states after the death of the last Ilkhan in 1335. While the Mongol tide eventually ebbed, leaving chaos and total disintegration in the east, a powerful political formation remained in Egypt, Syria and the Red Sea area, tightly and self-consciously organised around the 'house of Qalawun' and his son Muhammad, as well as around the memory of the sultanate's political continuity and military victory. Throughout most of the fourteenth century this Qalawunid sultanate of Cairo was the hegemonic mainstay in West Asian Islam, bustling with cultural and economic activity that connected east and west ever more closely in an era of polycentric post-Mongol territorial and political transformations.

However, the first decade of the fifteenth century was a time of chaos, political upheaval and extreme internecine violence for the sultanate. This was partly due to the socio-economic havoc unleashed by the Black Death, which affected the Middle East in 1348–9, and by subsequent epidemics and natural disasters; partly to the break-up of the Qalawunid dynasty and a series of less convincing replacements towards the end of the fourteenth century; and partly to Timur's brief but devastating passage through Syria in 1400. The sultanate was rebuilt by a generation of fresh *mamluk* sultans, notably al-Mu'ayyad Shaykh (1412–21), Barsbay (1422–37) and Jaqmaq (1437–53), strongmen of mostly Circassian origin. Together with local experts and administrators, in the early fifteenth century they managed to create what was in many ways – territorial and social – a new and different political order in the Syro-Egyptian region. In political, military and socio-economic terms it was no less successful than its predecessors, holding its own on the wider stage with the Ottomans, Timurids and various Turkmen leaderships. This regional hegemony pulsating out from the Citadel of Cairo did not substantially change until after the mid-fifteenth century.[53]

---

[52] For detail on the Mongol-Mamluk conflict: R. Amitai, *Mongols and Mamluks: The Mamluk-Ilkhanid War, 1260–1281* (Cambridge, 1995).

[53] J. Loiseau, *Reconstruire la Maison du Sultan, 1350–1450: ruine et recomposition de l'ordre urbain au Caire* (Cairo, 2010).

The gradual emergence in the era after Timur of powerful and ambitious political enterprises to the north and east, especially Uzun Hasan's White Sheep Turkmen and Mehmed II's Ottoman Turks, did pose a challenge to Cairo's hegemony and put a strain on its resources. This, in turn, affected the internal balance of power: between *mamluk* military entrepreneurs; sultans from their ranks such as Inal (1453–61), Khushqadam (1461–7), Qaytbay (1468–96) and Qanisawh (1501–16); their troops and wider entourages; various non-military groups such as courtiers and legal or financial experts; and the leaderships of diverse local communities in and beyond the urban centres of Egypt, Syria, south-eastern Anatolia, Cyprus and the Hijaz. Like anywhere else across fifteenth-century Muslim western Asia, this was a fragile equilibrium between ever-changing central and local interest-groups, political partners and opponents. And like anywhere else, this volatility defined the course of local and central politics throughout the fifteenth century. However, more than anywhere else, in Cairo this took place in a context of apparent structural continuity. The sultan's court, its agents and its offshoots grew into a new central pre-modern 'state': it represented at the same time a non-dynastic hegemony and a weighty bureaucracy, the latter set up to maintain the former, and vice versa.[54] But early in the sixteenth century, the balance of power shifted in an entirely new direction with the shocking appearance of Portuguese ships in the sultanate's backyard – the Red Sea. This showed up the central state's growing difficulty in accommodating change and loss of regional hegemony. When the new tide of Ottoman imperial ambition reached Syria and Egypt in 1516–17, the long-standing sultanate of Cairo was quite easily swept away. After almost nine centuries, Egypt and Syria were incorporated once more into the realm of the new 'emperor' of Constantinople.[55]

Political and Other Elites: War, Religion, Kinship – and Bureaucrats

Early Islam: Multiple Elites and Monarchy

The history of elite political culture in the early Islamic world is, above all, a history of imperial conquest and imperial transformation.[56] The first

---

[54] J. Van Steenbergen *et al.*, 'The Mamlukization of the Mamluk sultanate? State formation and the history of fifteenth century Egypt and Syria, part II: comparative solutions and a new research agenda', *History Compass* 14 (2016), 560–9 at 565.

[55] A point made by Humphreys, 'Egypt in the world system', 245. On this shifting of the internal balances of power: C. Petry, *Protectors or Praetorians: The Last Mamluk Sultans and Egypt's Waning as a Great Power* (Albany, NY, 1994).

[56] Note the comparisons with modern empire and migration in *SOH*, 30; also P. Crone, 'Introduction', in her *From Arabian Tribes to Islamic Empire: Army, State and Society in the*

conquering Arabian groups usually sought to live apart from the conquered populations in new garrison towns (*amsar*), such as Basra and
Kufa in Iraq. The monotheist Arabian settlers also sought to perpetuate
a separate identity by insisting that joining their monotheist group
entailed also becoming affiliated with an Arabian tribe. This was achieved
through the patronage of a member of that tribe (*wala'*, or 'clientage',
whence *mawali*, for this period, 'non-Arab Muslims').[57] Arabian armies
had replaced (and occasionally assimilated) Roman and Sasanian ones,
and the fiscal resources of the defeated empires were now collected for the
benefit of this new ruling minority. Payments were still largely made in
precious metal coin. Imperial political power was notionally centralised at
the somewhat peripatetic court of the Umayyad caliph in Greater Syria
(*Bilad al-Sham*), but the governors of the vast provinces into which the
empire was divided were also powerful figures, with their own regional
courts. These governors distributed the provincial tax revenues among
their local garrisons and passed only a small percentage on to the Syrian
centre.[58]

Within the provinces, power was also relatively devolved. The vast
majority of the population of the empire was non-Arabian and non-
Muslim. The indigenous peoples of the conquered provinces probably
accounted for well over 90 per cent of the population of the early eighth-
century Muslim empire.[59] As a result many local, pre-Islamic, political
structures persisted in some form, albeit transformed by interactions with
the new ruling elite. In Roman territories, these were local, provincial
structures. Higher levels of parts of Iranian society survived intact, since
flight to a surviving imperial centre was not an option. Such Roman and
Iranian notables are occasionally visible in the sources as the local leaders

Near East c. 600–850 (Aldershot, 2008), vii–xiii at vii; *eadem*, 'Imperial trauma: the case of
the Arabs', *Common Knowledge* 12 (2006), 107–16 at 116; repr. in her *From Arabian
Tribes to Islamic Empire*, no. 12.
[57] On clientage: J. Nawas and M. Bernards (eds), *Patronate and Patronage in Early and
Classical Islam* (Leiden, 2005).
[58] *SOH*, esp. 37–40; K. Morimoto, *The Fiscal Administration of Egypt in the Early Islamic
Period* (Kyoto, 1981); M. Morony, *Iraq after the Muslim Conquest* (Princeton, 1984);
C. F. Robinson, *Empire and Elites after the Muslim Conquest: The Transformation of North
Mesopotamia* (Cambridge, 2000), esp. 63–89. On the devolved nature of power in the
empire: A. Nef and M. Tillier, 'Introduction: les voies de l'innovation dans un empire
islamique polycentrique', *Annales islamologiques* 45 (2011), 1–19; for a close study of the
uniquely well-documented province of Egypt: P. Sijpesteijn, *Shaping a Muslim State: The
World of a Mid-Eighth Century Egyptian Official* (Oxford, 2013). For the channelling of
revenue streams to Constantinople: pp. 309–10, 418–20, 432–5; such channeling of
resources towards the ruler's power base only developed in the west in the later middle
ages: pp. 149, 150, 169, 382, 384, 405–6.
[59] R. Bulliet, *Conversion to Islam in the Medieval Period: An Essay in Quantitative History*
(Cambridge, MA,1979).

who negotiated with Muslim tax-collectors and governors and continued to function as authority figures in their communities.[60] Some people of non-Arabian heritage found their way to the centre of imperial power by virtue of their talents as politicians and administrators, usually as *mawali* – members of the new ruling groups associated with a particular Muslim patron[61] – or as power-brokers or interlocutors of some kind. Hence, figures such as the patriarchs of the various Christian churches or the *gaon* of the rabbinical Jews in Iraq gained from their association with caliphal power.[62] Other regions of the former empires escaped central control almost completely, largely by virtue of their remote or inaccessible character.[63]

The process of imperial conquest and the consolidation of imperial power led in turn to the formation of new Arabian tribal identities and a new sense of 'Arab' as an ethnic category, referring to a shared heritage and linguistic identity.[64] However, the hegemony of the conquering Arabian elite also began to lose ground. The eighth and ninth centuries witnessed processes of Arabisation and also Islamisation.[65] The hierarchies established in the seventh and early eighth centuries did not long survive the pressure of non-Arabians wanting to join Muslim society – an ambition that could be justified in some cases by claiming Arab ethnicity but increasingly could also be grounded in the universalist monotheism of Islam. Arab

[60] Morony, *Iraq*; Robinson, *Empire and Elites*; P. Sijpesteijn, 'Landholding patterns in early Islamic Egypt', *Journal of Agrarian Change* 9 (2009), 120–33; for some very suggestive discussion of late Roman structures and the formation of an Islamic state: M. Legendre, 'Neither Byzantine nor Islamic? The duke of the Thebaid and the formation of the Umayyad state', *Historical Research* 89 (2016), 3–18. For the survival and development of provincial elites in Byzantium: pp. 417–18. The outlook for power elites to the north of the Alps and the Rhône was generally more uncertain: pp. 143–5, 147–50.

[61] *SOH*, 51; A. J. Wensinck and P. Crone, *EI²*, s.v. 'Mawla'.

[62] For an early instance of caliphal intervention in Christian affairs: 'Extract from the *Maronite Chronicle* (AD 664+)', in A. Palmer et al. (eds), *The Seventh Century in the West-Syrian Chronicles* (Liverpool, 1991), 29–35 at 29–31; for interactions between the patriarch of Alexandria and the Muslim authorities in the seventh to ninth centuries: *The History of the Patriarchs of the Coptic Church of Alexandria*, ed. and tr. B. Evetts (Paris, 1904); on the *gaon*: J. Brand et al., 'Gaon', in M. Berenbaum and F. Skolnik (eds), *Encyclopaedia Judaica*, 2nd edn (Detroit, MI, 2007), vii:380–86. With thanks to Philip Wood.

[63] On Armenia: A. Vacca, *Non-Muslim Provinces under Early Islam: Islamic Rule and Iranian Legitimacy in Armenia and Caucasian Albania* (Cambridge, 2017); on Iran: P. Crone, *Nativist Prophets of Early Islamic Iran* (Cambridge, 2012).

[64] Webb, *Imagining the Arabs*; P. Webb, 'Identity and social formation in the early caliphate', in H. Berg (ed.), *The Routledge Handbook on Early Islam* (Abingdon, 2017), 129–58.

[65] For 'Arabisation' in Egypt: Sijpesteijn, 'Landholding patterns'; on the challenges in understanding Arabisation and Islamisation in Egypt in the early period: Y. Lev, 'Coptic rebellions and the Islamization of medieval Egypt (8th–10th century): medieval and modern perceptions', *JSAI* 39 (2012), 303–44.

ethnic identity became more closely bound to Islamic faith, as attested by disputes about the tax status of Christian Arab tribes and conversions of many of these groups in the later eighth century.[66] At the same time, however, Islamic faith became more open to groups that remained non-Arab in ethnic identity.

This success of a universalist Islam, detached to a significant extent from 'Arabness', saw the Muslim elites of Arabian heritage lose their exclusive power as a military and tax-collecting class. Various non-Arab regional populations adopted Islam as they took military and fiscal power, in the context of factional conflict at the imperial centre and the limited reach of the caliphal armies;[67] to become Muslim was to make a bid to participate in the benefits of belonging to the ruling elite of the Islamic world empire. The pre-eminent example of this process is the Abbasid Revolution of 750. Many of the soldiers of the revolutionary armies were drawn from Khurasan. They appear to have converted to Islam as they joined the movement, hoping to replace the existing Syrian military elite at the centre of the empire. Following the revolution's success, the Khurasanians and their descendants dominated at the imperial centre, in the army and in many of the provinces, for three generations, from the 750s until the 820s.[68]

Further factional conflict within the ruling Abbasid family led to the increasing use of soldiers recruited on the eastern frontiers, including many 'slave soldiers' (*ghulams*, *mamluks*), owned by the caliph or his close relatives. From the 820s these Transoxianan and Central Asian Turkish cavalry became the military mainstay of the caliphate. However, many of the Turks' commanders soon developed their own autonomous power – either at the centre, in the Iraqi capitals of Baghdad and Samarra, or in the provinces, notably in Egypt, which became an independent emirate under first the Tulunids (868–905) and then the Ikhshidids (935–69), which were both ruling groups of Central Asian heritage. With the complete collapse of the military and fiscal power of the Abbasid caliph in the 920s, further non-Arab groups moved into Iraq – including the Buyids, whose ancestors had probably converted to Shiʻi Islam in the highlands of Daylam. New groups that claimed Arabian

---

[66] For material which dates from the era of the Islamisation of groups perceived to be Arabs, see e.g. on the Christian Banu Taghlib: Abu Yusuf, *Kitab al-kharaj*, tr . A. Ben Shemesh, *Taxation in Islam: Abu Yusuf's Kitab al-Kharaj* (Leiden, 1969), 90–2, 141–2. With thanks to Simon Pierre.

[67] P. Crone, *Early Islamic Political Thought* (Edinburgh, 2004), 84–6.

[68] See pp. 458–9; E. Daniel, *The Political and Social History of Khurasan under Abbasid Rule* (Minneapolis, MN, 1979); S. S. Agha, *The Revolution which Toppled the Umayyads: Neither Arab nor Abbasid* (Leiden, 2003).

heritage also emerged in Iraq and Syria, such as the Hamdanids of Mosul and Aleppo.

Political ambition could also be expressed by bids for autonomy rather than bids for power at the centre. In western North Africa, large numbers of Berber tribesmen had already joined the ranks of the imperial military in the late seventh and early eighth centuries, and after the 730s new Berber groups formed independent Islamic polities in the Maghreb. Other North African Berbers had participated in the conquest and settlement of the Iberian peninsula and were found in the armies of the Spanish Umayyads after 756. The Kutama Berbers also supplied the initial military impetus for the foundation of the Fatimid empire at the turn of the ninth and tenth centuries. At the other end of the Islamic world, in Transoxiana, Samanid independence was built on a similar assimilation of Turkic peoples into the Muslim military on the eastern frontier; while notionally loyal to the Abbasid caliphs in Iraq, they ruled a large western Central Asian empire as an independent political elite with a distinctive Persian-language court culture.

Just as the Abbasids had made extensive use of slave soldiers and eunuch palace servants (*khadim*s), so did the tenth-century successor polities. Indeed, the use of military slaves would remain a distinctive feature of pre-modern Islamic political culture. In the early centuries of Islam, war on the frontiers brought North Africans, northern Europeans and Turks into the Muslim armies. Trade on the same frontiers brought peoples from further afield – notably Slavs, Sub-Saharan Africans and other people from the Caucasus and Central Asia. *Ghulam*s and *khadim*s were very high-status slaves and can certainly be considered part of the ruling elite. Although they were sometimes owned by their master, who was often the emir or the caliph, they were also sometimes freed to become his clients (*mawali*); others appear to have entered military service as vassals of their commanders, according to customs with roots in Central Asia. Freed or slave, they were quite different from the domestic slaves and servants of non-elite Muslims and still more so from agricultural slaves. Some gained great wealth and significant political and military power, making and unmaking emirs and caliphs.[69]

Despite the emergence of non-Arab populations, both slaves and free, as military and political elites in the ninth and tenth centuries, the formative

---

[69] On the ninth-century revolt of the agricultural slaves in Iraq: A. Popovic, *The Revolt of African Slaves in Iraq in the 3rd/9th Century*, tr. D. Waines (Princeton, 1998); for the first Turkish armies of the caliphs: M. Gordon, *The Breaking of a Thousand Swords: A History of the Turkish Military of Samarra (AH 200–275/815–889 CE)* (Albany, NY, 2001); for the Samanids: J. Paul, *The State and the Military: The Samanid Case* (Bloomington, IN, 1994); on eunuchs at Islamic royal courts: D. Ayalon, *Eunuchs, Caliphs and Sultans: A Study in Power Relationships* (Jerusalem, 1999); although largely focused on later periods, see also S. E. Marmon (ed.), *Slavery in the Islamic Middle East* (Princeton, 1999).

decades of Arabian Islam had been crucial in shaping Islamic political culture. Many of the new ninth- and tenth-century political entities had rulers that might be characterised in very broad terms as Berber, Persian or Turkish in ethnicity (or in the basis of their military and administrative power where the ruling political elite remained Arab). However, Arabic and New Persian were the languages in which formal public affairs were conducted in every one of them. Furthermore, various interpretations of Islam as a religion (and so also as political ideology and legal system) were the basis of political culture in them all. The movements led by Babak (d. 837) and Mardavij (d. 935) are the last major non-Muslim, or at least highly syncretic, political movements within the borders of the Muslim empire. (Notably, both were in post-Sasanian Iran, which had been completely absorbed by Islam and where flight was not an option.) Furthermore, these non-Muslim Iranian revolts were failures – the successful formation of new regional centres of power in the Islamic world always entailed the assertion of political identity in Islamic terms.[70] Where groups did sometimes resist centralised control in the deserts, marshes, steppes or mountains, they usually did so not as non-Muslims but as distinctive minority Muslim groups (albeit groups that could be characterised as heretics by their opponents) – Kharijites, Carmathians or Zaydi Shi'is.[71] None of the successor polities of the Muslim commonwealth were simple continuations of pre-Islamic political formations, and – with the one notable exception of Christian Armenia – none perpetuated a pre-Islamic religion as their political ideology.

The conversion of peoples who claimed a non-Arab ethnic identity appears to have accelerated from the second half of the eighth century; in many pre-Islamic urban centres, Muslims probably outnumbered non-Muslims for the first time at some point between the mid-eighth and the early tenth centuries.[72] The system of clientage in the sense of affiliation to an Arabian tribal group seems to have disappeared during the eighth

---

[70] Kennedy, 'Decline and fall'; R. Bulliet, *Islam: The View from the Edge* (New York, 1994).

[71] These regions were described by Xavier de Planhol as 'terres d'insolence': *Les Fondements géographiques de l'histoire de l'Islam* (Paris, 1968), 59. De Planhol elaborated the question of religious 'heresy' and terrain in his *Le Monde islamique: essai de géographie religieuse* (Paris, 1957), 79–91. For brief comments on this in an early Islamic context, and comparisons with historiography on Roman Christianities, see A. Marsham, '"Those who make war on God and His Messenger": some implications of recent scholarship on rebellion, banditry and state formation in early Islam', *Al-'Usur al-Wusta* 17 (2005), 29–31. Plain facts of geography and accessibility to hegemonial governing apparatus are no less important for understanding Byzantium and the Latin west: pp. 181–2, 140–1, 369–70.

[72] While the exact conclusions of R. Bulliet, *Conversion to Islam in the Medieval Period: An Essay in Quantitative History* (Cambridge, MA, 1979), are open to question, the broad outline remains highly suggestive. See also Bulliet, *Islam: The View from the Edge*.

and ninth centuries; by the tenth century, Islamic beliefs and practices were no longer the preserve of those claiming an exclusively, or even a partially, Arabian heritage.[73] Indeed, some of the pioneers of what was to become 'classical' Islamic thought were of non-Arabian or mixed heritage and would have been native speakers of Persian, among them the collector of Sunni *hadith*, al-Bukhari (d. 870); the religious scholar and historian al-Tabari (d. 923); and the polymaths Ibn Sina (d. 1037) and al-Biruni (d. 1050).

However, another manifestation of the importance of the first formative decades of Islam was the survival of the idea of west Arabian – and particularly post-Prophetic – monarchic authority for many centuries after the collapse of the Arabian empire. All the great caliphal dynasties of the early tenth century – the Abbasids, the Fatimids and the Umayyads of al-Andalus – traced their ancestry back to the early seventh-century Meccan tribe of Quraysh. The two major caliphates of the central Islamic lands, the Abbasids and the Fatimids, traced their heritage back to the Prophet's specific branch of Quraysh – the tribe of Hashim. It is also striking that the Sunni Abbasid caliph – now a figurehead in Iraq – was not replaced by his Shiʿi Buyid military protectors; his symbolic capital as the Imam of all Sunni Muslims was simply too great. Although religio-political universalism had triumphed over any tendency for ethnic exclusivity in early Islam, the formative imperial success of the Arabians, who were related to God's Prophet by close kinship, created Arabian caliphal elites whose position was unassailable by virtue of their Prophetic inheritance: no non-Arab military elite successfully had one of their own widely acknowledged as caliph until the Ottoman Turks in the 1540s, more than 900 years after the death of Muhammad (and then in very changed circumstances from the universal empire of the west Arabians in the 700s).

Elites in Early 'Medieval' Islam: Clans and Military Households

Thus many ethnic groups and cultural traditions were represented among Buyid and Seljuk elites in the tenth and subsequent centuries. Unlike the other two spheres discussed in this book, the elites that dominated the post-Abbasid Islamic world all had a 'marginal', tribal background, and they relied on martial prowess, notably as mounted archers, to control local resources and tap them to their own advantage. Traditional political organisation around clans and the military households of charismatic strongmen became the norm, and this did not change in essence until

[73] Wensinck and Crone, 'Mawla'.

the later sixteenth century.[74] However, the tribal, dynastic and politico-military elites themselves did. And as the period progressed, their claims to power no longer rested specifically on Sunni Islam and tribal heritage but embraced a much wider, more eclectic blend of Islamic, Berber, Turkish or Turco-Mongol frameworks of legitimisation.

What complicated matters, however, was the frequent existence of parallel administrative systems, both new and old, often working in concert but also in competition. Both the Buyids and Seljuks relied on an urban, military-based system of governance, yet each established their own administrative structures, borrowing from existing practices (for example, the vizierate) while adopting more complex systems of land tenure (such as the *iqta'*) to help pay their military and bureaucratic supporters.[75] The tensions that arose from ethnic and cultural rivalries, or from competing administrations, merely added to the problems associated with rule by loose family confederations and extensive use of political marriages among rivals.[76] The gradual revitalisation of the Abbasid presence in the region that started in the late tenth century never really threatened to overthrow the existing regional powers. But it did add a further twist to the tense and fragmenting nature of the period's larger political culture.

A few features of that political culture can be picked out from these tensions. The first of these relates to rule by a kind of family joint-enterprise. As already noted, the Buyids ruled the central Islamic lands in what amounted to a loose partnership, whereby territories were divided up among brothers, uncles and cousins.[77] Tribal customs prevailed: for

---

[74] Not that the household was wholly unknown to earlier Islamic regimes: pp. 115, 128. Military households were also an important element in western political culture: pp. 406–7. The household (*oikos*), in less martial form, is also of significance in Constantinople and more generally in the Palaiologan era: pp. 200–1, 438–41.

[75] For the *iqta'* system in Islamic politics: pp. 472, 484. Land was fundamental to acquisition and maintenance of power and the rewarding of supporters in the west: pp. 46–7, 51–2, 61–2, 67, 71, 73–4, 149–50, 369–70, 372, 380–1, 382–3, 409. Land mattered, but was not so all-important in Byzantium: pp. 200–1, 420, 432–5.

[76] On nomadic-sedentary relations: S. Heidemann, *Die Renaissance der Städte in Nordsyrien und Nordmesopotamian. Städtische Entwicklung und wirtschaftliche Bedingungen in ar-Raqqa und Harran von der Zeit der beduinischen Vorherrschaft bis zu den Seldschuken* (Leiden, 2002); J. Paul (ed.), *Nomad Aristocrats in a World of Empires* (Wiesbaden, 2013).

[77] On the concept of family confederations and an analysis of the social forces behind them: M. Dickson, 'Uzbek dynastic theory in the sixteenth century', in *Trudy 25-go Mezhdunarodnogo Kongressa Vostokovedov III* (Moscow, 1963), 208–17; J. Fletcher, 'Turco-Mongolian monarchic tradition in the Ottoman empire', in *Harvard Ukrainian Studies* 3 (1979–80), 236–51; see also Busse, *Chalif und Grosskönig*; Bosworth, 'Political and dynastic history', 1–3. Variations of family confederations can be found in the Latin west, e.g. the Angevin, Aragonese and Jagiellonian assemblages of principalities: pp. 75, 376, 383. They are also discernible in late Byzantium: pp. 321–4.

example, although Ahmad (Mu'izz al-Dawla) had taken control of the Abbasid caliphate, he did not assume the title of chief emir (*amir al-umara*'), used by other military leaders of the previous generation. Being the youngest, he deferred to the authority of his elder brother Ali (Imad al-Dawla). For the first generation, Imad al-Dawla had control over Fars and Kirman, basing himself in Shiraz; the middle brother Hasan (Rukn al-Dawla) was in control of much of Jibal and the cities of Rayy and Isfahan; while Mu'izz al-Dawla himself was based in Iraq and focused on the region around Baghdad.

This system of rule was largely patrimonial and familial as opposed to imperial or dynastic,[78] and, for the Buyids' opening years of power, it appeared to work to their benefit. There were, however, basic drawbacks, as the problems surrounding the second generation of Buyid rulers show. When Adud al-Dawla (949–83) attempted to secure his position as chief emir:

Neither primogeniture nor appointment by the caliph sufficed to establish supremacy; military force was the only guarantee. 'Adud al-Dawla had succeeded in associating the chief emirate with Baghdad and the protection of the caliph, but other than that the institution was fluid, depending completely on the personality and power of the incumbent.[79]

This encapsulates an inherent problem faced by many of the post-Abbasid successor polities. During the Buyid period, each of the candidates for the position of chief emir sought caliphal approbation, but in the end this legitimisation was not enough to secure their position. What was needed was someone who could inspire and coerce his support base; and this in turn required a leader who was able to provide a steady source of income. Complicating matters for the Buyids was their custom of dividing up their lands among the family, a system that would only become more convoluted over time. In the end, the Buyid polity succumbed to the simultaneous pressure of internecine warfare among Adud al-Dawla's successors and the new powers only too eager to take advantage of the vulnerable Buyid system. However, this mode of rulership – leaving open the issue of succession to power and legitimate authority for resolution by the sword – would continue to be a key feature of all patrimonial polities in the medieval *dar al-Islam*, from the Buyids by way of the Seljuks and other Turkish dynasties to the Jingizid Mongols and their successors. It was, in fact, the defining endemic source of tension, instability and fragmentation for the political elites of Islam until the early modern period.

---

[78] Cahen, 'Buyids/Buwayhids'.   [79] *BDI*, 92.

Another point, as salient as that of unstable family rule, concerns the limited scope for militant religious sectarianism at the apex of the political order. Even though the Buyids were Shiʿi, and even though they had little if any respect for the office of the Sunni Abbasid caliphs, Muʿizz al-Dawla nevertheless replaced al-Mustakfi with his cousin al-Muti (946–74). While the medieval Islamic historians claim that this was religious *Realpolitik*, some modern scholars argue that considerations of religious sectarianism did not play such a decisive role in the matter.[80] Easy as it is to represent the Sunni–Shiʿi schism as a major factor in political power-play, we should not place too much emphasis on the divisions. Although the Buyids were Shiʿi and promoted Shiʿi practices and rituals throughout their lands, they by no means forced conversion on the Sunni majority population, nor did they make Shiʿism an official tenet in their governance.[81] The practical necessities of maintaining order trumped adherence to any particular religious confession. In the case of the Fatimid caliphate, where the rulers were Ismaʿili Shiʿi, the leadership treated their belief system as something that was exclusive to the ruling elite of society. During the Buyid era, we find that a sense of ethnic identity and cultural pride was more likely to be a cause of civil and military strife. Although the chroniclers highlight religious divisions – both inter- and intra-faith – and make much of them in their narratives, modern scholarship has shown that the rise and fall of the Buyid dynasty was tied more intimately to their Persian ethnicity and their rule as a kind of family firm.

Later 'Medieval' Elites: Urban Administrators and Warlords from the Steppes

Although tribal traditions of charismatic leadership, family rule, personal power networks and violent succession continued to define regional and local elites in the Nile-to-Oxus region after the Mongols, their identities underwent thoroughgoing change, and local rule saw a range of continuities and disruptions. The most obvious bid for continuity was the reinvention in Cairo of the Abbasid caliphate, boosting the authority of

---

[80] For two medieval accounts of al-Mustakfi's deposition: Ibn al-Jawzi, *al-Muntazam fi taʾrikh al-muluk wa-l-umam*, ed. M. Ata, 18 vols (Beirut, 1992), xiv:45; Ibn al-Athir, *al-Kamil fiʾl-taʾrikh*, ed. C. J. Tornberg, 11 vols (Beirut, 1998), vii:206–7. The medieval view is that had the Buyids installed a Shiʿi as ruler, the military might have turned their full allegiance to this figure (see *BDI*, 16). For more on sectarian issues: C. D. Baker, *Medieval Islamic Sectarianism* (Leeds, 2019).

[81] The Buyids are said to have introduced the lamentation aspect to the Ashura commemoration of the martyrdom of Husayn, the cause of many riots between the Sunni and Shiʿi quarters in Baghdad, which the Buyids were forced to quell.

post-Mongol leaderships there. Although this reinvention was not accepted unequivocally, it confirmed the new realities of the later thirteenth century: Cairo was increasingly eclipsing other cities as a regional political centre. In 1261, an Abbasid pretender was acclaimed universal caliph of the Islamic community, establishing a new line of (supposedly) Abbasid caliphs in Cairo. Unlike their predecessors in Baghdad, however, they were no more than isolated puppets of the sultans and became increasingly irrelevant.[82] A more creative reinvention of that tradition of legitimate leadership of the Muslim community emerged in the writings of some contemporary scholars. They linked the new realities of Turco-Mongol and Berber power politics to the divine sanction of a lost caliphal heritage: the new instruments of divine guidance were none other than the various local military leaders, by dint of their positions of supreme power and authority. The sultans and their consorts of the fourteenth and fifteenth centuries were to be considered the caliphs of their time, a theory that eventually resulted in the Ottoman sultan's uncontested formal appropriation of the title of caliph in the 1540s.[83]

The post-Mongol transformation of the region's political landscape did not just affect its ideological backdrop. It also brought to power new, mainly Mongol and Oghuz Turkish military elites. During the thirteenth and fourteenth centuries, military muscle and an unmatched ability as mounted archers allowed Ilkhanid and Chaghadai military commanders, Turco-Mongol strongmen, and a medley of Turkish, Turkmen, Arab, Kurdish, Mongol and Iranian tribal chiefs to impose their authority: they filled the vacuum left by the relatively rapid disintegration of the Ilkhanid and Chaghadai dynasties. In the regions to the east and north of the Euphrates, many of these new leaders and their elaborate entourages practised some form of transhumance derived from Central Asian pastoralism. Timur purged all rival rulers in a series of campaigns and shaped an entirely new regional elite which would dominate western Asian politics for most of the fifteenth century – made up of Chaghadai commanders, Timur's descendants and their armies. However, nothing really changed in the basic Turco-Mongol outlook and organisation of local elites. What was new was Timur's policy of raising local potentates over more powerful regional competitors. At the local level, especially in

---

[82] S. Heidemann, *Das aleppiner Kalifat (AD 1261): Vom Ende des Kalifates in Baghdad über Aleppo zu den Restaurationen in Kairo* (Leiden, 1994); M. Banister, '"Naught remains of the caliph but his title": revisiting Abbasid authority in Mamluk Cairo', *MSR* 18 (2014–15), 219–46.

[83] This theory's most explicit proponent was Ibn Jama'a (1241–1333) in his *Tahrir al-ahkam fi tadbir ahl al-Islam*, but it can also be found in the writings of Ibn Taymiyya (d. 1327) and Ibn Khaldun (d. 1406): see *SGMI*, 138–77. See also pp. 353–4.

Anatolia, Azerbaijan and Iraq, this bolstered the fragmented political leaderships which had been vulnerable to subjection, absorption or outright annihilation by rising powers such as the Ottomans.

The politico-military elites of the Cairo Sultanate continued to be known as 'the Turks' throughout this period. They shared many defining characteristics with Turco-Mongol elites, going back to post-Seljuk-era traditions of family rule and political violence; most of them were, after all, military slaves of Turkish, Anatolian or Circassian origin. Even in their urban palaces and court citadels, these sultans, military commanders and their expanding entourages clung to distinctively Mongol lifestyles in the fourteenth century and Turkish in the fifteenth. They sometimes organised themselves around vague and inclusive ethnic labels, such as that of 'Circassians' in the fifteenth century.[84]

Perhaps surprisingly, the elite most affected in the very essence of its make-up was the most successful and stable of them all – politically at least. Ottoman elites and powerholders had emerged from the warbands that rallied around or merged with the long and successful leaderships of Osman's son Orkhan (c.1324–62), his son Murad (1362–89) and his grandson Bayezid (1389–1402). They were drawn from a variety of Anatolian and Balkan families and communities of Turkish, Turkmen and possibly also Turkicised stock. The glue that initially bound them was the individual qualities of Orkhan, Murad and Bayezid, although this increasingly morphed into loyalty to the Ottoman lineage in general along with its representatives, especially in western and central Anatolia and the Balkans. This growing Ottoman dynastic distinctiveness was, however, also linked to the drastically changing nature of Ottoman elites, especially after 1453 and the rise of a breed of 'new Ottomans' – *devshirme* recruits or other slaves from Ottoman lands who came to dominate the top offices of the realm. Having

distinguished themselves from ethnic Turks, functionally if the Turkish-born were fellow members of the elite as bureaucrats or *ulamâ* members, socially and politically from the urban and rural Turks, [they were] subjects of the Ottoman sultan as much as Greeks or Armenians or Arabs.[85]

One of the main reasons for this was that members of the traditional and largely hereditary Ottoman elite of Turkish stock were gradually relegated to secondary roles – in administration, cavalry and education, for example – and pushed away from positions of power and military

---

[84] Loiseau, *Les Mamelouks*, 143–204 ('L'identité mamelouke').

[85] M. Kunt, 'Ottomans and Safavids: states, statecraft, and societies, 1500–1800', in Y. Choueiri (ed.), *A Companion to the History of the Middle East* (Oxford, 2005), 191–205 at 199.

leadership. The Ottomans tightened their grip over their realm partly through the use of agents more closely connected with their dynasty. They selected from those captured on the battlefield, bought at the slave market or recruited from the rural Christian populations of the Balkans, and transformed them into new, Islamised, Turkicised and Ottomanised politico-military elites; prominent among these was the famous janissary infantry corps. Wives and concubines of similar origins were sought after by the Ottomans, as they were by the 'new Ottoman' officials and commanders. Thus by the early sixteenth century, the Ottoman empire's elites, including the dynasty itself, had absorbed the diverse former Byzantino-Balkan and Anatolian leaderships into their ranks rather more fully than the ever more emphatic adoption of a distinctively Turkish and Sunni Muslim identity might imply.[86]

Across the Nile-to-Oxus region, however, the diverse and transforming Turco-Mongol elites had to share power with many others. The Timurids' power bases have been likened to an 'archipelago within a sea of semi-independent regions, over which control was a matter of luck, alliance and an occasional punitive expedition',[87] but this description could just as well apply to the entire period and region. Administering urban communities, maintaining hierarchical order, and accumulating agricultural and commercial surpluses year in year out called for the sort of skills and resources that did not come naturally to military strongmen and tribal leaders. Thus long-standing local, Persianate administrative and intellectual elites survived in the east, despite the Mongol irruptions of the thirteenth century. So, too, did some of the military elites. They formed a crucial organisational backbone to all the Mongol, post-Mongol, Timurid and Turkmen political formations that came and went. They upheld Persian as a language of administration and culture in the regions east of the Euphrates, and they kept alive Persian traditions harking back to pre-Islamic times. Among these are the models of kingship found in the lively manuscript traditions of the *Shahnama* ('The Book of Kings').[88] Those Persian traditions that had entered western Asia Minor along with the Seljuks in the eleventh century proved somewhat less resilient, at least as far as the language was concerned: they were eventually rendered into and enriched by Turkish, albeit in the heavily Persianised form of Ottoman Turkish. In Anatolia, Istanbul and the

---

[86] Imber, *Ottoman Empire*; Kunt, 'Ottomans and Safavids'; L. Peirce, *The Imperial Harem; Women and Sovereignty in the Ottoman Empire* (Oxford, 1993); H. W. Lowry, *The Nature of the Early Ottoman State* (Albany, NY, 2003); K. Barkey, *Empire of Difference: The Ottomans in Comparative Perspective* (Cambridge, 2008).
[87] Manz, *Power, Politics*, 2.
[88] Firdawsi, *Shahnama*, ed. J. Khaliqi-Mutlaq *et al.*, 8 vols (New York, 1987–2007).

Balkans, where established local traditions of Sunni Muslim scholarship and learning were lacking, possession of Ottoman Turkish became a key marker of elite membership:

> Turkish was established as a legitimate, eventually the preferred language of expression in history writing, literary efforts, and other products of high culture, hitherto considered the exclusive domain of Persian. Even the *ulamâ* [...] replaced Arabic with their native Turkish not only in such mundane tasks as keeping court records and issuing legal documents, but also in legal discourse.[89]

In the lands of Egypt and Syria, a combination of these processes of wider elite formation occurred. Arabic remained the language of culture and administration, but Turkish (in its Qipchaq form) acquired an increasingly distinctive and valued status as a literary language, especially in the entourages of sultans and their military commanders. Here, too, local financial and legal elites continued to be gratefully employed, acquiring power and substantial resources in the process. Cairo and Damascus emerged as renowned centres of Arabo-Muslim learning and Sunni as well as Sufi religious authority. They attracted extensive patronage from the political elites as well as scholars and students from all over the Muslim world, including from Berber North Africa, Turkish Anatolia and the Persian east. Resources continued to be concentrated in the same urban centres through skilful management on the part of Syrian and Egyptian families of administrators, many of whom were of Arabicised (and occasionally Islamicised) Christian origin. Serving in the households of, and empowered by, the kaleidoscope of military commanders and sultans at the top of the sultanate's volatile political order, most of these families shared in their employers' fates. Indeed, a major transformation also marks out the administrators of the fourteenth century from those of the fifteenth.[90]

Conclusion

The roots of the Islamic world lay in the collapse of the great antique powers of Rome and Iran. However, in uniting the Mediterranean and Middle East, the Arab-Muslim tribesmen created a far larger zone of

---

[89] Kunt, 'Ottomans and Safavids', 197, 199.
[90] C. Petry, *The Civilian Elite of Cairo in the Later Middle Ages* (Princeton, 1981); M. Chamberlain, *Knowledge and Social Practice in Medieval Damascus, 1190–1350* (Cambridge, 1995); J. Berkey, *The Transmission of Knowledge in Medieval Cairo: A Social History of Islamic Education* (Princeton, 1992); B. Martel-Thoumian, *Les Civils et l'administration dans l'état militaire Mamluk (IXe/XVe siècle)* (Damascus, 1992); M. Eychenne, *Liens personnels, clientélisme et réseaux de pouvoir dans le sultanat mamelouk (milieu XIIIe–fin XIVe siècle)* (Beirut, 2013).

integrated politico-religious culture than either of their precursors had managed. The universalist potential of Islam allowed conquered peoples like the Berbers and Persians to seize a significant stake in the new world order. This new Islamic commonwealth was primarily shaped and given contours by settled urban elites; but crucially, it was open on two long borders to nomadic pastoralists – in the deserts of northern Africa and in the steppes of Central Asia. Just as Islam's success was a consequence of the unification and settling of Arabian nomadic pastoralists, its history up to the early modern period was one of interaction and also integration with other nomadic groups. However, none of Islam's nomadic conquerors brought with them anything like an effective alternative to the religion and culture of Islam, and each wave of conquerors successfully became an active partner of the ongoing formation of Islam. Between the tenth and the thirteenth centuries, this entailed the dividing up of authority between caliph and military warlord. After the crisis of the mid-thirteenth century, the religious scholars of Sunni Islam fully came to terms with the redundancy of the caliphate or, perhaps more accurately, with the success of their own claims to be the true heirs of the Prophet. A second consequence of all these waves of migration and conquest was the predominance of trans-regional, dynastic and familial practices of power at the very top throughout the period. Yet at the more local level, Islam gradually sank in and became the main religion: it made the transition from being a radical ideology of conquering elites to being the routine and deep-seated religion and culture across western Eurasia.

Part III

Norms, Values and Their Propagation

10 The Latin West
Expectations and Legitimisation

Björn Weiler

Figure 10.1 Earl Harold Godwinson in hunting mode sets out on a journey that would end up at the court of Duke William of Normandy; each would become England's king (scene from the Bayeux Tapestry); photo © Ministère de la Culture-Médiathèque de l'Architecture et du Patrimoine, Dist. RMN-Grand Palais/Jean Courbeix/Simon Guillot

Around 1040, Wipo composed the *Gesta Chuonradi imperatoris* ('Deeds of Emperor Conrad II'). We know little about the author: he probably originated from northern Italy and seems to have been a chaplain at the court of the western emperors.[1] His duties were administrative (writing,

---

[1] V. Huth, 'Wipo, neugelesen. Quellenkritische Notizen zur "Hofkultur" in spätottonisch-frühsalischer Zeit', in A. Bihrer *et al.* (eds), *Adel und Königtum im mittelalterlichen Schwaben: Festschrift für Thomas Zotz zum 65. Geburtstag* (Stuttgart, 2009), 155–68.

251

receiving and translating documents) as well as religious (celebrating mass and offering religious instruction). The *Gesta* traces the deeds and career of Conrad II (1024–39) and was written for his son and successor, Henry III (1039–56). It was not a biography. It had little to say about Conrad's upbringing and started instead with his election as king (an account that occupies nearly a third of the total narrative). But Wipo had not intended the *Gesta* to be a biography. Rather, he sought to provide Henry with a guide to kingship: to instruct him in the principles of royal lordship and warn him of the dangers facing those who erred from the path of righteousness.[2] In this regard, the *Gesta* was representative of a considerable corpus of materials especially popular in the eleventh and twelfth centuries that sought to use history both to provide a record of events and to instruct the reader in appropriate political and moral conduct.[3] These texts built on older traditions, but they foreshadowed ways of engaging with the norms and values of political conduct that emerged in the thirteenth century and later. They also hint at the variety of genres in which medieval authors thought and wrote about power. Historical writing was used alongside, drew on and in turn influenced genres as diverse as letters and letter collections, liturgical texts, commentaries on the Bible, vernacular romances, and treatises on a community's laws and customs.[4] But although contemporaries might have used different genres to convey their ideas, and context certainly shaped what aspects were discussed or how they were formulated, the underpinning principles remained fairly constant. Those in power were supposed to be just, pious, generous, humble and valiant. They were to protect those who could not protect themselves and to take the advice of wise and prudent

---

[2] S. Bagge, *Kings, Politics, and the Right Order of the World in German Historiography c.950–1150* (Leiden, 2002); J. Banaszkiewicz, 'Conrad II's *theatrum rituale*: Wipo on the earliest deeds of the Salian ruler (*Gesta Chuonradi imperatoris cap. 5*)', in P. Górecki and N. van Deusen (eds), *Central and Eastern Europe in the Middle Ages: A Cultural History* (London and New York, 2009), 50–81; B. Weiler, 'Describing rituals of succession and the legitimation of kingship in the west, *c.*1000–*c.*1150', in A. Beihammer *et al.* (eds), *Court Ceremonies and Rituals in Byzantium and the Medieval Mediterranean: Comparative Perspectives* (Leiden and Boston, 2013), 115–40.

[3] Bagge, *Kings, Politics*; B. Weiler, 'Tales of first kings and the culture of kingship in the west, *c.*1050–1200', *Viator* 46 (2015), 101–28.

[4] P. Buc, *L'Ambiguïté du Livre: prince, pouvoir, et peuple dans les commentaires de la Bible au Moyen Âge* (Paris, 1994); *idem*, 'Die Krise des Reiches unter Heinrich IV. mit und ohne Spielregeln', in C. Garnier and H. Kamp (eds), *Die Spielregeln der Mächtigen: mittelalterliche Politik zwischen Gewohnheit und Konvention* (Darmstadt, 2010), 61–94; L. Melve, *Inventing the Public Sphere: The Public Debate during the Investiture Contest, c. 1030–1122*, 2 vols (Leiden and Boston, 2007); M. Münster-Swendsen, '"Auf das Gesetz sei das Land gebaut": Zum Zusammenhang rechtlicher und historischer Diskurse im hochmittelalterlichen Dänemark', in G. Vercamer and N. Kersken (eds), *Macht und Spiegel der Macht: Herrschaft in Europa im 12. und 13. Jahrhundert vor der Hintergrund der Chronistik* (Wiesbaden, 2013), 85–102.

men. Then there were what might be termed secondary values: maintaining honour and standing, an emphasis on pedigree and precedent, and having a say in the interpretation and implementation of norms. Thus were we to focus exclusively on the norms, we would have to engage with variations so subtle that only those already familiar with the subject would benefit.

It will prove more fruitful to pursue a number of other aspects instead. Among these are the importance of debates for the development of thinking about power, the nature of those debates, and the wide range of materials containing evidence for political values. Thinking about power was never static. The norms invoked might have remained inherently conservative, but this reflected both a shared corpus of canonical sources and the inherently abstract nature of the norms themselves. The Bible, authors of classical antiquity, the Church Fathers, and an ever-changing body of medieval writers provided the models and conceptual framework for defining the purposes and limitations of power. But they offered a framework, not a rigid template, and debates turned not only on which norms should be obeyed but on what they meant, how to implement them and who should do this. To get a sense of these debates, we should focus less on the interpretation of ideals than on who had the resources and capabilities to interpret them. Institutions, groups and individuals laying claim to define values also invoked the right to participate in implementing them. And because actors were operating within a shared framework, the basis on which one group might claim pre-eminence could also be the basis for others to challenge those claims.[5] Such debates remain hidden if we focus solely on the norms themselves or on abstract expositions of political, legal or religious organisation. We will gain a better sense of what medieval men and women thought about power by looking at the whole range of media and genres at the disposal of medieval writers and focusing on the – often incidental – context within which norms were developed and debated.[6]

Scholarship on political ideas in the medieval Latin west tends to focus on the history of political thought.[7] Priority is given to abstract treatises on

---

[5] B. Weiler, 'Politics', in D. J. Power (ed.), *The Central Middle Ages, c.950–c.1320* (Oxford, 2006), 91–120 at 119–120.

[6] B. Weiler, 'Thinking about power before Magna Carta: the role of history', in F. Foronda and J.-P. Genet (eds), *Des Chartes aux constitutions: autour de l'idée constitutionnelle en Europe (XIIe–XVIIe siècles)* (Paris, 2019), 3–26.

[7] See e.g. W. Ullmann, *Medieval Political Thought* (Harmondsworth, 1975); A. J. Black, *Political Thought in Europe, 1250–1450* (Cambridge, 1992); M. Senellart, *Les Arts de gouverner: du regimen médiéval au concept de gouvernement* (Paris, 1996); *Fürstenspiegel des frühen und hohen Mittelalters*, ed. and tr. H. H. Anton (Darmstadt, 2006); F. Lachaud and L. Scordia (eds), *Le Prince au miroir de la littérature politique de l'Antiquité aux Lumières*

the fundamental principles of political and legal organisation, excluding even biblical exegesis, let alone the plethora of other texts in which medieval men and women engaged with questions of power and politics.[8] My concern here is more with political mentalities:[9] the framework within which debates over values unfolded, and the parameters that helped determine participation in these debates. Inevitably, some of the ideas that we will encounter were contradictory; not all were fully thought through or particularly sophisticated. How values were invoked and their meaning defined was often in response to concrete problems and challenges; and how abstract norms were interpreted in practice reflected changing social, cultural, religious and political patterns, the varying composition of political elites, and the availability of resources and means of communication.[10] But then, if we accept that values could shape political actions, we need to look at norms as they were used, not as they were abstracted. We can lament the resulting cacophony, or we can accept it as the inevitable by-product of a functioning political culture. Yet a political culture could only function if it shared a common framework – a basic agreement as to what values were worth invoking, even if their precise meaning remained contested. The framework could be tested, enhanced and revised, and this very malleability ensured its survival. All of which means we need to explore the factors that determined how values were interpreted.

I will use Wipo's *Gesta* as a case study of how writers in the west formulated their thinking about power. Although Wipo reflects a very specific moment in time (the mid-eleventh century), social group (Latinate clerics) and cultural milieu (the imperial court), he drew on concepts and a mode of delivery pervasive in the west. I will then consider some of Wipo's sources and the extent to which their values circulated beyond his particular milieu before turning to the broader group of actors and agents shaping the interpretation of political norms in the west.

(Rouen, 2007); C. J. Nederman, *Lineages of European Political Thought: Explorations Along the Medieval/Modern Divide from John of Salisbury to Hegel* (Washington, DC, 2009); J. Canning, *A History of Medieval Political Thought, 300–1450* (London, 1996).

[8] Important exceptions are: F. Lachaud, *L'Éthique du pouvoir au Moyen Âge: l'office dans la culture politique (Angleterre, vers 1150–vers 1330)* (Paris, 2010); J. W. Sabapathy, *Officers and Accountability in Medieval England, 1170–1300* (Oxford, 2014); M. S. Kempshall, *The Common Good in Late Medieval Political Thought: Moral Goodness and Material Benefit* (Oxford, 1999).

[9] T. Foerster, 'Political myths and political culture in twelfth-century Europe', in H. Brandt *et al.* (eds), *Erfahren, Erzählen, Erinnern: narrative Konstruktionen von Gedächtnis und Generation in Antike und Mittelalter* (Bamberg, 2012), 83–116; G. Vercamer and N. Kersken (eds), *Macht und Spiegel der Macht: Herrschaft in Europa im 12. und 13. Jahrhundert vor dem Hintergrund der Chronistik* (Wiesbaden, 2013).

[10] See also R. Kosselleck, *The Practice of Conceptual History: Timing History, Spacing Concepts* (Palo Alto, CA, 2002).

Wipo's 'Deeds of Conrad'

A sermon delivered by the archbishop of Mainz during Conrad's coronation forms a key episode in Wipo's narrative. Conrad, the metropolitan explained, had reached the highest dignity available to man: he had become the vicar of Christ. That also entailed duties:

> No one but his [Christ's] imitator is a true ruler. It is necessary that in this 'throne of the kingdom' you reflect on the perpetual honour. It is great felicity to rule in the world, but the greatest is to triumph in Heaven. Although God requires many things of you, He wishes most of all that you render judgement and justice, and peace for the fatherland, which always looks to you; and [He wishes] that you be a defender of churches and clerics, the guardian of widows and orphans. With these and other good [works] your throne will be firmly established here and forever.[11]

The sermon summarises key values of Christian rulership: the power to rule was granted by God to those he deemed most capable of exercising it. Indeed, the archbishop began his sermon by pointing out that Conrad had only been granted such power after his suitability for the throne had repeatedly been tested. Moreover, he had received the royal dignity not to satisfy his own desires but to serve the needs of his people. Conrad's success as ruler would depend on his willingness to protect the church and those who could not defend themselves. These duties were so important, their exercise so central to the concept of good royal lordship, that Wipo describes how Conrad performs them even en route to his coronation. Encountering a peasant, a widow and an orphan seeking justice, Conrad upbraids his entourage for trying to hurry him on:

> I remember that you have said often that not the hearers of the law, but the doers are made just. If, however, one must haste to the consecration, as you say, it behooves me to set my footsteps firmly in the work of God so much the more carefully as I know that I draw near that exacting dignity.[12]

The willingness to offer justice was a mark of Conrad's suitability, central to the office he would soon hold.

Other passages similarly recount Conrad's regal qualities: he appointed more prudent and suitable officials than any of his predecessors, confirmed the laws and customs of his people, and was generous yet consistent in his governance.[13] Indeed:

---

[11] GC[1] ch. 3, 548–9; GC[2], 67. Personal piety, righteousness, and defence of true religion and the church were also expected of the Byzantine emperor: pp. 293–4, 299–302, 304. Piety and a sense of justice were no less important to Islamic concepts of rulership, yet moving to a different beat: pp. 332–3, 342–3, 353–5, 360–2.
[12] GC[1] ch. 5, 554–5; GC[2], 70.   [13] GC[1] ch. 4, 550–1; GC[2], 68–9.

[...] every day he was held by all more outstanding than the day before, for the fastness of peace, more dear for the grace of benevolence, more honored for regal judgement. [...] It would arouse suspicion to tell how munificent he was, how agreeable; of what a constant, of how undaunted a soul; gentle to all good men, severe to evil; kindly towards subjects, harsh toward enemies; effective in action; indefatigable in his effort to be of the greatest service to the kingdom [...][14]

Once firmly established in Germany, Conrad turned his attention to Italy, Poland, Hungary and Burgundy,[15] defending the honour of each realm and performing the duties of his office in exemplary fashion. In Burgundy, Conrad let his subjects 'for the first time, taste the law, long disused and almost wiped from the books';[16] and in Pavia he upbraided the citizens for destroying a royal palace during the interregnum between Henry II's death and his own election: '"Even if the king died, the kingdom remained, just as the ship whose steersman falls remains."'[17] The realm existed independently of the ruler. It was the king's duty to maintain its integrity, to increase its honour, to preserve peace and justice within it.

However, virtuous rule was not solely a matter of virtuous action. It also required a virtuous mindset. Conrad was always humble and accessible: his subjects could approach him without fear, irrespective of status. He personified regal serenity: even the citizens of Pavia were chided calmly, and he kept his temper despite the many petitioners and princes attending his person. Conrad was a successful king because he acted like one.[18] But it was his innate virtue that allowed him to perform his duties in so outstanding a fashion: being the master of his emotions allowed him to discern what was just, to choose wise and prudent counsellors and to act as a true father and guardian of his people. Moral disposition and moral action were inextricably linked. An immoral ruler could not be a just and prudent king.

Conrad's actions and Wipo's reporting of them were steeped in biblical and Roman precedent. The archbishop's sermon contains echoes of Kings[19] and Proverbs,[20] while Conrad's demonstrative halting of the

---

[14] GC¹ ch. 6, 556–7; GC², 72.

[15] GC¹ chs 7–15, 21, 26–38, 558–71, 576–9, 582–607; GC², 73–8, 82–3, 85–97.

[16] GC¹ ch. 38, 606–7; GC², 97.   [17] GC¹ ch. 7, 560–1; GC², 73.

[18] T. Reuter, '*Regemque, quem in Francia pene perdidit, in patria magnifice recepit*: Ottonian ruler representation in synchronic and diachronic comparison', in *MPMM*, 127–146 at 127.

[19] 'Blessed be the Lord thy God, which delighted in thee, to set thee on the throne of Israel: because the Lord loved Israel for ever, therefore made he thee king, to do judgement and justice' (I Kings 10:9).

[20] 'The king that faithfully judgeth the poor, his throne shall be established for ever' (Proverbs 29:14).

procession to his coronation mirrors Jeremiah.[21] Wipo draws on antique authors, including Sallust, Horace, Vergil, Caesar and Ovid, as well as on classics of early medieval history such as Jordanes. He consults Sulpicius Severus' *Life of St Martin* and Macrobius: by the eleventh century, such texts had become the standard fare of ecclesiastical education, but they had originally emerged from the encounter of a triumphant Christianity with the culture of paganism in the centuries after the conversion of Constantine to Christianity in 312. In this, Wipo was by no means unusual. Antiquity provided a repertoire of learned precedent and a standard of educated composition in Latin, but it remained subservient to divine truth as espoused in the Old and New Testament, serving to flesh it out and to illustrate it further.[22]

Attention should also be drawn to the historical figures whom Wipo invokes. David and Solomon are mentioned – key Old Testament models of good kingship – as are Aeneas, the founder of Rome, and Superbus Tarquinius, its last king. However, as the narrative unfolds, they are soon overshadowed by the figure of Charlemagne. On Christmas Day 800, Charlemagne had revived the tradition of a western empire, and the rulers of Germany had come to see themselves as his successors. Such references are especially prominent in the chapter on Conrad's coronation:

If Charlemagne had been present, alive, with his scepter, the people would not have been more eager, nor could they have rejoiced more at the return of so great a man than at the first coming of this King.[23]

And when Conrad tours his new kingdom for the first time, observers are reported as saying: 'The saddle of Conrad has the stirrup of Charles [Charlemagne].'[24] By the eleventh century, the first western emperor had become a legendary ideal: Conrad not only proved a worthy successor but surpassed him in accomplishments.[25]

Thus, Wipo points to a key feature in western political culture: the desire to see values and norms ennobled by the patina of history. To be deemed worth upholding, ideas and practices were presented as rooted in precedent, in traditions either forgotten or wilfully set aside. Yet antiquity also bestowed obligations: being Charlemagne's successor provided a

[21] 'This is what the Lord says: Do what is just and right. Rescue from the hand of the oppressor the one who has been robbed. Do no wrong or violence to the foreigner, the fatherless or the widow, and do not shed innocent blood in this place' (Jeremiah 22:3).

[22] On the abundance of ecclesiastical sources: pp. 42–4.

[23] GC[1] ch. 3, 546–7; GC[2], 66. See also p. 143.   [24] GC[1] ch. 6, 556–7; GC[2], 72.

[25] See the essays collected in W. Purkis and M. Gabriele (eds) *The Charlemagne Legend in Medieval Latin Texts* (Woodbridge, 2016); M. Gabriele, *An Empire of Memory: The Legend of Charlemagne, the Franks, and Jerusalem before the First Crusade* (Oxford, 2011).

standard against which Conrad's performance could be measured.[26] Conrad might have emerged from this comparison with his reputation heightened. Others would not. Precedent established a source of prestige and pedigree but also a means to find wanting those who wielded power. More importantly, a regnal community transcended the lifespan of any one ruler: it existed through, but also independently of, the monarch. After all, that was the point which Conrad had made to the citizens of Pavia. His was an office received from God and exercised on behalf of people and realm.

But someone had to make sure that kings performed their functions, and this made all the more important the idea that the power of a true king was greater than that of a mere mortal.[27] Indeed, to Wipo it was a sign of divine favour that Conrad had been elected:

[. . .] without malice, without controversy; he, who, although he was inferior to no one in family and in valor and in allodial goods, nevertheless in comparison with such men [the assembled princes] held of the state but little in fief and in power.

While of equal pedigree to his peers, Conrad's power and resources did not exceed theirs. The lack of rivalry and open competition, indeed, the unanimous assent of all those present, therefore suggested 'that the good will of heavenly powers, indeed, was not absent from this election'.[28] Candidates more commonly claimed the throne because they possessed both the moral characteristics of a good king and the resources to perform the functions of one. Yet there always was a danger that the magnificence of royal power might lead them astray; they might succumb to ambition and lose sight of the moral underpinnings of their office.

Oversight was needed, particularly during the election of a king:

[. . .] a long disputation took place as to who ought to rule; and when age – too immature or, on the other hand, too greatly advanced – rejected one, untested valor, another; and a proven state of insolence, some others, few were chosen among many, and from the few two only were singled out [Conrad and his eponymous cousin].[29]

In the end, Conrad's suitability manifested itself in his concrete actions as a just and pious lord. His illustrious pedigree and the obligations this imposed also weighed in his favour, numbering as he did emperors, saints and popes among his forebears. Yet suitability could only be demonstrated by heeding clerical advice and counsel – hence the archbishop's

---

[26] See also pp. 53–4, 149.
[27] B. Weiler, 'Crown-giving and king-making in the west, ca. 1000–ca. 1250', *Viator* 41 (2010), 57–88.
[28] GC[1] ch. 2, 544–5; GC[2], 65.   [29] GC[1] ch. 2, 538–9; GC[2], 61.

sermon.[30] The new king needed to act like an ideal monarch precisely because he lacked the material resources of power. He acquired legitimacy and the ability to head off and discredit resistance to his governance by performing his kingly duties in a manner that was both exemplary and widely witnessed; because he had the moral outlook of a true king, he was able to act like one.

Wipo in Context

Works similar to Wipo's proved a popular genre in the eleventh century. Adalbold of Utrecht's *Life* of Henry II (1002–24) focuses on the emperor's exemplary performance of the royal office,[31] while Helgaud of Fleury's *Life* of Robert I of West Francia (987–1034) centres on the king's archetypal performance of penance.[32] And not long after 1066, an anonymous monk wrote the *Life* of Edward the Confessor (*Vita Edwardi*), celebrating the monarch's pious devotion and good deeds.[33] According to all three, royal power reflects both innate virtue and divine favour; it is a duty rather than an opportunity for power and self-enrichment. Comparable thinking can be found in abstract treatises such as the *Admonitions* attributed to King Stephen of Hungary (d. 1035) and the *Institutes of Polity* of Wulfstan of York (d. 1023), as well as in several letters.[34] In short, Wipo reflected wider contemporary thinking about power, its origins and its purpose.

These writers drew on a shared legacy of biblical, classical and patristic thought. The Old Testament proved important both for the ambiguity that surrounded its ideas of kingship and for the concrete models it provided.[35] Kingship may have been granted at the behest of the people, but they were also warned about the ruler's absolute power over them (1

[30] See also pp. 138–40, 171–3, 387–8.
[31] See www.geschichtsquellen.de/repOpus_00020.html (accessed 21 October 2018).
[32] S. Hamilton, 'A new model for royal penance? Helgaud of Fleury's *Life of Robert the Pious*', *EME* 6 (1997), 189–200.
[33] *The Life of Edward the Confessor who Rests at Westminster*, ed. and tr. F. Barlow, 2nd edn (Oxford, 1992).
[34] E. Nemerkenyi, *Latin Classics in Medieval Hungary: Eleventh Century* (Budapest and New York, 2005); R. Trilling, 'Sovereignty and social order: Archbishop Wulfstan and the Institutes of Polity', in A. T. Jones and J. S. Ott (eds), *The Bishop Reformed: Studies in Episcopal Power and Culture in the Central Middle Ages* (Aldershot, 2007), 58–85; B. Weiler, 'Clerical *admonitio*, letters of advice to kings and episcopal self-fashioning, c.1000–c.1200', *History* 102 (2017), 557–75.
[35] See S. Boynton and D. Reilley (eds), *The Practice of the Bible in the Middle Ages: Production, Reception and Performance in Western Christianity* (New York, 2011); J. L. Nelson and D. Kempf (eds), *Reading the Bible in the Middle Ages* (London, 2015); B. Smalley, *The Study of the Bible in the Middle Ages*, 2nd rev. edn (Oxford, 1952); F. Van Liere, *An Introduction to the Medieval Bible* (Cambridge, 2014).

Kings 8). Moreover, suitability trumped descent: the tallest of the
Israelites, Saul, was chosen as their first king, although his replacement
David was seemingly picked at random by the prophet Samuel; and
Solomon was the most suitable – rather than the oldest – of David's
sons.[36] Saul forfeited his claim to the throne by defying the will of God,
while David merited his through his quest for wisdom, the exemplary
penance he performed for his transgressions, and his willingness to heed
the counsel of wise and pious men. Some kings would rend asunder Israel
through harsh governance, ignoring the advice of wise men or endorsing
false idols; others would reunite the people of Israel and Judaea. Thus the
Bible provided a core set of principles with which the exercise of power
could be evaluated and interpreted: rulers were to defend the people
against foreign aggressors, to act as paragons of virtuous behaviour and
to heed the warnings of God's prophets. Equally, royal power, while
rooted in God, was a privilege and not a right. It could be withdrawn
either by God (through his prophets) or by the people (who would
abandon a cruel and unjust king).

Old Testament ideas have to be considered alongside New Testament
ones. A foundational text is Paul's Epistle to the Romans, which, superfi-
cially at least, postulates complete submission to secular authority.[37] Yet
it also provides a means of evaluating authority: taxes were paid to
maintain the ruler and justice, since the ruler yielded the sword of justice
entrusted to him by God. In some respects, even the Pauline understanding of power reflects elements of Old Testament ambiguity about, and the
complex interaction between, the king as instrument of divine will and as
chosen leader of a people.[38]

---

[36] J. Funkenstein, 'Samuel and Saul in medieval political thought', *Hebraic Political Studies* 2 (2007), 149–63.

[37] 'Let everyone be subject to the governing authorities, for there is no authority except that which God has established. The authorities that exist have been established by God. Consequently, whoever rebels against the authority is rebelling against what God has instituted, and those who do so will bring judgement on themselves. For rulers hold no terror for those who do right, but for those who do wrong. Do you want to be free from fear of the one in authority? Then do what is right and you will be commended. For the one in authority is God's servant for your good. But if you do wrong, be afraid, for rulers do not bear the sword for no reason. They are God's servants, agents of wrath to bring punishment on the wrongdoer. Therefore, it is necessary to submit to the authorities, not only because of possible punishment but also as a matter of conscience. This is also why you pay taxes, for the authorities are God's servants, who give their full time to governing. Give to everyone what you owe them: if you owe taxes, pay taxes; if revenue, then revenue; if respect, then respect; if honour, then honour' (Paul, Epistle to the Romans, 13:1–7).

[38] W. Affeldt, *Die weltliche Gewalt in der Paulus-Exegese. Röm.13, 1–7 in den Römerbriefkommentaren der lateinischen Kirche bis zum Ende des 13. Jahrhunderts* (Göttingen, 1969).

Classical Roman concepts were also frequently invoked by medieval writers, notably Cicero's *De officiis* ('On Duties') which focuses on the requirements, duties and obligations of those seeking office. Public service should not be for personal gain but to ensure the well-being of the republic by maintaining justice. Of particular importance is the behaviour and character of those seeking power: unmoved by excessive emotion, beholden to neither friend nor foe, but acting purely in pursuit of the public good.[39] Cicero, in turn, influenced a range of Church Fathers – early Christian writers, whose interpretation of the Bible itself became canonical.[40] Chief among them were Ambrose of Milan (*c.*339–97), whose *De officiis* applies Ciceronian concepts to church governance,[41] and St Augustine (354–430), who encapsulates patristic concepts of power thus: *prodesse, non praeesse* (those assuming authority over others should do so to serve, not to lead).[42] Augustine lists the virtues that a Christian emperor should seek to acquire: to rule with justice, maintain humility in the face of excessive praise, employ his power on God's behalf and be moderate in punishment. His power would make it all too easy to gratify his desires, yet he should practise self-restraint and act not out of desire for vainglory but to serve God.[43] Similar ideas are espoused by Isidore of Seville (560–638), whose *Etymologies* remained a standard point of reference in western Europe until the late twelfth century. Isidore employs an often fanciful etymology to explain deeper meanings: for example, the term 'king' implies to pursue what was right (*rex a rectum agere*), since a king did not rule if he did not correct the people given into his care (*non regit qui non corrigit*).[44] There are many other examples of medieval writers employing classical Roman concepts.[45]

---

[39] Cicero, *De officiis*, ed. and tr. W. Miller (Cambridge, MA, 1913); N. Wood, *Cicero's Social and Political Thought* (Berkeley, 1988).

[40] P. Boucheron and S. Gioanni (eds), *La Mémoire d'Ambroise de Milan: usages politiques d'une autorité patristique en Italie, Ve–XVIIIe siècle* (Paris, 2015); M. L. Colish, 'Cicero, Ambrose, and stoic ethics: transmission or transformation?', in her *The Fathers and Beyond: Church Fathers between Ancient and Medieval Thought* (Aldershot, 2008), 95–112; I. J. Davidson, 'A tale of two approaches: Ambrose, *De officiis* 1.1–22 and Cicero, *De officiis* 1.1–6', *Journal of Theological Studies* 52 (2001), 61–83; S. Fanning, '*Rex* and *tyrannus* in Roman historiographical tradition – Livy, Cicero, Josephus and Gildas', *Majestas* 6 (1998), 3–18.

[41] Ambrose, *De officiis*, ed. and tr. I. J. Davidson, 2 vols (Oxford, 2002).

[42] Augustine of Hippo, *De civitate dei*, ed. B. Dombart and A. Kalb, 2 vols, *CCSL* 47–8 (Turnhout, 1955), ii:686–7.

[43] Augustine of Hippo, *De civitate dei*, i:160.

[44] Isidore of Seville, *The Etymologies*, tr. S. A. Barney *et al.* (Cambridge, 2006), 200; B. Weiler, 'The *rex renitens* and the medieval ideal of kingship, *c.*950–1250', *Viator* 31 (2000), 1–42.

[45] M. Reydellet, *La Royauté dans la littérature latine de Sidoine Apollinaire à Isidore de Séville* (Paris, 1981).

Thus Wipo's concepts of kingship and of power drew on a rich ferment of biblical, classical and patristic thought. The ability to rule was granted by God. It could legitimately be exercised only by those who saw power as a means to advance the welfare of others. In particular, they should ensure that justice was done (especially to those who could not protect themselves), that judicial rigour was tempered by mercy and that God's will also be done. If a ruler failed – because he lacked moral strength, succumbed to the lures of power or surrounded himself with flatterers and sycophants – he betrayed both God and his people. By failing to set high moral standards or failing to correct abuses, a ruler encouraged depravity amongst his people and incurred divine wrath, resulting in foreign invasions, civil unrest and even bad harvests.

These ideas were adopted, elaborated and disseminated by early medieval writers.[46] Well into the twelfth century, one of the most widely read was Pseudo-Cyprian, in all likelihood a seventh-century Irish monk.[47] His *Twelve Abuses of the World* lists the several types of evil that could endanger a community's well-being, culminating in a people without law. Ninth was the unjust king. It was a ruler's duty to ensure that justice was done, since he who could not correct could not rule, but this also meant acting as moral exemplar. To neglect his duties risked forfeiting not only the benefits of good lordship – peace, tranquillity and justice – but his own position in the next world. All the sinners an unjust king had failed to correct would be closer to God than him.[48] In more sophisticated form, a similar amalgamation of patristic, classical and biblical thought dominated ninth-century Carolingian treatises on royal power.[49]

This shared inheritance provided the essential foundations on which most medieval writings about the norms of power would rest. Moreover, these concepts applied to anyone exercising power: bishops and abbots as well as knights, counts and dukes.[50] A few decades after Wipo wrote his *Gesta*, the religious reformer and cardinal Peter Damian berated Margrave Godfrey of Tuscany for indulging in the fruits of his power while shunning its duties. Holding the power of absolute judgement in his lands meant that

---

[46] M. Blattmann, '"Ein Unglück für sein Volk". Der Zusammenhang zwischen Fehlverhalten des Königs und Volkswohl in Quellen des 7.–12. Jahrhunderts', *Frühmittelalterliche Studien* 30 (1996), 80–102.

[47] A. Breen, 'Pseudo-Cyprian *De duodecim abusivis saeculi* and the Bible', in P. Ni Chithain and M. Richter (eds), *Ireland und die Christenheit: Bibelstudien und Mission / Ireland and Christendom: The Bible and the Missions* (Stuttgart, 1987), 230–45; J. Grigg, 'The just king and *De duodecim abusiuis saeculi*', *Parergon* 27 (2010), 27–51.

[48] *Vincent of Beauvais: The Moral Instruction of a Prince; and Pseudo Cyprian: The Twelve Abuses of the World*, tr. P. Throop (Charlotte, VT, 2011), 127–9.

[49] H. H. Anton, *Fürstenspiegel und Herrscherethos in der Karolingerzeit* (Bonn, 1968). See also p. 149.

[50] J.-P. Genet (ed.), *La Légitimité implicite*, 2 vols (Paris, 2015).

Godfrey would have to account before God for the use he had made of it. For Godfrey's subjects to be kept free of harm, he must exercise justice himself and must appoint officials who would maintain and enforce the law.[51] In the eleventh century, Wulfstan of York also designed a comprehensive framework for moral reform. In his *Institutes of Polity*, Wulfstan stresses repeatedly the importance of taking sound advice: by heeding the counsel of good men, kings would ensure peace and tranquillity for their people.[52] Foolish princes would cause untold suffering,[53] and it was therefore incumbent upon the virtuous ruler to be familiar with the teachings of books and 'wise men'.[54] Wulfstan never actually specifies that these wise men are prelates. Yet bishops are listed first among the king's natural counsellors, their role being to warn those who transgress and to instruct their flock untiringly in proper moral action.[55] The failure of kings to heed wise counsel – and of prelates to offer it – would inflict suffering on their people and their flocks respectively.[56]

Providing counsel also established status and signified proximity to power. The dynastic histories of noble families, which became popular in the twelfth century, frequently praised their ancestors for exercising 'royal' duties: defending their domains, protecting the church and exercising justice.[57] A family thus received both material and symbolic capital from past deeds, which each generation was called upon to preserve and to surpass.[58] The same applied to ecclesiastical elites. Bishops and abbots were lauded for maintaining, recovering and expanding their community's domains, rights and privileges, sometimes using means which differed little from those of their secular counterparts. Not long after his death, a cleric named Balderic composed an account of the deeds of Archbishop Albero of Trier (1131–52). Its early sections are taken up with Albero's many secret missions, frequently in disguise as a pilgrim, beggar, knight or woman, couriering messages between the papal court

---

[51] *Die Briefe des Peter Damian*, ed. K. Reindel, 4 vols (Hanover, 1983–93), nos 67–8.
[52] Trilling, 'Sovereignty and social order', 73–8.
[53] Wulfstan of York, *Die 'Institutes of Polity, Civil and Ecclesiastical'. Ein Werk Erzbischofs Wulfstans von York*, ed. and tr. K. Jost (Bern, 1959), 47, 57.
[54] Wulfstan, *Institutes*, ed. and tr. Jost, 49, 57.
[55] Trilling, 'Sovereignty and social order', 71–3; Wulfstan, *Institutes*, ed. and tr. Jost, 62.
[56] Wulfstan, *Institutes*, ed. and tr. Jost, 63–4, 67–71.
[57] S. Patzold, *Episcopus: Wissen über Bischöfe im Frankreich des späten 8. bis frühen 10. Jahrhunderts* (Ostfildern, 2008); T. Reuter, 'Nobles and others: the social and cultural expression of power relations in the middle ages', in *MPMM*, 111–26; B. Weiler, 'Kingship and lordship: kingship in "dynastic" chronicles', in K. Stopka (ed.), *Gallus Anonymous and his Chronicle in the Context of Twelfth-Century Historiography from the Perspective of the Latest Research* (Cracow, 2011), 103–23.
[58] N. L. Paul, *To Follow in Their Footsteps: The Crusades and Family Memory in the High Middle Ages* (Ithaca, NY, 2012).

and its German supporters.[59] But once Albero succeeded to the see of Trier, he quickly grew into his role, not only expanding its estates but also reinforcing its standing vis-à-vis the king. Lothar III (1125–38) was afraid to take action against him, and Albero was able to bribe the Saxons into supporting Conrad III (1138–52) by distributing cartloads of wine.[60] He also took on ecclesiastical rivals: on attending an imperial diet at Mainz, where the resident archbishop was an old enemy, Albero ordered his troops to unfold their battle banners and intone war songs, approaching the meeting 'with horns and trumpets, the clash of weapons, and the horrible sounding war-song of the men'.[61] Archbishop Albero was also a prince of the world.[62]

What makes the case of Trier all the more important is the town's almost unbroken sequence of archiepiscopal *Gesta*, beginning in the eleventh century. Balderic's narrative presented itself (and was preserved by its readers) as part of a continuous record that centred not only on the deeds of the see's incumbent but also the city of Trier and its religious institutions. Just as Conrad II's status was raised and expectations formulated by setting him in succession to rulers such as Theodosius and Charlemagne, so noble and ecclesiastical lords were placed in a line of tradition that denoted both honour and duty. Prelates were judged not only by their defence of their cathedral church and its rights, but also by their protection of the community over which they presided. A bishop who failed to uphold the privileges of his see also deprived those given into his care of the opportunity to stake claims, seek justice and win the means of enforcing their rights. By providing advice and counsel to kings, prelates fulfilled obligations towards their own people and dependants.

Standing could have value in its own right. It reflected divine benevolence, suitability and earthly might. All three were interdependent and mutually reinforcing. God only entrusted power to those capable of enacting His will. But power was also needed in order to do good: after all, one needed means in order to demonstrate suitability. Of course this also had

---

[59] *A Warrior Bishop of the Twelfth Century: The Deeds of Albero of Trier, by Balderich*, tr. B. A. Pavlac (Toronto, 2008), 37–40.

[60] *Warrior Bishop*, tr. Pavlac, 55.   [61] *Warrior Bishop*, tr. Pavlac, 71.

[62] J. Keupp, 'Die zwei Schwerter des Bischofs. Von Kriegsherren und Seelenhirten im Reichsepiskopat der Stauferzeit', *Zeitschrift für Kirchengeschichte* 117 (2006), 1–24; T. Reuter, '*Episcopi cum sua militia*: the prelate as warrior in the early Staufen era', in T. Reuter (ed.), *Warriors and Churchmen in the Middle Ages. Essays Presented to Karl Leyser* (London, 1992), 79–94; G. A. Smith, '*Sine rege, sine principe*: Peter the Venerable on violence in twelfth-century Burgundy', *Speculum* 77 (2002), 1–33. See, though, the forthcoming work by Ryan Kemp, which shows that the image of an especially warlike German episcopate owes more to modern historiographical convention than to high medieval evidence: R. Kemp, *Images of Kingship in Bishops' Biographies and Deeds in Twelfth-Century England and Germany* (unpublished PhD thesis, Aberystwyth University, 2018).

practical implications. Standing denoted the ability to exercise influence on one's own behalf and for the benefit of one's followers and dependants. Securing the material foundations of power was thus both a means to an end and a goal in its own right. It was testimony to virtue and capability in equal measure. Consequently, the acquisition of lands and territories, the overcoming of foes and rivals through trickery and force, became recurring themes.[63] The twelfth-century counts of Barcelona, for instance, claimed descent from Godfrey II, who had single-handedly liberated the city from a Muslim host,[64] while his son cemented the family's standing by abducting a princess of Carolingian descent.[65] The Welf dukes of Bavaria and Saxony took pride in their history of resistance to royal power and in having first acquired their lands by duping their imperial lords.[66] Similar motifs emerge in histories of regnal and urban communities. To Vincent Kadłubek, writing in Cracow around 1200, the Poles were actually Gauls: some of them had attacked and conquered Rome, while others had defeated the Danes before settling in Poland.[67] According to Simon de Kéza, writing some eighty years later, the Magyars were Egyptians who migrated to Persia after the fall of the Tower of Babel: forced into Scythia by over-population, they – or rather the Huns – had gone on to conquer most of Europe before eventually settling in Hungary.[68] Central to origin narratives

[63] See, generally, J. Banaszkiewicz, 'Slavonic *origines regni*: hero the law-giver and founder of monarchy (introductory survey of problems)', *Acta Poloniae Historica* 69 (1989), 97–131; T. N. Bisson, 'Unheroed pasts: history and commemoration in South Frankland before the Albigensian Crusades', *Speculum* 65 (1990), 281–308; A. Plassmann, *Origo gentis. Identitäts- und Legitimitätsstiftung in früh- und hochmittelalterlichen Herkunftserzählungen* (Berlin 2006). On the importance of landholding in underpinning power, see also pp. 150, 369–70.

[64] *Gesta Comitum Barcinonensium. Textos Llatí i Català*, ed. L. Barrau Dihigo and J. Massó Torrents (Barcelona, 1925), 5; P. Freedman, 'Cowardice, heroism and the legendary origins of Catalonia', *P&P* 121 (1988), 3–28 at 14–9; M. Zimmermann, 'Les origines de la Catalogne d'après les *Gesta Comitum Barcinonensium*. Mythe fondateur ou récit éthiologique?', in D. Barthélemy and J.-M. Martin (eds), *Liber Largitorius. Études d'histoire médiévale offertes à Pierre Toubert par ses élèves* (Geneva, 2003), 517–43.

[65] *Gesta Comitum*, ed. Barrau Dihigo and Massó Torrents, 3–5. Jaume Aurell has suggested an implied link with the Carolingians as a possible explanation for this fairly widespread topos: 'From genealogies to chronicles: the power of the form in medieval Catalan historiography', *Viator* 36 (2005), 235–64 at 244–5. See also *The Gesta Normannorum Ducum of William of Jumièges, Orderic Vitalis and Robert of Torigni*, ed. and tr. E. M. C. van Houts, 2 vols (Oxford, 1992–5), ii:128–31.

[66] *Historia Welforum*, ed. and tr. E. König, *Schwäbische Chroniken der Stauferzeit* 1 (Stuttgart, 1938; repr. Sigmaringen, 1978), 2–9; A. Plassmann, 'Die Welfen-Origo: ein Einzelfall?', in D. R. Bauer and M. Becher (eds), *Welf IV.: Schlüsselfigur einer Wendezeit. Regionale und europäische Perspektiven* (Munich, 2004), 56–83.

[67] *Die Chronik der Polen des Magister Vincentius*, ed. and tr. E. Mühle (Darmstadt, 2014), 94–7. On Vincent: D. von Güttner-Sporzyński (ed.), *Writing History in Medieval Poland: Bishop Vincentius of Cracow and the 'Chronica Polonorum'* (Turnhout, 2017).

[68] Simon de Kéza, *Gesta Hungarorum*, ed. and tr. L. Vészpremy and F. Schaer, with J. Sczücs (Budapest, 1999), 8–25.

of royal power was the theme of kingship claimed or awarded once a ruler had grown more powerful than any of his people, provided he used the power for the common good.[69]

Rank and standing had to be constantly displayed. Enacting power involved gift-giving, founding churches and hospitals, and feeding and housing the poor, as well as waging war, distributing plunder and persecuting evil-doers.[70] Such display emphasised both the moral excellence and the material wealth of the mighty: 'If you were perceived as a king, then you were one.'[71] Even when a king demonstratively laid aside the accoutrements of status – on pilgrimage, for instance, or when interacting with the needy in person, as Conrad II had done – the act was performative. Only the truly powerful could afford to suspend this constant demonstration of status, and then only temporarily.[72] By contrast, the inability to muster resources legitimised challenge. Einhard's caricature of the last Merovingian king is a case in point:

He had nothing that he could call his own beyond this vain title of King and the precarious support allowed by the Mayor of the Palace in his discretion, except a single country seat, that brought him but a very small income. There was a dwelling house upon this, and a small number of servants attached to it, sufficient to perform the necessary offices. When he had to go abroad, he used to ride in a cart, drawn by a yoke of oxen driven, peasant-fashion, by a ploughman [...].[73]

Possessing only an empty title, Childeric III was deposed and replaced by someone with the resources to be taken for a king – Pippin the Short, his Mayor of the Palace. Similar principles could be applied to princes, prelates and townsmen. A failure to demonstrate power signified the inability to hold authority over others; a more capable, and hence suitable, candidate should be found.

[69] Weiler, 'Crown-giving'.
[70] G. Algazi et al. (eds), *Negotiating the Gift: Pre-Modern Figurations of Exchange* (Göttingen, 2003); H. J. Orning, *Unpredictability and Presence: Norwegian Kingship in the High Middle Ages*, tr. A. Crozier (Leiden, 2008); H.-J. Schmidt, *Herrschaft durch Schrecken und Liebe: Vorstellungen und Begründungen im Mittelalter* (Stuttgart, 2018); L. Kjaer, *The Medieval Gift and the Classical Tradition: Ideals and the Performance of Generosity in Medieval England, 1100–1300* (Cambridge, 2019). On the importance of pious and charitable foundations, see M. Borgolte (ed.), *Stiftungen in Christentum, Judentum und Islam vor der Moderne: auf der Suche nach ihren Gemeinsamkeiten und Unterschieden in religiösen Grundlagen, praktischen Zwecken und historischen Transformationen* (Berlin, 2005); M. Borgolte (ed.), *Enzyklopädie des Stiftungswesens in mittelalterlichen Gesellschaften*, 3 vols (Berlin, 2014–17).
[71] Reuter, '*Regemque*', 129.
[72] P. Buc, 'Conversion of objects: Suger of St-Denis and Meinwerk of Paderborn', *Viator* 28 (1997), 99–143; N. Vincent, 'The pilgrimages of the Angevin kings of England, 1154–1272', in C. Morris and P. Roberts (eds), *Pilgrimage: The English Experience from Becket to Bunyan* (Cambridge, 2002), 12–45.
[73] Einhard, *Life of Charlemagne*, tr. A. J. Grant (Cambridge, ON, 1999), 5.

The need to display status was tempered by moral expectations. Power should not be desired but humbly accepted;[74] it should only be used to advance the common good, not to satisfy the desires of the mighty. Thus excessive display of power could be reason to reject the right to hold it. Profligacy denoted an abdication of responsibility, a desire for worldly goods that stood in direct conflict with the moral imperatives of wielding secular might. Spendthrifts and gluttons were tyrants in the making. The display of might was therefore guided by a set of unwritten expectations that changed over time and that could themselves become a means for demonstrating status. While the evidence is hard to come by for earlier periods,[75] from the tenth century we can observe the development of a moral and a behavioural code designed to encourage and signify adherence to ideals of righteous action. Courtliness favoured displays of restraint, wit and ease of manners, but it was embedded in a moral framework of admonishing the mighty and protecting the weak. Drawing on classical conventions of elite behaviour, courtliness required familiarity with tropes, conventions and allusions accessible only to those with resources to spend on education.[76] It existed, moreover, in a complex relationship with ideals of chivalry.[77] The two overlapped, but having its origins as a clerical code of conduct, courtliness provided a counterpoint to chivalric displays of martial prowess. In combination, they helped establish an ideal type of elite behaviour that manifested itself in norms of politesse: comportment, speech and clothing all expressed standing and regulated elite interaction. A certain type of knightly behaviour, largely divorced from the reality of life among the lower and middling aristocracy, was celebrated and inspired by fictionalised representations of noble conduct. Chivalry became an act of performance: for example, the *Frauendienst* ('Service of the Ladies') of

---

[74] Weiler, '*Rex renitens*' (which, its title notwithstanding, also deals with prelates and sections of the aristocracy).

[75] Y. Hen, *Roman Barbarians: The Royal Court and Culture in the Early Medieval West* (Basingstoke, 2007).

[76] C. S. Jaeger, *The Origins of Courtliness: Civilizing Trends and the Formation of Courtly Ideals, 939–1210* (Philadelphia, 1985); idem, 'Origins of courtliness after 25 years', *Haskins Society Journal* 21 (2009), 187–216; J. Fleckenstein (ed.), *Curialitas: Studien zu Grundfragen der höfisch-ritterlichen Kultur* (Göttingen, 1992); K. Beyer, *Witz und Ironie in der politischen Kultur Englands im Hochmittelalter. Interaktionen und Imaginationen* (Würzburg, 2012).

[77] J. Bumke, *Courtly Culture: Literature and Society in the High Middle Ages* (Berkeley, 1992); R. W. Kaeuper, *Chivalry and Violence in Medieval Europe* (Oxford, 1999); R. W. Kaeuper, *Holy Warriors: The Religious Ideology of Chivalry* (Philadelphia, 2009); J. Flori, *Chevaliers et chevalerie au Moyen Âge* (Paris, 2004); D. Crouch, 'Chivalry and courtliness: colliding constructs', in P. Coss (ed.), *Soldiers, Nobles and Gentlemen: Essays in Honour of Maurice Keen* (Woodbridge, 2009); J. Peltzer (ed.), *Rank and Order: The Formation of Aristocratic Elites in Western and Central Europe, 500–1500* (Ostfildern, 2015). See also pp. 139, 157–8.

Ulrich of Lichtenstein (*c.*1255), who travelled from Bohemia to Venice and fought a series of tournaments while dressed as the Goddess Venus.[78] Orders of chivalry proliferated in the later middle ages, enabling the highest aristocracy to imitate a heavily romanticised knightly way of life and thus project the moral probity of their founders and members.[79] Elite status manifested itself in the celebration of an idealised code of conduct. Yet it did so, in part at least, because this code was normative. It provided a means for celebrating status as well as a standard against which actions could be measured and by which they could be legitimised.[80]

Moreover, status was rooted in antiquity, which signified both legitimacy and distinctiveness. From the twelfth century on, towns and newly converted realms increasingly attempted to fashion narratives of ancient origins. In Iceland, *Landnámabók* ('Book of Settlement') and *Íslendigabók* ('Book of Icelanders') construct a narrative celebrating the differences that mark out the settlers on the island from their Norwegian homeland.[81] In Denmark, Saxo Grammaticus' *Gesta Danorum* (composed *c.*1200) centres on the antiquity of the Danish realm: predating Rome, its rulers not only ward off but defeat and subjugate their hostile southern neighbours.[82] And in twelfth-century Poland, Bohemia and

---

[78] Ulrich of Liechtenstein, *Service of the Ladies*, tr. R. Barber (Woodbridge, 2004).

[79] J. D. B. d'Arcy, *The Knights of the Crown: The Monarchical Orders of Knighthood in Later Medieval Europe, 1325–1520* (Woodbridge, 1987); H. E. L. Collins, *The Order of the Garter, 1348–1461: Chivalry and Politics in Late Medieval England* (Oxford, 2000); M. G. A. Vale, *The Princely Court: Medieval Courts and Culture in North-West Europe, 1270–1380* (Oxford, 2001); K. Stevenson, *Chivalry and Knighthood in Late Medieval Scotland, 1424–1513* (Woodbridge, 2004); K. Oschema *et al.* (eds), *Die Performanz der Mächtigen: Rangordnung und Idoneität in höfischen Gesellschaften des späten Mittelalters* (Ostfildern, 2015).

[80] T. Reuter, 'Nobles and others: the social and cultural expression of power relations in the middle ages', in *MPMM*, 113–26; R. Schnell, '"Curialitas" und "dissimulatio" im Mittelalter: zur Interdependenz von Hofkritik und Hofideal', *Zeitschrift für Literaturwissenschaft und Linguistik* 41 (2011), 77–138; C. Herrmann, 'Burgensymbolik im Rathausbau des Deutschordenslandes Preussen (Thorn, Marienburg)', in F. Biermann *et al.* (eds), *Castella Maris Balticae VII* (Greifswald, 2006), 51–9.

[81] H. Antonsson, 'The present and the past in the Sagas of Icelanders', in P. Lambert and B. Weiler (eds), *How the Past was Used: Historical Cultures, c.750–2000* (Oxford, 2017), 69–90; E. Mundal, '*Íslendigabók*: the creation of an early Icelandic Christian identity', in I. Garipzanov (ed.), *Historical Narratives and Christian Identity on a European Periphery: Early History Writing in Northern, East-Central, and Eastern Europe (c.1070–1200)* (Turnhout, 2011), 111–21; D. Whaley, 'A useful past: historical writing in medieval Iceland', in M. Clunies Ross (ed.), *Old Icelandic Literature and Society* (Cambridge, 2000), 161–202.

[82] S. Bagge, 'Ideologies and mentalities', in *CHS* 1, 465–86; O. Engels, 'Friedrich Barbarossa und Dänemark', in A. Haverkamp (ed.), *Friedrich Barbarossa: Handlungsspielräume und Wirkungsweisen des staufischen Kaisers* (Sigmaringen, 1992), 353–85; M. Groh, 'Das Deutschenbild in den historischen Büchern der *Gesta Danorum*', in T. Nyberg (ed.), *Saxo and the Baltic Region: A Symposium* (Odense, 2004), 143–60.

Hungary, chroniclers highlight the antiquity and distinctiveness of their communities by situating their origins in a distant past and stressing their traditional independence from outside forces.[83] We see comparable developments in Italy and the Rhineland, where urban communities revised religious origin narratives to show that the community predated the arrival of Christianity. In many cases, these communities had been in competition with the local bishop for power, gradually seizing it from him. Such accounts frequently adapt existing models by citing a Trojan pedigree, for example, but sometimes they go further still. In eleventh-century Trier, the city's origins are attributed to Trebeta, grandson of Ninus, king of the Assyrians 1,300 years before the foundation of Rome.[84] In each of these cases, modes of organisation and norms of political conduct that marked out a community as distinctive are traced to a distant or heroic past, thus establishing a means of assessing present-day affairs.[85]

Narratives of origin were not new, as surviving accounts by Jordanes and Paul the Deacon – of, respectively, the barbarian Goths and Lombards – suggest;[86] and more recent accounts often built on these, as well as on themes from classical antiquity and the Bible. The first indigenous account of Czech history, the *Chronica Boemorum* (*c*.1120), opens with their wanderings after the collapse of the Tower of Babel.[87] Yet compared to ecclesiastical or dynastic foundation narratives, we see a greater emphasis on and loyalty to the community in these later accounts – a loyalty predating and transcending any particular dynasty or even the adoption of Christianity. Hungarians and Poles existed long before there were Árpáds or Piasts, and long before the first missionaries arrived. Indeed, the early thirteenth-century *Gesta Hungarorum* stops just short of their conversion.[88] By the thirteenth century it is even possible to detect regnal identities which emphasise local, well-established laws and customs that were distinct from

---

[83] Banaszkiewicz, 'Slavonic *origines regni*'; L. Wolverton, *Cosmas of Prague: Narrative, Classicism, Politics* (Washington, DC, 2014).

[84] *Gesta Treverorum*, ed. G. Waitz, *MGH SS* 8 (Leipzig, 1848), 111–260 at 30.

[85] Foerster, 'Political myths'; Weiler, 'Tales of first kings', 101–28. See also pp. 160, 170.

[86] W. Goffart, *The Narrators of Barbarian History (AD 550–800): Jordanes, Gregory of Tours, Bede, and Paul the Deacon* (Princeton, 1988); H. Reimitz, *History, Frankish Identity and the Framing of Western Ethnicity, 550–850* (Cambridge, 2015).

[87] Cosmas of Prague, *Die Chronik der Böhmen des Cosmas von Prag*, ed. B. Bretholz with W. Weinberger, *MGH SRG* n.s. 2. (Berlin, 1923), 4–7.

[88] *Anonimi Bele regis notarii Gesta Hungarorum et Magistri Rogerii Epistolae in miserabile Carmen super destructione Regni Hungariae per tartaros facta*, tr. M. Rady *et al.* (Budapest and New York, 2010), 4–10; L. Veszprémy, '"More paganismo": reflections on the pagan and Christian past in the *Gesta Hungarorum* of the Hungarian Anonymous Notary', in Garipzanov (ed.), *Historical Writing*, 183–201; L. E. Scales, 'At the margin of community: Germans in pre-Hussite Bohemia', *TRHS* 6th series 9 (1999), 327–52.

those of surrounding lands;[89] and obligations of status start to extend from a dynasty, or a particular church and its saints, to the wider community. The people take the place of a lord's kin, *familia* and dependants – less through ties of lordship than through ruler and ruled alike belonging to a community which is identifiable by its shared laws, customs and even language.

This development of communal identity frequently goes hand in hand with an emphasis on the ruler's duties towards his people and the right of the people to oversee the ruler. Saxo Grammaticus' *Gesta Danorum* opens with the Danes deposing one ruler because of his ineptitude, replacing him with someone more capable.[90] The contemporaneous *Gesta Hungarorum* traces the Hungarians' origins to a mythical past. Just before their army sets out from Scythia to conquer new lands, the Seven Leaders (precursors of the Hungarian aristocracy) swear both to follow Álmos wherever he might take them and for ever more to elect one of his descendants as their lord. But they swear this on four conditions: that all land and booty should be divided equally; that the Leaders and their heirs should always advise their lord and participate fully in the honour and business of the realm (*honor regni*); that anyone seeking to sow discord should pay for this with his blood; and that, should Álmos, the Leaders or any of their descendants violate these terms, he would be cursed for all eternity.[91] Antiquity bestowed standing on a community, often independently of those leading it. The leader had a duty to maintain that status and to defend the reputation and standing of his people. But their subjects also had a duty to hold their leader to account and to ensure their righteous behaviour.

What we have seen so far are *ideals* – power as both a reward and a duty; the oversight of the rulers by the ruled; the importance of antecedent and tradition; and (as we shall see slightly later on) the distinctive role played by professional interpreters of holy texts – expectations as to how things should be and not accurate reflections of how they actually *were*. Yet even abstract values were not static: people adopted and revived previous generations' ideas, adapting them to the needs of a particular community at a specific moment in time, just as subsequent generations would revise and amend their approaches in turn. It is to the factors driving such change that we now must turn.

---

[89] A. Nedkvitne, 'Linguistic tensions between Germans and natives in Scandinavia compared to eastern Europe', in M. Mostert and A. Adamska (eds), *Uses of the Written Word in Medieval Towns, Medieval Urban Literacy 2* (Turnhout, 2014), 87–97.

[90] Saxo Grammaticus, *Gesta Danorum*, ed. K. Friis-Jensen, tr. P. Zeeberg, 2 vols (Copenhagen, 2005), i:86.

[91] *Anonimi Bele*, ed. and tr. Rady *et al.*, 16–19.

Changes and Challenges

Norms were open to interpretation. Even as elementary a principle as justice could encompass a multiplicity of meanings.[92] There was the maintenance of law: ensuring an agreed body of rules was upheld. Wipo describes Conrad as restoring the laws of Burgundy and confirming even the barbarous customs of the Saxons, simply because they reflected established law. Yet what did this mean in practice? At Pavia, both emperor and townsmen invoked shared legal principles: they simply disagreed as to how they should be applied. Law and justice also required that loyal and faithful servants should be duly rewarded. Yet one party's fair recompense was another's undue favouritism.[93] To complicate matters further, good lords were meant to protect those who could not protect themselves, even if this meant acting against the great and the good or aggravating their own dependants and allies. This is clearly central to Wipo's account of Conrad's coronation, and almost identical norms are invoked by an anonymous early twelfth-century cleric at the Polish ducal court, who writes about Bolesław I Chrobry, ruler of Poland from 992 to 1025, thus:

> [. . .] if some poor peasant or some ordinary woman came with a complaint against a duke or count, no matter how important the matters he was engaged in [. . .] he would not stir from the spot before he had heard the full account of the complaint and sent a chamberlain to fetch the lord against whom the complaint had been made.[94]

A ruler's responsibilities also extended to his servants, since the very agents of royal justice could prevent it from being carried out. Walter Map's *De nugis curialium* ('Courtier's Trifles') (*c.*1180) opens with a warning from the bishop of Lincoln to Henry II: royal agents endanger both the king's eternal salvation and their own.[95] It ends with a caveat to all kings: they must be ever-vigilant, never allowing their officials to act

---

[92] G. Melville *et al.* (eds), *Gerechtigkeit* (Cologne, 2014); S. Patzold, 'Consensus – Concordia – Unitas. Überlegungen zu einem politisch-religiösen Ideal der Karolingerzeit', in N. Staubach (ed.), *Exemplaris imago: Ideale in Mittelalter und Früher Neuzeit* (Frankfurt am Main, 2012), 31–56. See also the important case study on 'false peace' by J. Malegam, *The Sleep of Behemoth: Disputing Peace and Violence in Medieval Europe, 1000–1200* (Ithaca, NY, 2013).

[93] T. Reuter, 'Peace-breaking, feud, rebellion, resistance: violence and peace in the politics of the Salian era', in *MPMM*, 355–87.

[94] *Gesta Principum Polonorum: The Deeds of the Princes of the Poles*, ed. and tr. P. W. Knoll and F. Schaer, with T. N. Bisson (Budapest, 2003), 48–9.

[95] Walter Map, *De nugis curialium: Courtiers' Trifles*, ed. and tr. M. R. James, rev. C. N. L. Brooke and R. A. B. Mynors (Oxford, 1983), 10–11; Jaeger, *Origins of Courtliness*; E. Türk, '*Nugae Curialium*': le règne d'Henri II Plantagenêt (1145–1189) et l'éthique politique (Geneva, 1977).

without close supervision.[96] Finally, the relationship between rigour and compassion remained a matter of debate. Isidore of Seville viewed mercy as central to ruling and correcting,[97] as did Wipo and Walter Map.[98] But Peter Damian, writing to Godfrey of Tuscany in the 1060s, claims that showing compassion – acting like a loving mother to errant children – was a matter for priests. Secular princes, by contrast, were meant to punish evil-doers.[99]

All these readings were equally valid, and each drew on a shared framework of thinking about power and its uses. Collectively, they point to a defining feature and an equally defining tension in medieval thinking about power. The interpretation and implementation of abstract values reflected the needs of the specific moment in which justice was called for or done, as well as the often unique confluence of circumstance, necessity, actors and means. Furthermore, in each community, conflicting discourses of justice existed. Clerics involved in the realm's fiscal administration might hold different views from university scholars, and these might differ from ones espoused by friars, wandering preachers, parish priests or archbishops, all of whom might well disagree with each other. Theirs, in turn, might overlap with, but also be challenged by, kings, princes, knights, artisans and merchants. So who decided which values to invoke and how to interpret them? In most cases, there was no uncontested interpretative monopoly, no single body universally entrusted with defining the sole legitimate reading and application.[100] How norms were interpreted thus reflected a complex interplay of social, economic, political, cultural and religious factors, which could overlap, reinforce or exist in sometimes open and sometimes latent competition.

Paradoxically, this went hand in hand with expectations that put a premium on consensus and stressed unanimity as the ideal way of reaching

---

[96] Walter Map, *De nugis curialium*, ed. and tr. James *et al.*, 510–3.
[97] Isidore of Seville, *Etymologies*, tr. Barney *et al.*, 200.
[98] Walter Map, *De nugis curialium*, ed. and tr. James *et al.*, 442–6, 470–1.
[99] *Die Briefe des Peter Damian*, ed. Reindel, no. 67.
[100] A. de Benedictis (ed.), *Revolten und politische Verbrechen zwischen dem 12. und 19. Jahrhundert: rechtliche Reaktionen und juristisch-politische Diskurse* (Frankfurt am Main, 2013); T. Eckert, 'Nichthäretische Papstkritik in England vom Beginn des 14. bis zur zweiten Hälfte des 15. Jahrhunderts', *Annuarium Historiae Conciliorum* 23 (1991), 116–359; M. Kintzinger *et al.* (eds) *Gewalt und Widerstand in der politischen Kultur des späten Mittelalters* (Ostfildern, 2015); T. E. Morrissey, *Conciliarism and Church Law in the Fifteenth Century* (Farnham, 2014); H. Müller and J. Helmrath (eds), *Die Konzilien von Pisa (1409), Konstanz (1414–18), und Basel (1431–49): Institution und Personen* (Ostfildern, 2007); F. Oakley, *Natural Law, Conciliarism and Consent in the Late Middle Ages: Studies in Ecclesiastical and Intellectual History* (London, 1984); J. Rollo-Koster and T. M. Izbicki (eds), *A Companion to the Great Western Schism, 1378–1417* (Leiden, 2009). On the diversity of multiple loci of authority: pp. 148–56, 165–9, 171–5, 373–5, 400–2, 409.

decisions. For most of the middle ages, public disagreements were shunned.[101] Indeed until the fourteenth century,[102] the avoidance of dispute was central to the conduct of assemblies and legal proceedings.[103] Partisanship and the rise of factions were viewed as harbingers of civil strife. Urban communes went out of their way to establish mechanisms whereby factionalism could be, if not be wholly avoided, at least muffled. Of course, this expectation of unanimity did not reflect reality. Even Wipo had to admit that the archbishop of Cologne and the duke of Lorraine had been absent from Conrad's coronation; in fact, it could not take place at Aachen because of their opposition.[104] And while Wipo upheld Conrad as an exemplary ruler, his contemporary Ralph Glaber claimed that he had only become king with the devil's help![105] Still, unanimous consent remains central to the normative framework of power. Divergent views constitute a challenge to the right order of the world, partly because of a shared framework which is itself rooted in precedent and divine revelation. Either a disputed decision lacks God's blessing or those opposing it are driven by factionalism, greed and ambition. Thus, although many of our extant materials originate in an attempt to voice or to refute dissent, a defining feature of most of them is their claim to universality.

Literacy as a Case Study at the Heart of High Medieval Political Culture

Literacy provided both the framework for and the means of expressing shared norms. It was both a cultural and a social practice, a skill whose acquisition required resources and hence recognition as something worth supporting. Tracing how literacy was used and who used it should allow us to identify wider patterns. After all, using literacy to define norms also meant claiming a stake in their enforcement.

[101] B. Schneidmüller, 'Rule by consensus: forms and concepts of political order in the European middle ages', *Medieval History Journal* 16 (2013), 449–71.

[102] J. R. Maddicott, *The Origins of the English Parliament, 973–1328* (Oxford, 2012); J. Peltzer *et al.* (eds), *Politische Versammlungen und ihre Rituale: Repräsentationsformen und Entscheidungsprozesse des Reichs und der Kirche im späten Mittelalter* (Ostfildern, 2009).

[103] P. Barnwell and M. Mostert (eds), *Political Assemblies in the Earlier Middle Ages* (Turnhout, 2003); V. Epp and C. H. F. Meyer (eds), *Recht und Konsens im frühen Mittelalter* (Ostfildern, 2017); L. Melve, '"Even the very laymen are chattering about it": the politicization of public opinion, 800–1200', *Viator* 44:1 (2013), 25–48; L. Melve, 'Assembly politics and the "rules of the game" (ca. 650–1150)', *Viator* 41 (2010), 69–90; T. Reuter, 'Assembly politics in western Europe from the eighth century to the twelfth', in *MPMM*, 193–216.

[104] GC[1] chs 2–3, 544–7; GC[2], 65–6.

[105] Rodulfus Glaber, *The Five Books of the Histories*, ed. and tr. J. France (Oxford, 1989), 178–9.

Literacy had religious underpinnings since Christianity was a text-based religion, centred on divine revelation as recorded in a series of canonical scriptures, making the ability to read essential.[106] The emergence of an infrastructure to ensure the education of a literate caste of specialised interpreters of sacred scriptures was characteristic of the process of Christianisation in many societies.[107] Moreover, the adoption of Christianity established channels of communication linking the newly converted regions of Europe to an already Christianised core. In the eighth and ninth centuries, successive waves of missionaries helped to disseminate Carolingian concepts of power and how it should be exercised to the recently Christianised regions of Germany;[108] in the twelfth, the first narrative of Polish history was composed by Gallus Anonymus, plausibly a French cleric who had found his way to the ducal court;[109] and a century later, Albert Suerbeer of Cologne embarked on an ecclesiastical career spanning Germany, Ireland and Prussia.[110] This internationalisation of the religious sphere persisted well into the fifteenth century. It became a central feature of newly emerging religious orders, such as the Cistercians and Mendicants, but these channels of communication also ensured the circulation of heterodox ideas.[111]

However, the process of conversion could not succeed without the backing of those who controlled the material sources of power. Endowing churches was expensive, as was defending and protecting them, and patrons both exercised considerable control over and were in turn held responsible for their proper functioning. This could both reinforce and weaken their authority. The ninth century, in particular, witnessed vigorous efforts by rulers to ensure uniformity in script, textual standards and education, resulting in canonical compilations of texts that

---

[106] For the western church's hold on the technology of literacy: p. 388. Basic literacy was fairly evenly spread among laypersons and clergy in Byzantium: pp. 92, 97, 319, 427, 428; as also in the world of Islam: pp. 117–18, 126, 127, 128.

[107] N. Berend (ed.), *Christianization and the Rise of Christian Monarchy: Scandinavia, Central Europe and Rus', c. 900–1200* (Cambridge, 2007).

[108] M. J. Innes, *State and Society in the Early Middle Ages: The Middle Rhine Valley* (Cambridge, 2000); J. T. Palmer, *Anglo-Saxons in the Frankish World, 600–900* (Turnhout, 2009); I. Wood, *The Missionary Life: Saints and the Evangelisation of Europe 400–1050* (London, 2001).

[109] Z. Dalewski, 'A new Chosen People? Gallus Anonymus's narrative about Poland and its rulers', in Garipzanov (ed.), *Historical Writing*, 145–66; E. Mühle, '*Cronicae et gesta ducum sive principum Polonorum*: neue Forschungen zum so genannten Gallus Anonymus', *Deutsches Archiv für Erforschung des Mittelalters* 65 (2009), 459–96; Stopka (ed.), *Gallus Anonymus and his Chronicle*.

[110] M. Rohkohl, 'Albert Suerbeer, Erzbischof von Livland, Estland und Preußen', *Zeitschrift für Schleswig-Holsteinische Geschichte* 47 (1917), 68–90.

[111] M. Van Dussen and P. Soukup (eds), *Religious Controversy in Europe, 1378–1536: Textual Transmission and Networks of Readership* (Turnhout, 2013).

continued to be read and consulted into the twelfth century.[112] Similarly, on an aristocratic level, the defence and patronage of ecclesiastical institutions constituted a mark of dynastic legitimacy. Comparable conditions prevailed in towns and cities, where the responsibility of communal governments for the functioning of religious institutions led to frequent rivalry with ecclesiastical lords, as well as becoming a means of legitimising displacement of the latter.[113]

Yet such secular involvement also posed a dilemma: it was, after all, open to abuse. Ensuring the moral purity of ecclesiastical institutions by freeing them from secular entanglements was a common concern among religious reform movements. Hincmar of Rheims is perhaps the best-known example, but many reformists believed that the moral principles they expounded gave them a duty to oversee the high and mighty.[114] Ecclesiastical writers made recurring efforts to delineate the limits of secular involvement in spiritual matters. The matter of where precisely that line should be drawn formed a constant in medieval engagements with norms of power. It is worth noting that lay patrons were often the ones who helped realise ever stricter readings of what that freedom entailed: without them, there would have been no Cluniac monasticism, no Cistercians, no Mendicants and certainly no Reformation. Shifts in religious practice not only reflected debates among churchmen, monks, secular clergy, court clerics and university teachers but also the expectations of an equally diverse laity. They were initiated, discussed, embraced or rejected, modified, and adapted by clergymen and lay persons alike. And they echoed the increasing diversification of the church, the formalisation of ecclesiastical law, the emergence of new ways of thinking about and engaging with religious doctrine, and the arrival of scholasticism. The distinction between the secular and religious spheres,

---

[112] R. McKitterick, 'The Carolingian renaissance of culture and learning', in J. Storey (ed.), *Charlemagne: Empire and Society* (Manchester, 2005), 151–66; S. MacLean, 'The Carolingian past in post-Carolingian Europe', in J. Hudson and S. Crumplin (eds), *The Making of Europe: Essays in Honour of Robert Bartlett* (Leiden, 2016), 11–31; M. Teuween, 'Carolingian scholarship on classical authors: practices of reading and writing', in E. Kwakkel (ed.), *Manuscripts of the Latin Classics, 800–1200* (Leiden, 2015), 23–52; M. M. Tischler, *Einharts 'Vita Karoli': Studien zu Entstehung, Überlieferung und Rezeption*, 2 vols (Hanover, 2001).

[113] C. Dartmann, *Politische Interaktion in der italienischen Stadtkommune (11.–14. Jhdt.)* (Ostfildern, 2011); U. Grieme *et al.* (eds), *Bischof und Bürger: Herrschaftsbeziehungen in den Kathedralstädten des Hoch- und Spätmittelalters* (Göttingen, 2004); M. C. Miller, *The Bishop's Palace: Architecture and Authority in Medieval Italy* (Ithaca, NY, 2000).

[114] J. L. Nelson, 'Kingship, law and liturgy in the political thought of Hincmar of Rheims', *EHR* 92 (1977), 241–79; R. Stone and C. West (eds), *Hincmar of Rheims: Life and Thought* (Manchester, 2015).

so widely postulated in theory, was not always strictly adhered to in practice.[115]

Nor were these new actors united in their understanding of political norms. In England during the 1260s, Dominicans and Franciscans appear to have been highly supportive of those seeking to restrain royal power, whereas a decade later they emerged in Germany as ardent backers of King Rudolf I.[116] In both cases they were part of complex coalitions which pitched groups of barons and clergy against both their peers and the king. All too often, therefore, the spectrum of those promulgating and formulating readings of abstract political norms transcends simplistic categorisation into lay or clerical, reformist or conservative. Indeed, the term 'reform' is often used by medieval writers – and their modern readers – to label a range of such diverse goals that its precise meaning is impossible to determine.[117] At best, its popularity indicates that the desire to return to an ideal status quo ante was itself a cultural norm.[118]

We also need to take into account social and economic factors. From around the year 1000, western Europe underwent a period of rapid growth.[119] A considerable portion of the surplus thus accruing flowed

[115] P. Boucheron and J. Chiffoleau (eds), *Religion et société urbaine au Moyen Âge: études offertes à Jean-Louis Biget par ses anciens élèves* (Paris, 2000); S. Hamilton, *Church and People in the Medieval West, 900–1200* (Harlow, 2013); A. Nedkvitne, *Lay Belief in Norse Society, 1100–1350* (Copenhagen, 2009); T. Reuter, 'Pre-Gregorian mentalities', in *MPMM*, 89–99; B. Stock, *The Implications of Literacy: Written Language and Models of Interpretation in the 11th and 12th Centuries* (Princeton, 1983); A. Thompson, *Cities of God: The Religion of the Italian Communes, 1125–1325* (University Park, PA, 2005); O. Zumhagen, *Religiöse Konflikte und kommunale Entwicklung. Mailand, Cremona, Piacenza und Florenz zur Zeit der Pataria* (Cologne, 2001).

[116] J. B. Freed, *The Friars and German Society in the Thirteenth Century* (Cambridge, MA, 1977); J. Röhrkasten, *The Mendicant Houses of Medieval London, 1221–1539* (Münster, 2004).

[117] K.-F. Krieger, *König, Reich und Reichsreform im Spätmittelalter* (Munich, 2005); C. Leyser, 'Church reform – full of sound and fury, signifying nothing?', *EME* 24 (2016), 478–99; L. Melve, 'Ecclesiastical reform in historiographical context', *History Compass* 13 (2015), 213–21; M. C. Miller, 'Reconsidering reform: a Roman example', in D. C. Mengel and L. Wolverton (eds), *Christianity and Culture in the Middle Ages: Essays in Honour of John Van Engen* (Notre Dame, IN, 2015), 123–40; M. C. Miller, 'Reform, clerical culture and politics', in J. Arnold (ed.), *The Oxford Handbook of Medieval Christianity* (Oxford, 2014), 305–22; S. Vanderputten, *Reform, Conflict, and the Shaping of Corporate Identities: Collected Studies on Benedictine Monasticism in Medieval Flanders, c.1050–c.1150* (Berlin, 2013); S. Vanderputten, '*Magna rei restaurandae difficultas*: experiencing and remembering conflict over monastic reform (southern Low Countries, 10th–12th centuries)', *Saeculum* 66 (2016), 147–68.

[118] C. M. Belitto and D. Z. Flanagin (eds), *Reassessing Reform: A Historical Investigation into Church Renewal* (Washington, DC, 2012); G. B. Ladner, *The Ideas of Reform: Its Impact on Christian Thought and Action in the Age of the Fathers* (Cambridge, MA, 1959).

[119] U. Blum and L. Dudley, 'Standardised Latin and medieval economic growth', *European Review of Economic History* 7 (2003), 213–28; H. Steuer, 'Minting, silver routes and mining in Europe: economic expansion and technical innovation', in J. Heitzman and

into the endowment of religious institutions, leading to expansive building and rebuilding programmes of cathedral churches across Europe, as well as the establishment of new monastic sites and even of new orders.[120] The reforming movements of the period were made possible by this increasing wealth and became necessary because of it. Of particular importance is the resulting outburst in manuscript production, particularly around 1150, 1250 and 1400,[121] as well as the emergence of a greater variety of genres and an expansion of the institutional framework for reading and writing. Universities are perhaps the most visible manifestation of this phenomenon: they transformed not only expectations about what constituted a Latinate education but also the range of topics treated and the ways in which they could be discussed.[122] Yet they were modelled on older institutions that continued to remain active, chief among them cathedral schools and monastic scriptoria.[123]

Although literary patronage remained essentially an elite activity, it reflected the gradual diversification of the elite from the second half of the thirteenth century, with administrators, merchants, lawyers and urban officials playing an increasingly prominent role.[124] These developments were closely entwined with the rise of different types of literacy and

---

W. Schenkl (eds), *The World in the Year 1000* (Lanham, MD, 2004), 105–17; C. Wickham, *Medieval Europe* (Oxford, 2016), 121–40.

[120] I owe this point to Jonathan Shepard, 'Did anything happen in the eleventh century?' (unpublished research seminar paper, Aberystwyth, 9 November 2016). See also pp. 144–5, 150–1.

[121] E. Buringh, *Medieval Manuscript Production in the Latin West: Explorations with a Global Database* (Leiden, 2010).

[122] M. Kintzinger and S. Steckel (eds), *Akademische Wissenskulturen: Praktiken des Lehrens und Forschens vom Mittelalter bis zur Moderne* (Basel, 2015); K. U. Mersch (ed.), *Was als wissenschaftlich gelten darf: Praktiken der Grenzziehung in Gelehrtenmilieus der Vormoderne* (Frankfurt an Main, 2014); F. Rexroth, *Expertenweisheit: die Kritik an den Studierten und die Utopie einer geheilten Gesellschaft im Späten Mittelalter* (Basel, 2008); F. Rexoth, *Fröhliche Scholastik: die Wissenschaftsrevolution des Mittelalters* (Munich, 2018); S. E. Young (ed.), *Crossing Boundaries at Medieval Universities* (Leiden, 2011); S. E. Young, *Scholarly Community at the Early University of Paris: Theologians, Education and Society, 1215–1248* (Cambridge, 2014).

[123] J. G. Clark, *A Monastic Renaissance at St Albans: Thomas Walsingham and his Circle, c.1350–1440* (Oxford, 2004); S. Steckel, *Kulturen des Lehrens im Früh- und Hochmittelalter: Autorität, Wissenkonzepte und Netzwerke von Gelehrten* (Cologne, 2010); I. P. Wei, *Intellectual Culture in Medieval Paris: Theologians and the University, c.1100–1330* (Cambridge, 2012).

[124] M. Asenjo González (ed.), *Urban Elites and Aristocratic Behaviour in the Spanish Kingdoms at the End of the Middle Ages* (Turnhout, 2013); M.-A. Chevalier and I. Ortega (eds), *Élites chrétiennes et formes du pouvoir (XIIIe–XVe siècle)* (Paris, 2017); L. Coste (ed.), *Le Concept d'élites en Europe de l'Antiquité à nos jours* (Pessac, 2014); N. Gaul, 'Rising elites and institutionalization – ethos/mores – "debts" and drafts: three concluding steps towards comparing networks of learning in Byzantium and the "Latin" west, c.1000–1200', in S. Steckel et al. (eds), *Networks of Learning: Perspectives on Scholars in Byzantine East and Latin West, c. 1000–1200* (Berlin, 2015), 235–80.

different written languages. Pragmatic literacy grew in importance, documenting administrative, fiscal or juridical processes. Most common among such texts were charters recording property transactions, but the genre soon diversified.[125] In Aragon and Hungary, *arengae*, a charter's opening statement explaining why a grant was given, often performed the role that narrative sources such as chronicles and annals fulfilled elsewhere in western Europe,[126] while ninth-century Frankish capitularies presented a mixture of administrative instrument and rule-setting narrative.[127] From the twelfth century on, we find new ways of recording and administering fiscal resources, including cartularies (collections of property deeds, often interspersed with short narrative sections) and in England the pipe rolls (lists of royal officials' expenditure).[128]

Perhaps unsurprisingly, pragmatic literacy offered ways of formulating and enforcing norms. Traditionally, *arengae* rehearsed political values. These were often collaborative efforts between grantee and grantor: ecclesiastical institutions in particular would draft a privilege, which was then revised by the cleric or chancery of those nominally issuing it. There is some evidence, however, that rulers took a direct interest in how such values were framed.[129] Naturally, *arengae* tended to project an idealised

[125] F.-J. Arlinghaus *et al.* (eds), *Transforming the Medieval World: Uses of Pragmatic Literacy in the Middle Ages*, Turnhout, 2006); R. Britnell (ed.), *Pragmatic Literacy East and West* (Woodbridge, 1997); H. Keller *et al.* (eds), *Pragmatische Schriftlichkeit im Mittelalter: Erscheinungsformen und Entwicklungstendenzen* (Munich, 1992); A. Nedkvitne (ed.), *The Social Consequences of Literacy in Medieval Scandinavia* (Turnhout, 2004).
[126] A. J. Kosto, *Making Agreements in Medieval Catalonia: Power, Order, and the Written Word, 1000–1200* (Cambridge, 2007); A. J. Kosto, 'The elements of practical rulership: Ramon Berenguer I of Barcelona and the revolt of Mir Geribert', *Viator* 47 (2016), 67–94; L. Veszprémy, 'The invented eleventh century of Hungary', in P. Urbańczyk (ed.), *The Neighbours of Poland in the 11th Century* (Warsaw, 2002), 137–54.
[127] S. Patzold, 'Normen im Buch. Überlegungen zu Geltungsansprüchen sogenannter "Kapitularien"', *Frühmittelalterliche Studien* 41 (2007), 331–50; C. Pössel, 'Authors and recipients of Carolingian capitularies, 779–829', in R. Corradini *et al.* (eds), *Texts and Identities in the Early Middle Ages* (Vienna, 2006), 253–76.
[128] T. N. Bisson, *The Crisis of the Twelfth Century* (Princeton, 2009); W. C. Brown *et al.* (eds), *Documentary Culture and the Laity in the Early Middle Ages* (Cambridge, 2013); D. P. Bubalo, *Pragmatic Literacy in Medieval Serbia* (Turnhout, 2014); M. T. Clanchy, *From Memory to Written Record: England 1066–1307*, 3rd edn (Oxford, 2012); M. J. Innes, 'Memory, orality and literacy in an early medieval society', *P&P* 158 (1998), 108–36; J. Jarrett and A. S. McKinley (eds), *Problems and Possibilities of Early Medieval Charters* (Turnhout, 2013); M. Mostert, *Organising the Written Word: Scripts, Manuscripts and Texts* (Turnhout, 2013).
[129] H. Hoffmann, 'Eigendiktat in den Urkunden Ottos III. und Heinrichs II.', *Deutsches Archiv für Erforschung des Mittelalters* 44 (1988), 390–423; N. Vincent, 'The personal role of the kings of England in the production of royal letters and charters (to 1330)', in C. Feller and C. Lackner (eds), *Manu propria: vom eigenhändigen Schreiben der Mächtigen (13.–15. Jahrhundert)* (Vienna, 2016), 171–84. For a particularly splendid case study: P. Gorecki, *The Text and the World: The Henryków Book, Its Authors, and Their Region, 1160–1310* (Oxford, 2015).

image. They also remained fairly abstract and might, for instance, invoke proforma obligations of generosity and justice, of reward for faithful service, or a general duty to set right past injustices. They rehearsed rather than defined moral principles.[130] Still, they reflect a broad consensus about the purpose of power and the uses to which it ought to be put.

Pragmatic literacy also opened up new ways of enshrining values. It did so partly in the form of formal coronation-oaths, where a monarch issued a charter vowing to uphold general principles and to undertake concrete steps to remedy past abuses.[131] Abstract principles were increasingly translated into concrete privileges from the thirteenth century on, although building on earlier antecedents. Documents like Magna Carta in England, the Golden Bull in Hungary or the 1235 *Reichslandfrieden* in Germany combined redress to specific grievances with an outline of the basic principles of good governance and means for their enforcement.[132] Moreover, these documents gained significance from their frequent re-issues, which added, revised and adapted them to fit changing needs. In England, it was the 1225 version of Magna Carta that was reissued and revised, because it had been purged of the more radical steps envisaged a decade earlier.[133] In Hungary, by contrast, the 1232 re-issue of the Bull introduced mechanisms for complaints against royal officials to be investigated independently of the monarch.[134] The tradition continued into the later middle ages, with the Golden Bull (1356) of Charles IV perhaps the most striking example.[135] How secular power should be used and how its legitimacy was to be ascertained were frequently codified in documents which could then be invoked in order to justify resistance or to demand a role in the political process or oversight of those granting and implementing them.

---

[130] H. Fichtenau, *Arenga: Spätantike und Mittelalter im Spiegel von Urkundenformeln* (Graz, 1957); H. Hold, *Unglaublich glaubhaft: die Arengen-Rhetorik des Avignonenser Papsttums*, 2 vols (Frankfurt am Main, 2004).

[131] S. Haider, *Die Wahlversprechungen der römisch-deutschen Könige bis zum Ende des 12. Jahrhunderts* (Vienna, 1968); idem, 'Schriftliche Wahlversprechungen römisch-deutscher Könige im 13. Jahrhundert', *Mitteilungen des Instituts für Österreichische Geschichtsforschung* 76 (1968), 106–73; M. Clayton, 'The Old English *Promissio regis*', *Anglo-Saxon England* 37 (2008), 91–150; A. M. Spencer, 'The coronation oath in English politics, 1272–1399', in B. Thompson (ed.), *Political Society in Later Medieval England: A Festschrift for Christine Carpenter* (Woodbridge, 2015), 38–54.

[132] *Album Elemér Mályusz: Studies Presented to the International Commission for the History of Representative and Parliamentary Institutions, no. 56, Székesfehérvár, Budapest, 1972* (Brussels, 1976).

[133] *Magna Carta*, tr. D. A. Carpenter (London, 2015); J. C. Holt, *Magna Carta*, 3rd edn, rev. G. Garnett and J. Hudson (Cambridge, 2015).

[134] M. J. Rady, 'Hungary and the Golden Bull of 1222', *Banata* 24 (2014), 87–108.

[135] *Album Elemér Mályusz*; U. Hohensee (ed.), *Die Goldene Bulle: Politik – Wahrnehmung – Rezeption*, 2 vols (Berlin, 2009).

Such charters also document new political actors. It is partly thanks to pragmatic literacy that we get glimpses of non-literate actors. They left few manifestos, histories or expositions of power, and their values thus tend to be filtered through elite perspectives. But they were far less passive than this might suggest, and, in urban communities in particular, artisans, workers and tradespeople appear as political actors. Administrative and legal materials, such as trial and court records, offer a sense of the values they might have espoused, even if these are framed to tally with elite discourses.[136] Of course, such refashioning might genuinely reflect shared values. In eleventh-century Milan, the Pataria was a social and political as well as a religious movement. Issues of ecclesiastical and communal reform created a mutually reinforcing framework, driven by an emerging artisan and mercantile class.[137] Yet the evidence has largely come down to us through elite narratives. Two centuries later, the cult of Simon de Montfort in thirteenth-century England can help us to paint a far richer picture. Leader of a rebellion against Henry III, de Montfort seized power and even took the king captive before being killed in battle in 1265. His traitorous corpse was dismembered and displayed across the realm. Yet within a few years he had become the subject of an unofficial, popular cult, albeit one supported by some members of the ecclesiastical elite.[138] Trial records and jury proceedings reveal so broad a backing for his rebellion that de Montfort has been dubbed the first leader of a political movement in English history,[139] showing how pragmatic literacy widens our understanding of both actors and ideas.

[136] J. R. Maddicott, 'Politics and the people in thirteenth-century England', in J. Burton *et al.* (eds), *Authority and Resistance in the Age of Magna Carta, Thirteenth-Century England* 14 (Woodbridge, 2015), 1–14; P. R. Schofield, 'Peasants at the manor court: gossip and litigation in a Suffolk village at the close of the thirteenth century', *P&P* 159 (1998), 3–42; S. K. Cohn, *Lust for Liberty: The Politics of Social Revolt in Medieval Europe, 1200–1425 – Italy, France, and Flanders* (Cambridge, MA, 2006); S. K. Cohn, *Creating the Florentine State: Peasants and Rebellion, 1348–1434* (Cambridge, 1999); R. Köhn, 'Die Stedinger in der mittelalterlichen Geschichtsschreibung', *Niedersächsisches Jahrbuch für Landesgeschichte* 63 (1991), 139–202; M. Cassidy-Welch, 'The Stedinger Crusade: war, remembrance and absence in thirteenth-century Germany', *Viator* 44 (2013), 159–74; C. Wickham, 'Looking forward: peasant revolts in Europe, 600–1200', in J. Firnhaber-Baker and D. Schoenars (eds), *The Routledge History Handbook of Medieval Revolt* (Abingdon, 2017), 155–67. See also pp. 384–6, 402–4.
[137] O. Zumhagen, *Religiöse Konflikte und kommunale Entwicklung: Mailand, Cremona, Piacenza and Florenz zur Zeit der Pataria* (Cologne, Weimar and Vienna, 2001); C. Wickham, *Sleepwalking into a New World: The Emergence of Italian City Communes in the Twelfth Century* (Princeton, 2015).
[138] C. Valente, 'Simon de Montfort, Earl of Leicester, and the utility of sanctity in the thirteenth century', *Journal of Medieval History* 21 (1995), 27–49; J. St Lawrence, 'A crusader in a "communion of saints": political sanctity and sanctified politics in the cult of St Simon de Montfort', *Comitatus* 38 (2007), 43–68.
[139] D. A. Carpenter, 'Simon de Montfort: the first leader of a political movement in English history', *History* 76 (1991), 3–23.

In the long run, surplus resources and widening literacy helped new social groups to emerge and ensured this was documented across the Latin west. Increasingly wealthy urban communities needed administrators with at least basic legal training, and there developed professional, non-clerical groups whose status was rooted in their command of the conventions and practices of administrative and legal literacy.[140] Even in the twelfth century something akin to professional bureaucrats can be detected.[141] These new actors expressed and developed political norms quite unlike those of the traditional clerical and ecclesiastical elites, and in so doing they adapted, appropriated and ultimately transformed existing discourses.

Legal literacy provides a useful example. The use of law texts to express political norms was not, of course, a new phenomenon: the Book of Leviticus had done just that, and most early medieval attempts to codify the customary procedures of a people, the so-called Barbarian Laws, were as much aimed at projecting an image of good rulership as they were at codifying its practice.[142] Indeed, collating and preserving good laws as well as reforming bad ones were hallmarks of the truly exemplary ruler.[143] But even the rulers of England lacked the resources to turn such codifications into actual practice until the later twelfth century. Thus both the codex and the circumstances of its composition communicated conformity with an ideal, often with an imagined status quo ante. Writing in the 1180s, the Danish chronicler Sven Aggesen looked back to the reign of King Cnut (d. 1035) to portray exemplary practice of law in the royal

---

[140] H. Barak, 'The managerial revolution of the thirteenth century', in W. C. Jordan and J. R. Phillips (eds), *The Capetian Century, 1214–1314* (Turnhout, 2017), 143–50; A. Bérenger and F. Lachaud (eds), *Hiérarchie des pouvoirs, délégation de pouvoir et responsabilité des administrateurs dans l'Antiquité et au Moyen Âge. Actes du colloque de Metz, 16–18 juin 2011* (Metz, 2012); J. A. Brundage, *The Medieval Origins of the Legal Profession: Canonists, Civilians and Courts* (Chicago, 2008); G. Castelnuovo, 'Offices and officials', in A. Gamberini and I. Lazzarini (eds), *The Italian Renaissance State* (Cambridge, 2012), 368–84; J. Dumolyn, 'Nobles, patricians and officers: the making of a regional political elite in late medieval Flanders', *Journal of Social History* 40 (2006), 431–52; M. Häberlein and C. Jeggle (eds), *Praktiken des Handels: Geschäfte und soziale Beziehungen europäischer Kaufleute in Mittelalter und früher Neuzeit* (Constance, 2010); R. V. Turner, 'The judges of King John: their background and training', *Speculum* 51 (1976), 447–61; R. V. Turner, *Judges, Administrators and the Common Law in Angevin England* (London, 1994).

[141] U. Kypta, *Die Autonomie der Routine: wie im 12. Jahrhundert das Englische Schatzamt entstand* (Göttingen, 2014); Lachaud, *L'Éthique du pouvoir*; Sabapathy, *Officers and Accountability*.

[142] W. Davies and P. Fouracre (eds), *The Settlement of Disputes in Early Medieval Europe* (Cambridge, 1986); T. Lambert, *Law and Order in Anglo-Saxon England* (Oxford, 2017); V. Epp and C. H. F. Meyer (eds), *Recht und Konsens im frühen Mittelalter* (Ostfildern, 2017).

[143] Banaszkiewicz, 'Slavonic *origines regni*'; see also p. 59.

court;[144] the Golden Bull of 1222 purported to restore the good old laws of the first Christian king of Hungary, St Stephen (d. 1038); and the 1260s compilation of legal customs in the Latin kingdom of Jerusalem claimed to record practices as they had been under the kingdom's first ruler, Godfrey de Bouillon (d. 1101).[145]

We increasingly find individuals below the level of ruler credited with compiling secular legal texts. Many were practitioners – judges, officials and lawyers – such as Ralph de Glanville, justiciar to Henry II (1154–89), credited with compiling a systematic survey of the laws and customs of England;[146] the Saxon knight Eike of Repgow, who composed the *Sachsenspiegel* ('Mirror of the Saxons') around 1230;[147] Henry de Bracton, a judge who produced another survey of English law around 1240;[148] and the series of lawyers, nobles and churchmen who penned treatises on the laws and customs of the Latin kingdom of Jerusalem from around 1250. Towards the end of the thirteenth century, law books and guides to interpreting law proliferated across Europe, reflecting developments in canon law. The increasing interconnectedness of the western church, as well as demands for moral and clerical reform, needed a corpus of legal principles for settling disputes, and canon law increasingly impinged on lay lives as it extended to matters of inheritance, family and marriage law. Yet in the ecclesiastical sphere, too, the initiative was initially taken by individuals such as Bishop Burchard of Worms, whose early eleventh-century *decretum* was one of the most comprehensive accounts of ecclesiastical law of its time;[149] or Gratian, who around 1140 compiled what was to remain the definitive work of canon law scholarship well into the thirteenth century.[150] It was not until the pontificate of

[144] *The Works of Sven Aggesen, Twelfth-Century Historian*, tr. E. Christiansen (London, 1992); Münster-Swendsen, '"Auf das Gesetz sei das Land gebaut"'.
[145] John of Ibelin, *Le Livre des Assises*, ed. P. W. Edbury (Leiden, 2003).
[146] *The Treatise on the Laws and Customs of the Realm of England Commonly Called Glanvill*, ed. and tr. G. D. G. Hall (Oxford, 1993); J. C. Russell, 'Ranulf de Glanville', *Speculum* 45 (1970), 69–79.
[147] H. Lück, *Der Sachsenspiegel: das berühmteste deutsche Rechtsbuch des Mittelalters* (Darmstadt, 2017).
[148] P. A. Brand, 'The date and authorship of Bracton: a response', *Journal of Legal History* 31 (2010), 217–45; T. J. McSweeney, 'Creating a literature for the king's courts in the later thirteenth century: Hengham Magna, Fet Asaver, and Bracton', *Journal of Legal History* 37 (2016), 41–71.
[149] G. G. Austin, *Shaping Church Law around the Year 1000: The Decretum of Burchard of Worms* (Farnham, 2009); W. Hartmann (ed.), *Bischof Burchard von Worms 1000–1025* (Mainz, 2000).
[150] J. C. Wei, *Gratian the Theologian* (Washington, DC, 2016); A. Winroth, *The Making of Gratian's Decretum* (Cambridge, 2000).

Gregory IX (1227–39) that the papal curia nominally took charge of the process.[151]

We also see a shift in content, with an increasing emphasis on accountability: the enforcement of norms not only by but also against those in power.[152] Texts like the *Leges Henrici Primi* – which purports to record the legal customs of Henry I (1100–35) – sought to establish continuity even though the Anglo-Saxon customs it describes were no longer necessarily still applied in practice.[153] Such texts reflect a normative expectation that the ruler should be a law-giver, compiling and codifying the legal customs of his people. A century later, Henry de Bracton's survey includes a detailed section on how the ruler could be forced to abide by the law of the land and how law was created not by the king alone but in consultation with his barons.[154] Of course, such accounts still tried to propagate an ideal: of a society made exemplary because it adhered to an image of how the law should function. Nor were they free from postulating customs as normative that were no such thing. Eike of Regpow's *Sachsenspiegel* defines how a college of princes should elect the king some fifty years before the principle was applied in practice.[155] Legal texts conveyed what ideally should be, though precisely what that was clearly changed over time.

Eike and Henry reflect broader shifts in thinking about power that can also be seen in works of biblical exegesis. Just as rulers were meant to be law-givers, so should they be bound by law, and it fell to their subjects to ensure that they were.[156] These texts reflect a broadening social base for thinking and writing about power, and the general shift towards codification was shaped by the needs and cultural horizons of emerging elites. They foreshadow an intellectual tradition, which gained ground from the twelfth century on, of legal commentary as a form of political philosophy.[157] Over the course of the fourteenth and fifteenth centuries,

---

[151] W. Hartmann and K. Pennington (eds), *The History of Canon Law in the Classical Period, 1140–1234* (Washington, DC, 2008).

[152] Bisson, *Crisis*; Lachaud, *L'Éthique du pouvoir*; Sabapathy, *Officers and Accountability*.

[153] *Leges Henrici Primi*, ed. and tr. L. J. Downer (Oxford, 1972); N. J. Karn, 'Quadripartitus, *Leges Henrici Primi* and the scholarship of English law in the early twelfth century', *Anglo-Norman Studies* 37 (2015), 149–60.

[154] Bracton, *De legibus et consuetudinibus Angliae*, ed. G. E. Woodbine, 4 vols (New Haven, CT, 1915–42), ii:110. Senior Byzantine judges were less explicitly restrictive than the likes of Bracton, yet the upshot of their rulings was a corpus not lightly disregarded; see pp. 89–90, 296. The ruler's role in making and interpreting Islamic law was markedly different: pp. 104–5, 331–2, 334.

[155] P. Landau, 'Eike von Repgow und die Königswahl im Sachsenspiegel', *Zeitschrift der Savigny-Stiftung für Rechtsgeschichte: Germanistische Abteilung* 125 (2008), 18–49.

[156] Buc, *L'Ambiguïté du Livre*.

[157] M. Ryan, 'Roman law in medieval political thought', in D. Johnston (ed.), *The Cambridge Companion to Roman Law* (Cambridge, 2015), 423–51.

this helped to embed principles of oversight, leading to a legal and theological framework for the deposition of kings,[158] consultative assemblies[159] and Conciliarism.[160] It also resulted in a developing doctrine of sovereignty, where regnal power defined itself not only through tradition and ancestry but also through the ability to create law.[161] Of course each triggered its own countervailing movement, but even these were rooted in the literary forms outlined here. The exercise and interpretation of law became a means whereby established norms and conventions could be challenged as well as shaped.

Social and linguistic diversification accompanied one another, although we should beware of easy generalisations. There had always been writing in the vernacular. In the ninth century, the rulers of Wessex sought to establish Anglo-Saxon as the language of record-keeping, education, theology and historical writing,[162] and the vernacular had begun to replace Latin in Castile and Aragon by the later twelfth century,[163] while across Scandinavia Icelanders were renowned for their writings in Old Norse.[164] Yet a sound command of Latin remained a mark of cultural sophistication throughout Europe – and well into the second half of the twentieth century. In Norway, Latin historical writing started partly in order to claim membership of the community of civilised nations and to distinguish proper, Latinate writing from the 'the gabbling song of Icelanders'.[165] But until the fourteenth century, the patronage of vernacular writing in most of Europe was an aristocratic and piously pastoral pursuit rather than a quintessentially lay one. Most surviving

[158] E. M. Peters, *The Shadow King: rex inutilis in Medieval Law and Literature, 751–1327* (New Haven, CT, 1970); F. Rexroth, 'Tyrannen und Taugenichtse. Beobachtungen zur Ritualität europäischer Königsabsetzungen im späten Mittelalter', *Historische Zeitschrift* 278 (2004), 27–54; E. Schubert, *Königsabsetzung im deutschen Mittelalter: eine Studie zum Werden der Reichsverfassung* (Göttingen, 2005).

[159] J. Dücker, *Reichsversammlungen im Spätmittelalter: Politische Willensbildung in Polen, Ungarn und Deutschland* (Ostfildern, 2011); Peltzer *et al.* (eds), *Politische Versammlungen und ihre Rituale.*

[160] M. Decaluwé *et al.* (eds), *A Companion to the Council of Basel* (Leiden, 2016); Müller and Helmrath (eds), *Die Konzilien von Pisa*; H. Müller, *Die kirchliche Krise des Spätmittelalters: Schisma, Konziliarismus und Konzilien* (Munich, 2012); Oakley, *Natural Law.*

[161] W. Bain (ed.), *Medieval Foundations of International Relations* (London, 2017).

[162] T. Reuter (ed.), *Alfred the Great: Papers from the Eleventh-Centenary Conferences* (Aldershot, 2003); A. Scharer, *Herrschaft und Repräsentation: Studien zur Hofkultur König Alfreds des Großen* (Vienna and Munich, 2000).

[163] T. M. Ruiz, *From Heaven to Earth: The Reordering of Castilian Society, 1150 – 1350* (Princeton, 2004).

[164] S. Ghosh, *Kings' Sagas and Norwegian History: Problems and Perspectives* (Leiden, 2011).

[165] *Historia Norwegie*, ed. I. Ekrem and L. B. Mortensen, tr. P. Fisher (Copenhagen, 2003), 50–1; see also p. 67.

vernacular writing is religious,[166] while epic is commonly to do with aristocratic patrons.[167] In contrast, some of the earliest examples of historical writing by, or for, members of professional elites are in Latin: the *Chronicle of the Sheriffs of London*, produced by the son of German immigrants in the later thirteenth century,[168] or the *Codex Ellenhardi*, a compilation about Strasbourg's recent history from around the same time.[169] In short, secular did not always equal vernacular.

From the fourteenth century onwards, how a realm was defined began to shift: it became defined at least in part by language, rather than by a *gens* inhabiting a particular region. Thus writing in the vernacular could itself become a political act. In some instances, this meant harking back to a lost but glorious past. Most Icelandic sagas – part-fictionalised dynastic accounts of the settlement period (*c*.890–1030) – were written some 300 to 400 years later, after the community had come under Norwegian rule. They commemorate the creation of a political system which is defined by its independence and resistance to royal government, but one that lies irretrievably in the past.[170] The period after Edward I's conquest of Wales saw a revival of vernacular poetry, history and legal commentary, in part at least to preserve and commemorate a past increasingly viewed as ideal but irrevocably lost.[171] In other cases, such as fourteenth-century England, it was the expediency of English as the native tongue which helped vernacular literary writing to develop, as it had in France and Germany some centuries before. Meanwhile in

---

[166] W. Green *et al.* (eds), *The Oxford Handbook of Medieval Literature in English* (Oxford, 2010); D. Mieth and B. Müller-Schauenburg (eds), *Mystik, Recht und Freiheit: religiöse Erfahrung und kirchliche Institutionen im Spätmittelalter* (Stuttgart, 2012); R. G. Newhauser, 'Religious writing: hagiography, pastoralia, devotional and contemplative works', in L. Scanion (ed.), *The Cambridge Companion to Medieval English Literature, 1150–1500* (Cambridge, 2009), 37–56.

[167] M. Aurell, *The Lettered Knight: Knowledge and Aristocratic Behaviour in the Twelfth and Thirteenth Centuries* (Budapest and New York, 2016); J. Bumke, *Mäzene im Mittelalter: die Gönner und Auftraggeber der höfischen Literatur in Deutschland 1150–1300* (Munich, 1979).

[168] N. Fryde, 'Arnold Fitz Thedmar und die Entstehung der Großen Deutschen Hanse', *Hansische Geschichtsblätter* 107 (1989), 27–42; I. Stone, 'Arnold Fitz Thedmar: identity, politics and the city of London in the thirteenth century', *London Journal* 40 (2015), 106–22.

[169] D. Mertens, 'Der Straßburger Ellenhard-Codex in St Paul im Lavanthal' in H. Patze (ed.), *Geschichtsschreibung und Geschichtsbewußtsein im späten Mittelalter* (Sigmaringen, 1987), 543–80. See also the important case study by J. B. Smith, *Walter Map and the Matter of Britain* (Philadelphia, 2017).

[170] T. M. Andersson, 'The king of Iceland', *Speculum* 74 (1999), 923–34; T. M. Andersson, *The Growth of the Medieval Icelandic Saga, 1280–1350* (Ithaca, NY, 2006); Antonsson, 'The present and the past in the Sagas of Icelanders'.

[171] H. Pryce, 'Lawbooks and literacy in medieval Wales', *Speculum* 25 (2000), 29–67; H. Pryce, 'The context and purpose of the earliest Welsh lawbooks', *Cambrian Medieval Celtic Studies* 39 (2000), 39–62.

Bohemia, his inability to speak Czech was one of the factors that helped to marginalise King John I the Blind, a member of the Luxembourg dynasty.[172] People and realm were increasingly defined by a common tongue.[173]

Yet the vernacular did not replace Latin but operated alongside it;[174] and, regardless of the language used, later practice was built on earlier precedent. Although many of the Icelandic family sagas were associated with the abbey of Helgafell, the best-known writer was the landowner and lawyer Snorri Sturluson (d. 1240), author of *Heimskringla* (a history of the Norwegian kings), *Prose Edda* (an account of pagan religion) and *Egilssaga*.[175] Similarly in Wales, literary production moved from abbeys to lawyers like Iowerth ap Madog, who in the early decades of the thirteenth century oversaw the Penarth redaction of the *Cyfraith Hywel*, a compilation of Welsh laws;[176] and from professional court poets to lawyer noblemen like Dafydd ap Gwilym (d. 1350/70), perhaps the most famous medieval Welsh writer.[177] This linguistic diversity remains a striking feature of late medieval Europe, but its significance should not be overstated. Most audiences would have been capable of approaching materials in more than one language,[178] and writing in the vernacular did

---

[172] M. Pauly (ed.), *Johann der Blinde, Graf von Luxemburg, König von Böhmen 1296–1346* (Luxembourg, 1997).

[173] R. J. W. Evans, 'Language and politics: Bohemia in international context, 1409–1627', in E. Doležalová (ed.), *Confession and Nation in the Era of Reformations: Central Europe in Comparative Perspective* (Prague, 2011), 255–82; P. von Moos (ed.), *Zwischen Babel und Pfingsten: Sprachdifferenzen und Gesprächsverständigung in der Vormoderne (8.–16. Jahrhundert)* (Vienna, 2008); A. Ruddick, 'Ethnic identity and political language in the king of England's dominions: a fourteenth-century perspective', in L. S. Clark (ed.), *Identity and Insurgency in the Late Middle Ages, The Fifteenth Century* 6 (Woodbridge, 2006), 15–32; M. G. A. Vale, 'Language, politics and society: the uses of the vernacular in the later middle ages', *EHR* 120 (2005), 15–34.

[174] G. Briguglia (ed.), *Thinking Politics in the Vernacular: from the Middle Ages to the Renaissance* (Fribourg, 2011); J. Miethke, 'Politische Theorie in lateinischen und volkssprachlichen Dialogen des 14. Jahrhunderts: Publikum und Funktion der Texte', *Mittellateinisches Jahrbuch* 48 (2013), 229–60.

[175] S. Bagge, *Society and Politics in Snorri Sturluson's Heimskringla* (Berkeley, 1991); H. Beck *et al.* (eds), *Snorri Sturluson: Historiker, Dichter, Politiker* (Berlin, 2013); T. H. Tulinius, *The Enigma of Egill: The Saga, the Viking Poet, and Snorri Sturluson* (Ithaca, NY, 2014); K. J. Wanner, *Snorri Sturluson and the Edda: The Conversion of Cultural Capital in Medieval Scandinavia* (Toronto, 2008).

[176] T. M. Charles-Edwards, *The Welsh Laws* (Cardiff, 1989); H. Pryce, *Native Law and the Church in Medieval Wales* (Oxford, 1991).

[177] T. M. Charles-Edwards *et al.* (eds), *The Welsh King and his Court* (Cardiff, 2001); K. Hurlock, 'Counselling the prince: advice and counsel in thirteenth-century Welsh society', *History* 94 (2009), 20–35.

[178] M. E. Amsler, *Affective Literacies: Writing and Multilingualism in the Late Middle Ages* (Turnhout, 2011); M. Baldzuhn and C. Putzo (eds), *Mehrsprachigkeit im Mittelalter: kulturelle, literarische, sprachliche und didaktische Konstellationen in europäischer Perspektive; mit Fallstudien zu den 'Disticha Catonis'* (Berlin, 2011); A. Classen (ed.), *Multilingualism*

not imply a rejection of shared norms. Writers were most commonly concerned with identifying quite how the abstract principles underpinning the common framework could be applied in practice, not with revising the framework; how they might advance (or hold at bay) the concerns and expectations of new political actors; and how common norms could be enforced and their implementation overseen.

Conclusion

By the later fifteenth century, new actors, genres, audiences and even languages had emerged. More people were laying claim to participation in the political process, and more of them were thinking and writing about what they expected those in power to do, how they should do it, and to what ends. To put this more concretely: a present-day student of Wipo might be expected to have read all the published and many of the unpublished primary source materials covering the mid-eleventh century for much of western Europe. Most of these – with the partial exception of England – are in Latin and would most likely have emerged from a Latinate clerical elite. By c.1500 and, indeed, the mid-fifteenth century, such an approach would no longer be feasible, even for a single ruler's reign. The *Regesta imperii*, the multi-volume register of German royal acts, has some 300 entries for Conrad II's entire fifteen-year reign; in contrast, the volume covering the years 1424–37 of Sigismund II's rule contains over 6,000 entries – and this excludes most of his Bohemian and all of his Hungarian acts. To study imperial politics in the fifteenth century requires Latin, Middle Dutch, German, Czech, Italian, Hungarian and French. And while monasteries and even cathedrals continued to act as literary nexuses, they were now competing with universities – more than seventy were founded between the early thirteenth and mid-fifteenth centuries – municipal schools, literate lay patrons and authors.

When recounting the election of Conrad in 1024, Wipo could name most of the politically relevant actors in the realm – a list that remained comfortably within double figures. It consisted of prelates, dukes and counts. By the mid-fifteenth century, the leading ecclesiastical figures were the incumbents of the same sees; but new actors had emerged

in the Middle Ages and Early Modern Age: Communication and Miscommunication in the Premodern World (Berlin, 2016); M. Garrison *et al.* (eds), *Spoken and Written Language: Relations between Latin and the Vernacular Languages in the Earlier Middle Ages* (Turnhout, 2013); M. Selig and S. Ehrlich (eds), *Mittelalterliche Stadtsprachen* (Regensburg, 2016); D. A. Trotter, *Multilingualism in Later Medieval Britain* (Cambridge, 2000).

among the princes. Sigismund himself was king of Bohemia and Hungary: Bohemia's rulers did not acquire hereditary royal status until the thirteenth century, and Hungary was not even part of the western empire. The margraves of Brandenburg had joined the top tiers of the imperial aristocracy, while, further down the hierarchy, new players had emerged, like the Wettins of Anhalt or the Welfs of Brunswick and Wolfenbüttel. More important still was the emergence of towns:[179] in the later medieval empire, royal lordship was increasingly dependent on the backing of free imperial cities such as Nuremberg and Schweinfurt. Nuremberg first appeared on record *c.*1050; by the mid-fourteenth century, it had become a leading political actor in the German south-east; and a century or so later, it was a major intellectual and cultural centre. The German Hansa and the rise of Italian communal government had an equally significant impact on imperial rule. In short, the political landscape of western Europe was transformed beyond recognition.

However profound and wide-ranging these changes, we should not lose sight of the continuities and traditions. Even new actors drew on an established repertoire of norms and means of expressing them. Thus the thirteenth-century revival of treatises on power, of which Godfrey of Viterbo and Gerald of Wales are perhaps the most striking exponents, remains rooted in the intellectual practices of the twelfth.[180] They might seek to outline principles of good governance, but they did so in the guise of history. Of course, new approaches did emerge, foremost among them the discovery in the west of Aristotle; the influx of Greek texts after 1204; and the translation into Latin of the works of the twelfth-century Andalusian judge and philosopher Averroes. At first incorporated within an established framework of textual practice, new thinking only gradually supplanted familiar modes of expression and even then still drew on a familiar corpus of foundational texts. Martin Luther was as indebted to St Augustine and Gregory the Great as Wipo had been; Marsilius of Padua owed as much to Roman historians and orators as did Hincmar of Rheims. And they all referred back to the Bible. What changed was how these materials were used, who used them and how ideas travelled.

As we have seen, most authors drew on a long-standing conceptual framework of norms and values. In fact, the relative consistency of these norms is a central feature in medieval western thinking about power. Comparable principles underpin ninth-century Carolingian Mirrors for

---

[179] See also pp. 151–2.
[180] Gerald of Wales, *Instruction for a Ruler: De principis instructione*, ed. and tr. R. Bartlett (Oxford, 2018); R. Bartlett, *Gerald of Wales, 1143–1223* (Oxford, 1982); T. Foerster (ed.), *Godfrey of Viterbo and his Readers: Imperial Tradition and Universal History in Late Medieval Europe* (Farnham, 2015).

Princes and the *Reformatio Sigismundi*, a vernacular proposal for the reform of church and empire that began circulating in 1439. Debates thus centred not on the norms themselves but on what they meant: Who should hold the mighty to account? How could good law be identified and enforced? What was religious orthodoxy, who should enforce it and how? Each generation and each group of actors interpreted the abstract norms, fitting them to their audience's specific circumstances, and it was by drawing on these changing and historically contingent circumstances that new traditions were forged and new ideas emerged. Conciliarism and the doctrine of sovereignty were new, but they drew on modes of thinking anchored in earlier medieval practices and models; the old ideas provided the fertile soil out of which new readings emerged, as well as the means for interpreting, evaluating and channelling them.

Recognising this diversity is essential for understanding the political culture of medieval western Europe. There was no homogenous thinking that could be labelled 'medieval'. Just as Latin Christendom was never exclusively Latin or Christian but encompassed Eastern Christians, pagans, Jews and Muslims, as well as unbelievers and dissidents, so thinking about power was full of contradictions and rich in often bitter and violent disputes.[181] But neither these debates nor the differences that emerged from them map easily onto modern constructs like the nation state. It is worth bearing in mind that, if townsmen in Cologne, Antwerp and Milan had their own deep-rooted cultural practices and historically contingent patterns of thought, the problems they faced and sought to tackle reflected conditions transcending regnal boundaries. Members of urban communities probably had more in common with each other than with the peasants, courtiers and princes in their immediate vicinity. The same goes for the church. The inevitable effects of this diversity were a multiplicity of opinions on how shared norms were constructed and interpreted. This inherent flexibility and elusiveness, along with the often vigorous and even violent debates they engendered, define the norms and values of power in the Latin west.

---

[181] Cohn, *Lust for Liberty*; J. Dumolyn, 'Nobles, patricians and officers'; *idem*, 'The "terrible Wednesday" of Pentecost: confronting urban and princely discourses in the Bruges rebellion of 1436–1438', *History* 92 (2007), 3–20; J. Dumolyn *et al.* (eds), *The Voices of the People in Late Medieval Europe: Communication and Popular Politics* (Turnhout, 2014); Firnhaber-Baker and Schoenars (eds), *Routledge History Handbook of Medieval Revolt*; P. Lantschner, 'Revolts and the political order of cities in the late middle ages', *P&P* 225 (2014), 3–46; *idem*, *The Logic of Political Conflict in Medieval Cities: Italy and the Southern Low Countries, 1370–1440* (Oxford, 2015); Maddicott, 'Politics and the people'; B. Weiler, *Kingship, Rebellion and Political Culture: England and Germany, c.1215–1250* (London, 2007).

11 Byzantium
Imperial Order, Constantinopolitan Ceremonial and Pyramids of Power

Judith Herrin

Figure 11.1 Imperial lion hunt from the Troyes Casket, Constantinople (?), tenth- or eleventh-century Byzantine, dyed purple ivory, possible diplomatic gift (13x26x13 cm); Cathedral Treasury, Troyes; photo © Ministère de la Culture-Médiathèque de l'Architecture et du Patrimoine, Dist. RMN-Grand Palais/Luc Joubert

Byzantine ideology rested on the advantages of monarchy, supreme authority in the hands of one ruler. Even when, as was quite often the case, an emperor had co-emperors, the most senior was distinguished by the term *autokrator* (self-ruler). The idea of empire was embodied in his person. In fact, the very word for 'empire' could also denote the emperor, whose documents termed him *hemon basileia* (our majesty). This chapter will take their word for it and focus on the idea of empire, the various media by which

290

it was expounded and propagated, and the imperial hierarchy. The imperial court and Constantinople (its usual base) will take centre stage, given that reigning from 'the City' (as Constantinople was commonly known)[1] was the ultimate objective of any ambitious rebel in the period covered by this volume, at least until 1204.[2] Gaining or retaining favour within the established system of the City – founded as New Rome and known as *he polis basileousa* (the Ruling City or the Queen City) – was the way to the top in virtually every walk of life, including religious ones. Of course there could be other priorities for ascetic, self-effacing monks; and family connections and landed estates could assure one of status and a fair degree of informal influence, if not an official state position, especially in the provinces.[3] But since this chapter is dedicated to the public, formal face of Byzantium and its explicit aspirations, it is reasonable to concentrate on the court, the order which its ceremonies exalted and the hierarchies closely affiliated with it, although the provinces are not overlooked altogether.[4] The emperor's City housed the ultimate tribunal of the Roman law still in force, and it was where the doctrine and the principal regulations of the church were agreed and promulgated. Most, though not quite all, of the seven ecumenical councils of the church met in or near Constantinople, and the canons they put out in writing are still taken as benchmarks of religious orthodoxy in the eastern church and, to some extent, in the west. They are also a source of information about Byzantine ideology, since they were presided over by the emperor and their regulations were incorporated in civil law.[5]

We have, in addition, very many texts referring favourably to imperial power. These literary set pieces receive coverage in the next sub-section of this chapter, along with inauguration-ritual, theoretical treatises about the rights and duties of the emperor, and the rule of law he was supposed to personify.[6] Some of the clearest expressions of what was generally expected of the emperor come from writings about times of turmoil, when contenders for the throne criticised the incumbent and presented their own credentials. These expectations of the imperial office also belong to the first sub-section. Then the spotlight falls on Constantinople and the aura

---

[1] And still is, seeing that the modern name 'Istanbul' preserves the Greek term by which the imperial capital became known to the Turks, 'eis ten Polin' (literally 'in/to the City').

[2] J.-C. Cheynet, *Pouvoir et contestations à Byzance (963–1210)* (Paris, 1990).

[3] For the distinction between 'power' elite and 'general' elite: pp. 410–14; for the diverse elites of the other spheres: pp. 234–6, 241–7, 460–6, 474–82, 151–3, 156–60, 375–9, 389–91.

[4] For the distinction between 'formal' and 'informal': pp. 178–9, 199–203.

[5] J. Hussey, *The Orthodox Church in the Byzantine Empire*, rev. edn A. Louth (Oxford, 2010); M. G. T. Humphreys, *Law, Power, and Imperial Ideology in the Iconoclast Era, c.680–850* (Oxford, 2015).

[6] See pp. 84–7.

enshrouding and, in part, distancing the emperor from his people. Ceremonial, and the *un*written expressions of support for the imperial order and the monumental props upholding it, were at least as important to Byzantine political culture as the flowery speeches of court orators. Since these were concentrated in the capital in the form of cults and ceremonial, the City and its privileged inhabitants take up much of this chapter.

Several distinct hierarchies gravitated around the palace. Some, like civilian administrators and the supply chain of provisioners for the City, were employed there. But others, like the army, had bases far away or, in the case of churchmen, had an organisation reaching beyond the frontiers. These hierarchies nonetheless revolved around the capital, and *symphonia* (harmony) between the imperial ruler and senior churchmen was the order of the day. But points of principle and personal ambition could boil over between emperor and patriarch and lead to confrontations. And for generals, the armed forces regularly made a potential springboard to the throne. These tensions were important dynamics in Byzantine political culture until its fall to the Fourth Crusaders in 1204. Michael VIII Palaiologos restored Constantinople as the imperial capital in 1261, and the state of play for the empire's last centuries contains familiar features, the subject of the final sub-section. Things were, however, never quite the same again, for all the emphasis laid on continuity by the proponents of empire and doctrinal correctness. Some new approaches to political and social order were set out in tracts. But real innovation in political culture as a whole is more to be found in practice than writings, and this characteristic of Byzantium receives extensive coverage elsewhere in this volume.[7]

The Imperial Office: Theory, Expectations and Demands

The emperor's position was an office, not a bloodline, despite many attempts of emperors to keep the succession in their family. The emperor was expected to live up to the standards of his illustrious predecessors, particularly those of Constantine I (324–37), who founded the City, generating a mythic ideal over time.[8] Despite many shifts in political authority in Byzantium, the achievements of the first Christian Roman emperor cast a dominant influence for over a millennium. In the course of such a long period, political elites justified their hegemony in many

[7] See pp. 441–50.
[8] P. Magdalino (ed.), *New Constantines: The Rhythm of Imperial Renewal in Byzantium, 4th–13th Centuries* (Aldershot, 1994).

different ways, yet the patterns established in late antiquity continued to inform later traditions. The wisdom of the sixth century, encapsulated in documents connected with the emperor Justinian (527–65), as well as in the church of St Sophia, which that emperor rebuilt following the Nika riots of 532, remained a symbol of imperial government in a glorious period. It provided a touchstone for later commentators who insisted that a God-given monarchy was the most appropriate form of government. Serious challenges to this belief in imperial rule were few and largely unsuccessful.

Whatever their origin, however, emperors had to conform to a role deemed appropriate to the ruler of all the known world. It was their duty to lead armies to victory, to demonstrate God's approval through such victory, and to perform all the necessary acts and rituals to bring prosperity, orthodoxy, security and peace.[9] This imperial ideology of continuing the Roman empire through enjoyment of divine support – rule by emperors chosen by the Christian God to represent His authority on earth and prepare for a better world to come – represented a successful adaptation of ancient practice. The imperial court at Constantinople became a mirror of the court of heaven. It ensured an overarching system of universal Christian rule designed to last forever – or until God willed otherwise. Expectation of the apocalypse was ever-present, and prophesies of the end of world entailed the end of empire.[10] The fall of the City was widely supposed to trigger this chain of events.

While having an eye to the future and a sense that their empire held the key to it, Byzantines were not lost for words about their rulers. Occasionally *psogoi* – defamatory tracts about the emperor of the day – found their way into the narratives of later historians who had no reason to flatter him. This is a sign that an emperor's performance underwent constant scrutiny, behind the glassily smooth façade which official writings and established voices sought to maintain. The imperial ideology within whose framework they operated can be found in a vast array of speeches, sermons, panegyrics and instructions delivered by court orators, patriarchs, bishops and sometimes the emperor himself.[11] Being composed in the Attic Greek of classical literature, most were put down in writing. Of course, these orations changed over time, altering their focus to appropriate subjects. They

---

[9] M. McCormick, *Eternal Victory: Triumphal Rulership in Late Antiquity, Byzantium, and the Early Medieval West* (Cambridge, 1986).

[10] O. Treitinger, *Die oströmische Kaiser- und Reichsidee nach ihrer Gestaltung im höfischen Zeremoniell* (repr. Darmstadt, 1956), 228–32; H.-G. Beck, *Das byzantinische Jahrtausend* (Munich 1978); H. Ahrweiler, *L'Idéologie politique de l'Empire byzantin* (Paris, 1975). *IIPTB*, 1–15 gives a neat summary of this background.

[11] G. Dennis, 'Imperial panegyric: rhetoric and reality', in *BCC*, 131–40; E. Jeffreys (ed.), *Rhetoric in Byzantium* (Aldershot, 2003); see also p. 85.

showed concern with the poor in late Byzantine centuries, less noticeable earlier. But in the formulations of court orators, the power they exalted retained a universal and imperial character, marked by personal qualities: philanthropy, humility, mercy, generosity and other Christ-like attributes. They could vary their tone and emphases to suit the political agenda of the day, but they had firm points of reference in the treatises on rulership composed in the early Byzantine period.

Theoretical treatises on imperial rule and didactic texts instructing rulers, the so-called Mirrors for Princes, provided an ideal for emperors to emulate. The anonymous sixth-century *Dialogue on Political Science* and especially the *Ekthesis* addressed by Agapetos the Deacon to Justinian were much read, copied and imitated by later authors.[12] In the ninth century, the erudite and ambitious patriarch Photios added a more original analysis of the position of the emperor in relation to the church and the law in his *Eisagoge* ('Introduction'), and this influenced later legal compilations.[13] In the tenth century, the compendious collecting of material by Constantine VII Porphyrogennetos produced texts which fulfil a similar function to the mirror literature, most obviously in the *De administrando imperio* ('On Governing the Empire') dedicated to his son Romanos II.[14] Then, in the twelfth century, the canon lawyers contributed important observations on the relationship between church and civil law. And in the late Byzantine period, numerous authors devoted attention to the theoretical underpinnings of imperial power with notable innovations, for example, Manuel Moschopoulos.[15] All these more theoretical texts coexisted beside works of propaganda and aspiration embodied in forms of rhetoric, panegyric and dialogue. The sixth-century model set by Agapetos was

---

[12] *The Dialogue on Political Science*, tr. P. N. Bell, in *Three Political Voices from the Age of Justinian* (Liverpool, 2009), 123–88; Agapetos, *Mirror for Princes*, ed. R. Riedinger, *Der Fürstenspiegel für Kaiser Iustinianus von Agapetos Diakonos* (Athens, 1995); tr. Bell as 'Advice to the emperor Justinian', in *Three Political Voices*, 99–122; see also C. Pazdernik, 'Justinianic ideology and the power of the past', in M. Maas (ed.), *The Cambridge Companion to the Age of Justinian* (Cambridge, 2005), 185–212 at 195–6.

[13] E. Barker, *Social and Political Thought in Byzantium* (Oxford, 1957) with a translation of part of the *Eisagoge*; F. Dvornik, *Early Christian and Byzantine Political Philosophy*, 2 vols (Washington, DC, 1996).

[14] *DAI*. See also N. Gaul *et al.* (eds), *Center, Province and Periphery in the Age of Constantine VII Porphyrogennetos: From* De ceremoniis *to* De administrando imperio (Wiesbaden, 2018); B. Flusin, 'Un auteur impérial: Constantin Porphyrogénète', in R. Ceulemans and P. de Leemans (eds), *On Good Authority: Tradition, Compilation and the Construction of Authority in Literature from Antiquity to the Renaissance* (Turnhout, 2015), 23–41; P. Magdalino, 'Byzantine encyclopaedism of the ninth and tenth centuries', in J. König and G. Woolf (eds), *Encyclopaedism from Antiquity to the Renaissance* (Cambridge, 2013), 219–31.

[15] See the analysis by *IIPTB*, 310–47 and pp. 324–5.

reworked over the centuries and sustained into the late Byzantine period: over eighty manuscripts of his treatise survive.[16] The literary forms of court speeches were particularly developed from late antiquity onwards. A source of inspiration, they also imposed restrictions: formulaic styles of praise recur over and over again, sometimes without any connection to the individual being praised! So while propaganda varied with circumstances, rhetoric preserved unchanging elements.[17]

So, too, at a more mundane level did the operation of justice and the creation of deeds intended to be of permanent, uncontestable validity – wills, for example, and commercial contracts. All this was subject to and underwritten by Roman law, codified by Justinian's team of lawyers. Legal traditions inherited from Rome formed a vital ingredient of imperial ideology. In principle, Byzantine society was regulated by an independent judicial system to which all might have recourse. This meant that the position of the emperor in relation to the law was always debatable. Could the emperor set himself above the laws? Or was he subject to them? Was he the sole maker of new law? Or could the interpretation of lawyers challenge his authority? The constant revision and reissue of law-codes, however limited, suggests a concern to update and transform legal practice to meet new circumstances.

Emperors took responsibility for the codes, and Leo III (717–41) was not the only newcomer to try to bolster his regime by issuing one. The *Ecloga* ('Extracts') he promulgated in 741 represents an attempt to adapt Justinianic law to hard times and a predominantly agrarian economy. There is renewed emphasis on the personal morality of individuals, presumably with an eye to winning back God's support for a beleaguered empire.[18] Almost a century and a half later, another usurper, Basil I, commissioned a systematic collection of materials from Justinian's legal corpus, arranged by subject matter: the *Basilika*. This massive project was only brought to an end in the reign of his son and successor, Leo VI (886–912). Leo, too, took keen interest in legal matters and issued some 113 new ordinances – *novellae*. Leo's personal engagement emerges from, for example, *novella* 72, which reviews two possible strands of thought on what constitutes an enforceable agreement.[19] Leo's championing of, in

[16] Agapetos, *Mirror for Princes*.   [17] On late Byzantine orations: *IIPTB*, 161–80.
[18] Humphreys, *Law, Power, and Imperial Ideology*, 84–105, 128–9.
[19] Leo VI, *Novellae*, ed. P. Noailles and A. Dain, *Les Novelles de Léon le Sage* (Paris, 1944), 258–9 (no. 72); B. Stolte, 'The Byzantine law of obligations', in T. McGinn (ed.), *Obligations in Roman Law: Past, Present and Future* (Ann Arbor, MI, 2012), 320–33 at 326–7; M. L. D. Riedel, *Leo VI and the Transformation of Byzantine Christian Identity: Writings of an Unexpected Emperor* (Cambridge, 2018), 96–118. See also p. 91.

effect, the 'little people' against 'the strong' is echoed in his *Book of the Eparch* and many other imperial ordinances.[20]

The question of how far these pronouncements were borne out by provincial realities is very much harder to answer. In his 'Counsels and Tales', the eleventh-century commander and curmudgeon Kekaumenos presupposes that grandees and other prominent local figures will strive to prevail at law but will not invariably win.[21] A similar assumption pervades the collection of rulings from another eleventh-century figure, the senior judge Eustathios Romaios. Here, comparison with predators and peacemakers in the Latin west and the Islamic world should prove fruitful.[22] And scrutiny of the archives of the monasteries on Mount Athos and other texts can shed light on property matters at grassroots.[23] At any rate, there are hints of imperial attention to smallholders in the countryside even in the darkest days of Arab attacks. Both the *Ecloga* and the *Nomos georgikos* ('Farmer's Law'), which probably dates from a generation later, regularly refer to judges as *akroatai*, literally 'hearers'. These may have been itinerant local judges, who dealt mainly with petty disputes over loans, property and animals among country folk, offering immediate solutions while bringing a degree of equitableness to tax-collection. This, together with the citation of Justinianic laws by thirteenth- and fourteenth-century bishops and judges, implies a living tradition that survived throughout the Byzantine millennium.[24] In Constantine Harmenopoulos' mid-thirteenth-century compendium, another reworking of the ancient body of the law, along with extracts from more recent works like the *Peira*, this senior judge created a version so successful that it continued in use up to the nineteenth century.[25] These hints of a lasting predisposition towards law amassed within the imperial order help explain the circumspection that potentates like the Serbian ruler Stefan Dušan showed in appropriating Byzantine territories. Stefan did not demur when the monks of Athos insisted on praying for 'the emperor of the Romans' ahead of their prayers for himself and his regime.[26] Equally, Stefan's concern to maintain

[20] See pp. 424, 426, 429.
[21] L. Neville, *Authority in Byzantine Provincial Society, 950–1100* (Cambridge, 2004), 104–5. See also p. 97.
[22] See pp. 71–2, 161–2, 402–4, 347–9, 360–2.
[23] See pp. 422, 426–7, 446. On literacy and the maintenance of archives in the other spheres: pp. 46, 61–2, 273–4, 126–9.
[24] Demetrios Chomatenos, *Ponemata diaphora*, ed. G. Prinzing, CFHB 38 (Berlin and New York, 2002); R. Macrides, *Kinship and Justice in Byzantium, 11th–15th Centuries* (Aldershot, 1999). See now Z. Chitwood, *Byzantine Legal Culture and the Roman Legal Tradition, 867–1056* (Cambridge, 2017).
[25] *Constantini Harmenopuli: Manuale legum sive Hexabiblos*, ed. G. E. Heimbach (Leipzig, 1851).
[26] *Grčke povelje srpskih vladara*, ed. A. Solovjev and V. A. Mošin (Belgrade, 1936; repr. London, 1974), 32–3.

'Roman' laws and customs in the Byzantine provinces he took over was not sheer window-dressing. The law-code he issued in 1349 and subsequently amended drew heavily on a recent synthesis of Byzantine secular and church law by Matthew Blastaras and was intended to serve as a working document.[27]

All this reflects the prestige attached to the imperial office and the ancient legal framework it perpetuated. But it also points to the various expectations placed upon rulership.[28] Although there was no formal or written constitution, multiple norms were expected of the emperor: *to koinon* (the common good) should be his concern. The common good was a theme of the preambles to imperial edicts and laws. Its centrality to Byzantine political life is highlighted by the title of Anthony Kaldellis' book on the dynamics of lawmaking and power, *The Byzantine Republic*.[29]

There was also an underlying belief that the emperor should ceremoniously take office and receive recognition from other leading players in the political arena. Foremost among these was the head of the only Byzantine hierarchy that was virtually self-standing, the church. Its close co-operation with the emperor was deemed essential for imperial stability and success.[30] This gave the archbishop of Constantinople, usually called patriarch, a key position, notably in the inauguration of new rulers. Coronation in St Sophia, although not essential, became a regular feature from the reign of Leo I (440–61).[31] It enhanced other rites, such as acclamations by the soldiery and the crowning of a co-emperor by the existing emperor, an act going back to the first century CE. Anointing with chrism, however, does not appear to have become integral to coronation-ritual until the thirteenth century.[32] Through additional liturgies designed to enhance imperial authority, patriarchs tried to insist on their equal role in government. But since emperors retained the right to nominate the leader of the church, ultimate power remained in the ruler's hands. Although several prolonged

---

[27] See a version of the law-code translated into English by D. Krstić, *Dushan's Code: The Bistritza Transcript* (Belgrade, 1989); D. Obolensky, *The Byzantine Commonwealth: Eastern Europe, 500–1453* (London, 1971), 318–20; P. Angelini, 'The Code of Dušan 1349–1354', *Tijdschrift voor Rechtsgeschiedenis / Revue d'Histoire du Droit / The Legal History Review* 80 (2012), 77–93. For the alignment of other polities' elites and religious cultures with Byzantium: pp. 78–9, 185, 190–1.

[28] This may be compared with the expectations made of western rulers: pp. 255–62.

[29] For *to koinon*, see H. Hunger, *Prooimion: Elemente der byzantinischen Kaiseridee in den Arengen der Urkunden* (Vienna, 1964); A. Kaldellis, *The Byzantine Republic: People and Power in New Rome* (Cambridge, MA, 2015), 56–9.

[30] D. G. Angelov and J. Herrin, 'The Christian imperial tradition: Greek and Latin', in P. Fibiger Bang and D. Kołodziejczyk (eds), *Universal Empire: A Comparative Approach to Imperial Culture and Representation in Eurasian History* (Cambridge, 2012), 149–74.

[31] G. Dagron, *Emperor and Priest: The Imperial Office in Byzantium*, tr. J. Birrell (Cambridge, 2003), 61.

[32] Dagron, *Emperor and Priest*, 275–9.

conflicts occurred, co-operation was usually achieved by the emperor replacing an antagonistic patriarch.[33] No amount of inauguration-ritual or moral support from the patriarch could guarantee the survival of an emperor on the throne indefinitely. Paradoxically, the sheer attractiveness and renown of the imperial position made it tantalising to a wide variety of individuals and interest-groups. In fact, emperors were quite often killed in warfare, civil conflicts or military rebellions, which created an unstable tendency in the highest office in the empire. Specific conditions helped define how emperors gained and then exercised power. Sons inheriting their fathers' imperial status perpetuated dynastic rule. But such regimes often arose from rebellion and coups d'état and were ever open to challenge from fresh aspirants to the throne.[34]

The clearest sidelights onto the norms of rulership and the benefits an emperor was supposed to deliver come from times of crisis. It was when a challenger launched a takeover bid for the throne that the need arose to justify his move, gaining supporters by explaining the current regime's shortcomings or demonstrating the extraordinary leadership qualities that made him the obvious candidate. Qualities of derring-do and superb generalship were, for example, the essence of the personality cult promoted in the opening years of the reign of Manuel I Komnenos (1143–80): they helped to justify his leap-frogging onto the throne over his elder brother, Isaac, and also his uncle.[35] Each case of accession – even a peaceful one – had its own tensions and rivalries; as Gilbert Dagron has shown, this is registered by the nuances and emphases of the inauguration-ritual of the day.[36] But the rightful function of emperorship comes into sharpest relief from coups d'état. Broadly speaking, at least six methods of justification were employed by would-be wielders of imperial power.

The first and probably most common claim was to save the empire from bad government. Numerous emperors came to power on the basis of replacing a bad ruler by one approved by God, who would fulfil the tasks of the emperor better. These upstarts murdered, exiled or blinded and thus removed previous rulers by military force, which was necessary to overcome

---

[33] For further discussion of patriarchs and the patriarchate: pp. 312–14.

[34] Cheynet, *Pouvoir et contestations*; M. Whittow, 'Staying on top in Byzantium, 963–1210', in B. Caseau *et al.* (eds), *Mélanges Jean-Claude Cheynet* [= *TM* 21/1] (Paris, 2017), 807–30; A. J. Davidson, '*The Glory of Ruling Makes all Things Permissible': Power and Usurpation in Byzantium: Some Aspects of Communication, Legitimacy and Moral Authority* (unpublished PhD thesis, University of Birmingham, 2018). The high incidence of attempted coups, deposition and killing of emperors may often register the strength of central government during Byzantium's heyday and its requirement for an effective overseer, in a way comparable to later medieval England's: S. Bagge, 'The decline of regicide and the rise of European monarchy from the Carolingians to the early modern period', *Frühmittelalterliche Studien* 53 (2019), 151–89 at 168–74, 179–84. See also pp. 444–5, 69.

[35] *EMK*, 41–2, 192–5.   [36] Dagron, *Emperor and Priest*, 54–83, 113–14.

the imperial guard, normally loyal to the ruling emperor. Most of them therefore had a military background and drew on the support of their own provincial troops. However, not all were military figures, as Nikephoros I, the finance minister of Empress Eirene, demonstrated in 802. But his rebellion was planned in alliance with military officials, including some of the units (*tagmata*) associated with the defence of the city who tricked the palace guards into supporting it. Once in control of the Great Palace they proclaimed Nikephoros emperor and imprisoned the empress, who was living in her own palace called Eleutherios.[37] So most revolts relied on military clout.[38]

A second and subsequent justification lay in the success of such a coup, which allowed the incoming emperor to claim divine approval. Even in the case of Basil I, who ordered the murder of his predecessor in 867 and may have actually performed it himself, the fact that he succeeded so easily allowed him to insist on God's support for his strategy of saving the empire from the mad Michael III.[39]

A third justification might turn on the previous ruler's wrong belief, as in the case of Philippikos, who reinstated the monothelite doctrine in 711. Since monothelitism had been condemned as heresy by the Sixth Ecumenical Council in 680–1, its renewal was used as a legitimising strategy by his enemies. The count and *protostrator* of the Opsikion took the lead in replacing Philippikos by his secretary (*asekretis*) Artemios in a carefully planned coup, and as soon as Artemios had been installed as Emperor Anastasios II, he restored the orthodox definition.[40] Needless to say, Philippikos in 711 had justified his own coup against Justinian II (685–95, 705–11) as a necessary method of putting an end to a reign of terror (murders, brutal punishments and abuse of power, which amounted to a tyranny). And this revolt was subsequently legitimised by stories of predictions and astrological justifications to cover the plot against Justinian II and his eventual assassination.[41]

[37] Theophanes, *Chronographia* AM 6295, ed. C. de Boor, 2 vols (Leipzig, 1883–5), i:476–7; tr. C. Mango and R. Scott, *The Chronicle of Theophanes Confessor* (Oxford, 1997), 655.
[38] In contrast to the west, however, this was the preserve of the professional armed forces; on the nature of violence in the other two spheres: pp. 496–8.
[39] *Vita Basilii* chs 18, 19, 20–7, 28, 29, ed. and tr. I. Ševčenko, *Chronographiae quae Theophanis Continuati nomine fertur liber V quo Vita Basilii imperatoris amplectitur*, CFHB 42 (Berlin and New York, 2011), 70–3, 78–9, 80–109, 110–11, 112–15.
[40] Agathon, deacon and *chartophylax* of the Great Church, *Epilogos*, in *Concilium universale Constantinopolitanum tertium*, ed. R. Riedinger, *Acta conciliorum oecumenicorum*, series II, vol. 2.2 (Berlin, 1992), 898–901 at 900; J. Herrin, 'Philippikos and the Greens', in her *Margins and Metropolis: Authority across the Byzantine Empire* (Princeton, 2013), 179–91.
[41] Theophanes, *Chronographia* AM 6203, ed. de Boor, i:378–81; tr. Mango and Scott, 528–30; Nikephoros I, patriarch of Constantinople, *Short History* ch. 45, ed. and tr. C. Mango, CFHB 13 (Washington, DC, 1990), 110–13; W. E. Kaegi, *Byzantine Military Unrest, 471–843*

After the obligatory acclamation by army and people, a fourth way of securing a successful coup was for the new ruler to enhance his authority by marrying a member of the previous ruling family. In this way Michael II (820–9) sought out Euphrosyne; Romanos I (919–44) married his daughter Helena to Constantine Porphyrogennetos; Nikephoros Phokas (936–9) married Theophano, widow of his predecessor; and Alexios Komnenos (1081–1118) married Eirene Doukaina.[42] Usurpers could thus feel that they had acquired a more legitimate imperial status and hope to win over supporters of the previous dynasty.[43] They often proceeded to a fifth method of establishing power, by appointing a member of their own family to head the church, particularly if the incumbent opposed the coup. On occasion this was flagrantly abused, as when Romanos I put his sixteen-year-old son Theophylact on the patriarchal throne. But the emperor's power to nominate the leader of the church was usually limited by the need for a competent ally in charge of the church, an essential feature of successful imperial government.

Finally, once established, the new elites maintained their hegemony by exclusion: only their own good blood would guarantee imperial success. They proceeded to employ the full panoply of propaganda to justify and enhance their newly acquired power, doing so immediately on the coinage (a vital, often critical, signal of the change of ruler) and insignia (crowns, orb and sceptre, imperial robes and thrones and so forth) and issuing laws and practising philanthropy in true imperial fashion.

Virtually every emperor who managed to secure himself on the throne and sire a son tried to bequeath it to him, although this did not preclude bitter tensions, as when Basil I, founder of what became the Macedonian dynasty, had his eldest surviving son Leo VI thrown into gaol. To lay the foundations of a lasting dynasty, it was wise to go beyond pomp and circumstance and propaganda – indispensable though these were – and to tap into values and priorities resonating with broad sectors of society and their material interests, beliefs and fears.[44] A telling example is that of Leo III, an ambitious and resourceful army commander, who showed

(Amsterdam, 1981), 190. On the prophetic and astrological signs: P. Magdalino, *L'Orthodoxie des astrologues: la science entre le dogme et la divination à Byzance (VIIe–XIVe siècle)* (Paris 2006), 23–32; for a later period: Cheynet, *Pouvoir et contestations*, 179–83.

[42] Marriage-ties with members of a previous dynasty to legitimise regime change are not unknown in the Latin west, but attitudes about inheritance through the female line varied markedly: pp. 395, 397–8.

[43] Cheynet, *Pouvoir et contestations*, 337–44, on the turmoil generated by the failure of the daughters of Constantine VIII (1025–8) to provide heirs and the conflicts of Theodora's reign (1055–6).

[44] For other instances of a new dynasty or ruler attempting to appeal beyond their immediate supporters and interest-groups: pp. 59, 255–9, 271, 104–5, 116, 224–5, 334–6, 353–5.

determination in establishing what has become known as the Isaurian dynasty, after the region he came from, Isauria.[45]

After over twenty years of unstable government (from the first removal of Justinian II in 695 to Theodosius III's brief reign), Leo, the general commanding operations against the Arabs, seized the throne in 717. He ensured the succession of his son Constantine through a series of reforms dealing with military and legal matters and by issuing a new type of silver coin, the *miliaresion*, which bridged the gap between the very valuable gold *nomisma* and everyday copper pieces. Besides these practical steps to improve the lot of his subjects, under heavy Arab pressure Leo sought to provide for their spiritual welfare, too, launching a drive against the excessive veneration made to images for religious – or magical – purposes. While the pace and scale of the increase in recourse to icons in preceding centuries is uncertain,[46] it is clear that images and other items associable with holy persons had passionate devotees and that their cults and practices were not closely regulated. Equally, by the early eighth century, some churchmen and other pious persons were not merely concerned by these habits but saw them as the reason for the empire's defeats and humiliations at the hands of the Arab unbelievers. Their siege of Constantinople in 717–18 was thwarted by Leo, but the catastrophic eruption of the volcano of Santorini a few years later seemed to some to be a sign of God's wrath. Leo took the initiative, reportedly removing an image of Christ from over the entrance to the Great Palace and ordering senior churchmen to condemn icons as 'idols'. Like the Jews in the Old Testament, the Byzantines had erred and strayed, and their idolatry was costing them divine protection. Leo's regime was now bound up with restoring purer forms of worship and a new moral order to bring back God's favour.

Leo's son and heir, Constantine V (741–75), sought to systematise and justify the practice of iconoclasm with theological arguments by calling a universal church council. This he inaugurated with a vigorous propaganda campaign.[47] After significant victories, he was able to leave the throne to his son, Leo IV. Leo died early and was succeeded by his widow Eirene, who took over as Regent for their young son Constantine VI. At

---

[45] It is clear that Leo III's family had been moved from Germanikeia in northern Syria, and Leo is associated with Syria in our sources: Theophanes, *Chronographia* AM 6209, 6232, ed. de Boor, i:391, 412; tr. Mango and Scott, 542 and n. 1 on 547, 572.

[46] L. Brubaker and J. Haldon, *Byzantium in the Iconoclast Era, c.680–850: A History* (Cambridge, 2011), 70–83; A. Bryer and J. Herrin (eds), *Iconoclasm* (Birmingham, 1977); see also p. 185.

[47] A. Alexakis, *Codex Parisinus Graecus 1115 and its Archetype* (Washington, DC, 1996); A. Alexakis, 'The "Dialogue of the monk and recluse Moschos concerning the holy icons", an early iconophile text', *DOP* 52 (1998), 187–224.

the Council of Nicaea, held under the auspices of Eirene and Constantine in 787, iconoclasm was condemned, and the Council's canons reinstituted the veneration of icons while laying down guidelines on how this should be carried out. The abandonment of what had been the dynasty's signature policy, iconoclasm, did not spell disaster for it. In the early ninth century the family of Leo III finally came to an end, but by 815 condemnation of icons was official policy again, and it is notable that Leo's last descendant, Euphrosyne, was brought out of a monastery by the usurper Michael II (820–9), in the belief that he could strengthen his own rule by marrying her. She also played a role in arranging the marriage of his son Theophilos.[48]

After the iconoclast era came to an end in the mid-ninth century, individual emperors and their dynasties had their particular hallmarks, but none attempted to alter religious practices and elements of doctrine so drastically. They all found it desirable to identify closely with two features of political culture already highlighted: unbroken continuity from the time of Constantine the Great – ten subsequent emperors were named after him – and presiding over activities that dominated the City of Constantinople. These two elements brought substance to the claim that, in effect, the Roman empire was alive and well, with non-stop performance behind the walls of Constantinople. The question of how far a sense of being Roman percolated down to grassroots in provincial society may be open to question.[49] Some emperors made carefully choreographed journeys outside the City, to visit shrines, bathe in warm springs or just demonstrate their power accompanied by musicians and dancers. But that the leadership in Constantinople was at the controls of what had been a world empire was undeniable, and it was of the essence to Byzantine political culture never to let this fact go out of sight. Both the

---

[48] See p. 300.
[49] The view that self-identification as Roman was widespread across most strata of society (A. Kaldellis, *Hellenism in Byzantium: The Transformations of Greek Identity and the Reception of the Classical Tradition* (Cambridge, 2007), esp. 42–119) has come under challenge from I. Stouraitis, 'Roman identity in Byzantium: a critical approach', *BZ* 107 (2014), 175–220 esp. 198–206, 212–14. For the ongoing debate: J. Haldon, '*Res publica Byzantina*? State formation and issues of identity in medieval east Rome', *BMGS* 40 (2016) 4–16; A. Kaldellis, 'The social scope of Roman identity in Byzantium: an evidence-based approach', *Byzantina Symmeikta* 21 (2017) 173–210; I. Stouraitis, 'Reinventing Roman ethnicity in high and late medieval Byzantium', *Medieval Worlds* 5 (2017), 70–94; I. Stouraitis, 'Byzantine Romanness: from geopolitical to ethnic conceptions', in W. Pohl (ed.), *Transformations of Romanness: Early Medieval Regions and Identities* (Berlin, 2018), 123–39; A. Kaldellis, *Romanland: Ethnicity and Empire in Byzantium* (Cambridge, MA, 2019); A. Cameron, 'Commonwealth, empire or nation-state?', in J. Shepard *et al.* (eds), *Byzantine Spheres: The Byzantine Commonwealth Re-evaluated* (Oxford, forthcoming).

elite and ordinary inhabitants had reason to trumpet it, maintaining collective memory of what amounted to a cult of the City.

Constantinople and the Imperial Palace: Ceremonial, Space and Power

If Byzantium did not produce many theoretical treatises on imperial ideology between the sixth and the thirteenth centuries, it had in Constantinople a kind of substitute, a standing demonstration of the nature of imperial order and of its material and spiritual benefits. No one with high ambitions could afford to ignore it, whether they aimed for a leading military command or even the throne. At the same time, the relentless pressure of ceremonial and liturgies presided over by the emperor had an air of inevitability and – of course – divine endorsement, which it would be virtually impossible for individual dissidents to defy or dispel. Although centred on the Great Palace, these rites and processions encompassed the whole City. They even took in the theme of fierce competition, laid on in most spectacular style, with chariot races in the Hippodrome sited beside the palace, where the emperor distributed prizes to the winning team.[50]

From their Roman roots as the organisers of public entertainment, two circus factions – groups of entertainers named after the colour of their uniforms, the Greens and the Blues – remained in charge of the Hippodrome and were active in Byzantium until the late ninth century, when their roles became more ceremonial.[51] They continued to accompany the emperor whenever he left the Great Palace to perform ceremonies in the City, and their organs provided musical accompaniment to many events within the palace, such as imperial marriages. In the tenth-century *De cerimoniis* ('Book of Ceremonies'), they are responsible for arranging music, acrobatics and dancing to entertain diners at the banquets in the Hall of the Nineteen Couches. By this time, their public activity had been greatly reduced, but they were yet another group of citizens dedicated to the elevation of imperial power.[52]

In this worldview centred on the capital, historical awareness was deepened by annual commemorations, secular and religious. These

---

[50] G. Dagron, *L'Hippodrome de Constantinople: jeux, peuple et politique* (Paris, 2011), 126–34, 335–7. See now M. Featherstone, 'Public processions in Middle Byzantine Constantinople', in L. Brubaker and N. Sevčenko (eds) *Processions and Strategies of Civic Control in Byzantium: A Comparative Perspective* (Washington, DC, forthcoming).

[51] Alan Cameron, *Circus Factions: Blues and Greens at Rome and Byzantium* (Oxford, 1976).

[52] For the citizens' involvement in acclaiming and sustaining the emperor's rule: p. 86.

provided regular reminders of the past: events deemed essential to the historic role of the city, significant victories and evidence of God's support. The inauguration by Constantine I on 11 May 330 was marked every year by processions to the Hippodrome, followed by chariot races and feasting in honour of Constantinople's birthday. Although evidence for the most elaborate celebrations gradually faded, the public holiday carried on.[53] By the ninth century Constantine I had been acclaimed a saint in the Byzantine church.[54] The major feasts of the church calendar (Easter, Christmas and particular events such as the Dormition of the Virgin on 15 August) were observed, as shown by records of the tenth century.[55] A great victory over the Arabs in 718, which occurred on the same day, enhanced the feast of the Dormition yet further, although patriarchal sermons tended to stress the religious rather than the military element.[56] Similarly, the feast of Sts Constantine and Helena and the Finding of the True Cross (Exaltation, 14 September) permitted all the inhabitants of the city to venerate the relic, which was exposed for three days in St Sophia.[57] The lives of local saints Akakios and Mokios were observed by imperial processions to their shrines. And past emperors were remembered by rulers who went to the imperial mausoleum of the Holy Apostles to burn incense before the tombs, light candles and say prayers for the souls of their predecessors buried there. Even major earthquakes that had damaged key monuments in Constantinople were commemorated by liturgies designed to prevent similar catastrophes.[58]

Imperial ideology in all its forms was greatly enhanced by the settings of rituals and ceremonies, both secular ones of the court and ecclesiastical.

[53] *Chronicon paschale*, ed. L. Dindorf, *CSHB*, 2 vols (Bonn, 1832), i:529–30; tr. Michael Whitby and Mary Whitby (Liverpool, 1989), 17–18; John Malalas, *Chronicle* 13.8, ed. H. Thurn, Chronographia, *CFHB* 35 (Berlin and New York, 2000), 247; tr. E. Jeffreys *et al.*, *The Chronicle of John Malalas* (Melbourne, 1986), 175; *Parastaseis syntomoi chronikai*, ed. in and tr. A. Cameron and J. Herrin, *Constantinople in the Early Eighth Century: The Parastaseis syntomoi chronikai* (Leiden, 1984), 132–3 (text), 242 (commentary); *DC* I.70, i:340–9; J. Bardill, *Constantine, Divine Emperor of the Christian Golden Age* (Cambridge, 2012), 151.
[54] A. P. Kazhdan, '"Constantin imaginaire": Byzantine legends of the ninth century about Constantine the Great', *Byzantion* 57 (1987), 196–250.
[55] See e.g. the prescriptions for the Dormition of the Virgin in *DC* II.9, ii:541–4.
[56] P. Speck, 'Klassizismus im achten Jahrhundert? Die Homelie des Patriarchen Germanos über die Rettung Konstantinopels', *REB* 44 (1986), 209–27; English tr. in his *Understanding Byzantium: Studies in Byzantine Historical Sources*, ed. S. Takács (Aldershot, 2003), no. 11; McCormick, *Eternal Victory*.
[57] Arculf, *Relatio de locis sanctis*, ed. L. Bieler, *Itineraria et alia geographica*, *CCSL* 175 (Turnhout, 1965), 228. On the likelihood that this text does draw on information gained in Constantinople by a pilgrim en route to Jerusalem: R. G. Hoyland and S. Waidler, 'Adomnán's *De locis sanctis* and the seventh-century Near East', *EHR* 129 (2014), 787–807 at 800–7.
[58] G. Dagron, 'Quand la terre tremble . . . ', *TM* 8 (1981), 87–103.

After the construction of St Sophia, no church could rival its size, and visitors recorded their amazement at the structure where many critical ceremonial and political events were played out.[59] The high altar created asylum for those fleeing arrest, although soldiers regularly destroyed this hope by dragging men, women and children outside. In the Middle Byzantine period, a tradition of smaller buildings with more concentrated decoration in precious materials developed, for example the Nea Ekklesia of Basil I.[60] Since few of these survive, we are dependent on written descriptions of the impact they made on observers.

One sign that decorum was maintained, at least in Constantinople, is the variety of foreigners remarking upon it. One may note a couple of descriptions: an account of ceremonies in the palace complex and processions through the streets written by a Muslim prisoner-of-war, Harun b. Yahya, around the beginning of the tenth century; and Liudprand of Cremona's accounts of his experiences at court in the mid-tenth century.[61] Liudprand reports that in 968 his hosts took him to watch the emperor's procession from the palace to St Sophia, assigning him 'a vantage-point beside the chanters'. Requiring outsiders, especially prisoners-of-war from formidable enemies, to take part in such spectacles burnished the image of the imperial court as a locus of power, where all things were possible and where those participating voluntarily would themselves be empowered. Much of this can be usefully compared with Clifford Geertz's presentation of the sacred space and ritual, largely consensual, happenings over which rulers presided at nineteenth-century Bali's paramount negara.[62] Pressing invitations to court ceremonies and insistence that foreign envoys should attend are characteristic features of what Mary Helms terms 'superordinate centres'.[63] Such external validation was a useful means of impressing upon one's *own* subjects

[59] G. P. Majeska, 'The emperor in his church: imperial ritual in the church of St Sophia', in *BCC*, 1–11.
[60] P. Magdalino, 'Observations on the Nea Ekklesia of Basil I', *JÖB* 37 (1987), 51–64.
[61] A. A. Vasiliev, 'Harun ibn-Yahya and his description of Constantinople', *Seminarium Kondakovianum* 5 (1932), 149–63, with translation at 154–62; Liudprand of Cremona, *Relatio de legatione Constantinopolitana* 9, ed. P. Chiesa in *Liudprandi Cremonensis opera omnia* (Turnhout, 1998), 185–218 at 191; tr. B. Scott (London, 1993), 30; M. McCormick, 'Analyzing imperial ceremonies', *JÖB* 35 (1985), 1–20 at 9 n. 25.
[62] On *negara*, a term denoting palace, capital and state more or less interchangeably, and on the diverse *negaras*, in mutual competition yet acknowledging a titular capital of the whole island: C. Geertz, *Negara: The Theatre State in Nineteenth-Century Bali* (Princeton, 1980).
[63] Helms' concept of the superordinate centre amplifies Geertz's theory of the 'exemplary centre' of a 'system of superordinate political authority': Geertz, *Negara*, 4, 13–16, 109–20, 125–36. For the expectation that representatives of 'flawed outsiders' – barbarians – should bear witness to the superiority of the centre: M. W. Helms, *Craft and the Kingly Ideal: Art, Trade, and Power* (Austin, TX, 1993), 182, 183–5, 203.

and outside observers that the court stood at the centre of earthly things and of rightful order.[64] It is clear that St Sophia continued to impress: Mehmed II's immediate conversion of it into the main mosque of the conquered city reflects this dominance.

Although the court ceremonies of the Great Palace shifted from one hall to another as grander reception spaces were constructed and novel rituals designed to impress evolved, the sixth-century Chrysotriklinos ('Golden Hall') remained the venue for Easter receptions. Other receptions were held in the Triklinos of Justinian II, built at the end of the seventh century, or the Magnaura, housing the famous automata, where foreign embassies were received, while banquets were held in the Hall of the Nineteen Couches. In the church of St George attached to the Mangana Palace, constructed in the eleventh century, the imperial court celebrated the saint's feast every year on 23 April. On the feast of the Hypapante, the emperor and the patriarch met at the church of Blachernai, site of the famous relics of the Virgin since the fifth century, venerated the relics and icons, and then dined together in the palace. On other occasions the entire court would be transported to the palace and church at Blachernai, sometimes by boat or on horseback, with the emperors in procession. After venerating the relics, they lit candles in front of the many silver icons and bathed in the baths.[65] In the twelfth century, the Komnenoi moved the court to Blachernai on a permanent basis, leaving the Great Palace much less used, although specific functions still took place there and in the Hippodrome. Although Blachernai was not such a vast complex, western Crusaders were deeply impressed by how the panoply of imperial power was displayed at receptions.[66]

The imperial court and palace was the inner sanctum of the City. Yet it was never wholly sealed off from the rest of Constantinople or the wider world. The blend of ceremonial, worship, distribution of rewards and favours, and modish recreation that made up court culture drew in Byzantine provincials and rank outsiders.[67] Appearances, striking symbols, and ranking orders of merit and beauty were of the essence for imperial rulership. A whole category of persons, 'the theatrical profession', is employed for celebrating the emperor's birthday, triumphs and

[64] J. Trilling, 'Daedalus and the nightingale: art and technology in the myth of the Byzantine court', in *BCC*, 217–30 lays emphasis on 'the value of internal propaganda' (at 230).

[65] *DC* I.27, II.12, i:147–54 (Hypapante); ii:551–6 (bathing in the baths at Blachernai).

[66] Odo of Deuil, *De profectione Ludovici VII in orientem*, ed. and tr. V. G. Berry (New York, 1948), 65–6; R. Macrides, 'Constantinople: the crusaders' gaze', in R. Macrides (ed.), *Travel in the Byzantine World* (Aldershot, 2002), 193–212.

[67] *BCC*; H. Maguire, 'Images of the court', in *GOB*, 182–91.

other great occasions, according to the *Peri strategias* ('On Strategy').[68] Fine textiles, precious stones, gold and silver organs, and other well-wrought artefacts were essential to the emperor's image of his status when presented to his own subjects and to outsiders alike.[69] The importance of images for projecting the ruler himself, making him omnipresent across his empire and beyond, is the theme of a classic study.[70]

The accent was predominantly on piety: emperors were often shown holding crosses, or orbs topped with crosses, and with the image of Christ on the other side of their coins, when He was not actually crowning them. But the desire to convey imperial tranquillity and permanence might jar with political needs of the moment, as a mosaic in St Sophia suggests. This shows and names Empress Zoe, purple-born and thus of impeccable legitimacy, flanking Christ together with her third husband and co-emperor until her death in 1050, Constantine IX Monomachos. Constantine's handsome features have been substituted for those of an earlier husband of Zoe, and the accompanying legend altered to bear his name.[71] Keeping up appearances presupposed a certain topicality, and Constantine wished both to commemorate his recent donation to St Sophia and to supersede the earlier husband. More surprisingly, the mosaicist changed the faces of Christ and Empress Zoe, too. New emperors could emphasise the contrast between their courts and those of their predecessors. And from the time of the Komnenoi onwards, the court had a more military bearing, with swords, lances, shields and other military gear featuring as imperial attributes in Pseudo-Kodinos' treatise of the fourteenth century.[72] However, the

---

[68] *Peri strategias*, ed. in G. T. Dennis, *Three Byzantine Military Treatises*, CFHB 25 (Washington, DC, 1985), 1–136 at 18–19; the text also provides for what visiting envoys may be shown: *ibid.*, 124–5; see also *DAI* ch. 13, 64–77; see also p. 87.

[69] A. Muthesius, *Studies in Byzantine and Islamic Silk Weaving* (London, 1995); A. Muthesius, *Byzantine Silk Weaving: AD 400 to AD 1200*, ed. E. Kislinger and J. Koder (Vienna, 1997); N. Koutrakou, '"*Lithomanes hyparchon*": le revers de la médaille: pierres précieuses signe de prestige et d'injure', *Byzantion* 75 (2005), 250–76; M. G. Parani, 'Cultural identity and dress: the case of late Byzantine ceremonial costume', *JÖB* 57 (2007), 95–134.

[70] A. Grabar, *L'Empereur dans l'art byzantin: recherches sur l'art officiel de l'empire d'Orient* (Paris, 1936; repr. London, 1971).

[71] See e.g. R. Cormack, 'Interpreting the mosaics of S. Sophia at Istanbul', *Art History* 4 (1981), 131–49 at 141–5 and fig. 6; L. Rodley, *Byzantine Art and Architecture: An Introduction* (Cambridge, 1994), 232–3; A. Cutler and J.-M. Spieser, *Byzance médiévale, 700–1204* (Paris, 1996), 326–7, plates 260, 261. On the importance of female line of succession in some western polities: pp. 397–8.

[72] Pseudo-Kodinos, *Treatise on the Dignities and Offices*, ed. and French tr. J. Verpeaux, *Traité des offices* (Paris, 1966), 168.2–3, 171.8, 176.4, 183.12–13, 190.21, 196.16, 263.10–16, 273.14–15; tr. R. Macrides *et al.*, *Pseudo-Kodinos and the Constantinopolitan Court: Offices and Ceremonies* (Farnham, 2013), 72–3, 78–9, 88–9, 104–5, 118–19, 130–1, 226–7, 242–3. Hunting was also a feature of Komnenian, as of earlier imperial, pursuits (see Figure 11.1). For hunting as a mark of rulership in the Islamic world: pp. 107, 117, 118–19, 341, 358 and Figure 12.1. Hunting was, along with horsemanship and

repeated injunctions in manuals of court precedence (*tactica*) on the need to maintain *taxis* (good order) were not a dead letter, and they complement the various late Byzantine presentations of the liturgy quite well.[73] More often than not, emperors were still portrayed in court costume, not armour.

One important feature of the ceremonial life of the Byzantine court was its reliance on non-verbal actions.[74] Such unspoken aspects of propaganda were possibly the most significant because they were played out before the court – the senate, office holders, court officials and representatives of the circus factions – and they often involved processions to distant churches, in which the entire City population could participate. In many ceremonies speech was totally subordinated to gestures and actions that displayed authority without words.[75] When the emperor blessed the people in the Hippodrome, his hands conveyed the message that in his imperial capacity he could invoke God's blessing on them. Patriarchs, bishops and abbots did this all the time, but in the case of emperors it was a significant imperial attribute. Similarly, when emperors processed to the imperial mausoleum on the anniversaries of their predecessors, actions spoke louder than words. Their gestures were further enhanced by the authority symbols they carried and the coins they threw to the crowds along the route. In marriage ceremonies, coronations (including those of empresses and junior emperors) or the symbolic washing of the feet of the poor at Easter, no words were spoken.

This is not to say that prescriptions for and descriptions of court ceremonies were never written down. Someone wrote a full account of the route taken by Emperor Theophilos' triumphal procession in 837. This led from the Golden Gate across the City to St Sophia and the Great Palace, a reminder that the trails of ceremonies criss-crossed the whole

tourneying, an aristocratic attribute in the west that eventually spread even to urban elites: pp. 158–9 and Figure 10.1.

[73] R. F. Taft, 'At the sunset of the empire: the formation of the final "Byzantine liturgical synthesis" in the patriarchate of Constantinople', in P. Odorico (ed.), *Le Patriarchat oecuménique de Constantinople aux XIVe–XVIe siècles: rupture et continuité* (Paris, 2007), 55–71; see also p. 87.

[74] For the importance of gesture, image and ceremonial in societies irrespective of their literacy levels: pp. 57–8, 102–5, 109, 116, 338–40, 344–5, 352, 356–8, 359–64.

[75] L. Brubaker, 'Gesture in Byzantium', in M. Braddick (ed.), *The Politics of Gesture: Historical Perspectives* (Oxford, 2009), 36–56; J.-C. Schmitt, *La Raison des gestes dans l'Occident médiéval* (Paris, 1990); for the depiction in the 'Egbert Psalter' of gestures of the Polish-born Gertrude and her son, the Rus prince Iaropolk, before Christ and St Peter: J.-C. Schmitt, 'Circulation et appropriation des images entre Orient et Occident: reflexion sur le psautier de Cividale (Museo Archeologico Nazionale, ms. CXXXVI)', in *Cristianità d'Occidente e cristianità d'Oriente: (secoli VI–XI), Settimane di studio della Fondazione Centro Italiano di studi sull'alto Medioevo* 51, 2 vols (Spoleto, 2004), ii:1283–1318.

inhabited area, not just the palace complex.[76] The main compilation of records and of prescriptions for imperial ceremonies was done in the mid-tenth century, at the behest of Constantine VII. In his preface, Constantine equates regularity in the performance of ceremonies with orderliness in the empire, imputing neglect to Romanos I, the co-emperor who had replaced him for twenty-four years. Through his predecessor's failure to codify ceremonial, Constantine claims that 'one could behold the empire in truth unadorned and ugly', as if reflecting disorder in the state itself.[77] The sheer scale of the ceremonies put a premium on expert-ise of one sort or another, giving an advantage to those with intimate knowledge over the uninitiated, including emperors who had not been raised in the palace as Constantine VII had been. Thus the rituals and procedures which elaborated the solemn, public expression of the empire's claims and values were, to a large extent, carried in people's heads.

The Imperial Palace, Formal Hierarchies – Status, Competition and Tensions

Pecking Order, Pay and Hierarchies of Courtiers

The material advantages of access to the emperor and enjoyment of his favour were important and worth advertising. An empire-wide manifest-ation was the honours system, whereby a person could make a substantial down payment in return for a court-title, corresponding insignia and vestments, and an annual salary (*rhoga*) from the treasury.[78] Besides gaining visible association with the establishment, an individual would eventually recoup his initial outlay and receive an annuity for the rest of his days.[79] Holding a title and drawing a *rhoga* from this and from one's office brought not only wealth but also a place at court. It was, in part, a matter of positioning in the literal sense: who sat where at palace

---

[76] Constantine VII Porphyrogennetos, *Three Treatises on Imperial Military Expeditions*, ed. and tr. J. F. Haldon, *CFHB* 28 (Vienna, 1990), ll. 825–73 on 146–51; 57, 58 (introduction); M. McCormick, *Eternal Victory*, 146–8. On the scope of imperial 'events' across all Constantinople: J. Herrin, 'Byzance: le palais et la ville', *Byzantion* 61 (1991), 213–30 (English tr. 'Byzantium: the palace and the City', in her *Margins and Metropolis*, 159–78).

[77] '[A]kallopiston kai dyseide [. . .] ataxian [. . .] me taxei agomenou kai kyvernomenou': *DC* I (preface), ll. 6 and 9–12 on 4; see also p. 86.

[78] See also pp. 420–2.

[79] P. Lemerle, '"Roga" et rente d'État aux Xe–XIe siècles', *REB* 25 (1967), 77–100; repr. in his *Le Monde de Byzance: histoire et institutions* (London, 1978), no. 16; J.-C. Cheynet, 'Dévaluation des dignités et dévaluation monétaire dans la seconde moitié du XIe siècle', *Byzantion* 53 (1983), 453–77; repr. in *TBAMF*, no. 6.

banquets, and who took precedence. A manual compiled in 899 offers a set of instructions to clarify ranking order. Writing from experience, the master of ceremonies Philotheos envisages disruption to banquets and a general demeaning of titles in the event of uncertainty, and he seeks to pre-empt this.[80] The implication that the court was a cockpit of competing individuals chimes in with the court gossip relayed in the eleventh-century history of Michael Psellos. This continued even after Alexios I Komnenos (1081–1118) abolished many titles and resorted to non-monetary forms of remuneration, in a bid to keep his administration functioning and loyalties firm.[81] Ties of kinship at the top alongside the delegation to individuals, often family relatives, of sweeping quasi-governmental powers were now more important for sustaining the body politic. Yet the emperor's money-payments to officials and his grants of court-titles and concomitant access to court circles still counted for much.[82] These variations on the theme of the advantages arising from access to the emperor and his intermingled material and otherworldly resources played on, even after the empire's tax-base and territorial possessions shrank in the mid-fourteenth century.[83]

From earliest times, imperial propaganda had been sustained through oral traditions, and court eunuchs made themselves the keepers of these traditions. Their roles developed as the court became larger and monopolised tasks associated with the imperial family. The lists of officials invited to banquets document this hierarchy of 'unbearded men', recruited from all parts of the empire and even beyond.[84] They supervised the training of younger eunuchs who gradually worked their way up a hierarchy restricted to castrated men, in the same way as bureaucrats advanced their careers in the civil service and monks and priests gained

---

[80] Philotheos, *Kletorologion*, ed. and French tr. N. Oikonomides, *Les Listes de préséance byzantines des IXe et Xe siècles* (Paris, 1972), 83.21–4; P. Magdalino, 'Court society and aristocracy', in J. Haldon (ed.), *A Social History of Byzantium* (Chichester, 2009), 212–32 at 214–16; see also p. 86.

[81] N. Oikonomides, 'Title and income at the Byzantine court', in *BCC*, 199–216 at 210–14.

[82] See e.g. *TBA*; M. Angold, *The Byzantine Empire, 1025–1204: A Political History*, 2nd edn (London, 1997); *EMK*.

[83] M. A. Poliakovskaia, 'Pozdnevizantiiskii chin koronovaniia vasilevsa', *Vizantiiskii Vremennik* 68 (93) (2009), 5–24 at 21–4; R. Macrides, 'Ceremonies and the city: the court in fourteenth-century Constantinople', in J. Duindam *et al.* (eds), *Royal Courts in Dynastic States and Empires: A Global Perspective* (Leiden, 2011), 217–35. For further refinements, involving the showering of coins over an empress at her wedding: S. W. Reinert, 'What the Genoese cast upon Helen Dragash's head: coins not *confecti*', *Byzantinische Forschungen* 20 (1994), 235–46. See also pp. 443–5.

[84] S. Tougher, *The Eunuch in Byzantine History and Society* (London, 2008); S. Tougher (ed.), *Eunuchs in Antiquity and Beyond* (London, 2002); K. Ringrose, *The Perfect Servant: Eunuchs and the Social Construction of Gender in Byzantium* (Chicago, 2003); J. Herrin, *Byzantium: The Surprising Life of a Medieval Empire* (London, 2008), 160–9.

promotion to wealthy monasteries and bishoprics. Under particular rulers, the power of the leading eunuchs within the court might well be supreme, as Basil II (976–1025) found during his minority when his illegitimate relative-by-marriage Basil Lekapenos, the grand chamberlain, acted as effective ruler. By the twelfth century the eunuch cohort's prominence was fading, perhaps because the Komnenos dynasty wished to prevent any rivalry to its own authority. Besides, the Komnenian households seem to have set more store by their women, who did much to set the tone. Nonetheless, as overseers of ceremonial, eunuchs kept their role into the last centuries of the empire.[85]

In addition to the court hierarchy of unbearded men, there was a smaller but essential hierarchy of female courtiers (*koubikoulariai*). They attended the empress, who had a formal part in proceedings, as *augusta*.[86] These ladies-in-waiting assisted her in every daily routine – dressing, undressing and eating – and accompanied her wherever she went. The older ones with many years of experience accumulated knowledge of court ceremonial. So they played a critical role in preparing young brides for their imperial coronation, explaining what robes would be worn, the procedures of reception, acclamation, procession from one part of the palace to another, and so on. If a bride came from Khazaria or the west, or even from some distant province of the empire, she would have little or no understanding of rituals based on unwritten culture. Senior eunuch officials also participated in this induction and instruction, which brought foreigners to Byzantium and into the highest ranks of court society.[87]

The Church Hierarchy

It may seem strange to put the church hierarchy in this section, given its separateness from the secular hierarchy. But the patriarch played an important part in inauguration-ritual (see p. 297), was quite a frequent guest at palace banquets and lived, literally, next door, in the complex

---

[85] On the role of women in setting the tone of court life in the Latin west: pp. 55, 407; on eunuchs and procedures at Islamic courts: pp. 238, 480, 481.
[86] J.-C. Cheynet, 'Les impératrices byzantines et leurs réseaux (1028–1203)', in F. Chausson and S. Destephen (eds), *Augusta, Regina, Basilissa: la souveraine de l'Empire romain au Moyen Âge* (Paris, 2018), 141–58.
[87] Herrin, *Byzantium*, 172–4; on the role of eunuchs in educating foreign brides for their role: J. Herrin, 'Theophano: considerations on the education of a Byzantine princess', in her *Unrivalled Influence: Women and Empire in Byzantium* (Princeton, 2013), 238–60 at 243–5; see also pp. 203–4, 208; and for the role of women in elite political culture: pp. 21–3, 397–8.

adjoining St Sophia. By and large these close neighbours, emperor and patriarch, maintained a working relationship, and this 'political ortho-doxy', as it has been termed, provided essential coordinates for the empire.[88] In effect, the church provided additional support for unity, binding ecclesiastical and political control together, although bishops were not invariably deferential to the emperor of the day, and they mostly lacked the charisma of yet another grouping, the monks.

As an administrator, the patriarch had extraordinary powers. These ranged from the appointment of leading metropolitans (thereby control-ling recruitment to the top of the hierarchy) to the initiation of missionary activity, the maintenance of a supreme court of appeal for ecclesiastical cases, whose resolution could become a source of canon law, and the calling of councils to settle matters of dogma. In addition, the patriarch could intervene against imperial actions deemed immoral – such as, for example, Nicholas I Mystikos' condemnation of the fourth marriage of Leo VI (886–912) – and he could exercise *oikonomia* (prudent discretion) when necessary. Thus he could suspend the strict application of canon law to permit a person's divorce and remarriage. Some patriarchs took advantage of a power vacuum to assume quasi-imperial roles at court in critical moments, such as the death of an emperor whose son (or sons) was too young to exercise power. In 913 Nicholas Mystikos opposed Empress Zoe, the widowed mother of the young Constantine VII, and effectively took over the running of the empire. His negotiations with the Bulgarian leader Symeon may indeed have saved Byzantium. But his clashes with Leo VI – whom he had excluded from the church of St Sophia for nearly a year – split the church and rocked the government; this did, however, lead to Nicholas' deposition from office for the rest of Leo's reign.[89]

The fact that most patriarchs were highly educated men, steeped in classical education and able to speak the same language – literally – as the most cultivated mandarins, gave them standing in the imperial court and facilitated their participation in secular affairs. Their involvement in regencies was accepted practice and allowed them to assume leading political roles. But sometimes they appear to have permitted widowed mothers unusual prominence in imperial government. When the nomin-ally iconoclast patriarch Paul retired – or was persuaded to retire – Empress Eirene, who had virtually taken over the council of regency set up for her son Constantine in 780, proceeded to appoint to the post her own choice, a civilian administrator named Tarasios. Similarly, Empress

[88] H.-G. Beck, *Das byzantinische Jahrtausend* (Munich, 1978), 87–108.
[89] S. Tougher, *The Reign of Leo VI (886–812): Politics and People* (Leiden, 1997), 154–63.

Theodora insisted on the appointment of Methodios as patriarch once John Grammatikos (the Grammarian) had been removed. In this way, both widowed empresses increased their control over the church and brought about the return to icon veneration, in 787 and 843 respectively.[90] In this co-operation with their patriarchs, they faced down any opposition by loyal iconoclasts and saw through major change. These two episodes show that, when church and state worked together, they made for a very powerful combination.

The institutional hierarchy beneath the patriarch spanned the empire, and its synods and other assemblies gave an energetic holder of the office the chance to weave his own webs of patronage and, occasionally, take a public stand. A sizable proportion of prelates rallied together against Alexios I Komnenos, after he had infringed the church's property-rights and sacrality by melting down church vessels to raise resources for the war effort against the Normans in the opening years of his reign.[91] On the whole, bishoprics were not as well-endowed with lands and revenues as their counterparts in the Latin west, although the hierarchy of sees meant that Caesarea, Ephesos and Ankyra, among the highest-ranking, had considerable resources.[92] Various projects on Byzantine prosopography have shown how difficult it is to extract substantive information about an individual bishop from his surviving seals or a passing mention in a saint's

---

[90] See p. 204. For the scope for women acting as regents or royal spouses to affect policy: p. 23.

[91] See p. 207.

[92] For the status and material resources of bishops and their clergy: Hussey, *Orthodox Church*, 325–35; M. Angold, *Church and Society in Byzantium under the Comneni, 1081–1261* (Cambridge, 1995), 139–57; M. Angold and M. Whitby, 'The church: structures and administration', in *OHBS*, 571–82; B. Moulet, *Évêques, pouvoir et société à Byzance (VIIIe–XIe siècle)* (Paris, 2011), esp. 173–210, 291–348; K. Smyrlis, 'Priesthood and empire: ecclesiastical wealth and privilege under the early Palaiologoi', in C. Gastgeber *et al.* (eds), *The Patriarchate of Constantinople in Comparison and Context* (Vienna, 2017), 95–104. For the situation in the west. see e.g. T. Reuter, 'A Europe of bishops: the age of Wulfstan of York and Burchard of Worms', in L. Körntgen and D. Wassenhoven (eds), *Patterns of Episcopal Power: Bishops in Tenth and Eleventh Century Western Europe* (Berlin, 2011), 17–38; R. B. Ekelund *et al.*, 'The political economy of the medieval church', in R. M. McCleary (ed.), *The Oxford Handbook of the Economics of Religion* (Oxford, 2011), 305–22; G. E. M. Gasper and S. H. Gullbekk (eds), *Money and the Church in Medieval Europe, 1000–1200: Practice, Morality and Thought* (Farnham, 2015). A contrast between the increasing splendour of western bishops' vestments and the more modest clothing of their Byzantine counterparts can be adduced from M. C. Miller, *Clothing the Clergy: Virtue and Power in Medieval Europe, c.800–1200* (Ithaca, NY, 2014), 64–76, 177–83, 199–206. The vesture of Byzantine bishops did, however, become more elaborate, symbolising their more exalted status in the Palaiologan era: *ODB* i:291–2, s.v. 'Bishop' (A. Papadakis); iii:1526, s.v. 'Omophorion' (N. P. Ševčenko); iii:1830, s.v. '*sakkos*' (A. P. Kazhdan); W. T. Woodfin, *The Embodied Icon: Liturgical Vestments and Sacramental Power in Byzantium* (Oxford, 2012), 187–213.

Life. Even so, studies have highlighted the variety of situations of bishops across the empire: some, at least, were firmly integrated into local elites.[93]

Unlike civilian and military officials, who generally served for only a three-year term, bishops were for life and had to reside in their sees and look after the spiritual well-being of their diocese. They formed a lasting link between the margins and the metropolis of the empire, keeping in touch with patriarchal staff, visiting the capital to attend synods or to defend legal judgements, and complaining about abusive demands made by civilian and military administrators. Within each diocese, the archbishop appointed local clergy, administered church property and assisted in the education of local boys. Letters written by such educated men often reflect their distaste for provincial life, dull in comparison with Constantinople. They missed friends' stimulating conversation, court gossip, news from abroad and the richer, more varied, diet. Yet they also tried to resolve local problems and defended the interests of their parishioners against excessive imperial taxation or punishment.[94]

The attention paid by the imperial-ecclesiastical leadership to the setup at grassroots is shown by lists of bishoprics compiled periodically throughout the middle and later Byzantine periods, the *Notitiae*. They are proving rather more informative than their editor, the great French scholar Jean Darrouzès, was inclined to accept.[95] That, at least, is the conclusion drawn by students of different periods: for example, Marie-France Auzépy, studying evidence of new episcopal sees in the eighth and early ninth centuries; Stanislaw Turlej doing similar work on ninth- and tenth-century Greece; or Dimitri Korobeinikov, who has collated the *Notitiae* with the evidence of Christian communities persisting in Asia Minor under Turkish rule as late as the fourteenth century.[96] Their indications of shifting sees, merging and uncoupling according to

[93] Moulet, *Évêques, pouvoir et société*. See also *The Prosopography of the Byzantine Empire I (641–867)*, ed. J. Martindale (CD-ROM, Aldershot, 2001); *Prosopography of the Byzantine World, 2016*, ed. M. J. Jeffreys *et al.* (London, 2017), http://pbw2016 .kdl.kcl.ac.uk (accessed 8 August 2019); *PmbZ*[1]; *PmbZ*[2]. On bishops in the west: pp. 148, 149, 159–60, 167–8, 262, 263–4, 374–5, 398–400, 407.

[94] J. Herrin, 'Realities of Byzantine provincial government: Hellas and Peloponnesos, 1180–1205', *DOP* 29 (1975), 253–84; repr. in her *Margins and Metropolis*, 58–102; M. Mullett, *Theophylact of Ochrid: Reading the Letters of a Byzantine Archbishop* (Abingdon, 1997). See also p. 96.

[95] As the editor of scattered and disparate manuscripts, he had to contend with the absence of standardised names and 'the apparent anarchy of forms in the text': *Notitiae Episcopatuum ecclesiae Constantinopolitanae*, ed. J. Darrouzès (Paris, 1981), xii. This, and the fluctuations between successive *Notitiae*, made him cautious, while accepting the relative accuracy of certain lists, e.g. no. 12, datable to the era of the Komnenoi (*ibid.*, 130–5).

[96] SOE, 251–91 at 286; S. Turlej, *The Chronicle of Monemvasia: The Migration of the Slavs and Church Conflicts in the Byzantine Source from the Beginning of the 9th Century* (Cracow,

circumstances, match similar flexibility in secular administrative arrangements, at least in border areas or regions under external pressure. The involvement of the government in the setting up of new bishoprics, which Auzépy shows with the help of seals and prosopography,[97] also tells us something about Byzantine political culture. Metropolitans – like the governors of provinces – were regular attendees at court, judging by the provision for their placement at receptions and banquets in texts like the *Kleterologion*. In fact, they could hold court titles such as *proedros*.

The ecclesiastical hierarchy was, then, a distinct institution, but this never gave rise to fully fledged autonomy or an alternative ideology, in the style of the western papacy.[98] Factors like the size of Constantinople, the resources of some churches and the foundation charters of some monasteries permitted a few places to evade the dominance of patriarch and emperor. Although subscribing to the same imperial ideology, certain monasteries developed their own webs of power. In the case of the foundations on Mount Athos and a few other remote monasteries, the patrons who built them proceeded to appoint their leaders and often wrote the *typika* (charter of regulations) with the aim of keeping them free from outside control. Some houses under imperial patronage were provided with documents sealed by a *chrysoboullon* (golden seal) that established the independence of the monastery from patriarchal or episcopal rule and denied imperial officials the right to enter and levy taxes.[99]

In this way, the founders and patrons fostered a sprawling conglomerate of abbots and monks. If conflicts arose, or standards faltered, neither patriarch nor emperor found it easy to intervene. This was for one very good reason: Byzantines were taught to regard the monastic life as superior to their own lay existence. As Theodore the Studite put it in the ninth century, 'the monastic state is lofty and exalted, even angelic, pure of every sin on account of its perfect way of life'.[100] As a matter of course, then, all

2001), 105–7, 111–20; D. Korobeinikov, 'Orthodox communities in Eastern Anatolia in the thirteenth and fourteenth centuries, I: the two patriarchates: Constantinople and Antioch', *Al-Masaq* 15 (2003), 197–214; *idem*, 'Orthodox communities in Eastern Anatolia in the thirteenth to fourteenth centuries, II: the time of troubles', *Al-Masaq* 17 (2005), 1–29 at 5, 9–10, 16–18.

[97] SOE, 286. See also, on Nikephoros I's role in founding a metropolitan see at Patras, Turlej, *Chronicle of Monemvasia*, 110, 123–4, 147–8, 159–60.

[98] For insistence on the benefits of monarchy in most Byzantine and Islamic sources: pp. 80–2, 84–5, 87, 347–9; for diverse views about ideal forms of rulership in the Latin west: pp. 268–70, 283–4; and for ideas about the division of powers in the Islamic world, e.g. between sultan and caliph: pp. 110–14, 342–5, 348–9.

[99] See pp. 93, 425–7; on the social significance of land: p. 421.

[100] *'Testament* of Theodore the Studite for the Monastery of St John Stoudios in Constantinople', tr. T. Miller, in *BMFD*, i:67–83 at 76.

monks were to be admired, deferred to and supported. Their prestige far outshone that of secular clergy; even senior bishops, grand though they might be, were not held in such reverence as *hegoumenoi* (abbots), although they were often monks themselves. It was the way of life monks were believed to lead that raised their status in the eyes of their compatriots. This did not, however, make monks a standing counterweight to the imperial court or anything like an alternative hierarchy. On the contrary, it was the custom of prominent houses such as those on Athos to uphold prayers for 'the emperor of the Romans', as Stefan Dušan found in 1345. Monks might condemn the actions of individual emperors and their families but not systematically impugn the imperial order itself.

Status and Competition within the Imperial-Ecclesiastical Establishment: Military, Bureaucratic and Constantinopolitan Hierarchies

Issues of status, wealth and outright power could be contested by members of the various hierarchies making up the imperial-ecclesiastical complex. Each had its own mode of recruitment and promotion ladder, expressed by costumes and titles which grew more complex with an individual's progress through the grades. Meanwhile, the continuous and more or less effective functioning of the capital's law-courts up to the fall of Constantinople in 1204 provided a framework for working out differences of interests, property disputes and even personal rivalries. Along with the church and other institutions, the law provided not only an ideology but also practical means for upholding the imperial order.

Military structures were probably the most open to talent irrespective of birth or connections, in that they accepted soldiers who had displayed great courage, valour or strength and who could make careers based on experience in battle.[101] Their hierarchy played a critical role, as it not only safeguarded the frontiers but also launched military revolts. As in all premodern societies, force of arms could determine the imperial succession, and several families provided multiple contenders for the throne. Many were based in Anatolia, with most of their male members holding military posts.[102] By about 850, the families of Skleros, Phokas and Doukas (all of

---

[101] Thus prowess in violence and warfare had, within limits, its uses for advancement in Byzantium as well as the Latin west and the Islamic world: pp. 157–60, 165, 264–7, 376–8, 409, 25, 111–12, 115–16, 348–9, 358–9, 472–7, 482–3.

[102] E. Patlagean, 'Les débuts d'une aristocratie byzantine et le témoignage de l'historiographie: système des noms et liens de parenté aux IXe–Xe siècles', in *TBA*, 23–43; J.-C. Cheynet, 'The Byzantine aristocracy (8th–13th centuries)', in *TBAMF*, no.1, 1–43.

whom were to remain influential for centuries afterwards) appear frequently in the sigillographic and literary record.[103] Who were these families, and how had they come to prominence? A clue may perhaps be found in the *Taktika* (military handbook) of Leo VI (886–912), where the emperor remarked that '[generals] who have no ancestral renown desire to make up for the obscurity of their lineage by their own enthusiasm and are moved to undertake more dangerous activities'.[104] Given the military associations of most of these powerful families, when identifiable, their importance may be due to their immediate ancestors who provided local leadership and military expertise during the seventh and eighth centuries and were rewarded for their efforts with imperial titles.[105] An ethos of enthusiasm for action and fighting the good fight with celestial support ran through this milieu, and many senior officers showed warrior saints like George or Theodore on their seals.[106] It is no accident that notions of campaigning against the Muslims as being a battle for the faith circulated among them. It was a scion of one such family, Nikephoros II Phokas, who capped his ascent to the throne with a proposal for venerating the slain as 'martyrs'.[107] This bid to exalt the military way of life was blocked by the patriarch, and, although morale-boosting rhetoric and slogans along with bouts of war fever went so far as to present warfare on behalf of fellow Christians as meritorious and earning one a place in heaven, this did not match the passionate sense of personal loyalty to Christ manifested by Crusaders in the eleventh and twelfth centuries, in their zeal to reconquer and defend His Sepulchre and the Holy Land, or the Muslim promise of

[103] For the Skleros family: W. Seibt, *Die Skleroi: eine prosopographisch-sigillographische Studie* (Vienna, 1976); for the Doukas: D. I. Polemis, *The Doukai: A Contribution to Byzantine Prosopography* (London, 1968). See also pp. 421–3. Essential tools for the tracking of Byzantine families and their members include: *Prosopography of the Byzantine Empire I*, ed. Martindale; *Prosopography of the Byzantine World*, ed. Jeffreys *et al.*; *PmbZ¹*; *PmbZ²*.

[104] Leo VI, *Tactica* II.13, ed. and tr. G. T. Dennis, *The Taktika of Leo VI*, rev. edn, *CFHB* 49 (Washington, DC, 2014), 25; see also A. Kazhdan, 'The aristocracy and the imperial ideal', in *TBA*, 43–57 at 43.

[105] SOE, 272–3; I. Anagnostakis, 'Byzantium and Hellas: some lesser known aspects of the Helladic connection (8th–12th centuries)', in J. Albani and E. Chalkia (eds), *Heaven and Earth, II: Cities and Countryside in Byzantine Greece* (Athens, 2013), 192–209. See also pp. 418–21.

[106] J.-C. Cheynet, 'Par Saint Georges, par Saint Michel', *TM* 14 (2002), 115–34; J.-C. Cheynet, 'Le culte de Saint Théodore chez les officiers de l'armée d'Orient', in A. Avramea *et al.* (eds), *Vyzantio kratos kai koinonia: mneme Nikou Oikonomide* (Athens, 2003), 137–54; M. White, *Military Saints in Byzantium and Rus, 900–1200* (Cambridge, 2013). On warfare and religion as touchstones of a society and its political culture: pp. 19–21, 25–7.

[107] John Skylitzes, *Synopsis historiarum*, ed. H. Thurn, *CFHB* 5 (Berlin, 1973), 274; tr. J. Wortley, *John Skylitzes: A Synopsis of Byzantine History, 811–1057* (Cambridge, 2010), 263.

immediate entry to heaven for warriors killed in battle.[108] Nor did exalting the war effort ever really spin out of the control of the state apparatus. Even the warrior saints seem to have been primarily a top-down cult, promoted from the imperial court.[109] Equally it would be a mistake to see the army as an interest-group perpetually at odds with the central administration or hatching plots. Very many skilled commanders served loyally under more than one ruler and sustained the discipline of military life through difficult times. One has only to consider the iconoclast generals left in power by Eirene, or the family of Kekaumenos, which provided military expertise to several eleventh-century emperors.[110]

The civilian bureaucracy amounted to another hierarchy trained in Constantinople, where ambitious young men sought out the best teachers in order to qualify for entry to it. Both ecclesiastical and civilian hierarchies required classical education and significant rhetorical skill, though again some dedicated monks could be made patriarch without climbing step-by-step up the established ladder. Even a lawyer could become patriarch, since the emperor had the final choice for this post. The higher men progressed up the Byzantine administrative hierarchy (whether clerical or lay), the more they needed more than a modicum of learning. This was not only to fulfil the demands of the post but also to mark one out as belonging to a privileged, mutually admiring group.[111] Although voices were sometimes raised complaining that the fate of the empire was in the hands of people of no 'breeding' (by which the tenth-century poet John Geometres meant little education),[112] there is evidence to suggest that the

---

[108] On the various Byzantine concepts about warfare, as science, Christian endeavour and noble calling: J. Haldon, *Warfare, State and Society in the Byzantine World, 565–1204* (London, 1999); W. Treadgold, 'Byzantium, the reluctant warrior', in M. Yazigi and N. Christie (eds), *Noble Ideals and Bloody Realities: Warfare in the Middle Ages, 378–1492* (Leiden, 2006), 209–33; contributions to J. Koder and I. Stouraitis (eds), *Byzantine War Ideology between Roman Imperial Concept and Christian Religion* (Vienna, 2012), esp. J. Koder and I. Stouraitis, 'Byzantine approaches to warfare (6th –12th centuries): an introduction' (9–15) and A. Kolia-Dermitzaki, '"Holy War" in Byzantium twenty years later' (121–34). For jihad: pp. 26, 108, 112, 113, 359; for the Christian west: pp. 145, 172, 174, 379.

[109] White, *Military Saints*, 65–82.

[110] On Kekaumenos, see also pp. 97–8, 432; on Eirene: J. Herrin, *Women in Purple: Rulers of Medieval Byzantium* (London, 2001).

[111] For C. Wright Mills' views on 'mutual recognition' of members of elites: p. 410; for levels of learning and high culture in western clerical elites: pp. 41–5, 151, 171–3, 254–64, 274, 276–7, 388–9; for the *'ulama'* in the Islamic world: pp. 247, 340–3, 347–9, 362, 456, 464–6.

[112] On John Geometres' family, education and elitist outlook: E. van Opstall (ed. and French tr.), *Poèmes en hexamètres et en distiques élégiaques* (Leiden, 2008), 3–7, 10–13, 27–8; E. van Opstall and M. Tomadaki, 'John Geometres: a poet around the year 1000',

opposite was, in fact, the case. Ambitious parents (such as those of the future St Athanasios of Athos in the tenth century) were keen to send their sons to Constantinople to acquire a standard of education above the level of *ta grammata* (the learning of letters and basic literacy): they could obtain that familiarity with ancient Greek learning, especially literature, which came to mark out the administrative elite.[113] By the eleventh century, the days of the 'able illiterate' gaining high office were long gone; the cultural elite was inseparable from the court elite; figures such as Nikephoros Bryennios, Anna Komnene, and, later, Andronikos Palaiologos and John Kantakouzenos were all leading members of both.[114] Members could be immediately recognised by their ability to speak 'correct' Greek: Maria Skleraina, the mistress of the Emperor Constantine IX Monomachos (1042–55), 'in appearance not specially remarkable', won over the arch-snob Michael Psellos by her speech, 'which had the delicate beauty of expression, the rhythmic perfection of a scholar and [. . .] an unaffected sweetness of diction'.[115] The ability to express oneself in writing in Attic Greek rather than the contemporary vernacular was also prized. The Byzantine intellectual elite and its eager, socially ambitious audience revelled in what has been aptly described as 'educated chauvinism' and took every opportunity to display it.[116] Most civilian officials had to serve in whatever capacity the emperor, or his advisers, thought fit, and many travelled the length and breadth of the empire as junior officials. The lead seals used to guarantee their documents provide invaluable evidence for their career patterns.[117]

in W. Hörandner *et al.* (eds), *A Companion to Byzantine Poetry* (Leiden, 2019), 191–211; M. Lauxtermann, 'John Geometres, poet and soldier', *Byzantion* 68 (1998), 356–80.

[113] M. Lauxtermann, 'Byzantine poetry and the paradox of Basil II's reign', in P. Magdalino (ed.), *Byzantium in the Year 1000* (Leiden, 2003), 199–216. For the education of Abraamios (later St Athanasios) who became a famous teacher in Constantinople: P. Lemerle, *Byzantine Humanism*, tr. H. Lindsay and A. Moffatt (Canberra, 1986), 298–302.

[114] Basil I and, possibly, Romanos I Lekapenos were illiterate: G. Cavallo, *Lire à Byzance*, French tr. P. Odorico and A. Segonds (Paris, 2006), 24; Magdalino, 'Byzantine snobbery', in *TBA*, 58–78 at 66. For the role of scholars in court culture: pp. 53, 54, 58, 336–8, 341–2, 347–8, 352–3, 361–2.

[115] Michael Psellos, *Chronographia* VI.60, ed. D.-R. Reinsch, 2 vols (Berlin, 2014), i:130; tr. E. A. R. Sewter, *Fourteen Byzantine Rulers: The Chronographia of Michael Psellus* (Harmondsworth, 1966), 184.

[116] G. Page, *Being Byzantine: Greek Identity before the Ottomans* (Cambridge, 2008), 59–65; Magdalino (*EMK*, 335–56) discusses the importance of rhetoric in twelfth-century Constantinople.

[117] *MOB*, 1–2; *Studies in Byzantine Sigillography*, ed. N. Oikonomides et al., 12 vols to date (Washington, DC and Munich, 1987–). For a collection of seals of Cherson's *kommerkiarioi* illustrating the *cursus honorum* of individuals: N. Alekseyenko, *L'Administration byzantine de Cherson: catalogue des sceaux* (Paris, 2012).

Senior officials might parade the string of court titles they had attained alongside their current post, and one side of their seal would often show the saint after whom they were named or a saint revered by their families, most notably those with strong military connections. These seals tend to be grander and of superior design and execution than the seals of private individuals, which were also in use until lead seals in general went out of fashion in the twelfth century. From the later tenth century onwards, family names begin to appear on seals. This is sometimes taken for a sign of growing self-awareness on the part of great houses, especially army families, of alternative identities and sources of status.[118] It could, however, equally well register the need for precision, as the armed forces and the bureaucracy grew more elaborate in line with the empire's expansion. In other words, clarification of a person's identity may actually mark more extensive down-reach of the state.[119] In any case, neither the seals nor other types of medium or imagery show any emblems or other devices of the sort distinguishing noble families in the Latin west.[120] The accent and visual focus was decidedly on imperial institutions and on an individual's status accruing from service there.

Entry to official circles involving proximity to the ruling family was competitive, as the benefits of placing at court a child (male, female or eunuch) were considerable. Pages recruited to the equivalent court structure of bearded men could expect to work their way gradually up the hierarchy until, perhaps, appointment to the highest roles in the central imperial administration, such as Eparch (*eparchos*) of the City, or Keeper of the Imperial Inkpot (*ho epi tou kanikleiou*).[121] In theory, at least, promotion and rewards were proportionate to an individual's merit, and the heights to which he – sometimes she – rose were conditional upon loyalty to the emperor. Whether belonging to the armed forces, the central administration, or the various branches of the bedchamber and other parts of the imperial household (usually reserved for eunuchs), status was defined by one's title. This was shown on one's seal and set the place in ceremonies for all.

[118] P. Stephenson, 'A development in nomenclature on the seals of the Byzantine provincial aristocracy in the late tenth century', *REB* 52 (1994), 187–211.

[119] For the interplay between family, household and state service in aiding or obstructing an individual's advancement: pp. 201–3.

[120] On seals: J.-C. Cheynet, *La Société byzantine: l'apport des sceaux*, 2 vols (Paris, 2008); also p. 88; on chivalry in general: pp. 157–9, 267–8, 378–80, 390.

[121] In general: Oikonomides, *Listes de préséance*; *ODB* i:705, s.v. 'Eparch of the City' (A. Kazhdan); ii:1101, s.v. 'kanikleios' (A. Kazhdan); for an individual Keeper of the Imperial Ink pot's career: Nikephoros Ouranos, *Taktika* chs 56–65, ed. and tr. in E. McGeer, *Sowing the Dragon's Teeth: Byzantine Warfare in the Tenth Century* (Washington, DC, 1995), 88–163; E. McGeer, 'Tradition and reality in the *Taktika* of Nikephoros Ouranos', *DOP* 45 (1991), 129–40.

Beyond the palace walls, in the sprawling expanses of Constantinople itself, other hierarchies took formal responsibility for everyday life and entertainment. We have already encountered the Blues and Greens who ran the Hippodrome. Of even greater consequence for keeping the citizens well-fed and ensuring stability were the hierarchies of craftsmen, merchants, bankers and record certifiers, signed up as members of their respective guilds. The guilds organised and regulated the supply and sale of both luxuries and daily necessities in the metropolis, which required vast quantities of imported food to sustain the population.[122] While workers of gold, silver, ivory, precious stones and the finest woven silks represented the most prestigious crafts, they were subject to regulations recorded in the *Book of the Eparch*, like all Constantinople's other trades (soap-, leather- and candle-makers, bakers, butchers, and wine merchants, for instance). The Eparch had inspectors to make sure that accurate weights and measures were used and goods were sold at the correct price. He also had authority to punish those found guilty of breaching the rules, an integral part of imperial control and ideology.[123] The *Book of the Eparch* itself exemplifies this ideology. Yet so far as we can tell, it was a working document, subject to occasional updates. Its measures helped maintain a showcase for imperial splendour and – no less important for being intangible – continuity from the ancient Roman order. So long as the emperor reigned from his City, all could seem right with the world.

Political Thinking and Culture after 1204

A major political change, however, could turn things upside down. In 1204, participants in the Fourth Crusade swept away much of the Byzantine system of government, which was reconstructed in no less than three centres: the three successor states of Trebizond, Nicaea and Epiros; partly in the Latin Empire set up in Constantinople (until 1261), which adapted many of the same imperial structures; and eventually in other regional polities which borrowed some elements of Byzantine official political culture.[124] That elements of the same mechanisms resurfaced in such different centres is not only a tribute to Byzantine political culture but also

---

[122] J. Koder, 'The authority of the eparchos in the markets of Constantinople (according to the Book of the Eparch)', in P. Armstrong (ed.), *Authority in Byzantium* (Farnham, 2013), 83–108.

[123] Leo VI, *Book of the Eparch*, ed. and German tr. J. Koder, *Das Eparchenbuch Leons des Weisen*, CFHB 33 (Vienna, 1991); also p. 91.

[124] See also pp. 188, 190, 414–15, 438, 439.

revealing of the confidence and self-belief of Byzantine elites in their own familiar way of governing. Although Nicaea had the advantage of the patriarch's presence, Trebizond and Epiros/Thessaloniki persistently disputed its claims to represent the entire empire. These splinter states also generated novel discussions of the imperial office and how it should be preserved, notably in the writings of Demetrios Chomatenos, justifying Theodore Komnenos Doukas as Despot of Epiros, and the treatise written by Emperor Theodore II Laskaris (1254–8).[125]

While control of the metropolis was not utterly essential to the three alternative Byzantine imperial manifestations, Constantinople would reassert itself as the principal focus of late Byzantine political theory after 1261. Even more strikingly, it clearly helped the western conquerors to realise their own version of an empire, as the Crusaders and Venetians tried to weld some of their own ideas of government onto the imperial system they found.[126] This mixed political ideology acquired status through incorporating Byzantine ceremonial, but the rulers of the Latin Empire never mastered the potential of the imperial court, and they failed to attract sufficient manpower to survive. In 1261, after the Venetian fleet had sailed into the Black Sea, a naval commander from Nicaea found the city defences deserted and managed to recapture Constantinople. The Latin emperor and patriarch fled with as many supporters as could board the surviving ships. On the feast of the Dormition (15 August 1261) Michael VIII Palaiologos entered the city, walking behind an icon of the Virgin. From this restoration of Byzantine authority over the capital some reworking of political theory emerged, characterised by Dimiter Angelov as 'rival ideas and theories of kingship' produced by a variety of authors.[127]

Already, even before Michael's triumphal return to Constantinople, scholars and philosophers exiled in Nicaea had contemplated the reasons for their condition. At that time Nikephoros Blemmydes had reasserted the Mirror for Princes ideal that the ruler should embody imperial virtues, listing nineteen and laying emphasis on self-control and the avoidance of

---

[125] Demetrios Chomatenos, *Ponemata diaphora* nos 114, 110, ed. Prinzing, 370–8, 363–7. See *ibid.*, 23*–26* (introduction); R. Macrides, 'Bad historian or good lawyer? Demetrios Chomatenos and novel 131', *DOP* 46 (1992), 187–96; repr. in her *Kinship and Justice*, no. 12; *IIPTB*, 204–52. For Theodore Laskaris' treatise: n. 130.

[126] S. Burkhardt, *Mediterranes Kaisertum und imperiale Ordnungen: das lateinische Kaiserreich von Konstantinopel* (Berlin, 2014); T. Shawcross, 'Conquest legitimised: the making of a Byzantine emperor in Crusader Constantinople (1204–1261)', in J. Harris *et al.* (eds), *Byzantines, Latins, and Turks in the Eastern Mediterranean World after 1150* (Oxford, 2012), 181–219.

[127] *IIPTB*, 13.

luxury.[128] Similarly, in Epiros, Demetrios Chomatenos had advised Theodore Komnenos Doukas (1215–30) on the traditional duties of a good ruler.[129] The teaching of Synesius from the early fifth century continued to generate such instruction and preserved the ideas of the Mirror for Princes into the fifteenth century.

Yet during this period of exile the Nicaean emperor Theodore II Laskaris, son of John III, had himself written several works that differed fundamentally from these ideals of the philosopher-ruler.[130] In an original and effective analysis Theodore attacked the power of the aristocracy as a brake on reforms that were essential for the survival of the empire. To remove their hereditary hold on government offices and resulting influence, he began recruiting competent men from social backgrounds generally unconnected to the entrenched aristocratic families. Through personal friendship with them – they were often drawn from among the court pages with whom he had been raised – Theodore sought a different style of government based on friendship rather than family connections. His idea of an empire governed by reciprocal relations founded on mutual interest appears to have taken account of contemporary civil upheavals in Italy. In his epitaph for Frederick II Hohenstaufen, Theodore recognised that good actions might provoke blame rather than praise: 'hatred was the political price which the emperor had to pay for governing in the name of the public benefit', as Angelov puts it.[131]

Despite this prescient analysis, Theodore Laskaris' insights were not taken into account after 1261, and aristocratic rivalry for supreme control disrupted imperial rule within the restored empire of Constantinople. Many established families refused to accept the usurpation of Michael Palaiologos and supported the heir of the Vatatzes dynasty, John IV, who had been blinded by Michael VIII but lived on as a constant reminder.[132] Infighting among the many branches of the Palaiologan dynasty provoked two periods of civil war (1321–8, 1341–7); the latter was exacerbated by the very wealthy Kantakouzenos family and pitted its experienced

---

[128] Nikephoros Blemmydes, *Imperial Statue: A Moral Treatise*, ed. and tr. H. Hunger and I. Ševčenko, in *Des Nikephoros Blemmydes* Basilikos Andrias *und dessen Metaphrase von Georgios Galesiotes und Georgios Oinaiotes* (Vienna, 1986), 43–117 (text), 121–47 (English tr.); *IIPTB*, 191–2, 243–5.

[129] Demetrios Chomatenos, *Ponemata diaphora* no. 110, ed. Prinzing, 363–7; *IIPTB*, 187, 192–4.

[130] Theodore II Laskaris, *Opuscula rhetorica*, ed. A. Tartaglia (Munich, 2000). See now D. G. Angelov, *The Byzantine Hellene: The Life of Emperor Theodore Laskaris and Byzantium in the Thirteenth Century* (Cambridge, 2019).

[131] Theodore II Laskaris, 'Oratio funebris in Fridericum II', ed. Tartaglia in *Opuscula rhetorica*, 85–94 at 91; *IIPTB*, 241.

[132] T. Shawcross, 'In the name of the True Emperor: politics of resistance after the Palaiologan usurpation', *Byzantinoslavica* 66 (2008), 203–27.

statesman, acclaimed as John VI, against the regency set up for the much younger John V Palaiologos. Even after the fall of Constantinople to the Ottoman Turks and the death of Constantine XI, his brothers Demetrios and Thomas continued to dispute control over the Morea. Aristocratic and sibling rivalries appear to have become too deeply engrained within the politics of the later Byzantine centuries to allow for fundamental change.[133]

Some thinkers had foreseen these problems and considered possible improvements to imperial rule. In the first years of the fourteenth century, Manuel Moschopoulos, a famed teacher in Constantinople, composed a treatise on the social contract implicit in Byzantium drawing heavily on Plato's *Republic*.[134] He traced the oath of loyalty all subjects owed the emperor back to the earliest formation of the state and emphasised its power to guarantee peaceful government and to avoid plots and conspiracies. He further specified an imperial oath that courtiers engaged in imperial affairs should take as a form of contract for paid services to the state. Although the church prohibited oaths, Moschopoulos insisted that they fell within the secular sphere and should not be considered part of religious morality.[135] Since oaths had regularly been used in the empire to ensure the rights of imperial children to accede to their inherited power, ecclesiastical opposition could be overcome. But the innovation in Moschopoulos' use of the oath as a contract between the emperor and his subjects was its reciprocal nature, raising the possibility of serious opposition to unfettered monarchical power. Western influence and feudal relations dependent on similar oaths that increased throughout the thirteenth century may lie behind this reconfiguration of monarchical authority. Michael VIII had obliged the rulers of Thessaly and Epiros to pledge their loyalty to him by oath, and under Andronikos II its use was extended, as in, for instance, 1318 when the citizens of Ioannina elected to return to imperial control, a change marked by a chrysobull.[136] Moschopoulos, however, clearly conceived of the new contractual system of government as a way of diminishing the emperor's sacral aura as well as preventing civil

---

[133] On the aristocratisation of politics in the later period: pp. 202, 443–6.
[134] L. Levi (ed.), 'Cinque lettere inedite di Emanuele Moscopulo', *Studi italiani di filologia classica* 10 (1902), 55–72 at 64–8: tr. I. Ševčenko, 'The imprisonment of Manuel Moschopulos in the year 1305 or 1306', *Speculum* 27 (1952), 133–57 at 134–5.
[135] *IIPTB*, 321–6.
[136] *Das Register des Patriarchats von Konstantinopel* no. 110, ed. H. Hunger and O. Kresten, 3 vols to date (Vienna, 1981–), ii:94–104; *Les Régestes des actes du patriarcat de Constantinople*, ed. V. Grumel *et al.*, 7 vols (Paris, 1932–91), I.5 (no. 2180); *IIPTB*, 342–3. On oaths and fealty in the west: pp. 74–5.

wars.[137] His treatise arose from personal upheavals as well as the empire's plight. It features among the writings he penned while in prison. He had been implicated – unwittingly, he claimed – in a plot to overthrow Andronikos II for failure to cope with Turkish advances in Asia Minor and the influx of refugees into Constantinople; Andronikos' response to criticism had been to demand a loyalty oath to himself and his son.[138]

Moschopoulos' ideas may have provoked Thomas Magistros in Thessaloniki to write *Peri basileias* ('On Kingship'), which also drew on Synesius to stress the importance of imperial philanthropy, self-control, concern for the public good and the strict administration of justice.[139] In addition, the scholar and teacher urged Andronikos II to strive for peace but be prepared for war. He shared with other late thirteenth- and fourteenth-century authors deep disapproval of the disbanding of the Byzantine navy and the use of foreign mercenaries such as the Catalans. But he went much further in his critique of imperial taxation, corrupt city governors and even Empress Yolanda-Eirene's excessively luxurious life-style. Since she had made her home in Thessaloniki from 1303–17, Thomas Magistros was probably writing from first-hand observation. His most radical attack, however, was on imperial taxation, especially the extraordinary taxes imposed to finance warfare. These tirades against tax-collecting methods were related to his view that such funds were public and should remain under public control.[140] Further, he disapproved of emperors appointing their relatives to administrative positions, because this strengthened the notion of government by aristocratic privilege, rather than for the public good. While developing a more fundamental critique of Palaiologan government, he also lectured the citizens of his home town, Thessaloniki, on their duties toward the poor and less privileged in society.[141] In advocating a productive and compassionate life, honest dealings with labourers, the selection of suitably qualified and virtuous city guardians, and an urban militia to protect the city, the

---

[137] Levi (ed.), 'Cinque lettere', 64–8; *IIPTB*, 346–7. Ideas involving a more contractual relationship between the ruler and other sectors of society (if not the entire body politic) were gaining ground in the west from around this time on: pp. 36, 62–3, 67, 175, 278–84, 402–3, 409.

[138] Ševčenko, 'Imprisonment of Manuel Moschopoulos', 146–50; *IIPTB*, 318.

[139] Thomas Magistros, *Peri basileias*, PG 145, cols 447–96, esp. 451–66; *IIPTB*, 193–5; F. Tinnefeld, 'Intellectuals in late Byzantine Thessalonike', *DOP* 57 (2003), 153–72. See also N. Gaul, *Thomas Magistros und die spätbyzantinische Sophistik: Studien zum Humanismus urbaner Eliten der frühen Palaiologenzeit* (Wiesbaden, 2011), 288–98, 330–7, 406–7.

[140] K. Smyrlis, 'Financial crisis and the limits of taxation under Andronikos II Palaiologos (1282–1321)', in D. Angelov and M. Saxby (eds), *Power and Subversion in Byzantium* (Farnham, 2013), 71–82.

[141] In his treatise, *Peri politeias*, PG 145, cols 495–548.

local teacher set out an alternative to contemporary fourteenth-century practices that undercut imperial prerogative.[142]

Fascinating insight into Byzantine governance is provided by Theodore, the second son of Andronikos II, who was sent to Italy as a young man to secure his mother's legacy of Montferrat. As the marquis of that principality, he became aware of western developments in city communes and brought back his ideas to Constantinople during two visits in 1317–19 and 1325–8. In his treatise *On the Government of a Ruler* – originally written in Greek around 1326, then translated into Latin and finally into Old French, the only version that survives – he emphasises the benefit of consulting among citizens rather than relying on the guidance of one or two close advisers as Byzantine rulers did. Even if this does not constitute 'the role of parliament in government', it builds on the use of citizen assemblies to participate in decision-making in a novel fashion.[143] This is how cities rather distant from Constantinople, such as Ioannina, Trikkala and Monemvasia, decided to place themselves under imperial protection, and this was confirmed by chrysobull. In this way Theodore of Montferrat may have signalled a consultative feature that gradually influenced Byzantium. Nonetheless, it is striking that when Andronikos III challenged his grandfather, Andronikos II, during the first civil war, both emperors remained fixated on the supreme power of the autocrat.

Similar concern with the plight of the city of Thessaloniki had focused Thomas Magistros' attention on issues of social justice. These were elaborated upon and symbolised by Alexios Makrembolites in his powerful *Dialogue between the Poor and the Rich*. In denying the poor any role in city government run by the aristocrats, he illustrates many of the evils that fuelled opposition to the imperial administration.[144] Telling contrasts such as that between the funerals of wealthy and impoverished citizens may well have contributed to the Zealot revolt in Thessaloniki (1341–50) led by a powerful guild of seamen.[145] They formed a Council of Twelve

---

[142] *IIPTB*, 297–305

[143] T. Shawcross, 'Mediterranean encounters before the renaissance: Byzantine and Italian political thought concerning the rise of cities', in M. S. Brownlee and D. H. Gondicas (eds), *Renaissance Encounters: Greek East and Latin West* (Leiden, 2013), 57–93; C. Knowles, *Les Enseignements de Théodore Paléologue* (London, 1983); *IIPTB*, 198–200. On councils: D. Kyritses, 'The imperial council and the tradition of consultative decision-making in Byzantium (eleventh to fourteenth centuries)', in Angelov and Saxby (eds), *Power and Subversion*, 57–70, esp. 63–8; also A. Kiousopoulou, *Emperor or Manager: Power and Political Ideology in Byzantium before 1453*, tr. P. Magdalino (Geneva, 2011), 137–40 stressing the novelty of citizens as partners in government.

[144] I. Ševčenko, 'Alexios Makrembolites and his dialogue between the poor and the rich', *Zbornik Radova Vizantološkog Instituta* 6 (1960), 187–228.

[145] Herrin, *Byzantium*, 281–98; J. W. Barker, 'Late Byzantine Thessalonike: a second city's challenges and response', *DOP* 57 (2003), 5–26; *IIPTB*, 200–3.

that set up its own government and prevented imperial authorities and the new archbishop from entering the city for almost a decade. This example of communal government suggests a current of political thought in Thessaloniki that elevated the authority of local citizens, as against governors appointed by the emperor and duty-bound to maintain imperial ideology. Throughout Byzantine history emperors manifested a great fear of the power of the mob, a force described as *demokratia*, rule by the *demos*, a word closely related to *demes*, the Blues and Greens of Constantinople.[146] Members of the circus factions were authorised to generate popular approval of imperial actions in the capital and were never supposed to initiate critical movements. It remains possible that Byzantine crowds drew energy from an unwritten (and unspoken) communal tradition, and some inhabitants of Constantinople clearly nurtured antagonism to imperial ideology.[147]

In Thessaloniki, hostility to the emperor's autocratic power may have been increased by the reduction of the Byzantine navy, a factor unwelcome to the seamen of Thessaloniki. Like the issue of taxation, maintenance of a fleet in an empire so exposed to naval attack provoked much contemporary comment. Whether the Zealots represented a lower-class rebellion against the established power structure of old wealthy families or came under western influences, they were able to attract further support during the long civil war between John VI Kantakouzenos and John V Palaiologos. But after Kantakouzenos' recapture of the city in 1350 and the installation of Gregory Palamas as the new archbishop, Thessaloniki returned to imperial control under the Empress-Mother, Anna of Savoy. She ruled there for about fourteen years, acting with autonomy.[148] This communal experiment remained an isolated example of developed anti-monarchical political theory, which may suggest that any alternative political system needed a supporting substructure – in the

---

[146] S. Vryonis, 'Byzantine *demokratia* and the guilds in the eleventh century', *DOP* 17 (1963), 287, 289–314; Kiousopoulou, *Emperor or Manager*, 27–31, 111–14.

[147] A. Kaldellis, 'How to usurp the throne in Byzantium: the role of public opinion in sedition and rebellion', in Angelov and Saxby (eds), *Power and Subversion*, 43–56, esp. 50–3. Alternatives to monarchy occasionally surface in extant Byzantine writings: pp. 85, 205. However, the theory and practice of non-monarchical structures feature more fully in the west: pp. 150–5, 162, 171, 283–5, 409. For 'family confederations' in the Islamic world: p. 241.

[148] This episode illustrates the diffusion of power in late Byzantium, and the opportunities opening up for strong-minded women: E. Malamut, 'Jeanne-Anne, princesse de Savoie et impératrice de Byzance', in E. Malamut and A. Nicolaïdes (eds), *Impératrices, princesses, aristocrates et saintes souveraines* (Aix-en-Provence, 2014), 85–118; P. Melichar, *Empresses of Late Byzantium: Foreign Brides, Mediators and Pious Women* (Bern, 2019), 171–208.

form of schools and religious traditions that reinforced and made use of such learning. Despite the growing weakness of subsequent emperors, the monarchical ideal was reinstated and frequently repeated in late Byzantine political treatises, such as the advice given by Manuel II Palaiologos to his son John.[149]

Yet in the late fourteenth century George of Pelagonia elaborated a critique of what had become increasingly dynastic succession, insisting that some form of elective kingship would be much better than the inheritance of sons: their upbringing in the imperial court left them 'spoiled by luxury, ignoble flattery, empty conceit': in short, bad rulers. Instead, 'the praiseworthy emperor is not the one who inherits power from his father. Rather, it is the one who has proved himself worthy of the imperial office [. . .] and has come to occupy it in a just manner – elevated to power by the just judgement of the electors, not by usurping it in a tyrannical fashion.'[150] This was a serious side-swipe at the Palaiologan dynasty, which had come to power precisely by tyrannical usurpation.

In the highly changed circumstances of the fifteenth century, as the empire shrank drastically, conflicting theories of the best form of government continued to circulate. From Mistra, George Gemistos Plethon adapted a concern for social justice in his treatises addressed to the despot Manuel Palaiologos, stressing that 'all the land should be the common property of all inhabitants' and that the wealth of his small province should be more equitably shared among all.[151] His ideas for more effective administration were, however, linked with his determination to revive the pagan cult of Zeus. Since orthodox church leaders could not tolerate any theory that involved a return to the ancient gods, Plethon's works were condemned to be burnt, and very few examples survived the flames. Even so, ephemeral ideologies based on astronomical observations, astrological predictions or apocalyptic expectations continued to circulate. Even dream interpretation might possibly give birth to an ideology, though immeasurably weaker than the prevailing imperial concept.[152] The power of holy men was always acknowledged and might become a source of alternative authority in specific circumstances. Thus many usurpers of all periods had cloaked their military revolts behind a monk's

---

[149] *PG* 156, cols 320–84; Kiousopoulou, *Emperor or Manager*, 133–40.

[150] George of Pelagonia, '*Life* of John Vatatzes the Merciful', ed. A. Heisenberg, 'Kaiser Johannes Batatzes der Barmherzige: eine mittelgriechische Legende', *BZ* 14 (1905), 160–233 (text 193–233) at 196–7; tr. from *IIPTB*, 283.

[151] C. M. Woodhouse, *George Gemistos Plethon: The Last of the Hellenes* (Oxford, 1986), 104–5; Niketas Siniossoglou, *Radical Platonism in Byzantium: Illumination and Utopia in Gemistos Plethon* (Cambridge, 2011).

[152] E.g. M. Mavroudi, 'Plethon as subversive and his reception in the Islamic world', in Angelov and Saxby (eds), *Power and Subversion*, 177–203.

predictions of future glory, justified by a condemnation of the ruling emperor.

It is hard to argue, though, that there were substantial regional or communal and self-sustaining powers within the empire. Elements of such forces emerged whenever imperial control failed (as in the late twelfth century) and became more firmly installed in disparate regions after 1204. But it would be hazardous to grant them the status of alternate types of power and authority. For the surprising aspect of Byzantine political ideology is that, for centuries, philosophers, theorists and writers of imperial propaganda reinforced its central emphasis on divinely approved monarchy. Even in the last centuries of Byzantium, when the actual power of the emperor was most limited, the Palaiologoi brothers fought each other in pointless rivalry to hold the title that still represented supreme authority. And as Constantine XI faced the Turks in May 1453, his belief in the divine protection of the empire gave him courage to attack. This was one of the many inheritances of Constantine I, after whom he had been named, which was adapted and re-worked by Mehmed II the Conqueror.

12 The Islamic World
Community, Leadership and Contested Patterns of Continuity

Andrew Marsham, Eric Hanne and Jo Van Steenbergen

Figure 12.1 Detail of huntsman from the so-called 'Baptistère de Saint Louis', an important example of Mamluk art: hammered brass with gold, silver and niello inlay produced in Egypt or Syria around 1320–40 by Master Muhammad ibn al-Zayn (medallion diameter 10 cm); photo © Musée du Louvre, Dist. RMN-Grand Palais/Hughes Dubois

Monarchical Rulership in Early Islam

In the late antique Middle East, imperial monarchy, sanctioned by divine power, was the 'natural' form of political organisation, already predominant in a variety of forms for over 2,000 years. It is therefore unsurprising that this was the political structure adopted – in the form of the caliphate – by the early Muslims.[1] Much else, however, remained at stake. The four most important questions were: who was qualified for the office of caliph; how should the caliph be selected; what were the limits of the caliph's power and authority; and how should it be shared with other representatives of God's will on earth? In the late tenth and early eleventh centuries, these questions would be answered by Sunni scholars in a way that became accepted as 'orthodox' in Sunni Islam; Fatimid Shi'i scholars had already composed very different answers in the tenth century, and Twelver Shi'is had elaborated their own theory of how the imamate (*imama*) was transmitted to the true leaders of the Muslims. However, all these clerical interpretations of legitimacy were legalistic and ahistorical: they brought past history into the present, justifying current practice and orthodox theory as rooted in the practice of the Prophet and his Companions and the formative decades of Islam. All the evidence indicates that we should be very wary of accepting at face value these later clerical explanations for the formative period of Islam. Furthermore, they were under challenge and subject to changing political realities throughout the whole period.

The development of both political thought and political culture in the first three centuries of Islam was far more contingent and determined by events than summaries of these later 'classical' Sunni and Shi'i positions tend to suggest. The means by which the caliph was selected was in constant flux, shaped by the exigencies of *Realpolitik*. Likewise, the range and extent of caliphal power and authority was not fixed but constantly negotiated and contested. In some older scholarship, the *mihna* (inquisition) of 833–c.847 is pointed to as a turning-point, after which the Abbasid caliphs lost direct authority over law and religion. In the *mihna*, the caliphs and their senior advisors sought to impose a theology inspired by speculative reasoning on those scholars who worked for the Abbasid state, by force if necessary. However, resistance from those who rejected speculative reasoning and emphasised adherence to scriptural literalism was ultimately successful, and after 847 the caliphs

---

[1] The question of the character of early Islamic monarchy has been addressed in detail in A. Al-Azmeh, *Muslim Kingship: Power and the Sacred in Pagan, Christian and Muslim Polities* (London, 1997); P. Crone, *Medieval Islamic Political Thought* (Edinburgh, 2004); *RIM*. For ideals of monarchy in the other spheres, see e.g. pp. 255–60, 291–8.

began to align themselves with these *ahl al-hadith*, 'tradition-minded folk', or 'proto-Sunnis'. More recent work has nuanced this reading of the place of the *mihna*: on the one hand, even in the early-to-mid-eighth century, the caliphs were only one, albeit special, actor among many in interpreting religion; and on the other, long after the *mihna* the caliphs sometimes claimed special religious authority.[2]

Indeed, the caliphs' status as God's chosen rulers still remained a vital ideological resource, open to various interpretations, especially as their material power diminished during the tenth century. Where maximalist understandings of the caliphate remained particularly strong, unharmed by the practical consequences of ruling a complex empire, was in certain forms of Shiʿism: when the Fatimids rose to power in the tenth century, they made much of their claim to be truly the heirs of Muhammad and law-making representatives of God on earth. However, once the Fatimids had established an empire, they too were compelled to move towards a more institutionalised and limited form of monarchical authority.[3]

Other conceptions of legitimate power and status continued to interact (and sometimes compete) with caliphal and scholarly perspectives. The various clerical, scholarly, military and landowning elites all had their own politico-cultural traditions, which were reshaped and reinvented in the context of the new Islamic dispensation. Perhaps the most important influence was the heritage, both real and imagined, of Sasanian Iran. Indeed, just as 'classical' Islamic religion owed much to the absorption of large numbers of the peoples of the former Sasanian territories during and after the Abbasid Revolution, much of what became 'classical' Islamic political culture also derived from the accelerated assimilation and re-working and reinvention of Sasanian political theory and practice during the same period. The model of the Abbasid court then shaped those of all the ninth- and tenth-century successor states, including those of the Umayyads of al-Andalus and the Fatimids.

---

[2] J. P. Turner, *Inquisition in Early Islam: The Competition for Political and Religious Authority in the Abbasid Empire* (London, 2013). See also J. Nawas, 'The *mihna* of 218 AH/833 CE revisited: an empirical study', *Welt des Islams* 33 (1993), 161–81; *idem*, 'A reexamination of three current explanations for al-Maʾmun's introduction of the *mihna*', *IJMES* 26 (1994), 615–29.

[3] On state formation and its consequences in the Fatimid context, see e.g. S. Hamdani, *Between Revolution and State: The Path to Fatimid Statehood* (London, 2006). The sense of a sacred – God-sent – precursor whose monarchical status must be perpetuated coloured Byzantine ideas of rulership, too. On Constantine the Great's image: pp. 207, 292–3, 304, 328–9. Westerners could look to Charlemagne, or even to Constantine himself, but not without some regard for Rome and its popes: pp. 146, 155–6, 165–7, 257–8, 264, 373, 386–7, 399.

The formation of a distinctively Islamic ideology of legitimate leadership within this wider post-Roman and post-Sasanian context can be seen in each of the four main foundations of legitimate, divinely approved, power: kinship, piety, victory and justice. Each had pre-Islamic precursors, but each tended to be given a distinctively Islamic inflection through reference to the kerygmatic origins of Islam: kinship with the Prophet and his early Companions became salient; and claims to piety, victory and justice were all articulated in Qur'anic language. All four were also tied to the soteriology of Islam: the salvation of the community in both this world and the next was guaranteed by recognition of the correct leader, which was symbolically expressed in ceremonies of allegiance and obedience. However, all of these aspects of caliphal legitimacy also had much wider resonances, and we should be wary of viewing them exclusively through the lenses provided by our later scholarly Muslim sources; many of the caliphs' armies – Arabians, Iranians, Transoxianans and Turks – brought with them the ideological and cultural baggage of their pre-Islamic heritage.[4]

Of all the four main foundations of caliphal authority, heredity deserves special attention. Although Islamic scripture might be interpreted as being critical of hereditary rule, the idea that people were born into their station in fact remained central to political life in pre-modern Islam; equality before God was for the afterlife in the minds of most Muslims. In this, Islamic culture reflected that of late antiquity and the middle ages in western Eurasia more generally. However, the precise history of hereditary claims to the caliphate reflects the distinctive consequences of the origins of Islam in the mission of Muhammad.

Although later Sunni scholars would somewhat downplay heredity's importance relative to nomination by members of the ruling Muslim elite, saying only that the caliph must be a member of Quraysh, this was in fact *because* bloodline and kinship had been far more central to political thought and practice than election had been during the formative period. The evolution of Shi'i thought in the ninth and tenth centuries then forced a formulation of a contrasting Sunni position that emphasised nomination and election and not heredity. Notions of elective and consensual authority had indeed always been important, but, outside Kharijite circles, the idea that those with a right to choose the caliph should do so from within a particular kin-group appears to have been widely accepted from the outset: for the Umayyads, this kin-group was the *ahl al-bayt* (household) of the ruling family; for many of their rivals,

---

[4] On salvation and monarchy, and the sources of monarchic authority in early Islam, see n. 1.

including the Abbasids, it meant the household of the Prophet, variously defined.[5] The Umayyads ruled as descendants of the murdered third caliph, Uthman (644–56), and as members of the Meccan tribe of Quraysh, but they could claim no close blood relationship to the Prophet beyond membership of his tribe. As a result, closer kinship with the Prophet was an effective rallying cry for the Umayyads' political opponents.

Thus when the Abbasid dynasty replaced the Umayyads in 750, they did so as the beneficiaries of agnatically oriented ideas among supporters of both Arabian and Iranian heritage. However, the Abbasids' specific claim was rooted in a distinctive 'Hashimite' or 'proto-Shi'i' movement in favour of a branch of Quraysh that included the Prophet and the Abbasids but not the Umayyads.[6] Predictably, with Abbasid victory came opposition to the Abbasids, expressed through a still narrower definition of kin-based legitimacy. Descent from Ali b. Abi Talib (656–61), who was a first cousin of Muhammad and a son-in-law via the Prophet's daughter, Fatima, became determinative, in part because it excluded the Abbasid line and included the only male descendants of Muhammad himself. From these movements emphasising descent in this bloodline, the various strands of 'classical' Shi'i Islam were born; all of them highlighted the true religious leadership of the descendants of Ali and Fatima. The same developments contributed to the emergence of what became Sunnism. After the early ninth century, the Abbasid caliphs abandoned the somewhat 'proto-Shi'i' aspects of their claims for an alliance with the emergent Sunni movement. The Sunni scholars tended to accept the Abbasids' limited but legitimate religio-political authority. In Sunni thought the precedents of the Companions of the Prophet as interpreted by the Sunni scholars had gained a central place, diminishing the status of the caliphs as law-makers and spiritual guides but according them a key role as the legitimating figureheads of a united Muslim political community. Ultimately, the scholars rejected the significance attached to the Abbasids' Hashimite heritage, looking instead to ideas about legitimate nomination from within the wider kin-group of Quraysh. But this shift took place in a political context in which there was little doubt that the Abbasid dynasty should in practice continue to hold the caliphate, as it did for more than 500 years.

---

[5] For interesting observations on *ahl al-bayt*: M. Sharon, 'The Umayyads as *ahl al-bayt*', *JSAI* 14 (1991), 115–52 (although some of the hypotheses have now been discredited); on the Umayyads' attitudes to heredity and election: *RIM*; A. Alajmi, 'Ascribed vs. popular legitimacy: the case of Al-Walid II and Umayyad *'ahd*', *JNES* 72 (2013), 25–34.

[6] On the Abbasid Revolution: pp. 104, 218, 237.

Partly as a result of the Abbasid move towards an emergent Sunnism, Shi'ism remained a vehicle for the expression of political independence in regions remote from imperial power; many of Ali's descendants fled Abbasid persecution in the later eighth and mid-ninth centuries, and the success of Zaydi Shi'ism, in the highlands south of the Caspian and in Yemen, in southern Arabia, was a direct result of their flight. In contrast, many of the nomads of the central Arabian peninsula and southern Iraq adopted another variant of Shi'ism. These Isma'ili Shi'i Carmathians (*Qaramita*) presented a serious threat to Abbasid Iraq in the late ninth and early tenth centuries. Shi'ism also spread in the Abbasid heartlands, and, by the mid-tenth century, anti-Abbasid Shi'i religious orientation had two major manifestations in the urban centres of the central Islamic lands: the 'quietist' Shi'ism of the Twelvers (*Ithna-'ashar-iyya*) and more militant Isma'ili Shi'ism.

Twelver Shi'is such as the Buyids came to venerate a line of twelve descendants of Muhammad as the true leaders of the Muslims, only one of whom, Ali b. Abi Talib, had actually ever held the caliphate. They believed that their twelfth Imam, who had disappeared in Abbasid custody in 874, had in fact gone into hiding, to return (somewhat like Jesus in Christian – and Sunni – eschatology) on Judgement Day. By the mid-tenth century, a Twelver Shi'i scholarly elite who preserved, transmitted and interpreted the sayings and deeds of Muhammad and the Twelve Imams was well-established in Buyid Iraq. In Twelver thought, the Abbasids were not, therefore, the true leaders of the Muslims. However, a Sunni majority in Iraq and Iran and the enormous ideological capital of the Abbasids meant that the Buyids never sought to depose the caliphs.[7]

In contrast, the militant and millenarian Shi'ism of the Isma'ili Fatimids brought about a repetition of many of the patterns of the Abbasid Revolution, this time at the turn of the ninth and tenth centuries. As we have seen, a non-Arab army was recruited from the remote frontiers of the empire – this time from the Kutama Berbers of Ifriqiya. This army provided the military force to install a group who claimed kinship with the Prophet as the rightful imams of the Muslims. As such, the Fatimids claimed universal authority in the Islamic world, but as the direct descendants of the Prophet, not merely as his cousins. They said that they were not simply members of Muhammad's wider tribal group of Hashim but directly descended from him via Fatima, his daughter, and Ali, his son-in-law.

[7] On the formation of Twelver Shi'ism and its subsequent history: A. Newman, *Twelver Shi'ism: Unity and Diversity in the Life of Islam, 632–1722* (Edinburgh, 2013); on political culture in the Buyid period: R. Mottahedeh, *Loyalty and Leadership in an Early Islamic Society*, 2nd edn (London, 2000).

However, although heredity was essential to the claims of all the imperial caliphs, it was only one of the concepts in which legitimacy was couched.[8] Caliphs also sought to persuade their followers of their legitimacy through their claims to be the pious, victorious and just representatives of God on earth. Historians have learned from anthropologists that monarchy is something that is performed; ideological and symbolic power are communicative, and so it is the enunciations of caliphal legitimacy that should particularly interest us. Because these are acts of persuasion, knowledge of audience and interlocutor is also crucial to understanding what is said. These performances took all the forms that one would expect of monarchy: the patronage of poetry, philosophy, history, science and religion, leading prayers and pilgrimages, the maintenance of the law, the collection of taxes, and the building of cities, hospitals, palaces, mosques and fortifications.[9]

At the Caliph's Court

The pre-eminent location for the performance of royal power was the act of holding court, where various ceremonial expressions were given to the relationship between the caliph and his subjects, reiterating the ruler's claim to obedient allegiance in return for reward. The Umayyad caliphs had urban palaces, but the dynasty remained somewhat peripatetic, moving between royal centres in the countryside and towns of Greater Syria, where they could hold court among their tribal armies. After the Abbasid Revolution of 750, it came to be expected that the caliph and his court would reside at a single imperial capital, where his army was garrisoned and to which the caliph's subjects were expected to travel. Initially this capital was al-Hashimiyya, near Kufa, which al-Mansur (754–75) replaced by Madinat al-Salam (Baghdad) in 762. New palaces were founded by almost every subsequent Abbasid caliph. Many amounted to new cities: the original 'round city' of Baghdad was quickly eclipsed by the palaces outside its walls and the centre of the caliphate was completely relocated on three occasions, to the twin city of al-Raqqa/al-Rafiqa in northern Syria in 796–809, to Merv in north-eastern Iran in 813–19, and to Samarra, 100 kilometres north of Baghdad, in 836–92. These palace-cities were the primary stages for caliphal ceremonial in the

---

[8] Comparable tension between tendencies towards heredity and expectations of a 'God-chosen' (and, in effect, more meritocratic) ruler characterised Byzantine political culture: pp. 292–3, 298–301, 323–5, 328. Bloodlines counted for far more in the west, but were not unbreachable, and the idea of 'election' was never extinguished: pp. 58–9, 255–63, 394–8.

[9] On performance in Byzantium: pp. 84–7.

Abbasid period, although the eighth-century Abbasids, notably Harun al-Rashid (786–809), did sometimes travel elsewhere to lead the pilgrimage or to take personal charge of military campaigns. On these occasions, the palatial caliphal tent – a well-established symbol of Middle Eastern monarchy – became a substitute palace.

The rulers of the successor states also built similar urban centres. In North Africa, new cities included Sijilmasa (second half of the eighth century) and Fez, which was founded in 789 (and again in 808). The Aghlabid rulers of Ifriqiya (modern Tunisia) developed Qayrawan (Kairouan) as their capital.[10] The first Fatimid caliph, Ubayd Allah al-Mahdi, began construction of his new capital of al-Mahdiyya (200 kilometres south of Tunis) within three years of declaring his caliphate and publicly inaugurated it as his capital in 921. After the Samanids achieved pre-eminence in Transoxiana and Khurasan, they relocated their capital from Samarqand to Bukhara, where Nasr b. Ahmad II (914–43) built a new palace and administrative buildings in the previously open space at the centre of the city.[11] Madinat al-Zahra, outside Cordoba, was begun in 936, seven years after Abd al-Rahman III had proclaimed himself caliph.

At his royal court, the caliph was the centre of the universe and the 'shadow of God on earth'. This status was symbolically and materially expressed in caliphal ceremonial, which reprised in various ways the Qur'anic iteration of the ancient Middle Eastern equation, in which loyalty (*wafa'*) and obedience (*ta'a*) led to reward (*ni'ma*).[12] Perhaps the most complete surviving statements of the caliphs' assertions about their status are found in the panegyric poetry performed at their courts, which 'depicts the authority of the caliphs as resting on the heroic virtues of the ancient Arabs, the divine sanction of Islam and the mythic power of Near Eastern kingship'.[13]

> Through you the expanses of the land have become fertile.
> How can the world be barren when you are its protector?
> Whatever bounty [*nu'ma*] God guides towards us
> So that its onset and its beginning is ours (comes)
> From your face which joyfully shines on us
> And from your hand the gifts of which shower upon us.

[10] On developments in ninth-century North African material culture: G. D. Anderson *et al.* (eds), *The Aghlabids and their Neighbours: Art and Material Culture in Ninth Century North Africa* (Leiden, 2017).
[11] A. Petruccioli, 'Bukhara and Samarqand', in S. K. Jayyusi *et al.* (eds), *The City in the Islamic World*, 2 vols (Leiden, 2008), i:491–524.
[12] *RIM*, 54, 175–77, 312.
[13] S. Sperl, 'Islamic kingship and Arabic panegyric poetry in the early 9th century', *JAL* 8 (1977), 20–35 at 25.

You are forever a sea of sustenance to the needy among us!
How can this be, since you face us owning the world and all it holds?
God granted it to you as a right of which he saw you worthy,
And you by the right of God grant it to us.[14]

In these lines, from two of al-Buhturi's (d. 897) poems for al-Mutawakkil (847–61), the 'mythic power of Near Eastern kingship' is prominent, and much of the language and symbolism is also specifically Qur'anic, such as the term *nu'ma* for 'blessings' and the idea of a right (*haqq*), granted by God.

The ceremonial performance of such poetry at the royal court allowed for the ritual enactment of the same equation of authority, obedience and reward: here, the poet stood for a wider constituency – his tribe, or the Muslims in general – and his poetic declaration of loyalty was symbolically rewarded in public with gifts from the ruler. Of these gifts, the most symbolically weighted was the bestowal of ceremonial robes of embroidered silk (*khil'a*). Again, this was an inheritance from ancient Middle Eastern royal practice, which had become integral to the performance of monarchy throughout the region; investiture with 'robes of honour' can be traced back to the middle of the first millennium BCE in Iran, and by pre-Islamic times the same custom had become central to Roman imperial ceremonial, as well as to that of their Sasanian rivals.[15]

The early eleventh-century guide to Abbasid ceremonial by Hilal al-Sabi (d. 1056) 'The Protocols of the Caliphal Court' (*Rusum Dar al-Khilafa*) describes the robes given at the appointment of Abbasid military commanders:

The robes of honour given to army generals were as follows: a plain black turban, a black garment with a hoop, lined at the bottom, and another plain black robe without a hoop; red cloth from Sus [in southwest Iran, famous for silk], gilded or plain embroidery, and a loose, sleeveless garment from Dabiq [in Egypt, famous for clothes], open down the front; and a red-sheathed sword, ornamented with white and silver and with a silver-tipped hilt [...] They are also given two quivers for arrows, and a standard [...] When Adud al-Dawla took over the government

---

[14] From two panegyrics by al-Buhturi for al-Mutawakkil: Sperl, 'Islamic kingship', 24, 35.
[15] S. P. Stetkevych, 'Abbasid panegyric and the poetics of political allegiance: two poems of Al-Mutanabbi to Kafur', in S. Sperl and C. Shackle (eds), *Qasida Poetry in Islamic Asia and Africa*, 2 vols (Leiden, 1996), i:35–63; S. P. Stetkevych, 'Umayyad panegyric and the poetics of Islamic hegemony: Al-Akhtal's Khaffa Al-Qatinu ("Those that dwelt with you have left in haste")', *JAL* 28 (1997), 89–122; S. Stewart (ed.), *Robes and Honor: The Medieval World of Investiture* (New York, 2001), esp. contributions by D. Sourdel, 'Robes of honor in Abbasid Baghdad during the eighth to eleventh centuries' (137–45); P. Sanders, 'Robes of honor in Fatimid Egypt' (225–39); G. R. G. Hambly, 'From Baghdad to Bukhara, from Ghazna to Delhi: the *khil'a* ceremony in the transmission of kingly pomp and circumstance' (193–222); and C. F. Petry, 'Robing ceremonials in late Mamluk Egypt: hallowed traditions, shifting protocols' (353–77).

of Iraq (in 975), he was adorned with the robes of honour mentioned above, and with the jewelled collar and armbands, and a studded crown with a jewel-laden tassel was put on his head. The same was done for al-Afshin, in the days of al-Mu'tadid bi'llah (892–902),[16] to Badr al-Mu'tadidi in the days of al-Muktafi bi'llah (r. 902–8), to Mu'nis in the days of al-Muqtadir bi'llah (r. 908–32), to Ibn Yalbaq in the days of al-Qahir bi'llah (r. 932–4), to Bajkam in the days of al-Radi bi'llah (r. 934–40), to Tuzun in the days of al-Mustakfi bi'llah (r. 944–6).[17]

This early eleventh-century information accords quite closely with earlier sources for the ninth-century Abbasid caliphate: the Transoxianan commander al-Afshin does indeed appear to have been one of the first military commanders to be invested with a crown and belts (albeit sixty years earlier than al-Sabi thinks, in 837/8); al-Sabi might also have added the Turkish slave soldier Ashinas, who was crowned (*tawwaja*), enthroned (*ajlasa* [. . .] '*ala kursi*) and invested with belts (*washshaha*) on his appointment to the governorship of Egypt, Syria and northern Iraq in 840.[18]

For the fifteenth-century historian of the caliphate al-Suyuti (d. 1505), a similar coronation in 843 marked the first delegation of government (*sultan*) by the caliph.[19] He had a point – the coronation-ritual does appear to have developed at the time when military commanders were being granted increasingly plenipotentiary powers by the caliphs. It may also reflect a need to integrate new military and political elites into existing imperial structures. The coronations contrast with investiture with honorific robes, which had been employed at the caliphal court from Umayyad times, and the tying of banners at the appointment of commanders, which likely was a custom in Arabia before Islam and was continued by the Prophet and his immediate succcessors. The first surviving fragment of an Islamic robe of honour probably dates from the late 740s. The form of the new coronation-rituals, which began in the late 830s, appears to reflect the expectations of military commanders recruited from the post-Sasanian frontiers of Iran, where sub-kingship was a long-standing way of expressing devolved political relationships.[20]

Accession and Succession

Two of the key occasions for the expression of the relationship between caliph and subject were the accession of the caliph, and the appointment of

---

[16] This was, in fact, in the reign of al-Mu'tasim bi'llah (833–42).
[17] Hilal al-Sabi, *Rusum dar al-khilafa*, tr. E. A. Salem, *The Rules and Regulations of the Abbasid Court* (Beirut, 1977), 75–6.
[18] *RIM*, 268.
[19] M. Gordon, *The Breaking of a Thousand Swords: A History of the Turkish Military of Samarra (AH 200–275/815–889 CE)* (New York, 2001), 79.
[20] *RIM*, 267–71.

his successors. These ceremonies entailed a personal, binding pledge (*bay'a*) before God – 'You are bound in this by God's covenant and his compact', as the pledge of allegiance to al-Walid II and his sons in 743 is said to have concluded. Such pledges were also another sine qua non of Middle Eastern monarchy. However, perhaps both because of their particular importance in tribal and nomadic Arabian society and because of their use by the Prophet, they gained a particularly prominent place in Islamic political practice. By the eighth century, the pledge of allegiance was an indispensable element in the accession of a new caliph, and *bay'a* became the standard word for the caliphal accession ceremony as a whole. The oaths were replicated in the provincial capitals of the empire by the caliph's governors and were communicated to the caliph by the imperial post (*barid*) where a governor or commander was unable to give his allegiance in person.[21]

In the early Abbasid period, the documents composed at the nomination of the caliph's successors became increasingly complex. The most famous examples of such texts are those drawn up for the elaborate (and ultimately futile) ceremony that took place at the Ka'ba in Mecca on the pilgrimage in 802, where Harun al-Rashid sought oaths from all the senior military commanders and bureaucrats at the Abbasid court that they and his two heirs would respect his succession arrangements. This ceremony had various less well-known precedents from the decades after the revolution (and some roots in pre-revolutionary Umayyad practice). The early Abbasid succession ceremonies reflect a response to anxiety about securing a smooth accession in a violent and factional political culture. The exact form of the response to this anxiety was shaped by the ideologies of the new class of caliphal scribes and the rising class of *'ulama'*. The two groups brought both the Iranian reliance on written oaths in politics and the developing 'Islamic' theory of contract into Islamic political culture. The first surviving copy of a document said to have been written for the *accession* of a caliph (as opposed to for the arrangements for *succession*) is said by al-Tabari to have been composed at Samarra in 861: the formula used there was then adopted at most subsequent accessions, and it became the 'classical' formula for the pledge of allegiance to the caliph.[22]

Mosque and Palace

Besides accessions and investitures, other regular encounters between the caliph and his subjects ranged from the daily, such as private evening

---

[21] *RIM*, 21–180; E. Landau-Tasseron, 'The religious foundations of political allegiance: a study of *bay'a* in pre-modern Islam', *Hudson Institute Research Monographs on the Muslim World* Series 2 no. 4 (Washington, DC, 2010).

[22] *RIM*, 181–317.

wine-drinking sessions (again, an inheritance from Sasanian Iran); through the weekly, such as the leadership of Friday prayers and appearances at more public audiences, as well as at the hunt and (in Samarra at least) at the races; to the annual, such as the leadership of the *hajj* pilgrimage and military campaigns. The involvement of the caliph in each of these varied over time. In general terms, the caliphs probably became less publicly visible: whereas in the eighth century, caliphs sometimes led the *hajj*, they began to delegate it to members of their family or to other leading figures in the government during the ninth century. Likewise, few caliphs were personally involved in military campaigns in the ninth century. Changing palace design also appears to reflect the changing status of the caliph: eighth-century palaces – both Umayyad and Abbasid – were built adjacent to the main congregational mosque, and caliphal ceremonial took place in both locations. In ninth-century Samarra (and tenth-century Madinat al-Zahra), by contrast, the congregational mosque was entirely separate from the palace; at Samarra this coincided with the end of assembly at the mosque as an element in the accessional ceremonial of the Abbasid caliph, which now took place exclusively inside the palace.[23]

This division between mosque and palace reflects the growing specialisation of the political classes. The caliph's religious authority was now shared with the '*ulama*', who laid claim to the leading role in the interpretation of scripture. The literary output of the caliphal courts also reflects this specialisation and the growing importance of the '*ulama*' in maintaining the legitimacy of the caliphs. Whereas the earliest Mirrors for Princes, such as those by Abd al-Hamid (d. 750) and Ibn al-Muqaffa (d. 756), are clearly the product of the post-Sasanian scribal class and do not necessarily manifest all the features of what we might now recognise as an Islamically inflected political discourse, the later eighth- and early ninth-century examples, such as the 'Book of the Land Tax' by Abu Yusuf (d. 798) and the Tahirid epistle of 821, are replete with the Qur'anic citations and the *hadith* which had become the markers of 'classical' Islam, with which rulers now wished to associate themselves and upon the transmission and interpretation of which the scholarly elite based their growing, and resilient, ideological power.[24]

---

[23] *RIM*, 256–8.

[24] On these Mirrors for Princes, see I. Abbas, *Abd al-Hamid al-Katib* (Amman, 1988); C. Pellat, *Ibn al-Muqaffa mort vers 140/757 – 'Conseilleur de Calife'* (Paris, 1976); Abu Yusuf, *Taxation in Islam: Abu Yusuf's* Kitab al-Kharaj, tr. A. Ben Shemesh (Leiden, 1969); C. E. Bosworth, 'An early Arabic Mirror for Princes', *JNES* 19 (1970), 25–41. For a short survey discussion to the eleventh century, see Crone, *Medieval Islamic Political Thought*, 148–64. On later mirrors, see L. Marlow, *Counsel for Kings: Wisdom and Politics in Tenth-Century Iran* (Edinburgh, 2016); also n. 53 and pp. 110–11. Mirrors for Princes were (in various forms) a persistent literary genre in the west: pp. 54, 67, 255–7, 261–2, 288–9. Fresh compositions were, however, less in

Monarchical Rulership in 'Medieval' Islam: Sharing the Burden?

Caliphs and Sultans: Authority and Power

[...] religion and kingship are two brothers, and neither can dispense with the other. Religion is the foundation of kingship, and kingship protects religion. For whatever lacks a foundation must perish and whatever lacks a protector disappears.[25]

This quotation, relating directly to Sasanian monarchical tradition, comes from the *Muruj al-dhahab wa-ma'adin al-jawhar* ('Meadows of Gold and Mines of Gems') written by the renowned tenth-century historian al-Mas'udi, who influenced generations of post-Abbasid, or 'medieval', scholars. Ann Lambton argues that this passage 'was incorporated in the medieval theory of state in the Eastern Muslim world', as it addresses both the theoretical and the practical aspects of medieval Islamic rule.[26] By pointing to the symbiotic relationship between the ideal and the political manifestation of that ideal, al-Mas'udi not only implicitly addresses the political realities of his day but also explicitly reinforces the views held by most medieval scholars: legitimate rule in the Muslim world derived ultimately from revelation. The concepts implied in al-Mas'udi's statement include the quest for legitimacy, the delegation of authority and the protection of the social order. But how should the relationship between religion (*din*) and the state (*dawla*) be understood? For Muslims, the two had coexisted from the beginning in the form of the Prophet and the early community; subsequent caliphs continued this relationship by symbolising a unified Muslim community.[27] Now that the caliphate had lost its ability to function as

favour as literature in Byzantium between the sixth and thirteenth centuries: pp. 84–5, 294, 322–6.

[25] Al-Mas'udi (d. 956), *Muruj al-dhahab*, ed. C. Pellat, *Muruj al-dhahab wa-ma'adin al-jawhar*, 7 vols (Beirut, 1966–79), i:189; French tr. C. Barbier de Maynard and A. Pavel de Courteille, rev. C. Pellat, *Les Prairies d'or*, 5 vols (Paris, 1962–97), i:220. See also p. 19.

[26] A. K. S. Lambton, 'Justice in the medieval Persian theory of kingship', *Studia Islamica* 15 (1962), 96. Lambton wrote extensively on the nature of medieval Islamic political culture. Some of her most important works on this subject include: 'Quis custodiet custodes? Some reflections on the Persian theory of government', *Studia Islamica* 5 (1956), 125–48; 'Islamic political thought', in J. Schacht (ed.), *The Legacy of Islam*, 2nd edn (Oxford, 1974), 404–24; *SGMI*; 'Concepts of authority in Persia: eleventh to nineteenth centuries AD', *Iran* 26 (1988), 95–103.

[27] On this concept, see P. Crone and M. Hinds, *God's Caliph: Religious Authority in the First Centuries of Islam* (Cambridge, repr. 2003). More generally, P. Crone, *God's Rule. Government and Islam: Six Centuries of Islamic Political Thought* (New York, 2004), esp. 219–55; A. Black, *The History of Islamic Political Thought* (New York, 2001).

a temporal polity, what was to be done? Instead of rejecting the role that kingship could play in society, al-Mas'udi opens the door to wider discussion of the relationship between power and authority.

It is a mistake to use the terms *potestas* (power) and *auctoritas* (authority) interchangeably when discussing political culture: power is, after all, a 'fluid concept, manifesting itself in any number of social relationships',[28] while authority, as derived from the social mores of a community, is a less malleable concept. As we shall see, however, the *'ulama'* found a way of effectively bridging *potestas* and *auctoritas* from the tenth century onwards. In the Islamic *umma*, a society where all authority came from the unchanging *shari'a*, the idea of power (*sultan*) generally had to adapt to the parameters set by divine revelation. Power could only be legitimised by derivation from, or sanction by, an accepted source of authority. Yet to realise authority, you also need the ability to do this here and now: power and authority are in symbiosis just as religion and kingship are according to al-Mas'udi. Focusing on the eleventh- and twelfth-century Muslim world and the dynamic relationship between caliphate and sultanate,[29] George Makdisi argues in a key article that:

Authority and Power [...] are two different things: Power is the force by which you obligate others to obey you. Authority is the right to lead and command, to have others listen and obey. Authority requires power. Power, without authority, is tyranny.[30]

This relationship created a magnetic attraction between caliphs and sultans that would last well into the Ottoman era[31] and which manifested itself in the variety of methods used by caliphs, emirs and sultans to legitimise their position vis-à-vis one another and in the eyes of the masses.

Acts, Rites and Symbols: Legitimising Leadership of Caliphs, Sultans – and Others

In 'medieval' Islam – as in early Islam, but becoming more widely practised as powerbases proliferated – methods of legitimisation included

---

[28] E. J. Hanne, *Putting the Caliph in His Place: Power, Authority, and the Late Abbasid Caliphate* (Madison, WI, 2007), 40.

[29] G. Makdisi, 'Authority in the Islamic community', in G. Makdisi et al. (eds), *La Notion d'autorité au Moyen Âge: Islam, Byzance, Occident* (Paris, 1982), 117–26; G. Makdisi, 'The marriage of Tughril Bek', *IJMES* 1 (1970), 259–75; G. Makdisi, 'Les rapports entre calife et sultân à l'époque saljûqide', *IJMES* 6 (1975), 228–36.

[30] G. Makdisi, 'Authority in the Islamic community', 117, who discusses Jacques Maritain's *Man and the State* (Chicago, 1951) and *Scholasticism and Politics* (London, 1954)

[31] G. Makdisi, 'Authority in the Islamic community', 120.

giving oaths of loyalty (*bay'a*); using honorific titles (s. *laqab*/pl. *alqab*); bestowing robes of honour (*khil'a*); granting the right to be named on the coinage (*sikka*); and having one's name recited in the Friday prayer (*khutba*).[32] Of these, the *bay'a* ceremony in which individuals swore their allegiance to each other is most closely associated with the Qur'anic message:

Allah's Good Pleasure was on the Believers when they swore Fealty to thee under the Tree: He knew what was in their hearts, and He sent down Tranquillity to them; and He rewarded them with a speedy Victory.[33]

By the tenth century, the act of swearing an oath of fealty before God had become an important means of formalising relationships in Muslim society.[34] At elite level, the *bay'a* ceremony was used on a number of occasions: to solemnise the appointment of an heir-apparent (*wali al-'ahd*, 'recipient of the pact'); when the new caliph ascended the throne; and when two powers recognised one another. Most involved both private and public ceremonies, at which whole groups – members of the public (*'awwam*), for example, or the military – would collectively swear allegiance to a particular ruler. In the case of relations between caliph, emir and sultan, the individuals did not necessarily meet in person; a caliphal official or a member of a ruler's entourage might be sent to represent their respective ruler at the *bay'a* ceremony. The caliphate's position of almost complete impotence did not diminish the desire of other powers to formalise their relations with it. The medieval chronicles attest the ubiquity of this particular ceremony, often providing full and precise details as to who exactly was in attendance and what was said and done. The *bay'a* ceremony was often, but not always, accompanied by the granting of *laqab*s, the bestowal of robes of honour (*khil'a*), and the instigation of the rights of *sikka* and the *khutba*.

Whereas the Rashidun ('Rightly Guided') and Umayyad caliphs went by their birth names, the Abbasid caliphs adopted honorific titles to set themselves apart from the community at large and to augment their religious status in the public's eyes.[35] The *laqab*s, which were seen by many to represent the transmission of caliphal authority to the recipient, often

---

[32] Both the Buyids and Seljuks introduced new symbols of rule tied to their historical traditions; see W. Madelung, 'The assumption of the title shahanshah by the Buyids and the "Reign of the Daylam (*Dawlat al-Daylam*)"', *JNES* 28 (1969), 84–108; *GSE*, 3.

[33] Qur'an 48:18 (Yusuf Ali translation).   [34] See Mottahedeh, *Loyalty and Leadership*.

[35] H. F. Amedroz, 'On the meaning of "al-Saffah" as applied to the first Abbasid caliph', *JRAS* (1907), 660–63; see also C. E. Bosworth, *EI²* s.v. 'lakab'; E. Tyan, *Institutions de droit public musulman*, 2 vols (Paris, 1954–7). For an interesting glimpse into the late Abbasid court, see Hilal al-Sabi, *Rusum dar al-khilafa*, tr. Salem.

expressed a personal relationship between the individual honoured and the larger Muslim community. Three examples may help to explain the use of *laqab*s. As we have seen, before deposing the Abbasid caliph al-Mustakfi in 945, Ahmad b. Buya had demanded from him – and had received in person – honorific titles for himself and his two brothers. According to the historical accounts, it was only *after* receiving this official recognition that the Buyids took complete control of the caliphate. You often have to search through necrologies to find rulers' birth names: the chroniclers tend to use rulers' honorific titles or, confusingly, the birth name in one passage and the *laqab* later on. When Mahmud of Ghazna won victories over the Samanid forces in the late tenth century, he sent the caliph, al-Qadir, news of his success along with gifts and a pledge of loyalty to the Sunni leader. In return, al-Qadir bestowed the title Yamin al-Dawla ('Right Hand of the State') on the Ghaznavid warlord, recognising his efforts on his behalf.[36] During the Seljuk period, *laqab*s became more complex, spelling out the relationship between the caliphate and the sultanate. For example, Barkyaruq b. Malikshah was given the title Rukn al-Dunya wa-l-Din ('Pillar of the World and the Religion'). It would be rash to read too much into this change, as not all the Seljuk sultans used similar forms of *laqab*s; in their case, and that of the Buyids, rulers would often assume titles of their own without having secured prior approval or sanction from the caliph.[37] In comparison with the details provided for the *bay'a* ceremony and the granting of *laqab*s, the third method of publicly recognising rulers – the granting of robes of honour (*khil'a*) – receives less coverage in the sources. The chroniclers often refer in passing to the bestowal of *khil'a* in the context of a developing relationship between the caliph and other rulers; in some cases, the robes of honour accompany other gifts, and they appear to be part of a larger bid to normalise relations.[38]

The right to have one's name and titulature inscribed on the coinage (*sikka*) and also recited in the Friday prayers (*khutba*)[39] – collectively dubbed the concrete symbols of authority – were the most public acts of legitimisation in medieval Islam, and the ones where we see the most variation. Everyone, from the elites down to the level of the common man, came into contact with coins or heard the names recited by the *khatib* on Fridays. Both *sikka* and *khutba* were essential to maintain one's position

---

[36] On Mahmud's arrogation of the term 'sultan', see C. E. Bosworth, *The Ghaznavids: Their Empire in Afghanistan and Eastern Iran, 994–1040* (Edinburgh, 1963).

[37] See H. F. Amedroz, 'The assumption of the title shahanshah by Buwayhid rulers', *The Numismatic Chronicle* 4th series 5 (1905), 393–9; Madelung, 'Assumption of the title shahanshah'; L. Richter-Bernberg, 'Amir–malik–shahanshah: Adud al-Daula's titulature reexamined', *Iran* 18 (1980), 83–102.

[38] On the use of robes of honour, see p. 338.   [39] A. J. Wensinck, *EI*² s.v. 'khutba'.

in the fractious political arena, and both were fiercely contested. Our textual sources mention the *khutba* more often: when a figure ascended to power, he would ensure that his name was recited in the Friday prayer, while in times of crisis the *khutba* could change from week to week in a city. A break in the *khutba* could signal a decline in regional power. In 1076 an ally of the Seljuks, Atsiz, seized Damascus from the Fatimids and had the name of the Abbasid caliph, al-Muqtadi, replace that of the Fatimid caliph, al-Mustansir.[40] Although the Fatimids controlled Egypt for another century, according to the chroniclers an increasing number of cities changed the Fatimid *khutba* to an Abbasid one, clear evidence of waning Fatimid power.

Unlike the narrative accounts concerning a city's *khutba*, we find little mention in our sources of the right of *sikka* or coinage in general. The chroniclers offer the occasional rare statement that such-and-such a ruler had their name put on the currency; more often, it is riots erupting over the debasement of the coinage or a change in the control of a city's mint (*dar al-darb*) that catches their attention. We must rely on the material evidence, and in many ways the extant coins from this period provide more concrete evidence of political affairs in a region than our written accounts do. Coins give their mint-city and year: they can be definitively placed and are not filtered through the medieval historian's lens. Although the reading of these coins is open to varying interpretation, there has been a gradual expansion of their use in historical research. A ground-breaking study of the coinage of Rayy reconstructed the financial and political history of this medieval city,[41] while investigation of the names and titles on Abbasid coins – as well as their placement – has helped us rank individuals and added to our understanding of Abbasid rule.[42] Research into the tenth-century Ikhshidid coinage from Egypt and the Levant shows how this material can shed invaluable light on political and financial events.[43] Similar work on the coins from the Buyid and Seljuk eras underscores the importance of the right of *sikka* as a method by which the political elite could promote their status to a much wider audience.[44]

---

[40] 'And that was the last *khutba* to the Egyptian Alawis': Ibn al-Athir, *al-Kamil fi 'l-ta'rikh*, ed. C. J. Tornberg, 11 vols (Beirut, 1998), viii:410.

[41] G. C. Miles, *The Numismatic History of Rayy* (New York, 1938).

[42] M. Bates, 'Islamic numismatics', *Middle Eastern Studies Association Bulletin* 12(2) (1978), 1–16; 12(3) (1978), 2–18; 13(1) (1979), 3–21; 13(2) (1979), 1–9; idem, 'The Abbasid coinage system, 833–946', paper presented at the annual meeting of the Middle East Studies Association (1996).

[43] J. Bacharach, *Islamic History through Coins: An Analysis and Catalogue of Tenth-Century Ikhshidid Coinage* (Cairo, 2006). See also p. 103.

[44] W. L. Treadwell, *Buyid Coins: A Corpus* (Oxford, 2001); W. L. Treadwell, 'Shahanshah and al-Malik al-Mu'ayyad: the legitimization of power in Samanid and Buyid Iran', in

Fitting New Facts to Faith and Theory: the 'Ulama''s Task[45]

So how did the *'ulama'* reconcile their understanding of the ordering of society with the new challenges posed by the caliphate's decline and the rise of all these self-promoting warrior dynasties? It seems somewhat ironic that, at a time when the central institution of Islamic rule – the caliphate – was at its supposed nadir, we find the *'ulama'* as its ideological champion. Yet, just as the political arena had altered drastically, so too had the relationship between caliphs and scholars.

Part of the reason for this may stem from the actions of the Buyid-era caliphs, notably al-Qadir (991–1031) and his son al-Qa'im (1031–75). In 1017, al-Qadir launched a programme of theological reform calling for 'innovators to repent' and forcing Mu'tazili Hanafi theologians and jurists to recant their views in writing before they could continue with their activities. A decade later, he went a step further: at a series of ceremonies in the caliphal palace (the *Dar al-Khilafa*), al-Qadir had a creed of orthodox belief recited, to which the assembled notables and scholars had to sign their adherence.[46] The promulgation of this creed continued under al-Qa'im, and at one point near the end of his reign, in 1067, we find the scholars of Baghdad entreating the caliph to disseminate the creed again, in order to quell the riots amongst various scholarly groups.[47] This assertion on the caliph's part of his spiritual role within the larger Islamic community appears to have been embraced by the scholars of the day, but whether this was support for the caliph as an individual (for the stability his presence as an effective 'heavyweight' helped to foster) or as the representative of a divinely sanctioned institution of rule (in accepting his role in determining orthodoxy) is open to question. One promising source of answers to that question is the series

---

F. Daftary and J. Meri (eds), *Culture and Memory in Medieval Islam: Essays in Honor of Wilfred Madelung* (London, 2003), 318–37; N. Lowick, 'Seljuq coins', *The Numismatic Chronicle* 7th series 10 (1970), 241–51; E. J. Hanne, 'Death on the Tigris: a numismatic study of the breakup of the Great Saljuqs', *American Journal of Numismatics* 16–17 (2005), 145–72.

[45] The *'ulama'* were peculiar to the Islamic sphere, but churchmen and lawyers were pivotal to determining norms and ideology in the west: pp. 52–4, 63–4, 152, 159–60, 172–3, 259–63, 282–4, 386–9, 401–2. In Byzantium, expectations of the imperial office stemmed from the legal system, as well as churchmen and senior administrators, and the army: pp. 292–7, 312, 316–18. For the *'ulama'*, see also pp. 464–6.

[46] Hanne, *Putting the Caliph in His Place*, 70–2; E. Glassen, *Der Mittlere Weg: Studien zur Religionspolitik und Religionstät der späteren Abbasiden-Zeit* (Weisbaden, 1981), 9–62; H. Laoust, 'La pensée et l'action politiques d'al-Mawardi', *Revue des études islamiques* 36 (1968), 11–92 at 63–72; G. Makdisi, *Ibn Aqil: Religion and Culture in Classical Islam* (Edinburgh, 1997), 10.

[47] Hanne, *Putting the Caliph in His Place*, 112.

of works they collectively helped to create, known as 'the classical theory of the caliphate'.[48]

Many medieval scholars devote sections or entire works to the institution of the caliphate, under its more correct name of the imamate (*imama*),[49] and they include al-Baqillani (d. 1013), al-Mawardi (d. 1058), Abu Ya'la b. al-Farra (known as both Abu Ya'la and Ibn al-Farra; d. 1066), al-Juwayni (d. 1085) and al-Ghazali (d. 1111).[50] Of these, al-Mawardi has received the most attention in modern scholarship, perhaps simply because his work *al-Ahkam al-Sultaniyya* ('Ordinances of Government') was one of the first to be translated into a western language.[51] Another reason could be the methodical way in which he and his contemporary Abu Ya'la wrote. Their similarly titled works follow much the same pattern: after determining the nature and necessity of the imamate (does it come from reason or revelation?), they outline the process for selecting the imam (what qualities are needed, how is the winning candidate selected and who is qualified to perform the selection?), then move on to the duties of the imam and to his ability to delegate his powers, before winding up with the tricky question of how to replace him.

The scholars' responses to these questions draw heavily on *shari'a* and on historical precedent. What makes these works fascinating is the fact that their authors are grappling with the political realities of the day, finding ways of legitimising the rise of military rulers over the community. The main thrust of their arguments concerns the delegated nature of the power held by these rulers who were not themselves caliphs. Al-Mawardi

[48] This term was coined by H. A. R. Gibb, 'Al-Mawardi's theory of the Khilafah', *Islamic Culture* 11 (1939), 291–302; *idem*, 'Some considerations on the Sunni Theory of the Caliphate', *Archives d'histoire du droit oriental* 3 (1939), 401–10.

[49] W. Madelung, *EI²* s.v. 'Imama'; also D. Sourdel *et al.*, *EI²* s.v. 'Khalifa', which focuses on the institution's political history. The inclusion in the *Encyclopaedia* of two separate entries on the subject is suggestive in itself.

[50] Titles are not included here, but key works that address their views on the imamate include Y. Ibish, *The Political Doctrine of al-Baqillani* (Beirut, 1966); W. M. Watt, 'Authority in the thought of al-Ghazali', in Makdisi *et al.* (eds), *La Notion d'autorité*, 57–68; W. Hallaq, 'Caliphs, jurists and the Saljuqs in the political thought of Juwayni', *MW* 74 (1984), 26–41.

[51] On al-Mawardi: Gibb, 'al-Mawardi's theory'; *idem*, 'Some considerations'; Laoust, 'La pensée et l'action'. See also E. J. Hanne, 'Abbasid politics and the classical theory of the caliphate', in B. Gruendler and L. Marlow (eds), *Writers and Rulers: Perspectives on Their Relationship from the Abbasid and Safavid Times* (Wiesbaden, 2004), 49–71; H. Mikhail, *Politics and Revelation* (Edinburgh, 1995); D. Little, 'A new look at *al-Ahkam al-Sultaniyya*', *MW* 64 (1974), 1–15; D. Sourdel, 'L'autorité dans le monde sunnite', in Makdisi *et al.* (eds), *La Notion d'autorité*, 101–16. On al-Mawardi and Abu Ya'la and the larger 'Sunni revival': C. Melchert, 'Mawardi, Abu Ya'la, and the Sunni revival', in K. Kościelniak (ed.), *Prosperity and Stagnation: Some Cultural and Social Aspects of the Abbasid Period (750–1258)* (Cracow, 2010), 37–61. See also pp. 107–11.

is more emphatic than most in arguing that, when difficult questions arise, they should be decided by the 'judgement of the time' (*hukm al-waqt*). Although this view appears to favour arbitrary decisions as to who should rule over the community and what form that rule should take, it is clear that al-Mawardi's overarching concern was for the welfare of the *umma* and the avoidance of conflict, a view shared by the other scholars mentioned. Al-Ghazali was, perhaps, most wedded to the idea of ruler-ship as key to the community's salvation. In essence, he states that the *umma*'s salvation rests on the right ordering of religion (that is, the message and example of the Prophet), which is itself possible only when society is rightly ordered. And in turn, the right ordering of society is only possible when there is a leader who is obeyed and who ensures that his orders are followed. The logical conclusion to this argument is that, for a society to achieve salvation, it must have a ruler – an imam – who is obeyed.[52]

This overview does not address all the methods used by the political and intellectual elites to format medieval political culture in Islam, aiming merely to raise a few points for discussion. What is worth underlining is that scholars in the tenth to thirteenth centuries did not focus solely on the caliphate when dealing with aspects of political culture. Theological and juridical treatises shared the intellectual stage with Mirrors for Princes and suchlike advice literature, as well as with works focusing on concepts of justice, equality and exemplary rulers from the past.[53] The period also saw the crystallisation of Shiʿi beliefs and voluminous scholarly output on the subject, including works touching on political culture.[54] While modern scholarship has taken account of many of these works, we are still far from mastering the politico-cultural contours of the world taking shape after the implosion in Baghdad in the mid-tenth century.

---

[52] Watt, 'Authority in the thought of al-Ghazali'. Al-Ghazali's work on this subject is *al-Iqtisad fi 'l-iʿtiqad* ('The Just Mean in Belief').

[53] See Al-Azmeh, *Muslim Kingship*; Gruendler and Marlow (eds), *Writers and Rulers*; L. Marlow, *Hierarchy and Egalitarianism in Islamic Thought* (New York, 1997); *eadem*, 'Kings, prophets and the ʿulamaʾ in mediaeval advice literature', *Studia Islamica* 81 (1995), 101–20; A. Afsaruddin, *Excellence and Precedence: Medieval Islamic Discourse on Legitimate Leadership* (Leiden, 2002); O. Safi, *The Politics of Knowledge: Negotiating Ideology and Religious Inquiry* (Chapel Hill, NC, 2006); D. Ephrat, *A Learned Society in a Period of Transition: The Sunni ʿUlamaʾ of Eleventh-Century Baghdad* (Albany, NY, 2000); A. K. S. Lambton, 'The dilemma of government in Islamic Persia: the *Siyasat-nama* of Nizam al-Mulk', *Iran* 22 (1984), 55–66; Y. Tabbaa, *The Transformation of Islamic Art during the Sunni Revival* (Seattle, 2001).

[54] S. A. Arjomand, 'The crisis of the imamate and the institution of occultation in Twelver Shiʿism: a sociohistorical perspective', *IJMES* 26 (1996); 491–515; A. Bausani, 'Religion in the Saljuq period', in *CHI* 5, 283–303; W. Madelung, 'Authority in Twelver Shiism in the absence of the imam', in Makdisi *et al.* (eds), *La Notion d'autorité*, 163–73.

The Age of Turco-Mongol Hegemons: New Blood, New Thinking, Old Rites and Observances

Throughout the period of Turco-Mongol domination in the Nile-to-Oxus region, from the Mongol invasions of the thirteenth century to the rise of early modern empires, elites and rulers continued to draw on varied sources in very varied ways to provide an 'ideology of kingship'.[55] Traditions from the glorious past continued to be crucial ingredients in such claims. However, the spectrum of pasts had widened substantially with the arrival of Turkish pastoral nomads in the eleventh century and the Mongol invasions of the thirteenth. Long-standing Iranian, Hellenic and Islamic concepts and ideals of divine providence, universal rule, sacral kingship, wisdom, justice and social order were thrown in with Turco-Mongol nomadic virtues of strong leadership, good fortune and royal genealogy. This mix led to the fluid, composite ideologies that now informed, and were informed by, the political landscape's elite constellations. The extinction of the caliphate and the spell of Mongol domination before their conversion to Islam in the thirteenth century meant that nomadic leadership virtues often took precedence in most parts of the Islamic world. Turco-Mongol ideologies of power took remarkably creative messianic and millenarian forms, increasingly incorporating neoplatonic ideas about the relationship between power and knowledge.

Arguably the strongest idea to inform claims to sovereignty and symbols of rulership was the 'golden dynasty': the natural, even divine, right of a royal line to rule – notably the clan's most capable males.[56] This idea of a select vanguard was omnipresent and had a deep impact on how other ideas of hegemony were valued, as well as on the practices and organisation of power politics. Essentially, this concept of the 'golden dynasty' was – and remained – strongly rooted in Turco-Mongol elite origins. Its very vagueness encouraged their tendencies towards fragmentation rather than checking them. Jingizid imperial ideology was undoubtedly the most powerful exponent of this idea. It stressed the divine destiny of the Jingizids, by dint of their forefather Jingiz Khan's mighty leadership, to rule the entire world; in some respects their lineage would survive into the nineteenth century as a result of this powerful idea. Variants could be found in all the courts of this period, harking back to the successes and fortunes of their early military

---

[55] 'The set of ideas by which a ruler defines himself as a sovereign [. . .] [which] gave rulers models for their behaviour, and helped them both assert the legality and legitimacy of their reigns, and maintain their claims to rule in the eyes of various, often overlapping audiences, frequently in opposition to the claims of others': *KI*, 6.

[56] The sense of hereditary right to rule existed in Byzantium, but was less pronounced: pp. 298–301, 323–4, 328. As ever, there was variation in the west: pp. 258–9, 371, 393, 394–8.

leaders, who had managed to carve out a political space for themselves and their clans or warbands in Islamic western Asia. These pioneering heroes included Hülegü and Temür (Timur) in the east, Baybars and Qalawun in Egypt, and Osman and his son Orkhan in western Anatolia, as well as many other, similarly successful and charismatic strongmen in the constantly changing archipelagos of claims to local or regional sovereignty within the stormy sea of Muslim western Asia. Most of these strongmen saw their own leadership narratives develop. They all tended to follow a similar pattern, charting their protagonist's rise from rags to riches, or rather from social marginality and petty brigandage to extraordinarily successful regional leadership. Equally important in such narratives was the restoration by our hero's own hand of special lineages or a particular social or religious order now fallen on hard times.[57] In the course of the fifteenth century, genealogies of Osman and Orkhan even pushed their claim to be a golden dynasty, lording it over other Turkish and post-Mongol ruling families in newly conquered territories. Osman, it was suggested, had links not only to the first and longest-ruling Turkish sultans of Asia Minor, the Seljuks of Rum, but also to a mythical ruler of the Western Turks Oghuz Khan, grandson of Noah and ancestor of the western Turkish tribes that spread over Islamic western Asia.[58] For many other clans and confederations, particularly among the Arabs, Kurds, Mongols and Turkmen of Asia Minor, Azerbaijan, Iraq and western Iran, such tribal affiliations remained key to building and justifying durable leadership structures. For example, White Sheep Turkmen leadership was believed to have originated from the association of as many as fifty Turkish, Arab and Kurdish confederate clans with the paramount clan of Oghuz Turkmens.[59]

Tribal affiliations had rather less impact in Egypt and the sultanate. It was the *mamluk* emir and sultan Qalawun (1279–90) who was first successfully metamorphosed into a mythical ancestor for the fourteenth-century Qalawunid dynasty. The entourages of his predecessor Baybars (1260–77) and his successor – the usurper of Qalawunid power Barquq (1382–99) – tried to conjure up the same aura for their masters but with far less success. In the fifteenth century, however, when succession to the sultanate failed time and again, stepping into the shoes of the Turkish *mamluk* sultan Baybars or the Circassian *mamluk* sultan Barquq seems to have become a substitute for one's lack of dynastic ties. For many a sultan, Baybars and Barquq became remarkably referential in expressing leadership ideology, on

---

[57] B. Manz, 'Tamerlane and the symbolism of sovereignty', *Iranian Studies* 1–2 (1988), 105–22.
[58] C. Imber, *The Ottoman Empire, 1300–1650: The Structure of Power*, 3rd edn (London, 2019), 95–7.
[59] J. Woods, *The Aqquyunlu: Clan, Confederation, Empire*, rev. edn (Salt Lake City, UT, 1999), 11.

the basis of shared *mamluk* status or alleged Circassian roots. As with the Ottomans, tribal genealogies appeared, purporting to link up fifteenth-century *mamluk* sultans, especially those of non-Turkish Circassian origin, with mythical tribal ancestors including the inevitable Oghuz Khan.[60] Such mythical figures became as ideologically important to post-Abbasid Turkish elites in western Asia as those of Jingiz Khan and his sons – and eventually the 'new Jingiz', Temür – became among Mongol and post-Mongol elites of the period. These origin stories and mythical genealogies all tapped into the same ideas of rulership and hegemony, blending blessed origins, royal lineage and successful leadership. Arguably this started to shape other ideas of legitimate power across Muslim western Asia, including the more traditional Islamic ones.

As we have seen, the caliphate was definitively lost in 1258, yet the *mamluk* sultan Baybars explicitly 'resurrected' its ostensible successor in Cairo for ideological purposes. Baybars' own ancestry had been all but erased during his time as a slave and in military service. He therefore needed to attach himself to an established pedigree – in this case, the Abbasid one – that could compete with the Ilkhanids' ideology of Jingizid imperial descent. Thus for a long time the traditional Muslim accession ritual was maintained in Cairo: the oath of allegiance (*bay'a*), whereby the Abbasid caliph delegated his divinely sanctioned authority to the sultan. Even though it was clear that these Abbasids were puppets of the Cairo sultans, Muslim rulers from as far away as the Indian peninsula and Sub-Saharan Africa continued to regard Abbasid acknowledgment of their accession as a necessary condition for public authority.[61] Above all, the ritual display of continuity confirmed the sultan's court as the main political centre of the *umma* and added an overlay of Islamic sovereignty to the sultan's position. To many the sultan appeared, as protector of the Abbasids, to be heading the virtual hierarchy of West Asian Muslim power-holders. The highly formalised correspondence and exchanges between the court at Cairo and other regional and local rulers attached great importance to this symbolic hierarchy. The rules of scribal protocol, which framed these multi-lingual acts of political communication, often presented themselves as objects of fierce competition and confrontation.[62] Historical writing was another important and burgeoning product of these late

---

[60] P. M. Holt, 'Literary offerings: a genre of courtly literature', in T. Philipp and U. Haarmann (eds), *The Mamluks in Egyptian Politics and Society* (Cambridge, 1998), 3–16, esp. 8–12.

[61] M. Hassan, *Longing for the Lost Caliphate: A Transregional History* (Princeton, 2017).

[62] D. Behrens-Abouseif, *Practising Diplomacy in the Mamluk Sultanate: Gifts and Material Culture in the Medieval Islamic World* (London, 2014); C. Y. Muslu, *The Ottomans and the Mamluks: Imperial Diplomacy and Warfare in the Islamic World* (London, 2014); M. Dekkiche, 'Crossing the line: Mamluk response to Qaramanid threat in the fifteenth

medieval West Asian court cultures. Their Arabic and Persian scribes actively engaged with the competing claims of political order and hierarchy, particularly in the Arabic tradition of how the relationship between caliphate and sultanate should be organised.[63]

Ultimately, though, the Abbasid connection was reduced to just one among many contested factors informing ritual observances and ideas of sovereignty in western Asia after 1258. A royal panegyric, written in Arabic at the court in Cairo in the 1340s, creatively melds Islamic and Turco-Mongol ideas to show how discourses of legitimate rule could now do very well without the caliphate. Divine sanction and fortunate lineage join forces in the accession of a new Qalawunid sultan, who is tellingly identified in both worldly and religious terms: 'The sultan, son of the sultan, son of the sultan; the imam, son of the imam, son of the imam.' The author further explains:

> [...] 64 years and 10 months after God, the exalted, had assigned the sublime kingship to this noble house [of Qalawun], God, the exalted, gave our lord the sultan royal authority over the regions, executing through the continuance of royalty in him and in his offspring the divine decree, ensuring the execution of his commands and prohibitions in all of the cities, and assisting him with supporters from his favourite angels, for as long as night and day succeed each other.[64]

Shadow of God, Alexander of the Age: New Roles for Military Strongmen

In this era, an increasingly powerful and mainstream ideology developed across western Asia. It argued that the role and authority of the caliphs of old had been taken over by military strongmen – sultans, khans, padishahs, beys and emirs – even suggesting that their legitimacy derived entirely from their ability to create and maintain conditions conducive to the rule of God's law (*shariʿa*) over His community.[65] Qalawunid claims to the title of imam and to divine election in the mid-fourteenth century are both significant and representative of this, as are the rulership qualities highlighted by the same panegyric: 'sultan of Islam', 'imam of mankind', 'God's shadow on earth', 'lord of the two prayer directions' (Mecca and Jerusalem),

---

century according to MS ar. 4440 (BnF, Paris)', *BSOAS* 80 (2017), 253–81; F. Bauden and M. Dekkiche (eds), *Mamluk Cairo: A Crossroads for Embassies* (Leiden, 2018).

[63] K. Hirschler, *Medieval Arabic Historiography: Authors as Actors* (London, 2006); J. Van Steenbergen, *Caliphate and Kingship in a Fifteenth-Century Literary History of Muslim Leadership and Pilgrimage* (Leiden, 2016). See also pp. 115–16, 118–19.

[64] J. Van Steenbergen, 'Qalawunid discourse, elite communication and the Mamluk cultural matrix', *JAL* 43 (2012), 1–28 at 12, 13.

[65] *SGMI*; Hirschler, *Authors as Actors*; O. Anjum, *Politics, Law and Community in Islamic Thought: The Taymiyyan Moment* (New York, 2012).

'servant of the two noble precincts' (Mecca and Medina), and 'reviver of justice in the world'.[66] Such titles are already attested for pre-Qalawunid rulers in Cairo such as Baybars, and they continued to mark out the sultans' special qualities after the end of the Qalawunid dynasty in the 1380s. They also resonate remarkably well with the ambitious claims that were made for Temür towards the end of the fourteenth century – 'pole of Islam and Muslims' (*qutb al-Islam wa-l-Muslimin*) – and for his son and successor Shah Rukh (1405–57), who allegedly even claimed the title of caliph itself in the 1420s.[67] Half a century later, echoes of these titles and claims are found in the ambitious styling of Uzun Hasan (1457–78), ruler of the White Sheep Turkmen. In a treatise on politics composed for him, he is described as 'the shadow of God, the caliph of God, and the deputy of the Prophet', and as 'the just imam [. . .] emperor of Islam, shadow of God over mankind' in an inscription on the main mosque of Yazd.[68] Ottoman and Safavid rulers would systematically adapt and repeat such claims to Muslim sovereignty and divine sanction in ever more ambitious formats from the sixteenth century on. In many ways this was a long-term effect of the remarkable ideological transformation that had affected Turco-Mongol elites across western Asia 300 years earlier.

However, this radical transformation of ideas about Muslim political order was not simply a binary fusion of Islamic and nomadic leadership ideals. It is a measure of the contest and debate between Turco-Mongol rulers, their supporters and opponents, as well as among wider groups of Muslim intellectuals.[69] It also took place when the relationship between power and knowledge was gradually transforming, when the boundaries of knowledge itself were expanding.[70] One of the more intriguing titles claimed for its Qalawunid dedicatee by the Arabic panegyric mentioned earlier is 'the Alexander of the Age' (*Iskandar al-Zaman*).[71] In fact by the mid-fourteenth century, this appeal to both Hellenic ideal and Qur'anic hero was quite

[66] Van Steenbergen, 'Qalawunid discourse', 8–9. More general assessment: C. A. Markiewicz, *The Crisis of Kingship in Late Medieval Islam: Persian Emigres and the Making of Ottoman Sovereignty* (Cambridge, 2019).
[67] M. Dekkiche, 'New source, new debate: re-evaluation of the Mamluk-Timurid struggle for religious supremacy in the Hijaz (Paris, BnF MS ar. 4440)', *MSR* 18 (2014–15), 247–71 at 260–1; J. E. Woods, 'Shahrukh's caliphate' (unpublished paper).
[68] Woods, *The Aqquyunlu*, 105, 106.
[69] J.-C. Garcin, 'Histoire, opposition politique et piétisme traditionaliste dans le Husn al-muhadarat de Suyuti', *Annales islamologiques* 7 (1967), 33–90; M. Banister, '"Naught remains of the Caliph but his title": revisiting Abbasid authority in Mamluk Cairo', *MSR* 18 (2014–15), 219–45; M. Banister, 'Casting the Caliph in a cosmic role: examining al-Suyuti's historical vision', in A. Ghersetti (ed.), *Al-Suyuti: A Polymath of the Mamluk Period* (Leiden, 2016), 98–117.
[70] See especially Markiewicz, *Crisis of Kingship*.
[71] Van Steenbergen, 'Qalawunid discourse', 8–9.

common practice in the sultanate. Such qualities had been claimed since the reign of Sultan Baybars, if not before, and found echoes everywhere, not least among the Ottomans.[72] Baybars is thus described in a handful of public texts, including royal inscriptions on a citadel, mosque and two commemorative mausolea in Syria, dated to the middle of his reign, between 1265 and 1269. In each case, the proud title 'the Alexander of the Age' is accompanied by 'Lord of the Auspicious Conjunction' (*sahib al-qiran*).[73] Rooted in pre-Islamic Iranian ideas of kingship, the latter proved an extremely popular and powerful mediator of charismatic power, and the title was claimed for various thirteenth-century Mongol, Ilkhanid and Anatolian Seljuk rulers, becoming increasingly prominent in the formal titulature of Temür and his successors in the fifteenth century and beyond.[74] Styling oneself Lord of the Auspicious Conjunction fused the astrological and the messianic, widely shared interests at the Turco-Mongol courts after 1258. Its growing centrality in Turco-Mongol leadership ideologies attests to the widespread popularity of millenarian ideals and the gradual integration of occult sciences into mainstream knowledge. The science of letters (*'ilm al huruf*), geomancy and the interpretation of dreams became increasingly important in royal patronage, the political instrumentalisation of stories, and the activities of soothsayers and Sufi masters. Together with ideas of divine election and sacred kingship, astrology, messianism and the like were enlisted to represent the privileged relationship between Turco-Mongol rulers, divine wisdom and truth. In the shifting vocabularies and ideals of Turco-Mongol sovereignty, the ancient images of the philosopher- and scientist-king regained prominence, especially in Timurid and post-Timurid lands, as did that of the secretary-king at the Yemeni Rasulid court between the mid-thirteenth and early fifteenth centuries, or that of the poet-king at the early sixteenth-century court in Cairo.[75]

---

[72] D. Kastritsis, 'The Alexander Romance and the rise of the Ottoman empire', in A. C. S. Peacock and S. N. Yıldız (eds), *Islamic Literature and Intellectual Life in Fourteenth- and Fifteenth-Century Anatolia* (Würzburg, 2016), 243–83.

[73] A.-M. Eddé, 'Baybars et son double: de l'ambiguïté du souverain idéal', in D. Aigle (ed.), *Le Bilad al-Šam face aux mondes extérieurs: la perception de l'autre et la représentation du souverain* (Damascus and Beirut, 2012), 73–86.

[74] N. S. Chann, 'Lord of the Auspicious Conjunction: origins of the *Sahib-Qiran*', *Iran and the Caucasus* 13 (2009), 93–110; A. A. Moin, *The Millennial Sovereign: Sacred Kingship and Sainthood in Islam* (New York, 2012).

[75] M. Melvin-Koushki, 'Astrology, lettrism, geomancy: the occult-scientific methods of post-Mongol Islamicate imperialism', *Medieval History Journal* 19 (2016), 142–50; E. Vallet, 'Des "sultans-secrétaires"? Pratique de l'archive et savoirs encyclopédiques dans l'État rasulide (VIIe–IXe/XIIIe–XVe siècles)', in I. Bierman and S. Denoix (eds), *L'Exercice de pouvoir à l'âge des sultanats: production, manifestation, réception* [= *Annales islamologiques* 46] (Cairo, 2012), 229–54.

Acts, Rites and Symbols: Legitimising and Performing Leadership from Cairo to Delhi

Just as the vocabularies of sovereignty shifted over time, various traditional ceremonial practices – other than those which had featured the caliph – took on symbolic importance for the proliferating claimants to dominion. Mentioning the ruler's name in the weekly Friday prayer (*khutba*) and, especially, his right to mint coins bearing his name and titles (*sikka*) became two far more important and visible symbols of sovereignty than anything the caliphal model could offer. When the Ilkhanid elites in Iraq fragmented in the 1330s, for instance, in return for military support various pretenders to local rule offered the Qalawunid sultan in Egypt the right to have the Friday prayer in Baghdad, Mosul and Diyarbakr delivered in his name. Al-Nasir Muhammad (1293–1341) happily accepted these competing offers, thus extending his authority over the territory of the sultanate's former arch-enemy, with all the telling symbolism this entailed for various audiences inside and outside his actual sphere of influence.[76] Although it came to naught, this episode does illustrate how this long-standing observance continued to carry a powerful meaning. The same goes for the minting of coins. Temür is reported to have taken a campmint with him while raiding westwards. Whenever his armies captured another urban centre, new coins were minted bearing Temür's name as well as the name of the newly conquered city, resulting in a whole range of different coins that kept track of the geography of his conquests and that preserved, in a very tangible and visible manner, the public memory of his glory and success.[77] Long-standing symbolic observances of Islamic sovereignty such as the minting of coins were also used to legitimise, or support, the ruler's claims to legitimacy on the basis of royal descent and family membership. For example, unlike earlier *mamluk* sultans and other contemporary dynasties, the later Qalawunids frequently included the sultan's lineage right back to Qalawun, even on coins of lesser value.[78]

In his biography of the Syro-Egyptian sultan Jaqmaq (1438–53), the courtier and historian Ibn Taghri Birdi (1411–70) noted:

As a result of his asceticism, he abolished many of the ceremonies of royal authority (*shiʿar al-mamlaka*), such as the procession of the *hajj* palanquin

---

[76] P. Wing, 'The decline of the Ilkhanate and the Mamluk sultanate's eastern frontier', *MSR* 11(2) (2007), 77–88.

[77] S. Heidemann, 'Timur's campmint during the siege of Damascus in 803/1401', in R. Gyselen and M. Szuppe (eds), *Matériaux pour l'histoire économique du monde iranien* [= *Cahiers de Studia Iranica* 21] (Leuven, 1999), 179–206.

[78] *KI*, 147–8.

(*mahmal*), the hunting party with the birds of prey, the public service (*khidma*) in the audience hall (*iwan*), the court of justice (*hukm*) at the chain gate of the sultan's stable, the guard of the Lady (*nawbat khatun*) that used to beat the drums from the Citadel of the Mountain at sunrise and sunset, and many similar things. [...] He used to resent those things because of the immoral acts they entailed.[79]

This reference to a sultan's alleged ritual iconoclasm in mid-fifteenth-century Cairo is striking, even though it neither caught on nor survived his reign. It is noteworthy that Sultan Jaqmaq's iconoclasm focused on a wide variety of ritual practices (and the ideas underlying them) which were, in a sense, innovations in Islamic western Asia. Ubiquitous among the post-1000 elites of the Nile-to-Oxus region, and rooted in a Turco-Mongol past with its emphasis on the worldly virtues of chieftainship and royal splendour, many of these rituals were difficult to digest for strict adherents of Muslim tradition, especially ascetics like Sultan Jaqmaq. Yet these rituals were a powerful means of symbolic communication among the huge cast of actors involved in western Asian regional and local politics. Ibn Taghri Birdi's listing of the 'ceremonies of royal authority' therefore makes a useful starting point for reviewing the diverse rituals and ideas that were as much defining features of the era's political practices as were the shifting vocabularies of sovereignty or being named in Friday prayers and on coins.

The procession of the *hajj* palanquin (*mahmal*) involved a lavishly decorated yet empty palanquin being paraded through the city of Cairo, before accompanying the main caravan of pilgrims on the annual *hajj* to Mecca. Allegedly introduced by Sultan Baybars in the 1260s,[80] it was a brilliant amalgamation of rituals of good Muslim practice (the *hajj*); of legitimate authority over Islamic subjects (enabling the performance of religious duties); and of Turco-Mongol style military leadership (which called for the proximity of the ruler to his subjects). In Cairo, along the pilgrimage route and among the many visitors and pilgrims to Mecca, the *mahmal* represented the omnipresence of the rulers of Egypt. Being such a powerful symbol of sovereignty, the *mahmal* was soon incorporated into many other pilgrimage caravans connecting cities and regions to Mecca, including those of the sultanate's rivals in Iraq and Yemen.[81]

[79] Translation from RPCMC, 228.
[80] J. Meloy, 'Celebrating the *Mahmal*: the Rajab festival in fifteenth-century Cairo', in J. Pfeiffer and S. Quinn (eds), *History and Historiography of Post-Mongol Central Asia and the Middle East* (Wiesbaden, 2006), 404–27; D. Behrens-Abouseif, 'The *Mahmal* legend and the pilgrimage of the ladies of the Mamluk court', *MSR* 1 (1997), 87–96.
[81] Van Steenbergen, *Caliphate and Kingship*, 18–19.

Acclaimed sovereignty was further visualised in Mecca by the *kiswa* or black cover of the Ka'ba. Brought from Cairo and renewed annually during the *hajj*, this powerful symbol of patronage over the region and its leaders symbolised pre-eminence in the hierarchy of Muslim rulers. Until 1258, the privilege of donating the *kiswa* had been a prerogative of the Abbasid caliphs of Baghdad, and it became the subject of lively competition between the sultans in Cairo and their rivals in Ilkhanid Iraq, Timurid Iran and Rasulid Yemen. In the 1320s, the Ilkhanid leader tried to enforce the right to have his own *kiswa* covering the Ka'ba. The reaction from Cairo was fierce: Sultan al-Nasir Muhammad undertook the *hajj* in person to ensure his authority remained intact. He would make the pilgrimage three times between 1312 and 1332, becoming the first Muslim ruler of regional status repeatedly to perform this key public ritual of Muslim good practice in almost four centuries. *Kiswa* competition resurged under Sultan Barsbay (1422–38), when the Timurid ruler Shah Rukh sent his own *kiswa* to Mecca and backed this up with substantial displays of Timurid pomp. Eventually it was the Ottoman sultans and their representatives who appropriated these privileges of *mahmal*, *kiswa* and *hajj* in the early sixteenth century, upon their conquest of Egypt.[82]

Ibn Taghri Birdi's list of royal ceremonies features an even more pragmatic fusion of Turco-Mongol and Muslim traditions: the hunting party with birds of prey. Throughout the pre-modern world, courts indulged in hunting parties whenever time and circumstances allowed, and the Turco-Mongol elites of the Nile-to-Oxus region were no exception – from Cairo and Bursa to Tabriz, Sultaniyya, Herat and Samarqand. As a ritual of kingship, hunting parties appealed to ideas of virility, martial prowess and strong leadership. They offered a useful stage to impress audiences at the centre and on the peripheries of power with the size and splendour of the ruler's following and encampments. And for the Mongols in particular, hunting parties also functioned as military training camps, where horsemen could practise their individual and collective fighting skills.[83]

This is also where the connection with Muslim traditions comes in. These hunting parties were, in fact, little more than a ritualised enactment of the raiding parties and military campaigning so characteristic of the period. If not in reality, then certainly ideologically, the endless pursuit of violence among the highly competitive and constantly fragmenting Turco-Mongol elites of the Nile-to-Oxus region could be explained as

---

[82] *KI*; Dekkiche, 'New source, new debate'; S. Faroqhi, *Pilgrims and Sultans: The Hajj under the Ottomans, 1517–1683* (London, 1994); J. Jomier, *Le Mahmal et la caravane égyptienne des pèlerins de La Mecque (XIIIe–XXe siècles)* (Cairo, 1953).
[83] T. T. Allsen, *The Royal Hunt in Eurasian History* (Philadelphia, 2006).

warfare at the frontiers of political authority, often with religious and sectarian overtones.[84] As in preceding centuries, these violent realities contributed to the formulation and formation of discrete other identities (including Sunni Islam) and to the refinement of ideas of rulership and order. The most powerful of these was the complex notion of jihad. This flexible Qur'anic concept was increasingly seen in very practical terms as defensive – even offensive – warfare against a variety of 'others' for the sake of God's rule and Islam's dominion on earth.[85] Military leaders engaging in frontier warfare and able to appeal convincingly to the idea of jihad had a powerful weapon at their disposal: to 'other' their opponents, rally peers and subordinates, and claim sovereignty on moral grounds. In the thirteenth century, Latin Franks and infidel Mongols offered myriad opportunities for Muslim leaders to instrumentalise their campaigns against both infidel and Muslim others under the powerful banner of jihad. Thereafter such clearcut frontiers dried up, especially in Syria, and the idea of the ruler as warrior-king and champion of Islam gradually lost some of its appeal. However, it never disappeared entirely, not least because it tied in so well with the era's basic idea of successful leadership, fortunate genealogy and royal lineage, and offered further opportunities for the fusion of Muslim and Turco-Mongol traditions. On the frontier zones of Muslim western Asia, particularly among the marcher lords of Asia Minor where social and ideological realities were fluid, this pragmatic fusion of traditions continued to be more actively invoked. In Anatolia and the Christian Balkans in the fourteenth and especially the fifteenth centuries, the tradition of the Muslim frontier emerged alongside the related title of *ghazi* (holy warrior). For a long time the subject of intense academic debate, this blend may help to explain in mainstream Islamic terms the momentum of Ottoman raiding, campaigning and conquest against a great variety of local and regional leaderships on the Anatolian peninsula and beyond. It thus proved as successful an ideological instrument for the Ottomans as it had once done for sultans such as Baybars and Qalawun.[86]

---

[84] M. Chamberlain, 'Military patronage states and the political economy of the frontier, 1000–1250', in Y. M. Choueiri (ed.), *A Companion to the History of the Middle East* (Chichester, 2008), 135–53.

[85] R. S. Humphreys, 'Ayyubids, Mamluks, and the Latin East in the thirteenth century', *MSR* 2 (1998), 1–17; the flexibility of the concept has also been highlighted by K. Goudie, *Reinventing Jihad: Jihad Ideology from the Conquest of Jerusalem to the End of the Ayyubids (c. 492/1099–647/1249)* (Leiden, 2019).

[86] C. Kafadar, *Between Two Worlds: The Construction of the Ottoman State* (Berkeley, 1996); A. Fuess, 'Ottoman Gazwah – Mamluk Gihad: two arms on the same body?', in S. Conermann (ed.), *Everything is on the Move: The Mamluk Empire as a Node in (Trans-) Regional Networks* (Bonn, 2014), 269–82.

Ibn Taghri Birdi's concluding references to 'ceremonies of royal authority' lead us away from pulpits, markets, texts, battlefields and hunting grounds towards other, more circumscribed, platforms for the ritual performance of late medieval rulership in western Asia: their often peripatetic courts. The three final ceremonies on his list represent more regular, organised and thus – in a sense – hardcore rituals of political power and authority that were shared by Turco-Mongol elites across the region. In mid-fifteenth-century Cairo, a great hall (*iwan*) in the Citadel of the Mountain was used for the *khidma*, a regular public service led by the sultan. The nature of the rituals performed on such occasions is shown in a handful of Arabic texts on court protocol from the fourteenth and fifteenth centuries. One early fourteenth-century manual from the court of the Qalawunid sultan al-Nasir Muhammad gives a full description:

It was the habit of this sultan [al-Nasir Muhammad] to hold a session on Monday morning at the *iwan* outside his palace, near its gate. This is a wide open hall with a high ceiling, in front of which there is a spacious square. It is known as the 'court of justice' (*dar al-'adl*) and is used for the public service (*al-khidma al-'amma*) and – in most cases – for the reception of rulers' envoys. But when [the sultan] sits down to redress wrongs (*al-mazalim*), he takes his place on a chair which is erected next to the pulpit (*al-minbar*) that is the throne of kingship [. . .] when he sits on it, his feet almost touch the ground. The chief judges of the four schools of law sit to his right, with the commissioner for the public treasury and the market inspector next to them; the secretary sits to his left, and before him there are the supervisor of the army bureau and all the clerks, completing a full circle. [. . .] Behind the sultan, *mamluk* weapons-bearers, robe-bearers and personal guards stand in two rows, to his right and left. At a distance of about fifteen cubits on his right and on his left sit the veterans from among the great 'amirs of 100' [*mamluks*], who are the amirs of the advisory council. Next to them stand the great amirs and office-holders of lower rank. The rest of the amirs stand behind the advisory council. At the back of this circle around the sultan stand the gatekeepers and the keepers of the inkwell, bringing forward the petitions of wretched people [that have been selected] to be read out to him. He consults with the judges in cases that require their consultation, he speaks with the lord chamberlain and the secretary of the army on cases that concern the army, and he commands as he sees fit in all other cases.[87]

This regular public session was the main ritual performance by the sultanate's ruling elite of their claims to authority and status within the sultanate's hierarchies of power. The very public enactment of current power relationships resulted in a detailed protocol which allocated specific places, roles and privileges to all, in keeping with their positions in the

---

[87] Ibn Fadl Allah al-'Umari, *Masalik al-Absar fi Mamalik al-Amsar: Mamalik Misr wa-l-Sham wa-l-Hijaz wa-l-Yaman*, ed. A. F. Sayyid (Cairo, 1985), 36–7; N. Rabbat, *The Citadel of Cairo: A New Interpretation of Royal Mamluk Architecture* (Leiden, 1995), 252–6.

ruler's entourage and thus at his court. Similar sessions were organised on a weekly basis at all the main urban centres across the sultanate, with the sultan symbolically represented by an empty throne and his role undertaken for most of the time by his local representative.

Such Turco-Mongol court ritual was replicated throughout not only the sultanate but late medieval western Asia.[88] An early fifteenth-century protocol text from Cairo recounts how – far away, in India – the Turkish ruler of Delhi, Muhammad b. Tughluq (1325–51), had two kinds of public sessions organised for him:

One of them was the daily session, which meant that every day the table was set up in the sultan's palace, from which 20,000 people would eat: chiefs, kings, amirs, commanders and leading military men. A special table was set up for the sultan, at which he was joined for lunch and supper by 200 scholars of jurisprudence [who were expected] to eat with him and to debate and discuss in his presence. The second was the public session [. . .] every Tuesday, this sultan would have a general session on a massive, wide square, where a large royal enclosure was set up for him, at the front of which he would sit on a lofty throne with a golden ceiling, with the lords of the dynasty standing around him on the right and left and the weapon-bearers behind him, with the officeholders standing in front of him arranged according to their ranks – only the chiefs, the chief judge and the secretary were allowed to sit down – and with the chamberlains standing immediately before him. A general announcement would then be proclaimed: 'whoever has a complaint or need, has to come forward'; thereupon anyone who had a complaint or need would come forward and stand before him, and he would not go away until his case was solved and the sultan had issued his command on it.[89]

This imagining of public sessions at the fourteenth-century Tughluqid court does not just remind us of the many ideas and rituals of power that connected late medieval Cairo and Delhi. With its references to audiences, receptions and banquets, it adds to our understanding of when and how royal public sessions were organised across the Nile-to-Oxus region. They offered the perfect environment to display a ruler's sovereignty and his control of resources. Public sessions were the convenient occasion for soldiers to receive their salaries in cash and kind; for commanders to receive rank and income; and for officials to receive titles and assignments. They involved conferring robes of honour, military gear or fully equipped horses, as well as many other lucrative gifts and symbols of the

[88] Manz, 'Tamerlane and the symbolism of sovereignty', 119–21; B. O'Kane, 'Architecture and court cultures of the fourteenth century', in F. B. Flood and G. Necipoğlu (eds), *A Companion to Islamic Art and Architecture, II: From the Mongols to Modernism* (Hoboken, NJ, 2017), 585–615.

[89] Ahmad b. Abd Allah al-Qalqashandi, *Subh al-a'sha fi sina'at al-insha'*, 14 vols (Cairo, 1913–19), v:95.

sultan's favour and social status. Public sessions were also the perfect stage to formalise and confirm support for a new ruler's accession: he would literally ascend to the throne, or royal dais, with oaths of loyalty sworn by the elites and all duly rewarded. And each manifestation of this intense gift economy ended with a lavish banquet, befitting the ruler's claims to beneficial sovereignty.[90]

Public sessions were also used to enact another important aspect of ideal rulership held in common by the Perso-Islamic and Turco-Mongol worlds: the performance of royal justice. The concept of the circle of justice was well known from ancient times and tied in well with tribal notions of the chief as responsible for the tribe's well-being. The ruler created conditions under which his subjects could flourish, and, in turn, he could expect such conditions from them. As the guarantor of safety and justice, he had a duty to enhance his coercive force, raise revenues through fiscal and administrative arrangements, and require his subjects to generate sufficient surplus resources – all of which required safety and justice. Royal (*mazalim*) justice had embodied this ideal since the early days of Islam: ad hoc rulings to redress wrongs which, in theory, a ruler's subjects could have suffered at the hands of his representatives and entourage.[91] This type of royal justice was not defined by religious law. Sessions of this sort were performed in various ways in towns throughout Muslim Western Asia, generally by military agents of the ruler, whether it was labelled *mazalim* or by its Mongol variant, known as Jingiz Khan's laws of the *yasa*. The presence of religious scholars and judges at these public sessions where the royal justice was formally enacted led to boundaries between the two legal systems of *mazalim* and *shariʿa* becoming ever more blurred. This eventually resulted in the pragmatic co-existence of religious and royal law, as codified during the early modern Ottoman sultanate.[92]

The final reference by Ibn Taghri Birdi in his list of traditional ceremonies is to 'the guard of the Lady (*nawbat khatun*) that used to beat the drums from the Citadel of the Mountain at sunrise and sunset'. This hints

---

[90] A. Levanoni, 'Food and cooking during the Mamluk era: social and political implications', *MSR* 9(1) (2005), 1–22; W. Flinterman and J. Van Steenbergen, 'Al-Nasir Muhammad and the formation of the Qalawunid state', in A. Landau (ed.), *Pearls on a String: Artists, Patrons, and Poets at the Great Islamic Courts* (Baltimore and Seattle, 2015), 86–113.

[91] See also pp. 103–5.

[92] L. T. Darling, *A History of Social Justice and Political Power in the Middle East: The Circle of Justice from Mesopotamia to Globalization* (London and New York, 2013), esp. 103–25; G. Burak, 'The second formation of Islamic law: the post-Mongol context of the Ottoman adoption of a school of law', *Comparative Studies of Society and History* 55 (2013), 579–602. On royal justice in the west: pp. 68–71.

at a set of rituals that was designed to bind the citadels and palaces of the court more closely to the town in which they were mostly set, without relinquishing the Turco-Mongol heritage of their elites. The obituary of an Egyptian emir reminds us how fashionable the Mongol lifestyle had become in fourteenth-century Cairo. His chronicler explains how the emir 'used to ride out with three hundred horsemen, organised in two lines, each one preceded by a man who beat the *qubuz*, just like the Mongol kings'.[93] The court-citadel truly flourished as a centre of power in the eastern Mediterranean. Although Turco-Mongol elites had come to take over the cities they found there, these cities were also adopted and adapted as extensions of the rulers' courts. Cities served as stages for a wide variety of ritual performances of power and authority, allowing rulers to reach a far wider audience than during their public sessions. This also left a deep mark on the urban development of cities like Cairo, Damascus and Aleppo, as it did on public life there, too.[94] We know less about this urban aspect of late medieval rulership in Ottoman Bursa, Ilkhanid Tabriz, Timurid Samarqand and Herat, or the other regional or local political centres of late medieval western Asia. But it is likely that ritual practices and ideas were similar – even though more mobile, tented and itinerant – across this deeply interconnected land mass.[95]

Early fourteenth-century Cairo witnessed the mushrooming of massive palaces between the court-citadel and the city proper, an area that was urbanised as a result. These palaces were either built by or given to the most powerful emirs in the Qalawunid sultan's entourage, and their position between city and court can be interpreted as a telling representation and performance of the power relations of the time.[96] Each of these palaces was, in itself, a stage both in Cairo and elsewhere in Egypt and Syria, judging by a fifteenth-century description paraphrased by David Ayalon:

As for the amir's court, it was a copy on a reduced scale of the court of the sultan. He had a coat of arms, with a special design serving as his emblem, such as a cup, an inkwell, a napkin, a fleur-de-lis, and the like. This coat of arms, which bore

[93] J. Van Steenbergen, 'The amir Qawsun, statesman or courtier? (720–741 AH/1320–1341 AD', in U. Vermeulen and J. Van Steenbergen (eds), *Egypt and Syria in the Fatimid, Ayyubid and Mamluk Eras III* [= *Orientalia Lovaniensia Analecta* 102] (Leuven, 2001), 449–66, esp. 454.

[94] RPCMC, 227–76; D. Behrens-Abouseif, *Cairo of the Mamluks: A History of the Architecture and its Culture* (Cairo, 2007); K. Hirschler, 'Riten der Gewalt: Protest und Aufruhr in Kairo und Damaskus (7./13. bis 10./16. Jahrhundert)', in S. Conermann and S. von Hees (eds), *Islamwissenschaft als Kulturwissenschaft, I: Historische Anthropologie. Ansätze und Möglichkeiten* (Schenefeld, 2007), 205–33.

[95] O'Kane, 'Architecture and court cultures'; L. Golombek and D. Wilber, *The Timurid Architecture of Iran and Turan* (Princeton, 1988).

[96] J. Loiseau, *Les Mamelouks (XIIIe–XVIe siècle): une expérience de pouvoir dans l'Islam médiéval* (Paris, 2014), 207–40, esp. ch. 5, 'La demeure des émirs'.

a colour of the amir's choice, was painted on the gates of his house and his other possessions, such as the grain storehouses, the sugar refineries, the ships, as well as on his sword, his bow, and the caparisons of his horses and camels. When the amir rode out of his house, the important members of his corps would escort him as follows: the head of the guard, the secretary, the organizer of his public session, and other high-ranking officeholders would precede him; the masters of his wardrobe would follow him, and the supervisor of his stable would come last, leading the reserve horses. The sultan rode in the same manner.[97]

Just as they were at the citadel of the sultan, drummers and other musicians would be stationed at the palace gates, announcing events and visitors to inhabitants and passers-by alike. They might also accompany the emir when he paraded through the city. Not much is known about these parades between elite residences and the city centre, apart from one regular, major procession that was made by the ruler and his court, the *mawkib*. This mostly preceded public court-sessions and took the entire court – arranged by rank and status and following a protocol similar to that of the public session – from the courts in Cairo, Damascus, Aleppo or elsewhere to a politically meaningful urban space. Following prescribed ceremonial routes through the densely packed cities of Egypt, Syria and probably elsewhere in western Asia, such royal processions and their more modest offshoots presented yet another major performance of the Turco-Mongol strongman's splendour and power. They also allowed such strongmen to connect directly with the city and its diverse populations, obliging the latter to participate, however reluctantly, in the construction of the political order.

---

[97] D. Ayalon, 'Studies on the structure of the Mamluk army – II', *BSOAS* 15(3) (1953), 448–76, esp. 461–2.

Part IV

Practice and Organisation

13 The Latin West
Multiple Elites and Overlapping Jurisdictions

Daniel Power

Introduction

In contrast to the Byzantine and Islamic spheres, it is difficult to tell a single narrative of the development of political organisation in Latin Christendom between the eighth and fifteenth centuries. It is true that both the legacies and the memories of the Christian Roman empire persisted in medieval Europe, with vast consequences even for kingdoms such as Bohemia or Scotland that had never been under Roman rule. It is also true that, early in this period, a majority of the Latin Christian population came under the rule of a single polity, the Carolingian empire, which left a very durable mark upon political organisation across Latin Christendom: its influence was felt beyond the reach of direct Carolingian authority, notably in Anglo-Saxon England.[1] Above all, the defining characteristic of Latin Christendom was its acknowledgment of the claims and institutions of the Catholic church, the source of a common sense of identity from the early middle ages that would be reinforced by common Latin Christian ventures such as the Crusades as well as by the transformation of the Roman church itself from the eleventh century onwards – a process that created an elaborate set of structures binding the furthest reaches of Latin Christendom to the papal curia. By the late middle ages, the monarchies of western Europe were exerting a growing sway over the churches in their kingdoms, while papal authority was further weakened by the rifts caused by the Great Schism (1378–1417), when support for rival popes in Rome and Avignon mirrored the dynastic conflicts of Latin Christendom; nevertheless, it was only from the 1520s onwards, as the Protestant Reformation took root, that this common Catholic identity was shattered permanently. Yet fragmentation was an essential feature of Latin Christian temporal political culture, especially after the disintegration of the Carolingian empire in the late ninth and tenth centuries.[2] This produced much diversity in the political

---

[1] See also pp. 54, 59–61, 62, 149, 257, 264–5.   [2] See also pp. 143–4, 149–50.

Figure 13.1 King Wenceslas II of Bohemia on the throne in the midst of his court; from the *Codex Manesse* (or *Great Heidelberg Book of Songs*, Zurich, *c*.1300–40); reproduced by kind permission of Heidelberg University Library, Codex Manesse, Cod. Pal. germ. 848, fol. 10 r

organisation of the Latin sphere. A recurring theme during the period is the contrast between the experiences of the lands bordering the Mediterranean, especially Italy, on the one hand, and of Europe north of the Alps on the other; but there were also strong disparities within transalpine Europe.

Geography

Geography played an important part in shaping Latin Christendom's political culture. Although there were enormous shifts in the extent and location of Latin Christendom between the eighth and fifteenth centuries, some common effects upon political organisation throughout the period can be identified. With the conversion to Christianity of the populations of much of east-central Europe between the eighth and eleventh centuries, Latin Christendom came to extend as far as the Russian forests and the edge of the Eurasian steppe, and henceforth it comprised a region with three main climatic zones (Atlantic, Mediterranean and Continental) and diverse vegetation and topography. These inevitably affected the nature of political organisation. A rich fertile core, suitable for growing crops, lay at the heart of the kingdoms of England, Scotland, France, Denmark, Sicily and Castile, amongst others, providing their rulers with the income to dominate neighbouring poorer, often upland areas. Conversely, the loss of arable regions by the indigenous rulers of Wales to Anglo-Norman invaders or the lack of a large fertile core in Ireland hindered strong kingship in those countries, although more effective princely exploitation of the fertile island of Anglesey played a crucial part in the rise of the otherwise mountainous and impoverished principality of Gwynedd in North Wales in the thirteenth century.[3] At a micro-level, too, the abundance or shortage of good farming land exerted a major influence upon political and legal structures. Across Latin Christendom, opportunities for land reclamation and for migration to new towns and villages helped to define the extent of freedom both of individuals and of communities and to undermine seigneurial control, whether of labour, natural resources such as forests and waterways, or the means of production such as mills. In the fourteenth century, the catastrophic collapse of populations in the wake of the Great Famine (1315–22) and the Black

---

[3] R. R. Davies, *The Age of Conquest: Wales 1063–1415* (Oxford, 1991), 236–8. For the maritime societies and polities that looked on to the North and Irish Seas and drew their livelihood from activities there: B. W. Cunliffe, *Facing the Ocean: The Atlantic and its Peoples, 8000 BC–AD 1500* (Oxford, 2001), 482–553; J. H. Barrett and S. J. Gibbon (eds), *Maritime Societies of the Viking and Medieval World* (Leeds, 2015).

Death (1347–51) and subsequent plagues had the twin effects of reducing pressure upon land and of creating labour shortages, both of which had a major political impact as well as social and economic effects. It is striking, however, that the most famous popular uprisings in the generation after the Black Death, the Jacquerie in northern France (1358) and the Peasants' Revolt in England (1381), despite their many differences in origins, objectives, and outcomes, both took place in areas of relative agricultural prosperity: although the Jacquerie was in part provoked by the depredations of the Hundred Years War, both revolts arose not only from the desperation of distressed serfs but also from the resentments of more prosperous peasants who inhabited fertile regions but were constrained by the structures of lordship.[4]

The determining influence of agricultural wealth upon political organisation should not be exaggerated, however. Successful rulership required favourable political organisation if it was to extract the wealth of arable heartlands, and many Latin Christian rulers failed to establish such structures. In the twelfth century the counts of Toulouse exerted a notional lordship over a vast area, but they rarely succeeded in imposing their hegemony over the very fertile upper Garonne basin: instead they had to share control of the region and its wealth with the towns, abbeys and petty lords of Languedoc.[5] The relationship between arable land and power was also complex in Italy, where the commercial wealth of cities throughout the period offset the natural poverty of much of the peninsula: from the eleventh century onwards, these cities came to dominate the peninsula's political landscape.[6] Across Latin Christendom, political success often appears to have owed less to environmental factors than to genealogical accident, which usually determined the location of the domains that lay at the base of most dynastic power. The political centre of gravity of a polity could sometimes shift remarkably through changes of dynasties.

---

[4] For the Great Famine: W. C. Jordan, *The Great Famine: Northern Europe in the Early Fourteenth Century* (Princeton, 1988); for a nuanced discussion of the origins and purpose of 'popular' revolts after the Black Death: S. K. Cohn, *Lust for Liberty: The Politics of Social Revolt in Medieval Europe, 1200–1425. Italy, France and Flanders* (Cambridge, MA, 2006), 211–42; for the Jacquerie: L. Feller, *Paysans et seigneurs au Moyen Âge VIIIe–XVe siècles* (Paris, 2007), 260–7.

[5] J. H. Mundy, *Liberty and Political Power in Toulouse, 1050–1230* (New York, 1954). However, L. Macé, *Les Comtes de Toulouse et leur entourage XIIe–XIIIe siècles* (Toulouse, 2000) argues for a strong process of comital consolidation by 1200.

[6] E. Coleman, 'Cities and communes', in D. Abulafia (ed.), *Italy in the Central Middle Ages* (Oxford, 2004), 27–57; G. Raccagni, *The Lombard League, 1167–1225* (Oxford, 2010), 12–25.

Nowhere is this more apparent than in the kingdom of Germany. Before the accession of the Carolingians to the Frankish throne in 751, that dynasty's most important domains had lain in Austrasia (roughly north-eastern France, Belgium, Lorraine and the western Rhineland today). Internecine strife amongst the descendants of Charlemagne after 840 led to the partition of Austrasia: the eastern part went to the Carolingian kings of the East Franks, while the remainder – known henceforth as the kingdom of Lotharingia or Lorraine – came to form a bone of contention between the different branches of the Carolingian dynasty.[7] With the extinction of the East Frankish branch of the family in 918, power in East Francia passed further north to the Saxon Ottonian dynasty. The Ottonians were followed as rulers of East Francia by the Salians in 1024, whose chief strength lay in the Rhineland, and they in turn were superseded in 1138 by the Hohenstaufen, whose power lay primarily in what is now southern Germany, Switzerland and eastern France.[8] With the end of Hohenstaufen rule in 1254, candidates from a succession of dynasties, including from the ruling lines of England, Castile and Holland, were elected as kings of Germany, some of them with little or no domain land within the empire. In the fifteenth century the most successful dynasty was the house of Luxembourg, based in the eastern territories of Bohemia, Silesia and Brandenburg as well as Luxembourg itself;[9] in the fifteenth century this accolade passed to the house of Hapsburg, a dynasty of Swiss origin that built up an unrivalled power base in the south-east of the kingdom of Germany in what is now Austria and Slovenia. The Hapsburgs first acquired the royal title as early as 1273, only to lose it again in 1291, but the dynasty secured a permanent grip on the German throne from 1437, and it retained the imperial title until the formal dissolution of the Holy Roman empire in 1806 (although it had been humiliatingly driven from its Swiss homeland by the embryonic Swiss Confederation in the early fifteenth century). For six centuries the geographical focus of royal power thus shifted back and forth across the empire before becoming permanently lodged in its south-eastern corners.

---

[7] J. Schneider, *Auf der Suche nach dem verlorenen Reich: Lotharingien im 9. und 10. Jahrhundert* (Cologne, 2010); M. Gaillard *et al.* (eds), *De la mer du Nord à la Méditerranée. Francia Media: une région au coeur de l'Europe (c. 840–1050)* (Luxembourg, 2011).

[8] For the Ottonian and Salian kings: J. W. Bernhardt, *Itinerant Kingship and Royal Monasteries in Early Medieval Germany, c. 936–1075* (Cambridge, 1993), 60–70.

[9] The medieval county (later duchy) of Luxembourg comprised a much larger area than the modern state of Luxembourg, including parts of modern Belgium, France and Germany. See also p. 64.

This changing regional focus deserves emphasising because it went a long way to shaping the political culture and institutional basis of the western empire. Successful rule there relied upon the emperor's charismatic presence as he toured his realms, rather than upon institutions based upon authority delegated to officials. This itinerant lifestyle could pose huge practical problems for effective imperial rule: in the 1090s, Henry IV was trapped in Italy for over four years when rebels prevented him crossing the Alps to visit his German territories.[10] By contrast, between the late tenth and the early thirteenth centuries, the Capetian kings of France based their power upon a concentration of lands between the Paris Basin and the Middle Loire around Orléans: although much more localised,[11] this reliance upon a trusted core gave Capetian rule a solidity that their imperial counterparts could never equal. The subjugation of the aristocracy within this core territory by the mid-twelfth century provided them henceforth with a reliable source of knights for wars against their neighbours and for the governance of their lands.[12] Capetian attempts to expand further afield long proved fruitless; the kings of France twice inherited the duchy of Burgundy in the first half of the eleventh century, only to cede it to cadet members of their dynasty to satisfy the claims of younger sons upon the family inheritance, rather than retain it for the royal domain.[13] By the beginning of the thirteenth century, by contrast, Capetian power was sufficiently robust to enable Philip Augustus to annex large parts of western and northern France to his domain at the expense of the Angevin kings of England and the counts of Flanders, and although Artois, Maine, Anjou and Poitou were granted as apanages to Philip's grandsons, the French crown retained vast dominions in Normandy, Languedoc and elsewhere that provided sufficient resources to ensure hegemony within their kingdom.

Forms of Political Organisation

In the papacy and the empire, Latin Christendom had two forms of universal rulership, complementary but competing. The rise of 'papal

[10] I. S. Robinson, *Henry IV of Germany* (Cambridge, 1999), 285–96.
[11] For the itineration of Philip I of France and Henry IV of Germany: A. Mackay *et al.* (eds), *Atlas of Medieval Europe*, 2nd edn (London, 2007), 51–2. Itinerancy was also practised by many powerful Islamic rulers from the eleventh century on: pp. 110, 114, 363, 470, 476–7. For the Byzantines, in contrast, occupation of the city of Constantinople was an attribute of rulership up to 1204, at least: pp. 303–9.
[12] J.-F. Lemarignier, *Le Gouvernement royal au premiers temps capétiens (987–1108)* (Paris, 1965); E. Bournazel, *Le Gouvernement royal au XIIe siècle 1108–80* (Paris, 1975); for the aristocracy of the royal domain, see N. Civel, *La Fleur de France: les seigneurs d'Île-de-France au XIIe siècle* (Turnhout, 2006).
[13] A. W. Lewis, *Royal Succession in Capetian France* (Cambridge, MA, 1981), 8–9, 24–8.

monarchy' will be discussed later in this chapter.[14] The rulers of the successor kingdoms to the Roman empire in the west made fitful acknowledgment of the Byzantine *basileus* until the eighth century. However, from the coronation of Charlemagne in 800 onwards, the western emperors came to be regarded instead as the legitimate ones, an acknowledgment justified by the notion of *translatio imperii*.[15] The western emperors were thereafter held to be universal rulers, even outside the empire itself. Otto, bishop of Freising and biographer of his nephew Emperor Frederick (I) Barbarossa (1152–90), stated that Frederick's imperial crown conferred 'sole rule over the world and the City [of Rome]' (*orbis et urbis*). But this view was also current outside the empire: in 1198, when Otto of Brunswick was elected as 'king of the Romans', or emperor-designate, a Norman monk recorded that Otto had been elected to rule the 'empire of the whole world'.[16]

From the 1030s, when Conrad II absorbed the kingdom of Burgundy into his *Reich*, at least in name,[17] the empire had relatively well-defined and stable external borders with other Christian kingdoms. By contrast, the framework of early medieval Christian kingdoms was very unstable, as kingdoms rose and fell in Britain and Ireland, while conversion to Christianity led to the expansion of Latin Christendom into east-central Europe and Scandinavia and the establishment of new kingdoms based around the converted peoples such as the Danes, Norwegians, Poles, Czechs and Hungarians.[18] From the eleventh century, the borders of kingdoms in most of Latin Christendom stabilised; but Latin Christian expansion in southern Europe and the Mediterranean lands led to the later establishment of new kingdoms and other polities there, such as the kingdoms of Castile (1065), Jerusalem (1099–1100), Sicily (1130) and Portugal (1139); the principality of Antioch (1098); and the Latin Empire

---

[14] See pp. 386–9; also pp. 146, 155–6, 165–8, 173–6.
[15] W. Goez, *Translatio imperii: ein Beitrag zur Geschichte des Geschichtsdenkens und der politischen Theorien im Mittelalter und in der frühen Neuzeit* (Tübingen, 1958).
[16] Otto of Freising, *The Deeds of Frederick Barbarossa*, tr. C. C. Mierow (New York, 1953), 135; *Les Annales de l'Abbaye Saint-Pierre de Jumièges*, ed. and tr. J. Laporte (Rouen, 1954), 77.
[17] H. Wolfram, *Conrad II, 990–1039: Emperor of Three Kingdoms*, tr. D. A. Kaiser (Philadelphia, 2003), 239–46. The kingdom of Burgundy comprised the south-eastern parts of modern France east of the rivers Saône and Rhône (the historical regions of Provence, Dauphiné, Savoy and Franche-Comté), as well as western Switzerland. It should be distinguished from the duchy of Burgundy, mentioned earlier, west of the river Saône. For an entertaining discussion of the various regions known as Burgundy in history: N. Davies, *Vanished Kingdoms: The History of Half-Forgotten Europe* (London, 2011), 90–149. See also Map 4 (inset).
[18] See especially N. Berend (ed.), *Christianization and the Rise of Christian Monarchy: Scandinavia, Central Europe and Rus' c. 900–1200* (Cambridge, 2007).

of Constantinople (1204).[19] Other polities, notably the Iberian kingdoms of León (frequently united with Castile) and Aragon, grew enormously in extent, chiefly at the expense of the peninsula's Muslim states. The emergence of new kingdoms along the northern, eastern and southern fringes of Christendom was matched by the gradual disappearance of kingdoms and even the title of king itself in Ireland, Wales, and the Highlands and Islands of Scotland. Ireland is a case of particular interest because its norms of kingship contrasted so strongly with the rest of Latin Christendom. 'In Ireland kings were as numerous as earls were elsewhere', one Anglo-Norman commentator observed;[20] but in fact Irish kingship existed on several levels, from the *ard-rí* or high king to the provincial kings of Leinster, Munster or Connacht and to the local kingdoms whose dynasties provided the candidates for the provincial and high kingship.[21] In Wales, Moray and the Scottish Isles, kings persisted until the twelfth century (and in the Isle of Man until the thirteenth),[22] but pressure from the kings of England and Scotland, combined with lack of recognition from the papacy, eventually deprived the ruling dynasties in these regions of royal status. In Ireland, by contrast, various levels of kingship survived, despite their endemic weakness, until the Tudor reorganisation of the island in the 1540s.

If the dynastic kingdom remained the norm in Latin Christendom throughout the middle ages and beyond, actual forms of political organisation became much more diverse during the period. Dynastic kingdoms came to share the continent with autonomous city states governed by communes, of which the most potent examples were the Italian maritime republics, such as Venice, Genoa and Pisa, and the great cities of the Lombard plain; with ecclesiastical lordships, ranging from archiepiscopal and episcopal counties to the Teutonic Knights' *Ordenstaat* in the Baltic

---

[19] R. Bartlett, *The Making of Europe: Conquest, Colonization and Cultural Change, 950–1300* (London and New York, 1993), 39–43; for this process, see Berend (ed.), *Christianization*.

[20] *The Deeds of the Normans in Ireland / La Geste des Engleis en Yrelande*, ed. and tr. E. Mullally (Dublin, 2002), 108 (ll. 2189–90). However, the author continues (ll. 2191–6): 'but whoever holds Meath, Leinster, Desmond, Munster, Connacht and Ulster [...] are the chief kings of Ireland, according to the Irish' (my translation). For the norms of kingship in continental Latin Christendom, see pp. 251–89.

[21] E.g. Diarmuid MacMurchada, king of Leinster and contender for the high kingship, whose hereditary power base was Uí Chennselaig – approximately modern Co. Wexford: M.-T. Flanagan, 'Strategies of lordship in pre-Norman and post-Norman Leinster', *Anglo-Norman Studies* 20 (1998), 107–26, esp. 111–14.

[22] D. Crouch, 'The slow death of kingship in Glamorgan, 1067–1158', *Morgannwg* 29 (1985), 20–41; *The Acts of Welsh Rulers 1120–1283*, ed. H. Pryce and C. Insley (Cardiff, 2005); R. A. McDonald, *The Kingdom of the Isles: Scotland's Western Seabord, c.1100–c.1336* (East Linton, 1997).

and the dominion of the Knights Hospitaller in Rhodes;[23] and with later medieval leagues such as the Swiss Confederation and the Hanseatic League. In some regions, power was effectively devolved to the level of castle-based lords who acknowledged no effective superior. However, by far the most widespread form of political organisation below the level of the kingdom, from the tenth century onwards, was the dynastic principality.[24] Regional aristocracies were the chief heirs of the Carolingian political order, and the emergence of territorial principalities as Carolingian dynastic control fragmented in the ninth and tenth centuries is one of the most important developments for medieval Latin Christian political culture. The territorial prince aimed for military, legal and fiscal control over his whole territory, including over the church, and usually aspired to exercise many if not all the same powers as contemporary crowned heads. Principalities coalesced through a mixture of dynastic claims and marriage alliances, seigneurial protection and brute force: the aggrandisement of the Plantagenet dynasty has been called 'an unholy combination of princely greed and genealogical accident'.[25] It was at this level that women were most likely to be found inheriting and exercising power, since female succession to a county did not pose the same ideological or theological difficulties as the succession of women as queens.[26] The territorial princes varied immensely in status and power: we might include amongst their numbers not only the dukes and counts of much of Latin Christendom but also the great barons of thirteenth-century Ireland and the Welsh March, or the *signori* (despots) of later medieval Italy.[27] Nevertheless, their political culture had many characteristics in common: their households comprised military retinues but also, from the twelfth century onwards, princely courts emerged as the focus for politics and as centres for patronage of the church and the arts.

---

[23] See also pp. 151–5, 169–70.

[24] See also pp. 64, 74–5, 149–50, 152–3. Comparable, although operating to very different scales and dynamics, are the regional dynasties and powers that emerged from the Abbasids' relicts: pp. 220–2. Byzantium did not see quite such a proliferation, even after 1204 and the emergence of new empires and statelets: pp. 438–40, 443–7.

[25] J. C. Holt, 'The end of the Anglo-Norman realm', *Proceedings of the British Academy* 61 (1975), 223–65 at 239–40.

[26] The succession of women as queens in their own right (rather than as widows and regents for children) is rare in Byzantium as well as the west: see pp. 397–8; also pp. 21, 55, 203–4, 299, 300, 307, 312–13. Female sultans and suchlike powerholders are known, albeit only very rarely, in the Islamic sphere: pp. 232, 504.

[27] For the *signori*: B. Paton and J. Law (eds), *Communes and Despots in Medieval and Renaissance Italy* (Farnham, 2010); T. Dean, 'The rise of the *signori*', in *NCMH* 5, 458–78.

Since their territories were regarded as units of inheritance, dynasties frequently held several principalities at once. Such multiple inheritances posed considerable challenges for political organisation, including for their ideological framework, for judicial and fiscal organisation, for methods of patronage and reward, and for court culture. In the twelfth century, the counts of Anjou accumulated their Angevin (or Plantagenet) empire (1144–1204) that came to comprise the kingdoms of England and Ireland, the duchies of Normandy, Aquitaine and Brittany, and the counties of Anjou and Maine. About the same time the royal dynasty of Aragon came to rule the counties of Barcelona and Provence, acquiring extensive rights and claims along the southern littoral of modern France, while in the thirteenth century members of the same family also acquired the kingdom of Sicily, Sardinia, and the Balearic Islands through a mixture of inheritance claims and conquest.[28] The changing fortunes of such collections of principalities shows the need to avoid focusing primarily upon kingdoms: the political organisation of the period was characterised by a constantly shifting mosaic of dynastic territorial principalities overlaid by a remarkably conservative matrix of kingdoms, most of them associated with particular *gentes*.

The Sources of Hegemony

Military Power

In 1500 as in 700, power in most of Latin Christendom lay with the landowning elite, but during this period there were great shifts in the distribution of power within that elite: in the relationships between temporal and ecclesiastical power; in the function and nature of patronage and office-holding; and in the material and cultural resources from which power was derived. Moreover, as trading networks grew and became more complex, especially from the tenth century onwards, an alternative source of power emerged in the form of commercial wealth. It allowed urban oligarchies in Italy to challenge imperial hegemony as early as the eleventh century and ensured that urban communities played a considerable role in the political culture of later medieval transalpine Europe as well.[29]

---

[28] For convenient summaries: T. N. Bisson, *The Medieval Crown of Aragon: A Short History* (Oxford, 1986); D. Abulafia, *The Western Mediterranean Kingdoms, 1200–1500* (London, 1997).

[29] Raccagni, *Lombard League*; D. Nicholas, *The Growth of the Medieval City from Late Antiquity to the Early Fourteenth Century* (London, 1997); D. Nicholas, *The Later Medieval City, 1300–1500* (London, 1997).

The dominance of military elites took several forms. The most important was the organisation of property, labour and economic resources in support of the elite. While debates about the nature and significance of 'feudalism' and 'feudal society' will continue to rage for many more years,[30] there can be no doubt that property relations and labour across much of Europe in the early and central middle ages came to be organised primarily to provide the military elite with the resources needed for its arms and armour, fortresses, horses, lifestyle, and culture of patronage.

The aristocratic monopoly of force varied in nature across Latin Christendom, but three aspects can serve as criteria for analysis and comparison and as barometers of effectiveness, and were the focus for negotiation – and frequently for conflict. The first of these is the degree of control that rulers exerted over the fortifications within their territory. Where subordinates were allowed to fortify on their own account, certain procedures ensured that the ruler retained overall control: these might include maintaining a right of entry into subordinates' castles (rendability) and requiring their subordinates to seek licences to fortify.[31]

A second indicator of a ruler's power is duties of military service. Some princes could rely upon a general summons of men fit to bear arms, regardless of whether the rulers were immediate lords of these warriors: examples include Henry II of England's Assize of Arms (1181), the *arrière-ban* or *retrobannum* in late Capetian France, and the general summons of the fourteenth-century kings of Hungary.[32] However, duties of service were often much more constrained and owed only by subordinates to their immediate lords. The disappearance, on either side of the millennium, of a free peasantry with the right to bear arms in much of southern Europe seems to indicate a great shift in the political organisation and mores of this part of Christendom.[33] The quantification of service was another aspect of military culture that required political negotiation, especially where obligations of military service began to be commuted

---

[30] S. Reynolds, *Fiefs and Vassals: The Medieval Evidence Reinterpreted* (Oxford, 1994).

[31] For a wide-ranging discussion of castle customs and 'rendability': C. Coulson, *The Castle in Medieval Society: Fortresses in England, France and Ireland in the Central Middle Ages* (Oxford, 2003).

[32] *English Historical Documents, II: 1042–1189*, ed. D. C. Douglas and G. W. Greenway, 2nd edn (London, 1981), no. 27; J. R. Strayer, *The Reign of Philip the Fair* (Princeton, 1984), 372–9, esp. 376; X. Hélary, *L'Armée du roi de France: la guerre de Saint Louis à Philippe le Bel* (Paris, 2012), 111–72; P. Engel, *The Realm of St Stephen: A History of Medieval Hungary, 895–1526*, tr. T. Pálosfalvi, ed. A. Ayton (London, 2001), 183–5. The idea that the Anglo-Saxon *fyrd* was a similar general levy was largely disproved by R. Abels, *Lordship and Military Obligation in Anglo-Saxon England* (Berkeley, 1988).

[33] P. Bonnassie, *From Slavery to Feudalism in Southwest Europe*, tr. J. Birrell (Cambridge, 2000), 217–37; P. Freedman, *The Origins of Peasant Servitude in Medieval Catalonia* (Cambridge, 1991).

for cash. Under Henry II of England, for instance, inquests were held in England in 1166 and in Normandy in 1172 to determine and record exact quotas of military service. Such quotas served as a means of defining political relations between ruler and subject as much as a means of mustering armies. Late in Henry II's reign, the king, under grave pressure from his enemies, wrote to the English baron William Marshal ordering him to hasten to France with as many knights as he could bring – there was no mention of quotas or fixed obligations.[34]

Thirdly, the ways in which elites chose to limit the use of their military powers is very revealing of the social constraints that underpinned their culture. In particular, warfare in Latin Europe witnessed a growing disparity between military technology and social status. Historians of warfare have dispelled the myth of the military (as opposed to social) dominance of heavy cavalry before 1300,[35] but the concerted deployment of lowborn infantry, armed with crossbows, longbows or pikes, to defeat noble cavalry becomes a much more prominent feature of warfare from the late thirteenth century onwards. The change reflected not so much advances in military technology as shifting social attitudes and new forms of recruiting and funding armies. On the one hand, noble commanders were becoming less inhibited in using the skills of their lowborn foot soldiers to inflict defeat upon their noble rivals: hence Edward III and his son Edward, prince of Wales (the Black Prince), were prepared to allow their archers to shoot down the flower of French chivalry at the battles of Crécy (1346) and Poitiers (1356).[36] On the other hand, developments in the fiscal apparatus available to rulers now allowed them to raise mercenaries and to rely upon soldiers recruited through contractual rather than feudal service. The more organised mercenary bands could sometimes become independent agents in political culture. In the early fourteenth century, mercenaries previously in Aragonese employ, known as the Catalan Company of the East, established their own small state in central Greece. During the Hundred Years War, the Free Companies from the disbanded royal armies took over parts of central and southern France after the kings of England and France made peace in 1360; while later medieval Italian politics was dominated by the *condottieri* who served the warring cities of northern and central Italy.[37]

---

[34] N. Vincent, 'William Marshal, King Henry II, and the honour of Châteauroux', *Archives* 25 (2000), 1–15.

[35] M. Bennett, 'The myth of the military supremacy of knightly cavalry', in M. J. Strickland (ed.), *Armies, Chivalry and Warfare* (Stamford, 1998), 304–16.

[36] C. J. Rogers, 'The age of the Hundred Years War', in M. Keen (ed.), *Medieval Warfare: A History* (Oxford, 1999), 136–60 at 141–6.

[37] K. Fowler, *Medieval Mercenaries* (Oxford, 2001); J. France (ed.), *Mercenaries and Paid Men: The Mercenary Identity in the Middle Ages* (Leiden, 2008); for the Catalan Company: P. Lock, *The Franks in the Aegean, 1204–1500* (London, 1995), 104–6, 111–27; D.

The Christian duties of keeping the peace, and of protecting the weak and the church, could assist rulers in maintaining their hegemony. Throughout the period, rulers used a discourse of maintaining peace as a justification for imposing their authority by force over their territory – and indeed for intervening in neighbouring territories on occasion. While it was primarily monarchs and princes who benefited from the peace discourse in this way, the Peace Movements of late tenth- and eleventh-century France are examples of associations of local landowners, church-men, and possibly even more low-born arms-bearers that were formed to reduce aristocratic violence. Although the purpose, coherence, social context and historical importance of the Peace and Truce of God are all much debated,[38] the associative political structures that produced these events contrast strongly with princely or royal attempts to enforce their authority through a discourse of peace. Nevertheless, in the hands of an ambitious prince, peace proclamations could become a method for con-solidating power, as in the example of William the Conqueror in Normandy (1047), or the *Landfrieden* for the princes of the empire in the twelfth and thirteenth centuries.[39] However, the Norman example should come as a warning not to take these solemn declarations at face value. For instance, by 1190 the dukes' chief concern regarding the Truce of God in Normandy was primarily as a source of revenue;[40] while the effectiveness of the *Landfrieden* in bringing peace to Germany was limited. The Peace Movements also served an ecclesiastical purpose for the reordering of Christendom: it is no coincidence that Pope Urban II extended the peace decrees to the whole of Christendom at the Council of Clermont (1095), at which he also launched the expedition that we know as the First Crusade.[41] The discourse of peace continued to play a part in papal policy: in the early thirteenth century, the suppression of

---

Jacoby, 'The Catalan Company in the east: the evolution of an itinerant army (1303–1311)', in G. I. Halfond (ed.), *The Medieval Way of War: Studies in Medieval Military History in Honor of Bernard S. Bachrach* (Farnham, 2015), 29–46.

[38] T. Head and R. Landes (eds), *The Peace of God: Social Violence and Religious Response in France around the Year 1000* (Ithaca, NY, 1992); D. Barthélemy, *L'An mil et la paix de Dieu: la France chrétienne et féodale 980–1060* (Paris, 1999); J. A. Bowman, 'Councils, memory and mills: the early development of the Peace of God in Catalonia', *EME* 8 (1999), 99–129. On more associative forms: pp. 154–5, 174, 175.

[39] D. Bates, *Normandy before 1066* (London, 1982), 163–4, 176, 179; B. Arnold, *Princes and Territories in Medieval Germany* (Cambridge, 1991), 43–6; W. C. Brown, *Violence in Medieval Europe* (Harlow, 2010), 223–5, 228–32, 238.

[40] Rouen, Archives de la Seine-Maritime, G 4484 (*Calendar of Documents Preserved in France, I: AD 918–1206*, ed. J. H. Round (London, 1899), no. 55): regulation by King Richard I of fines for homicide on account of the Truce, renewing an earlier grant by Henry I of England in 1135 (*ibid.*, no. 290). See also pp. 278–9.

[41] H. Hoffmann, *Gottesfriede und Treuga Dei* (Stuttgart, 1964), 220–5.

heresy in Languedoc was always known in Rome as 'the business of peace and the faith'.[42]

If the discourse of 'peace' formed an integral part of political culture, so did its opposite, 'violence'. The meaning and nature of violence in many medieval sources is bound up with clerical discourses of legitimate property-ownership or authority, so that it was the violation of property-rights, rather than physical brutality, that constituted violence;[43] it is therefore difficult to quantify its extent, and consequently its form and purpose varied according to context. For some historians it was a creative tool of seigneurial political culture; for others, notably Thomas Bisson, it was an 'anti-political' disruption of the legitimate order that was curbed by the rise of administrative monarchies in the twelfth century. The discourse of violence concerned the legitimacy as much as the nature of such violations, in the eyes of both their perpetrators and their victims (at least where the latter formed part of the elite, especially ecclesiastical institutions). In areas without strong princely rule, it is now recognised that compromise and arbitration prevailed rather than anarchy,[44] but, even where rulers did exercise coercive authority, noble expectations of using violence, even open warfare, to resolve their disputes remained strong.[45] Political culture also included cycles of physical violence provoked by the desire, or need, for vengeance, especially feuds: here, too, specific norms prevailed, usually conditioned by codes of honour, networks of political affiliation, and often – but not always – kinship.[46]

---

[42] M. Zerner, 'Le *negotium pacis et fidei*, ou l'affaire de paix et de foi: une désignation de la Croisade albigeoise à revoir', in R. M. Dessi (ed.), *Prêcher la paix et discipliner la société: Italie, France, Angleterre (XIIIe–XVe siècle)* (Turnhout, 2005), 63–101.

[43] On this discourse of violence and justice, and on the rhetoric of reform, see pp. 262–3, 271–2, 276.

[44] P. Geary, 'Vivre en conflit dans une France sans État: typologie des mécanismes de règlement des conflits (1050–1200)', *Annales: économies, sociétés, civilisations* 41 (1986), 1107–33; S. D. White (ed.), *Feuding and Peacemaking in Eleventh-Century France* (Aldershot, 2005). For important discussions about the political exercise of 'violence', include the debate concerning the 'feudal revolution': *P&P* (1994–7); G. Halsall (ed.), *Violence and Society in the Early Medieval West* (Woodbridge, 1998); R. W. Kaeuper, *Chivalry and Violence in Medieval Europe* (Oxford, 1999); R. W. Kaeuper (ed.), *Violence in Medieval Society* (Princeton, 2000); T. N. Bisson, *The Crisis of the Twelfth Century* (Princeton, 2009); Brown, *Violence in Medieval Europe*. For a useful summary of the scholarship concerning both 'political' and 'interpersonal' violence: H. Skoda, *Medieval Violence: Physical Brutality in Northern France, 1270–1330* (Oxford, 2013), 2–8. See also W. C. Brown and P. Górecki (eds), *Conflict in Medieval Europe: Changing Perspectives on Society and Culture* (Aldershot, 2003).

[45] J. Firnhaber-Baker, *Violence and the State in Languedoc, 1250–1400* (Cambridge, 2014).

[46] R. Fletcher, *Bloodfeud: Murder and Revenge in Anglo-Saxon England* (London, 2002); P. R. Hyams, *Rancor and Reconciliation in Medieval England* (Ithaca, NY, 2003); White (ed.), *Feuding and Peacemaking*; S. A. Throop and P. R. Hyams (eds), *Vengeance in the Middle Ages: Emotion, Religion and Feud* (Burlington, VT, 2010); D. Barthélemy *et al.*

Economic Power

Although it is a truism that land equalled power in medieval Europe, the equation between land and power varied considerably across the continent.[47] To begin with, the social significance of land was far from constant. Barbara Rosenwein has argued that the rise of the Cluniac order in the tenth and eleventh centuries helped to provoke a fundamental shift in attitudes towards land, from primarily social to chiefly economic significance. She has sought to demonstrate that early medieval noble families and the monasteries that they patronised held land in common as a mark of social status and shared political interests as much as a source of income. The Cluniacs, however, defined rights to lands much more exclusively, treating grants to them as perpetual and denouncing as 'violence' the attempts by donor families to recover or maintain their claims in this land. We might even characterise this as a Cluniac revolution in land that virtually invented the concept of landed property. Its social, political, economic and legal consequences were profound.[48]

More generally, the control of economic resources was an intrinsic aspect of lordship across much of Latin Christendom throughout the period. Forests (with their timber, grazing rights and game), waterways and mills held pride of place amongst seigneurial assets, along with places where tolls could be levied such as bridges, ports and town gates. But other material resources could offset agrarian poverty, such as the ore mines which supported *seigneuries minières* in Languedoc and filled English royal coffers in Cornwall and Cumberland, or the coal which bolstered the revenues of the lords of Gower in south Wales.[49] In the later middle ages, rights over mills and similar resources were sometimes

---

(eds), *La Vengeance, 400–1200* (Rome, 2006). Definitions of the feud vary significantly within this corpus.

[47] On land in general: pp. 150, 152–3, 158; on the situational dimension to so much in political thinking: pp. 254, 259–64, 288–9. For the importance of land-rights in providing income, enhancing status yet not being pivotal to political advancement in Byzantium: pp. 200–1, 420–3, 427–8, 434–5. Grants of land-rights and -revenues in the Islamic sphere operated on rather different, yet recognisable, patterns: pp. 241, 464, 484.

[48] B. H. Rosenwein, *To Be the Neighbour of St Peter: The Social Meaning of Cluny's Property, 909–1049* (Ithaca, NY, 1989). See also the comments by R. I. Moore, *The First European Revolution, c.970–1215* (Oxford, 2000), 81–6.

[49] H. Débax, *La Féodalité languedocienne XIe–XIIe siècles* (Toulouse, 2003), 294–6; M.-C. Bailly-Maître, 'Mines et monnaies: les sources du pouvoir dans le Languedoc occidental', in M. Bourin (ed.), *En Languedoc au XIIIe siècle: le temps du sac de Béziers* (Perpignan, 2010), 125–42; F. Madeline, 'Le don de plomb dans le patronage monastique d'Henri II Plantagenêt: usages et conditions de la production du plomb anglais dans la seconde moitié du XIIe siècle', *Archéologie médiévale* 39 (2009), 31–51; G. R. Lewis, *The Stannaries: A Study of the Medieval Tin Miners of Cornwall and Devon* (Truro, 1965); for the lord of Gower's coal mines in the Clyne valley near Swansea (1319), see *Cartae et alia*

partitioned amongst the offspring of aristocratic families, both as a ready source of cash and as a badge of shared status in face of social challenges from those regarded as of lesser birth.[50]

One of the most varied powers in Latin Christendom was the ability to raise direct taxation. Although some examples occur in the early middle ages, such as the *geld* levied by the late Anglo-Saxon kings of England, direct taxation mainly developed in the later middle ages. Even strong monarchies found such powers to be a cause of great political tension, and rulers were invariably forced into concessions in return for the consent of their great subjects and, sometimes, of more broadly based assemblies as well.

To avoid these difficulties, rulers continued to rely upon their domain estates as the prime source of their hegemony, and efforts to secure such lands remained a recurrent source of political conflict: examples include the disputes over the inheritance of Matilda of Tuscany in the twelfth-century empire; Frederick Barbarossa's attempts to consolidate his control over comital Burgundy in the mid-twelfth century; Philip Augustus' angling for the Vermandois-Valois inheritance and for French Flanders (Artois) in the 1180s and 1190s; and repeated attempts by the late medieval kings of England to divert earldoms and, later, dukedoms into the crown estates.[51] However much the rulers accumulated such domains, they were faced by the unending need to endow their younger sons and non-inheriting daughters. The role of the kin-group in the perpetuation of dynastic hegemony is discussed in the later section on 'Lay Succession', but it is worth mentioning here the difficulty of keeping all domains in the ruler's hands against the claims of their kin. The Capetian kings of France twice had to cede their valuable acquisition of ducal Burgundy to stave off the claims of a cadet branch upon their dynastic lands (in 1002 and 1031–2);[52] after the Barons' War (1258–65), Henry III of England acquired the

---

munimenta quae ad dominium de Glamorgancia pertinent, ed. G. T. Clark, 6 vols (Cardiff, 1910), iii:1067 (no. DCCCXCIII).

[50] E.g. the fief of Gervase de Montgaroult (dépt. Orne, cant. Magny-le-Désert) in Normandy was shared amongst his four daughters *c.*1190, one of whose sons, Richard du Douit, had inherited one-sixteenth of the mill by 1223, suggesting that the rights over the mill were partitioned between all Gervase's heirs: Alençon, Archives de l'Orne, H 6636; D. Power, 'Le régime seigneurial en Normandie (XIIe–XIIIe s.)', in M. Aurell and F. Boutoulle (eds), *Les Seigneuries dans l'espace Plantagenêt (c.1150–c.1250)* (Bordeaux, 2009), 117–36 at 128–9.

[51] P. Munz, *Frederick Barbarossa: A Study in Medieval Politics* (London, 1969), 326–8, 352–8 (Mathildine estates), 116–19 (Burgundy); J. W. Baldwin, *The Government of Philip Augustus: Foundations of French Royal Power in the Middle Ages* (Berkeley, 1986), 17–19, 24–6, 80–2; K. B. McFarlane, 'Had Edward I a policy towards the earls?', *History* 1 (1965), 145–59; H. Castor, *The King, the Crown, and the Duchy of Lancaster: Public Authority and Private Power, 1399–1461* (Oxford, 2000), e.g. 25–50.

[52] See p. 372.

earldoms of Leicester and Derby from the downfallen families of Montfort and Ferrers, only to use them to bolster the endowment of his younger son, Edmund of Lancaster;[53] and the Welsh kingdoms of Gwynedd and Deheubarth were fatally compromised in the thirteenth century by the need to partition the estates in order to meet the claims of the ruling dynasties' cadets.[54] The kingdom of Poland disintegrated completely in the late twelfth century, remaining divided amongst different branches of the Piast dynasty for over a century, with unity maintained only by the church.[55] In the Iberian peninsula, meanwhile, the inheritance of the kings of León and Castile was repeatedly partitioned and reunited amongst the royal sons in the central middle ages, but perhaps the most complex arrangements concerned the later medieval lands of the ruling house of Aragon: at various times between the twelfth and fifteenth centuries Aragon-Catalonia, Provence, Roussillon, Majorca, Naples and Sicily were divided or re-divided as part of dynastic policies.[56] Under the later Capetian and Valois kings of France, conversely, the kingdom itself was never divided, but the needs to provide adequate apanages for the princes of the blood meant that these cadets constructed very substantial power bases. Most famous of these were the Valois dukes of Burgundy who, by the mid-fifteenth century, had established a vast set of domains straddling the Franco-imperial border that made them amongst the most powerful and charismatic rulers in Europe.[57]

In the central and later middle ages, economic power of a different sort was exercised by the wealthier citizens of Latin Christendom's cities and towns. Individual merchants and financiers could influence monarchs,[58] but the rise of banking corporations such as those of the Riccardi, Frescobaldi, Bardi and Peruzzi gave these organisations unprecedented

---

[53] S. Lloyd, 'Edmund [called Edmund Crouchback], first earl of Lancaster and first earl of Leicester (1245–1296)', *ODNB*.

[54] See p. 394.

[55] W. F. Reddaway *et al.* (eds), *The Cambridge History of Poland* (Cambridge, 1950), 43–59, 85–124; J. Wyrozumski, 'Poland in the eleventh and twelfth centuries', in *NCMH* 4, 277–89; S. C. Rowell, 'The central European kingdoms', in *NCMH* 5, 754–78; C. Michaud, 'The kingdoms of central Europe in the fourteenth century', in *NCMH* 6, 735–63 at 743–56; N. Berend *et al.*, *Central Europe in the High Middle Ages: Bohemia, Hungary and Poland, c. 900–c. 1300* (Cambridge, 2013), 172–6, 418–25.

[56] Bisson, *Medieval Crown of Aragon*; Abulafia, *Western Mediterranean Kingdoms*; D. Abulafia, *A Mediterranean Emporium: The Catalan Kingdom of Majorca* (Cambridge, 1994), 9–17; N.-Y. Tonnerre and É. Verry (eds), *Les Princes angevins du XIIIe au XVe siècle: un destin européen* (Rennes, 2004).

[57] See also pp. 147, 169, Map 4 (inset). In Byzantium, the indivisibility of the empire remained paramount until 1204, and even the Palaiologan empire had its centripetal forces: pp. 188–9, 202, 443–5, 446–7. Political formations were more fluid in the Islamic world, especially from the tenth century onwards: pp. 220–6, 228–31, 350–3, 472–7.

[58] For the example of the De la Poles of Kingston-upon-Hull: p. 391 and n. 88.

power thanks to the size of their funds and the invention of instruments such as bills of exchange that enabled them to transfer vast sums of money across Europe. Without such Italian finance, Edward III's early campaigns in the Hundred Years War would have been unaffordable, although he bankrupted his sponsors in the process; in return for giving such support, bankers received advantageous trade concessions and control of customs duties or even lands.[59] Merchants also played an important role in diplomacy: for instance, in 1217 merchants from Saint-Omer in Flanders smoothed the negotiation of peace between the future Louis VIII of France – who had invaded England in support of rebel barons – and the regency of Henry III of England by acting as a conduit for payment of a large English indemnity to Louis.[60] Economic power found a different form through the emergence of craft and town guilds, whose monopolistic practices could dominate the conduct of trade but also exert great influence over broader municipal affairs.[61]

If rulers were to maximise their economic power, they required reliable and efficient officers who could be held to account for income and expenditure. The emergence of the revocable, often salaried official in the central middle ages was an important aspect of the political culture of Latin Christendom and was accompanied by far-reaching changes in administrative procedures for both monarchs and local landowners. Such officials were desirable for more than just economic reasons; the shift to a stronger culture of accountability also reflected more general changes in the nature of rulership and lordship in the later middle ages, changes that were infused with ideas drawn from theology and literature as well as law.[62]

Judicial Power

Throughout the period, judicial powers were sources of legitimacy, domination and cash income across Latin Christendom.[63] The workings of

---

[59] R. W. Kaeuper, *Bankers to the Crown: The Riccardi of Lucca and Edward I* (Princeton, 1972); E. S. Hunt, *The Medieval Super-Companies: A Study of the Peruzzi Company of Florence* (Cambridge, 1994).

[60] *Patent Rolls of the Reign of Henry III Preserved in the Public Record Office, I: 1216–1225* (London, 1901), 114–15 (Florentin le Riche and his son William).

[61] Nicholas, *Growth of the Medieval City*, 129–46.

[62] Important studies include Bisson, *Crisis of the Twelfth Century*, esp. 316–49; J. Sabapathy, *Officers and Accountability in Medieval England, 1170–1300* (Oxford, 2014), with numerous comparisons from other parts of Latin Christendom and beyond; for shifts in the broader mentality of accountability, see also R. F. Berkhofer III, *Day of Reckoning: Power and Accountability in Medieval France* (Philadelphia, 2004). See also pp. 279–80, 283–4, 289.

[63] See for Byzantium: pp. 291, 295–7, 299–303, 323, 325.

tribunals are an invaluable guide to the distribution of power: the role of 'custom' and the ways in which judicial decisions were reached and judgements were imposed are important indications of the power and function of the ruler. The tensions within legal cultures are an important aspect of the changing political organisation of Latin Christendom. At various times customs could mean unwritten social norms, semi-codified written law, fiscal exactions or all three. The creative interaction between 'Germanic' custom, royal 'legislation', Roman law and canon law shaped the various political roles of law in different parts of Latin Europe.

One of the touchstones for the nature and effectiveness of judicial power was the ability to compel attendance in court – known in English law as suit of court – and to enforce punishment for non-attendance or failure to observe agreements. Where there was no strong coercive authority, adherence to judgements or contracts had to be enforced by social pressure, for instance by neighbours or kin.[64] Of particular significance are the changing roles of sureties: in the early middle ages, suretyship functioned as a way of enforcing attendance in the absence of coercive power, whether at the level of a kingdom or at a local level; by contrast, as princely adminstrative rulership developed from the twelfth century onwards, suretyship became primarily a way of indemnifying parties affected by non-attendance in court or failure to pay debts. The practice of giving sureties is therefore a barometer for the strength of coercive power and its relationship to the enforcement of judicial decisions: its political role declined in proportion to the growth of princely judicial power.[65]

Another aspect of judicial power that needs consideration is the contradiction between the universal desire for impartiality in theory and the role of affective lordship in justice in practice. Across the period, the lord's (or lady's) public demonstration of emotions served an integral function in politics. When in 1214 King John of England secured the adherence of a Norman noble who had deserted his allegiance for that of the king of France ten years earlier, he announced that 'we have remitted to Fulk Paynel all fury, rancour, anger, and evil will which we have conceived

---

[64] See White (ed.), *Feuding and Peacemaking*.

[65] For 'suretyship for performance' and 'indemnifying suretyship': D. A. Binchy, 'Celtic suretyship, a fossilized Indo-European institution?', *Irish Jurist* n.s. 7 (1972), 360–72; J. Gilissen, 'Esquisse d'une histoire comparée des sûretés personnelles', *Recueil de la Société Jean Bodin* 28 (1974), 5–127; D. B. Walters, 'The general features of archaic European suretyship', in T. M. Charles-Edwards *et al.* (eds), *Lawyers and Laymen: Studies in the History of Law Presented to Professor Dafydd Jenkins on his Seventy-Fifth Birthday* (Cardiff, 1986), 92–116; D. Power, *The Norman Frontier in the Twelfth and Early Thirteenth Centuries* (Cambridge, 2004), 250–62. For sureties and hostages in general: A. J. Kosto, *Hostages in the Middle Ages* (Oxford, 2012).

against him from times gone by'.[66] Such public emotions also played a role in judicial cases. Rulers could be 'moved to mercy' when acting as judges, just as their *vis et voluntas* (force and will) played a dynamic role in political culture.[67]

The Church

Finally, any discussion of sources of hegemony needs to consider the church: both the exercise of the church's power on its own account; and the dominance and exploitation of its property, offices and powers of legitimation by temporal rulers. Also significant is resistance to ecclesiastical power, whether orthodox or heterodox, and the place of non-Christian minorities, most often Jews[68] but also Muslims in the Christian kingdoms of Sicily, Iberia and the Latin East, as well as Muslims and pagans in the kingdom of Hungary.[69]

The Roman church was transformed in the early and central middle ages. In 700, there were few parish churches and no system of territorially defined parishes. Over the next few centuries, a system of parish churches, defined parish boundaries and churchyards, advowsons (control of appointments to benefices), tithes and glebes (land to support the parish priest) gradually developed across most of Christendom, and the tools of ecclesiastical power were developed through the elaboration of church courts, judicial offices such as archdeacons, and canon law, which was especially significant for such areas of temporal life as marriage, consanguinity, and (il)legitimacy of offspring.[70] The papacy's means of influencing the church at a local level were greatly extended through the use of legatine powers and judges-delegate, from the eleventh and twelfth

[66] *Rotuli Chartarum in Turri Londinensi asservati (1199–1216)*, ed. T. D. Hardy (London, 1837), 207b.
[67] B. H. Rosenwein (ed.), *Anger's Past: The Social Uses of an Emotion in the Middle Ages* (Ithaca, NY, 1998); for the role of royal *vis et voluntas*: J. E. A. Jolliffe, *Angevin Kingship*, 2nd edn (London, 1963).
[68] For a summary of the position of medieval Jews: R. Chazan, *Reassessing Jewish Life in Medieval Europe* (Cambridge, 2010).
[69] N. Berend, *At the Gate of Christendom: Jews, Muslims and 'Pagans' in Medieval Hungary, c.1000–c.1300* (Cambridge, 2001). She shows, however (244–64), that the 'pagan' Cumans outwardly accepted Christianity after their admission into the kingdom of Hungary, although they retained many of their previous religious practices for generations.
[70] Important treatments of these developments include F. D. Logan, *A History of the Church in the Middle Ages* (London, 2002); C. Morris, *The Papal Monarchy: The Western Church from 1050 to 1250* (Oxford, 1989); I. S. Robinson, *The Papacy, 1073–1198: Continuity and Innovation* (Cambridge, 1990); S. Hamilton, *Church and People in the Medieval West, 900–1200* (London, 2013).

centuries respectively,[71] and through greater papal influence upon ecclesiastical appointments. It took the papacy and senior clergy nearly 200 years to enforce celibacy upon its clergy, and this campaign was never wholly successful; however, it did break the link between family inheritance and church property.[72]

The church also developed excommunication and interdict as weapons of enforcement, and, although frequently limited in their effectiveness, these became a crucial aspect of the church's power from the late eleventh century onwards. Most dramatically, the excommunication of King Henry IV of Germany in 1076 led to the future emperor's submission at Canossa to Pope Gregory VII the following year: whatever the short-term benefits to the emperor, the symbolism of this event had incalculable consequences for the balance of power between *regnum* and *sacerdotium*.[73] The repeated papal and episcopal excommunications of Counts Raymond VI and Raymond VII of Toulouse dealt heavy blows to the counts' authority that seriously hampered their ability to resist the Albigensian Crusade (1209–29).[74] Yet although churchmen frequently used excommunication and interdict to humble or restrain individual rulers and landowners, these weapons also came to be used, paradoxically, to bolster temporal power. Rebels routinely faced excommunication by churchmen loyal to the ruler, for, as the Old Testament put it, 'rebellion was as the sin of witchcraft',[75] and the fierce condemnation in the two books of Samuel of any assault against the king as the 'Lord's Anointed' bolstered royal authority against revolt.[76] In 1216, after the death of King John of England, the papal legate Guala used the sentence of anathema to prevent the future Louis VIII of France from snatching the English crown, despite his control of London and several other centres of royal power; it was universally accepted that no

---

[71] For regional studies of judges-delegate: J. Sayers, *Papal Judges Delegate in the Province of Canterbury, 1198–1254: A Study in Ecclesiastical Jurisdiction and Administration* (Oxford, 1971); H. Müller (ed.), *Päpstliche Delegationsgerichtsbarkeit in der Normandie (12. und 13. Jahrhundert)*, 2 vols (Bonn, 1997).

[72] For the impact of Gregorian reform upon the complex relations between churches and property: S. Wood, *The Proprietary Church in the Medieval West* (Oxford, 2006), esp. 851–921.

[73] H. S. J. Cowdrey, *Pope Gregory VII, 1023–1085* (Oxford, 1998), 153–67. Robinson, *Henry IV of Germany*, 143–64 emphasises the benefits that accrued to the king through his submission.

[74] M. Roquebert, *L'Épopée cathare*, 5 vols (Paris, 1970–98; repr. 2007), e.g. i:288–93, 515–35; iii:286–8; R. Kay (ed.), *The Council of Bourges, 1225: A Documentary History* (Aldershot, 2002), 117–22.

[75] 1 Samuel (1 Kings), 15:23.

[76] 1 Samuel (1 Kings), 24:6–10, 26:23; 2 Samuel (2 Kings), 1:13–16. See M. Strickland, 'Against the Lord's anointed: aspects of warfare and baronial rebellion in England and Normandy, 1075–1265', in G. Garnett and J. Hudson (eds), *Law and Government in Medieval England and Normandy* (Cambridge, 1994), 204–57.

excommunicate could be validly crowned, and the legate ensured that John's young son was crowned instead and that Louis felt the full weight of papal opposition.[77] In 1171 Frederick Barbarossa and Louis VII agreed to expel all the unruly mercenary bands known as Brabançons or *Coterelli* from a vast area bounded by the Rhine, the Alps and Paris. Yet their proclamations calling for the expulsion of the hated mercenaries within this vast region largely relied upon excommunication or the actions of local magnates for enforcement, continuing older practices derived from the peace associations of the previous century. This was a tacit admission of the ineffectiveness of both imperial and French royal power, but it also underlined the church's central role in maintaining the temporal political order.[78] The heyday of excommunication as a political weapon for the church was the thirteenth century, and in the later middle ages both the papacy and local churchmen would prove increasingly impotent in the face of lay defiance. Nevertheless, it still had sufficient force to have grave political consequences when the papacy pronounced sentences of excommunication against Henry VIII of England in the 1530s and his daughter Elizabeth I in 1570.

The church's domination was reinforced through its near-monopoly of the technology of literacy across most of the period; consequently, ecclesiastical chroniclers and writers of history were also the chief custodians of historical memory. Both these monopolies were loosened in the later middle ages, as lay literacy increased across Europe and lay chronicles became more common; the appearance of literate laymen in princely administrations was a particularly significant development.[79] However, the church's ideological power was reinforced through two developments of the twelfth and thirteenth centuries: the emergence of universities, allowing for a much more systematic approach to theology and providing clerical elites with more rigorous training in canon law; and a more systematic approach to religious dissent, especially through the development of the Inquisition. Although the medieval 'inquisition' should be seen as a process rather than an institution, and its effectiveness was always subject

---

[77] *The Historical Collections of Walter of Coventry*, ed. W. Stubbs, 2 vols (London, 1872–3), ii:232–3; C. Petit-Dutaillis, *Étude sur la vie et le règne de Louis VIII* (Paris, 1894), 115–16; *The Letters and Charters of Cardinal Guala Bicchieri, Papal Legate in England 1216–1218*, ed. N. Vincent (Woodbridge, 1996), xxxix–xlii.

[78] *Recueil des Historiens des Gaules et de la France*, ed. D. Bouquet *et al.*, 24 vols in 25 (Paris, 1738–1904), xvi:697–8; M. Strickland, *War and Chivalry: The Conduct and Perception of War in England and Normandy, 1066–1217* (Cambridge, 1996), 300.

[79] R. V. Turner, 'The *miles literatus* in twelfth- and thirteenth-century England: how rare a phenomenon?', *American Historical Review* 83 (1978), 928–45; M. Aurell, *Le Chevalier lettré: savoir et conduite de l'aristocratie aux XIIe et XIIIe siècles* (Paris, 2011). On literacy in the later middle ages: pp. 277–8, 281–4.

to lay veto, it nevertheless represents a major qualitative advance in the church's sources of power: indeed, James Given and John Arnold have argued that the Inquisition reshaped the *mentalités* of the people who were interrogated. More mundanely, the penalties handed out by the Inquisition with the support of lay powers, notably the use of long-term imprisonment in prisons (known in France as *murs*, literally walls), humiliating penances, and exclusion from public life, served to enforce the ecclesiastical authority. The activities of the Inquisition were restricted in both time and space, but they are the most dramatic demonstration of the social domination that the medieval church could achieve.[80]

The Continuation of Elite Hegemony

The Enforcement of Status

The elites of Latin Christendom used several methods to shore up their hegemony. First, throughout the period the emphasis upon noble birth was more or less universal, regardless of the very different social structures across Europe; and conversely, both rulers and chroniclers frequently expressed anxieties about those of 'servile' or 'ignoble' birth unduly exercising power and about the penetration of 'new men' into the ranks of the aristocracy. In 1127, when Count Charles the Good of Flanders attempted to reimpose servile status upon some officials who were allegedly of servile descent or had married female serfs, they assassinated him rather than suffer the legal and fiscal consequences of his claims upon them.[81] Late medieval sumptuary laws varied significantly between northern and southern Europe, notably in the matter of gender, but all were intended to enforce social distinctions through dress and display.[82]

---

[80] J. B. Given, *Inquisition and Medieval Society: Power, Discipline, and Resistance in Languedoc* (Ithaca, NY, 1997); J. H. Arnold, *Inquisition and Power: Catharism and the Confessing Subject in Medieval Languedoc* (Philadelphia, 2001). For the repercussions of inquisitorial procedures, especially in Italian cities: G. Geltner, *The Medieval Prison: A Social History* (Princeton, 2008). One may compare these with the ideas about the custodianship and advocacy of correct belief and religious law in the Islamic sphere: pp. 104–5, 110–11, 126–7, 331–6, 341, 347–9. The Byzantine church had an important but not monopolistic role in determining orthodoxy: pp. 293, 299, 301–2, 311–13.

[81] Galbert of Bruges, *The Murder of Charles the Good, Count of Flanders*, tr. J. B. Ross, 2nd edn (New York, 1967), esp. 96–100.

[82] C. Kovesi Killerby, *Sumptuary Law in Italy, 1200–1500* (Oxford, 2000); for a comparison between Florence, Nuremberg and London: A. Hunt, *Governing of the Consuming Passions: History of Sumptuary Law* (New York, 1996), 25–33, 201–13; F. Lachaud, 'Dress and social status in England before the sumptuary laws', in P. Coss and M. Keen (eds), *Heraldry, Pageantry and Social Display in Medieval England* (Woodbridge, 2002), 105–23.

The need to make such laws is, of course, an indication that social ranks were more open in practice than in theory. Louis IX's biographer, Jean de Joinville, claimed to have berated Robert de Sorbon, founder of the Collège de Sorbonne, for wearing finer woollen clothing than the king himself, despite being of peasant birth, whereas Joinville, a leading noble of Champagne, had inherited the right to wear furs; but Sorbon's humble origins had not prevented him from becoming one of the most influential figures in thirteenth-century Paris.[83] It is also true that definitions and concepts of nobility altered across the period:[84] if, in the early middle ages, to be noble was primarily a moral concept, and one that evaluated people by degrees (*nobiliores, nobilissimi*), by the late middle ages nobility had acquired formal legal status and was a quality that could be formally conferred by royal grant.[85]

Another restriction upon entry to the elite was the emergence of a defined concept of knighthood between the eleventh and thirteenth centuries. While there is much debate regarding the origins and nature of knighthood and its relationship to the concept of nobility, what is clear is that, by the thirteenth century, entry to the ranks of the knights was restricted both by the methods and ceremonies for entry and by the greater costs of membership.[86] The restrictions meant that many men who were eligible for knighthood on social grounds – usually because they were eldest sons of knights – deferred taking on the burdens of knighthood, forming a class of squires who were the bedrock of 'gentry' society across much of western Europe.[87]

[83] Joinville was dressed 'de vair et de vert', Sorbon was 'vestu de plus riche camelin que le roy n'est': Joinville, *Vie de Saint Louis* § 35–6, ed. and French tr. J. Monfrin (Paris, 1995), 16–19; *Chronicles of the Crusades*, tr. M. R. B. Shaw (Harmondsworth, 1963), 170–1.
[84] This is clear from P. Contamine (ed.), *La Noblesse au Moyen Âge* (Paris, 1976); A. J. Duggan (ed.), *Nobles and Nobility in Medieval Europe* (Woodbridge, 2000).
[85] D. Crouch, *The Birth of Nobility: Constructing Aristocracy in England and France, 900–1300* (Harlow, 2005); C. S. Jaeger, *The Origins of Courtliness: Civilizing Trends and the Formation of Courtly Ideals, 923–1210* (Philadelphia, 1985).
[86] The bibliographies for knighthood and its relationship to the concept of nobility are immense, comprising both pan-European and regional studies. See, amongst many works, Contamine (ed.), *La Noblesse au Moyen Âge*; G. Duby, *The Chivalrous Society*, tr. C. Postan (London, 1977); T. Hunt, 'The emergence of the knight in France and England 1000–1200', in W. H. Jackson (ed.), *Knighthood in Medieval Literature* (Woodbridge, 1981), 1–22; J. Bumke, *The Concept of Knighthood in the Middle Ages*, tr. W. T. H. and E. Jackson (New York, 1982); Strickland, *War and Chivalry*, 19–23, 142–9; J. Flori, *Chevaliers et chevalerie au Moyen Âge* (Paris, 1998); Crouch, *Birth of Nobility*; D. Barthélemy, *La Chevalerie: de la Germanie antique à la France du XIIe siècle* (Paris, 2007); Aurell, *Le Chevalier lettré*.
[87] Crouch, *Birth of Nobility*, 248–52; for continental developments: D. Crouch, *The English Aristocracy, 1070–1272: A Social Transformation* (New Haven, CT, 2011), 55–9; for regional examples: A. Chédeville, *Chartres et ses campagnes (XIe–XIIIe siècles)* (Paris, 1973), 322–3; T. Evergates, *The Aristocracy in the County of Champagne, 1100–1300*

As the harsh suppression of urban revolts frequently demonstrated, for most of the period urban oligarchies had much less legitimacy in the eyes of the military elites, especially north of the Alps. By the thirteenth century, however, merchants were becoming integrated into representative institutions from England to Spain, a recognition of their political as well as commercial power. The role of the Parisians in the Burgundian-Armagnac struggles of the early fifteenth century, or of the London oligarchy in the parliaments and court factions under Edward III and Richard II, demonstrates how urban elites had achieved a prominence in the political structures of late medieval northern Europe that would have been unthinkable a couple of centuries earlier. The rise of the de la Pole family in England shows the extent to which successful merchants could enter the political elite. William de la Pole (d. 1366) began his career as a merchant of Kingston upon Hull, but thanks to his activities as financier to Edward III, his family was so successfully established in the English aristocracy that his son Matthew was made chancellor of England and earl of Suffolk by Richard II. In the following century, a marriage alliance with the royal House of York brought a ducal title and royal blood to the earls of Suffolk, and three de la Pole brothers perished on the battlefield or the executioner's block as successive Yorkist candidates for the English throne.[88] In five generations, the de la Poles had risen from being merchants from a provincial port to contenders for the throne of England. If this family's success was exceptional, it nevertheless demonstrates that, in order to shore up their hegemony, the elites of later medieval Europe were prepared to accept newcomers on account of their wealth.

Lower down the social scale, certain groups remained effectively excluded from power. While slavery had disappeared from most of Latin Christendom by the end of the twelfth century, serfdom remained a prominent aspect of rural society, and much of the practice of lordship was dedicated to enforcing the inferior legal status and onerous services of the unfree. More general political action was sometimes taken to ensure this, perhaps most dramatically in the concession by Peter II of Aragon of

(Philadelphia, 2007), 52–3; L. Paterson, *The World of the Troubadours: Medieval Occitan Society, c.1100–c.1300* (Cambridge, 1993), 49–51 (for Occitanian *donzels*); for the term 'squire' in England, where it was less prestigious: P. Coss, 'Knights, esquires and the origins of social gradation in England', *TRHS* 6th series 5 (1995), 155–78. See also p. 158.

[88] John de la Pole, earl of Lincoln, possibly acknowledged by his uncle King Richard III as his heir in 1485, killed at the battle of Stoke Field, 1487; Edmund, duke (later earl) of Suffolk, executed 1513; Richard, nicknamed '*Blanche Rose*' as a Yorkist claimant, slain in battle while an exile at the French court (1525). For the family: A. S. Harvey, *The de la Pole family of Kingston upon Hull* (Beverley, 1957); R. Horrox, *The de la Poles of Hull* (Beverley, 1983); E. B. Fryde, *William de la Pole, Merchant and King's Banker* (London, 1988); and the relevant articles in the *ODNB*.

the right of the nobles of Catalonia to 'maltreat their peasants' (1202), and in the English Statute of Labourers (1351) that was issued in the wake of the Black Death's devastating impact upon the labour supply.[89] Yet against such concerted actions to tighten seigneurial domination must be set countless actions that weakened it. Prosperous unfree peasants could exploit aristocratic impoverishment by buying their way out of servitude, either through manumission – the release of individuals – or through the enfranchisement of whole communities.[90] Unfree status did not always exclude people from power. In parts of the empire in the central and later middle ages, even many knights – known as *ministeriales* – were unfree, so that their marriages and rights of residency were controlled by their lords. Nevertheless, they could often hold important offices and formed an influential group in German society.[91]

Exclusion from power of a different sort can be seen in the restrictions imposed upon Jews in much of Latin Christendom, especially from the eleventh century onwards. James Campbell has speculated that the absence of Jews in pre-Conquest England was a consequence of royal proclamation.[92] It is easier to demonstrate exclusion of Jews from political power in later centuries. An interesting exception is Languedoc, where the twelfth-century counts of Toulouse and viscounts of Béziers-Carcassonne permitted Jews to hold office; church denunciations led to the suppression of this practice by the French during the Albigensian Crusade. That crusade also led to the systematic exclusion of heretics and their descendants from holding office in Languedoc.[93]

---

[89] Bisson, *Crisis of the Twelfth Century*, 511–12; B. H. Putnam, *The Enforcement of the Statutes of Labourers during the First Decade after the Black Death, 1349–1359* (New York, 1908).

[90] R. H. Hilton, *Bond Men Made Free: Medieval Peasant Movements and the English Rising of 1381* (London, 1973), 72–95; W. C. Jordan, *From Servitude to Freedom: Manumissions in the Sénonais in the Thirteenth Century* (Philadelphia, 1986); L. Feller, *Paysans et seigneurs au Moyen Âge, VIIIe–XVe siècles* (Paris, 2007), 172–6.

[91] B. Arnold, *German Knighthood, 1050–1300* (Oxford, 1985); J. B. Freed, *Noble Bondsmen: Ministerial Marriages in the Archdiocese of Salzburg, 1100–1343* (Ithaca, NY, 1995). Warriors who were (unlike the *ministeriales*) outright slaves feature prominently in Islamic polities from the Abbasid era onwards and are most prominent in Qalawunid Egypt, where *mamluk*s provided the political leadership: pp. 232–5, 237–8, 245, 339, 459–60. Slave soldiers were not a feature of Byzantine military life, although exotic slaves were sometimes on show in the Great Palace.

[92] J. Campbell, 'Was it infancy in England? Some questions of comparison', in M. Jones and M. Vale (eds), *England and Her Neighbours, 1066–1453* (London, 1989), 1–17; repr. in his *The Anglo-Saxon State* (London, 2000), 179–99 at 195.

[93] H. Gilles, 'Commentaires méridionaux des prescriptions canoniques sur les juifs', in M.-H. Vicaire and B. Blumenkranz (eds), *Juifs et judaïsme de Languedoc XIIe siècle–début XIVe siècle* (Toulouse, 1977), 23–50 at 33–4; C. Duhamel-Amado, 'Les juifs à Béziers avant 1209: entre la tolérance et la persécution', in C. Iancu (ed.), *Les Juifs à Montpellier et dans le Languedoc à travers l'histoire: du Moyen Âge à nos jours* (Montpellier, 1988), 145–56 at

Lay Succession

The arrangements made by lords and rulers for the transmission of power to their successors reveal much about the practice of politics in Latin Christendom. The issues at stake include whether the ruler or lord wished to pass his or her power to an heir (or several heirs) and, if so, how this heir was selected and affirmed. Studies of early medieval monarchies, notably by Karl Leyser for the Ottonians and Andrew W. Lewis for the early Capetians, have emphasised the importance of the dynastic kin-group both as a source of power for the ruler and as a constraint upon the ruler's actions.[94] The broad outlines of Georges Duby's argument for a shift in aristocratic family structure either side of 1000, from sprawling clans to more narrowly defined patrilineal dynasties, have been accepted, but the details significantly qualified.[95] Constance Bouchard, for instance, has noted the attempts by Carolingian nobles to establish the succession of their eldest sons to the exclusion of other kin at a much earlier date than Duby maintained; conversely, Lewis' study of the Capetians shows how the claims of the broader kin-group could still exert a strong influence upon dynastic policy long after 1000.[96] In southern Italy under the rule of the Norman kings of Sicily, the nobility adopted a variety of inheritance practices, but their consistent aim appears to have been the maintenance of the integrity of the patrimonial property, whether concentrated in the hands of a principal heir or shared amongst a much broader section of a kin-group.[97]

Economic variations between the regions of Europe may have influenced the ways in which succession practices evolved differently across Latin Christendom. The availability of land in the depopulated plateaux

147 (Carcassonne); Mundy, *Liberty and Political Power in Toulouse*, 53, 266 n. 41, although he notes (p. 9) that Jews still faced bars on participating in Toulouse's political life; Paterson, *World of the Troubadours*, 175–82. The Statute of Pamiers (1212), ch. XIV, banned heretics, former heretics and Jews from offices: *Histoire générale de Languedoc*, ed. C. Devic and J. Vaissete, 2nd edn, 16 vols (Toulouse, 1872–1905), viii:col. 628.

94 K. J. Leyser, *Rule and Conflict in an Early Medieval Society: Ottonian Saxony* (London, 1979): Lewis, *Royal Succession*, esp. 7–64.

95 Duby, *Chivalrous Society*, developing ideas originally proposed by Karl Schmid in 'The structure of the nobility in the earlier middle ages', in T. Reuter (ed. and tr.), *The Medieval Nobility: Studies on the Ruling Classes of France and Germany from the Sixth to the Twelfth Century* (Amsterdam, 1979), 37–59. For a restatement of the shift from broad *Sippe* to hierarchical *parentèle* between the seventh and eleventh centuries: R. Le Jan, *Famille et pouvoir dans le monde franc (VIIe–Xe siècle): essai d'anthropologie sociale* (Paris, 2002), 381–427.

96 C. B. Bouchard, *'Those of My Blood': Constructing Noble Families in Medieval Francia* (Philadelphia, 2001), 59–97; Lewis, *Royal Succession*. See also, for twelfth-century Germany, J. R. Lyon, *Princely Brothers and Sisters: the Sibling Bond in German Politics, 1100–1250* (Ithaca, NY, 2013).

97 J. Drell, *Kinship and Conquest: Family Strategies in the Principality of Salerno during the Norman Period, 1077–1194* (Ithaca, NY, and London, 2002), esp. 97–121.

of Castile and León in the twelfth century may have slowed down the adoption of primogeniture there, since a landowning family could prosper without having to concentrate all its resources in the hands of a single son.[98] In another Iberian region, Catalonia, the opportunities offered by economic growth probably encouraged the urban patriciate of Barcelona to resist patrilineal inheritance strategies until the thirteenth century – and to continue to show much creativity in the disposition of property by both men and women thereafter. In the Catalan countryside, in contrast, greater pressure upon landed resources probably restricted the opportunities for endowing younger sons and daughters, although the stronger influence of Frankish culture in Catalonia than in Castile may have also played a part.[99] Yet paucity of resources did not necessarily encourage the concentration of resources in the hands of a single heir. In Wales, division of inheritance amongst the leading adult males of the princely dynasties remained the custom, despite the poverty of the Welsh economy. This practice of division was often matched by vicious internecine strife, and, although this became less murderous from the late twelfth century onwards, attempts by the most successful dynasty, the princes of Gwynedd, to introduce impartible succession to their lands proved only partly successful: Llywelyn ap Iorwerth's only legitimate son, Dafydd (d. 1246), was challenged by his older illegitimate brother Gruffudd, and after Dafydd's death, Gruffudd's second son Llywelyn (the Last, d. 1282), after imprisoning his elder brother Owain, never shook off the claims of his younger brother Dafydd. The other major principalities, Deheubarth and Powys, had both been permanently partitioned amongst competing heirs by the early thirteenth century.[100]

Various methods were employed by early medieval rulers to ensure the recognition of their heirs, including designation, naming patterns, oath-taking, and (especially for kings) anointing and anticipatory coronation. The ceremonies of designation and coronation appear to have become more elaborate across the period, and chroniclers were quick to note when they went wrong.[101] Timothy Reuter also argued that nationality

---

[98] S. Barton, *The Aristocracy in Twelfth-Century León and Castile* (Cambridge, 1997), 38–46.

[99] S. P. Bensch, *Barcelona and its Rulers, 1096–1291* (Cambridge, 1995), 234–76; J. Shideler, *A Medieval Catalan Noble Family: The Montcadas 1000–1230* (Berkeley, 1983), 56–61. Catalonia was notionally part of the kingdom of France until 1258.

[100] Davies, *Age of Conquest*, 218–51, 308–54; J. B. Smith, *Llywelyn ap Gruffudd: Prince of Wales*, 2nd edn (Cardiff, 2014); D. Stephenson, *Medieval Powys: Kingdom, Principality and Lordships, 1132–1293* (Woodbridge, 2016), 58–96, 215–33.

[101] See e.g. the future King John of England's disastrous investiture as duke of Normandy, as recorded in *Magna Vita S. Hugonis: The Life of St Hugh of Lincoln*, ed. D. L. Douie and D. H. Farmer, 2 vols, 2nd edn (Oxford, 1985), ii:144. For coronation-rituals: J. Dale, *Inauguration and Liturgical Kingship in the Long Twelfth Century* (Woodbridge, 2019).

was a crucial aspect of succession to the empire, for it effectively excluded potential foreign claimants in 1002 and 1024, including in the minds of these foreign contenders themselves.[102] In 987 a similar preference for a man based in the West Frankish kingdom appears to have favoured Hugh Capet over his main rival for the throne, Charles of Lorraine, even though the latter was a scion of the Carolingian dynasty.[103] However, several eleventh-century kings of Denmark and Norway as well as Duke William of Normandy felt no such compunction about claiming the English throne; and the reluctance of foreign claimants to seek the imperial throne had vanished by the 1250s, when candidates from the royal houses of Castile, France and England sought election as king of the Romans and received substantial local support.

In France, meanwhile, the gradual emergence of the concept of 'princes of the blood' excluded all who were not descended in the male line from the royal dynasty, and this played a decisive role in the succession to the last Capetians: between 1316 and 1328 the daughters of Louis X, Philip V and Charles IV, along with Edward III of England, who had a claim through the female line, were all passed over for the French crown, which eventually went to Charles IV's nearest relation in the male line, Philip of Valois, in 1328.[104] In England, Richard II attempted to treat the other descendants in the male line of Edward III in a comparable way to the French princes of the blood,[105] and in the fifteenth century the cadet Plantagenet lines of York and Beaufort enjoyed the same status in all but name; nevertheless, as we have seen, royal succession through the female line remained acceptable in England, where members of the families of Mortimer, Holland, Stafford and de la Pole were all regarded as potential claimants to the throne. Eventually, against all the odds, it passed through

---

[102] T. Reuter, 'The making of England and Germany: points of comparison and difference', repr. in *MPMM*, 284–99 at 291.

[103] Another obstacle was the humble birth of Charles' wife, allegedly from the family of a *miles* ('uxorem de militari ordine sibi imparem', as if 'de suis militibus feminam sumptam'): Richer of Reims, *Histoire de France (888–995)*, ed. R. Latouche, 2 vols (Paris, 1930–7), ii:160–2.

[104] For the 'princes of the blood': Lewis, *Royal Succession*, 155–92; for the last Capetians and the Valois succession: E. M. Hallam and C. T. Wood, *The French Apanages and the Capetian Monarchy, 1224–1328* (Cambridge, MA, 1966), 52–66, 89; E. M. Hallam and J. Everard, *Capetian France, 987–1328*, 2nd edn (Harlow, 2001), 364–6, 421–2; C. Taylor, 'Edward III and the Plantagenet claim for the French throne', in J. S. Bothwell (ed.), *The Age of Edward III* (York, 2001), 155–69. Edward's claim began at the death of Charles IV in 1328, as his nearest male relation – but through the female line. Succession to the throne in the female line was very rare, albeit not wholly unthinkable, in Byzantium: pp. 203–4, 300, 301–2, 307. Lines of female succession in the Islamic sphere await full investigation: pp. 22, 23.

[105] M. J. Bennett, 'Edward III's entail and the succession to the crown, 1376–1471', *EHR* 113 (1998), 580–609; I. Mortimer, 'Richard II and the succession to the crown', *History* 91 (2006), 320–36.

the female line from the Beauforts to Henry Tudor, an offshoot in the male line not of the English nobility but the Welsh *uchelwyr* (or squire-archy, but often of princely descent).

Despite the emphasis upon lineal descent, royal succession across Europe usually retained an elective element. Although often regarded as a source of weakness and discord, royal election had some advantages for both monarchies and their subjects, since it ensured the succession of a competent adult male.[106] In the course of the period the elective character weakened in most monarchies but strengthened in the empire (and, of course, the papacy). The Golden Bull issued by Emperor Charles IV in 1356 regularised a long-accepted electoral principle, fixing the right upon seven hereditary 'electors'. However, we should avoid drawing too strong a contrast between elective and hereditary succession. The eligibility of candidates for the imperial throne was primarily determined by member-ship of a dominant family: the Ottonians from 918 to 1024, the Salian dynasty thereafter until 1125, the Hohenstaufen for most of the period from 1137 to 1254, and predominantly the Luxembourg and Hapsburg dynasties in the late middle ages.[107] Conversely, the supposedly heredi-tary monarchies still required designation and acclamation of the succes-sor – and even direct election in some circumstances. In England, strict primogeniture was followed on only two out of seven occasions between 1066 and 1216, and on both occasions – the accessions of Richard I in 1189 and of Henry III in 1216 – during or after a struggle and threat from a rival candidate. Thereafter, the eldest surviving son or grandson of the king of England succeeded at each royal death until 1377, when Richard II succeeded Edward III as the son of the deceased eldest son, Edward the Black Prince, in preference to his uncle, John of Gaunt. Nevertheless, the growing legitimacy of primogeniture did not prevent the deposition of Edward II in favour of his adolescent son in 1327, and the deposition of Richard II in 1399 reintroduced dynastic uncertainty and election into the English crown that was not completely resolved until the Stuart accession in 1603. In Scotland, primogeniture prevailed from the early twelfth century onwards, displacing older practices of electing the most suitable member of the royal kin-group, but the aristocracy retained a say. In the 1190s, the nobles made clear to King William I (the Lion) that, if he died without a son, they would prefer his younger brother, Earl David of

---

[106] J. Gillingham, 'Elective kingship and the unity of medieval Germany', *German History* 8 (1991), 124–35 at 128–9.
[107] Gillingham, 'Elective kingship', 128. For broader European patterns: F. Lachaud and M. Penman (eds), *Making and Breaking the Rules: Succession in Medieval Europe, c.1000–c.1600 / Établir et abolir les normes: la succession dans l'Europe médiévale, vers 1000–vers 1600* (Turnhout, 2008).

Huntingdon, as king rather than one of his daughters married to a foreign husband. A century later, the total extinction of William I's legitimate line gave the aristocracy a strong say in deciding which of Earl David's descendants should inherit the crown, although they turned eventually to the king of England to arbitrate between the claimants by primogeniture (John Balliol) and nearness of degree (Robert Bruce the Competitor) respectively.[108]

As the disbarment of Capetian princesses from the French royal succession, discussed earlier, shows,[109] female succession to monarchical rule was frequently opposed in Latin Christendom. Nevertheless, women were accepted as the rightful rulers between the twelfth and fifteenth centuries in Jerusalem, Iberia, Naples, Poland, Scandinavia and (briefly) Scotland. The small number of queens regnant (that is, ruling in their own right rather than as consorts or regents) precludes generalisations about the rights of women to succeed to royal authority, as the differing fortunes of three royal heiresses in the first half of the twelfth century demonstrate. Urraca of León and Castile (1109–26) and Melisende of Jerusalem (1131–53) were both accepted as queens by the barons and leading churchmen of their kingdoms in the absence of male heirs, whereas Matilda, the only legitimate daughter of Henry I of England and eventually his sole heir after her brother's death in 1120, failed to win the English throne when her father died in 1135. Despite Henry's designation of Matilda as his successor and his strenuous efforts to secure baronial acceptance of her as his heir, a majority of nobles and prelates in England and Normandy opted instead to be ruled by her cousin Stephen of Blois, preferring a male claiming through the female line to the deceased king's daughter.[110] It is noteworthy that three of the most prominent examples of later medieval queens regnant were already royal consorts in other kingdoms, further enhancing their regal status: Berenguela, queen of Castile (1217–46), who had previously been queen consort of León; Margaret I, regent or queen regnant of Denmark from 1376 to 1412, as well as queen consort but eventually also queen regnant of Norway and Sweden; and Isabella I, queen of Castile (1474–1504), who at her accession was consort of the king of Sicily and heir of Aragon (and who displaced a rival female claimant, her

---

[108] K. J. Stringer, *Earl David of Huntingdon: A Study in Anglo-Scottish History* (Edinburgh, 1985), 42–3; *Edward I and the Throne of Scotland, 1290–1296: An Edition of the Record Sources for the Great Cause*, ed. E. L. G. Stones and G. G. Simpson, 2 vols (Oxford, 1978).

[109] See p. 395.

[110] B. F. Reilly, *The Kingdom of León-Castilla under Queen Urraca, 1109–1126* (Princeton, 1993); N. R. Hodgson, *Women, Crusading and the Holy Land in Historical Narrative* (Woodbridge, 2007), 75–7, 182–8, 213; M. Chibnall, *The Empress Matilda: Queen Consort, Queen Mother and Lady of the English* (Oxford, 1991).

half-niece Juana, to succeed to her kingdom). The successions of Berenguela of Castile and Margaret of Denmark were also assisted by the fact that they had initially assumed and long exercised royal power as regents for young male kinsmen. All three women played a major part in the establishment of long-lasting dynastic unions between the different kingdoms where they were rulers and consorts.[111]

Ultimately, royal and princely succession was determined by a balance between a number of different factors, including not only the ancestry and sex but also the age, wealth, character and political alliances of potential claimants. Succession was also invariably more complicated and contested where it involved multiple inheritances, such as the Anglo-Norman realm and Angevin empire, ruled by the kings of England, and the various territories accumulated by the ruling dynasty of Aragon and the Angevin branch of the Capetian dynasty in the thirteenth and fourteenth centuries: in such dynastic accumulations, the inheritance rights of eldest sons against those of their younger brothers were inevitably much less clear-cut.[112]

Ecclesiastical Succession

The reinforcement of hegemony through succession to ecclesiastical office gave rise to one of the great shifts in political organisation during the period, at least in theory, as the leaders of the church sought to establish its 'freedom' from lay domination. For the papacy itself, the crucial change was the election decree of 1059, which formalised the process of election by cardinals. Thereafter, there were many election disputes and emperors frequently nurtured more sympathetic candidates who were subsequently regarded as antipopes; but the move to election by cardinals helped to transform the papacy, vastly reducing the influence of both the imperial monarchy and local Italian nobles upon papal succession and consequently upon the whole institution.[113]

A more prolonged contest was waged over other senior ecclesiastical appointments, especially to bishoprics and abbacies. By the mid-twelfth century, theologians and canon lawyers had developed an elaborate set of procedures to ensure the probity and independence of episcopal elections.[114] Yet the reality was very different. Although systemic clashes between the

---

[111] On Berenguela, see n. 154; on Margaret of Denmark: H. Schück, 'The political system', in *CHS* 1, 677–709, esp. 682–91; J. Olesen, 'Inter-Scandinavian relations', in *CHS* 1, 710–70, esp. 717–29; on Isabella of Castile: J. Edwards, *Ferdinand and Isabella* (Harlow, 2004).

[112] See pp. 376, 383.   [113] Robinson, *Papacy*, 33–90.

[114] J. Peltzer, *Canon Law, Careers, and Conquest: Episcopal Elections in Normandy and Greater Anjou, c.1140–c.1230* (Cambridge, 2008), 20–72.

rivalry of the papacy and imperial monarchy concerned far more than ecclesiastical elections, these became the touchstone of relations between *regnum* and *sacerdotium*. The chief struggles were in the empire, where Gregory VII's decree on elections (1078), Paschal II's two radically different attempts at reconciliation with Emperor Henry V (1111), and the eventual compromise between Pope Calixtus II and Henry V known as the Concordat of Worms (1122) mark stages in the definition of the extent and limitations of lay influence.[115] In England, Anselm of Aosta, archbishop of Canterbury, waged a parallel struggle with Henry I of England in the opening years of the twelfth century.[116] In both the empire and England, the concordats theoretically reduced the ruler to a secondary role in episcopal appointments, with the right to present suitable candidates, veto unacceptable ones and take the homage of appointees for temporal domains; the formal election was to be made by the cathedral clergy. In practice, rulers across Europe continued to exercise huge influence over prelatial appointments, to use these to reward loyal clerks and chaplains for their service, and to influence elections indirectly where they could make appointments to canonries within cathedral chapters as well. The ironies of this situation are most clearly demonstrated in the actions of two thirteenth-century kings with strongly contrasting reputations in their dealings with the church. Between 1206 and 1213, King John of England fought a bitter battle with Pope Innocent III over the see of Canterbury, at the end of which the king had to submit to the pope and accept the papal candidate, Stephen Langton. Innocent's six-year interdict on English and Welsh priests made John a byword for oppression of the church; yet John's submission allowed him to promote many of his most loyal clerks to the sees that had fallen vacant during the interdict.[117] By contrast, Louis IX of France (1226–70) acquired a reputation as a model of royal piety in his lifetime and was canonised within a generation of his death; yet during his reign he tightened royal control of episcopal elections, notably in the territories conquered from the Angevins.[118]

Consequently the attempts of churchmen to secure autonomy for ecclesiastical appointments were only partially successful. Quasi-hereditary or princely control of church offices did not wholly disappear, and by the end of the period monarchies were, if anything, strengthening their ability to determine appointments within their kingdoms and to use clerical benefices as outlets for patronage and reward. Furthermore,

---

[115] Robinson, *Papacy*, 398–441.

[116] M. Brett, *The English Church under Henry I* (Oxford, 1975); J. A. Green, *Henry I: King of England and Duke of Normandy* (Cambridge, 2006), 108–9.

[117] C. Harper-Bill, 'John and the Church of Rome', in S. D. Church (ed.), *King John: New Interpretations* (Woodbridge, 1999), 289–315 at 309–10.

[118] Peltzer, *Canon Law*, esp. 238–52.

granting monasteries *in commendam* in France, Scotland and elsewhere became more commonplace in the later middle ages, undermining their independence and foreshadowing their widespread secularisation in both Protestant and Catholic Europe during the Reformation.[119] Yet ecclesiastical succession had changed in another very significant way from the early middle ages, for in much of Europe the pool of candidates had widened in social terms as burgeoning princely and ecclesiastical administrations and universities allowed talented men of humble birth to rise to the most senior positions – a strong contrast with the almost exclusively noble character of the early medieval episcopate.

The Organisation and Reach of Political Power

Public Organisation of Power

The concept of the 'public' is problematic for early medieval Latin Christendom. An older historiographical tradition, best known from the early, ground-breaking work of Georges Duby, asserted that the Carolingian empire had a strong concept of public authority; but that this was subverted from the tenth century onwards by 'private' aristocratic power, as castle-based lordship spread across the landscape, eventually undermining the public forum or *mallus* which maintained the Carolingian public order long after the division of the empire. According to this view, public authority then re-emerged with the evolution of strong bureaucratic monarchy and the spread of Roman law from the twelfth century onwards.[120] There is now much less certainty about the public character of Carolingian empire than amongst historians of earlier generations; in any case, such a model relies heavily upon evidence from parts of central and southern France, Catalonia and Italy, since the collapse of political order is hard to demonstrate in many other parts of Europe, where royal or princely authority remained robust.[121]

---

[119] For grants of monasteries *in commendam*: J. G. Clark, *The Benedictines in the Middle Ages* (Woodbridge, 2011), 294–5; for Scotland: I. B. Cowan, *The Medieval Church in Scotland*, ed. J. Kirk (Edinburgh, 1995), 166–7, 196–200; A. D. M. Birrell, *Medieval Scotland* (Cambridge, 2000), 246–8.

[120] The most famous exposition of this interpretation was G. Duby, *La Société aux XIe et XIIe siècles dans la région mâconnaise*, 2nd edn (Paris, 1971). For a survey of studies written under its influence: T. N. Bisson, '*La terre et les hommes*: a programme fulfilled?', *French History* 14 (2000), 322–45; and for an overview: J.-P. Poly and E. Bournazel, *The Feudal Transformation, 900–1200*, tr. C. Higgitt (New York, 1991).

[121] In general, see the debate in *P&P* 144 (1994), 6–42; 152 (1996), 196–223; 155 (1997), 177–225; D. Barthélemy, *La Mutation de l'an mil a-t-elle eu lieu? Servage et chevalerie dans la France des Xe et XIe siècles* (Paris, 1997); P. Bonnassie and P. Toubert (eds), *Hommes et sociétés dans l'Europe de l'an mil* (Toulouse, 2004).

The assumption that 'lordship' was antithetical to public order, still very firm in one major synthesis,[122] also raises as many questions as it answers.

Early medieval Europe certainly had processes and events that look as if they have a public character, such as the assemblies and great ceremonies of the early medieval monarchies, designed to achieve consensus.[123] Yet such gatherings did not vanish with the disintegration of Carolingian hegemony. It would also be difficult to prove that the small courts of castle-based lordships in eleventh-century France were regarded as in any way less public. What had often changed was not the loss of a concept of the public but the widespread diminution in scale of the area for which assemblies gathered and courts pronounced judgement.[124] Furthermore, where princely power declined – as it undoubtedly did in many parts of the former Carolingian empire – arbitration often replaced coercion as the means of enforcing agreements.[125] Other mechanisms were found for maintaining the status of public authority. Reuter has noted the greater importance of symbolic gestures in Germany than England, which compensated for the empire's lack of administrative structures comparable to those developed by the English monarchy.[126]

Yet a stronger sense between public and private did evolve by the later middle ages, under the influence of Roman law. The best-known demonstration of this is in the increasing distinction made between the king as man and as monarch.[127] In addition, both early and late medieval rulers frequently made great play of their accessibility to their subjects, and their subjects also indulged in what has been dubbed a 'fantasy of access', imagining that they could appeal directly to their rulers for the redress of wrongs.[128] The narrative sources make much of encounters between princes and the poor or humble of their domain. In a highly literary passage, John of Marmoutier, biographer of Geoffrey Plantagenet, count of Anjou (d. 1151), described how the count discovered the oppressions of his officials when, unrecognised, he had a chance encounter with a peasant in a forest.[129] In John's narrative, Geoffrey duly made

---

[122] Bisson, *Crisis of the Twelfth Century*.

[123] See especially J. L. Nelson, *Politics and Ritual in Early Medieval Europe* (London, 1986); P. S. Barnwell and M. Mostert (eds), *Political Assemblies in the Early Middle Age* (Turnhout, 2003).

[124] On miniaturisation: pp. 149–52, 176–7.   [125] For relevant historiography: n. 44.

[126] Reuter, 'Making of England and Germany', 290–2.

[127] The classic study of this remains E. H. Kantorowicz, *The King's Two Bodies: A Study in Mediaeval Political Theology* (Princeton, 1957).

[128] Sabapathy, *Officers and Accessibility*, 223.

[129] *Chroniques des comtes d'Anjou et des seigneurs d'Amboise*, ed. L. Halphen and R. Poupardin (Paris, 1913), 183–91; cf. Bisson, *Crisis of the Twelfth Century*, 322–6. On the qualities of the ruler: pp. 256–9, 261–3.

amends. By contrast, Gerald of Wales attributed the political difficulties of Geoffrey's son, Henry II of England, to his failure to heed the warnings of a lowborn prophet who accosted the king as he journeyed through Wales to reprove him for allowing his subjects to work and trade on Sundays.[130] Other tales coupled the simple manners and tastes of Louis VII (d. 1180) and Louis IX (d. 1270) of France with their accessibility to their humbler subjects who needed justice.[131] Also significant were the emergence of events or institutions which allowed more regular communication between the ruler and his subjects: assemblies of 'estates' such as Parliament in England or the *cortes* in Castile. These were often no mere ciphers but exercised a real influence upon the conduct of politics and upon the powers and actions of rulers. The extension of political inclusion for urban elites has already been noted, but it also occurred more broadly: the participation of the 'commons' in late medieval English politics, for instance, raised many anxieties amongst the elite, but it clearly had a major impact during some of the great political crises.[132]

Two very different matters, the administration of justice and the circulation of coinage, each illustrate the role of the public and its limitations. In matters of justice, the balance between the ruler's courts and seigneurial courts is a useful indication of the extent of the public organisation of power. In the twelfth century, customary law became increasingly territorialised, and the jurisdictions that evolved usually formed within the territorial framework of political divisions. Indeed, the customary jurisdictions tell us much about that framework: the fact that England developed a 'common law of the realm' by the end of the twelfth century, whereas in France custom was conceived primarily in terms of the region rather than the kingdom, reveals much about the different political cultures of the two kingdoms. The same contrast can be seen in the attempts to constrain royal power in the two kingdoms: attempts to constrain the power of the thirteenth-century kings of England conceived of a single 'community of the realm', whereas the reaction to the rule of Philip IV and Louis X in 1314–15 was organised along provincial lines and was met with charters which in most regions

---

[130] *Giraldi Cambrensis Opera*, ed. J. S. Brewer *et al.*, 8 vols (London, 1861–91), vi:64–6; repeated by the same author in Gerald of Wales, *Instructions for a Ruler: De Principis Instructione*, ed. and tr. R. Bartlett (Oxford, 2018), 484–7.

[131] E.g. Walter Map, *De nugis curialium: Courtiers' Trifles*, ed. and tr. M. R. James, rev. C. N. L. Brooke and R. A. B. Mynors (Oxford, 1983), 452–7; Joinville, *Vie de Saint Louis* § 59–60, ed. and tr. Monfrin, 30–1 (*Chronicles of the Crusades*, tr. Shaw, 177).

[132] J. Watts, 'Public or plebs: the changing meaning of "the commons", 1381–1549', in H. Pryce and J. Watts (eds), *Power and Identity in the Middle Ages: Essays in Memory of Rees Davies* (Oxford, 2007), 242–60. See also pp. 36, 69, 161–4, 280, 283–4.

confirmed the elite privileges.[133] Attitudes to custom also formed part of the public dialogue between rulers and ruled, as can be seen in the contrasting treatment of the Normans with the people of Languedoc when both regions were conquered by the French in the opening decade of the thirteenth century. As he subjugated Normandy in 1204, Philip Augustus agreed to respect the *usus et consuetudines Normannie* and was able to use this compromise as a way of establishing his authority there. By contrast, in 1212 Simon de Montfort, leader of the Albigensian Crusade, unilaterally imposed the *usus et consuetudines Francie circa Parisius* (uses and customs of France around Paris) in Languedoc for inheritance matters, a neat demonstration of the rupture between the order he wished to impose and the existing political structures of the subdued region.[134]

The nature of the 'public' sphere in justice can also be seen in the ways in which communal gatherings such as courts or assemblies were used to validate 'private' agreements. As the use of written documents to record contracts increased across Europe in the central middle ages, the problem arose as to how and where these precious records could be kept. One obvious solution, often adopted, was for lay parties to agreements to deposit the deeds in religious houses for safe-keeping, taking advantage of ecclesiastical archival practices.[135] However, other means also developed from the twelfth century onwards which gave public validity to private contracts. In Italy and other parts of southern Europe, a vibrant notarial culture emerged. In some northern European towns and cities, it became a civic responsibility to maintain communal chests or similar repositories. Elsewhere, royal or princely confirmation became an ever more desirable solution. The use of collusive, fictitious pleas in law-courts was one solution: parties to an agreement posed as litigants against each other in order to secure the formal court record of the 'judgement' that awarded the property in accordance with the terms of the agreement that they were making in reality. The rehearsal of such agreements in public, as much as the transcription of their terms into rolls or registers, was what gave them 'record' and shows the importance of an emerging 'public'

[133] J. C. Holt, *Magna Carta*, 3rd edn, rev. G. Garnett and J. Hudson (Cambridge, 2015), 237–9.

[134] J. Metman, 'Les inféodations royales d'après le *Recueil des actes de Philippe Auguste*', in R.-H. Bautier (ed.), *La France de Philippe Auguste: le temps des mutations* (Paris, 1982), 503–17. Statute of Pamiers (1212), chs XII, XLIII and codicil: *Histoire générale de Languedoc*, ed. Devic and Vaissete, viii:cols 628, 633–4. For this contrast as well as Philip Augustus' Norman enfeoffments: Power, *Norman Frontier*, 153–78.

[135] D. Crouch, 'A Norman *conventio* and bonds of lordship in the middle ages', in Garnett and Hudson (eds), *Law and Government*, 299–324 at 299–300 (see 299 n.1 for amusing consequences of this practice).

sphere. The clearest example of this impugnable status can be found in the English final concord made in the royal courts, a procedure that developed from the 1160s,[136] and this was reinforced from 1194 by the recording of such fines in (unsealed) tripartite chirographs, with one of the three copies of the document being retained by the royal officers who presided over the assizes where these fines were invariably concluded.[137]

Equally revealing of political structures are legal cultures that did not develop as an aspect of a particular polity but transcended political divisions. Wales and Ireland are two very obvious examples, for both countries were notoriously fragmented in political terms, yet each fostered a common legal culture that transcended the divisions between the different kings or princes.[138] The use of Roman law in the highly fragmented regions of central and southern France (the *pays du droit écrit*) could be seen in the same light.[139] In eleventh-century western France, peacemaking by arbiters could often maintain social order in the absence of strong monarchy – a far cry from the 'feudal anarchy' beloved of older generations of French historians.[140] In such cultures, the ruler had much less say in devising and upholding the law, in contrast to the better-known, more hierarchical, concentric systems of justice.

Another area where public power varied enormously was in matters of coinage. The exceptionally pure coinage and efficient minting regime of late Anglo-Saxon England attests to the strong public character of the

---

[136] See the declaration of a parliament of Edward I in January 1291 (*The Parliament Rolls of England, 1275–1504*, ed. C. Given-Wilson *et al.*, 16 vols (Woodbridge, 2005), i:247): 'nec in regno isto provideatur, vel sit aliqua securitas major seu solempnior per quam aliquis vel aliqua statum certiorem habere possit, vel ad statum suum verificandum aliquid solempnius testimonium producere, quam finem in curia domini regis levatum; qui quidem finis sic vocatur, eo quod finis et consummacio omnium placitorum esse debet'. ('In this realm no greater or more solemn security has been provided or exists, through which anyone can have a more sure estate, or produce any more solemn testimony to prove their estate, than a fine levied in the court of the lord king; which fine indeed is so called, because it should be the end and termination of all pleas, and was ordained for this reason'.)

[137] In general and for sources: D. Power, 'En quête de sécurité juridique dans la Normandie angevine: concorde finale et inscription au rouleau', *Bibliothèque de l'École des Chartes* 168 (2010 [2011]), 327–71. See also pp. 277–8. Public, legally binding, records were no less important in Byzantium: pp. 92–4, 97, 425–7, 433–6. The written record was of somewhat less decisive significance in Islamic law regarding property: pp. 126–7, 129.

[138] T. G. Watkin, *The Legal History of Wales*, 2nd edn (Cardiff, 2012), esp. 37–43, 47; *The Law of Hywel Dda: Law Texts of Medieval Wales*, ed. and tr. D. Jenkins (Llandysul, 1986); D. Ó Cróinín, *Early Medieval Ireland, 400–1200* (Harlow, 1995), 110–46; for comparisons: R. R. Davies, 'The peoples of Britain and Ireland 1100–1400, III: Laws and customs', *TRHS* 6th series 6 (1996), 1–23 at 9–10.

[139] M. Boulet-Sautel, 'Le droit romain et Philippe Auguste', in Bautier (ed.), *La France de Philippe Auguste*, 489–501; Paterson, *World of the Troubadours*, 173–4, 222–3, 231.

[140] See p. 380 and n. 44, p. 401.

English monarchy as well as to its power and intrusiveness; conversely, the appearance of baronial coinages in England and the Welsh March under King Stephen (d. 1154) attests to the political disruption of his troubled reign. The design and production of late Anglo-Saxon coins was linked closely to the individual monarch.[141] In France, by contrast, coins were usually 'immobilised', often bearing ancient legends and remaining unchanged at the death of a ruler; and although many coinages had been established by royal action, by 1100 most mints across France and the empire were in the hands of local lay or ecclesiastical magnates.[142] Nothing brings out more clearly both the heterogeneity of the Angevin (Plantagenet) empire and the limitation of the attempts at political and administrative unity than its coinage and accounting systems. By 1184, after thirty years of dynastic union, the exchange rates between the money of England (sterling), Maine and Anjou had entered a fixed relationship, suggesting substantial organisation by the ruling power; but the coins of Anjou continued to bear images of Henry II's grandfather Fulk V, while non-Plantagenet coins circulated widely in Henry's French lands and were often accepted as units of account as well as in the marketplace. Even English coinage came to be immobilised when, after Henry II's death in 1189, his successors continued to mint his second coinage of 1180 until 1247. Further south, in Aquitaine, minting was more fragmented still, in parallel to the weaker power of the Plantagenet dukes of Aquitaine.[143] The close connection between English silver coins and the power of the Angevin kings of England in European politics was clear to contemporaries: Philip Augustus, king of France (1180–1223), accused a cardinal whom he regarded as too favourable to Henry II of England as 'already smelling the king's sterlings'.[144] Philip Augustus himself did much to make the minting of coinage an effective tool and demonstration of his power, by suppressing local coinages: but the extent of compromise can be seen in his use of a western French coinage, the *denier tournois*, rather than Parisian money as a way to extend a royal quasi-monopoly of minting and circulation of

[141] J. J. North, *English Hammered Coinage, I: Early Anglo-Saxon to Henry III c.600–1272*, 2nd edn (London, 1980), 98–147; M. Blackburn, 'Coinage and currency', in E. King (ed.), *The Anarchy of King Stephen's Reign* (Oxford, 1994), 145–205.

[142] P. Spufford, *Money and its Use in Medieval Europe* (Cambridge, 1988), 55–7, 99–105. The most comprehensive survey of French medieval coinage remains *Manuel de Numismatique Française*, ed. A. Blanchet and A. Dieudonné, 4 vols (Paris, 1912–36).

[143] B. Cook, '*En monnaie aiant cours*: the monetary system of the Angevin empire', in B. Cook and G. Williams (eds), *Coinage and History in the North Sea World, c.500–1250: Essays in Honour of Marion Archibald* (Leiden, 2006), 617–86 (631–41 for coins of Angers).

[144] 'Adjecit etiam quod praenominatus cardinalis jam sterlingos regis olfecerat': *Gesta Regis Henrici Secundi et Ricardi Primi*, ed. W. Stubbs, 2 vols (London, 1867), ii:66–7.

coin across western France.[145] From the twelfth century onwards, rulers also experimented with heavier coins; the minting of gold coins alongside silver, always rare in the early middle ages and abandoned in Latin Christendom in the ninth century, was also revived with mixed success before 1300.[146]

The Devolution of Political Power: the Household, Patronage and Office

Throughout the period, princely households formed a focus of patronage. The lament of the twelfth-century Anglo-Welsh royal clerk Walter Map about the mutability of the court's composition would have been familiar to courtiers across the period:

> In the court I exist and of the court I speak, and what the court is, God knows, I know not [...] When I leave it, I know it perfectly; when I come back to it I find nothing or but little of what I left there. I am become a stranger to it, and it to me. The court is the same, its members are changed.[147]

The capricious character of court culture is reflected in the literary trope of the *losengiers*, the deceivers or flatterers who conspire against the heroes of romances, and also historical characters such as the eponymous hero of the *History of William the Marshal*.[148] The military and political importance of princely martial retinues, such as the household knights of the Anglo-Norman kings of England or the *teuluoedd* of the Welsh princes, has also been recognised: in societies that mostly lacked standing armies, the presence of a small but permanent military force at the ruler's command could play a decisive role in time of crisis, and so its leading members also tended to enjoy high political favour, receiving rewards not only in military commands such as the constableship of castles or fiscally through salaries, pensions or money-fiefs but also through advantageous marriages, wardships or offices.[149] If such household forces can

---

[145] F. Dumas, 'La monnaie dans le royaume au temps de Philippe Auguste', in Bautier (ed.), *La France de Philippe Auguste*, 541–74 at 546–8.

[146] Spufford, *Money and its Use*, 50–1, 176–86.

[147] Walter Map, *De nugis curialium*, ed. and tr. James *et al.*, 3 (playfully adapting St Augustine of Hippo's comments upon the nature of time). For the Plantagenet court: M. Aurell (ed.), *La Cour Plantagenêt (1154–1204)* (Poitiers, 2000).

[148] 'Vos menzongiers, voz traitors, vos losengiers': *History of William the Marshal*, ed. A. J. Holden, tr. S. Gregory, comm. D. Crouch, 3 vols (London, 2002–6), vol. 1, ll. 5152, 5420, 5722, 5849, 6419–54, esp. 6427–8.

[149] J. O. Prestwich, 'The military household of the Norman kings', *EHR* 96 (1981), 1–35; S. D. Church, *The Household Knights of King John* (Cambridge, 1999); S. Davies, *War and Society in Medieval Wales, 633–1283* (Cardiff, 2004), esp. 14–49. Cf. Abels, *Lordship and Military Obligation*, 161–75 for the military retinues of Anglo-Saxon kings.

be firmly traced only from the eleventh century, the warrior retinues of early medieval kings also exerted a strong political influence.[150] The ecclesiastical counterparts to household knights, the clerks, chaplains, almoners and other functionaries, were similarly well placed to benefit from princely largess: if only a fortunate few received the greatest reward of promotion to a bishopric, there were many lesser rewards that allowed curialist churchmen to advance their careers and political influence through their loyal service at court.

If the court, household or retinue played a central role in political culture across the period, this was less significant than in the Byzantine or Islamic worlds. In general, the princely courts of Latin Christendom lacked the protocols and rigidity of their eastern and southern counterparts. Nevertheless, the late medieval courts enjoyed a sophisticated culture, characterised by the use of display, heraldry and ceremony to communicate power, status and favour.[151] Although Geoffrey Koziol has shown how court ritual could often descend into farce, and Philippe Buc has delivered a cogent critique of highlighting ritual as a category,[152] the role of court ceremony and protocol in political culture should not be underestimated. It has also been cogently argued that later medieval princely courts had a 'civilising' effect, propagating a culture of *mansuetudo* (restraint) ultimately derived from clerical education but adapted for lay culture.[153] A specific political role was accorded to the households of royal consorts. Since queens were frequently from other royal or princely dynasties, often rival ones, their households and courts were frequently mistrusted for allowing undue influence to foreigners. Notwithstanding such suspicion, these played an important part in princely political culture in the central and later middle ages.[154]

---

[150] J. L. Nelson, 'Ninth-century knighthood: the evidence of Nithard', in C. Harper-Bill *et al.* (eds), *Studies in Medieval History Presented to R. Allen Brown* (Woodbridge, 1989), 255–66.

[151] M. Vale, *The Princely Court: Medieval Courts and Culture in North-West Europe, 1270–1380* (Oxford, 2001). For Byzantine courts' projection of status and ideology: pp. 85–7, 303–11. For the Islamic world: pp. 336–9, 356–63.

[152] G. Koziol, 'England, France, and the problem of sacrality in twelfth-century ritual', in T. N. Bisson (ed.), *Cultures of Power: Lordship, Status and Process in Twelfth-Century Europe* (Philadelphia, 1995), 124–48; P. Buc, *The Dangers of Ritual: Between Early Medieval Texts and Social Scientific Study* (Princeton, 2002).

[153] Jaeger, *Origins of Courtliness*; Aurell, *Le Chevalier lettré*. For an example of female agency in cultivating ideas of correct behaviour for royal and noble women: N. Silleras-Fernandez, *Chariots of Ladies: Francesc Eiximenis and the Court Culture of Medieval and Early Modern Iberia* (Ithaca, NY, 2015).

[154] For examples of prominent royal consorts and their courts and patronage: J. Martindale, 'Eleanor of Aquitaine and a "queenly court"?', in B. Wheeler and J. C. Parsons (eds), *Eleanor of Aquitaine: Lord and Lady* (Basingstoke, 2003), 423–39; L. Grant, *Blanche of*

Rulers and Local Affairs

To what extent did rulers intervene in the local affairs of their territories? There is a strong contrast here between Germany, where rulers were rarely involved directly in such matters, and England, where the crown intervened at a local level through the sheriff and shire court from as early as the eleventh century, and this was strengthened by the development of common law procedures under the Angevin kings. This contrast persisted to the end of the middle ages and beyond.

In France, meanwhile, very significant shifts took place during the late twelfth and thirteenth centuries that greatly increased French royal involvement in the local affairs of their kingdom. In the early eleventh century, Ralph Glaber had described Brittany as long enjoying 'freedom from the public fisc' (*libertas fisci publici*), but, by the time he wrote, this was true for most of West Francia, for effective royal authority was restricted to only a small part of the kingdom.[155] The participation of the kings of France in local affairs outside the Paris-Orléans region was spasmodic, opportunistic and rarely sustained. True, participants in local disputes were prepared to invoke the concept of French royal authority and even seek royal confirmations, so that Louis VI (1108–37) and Louis VII (1137–80) issued confirmatory acts concerning Languedoc, even though until the 1220s the Capetian kings had no way of enforcing their acts concerning the far south of their kingdom.[156] By then, Capetian power had been asserted across much of the rest of their realm, largely by force of arms but legitimised by the assertive actions of the king's court. The extension of Capetian judicial power also profited from the convenience for local powers of using the French king's court to arbitrate between them during conflicts; by the extensive use of royal rights over regalian bishoprics and abbeys; by the assertion of royal claims over great noble wards; and by royal marriage alliances with great subjects such as the counts of Blois, Champagne, Toulouse, Flanders and Ponthieu. In contrast to the king of England's systematic reliance upon the shire courts

Castile, Queen of France (New Haven, CT, 2016); M. Howell, *Eleanor of Provence: Queenship in Thirteenth-Century England* (Oxford, 1997); J. C. Parsons, *Eleanor of Castile: Queen and Society in Thirteenth-Century England* (Basingstoke, 1994). J. Bianchini, *The Queen's Hand: Power and Authority in the Reign of Berenguela of Castile* (Philadelphia, 2012), analyses a unique example of a queen regnant (of Castile, 1217, after acting as regent for her brother since 1214), consort (of León, 1197–1204) and co-ruler (of Castile, 1217–46, and of León, 1230–46, in both kingdoms with her son Ferdinand III); see also M. Shadis, *Berenguela of Castile (1180–1246) and Political Women in the High Middle Ages* (New York, 2009).
[155] Rodulfus Glaber, *The Five Books of the Histories*, ed. and tr. J. France (Oxford, 1989), 58.
[156] E.g. A. Luchaire, *Louis VI le Gros: annales de sa vie et de son règne (1081–1137)* (Paris, 1890); M. Pacaut, *Louis VII et son royaume* (Paris, 1964), 99–101.

and legal procedures to extend royal authority in the localities, the Capetian advance was more opportunistic.

Conclusions

Political organisation in Latin Christendom between 700 and the end of the fifteenth century varied enormously from region to region, but some common developments can be identified. By the later middle ages there were many more forms of political organisation than in earlier centuries, but monarchies, principalities, ecclesiastical polities and city states alike relied upon complex procedures using written instruments, and the customs and laws that underpinned these processes had become much more elaborate. In such a culture, knowledge of law and access to the ruler through his or her court lay at the foundations of the elite's hegemony alongside traditional military power.[157] The nature of that military power had been transformed, however, as the means of raising armies and war taxation had become far more sophisticated.

At the end of the middle ages, nobility of lineage and possession of land were still the sine qua non for participation in politics in theory, and noble status was reinforced by ever more elaborate laws. Martial prowess and display remained an integral aspect of political culture. Yet by then urban leaders and the commons had forced their way into the political community in many parts of Latin Christendom, and commercial wealth – and access to it – was playing an increasingly important role in politics. So, too, was the social power that education conferred upon those who wished to make their way in the world through administrative service or the law. Political organisation therefore remained dominated by social rank, yet in practice these ranks were far from rigid castes. For all the attempts of aristocratic military elites to shore up their hegemony, the political culture of most of Latin Christendom remained sufficiently flexible to enable parvenus to enter those elites: by the end of the period, merchants, lawyers and scholars were able to take their place within the elite in ways that would have been unimaginable in the early middle ages. In all spheres of political life, Latin Christian culture had become far more complex than several centuries earlier.

---

[157] On the development of pragmatic literacy: pp. 277–80.

14 Byzantium
'To Have and To Hold' – The Acquisition and Maintenance of Elite Power

Rosemary Morris

Definitions and Contexts

What's in a Name?

The concept of elites, familiar enough to modern political scientists, was not a notion familiar to Byzantines. Nonetheless, the identification of the 'power elite', as delineated by Charles Wright Mills, has proved alluring to writers on Byzantine social history.[1] John Haldon, for instance, distinguishes between a 'general elite' and a 'power elite': the former an 'economically distinct group in control of the basic means of production', which thus ensures its political power, and the latter an inner, or ruling, elite, which controls political authority.[2] Wright Mills' power elite consists of a 'series of overlapping, small but dominant groups' sharing decisions having national consequences and identifiable as members of larger political, economic and military circles. Networking is crucial to career progression and the maintenance of one's influence; clubs provide an important – and exclusive – venue for making and maintaining all kinds of useful contacts. Amongst members they 'accept one another, understand one another and marry one another [. . .] [T]hey tend to work and to think, if not together, then at least alike.'[3]

The concept of the power elite being opposed to the general elite is attractive to Byzantinists, not least because it helps to categorise and thus make sense of the variety of ways in which Byzantines themselves (or at least the literate ones whose records we have)[4] perceived what might

---

[1] C. Wright Mills, *The Power Elite* (Oxford, 1956; repr. with an afterword by A. Wolfe, New York, 1999).
[2] J. Haldon, 'Social elites, wealth and power', in J. Haldon (ed.), *A Social History of Byzantium* (Chichester, 2009), 168–211 [hereafter SEWP] at 170.
[3] Wright Mills, *Power Elite*, 4–5.
[4] Functional literacy in Byzantium was probably more widespread than the amount of surviving documents leads one to expect: pp. 92–4, 96–7. For levels in other spheres: pp. 61–2, 175, 274–87, 107, 109, 126, 127–8.

Figure 14.1 Emperor Nikephoros III Botaneiates flanked by four court officials, and with representations of the imperial virtues of Truth and Justice above, *c.*1078: one of the opening miniatures from a manuscript of the 'Liturgical Homilies of John Chrysostom', originally made for Michael VII and repainted to show his successor; reproduced by kind permission of the Bibliothèque nationale de France, Paris; MS Coislin 79, fol. 2 r

loosely be described as the economically and socially privileged and those able to wield power in all its aspects.[5] The words they use are general, vague or, indeed, archaic. Words like *archon* (pl. *archontes*, leading men), *proteuon* (pl. *proteuontes*, first, but referring to a leading man or men), *dynatos* (pl. *dynatoi*, powerful) and *dynastes* (dynast, ruler) frequently appear in the sources but give us little help in deciding what they meant or implied.[6] But then, our modern English usages of 'upper class' and 'top people' are scarcely more helpful! At the other end of the scale, terms which originally denoted subservience such as *oikeios* (belonging to the household of), *anthropos* (man, but denoting subordination as in 'the lord and his men') and even *doulos* (slave) had, by the late eleventh century, become honorific epithets when nothing was deemed more honourable than to describe oneself as the *oikeios* or *doulos* of the imperial family of the Komnenoi.[7] Family terms could also have a range of meanings: *gambros*, for instance, although in its narrowest sense meaning son-in-law or brother-in-law, was often used to mean any male with whom one had, or wished to have, a relationship of mutual friendship and support. Blood relationships, sometimes very distant, were often being alluded to here, but so were spiritual relationships based on the ties of baptism. Byzantine canon law deemed godparents and godchildren to be related in the same way as blood parents and children; monastic 'spiritual fathers' looked to the spiritual welfare of their 'spiritual children' by not only undertaking their moral and religious guidance but also by generally looking out for their interests.[8] So one is always left to deduce from the context what the implications and nuances of such words were at any given moment in the long history of Byzantium. In these opaque circumstances, the application of some theoretical frameworks seems not only helpful but essential.

But before doing so, it is important to establish what sort of people, in Byzantine eyes, could *never* constitute or gain access to an elite – however loosely defined. Gender was no barrier: women and eunuchs each provided

---

[5] 'Power' is taken to mean 'the ability to influence the behaviour of others according to one's own intentions': H. Goldhamer and E. Shils, 'Power and status', in E. Shils, *Center and Periphery: Essays in Macrosociology* (Chicago, 1975), 239–48 at 239. Goldhamer and Shils identify three major forms of power: 'force', 'domination' and 'manipulation'.

[6] Despite the brave attempts of the contributors to the *Oxford Dictionary of Byzantium*; see e.g. *ODB* i:160, s.v. 'archon' (A. Kazhdan).

[7] P. Magdalino, 'Byzantine snobbery', in *TBA*, 58–78 at 64.

[8] See the work of Ruth Macrides, esp. 'Families and kinship', in *OHBS*, 652–60; and *eadem*, 'The Byzantine godfather', *BMGS* 11 (1987), 139–62; *eadem*, 'Kinship by arrangement: the case of adoption', *DOP* 44 (1990), 109–18; repr. in her *Kinship and Justice in Byzantium, Eleventh–Fifteenth Centuries* (Aldershot, 1999), nos 1 and 2. On non-blood relationships: C. Rapp, *Brother-Making in Late Antiquity and Byzantium: Monks, Laymen and Christian Ritual* (Oxford, 2016); for spiritual fatherhood: *MLIB*, 90–102; see also pp. 203–5, 208, 210.

their own groups of 'powerful'. Nor was an ecclesiastical career.[9] Religion and language were the most important means of defining those irredeemably beyond the pale. To advance in Byzantine society one had to be Greek-speaking, Christian and orthodox at that, although precisely what beliefs and teachings the term 'orthodoxy' meant varied over time. To remain Jewish, Muslim or otherwise non-Christian was, therefore, to bar oneself from any prospect of high social advancement in Byzantium. To be a barbarian, an un-baptised member of the *ethne* (peoples or tribes) living usually outside of the empire but sometimes in small enclaves within its frontiers, was to remain savage and uneducated in the most profound sense. To remain resolutely provincial, either in domicile or manner, especially if one was monoglot in a language other than Greek, was to deny oneself access to the highest echelons of power and to risk the scorn of increasingly powerful groups of urban sophisticates whose main field of activity lay in Constantinople. Or at least it was until 1204, when the Latin conquest of the City and the subsequent establishment of a number of Byzantine 'successor states' elsewhere forced a dramatic re-thinking of notions of capital and provinces.[10]

If Byzantium, in one of its most Roman manifestations, made consistent claims to governance with a hierarchy of officials and administrators centred on an imperial court,[11] it is possible to conceive of this as a power elite whilst still allowing for the existence of other, more locally based, elites in the towns, villages and rural estates of the provinces. Haldon certainly advocates the notion of a 'special interest group within a broader privileged stratum', its members all coming from a similar social and cultural background, sharing the same attitudes, recognising common interests and, crucially, willing to work together – an analysis similar to that of Wright Mills. These groups were not mutually exclusive; individuals could move from provincial to central – until 1204 Constantinopolitan – circles of power or operate in both at the same time. They also could, of course, remain primarily big fish in small ponds and never leave a restricted geographical location.[12]

---

[9] See pp. 201, 203–4, 306, 310–11, 312–14. For western women's ability to manage property and exercise various shades of political power: pp. 55, 72, 375, 397–8, 407; and for the Islamic sphere: pp. 222–3, 504.

[10] G. Page, *Being Byzantine* (Cambridge, 2008), 48–9.

[11] See pp. 318–19, 320. A. Kaldellis, *The Byzantine Republic: People and Power in New Rome* (Cambridge, MA, 2015) postulates strong Roman influences on Byzantine political society.

[12] SEWP, 170–1, 180; also J. Haldon, 'Provincial elites, central authorities: problems in fiscal and military management in the Byzantine state', in B. Forsén and G. Salmeri (eds), *The Province Strikes Back: Imperial Dynamics in the Eastern Mediterranean* (Helsinki, 2008), 157–85 (an adapted version of SEWP).

Both general elites and power elites shared certain characteristics. Haldon emphasises that belonging to a broadly conceived upper class was subject to a number of variables: access to sources of wealth and land (and the maintenance of control over them); an imperial office or title; closeness to the emperor and relationships with other elite families.[13] Chris Wickham, analysing the early Byzantine social hierarchy in the context of a much broader study of early medieval socio-economic history, comes to similar conclusions, emphasising landed wealth, position in an imperial hierarchy, imperial or royal favour, and recognition by one's peers. Distinction of ancestry and lifestyle are also criteria which help to identify membership of elite groupings. Such an analysis, by a primarily western medievalist, highlights a key point: Byzantine elites had much in common with other medieval upper classes. Where they differed was in the importance laid on the various elements constituting elite-ness at any given moment.[14] Emerging from both analyses are certain themes: the origins and foundations of elite power; the ways in which power and influence could be exercised or manifested; the role of lineage and the part played by other kinds of personal relationships and networks in the creation of and accession to the ranks of 'the powerful'; and the strategies for maintaining and passing on privileged status.

Human agency was, of course, the prime mover in the creation and maintenance of elites, although, as Mark Whittow pointed out, 'geography is the key to the history of the Byzantine world'.[15] Its disjointedness and inherently centrifugal biases feature elsewhere in this volume, together with the ebb and flow of enemy invasion and counter-attack.[16] Despite these geopolitical constraints, the imperial centre held fast until the disasters of the later eleventh century. After that point Byzantium was built around what Paul Magdalino has termed a central block surrounding the Aegean and the Black Sea with only a few 'hot spots' directly under imperial control.[17] For him, the empire of the Komnenoi territorially matched the limits imperial forces could reach without help from allies: from the Danube to the Adriatic, but no longer east of central Anatolia or westwards into Italy.[18]

The catastrophe of 1204, however, disrupted this forever. Separatist tendencies were formalised by the Byzantine successor states which

---

[13] SEWP, 169.
[14] C. Wickham, *Framing the Early Middle Ages: Europe and the Mediterranean, 400–800* (Oxford, 2006).
[15] M. Whittow, 'Geographical survey', in *OHBS*, 219–31.   [16] See pp. 180–2, 185–9.
[17] SOE, 251–91; P. Magdalino, 'The empire of the Komnenoi', in *CHBE*, 627–63.
[18] Magdalino, 'Empire of the Komnenoi', 653.

emerged after the conquest of Constantinople by the Fourth Crusade. Geographical determinants played a part, as mini-states based on the plains of northern Greece (at Epiros and Thessaly), across the Bosphoros (at Nicaea) and beyond the Pontic Alps (at Trebizond) vied with each other for the imperial title and, in the process, created more localised *foci* for the activities of elites. In the fourteenth and fifteenth centuries, even the recovery of Constantinople by the rulers of Nicaea in 1261 and the progressive integration of some (though not all) of the successor states into a newly constituted empire presented a serious contradiction: ideologically and diplomatically, the Byzantine empire, its rulers and its Constantinopolitan-based elites continued to posit centralist and, indeed, universalist notions of authority and government. In reality, long-term 'decentralising tendencies' presented a fragmented geopolitical reality.[19] Although 1204 is commonly seen as a turning-point, we still lack an overarching study of the new world in which Byzantines found themselves, a world not only of territorial shrinkage but also where non-Byzantine occupation and government – by Latins or Turks – were a fact of life for many Greek groups still aspiring to local, if not imperial, power and influence.[20] Our literature is skewed towards the earlier period. Comparisons and contrasts across the events of 1204 are thus difficult to make.

What follows has two aims. First, it will examine the aspects of elite power and forms of influence that seem to have crystallised at one critical juncture, between the seventh and the ninth centuries. This entails looking at the status and the material resources of individuals and families and at how far these derived from the holding of public offices and, ultimately, the emperor's favour. Of particular concern will be the state of affairs beyond Constantinople and its hinterland, in the outlying regions which came under heavy barbarian pressure. Tracing the positions, possessions and political horizons of elite individuals and families, and gauging change over time, constitutes our second aim. They seldom receive very detailed coverage in our sources, but we may still piece together a picture

---

[19] A. E. Laiou, 'The Palaiologoi and the world around them (1261–1400)', in *CHBE*, 803–33; for the geopolitics: pp. 188–9; and for the ideological positioning of the post-1261 Byzantine world: pp. 322–6.

[20] In 'Social elites', John Haldon ends his discussion in 1204. The studies in *TBAMF* focus on the eleventh century. The balance has been somewhat redressed by D. Kyritses, *The Byzantine Aristocracy in the Thirteenth and Early Fourteenth Century* (unpublished PhD thesis, Harvard University, 1997; repr. Ann Arbor, MI, 2008) [hereafter *BATEFC*] which deserves to be much more widely known, and by the helpful short survey of D. Stathakopoulos, 'The dialectics of expansion and retraction: recent scholarship on the Palaiologan aristocracy', *BMGS* 33 (2009), 92–101. For discussion of the problem of framing a chronology for the Byzantine world: pp. 183–94.

of what sort of people – provincials and Constantinopolitans – lurk behind terms like *archon* and *dynatos*, their stake in the state apparatus and the strings this could help them to pull, noting their widespread tendency, at least in the ninth to eleventh centuries, to put money into land. No sharp line will be drawn between lay and ecclesiastical examples. But particular attention will be paid to the monastic life, a life which, Byzantines believed, was lived on a higher plane and represented the closest example on earth to the 'life of the angels' within the heavenly hierarchy of which human social order was but a pale *mimesis*.[21]

Continuity or Cataclysm (up to 1204)

New Families, New Elites

The years from 700 to 900, the so-called Byzantine dark age, mark a period when power was summarily wrenched from some previously powerful and privileged groups and shifted to new groupings. The old Roman elites based on the senates in Rome and Constantinople; on the councils of the cities from whom the senatorial aristocracy was drawn; on the great land-owners of the provinces; and on the imperial administration were disrupted. Some disappeared.[22] By *c.*750 senatorial rank was no longer recorded on lead seals; although a senate continued in Constantinople, it became more and more the creature of the emperor, and its members were appointed by him.[23] While the changing fortunes of the provincial cities of the empire in this period are much debated, long periods of warfare, siege and economic disruption undoubtedly isolated them from Constantinople and changed the nature of their government.[24] We know equally little about the survival, or otherwise, of Anatolian or Balkan *villae* in the dark age; it is often assumed that provincial landowners in this period were city dwellers and that the fall of the cities dragged them down too. Written sources for the period are sparse. Some early ninth-century hagiographies give hints about rural landholding in the previous century, especially in Bithynia and the western coastal regions which escaped frequent attack. But if the *Life* of Theodore of Sykeon (d. *c.*613), written after 641, still

---

[21] *MLIB*, 32.
[22] See Wickham, *Framing the Early Middle Ages*, 155–6. For a general historical survey emphasising change, see A. Louth, 'Byzantium transforming', in *CHBE*, 221–48.
[23] SEWP, 176–7.
[24] J. Haldon, *Byzantium in the Seventh Century: The Transformation of a Culture* (Cambridge, 1997), 92–124 discusses the arguments. See also W. Brandes, 'Byzantine cities in the seventh and eighth centuries – different sources, different histories', in G. P. Brogiolo and B. Ward-Perkins (eds), *The Idea and Ideal of the Town between Late Antiquity and the Early Middle Ages* (Leiden, 1999), 25–57.

portrays a world of locally focused landowning in Galatia, the interior of Asia Minor and the Balkans in the following two centuries are, in extant writings, largely blank.[25]

Two questions emerge: first, how far did any identifiable aspects of the life and function of elites in towns other than Constantinople and Thessaloniki carry on; and second, what became of the landowning rural elites? Both these questions can be answered by reference to the prevailing social experience of the dark ages: war. All citizens from the highest to the lowest – significantly, often led by senior churchmen and those in charge of sections of their walls – united to defend Thessaloniki and Constantinople. But what of the provincial towns? Here the prevalent archaeological model is of abandonment and contraction. Cities such as Ankyra, Amorion, Side and Sardis provide instances where the original confines of the city were abandoned and populations re-located to their citadels or other refuges on higher ground. When re-conquest began, new urban units were created: smaller *kastra* (fortified settlements), such as those established in Constantine V's reign (741–75) at Pribaton and Bulgarophygon in Thrace. But the very need to respond and reorganise in times of crisis may have given scope both for action and leadership by individuals who had always had a leadership role to play – bishops, men with practical experience, local area 'bosses' – and for the emergence of new leaders, cool heads in times of crisis.[26]

One example of this kind of activity may be seen in the construction or repair of city walls and other fortifications. The walls of Nicaea, as inscriptions record, were 'repaired by' Leo III (717–41) and Michael III (842–67), but the work was obviously organised locally by men such as the *strator* Isaac (in later monastic life the chronographer Theophanes Confessor) who was responsible for the repair of the walls of Kyzikos.[27] He himself was a military official sent by the emperor, but organisation of the manpower and necessary supplies will have required the co-operation of leading men in the locality. There are other hints that activities traditionally associated with urban 'leading men' may not have entirely ceased. Judging from the *Notitiae episcopatuum* (list of bishoprics), it would appear that many bishops remained in post.[28] Marie-France Auzépy characterises the Byzantine city at this period as 'a local branch

---

[25] *ODB* iii:2045–6, s.v. 'Theodore of Sykeon' (A. Kazhdan). See L. Brubaker and J. Haldon, *Byzantium in the Iconoclast Era (ca. 680–850): The Sources. An Annotated Survey* (Aldershot, 2001) for detailed discussion of dark age sources.

[26] For bishops: pp. 313–14.

[27] SOE, 263–5. See C. Foss and D. Winfield, *Byzantine Fortifications: An Introduction* (Pretoria, 1986), 79–117 for the walls of Nicaea.

[28] *Notitiae episcopatuum ecclesiae Constantinopolitanae*, ed. J. Darrouzès (Paris, 1981): notices 1–3 can be dated to before the end of the ninth century.

of the state': nothing more than a garrison, a refuge and the residence of a bishop. But even she admits there are signs of economic continuity (or restoration) such as the great fair at Ephesos reportedly taking place in 795.[29] Indeed, thorough excavations at Amorion provide a cogent warning against the cataclysm thesis: after short-lived periods of disruption in the seventh and eighth centuries, its sack as late as 838 was probably the major cause of its sudden contraction. Until then a bishopric seems to have survived – and risen in status – and there was continuous restoration and even erection of public buildings, defences and churches.[30] It is difficult to believe that all this was organised solely by imperial officials. Far away from sustained attack, it may even have been possible for late antique civic elites to remain virtually unchanged. The Crimean city of Cherson, for example, has excited interest because of the discovery of seals dating to the tenth century belonging to a *proteuon*, a term for the leading man in late antique civic government. Jean-Claude Cheynet has pointed to the occurrence of the surname Proteuon in the Middle Byzantine period. The name might, he suggests, have emerged 'where municipal institutions were preserved from antiquity and where members of the curial class received this name'.[31]

It is, however, to the influence of the imperial administration, particularly its ever more militarised aspect, that the emergence of a new provincial elite can be ascribed.[32] As the imperial power reorganised its military and fiscal offices to cope with the enemy threat, a new provincial organisation emerged. The debate about origins of the themes and their purpose still continues, but it is clear, first, that they gradually evolved over the period from the mid-seventh to the ninth centuries; and second, that they had a primarily military function. Each theme was led by a military governor (*strategos*) assisted by a corps of locally based officers and administrative staff.[33] These officials were not only designated with

---

[29] SOE, 264.
[30] C. Lightfoot, 'The survival of cities in Byzantine Anatolia, the case of Amorium', *Byzantion* 68 (1998), 56–71; E. A. Ivison, 'Amorium in the Byzantine dark ages (seventh to ninth centuries)', in J. Henning (ed.), *Post-Roman Towns, Trade and Settlement in Europe and Byzantium*, 2 vols (Berlin, 2007), ii:25–60. See also C. S. Lightfoot, 'Amorium', in P. Niewöhner (ed.), *The Archaeology of Byzantine Anatolia* (Oxford, 2017), 333–41.
[31] See J.-C. Cheynet, 'Official power and non-official power', in A. Cameron (ed.), *Fifty Years of Prosopography* (Oxford, 2003), 137–51 at 141; repr. in *TBAMF*, no. 7. See also J. Shepard, 'Closer encounters with the Byzantine world: the Rus at the Straits of Kerch', in K. L. Reyerson et al. (eds), *Pre-Modern Russia and its World: Essays in Honor of Thomas S. Noonan* (Wiesbaden, 2006), 15–78 at 28; N. Alekseyenko, *L'Administration byzantine de Cherson: catalogue des sceaux* (Paris, 2012), 42–3, 65–70.
[32] SEWP, 176–9; see also pp. 316–18.
[33] SOE, 266–8. For the evolution of the theme system: J. Haldon, *Warfare, State and Society in the Byzantine World, 565–1204* (London, 1999), 74–85; also J. Haldon, 'A context for two "evil deeds": Nikephoros I and the origins of the *themata*', in O. Delouis et al. (eds),

ranks reflecting their function but also – and a feature harking back to late antiquity – given court titles. Both types of title received a *rhoga* or imperial salary.[34] It is access to these two forms of influence (a foot on the imperial administrative ladder potentially leading to a successful career, especially in the military, and the acquisition of monetary wealth) which Wickham sees as offering new opportunities to those whose previous sole reliance on landowning was disrupted by attack: 'any surviving city-level landowner of even medium ambition would have found himself in the thematic hierarchies by the eighth century'[35] – a bold statement, perhaps, but one which attempts to explain the emergence of new provincial elite groupings. From now on, access to the court and the imperially appointed hierarchy (both clerical and lay), along with the moveable wealth this yielded, would become the dominant method of attaining elite status.[36]

By the eighth century, important family groupings seem to be emerging, often based in Anatolia.[37] Their names, unlike the lengthy nomenclature of the late Roman upper crust, usually consist simply of forename and surname, alongside the office held.[38] The *Chronicle* of Theophanes, for example, mentions the *patrikios* Sisinnios, surnamed Rendakis, active in Greece, under the year 719.[39] But Asia Minor provides the clearest examples of families that combined generations of military service against the Arabs with amassment of landed estates and local status and influence.[40] One cannot rule out the possibility that some could trace their lineage far back, perhaps to the sort of provincial worthies who had prospered off their landholdings and local markets in the era before the Arabs struck. Leo VI's *Taktika* (*c*.900) presupposes their existence, but

Le Saint, le moine et le paysan: mélanges d'histoire byzantine offerts à Michel Kaplan (Paris, 2016), 245–65.

[34] P. Lemerle, '"Roga" et rente d'Etat au Xe–XIe siècles', *REB* 25 (1967), 77–100; repr. in his *Le Monde de Byzance: histoire et institutions* (London, 1978), no. 16; J.-P. Cheynet, 'Dévaluation des dignités et dévaluations monétaire dans la seconde moitié du XIe siècle', *Byzantion* 53 (1983), 453–77; repr. in *TBAMF*, no. 6; see also pp. 198–201, 309–11.

[35] Wickham, *Framing*, 239.   [36] Haldon, 'Provincial elites', 160–1.

[37] E. Patlagean, 'Les débuts d'une aristocratie byzantine et le témoignage de l'historiographie: système des noms et liens de parenté aux IXe–Xe siècles', in *TBA*, 23–43; J.-C. Cheynet, 'The Byzantine aristocracy (8th–13th centuries)', in *TBAMF*, no. 1, 1–43. For Anatolia: L. Andriollo, *Constantinople et les provinces d'Asie Mineure, IXe–XIe siècle: administration impériale, sociétés locales et rôle de l'aristocratie* (Leuven, 2017), 355–402.

[38] J.-C. Cheynet, 'Aristocratic anthroponimy in Byzantium', in *TBAMF*, no. 3, 1–30.

[39] Theophanes, *Chronographia* AM 6211, ed. C. de Boor, 2 vols (Leipzig, 1883–5), i:400; tr. C. Mango and R. Scott, *The Chronicle of Theophanes Confessor* (Oxford, 1997), 552 and n. 10 on 553.

[40] See Andriollo, *Constantinople et les provinces*, 319–54.

significantly the context is one of military service. And, the emperor comments condescendingly yet approvingly, it is those generals lacking in 'ancestral renown' who make up for it by undertaking 'more dangerous activities'.[41] Leo's military handbook, like some of the writings attributed to his son, Constantine VII, gives us a glimpse of the essentially merito-cratic considerations governing imperial attitudes towards promotion in the armed forces.[42] So long as the state of emergency lasted, agricultural rhythms were liable to disruption, and anyway the urban markets for produce were, at best, of limited purchasing-power. Service with the armed forces amounted to a kind of insurance policy for one's lands and also pathways to prominence. It is no accident that the Argyros, Phokas and Maleïnos families, all of significance from the late ninth century onwards, were major landowners in Cappadocia, the front line against Muslim forces.[43] Their landed estates do not seem to have been ancestral and will anyway have been at risk from enemy raids.

What gave them the ability to rise from merely provincial to empire-wide significance was their possession of moveable wealth, and this was primarily derived from their *rhogai*.[44] The quite commonly held dignity of *magistros*, for example, befitting an officer at the height of his career, brought him a *rhoga* of 16 pounds of gold per annum (equivalent to 1,152 *nomismata*) as well as his military salary, which could be as much as 40 pounds of gold per annum, equal to 2,880 *nomismata*, and a share of any booty acquired on campaign.[45] Even though many offices had to be bought, the yield on capital was often as high as 20 per cent.[46] To put this in perspective, the cost of an *oikos* (residence, not just house) in tenth-century Constantinople is noted as 2,160 *nomismata*; that of a *modios* ($^1/_{10}$ $^1/_{12}$ of a hectare) of arable land, ½ *nomisma*; that of a sheep, $^1/_6$ *nomisma*; and that of a manuscript, 26 *nomismata*.[47] Such men were seriously rich,

---

[41] Leo VI, *Tactica* II.16, ed. and tr. G. T. Dennis, *The Taktika of Leo VI*, rev. edn, *CFHB* 49 (Washington, DC, 2014), 24–5; see also A. Kazhdan, 'The aristocracy and the imperial ideal', in *TBA*, 43–57 at 43; pp. 316–17.

[42] See pp. 317–18.

[43] M. Kaplan, ' Les grands propriétaires de Cappadoce', in *Le aree omogenee della Civiltà Rupestre nell'ambito dell'Impero Bizantino: la Cappadocia* (Galatina, 1981), 125–58; repr. in his *Byzance: villes et campagnes* (Paris, 2006) [hereafter *BVC*], 100–22.

[44] For texts and discussion on the challenge of 'the powerful' in the tenth century: *The Land Legislation of the Macedonian Emperors*, tr. E. McGeer (Toronto, 2000).

[45] Cheynet, 'Devaluation des dignités', 457 n. 15.

[46] N. Oikonomides, 'Title and income at the Byzantine court', in *BCC*, 199–215 at 202; repr. in his *Social and Economic Life in Byzantium*, ed. E. A. Zachariadou (Aldershot, 2004), no. 27, estimates that even middle-ranking officials could gain returns of 6%–20% on their capital outlay if they received annual salaries in the region of 300 *nomismata* (4 pounds of gold = 288 *nomismata* of 23 carats fine).

[47] J.-C. Cheynet *et al.*, 'Prix et salaires à Byzance (Xe–XVe siècles)', in V. Kravari *et al.* (eds), *Hommes et richesses dans l'empire byzantin*, 2 vols (Paris, 1989–91), ii:339–74 at

as often too were their wives, holders of offices in their own right and holders under Roman law of inherited or dower land and moveable wealth.[48] These high-flyers would maintain a residence in the City (as Constantinople was known) while keeping up their estates far away in the country.[49] And individuals went beyond this to make a bid for the throne itself, drawing on their military reputation and connections. Nikephoros and Bardas, members of the Phokas family in the tenth century, are obvious examples, the one succeeding in becoming emperor in 963; the other rebelling unsuccessfully against both John Tzimiskes and Basil II in subsequent decades. Both had the backing of members of the Maleïnos family. Another contender, Bardas Skleros, came from another army family of relatively recent ascent holding properties in Asia Minor.[50]

Individuals like the two Bardases, Phokas and Skleros were the exception, not the rule. Many senior commanders in their respective families served the empire loyally, as did countless officers without any pretension even to become players in the power elite. We know next to nothing about them, because they never did anything heinous or spectacular enough to earn mention in a chronicle, and archival evidence of their activities is virtually non-existent. What is, however, clear is that the assortment of persons owing status and substance to some sort of state connection or patronage were predisposed to put their wealth into landed property. The imperial legislation of the tenth century inveighs against their intervention in the land markets; it dubs them the powerful, as against the poor – the little people, lacking such connections and income streams, whom the emperor purports to be standing up for.[51] It is a measure of the lucrativeness of the state apparatus that this legislation identifies the powerful primarily as all holders of imperial posts and rank. Even a low thematic military rank, such as that of *komes*, was entitled to a *rhoga* of 6 *nomismata* during a campaign against Crete in 949, and a civilian judge or tax-collector could also expect to receive imperially sanctioned *synetheiai* (fees) in cash or in kind from the communities in which they were

344–5, 350, 353; V. Kravari, 'Note sur le prix des manuscrits (IXe–XVe siècle), in *ibid.*, ii:375–84 at 381.

[48] M. Kaplan, 'L'aristocrate byzantin et sa fortune', in S. Lebecq *et al.* (eds), *Femmes et pouvoirs des femmes à Byzance et en Occident (VIe–XIe siècles)* (Villeneuve d'Ascq, 1999), 205–26; repr. in *BVC*, 184–204.

[49] See p. 200.

[50] R. Morris, 'The two faces of Nikephoros Phokas', *BMGS* 12 (1988), 83–115; for the revolts of the Bardases Phokas and Skleros: C. Holmes, *Basil II and the Governance of Empire* (Oxford, 2005), 240–98; for the revolt of a younger Nikephoros in the early 1020s: *ibid.*, 515–25; on the Maleïnoi: J.-C. Cheynet, 'Les Maleïnoi', in his *La Société byzantine: l'apport des sceaux*, 2 vols (Paris, 2008), ii:511–24.

[51] R. Morris, 'The powerful and the poor in tenth-century Byzantium: law and reality', *P&P* 73 (1976), 3–27.

active.[52] In a system where tax-farming was prevalent and where payments even for access to justice were normal, there was profit to be made even from the lowliest office. The same went for the great monastic houses of the empire, such as those on Athos, where, again, imperial *rhogai* were granted to the monks on a yearly basis, thus integrating them into the imperial hierarchies of dependence.[53] The lists of the powerful included high churchmen, *hegoumenoi* (abbots) and the 'supervisors of pious or imperial houses' (*euages oikoi*, charitable institutions) with good reason, for many of them received imperial bounty.[54]

What could be done with *rhogai*? Here we are at something of a loss. Although we know that office-holders invested in shops and workshops in Constantinople as well as property, not much is known of the investment strategies of Byzantine provincial lay landowners.[55] But if one were to look at another type of *oikos*, the monastery, the uses of liquid assets become much clearer. The archives of powerful Athonite monasteries such as the Great Lavra and Iviron reveal a steady process of land and property accumulation, centred around the fertile agrarian regions of northern Macedonia and Thrace and the city of Thessaloniki which, in its turn, provided a steady income in the form of the sales of surplus produce or rents.[56] The cases of disputed land acquisition involving some of the big names of the provinces (the Skleros family, for example) that were recorded in the eleventh-century legal compilation of the *Peira* would indicate that powerful lay landowners aimed to extend their holdings in much the same way. Indeed, at the end of the eleventh century the widow Kale-Maria Pakourianos was able to donate an entire village, Radolibos in Thrace, to the Monastery of Iviron and still have other holdings and assets to bequeath elsewhere.[57]

---

[52] Cheynet *et al.*, 'Prix et salaires', 367; *ODB* iii:1993, s.v. '*synetheia*' (N. Oikonomides and M. Bartusis).

[53] For a table of imperial *rhogai* and *solemnia* (diverted fiscal revenues) to monastic houses in the period *c.*900–*c.*1100: *MLIB*, 194.

[54] *Land Legislation*, tr. McGeer, 55 (Doc. C: *novella* of Romanos I, 934).

[55] See pp. 425–6; for the discussion of an eleventh-century 'diversified portfolio', that of Michael Attaleiates: M. Kaplan, 'Les artisans dans la société de Constantinople', in N. Necipoğlu (ed.), *Byzantine Constantinople: Monuments, Topography and Everyday Life* (Leiden, 2001), 245–60 at 256; repr. in *BVC*, 297–307.

[56] *MLIB*, 200–40.

[57] Kale-Maria Pakourianos' initiative illustrates the resources and agency exercised by women below the topmost level of formal authority, where ideological constraints applied: pp. 88, 311, 434. See for the west: pp. 72, 375; and for elite women and female property-holders in the Islamic world: pp. 21–2, 471, 501. For the will of Kale-Maria Pakourianos: *Actes d'Iviron*, ed. J. Lefort *et al.*, 4 vols to date (Paris, 1985–), ii:178–83 (no. 47, dated 1098); for the donated village: J. Lefort, 'Radolibos: population et paysage', *TM* 9 (1985), 195–234. See also pp. 97–8, 202–3.

But imperial largesse to the favoured came in other ways, too. One of the few detailed descriptions of a lay estate from the eleventh century, the so-called *Praktikon* of Andronikos Doukas, notes the gift of an imperial *episkepsis* (estate or group of estates) by his cousin, the emperor Michael VII Doukas (1071–8), which formed the core of his extensive landholding in the Maeander Valley in western Asia Minor.[58] One has, however, to remember that what the emperor gave he could also take away. Basil II, for instance, confiscated enough properties from his enemies after the revolts of Phokas and Skleros families to create a series of imperial *episkepseis* in Asia Minor; indeed, the main farm (*oikoproasteion*) of Andronikos Doukas' new estate of Alopekai had once belonged to a member of the Parsakoutenos family, one-time supporters of the Phokas clan but now, as Peter Thonemann trenchantly puts it, 'in terminal decline'.[59] But though possession of land was useful and – despite protestations that autarky was the only 'proper' stance for a landowner of standing – could often be profitable, it could also fall victim to the vagaries of climate or agrarian mishap.[60] To retain influence, one needed access to public office and the rewards that came with it. As Catherine Holmes has shown, the rebel Eustathios Maleïnos, though allowed to keep his estates, was 'politically neutered' after his revolt against Basil II by being kept 'like a wild beast in a cage' under house arrest in Constantinople.[61]

Display, conspicuous consumption and keeping up appearances were some of the most lasting behavioural characteristics of Byzantine elites, both on an imperial level and in a provincial context. The lead was clearly given by the fashions and styles of the imperial house, but it is clear that this percolated down through the provinces and, indeed, across Byzantium's borders.[62] Display was crucial to the maintenance of social position. It manifested itself in an increasing diversity in material culture visible from the eleventh century onwards. The wills of successful imperial servants in

---

[58] *Praktikon* of Michael VII Doukas: *Vyzantina engrapha tes Mones Patmou*, ed. E. Vranouse *et al.*, 3 vols (Athens, 1980–2016), ii:3–35 (no. 50); for detailed discussion: P. Thonemann, *The Maeander Valley: A Historical Geography from Antiquity to Byzantium* (Cambridge, 2011), 259–70.

[59] J.-C. Cheynet, 'Basil II and Asia Minor', in P. Magdalino (ed.), *Byzantium in the Year 1000* (Leiden, 2003), 1–38; repr. in *TBAMF*, no. 7; Thonemann, *Maeander Valley*, 261.

[60] M. Kaplan, *Les Hommes et la terre à Byzance du VIe au XIe siècle: propriété et exploitation du sol* (Paris, 1992), 493–522. For the argument that 'aristocratic self-sufficiency' was a brake on Byzantine economic activity: M. Whittow, 'The middle Byzantine economy (600–1204)', in *CHBE*, 465–92 at 488. But it is clear that even Athonite houses had estates which produced for the market, presumably emulating the practices of contemporary lay landowners: see p. 431.

[61] C. Holmes, 'Political elites in the reign of Basil II', in Magdalino (ed.), *Byzantium in the Year 1000*, 35–69; SEWP, 194.

[62] J. Shepard, 'Invisible Byzantiums', in M. Grünbart *et al.* (eds), *Material Culture and Well-Being in Byzantium (400–1453)* (Vienna, 2007), 225–34, esp. 231–2.

the eleventh century, such as the Georgian general Gregory Pakourianos and the administrator Michael Attaleiates, mention silk clothing (often given as imperial rewards); those of Symbatios and Kale-Maria Pakourianos mention silver plate to the value of 50 pounds of gold, books, icons, gold jewellery, and gold-decorated harnesses as well as coin.[63] The 'repertoire of tableware' depicted in frescoes increased dramatically from the eleventh century onwards.[64] The availability of silk clothing, once the prerogative of the imperial house, is a particularly interesting indicator of more widespread wealth and the ambition to display it publicly. Even as early as the tenth century, the *Book of the Eparch*, dealing with the regulation of commerce in Constantinople, was concerned that *archontes* were attempting to buy certain 'imperial quality' types of silk for their own private use and, tellingly, that garment merchants were attempting to buy valuable silk garments *from* them. An unregulated market for expensive silks clearly already existed.[65] By the eleventh century, silk was being produced outside Constantinople; in Thessaloniki, Athens, Thebes and Corinth in Greece; and also in the Byzantine provinces of southern Italy, testifying to a growing provincial market for luxury clothing.[66] In this provincial setting, the urge to stand out could give rise to lavish buildings such as those of the eleventh-century 'manorial' complex at Baris in the lower Maeander Valley, described in the *Praktikon* of Andronikos Doukas, with its domed church, domed cruciform hall with living rooms opening off it, and bath house. As for the residence of Constantine Doukas (son of the emperor Michael VII) at Pentegostis near Serres, the rooms were 'big enough to receive an emperor as guest'.[67]

---

[63] A. Muthesius, 'Textiles and dress in Byzantium', in Grünbart *et al.* (eds), *Material Culture*, 159–69 at 160. See '*Typikon* of Gregory Pakourianos for the Monastery of the Mother of God *Petritzonitissa* in Bačkovo', tr. R. Jordan in *BMFD*, ii:507–63 at 553; '*Rule* of Michael Attaleiates for his Almshouse in Rhaidestos and for the Monastery of Christ *Panoiktirmon* in Constantinople', tr. A.-M. Talbot in *BMFD*, i:326–76 at 359–60; *Actes d'Iviron*, ed. Lefort *et al.*, ii:154 (no. 44, ll. 4–8, dated 1090); ii:179–81 (no. 47, ll. 21–47, dated 1098).

[64] M. G. Parani, 'Byzantine material culture and religious iconography', in Grünbart *et al.* (eds), *Material Culture*, 181–92 at 185.

[65] See J. Koder, 'The authority of the eparchos in the markets of Constantinople (according to the Book of the Eparch)', in P. Armstrong (ed.), *Authority in Byzantium* (Farnham, 2013), 83–108 at 94–5 and nos 31–3 on 105. In tenth- to eleventh-century Egypt, one pound of raw silk cost the equivalent of 2.5 *dinars*, enough to feed a family for a month: Muthesius, 'Textiles and dress', 159. See also p. 321.

[66] For a general survey of silk manufacture: *ODB* iii:1896–7, s.v. 'silk' (A. Gonosová and N. P. Ševčenko).

[67] For Baris: P. Magdalino, 'The Byzantine aristocratic *oikos*', in *TBA*, 92–111 at 95; Thonemann, *Maeander Valley*, 266; for Pentegostis: Anna Komnene, *Alexiad* IX.5.4, ed. D. R. Reinsch and A. Kambylis, 2 vols (Berlin and New York, 2001), i:269; tr. E. R. A. Sewter, rev. P. Frankopan (Harmondsworth, 2009), 247. Pentegostis was visited by Alexios I Komnenos in 1094: D. I. Polemis, *The Doukai: A Contribution to Byzantine Prosopography* (London, 1968), 63. But see also the description of what might be a much

These examples come from records about members of the power elite, but they suggest how pervasive was the imperial reach – and hopes of that reach. The question arises of whether this Constantinopolitan-centric axis was the only significant coordinate among the general elite or whether other connections counted – kinship, for example. Here again, one must resort largely to monastic texts for information, and members of the power elite loom large in them. But many of the social values of the secular world are reflected in these texts, and they show abiding concern with family, property and continuity. They also tell us about property differentials and pecking orders at local level.

Big Fish in Smaller Ponds

Most of the surviving *typika* (monastic foundation documents) place great emphasis on commemoration of members of the founder's family. Some houses, such as the Georgian Monastery of Iviron on Mount Athos, were clearly thought of as family property, where succeeding *hegoumenoi* were to be drawn from close relatives of the founder.[68] In others, such as the nunnery of the Theotokos Kecharitomene, founded *c.*1110 in Constantinople by Eirene Doukaina, wife of Alexios I Komnenos, alongside the family commemorations elaborate provisions were made for members of the empress's family to live in the house and be buried there.[69] Such monasteries often replicated the elite hierarchies of the world, serving to perpetuate the memory and indeed power of these important kinship groups. In economic terms, too, foundation and patronage of a family house could serve to protect and even increase family property, since no lands and buildings alienated to the church could be confiscated or sold. For instance, by founding a complex of monastery and hospice in Rhaidestos and Constantinople, Michael Attaleiates ensured for his son Theodore and his descendants a continuing stream of revenue when he decreed that any revenue received 'in excess' of monastic and charitable needs should be divided: one-third to the monastic treasury, but two-thirds to his heirs.[70] This formula neatly avoided the accusation that he was

---

more modest aristocratic *oikos* near Butrint in southern Albania: S. Greenslade and R. Hodges, 'The aristocratic *oikos* on the Vrina Plain, Butrint *c.* AD 830–1200', *BMGS* 37 (2013), 1–19.

[68] The founder and first three *hegoumenoi* of Iviron were all related: *Actes d'Iviron*, ed. Lefort *et al.*, i:93–4.

[69] '*Typikon* of Empress Irene Doukaina Komnene for the Convent of the Mother of God *Kecharitomene* in Constantinople', tr. R. Jordan in *BMFD*, ii:649–724, chs 4, 71, 76, 80 on 670–1, 700–2, 704–5, 709–11.

[70] '*Rule* of Michael Attaleiates', tr. Talbot, ch. 24 on 345; M. Kaplan, 'Les monastères et le siècle à Byzance: les investissements des laïques au XIe siècle', *Cahiers de Civilisation*

embezzling consecrated funds: who was to decide what constituted 'excess' is not made clear in the foundation document! In short, lay elites patronised monastic houses as a matter of course, and this was as true in the far-flung corners of the Byzantine provinces as it was in Constantinople.

Important monastic communities exerted influence over a wide area – in the case of holy mountains like Athos, Galesion and Latros, empire-wide. But even the inhabitants of small, local houses provided local spiritual and communal leadership. The monks of the Monastery of St John Kolobos in the small *kastron* (fortified town) of Hierissos, just outside the borders of Mount Athos, played their part with the lay inhabitants in attempting to stop the encroachments of the Athonite monks onto communally held lands in the region in the early tenth century. And the small rural chapels served by eight to ten monks which featured in a *novella* of Basil II (996) were clearly thought worthy of protection by the emperor from the encroaching hands of bishops.[71] This was not just for spiritual reasons. In their attempts to control the activities of the provincial powerful, emperors could look to village leaders, whether clerical or lay, and to village institutions as potential allies against the *dynatoi*: they might be expected to support and implement imperial edicts against the latter.[72]

Unfortunately, we know little about the rural clergy in the period before 1204.[73] The popularity of Theodore of Sykeon, who was frequently called upon in the seventh century to lead religious processions as well as settle disputes or cast out demons, may indicate that few rural clergy were available to carry out such rituals.[74] But by the tenth and eleventh centuries, at least in those areas for which we have documentation, village priests appear. More often than not they were completely integrated into village society, and their frequent appearance in witness lists, alongside

---

Médiévale 27 (1984), 71–83 at 79; repr. in *BVC*, 123–37 at 132–3. See also pp. 93, 207–9, 315–16.

[71] R. Morris, 'Dispute settlement in the Byzantine provinces in the tenth century', in W. Davies and P. Fouracre (eds), *The Settlement of Disputes in Early Medieval Europe* (Cambridge, 1986), 125–47 and Appendix XXI; *Land Legislation*, tr. McGeer, 122–7 (Doc. O).

[72] Michel Kaplan argues that Constantine VII's *novella* of 947 was particularly aimed to protect 'cette élite villageoise': *Hommes et la terre*, 231. For the dynamics of making appeals and dispute-settlement available to those dissatisfied with their local courts and lords in the Latin west: pp. 68–70, 71–2, 278–9, 401–3, 408–9.

[73] No legal or canonical text deals with the subdivisions of Byzantine bishoprics, and the meaning of the word *paroikos* (only in some cases 'parish') also presents problems: M. Kaplan, 'Le village byzantine: naissance d'une communauté chrétienne', in *Villages et villageois au Moyen Âge* [= *Actes des congrès de la Société des historiens médiévistes de l'enseignement supérieur public* 21] (Paris, 1992), 15–25; repr. in *BVC*, 79–87.

[74] Kaplan, *Hommes et la terre*, 202.

more prosperous lay members of the community, suggests they formed part of the village elite.[75] Beside them – when land transactions needed to be witnessed, when the defence of village rights had to be undertaken, or when information about landholdings had to be given to imperial fiscal administrators or judges – can be found the *oikodespotai* (heads of households), the larger village landowners found in the rural *choria* (villages or, generally, lands) of the *Life* of Theodore of Sykeon, in the documents of the Athonite archives and in the so-called *Marcian Treatise* (tenth–twelfth century), a guide for tax officials, where they are contrasted with 'simple villagers'.[76] Thus even at the very local level, Byzantine commentators were conscious of the existence of 'greater' and 'lesser' individuals; it was often the case, indeed, that the imperial power sought to protect these local village leaders and headmen (for they were always men) from the activities and ambitions of those who were greater in larger spheres. What was common to both groups, however, was a degree of landholding and an involvement in the administrative life of the empire and in the drawing up of the documentation upon which it depended. The literate, however stumbling they might be, themselves formed a kind of elite.[77]

What these various elites had in common was concern with the land and who had the rights to till or graze it. And unofficial networks and groupings are obvious enough, whether of family or the better-off households in village communities. No less clear are the tensions within communities and, indeed, between the imperial lawmakers and their many minions intent on putting the fruits of office into landed property. These findings are in line with our earlier considerations, that state office was the primary source of serious money and, conversely, that possession of the estates this might buy would be all the more secure thanks to one's official status. To that extent, state institutions and family interests and local networks could interact indefinitely, and positively, for all their inherent frictions.[78] But this begs the question of whether substantial economic benefits could accrue from landed estates, alongside individual status and familial influence. And this opens up issues of production and manufacturing for profit, of rural

[75] Kaplan, *Hommes et la terre*, 202–3, 227–31.
[76] See C. M. Brand, 'Two Byzantine treatises on taxation', *Traditio* 25 (1969), 35–60 at 49 (where *oikodespotai* is translated as 'house-owners'). On evidence for village social structures to be deduced from witness lists and for *oikodespotai* acting as village representatives in disputes: L. Neville, 'Organic local government and village authority', in Armstrong (ed.), *Authority in Byzantium*, 285–95.
[77] For both the acquisition of literacy, and the formal deployment of it, particularly in public reading: G. Cavallo, *Lire à Byzance* (Paris, 2006); on literacy and access to justice at grassroots: pp. 97, 296. See also (for the west), pp. 273–83.
[78] See also pp. 201, 203.

and urban markets, and of local, regional and trans-regional trade, activities that might be expected to rebound once the pressure from Arab attackers eased. Did these provide new means of making serious money, or did they fit into the existing imperial order?

Merchants and Money Men: a New Elite?

The wide availability of oriental-influenced textiles, perfumes, pottery and glass from the tenth century onwards points to lively trade in luxury goods and flourishing markets for them in the major cities of the empire. The Muslim and Jewish traders who brought them from the east are well known to scholars.[79] But what of the Byzantine merchants who bought from them? How far did this elite overlap with the administrative and military groups whose power and influence is much more obvious?

A lack of source material lies at the root of the difficulty of identifying those Byzantines who gained wealth and influence from trade. In contrast with Genoa, for example, virtually no Byzantine contracts have survived. Yet they must have existed, since the *Rhodian Sea Law*, probably dating from the later eighth century, contains a number of clauses insisting on the drawing up of contracts in writing if they are to be binding.[80] A further difficulty lies in the fact that contemporary Byzantine historians devoted little space to the doings of townspeople in general and their mercantile and banking activities in particular.[81] But enough clues are there to support the view that those involved in trade or other financial activity grew in significance in the politics of larger cities, especially Constantinople and Thessaloniki.[82]

Scholars have been wary of placing this development much before the eleventh century, associating it with the admission by Constantine IX Monomachos (1042–55) and Constantine X Doukas (105 9–67) of, as Michael Psellos put it, 'nearly all the people of the market and vagabonds' to the ranks of the senate and thus breaking the long-established legal

[79] M. Mundell Mango (ed.), *Byzantine Trade, 4th–12th Centuries* (Farnham, 2009); for Jewish traders: S. D. Goitein, *A Mediterranean Society: The Jewish Communities of the Arab World as Portrayed in the Documents of the Cairo Geniza*, 6 vols (Berkeley, 1999); N. M. El-Cheikh, *Byzantium Viewed by the Arabs* (Cambridge, MA, 2004), 139–88.
[80] See S. A. Epstein, *Genoa and the Genoese, 958–1528* (Chapel Hill, NC, 1996), 55–66. The *Rhodian Sea Law*, tr. M. Humphreys in *The Laws of the Isaurian Era: The Ecloga and its Appendices* (Liverpool, 2017), 113–28, ch. 20 on 122: 'Whoever hires a ship, the agreement must be written and sealed [or subscribed] to be effective.'
[81] For the Justinianic prohibition (re-iterated in the late ninth-century *Basilika*) on the holders of titles and 'those of good birth' undertaking commercial activity: M. Gerolymatou, 'L'aristocratie et le commerce (IXe–XIIe siècles)', *Symmeikta* 15 (2002), 77–89 at 77.
[82] See pp. 326–7.

prohibition on 'artisans' entering it.[83] Psellos was exaggerating, but this was a significant step, marking the moment when the old legal demarcation line between those who were 'senatorial' and those who were not was breached.[84] Individuals and groups drawing their wealth primarily from commerce can, however, be identified earlier than this period; and, more significantly, individual members of the senatorial class were themselves clearly involved in private trading enterprises.[85] The *Book of the Eparch* mentions the *argyropratai* of Constantinople, the goldsmiths who provided not only luxury items but also credit. The emperor Romanos I Lekapenos (920–44) is reported to have bought promissory notes (*semadia*) from the goldsmiths and had these ceremoniously burnt outside the Church of Christ of the Chalke, thus freeing many of the citizens of Constantinople of their debts.[86] Indeed, as early as seventh century the *Miracula S. Demetrii* mentions a group of *archontes* who sold grain at high prices for export while Thessaloniki was under siege and whom Paul Lemerle identified as 'great merchants who held municipal offices'.[87] They could equally well have been primarily provincial office-holders who, like the *kommerkiarioi* of the same period, bought up provisions on behalf of the state but also made a profit on the side for themselves.[88] Such trading activity on the part of members of the administrative elite is also evident in the *Book of the Eparch*. There, *archontes* not only participate in the silk trade but also buy animals directly from livestock dealers, clearly participating in the cattle trade.[89] Nicholas Oikonomides was

---

[83] G. Dagron, 'The urban economy, seventh–twelfth centuries', in *EHB*, ii:393–461 at 415 and n. 18. Constantine X Doukas was reported to have observed that there was no need only to consider those of high birth or those from the existing senatorial families when recruiting to the senate, since this might well limit access only to imbeciles.

[84] Gerolymatou, 'L'aristocratie et le commerce', 77, 87; Dagron, 'Urban economy', 415–16. Alexios Komnenos attempted to turn back the tide by legislating that only those senators *not* enrolled in a guild (i.e. not engaging in commerce) could enjoy the old privilege of taking legal oaths in their own homes, but the die was cast, and this atavistic response does not seem to have stopped the trend towards a less socially exclusive senate.

[85] Any rank above that of *protospatharios* was considered 'senatorial' in the tenth and eleventh centuries: Cheynet, 'Byzantine aristocracy', 3.

[86] *Book of the Eparch* ch.2, ed. and German tr. J. Koder, *Das Eparchenbuch Leons des Weisen*, CFHB 33 (Vienna, 1991), 84–9; tr. E. H. Freshfield, *Roman Law in the Later Roman Empire: Byzantine Guilds, Professional and Commercial: Ordinances of Leo VI c. 895 from the Book of the Eparch* (Cambridge, 1938), 10–13; Dagron, 'Urban economy', 438 n. 249.

[87] A. E. Laiou, 'Exchange and trade, seventh–twelfth centuries', in *EHB*, ii:697–770 at 701–2, citing *Les Plus anciens recueils des miracles de saint Démétrius et la pénétration des Slaves dans les Balkans*, ed. P. Lemerle, 2 vols (Paris, 1978–80), i:211–12; ii:118.

[88] A. Dunn, 'The *kommerkiarios*, the *apotheke*, the *dromos*, the *vardarios* and the west', *BMGS* 17 (1993), 3–24.

[89] See *Book of the Eparch* ch. 6.10, ed. Koder, 98–9; tr. Freshfield, 22, where members of the guild of *metaxopratai* (raw silk merchants) are forbidden to sell to an *oikeios* (in this case

able to demonstrate that holders of offices and ranks invested in commercial property – shops and workshops – in Constantinople in the tenth century, although appointing slaves as frontmen to run workshops was common, perhaps an attempt to disguise such activity.[90] The well-known anecdote of Emperor Theophilos (829–42) ordering a ship apparently belonging to his wife Theodora to be burnt has received an interesting reinterpretation in terms of gender politics: what was perfectly proper activity for an emperor was not proper for his wife.[91] Yet it has taken some time for the scholarly consensus that the Byzantine aristocracy did not indulge in undignified mercantile activity to be eroded.[92] So it is worth citing another instance of someone at the top of the power elite using their position to profit from the market. Leo Phokas, the brother of the emperor Nikephoros II Phokas (963–9), was accused of making a profit out of grain sales at a time of dearth in Honorias and Paphlagonia and condemned for his association with *sitokapeloi* (speculators in grain).[93]

Two centuries later, there seems to have been little social opprobrium attached to active participation in trading ventures by the emperors themselves. Indeed Isaac II Angelos (1185–95) requested the commune of Genoa to punish one Guilelmo Grasso, a pirate who had attacked ships carrying Byzantine envoys to Saladin and their Muslim counterparts to Constantinople. He claimed damages for himself and his brother, the *sebastokrator* Alexios (later Alexios III Angelos), as well as the imperial *mystikos* (secretary) and other merchants. Isaac's property was valued at 6,675 *hyperpera*; that of his brother at 50,000 *hyperpera* (eclipsing the total

---

meaning 'member of the household') of a 'powerful person' (*dynatos*); see also *ibid.* ch. 16.2–5, ed. Koder, 124–7; tr. Freshfield, 40, for the livestock trade. For discussion: Gerolymatou, 'L'aristocratie et le commerce', 77; Dagron, 'Urban economy', 442, 457.

[90] For examples of aristocratic investment in shops in the capital in the tenth century: N. Oikonomides, 'Quelques boutiques de Constantinople au Xe s.: prix, loyers, imposition (*Cod. Patmiacus* 171)', *DOP* 26 (1972), 345–56; repr. in his *Byzantium from the Ninth Century to the Fourth Crusade: Studies, Texts, Monuments* (Aldershot, 1992), no. 7; for slaves running *ergasteria* ('workshops') on behalf of their masters: Dagron, 'Urban economy', 421.

[91] Genesios, *Regum libri quattuor* III.20, ed. A. Lesmüller-Werner and H. Thurn, *CFHB* 14 (Berlin, 1978), 53; tr. and comm. A. Kaldellis, *On the Reigns of the Emperors* (Canberra, 1998), 69; J. H. Pryor, 'Shipping and seafaring', in *OHBS*, 482–90 at 482–3. On the question of women's property-holding and involvement with business in the Byzantine and other spheres: p. 72 n. 132, pp. 201, 203, 434, 502, 24–5.

[92] Dagron, 'Urban economy', 416 interprets the anecdote in a more traditional way: what was suitable activity for a person of lower social standing was not suitable for an emperor.

[93] Leo the Deacon, *History* IV.6, ed. C. B. Hase, *Historiae libri decem*, *CSHB* (Bonn, 1828), 64; tr. A.-M. Talbot and D. F. Sullivan, *The History of Leo the Deacon: Byzantine Military Expansion in the Tenth Century* (Washington, DC, 2005), 112 and n. 49; John Skylitzes, *Synopsis historiarum*, ed. H. Thurn, *CFHB* 5 (Berlin and New York, 1973), 278, ll. 66–7; tr. J. Wortley, *John Skylitzes: A Synopsis of Byzantine History, 811–1057* (Cambridge, 2010), 266–7.

of 39,193 *hyperpera* claimed by all the other merchants) and that of the *mystikos* at 700 *hyperpera*.[94] By this time, the end of the twelfth century, new men with a status based on wealth more than on blood had, as we have seen, long been allowed into the senatorial ranks, thus crossing this barrier from outside. But existing insiders were finding new ways of making money and began to expand their activities from land exploitation into areas like participation in trading enterprises at home and overseas.[95]

This process of diversification of elite activity is also evident among the more powerful monasteries. Like their lay counterparts, monastic landholders had always traded to a certain extent, but it is noticeable that, by the mid-eleventh century, conflicts on Athos about the possession of boats (clearly intended to convey and acquire produce beyond the mountain) were rife. By the end of the century, the estates of such houses as the Great Lavra and Iviron stretched far into Macedonia and Thrace and were organised to provide agrarian surpluses sellable for profit. Possession of property including workshops and shops, particularly in Thessaloniki, also gave access to urban markets.[96] The evolution towards justifying the acquisition of wealth by citing the needs of ever-growing monastic numbers is mirrored by the disputes over both principles and practice this engendered and by the compromises which the imperial regulatory chrysobulls for the Holy Mountain struck.[97] By the late eleventh century, monastic founders had also lost any lingering sensitivity about profitable activity. Gregory Pakourianos proudly listed the estates with which he intended to endow his foundation at Bachkovo; the updated versions of the *Hypotyposis* of the Monastery of the Theotokos Evergetis near Constantinople took care to include commemorations for benefactors who had given land and monetary donations to the house.[98]

Seen in this light, the view of many scholars that autarky was the prevailing attitude amongst tenth- and eleventh-century Byzantine landowners looks

---

[94] F. Miklosich and J. Müller (eds), *Acta et diplomata graeca medii aevi sacra et profana collecta*, 6 vols (Vienna, 1860–90), iii:37–40; Gerolymatou, 'L'aristocratie et le commerce', 87; Laiou, 'Exchange and trade', 750. The *hyperperon* (*nomisma*) was a gold coin introduced by Alexios I in 1092. The term continued to be used as a money of account after gold coins ceased being struck in Byzantium in the mid-fourteenth century: *ODB* ii:964–5, s.v. '*hyperperon*' (P. Grierson).

[95] Oikonomides, 'Quelques boutiques de Constantinople' mentions the names of five holders of court rank who invested in commercial property.

[96] For monastic shipping: K. Smyrlis, *La Fortune des grands monastères byzantins (fin du Xe– milieu du XIVe siècle)* (Paris, 2006), 106–16; for buildings: *ibid.*, 118–24.

[97] For the regulation of Athonite boats: '*Typikon* of Emperor Constantine IX Monomachos', tr. T. Miller, in *BMFD*, i:281–93.

[98] '*Typikon* of Gregory Pakourianos', tr. Jordan, chs 2, 33 and D–E at 524–7, 551–2, 555–7; *The* Hypotyposis *of the Monastery of the Theotokos Evergetis, Constantinople (11th–12th Centuries)*, tr. R. H. Jordan and R. Morris (Farnham, 2012), ch. 36, 201–3 at 202.

bizarre. Certainly, this is a view promoted by the eleventh-century writer Kekaumenos but, as so often with obviously didactic texts such as his, this might well be a case of 'do what I say, not what I do'.[99] However, without the evidence that we need – the nuts and bolts of trading contracts, bills of lading, documents dealing with the settlement of debts and so on – we are left with many questions to answer about the commercially profitable activities of elite individuals and institutions in the period before 1204.

Old and New Rewards

The opening up of the senatorial ranks to urban traders and merchants and to those, like Michael Attaleiates, who confessed themselves of 'foreign [i.e. provincial] and humble origins' meant that they, too, could enjoy the social cachet which membership brought, at least up to 1204.[100] In theory, therefore, these newcomers could also enjoy the cash *rhoga* payable to holders of court ranks. But this source of reward was already under threat by the middle of the eleventh century. It was certainly gone by the end of Alexios I Komnenos' reign.[101] Rewards in moveable form were still forthcoming, however, in the form of imperial gifts, monetary 'tips' on taking office and valuable regalia (such as costumes) associated with office-holding. But the emphasis changed from a system of cash rewards for office-holders to that of grants of the revenues from state institutions, of diversion of – or exemptions from – taxation and, in some cases, of gifts of land. Whatever the reason for the discontinuation of *rhogai* – Oikonomides connected it with a shortage of precious metal and

[99] 'Make self-sufficient investments for yourself': Kekaumenos, 'Counsels and tales', ed. and Russian tr . G. G. Litavrin, *Sovety i rasskazy Kekavmena*, 2nd edn (St Petersburg, 2003), 204–5; tr. C. Roueché, 'Consilia et narrationes', (2013) www.ancientwisdoms.ac.uk/library/kekaumenos-consilia-et-narrationes/ (accessed 25 July 2019), 36.13; 'Concern yourself first with the essentials for your household': ed. and tr. Litavrin, 236–7; tr. Roueché, 51.11. See also pp. 97–8.

[100] '*Rule* of Michael Attaleiates', tr. Talbot, 333. There is no mention of a senate or senators in the empire of Nicaea, and after the restoration of 1261 the term *synkletos* is generally used to denote the highest echelon in society rather than a specific group, though it did have a more specialised meaning in the sense of those holding high enough positions to allow them to be employed as judges. See *BATEFC*, 54–64, 66–71.

[101] *BATEFC*, 52, 144. Oikonomides cites a remark of Zonaras that Alexios I Komnenos 'being short of money, to begin with cut off the habitual yearly gifts to those holding ranks (*axiomata*)' (though note that Zonaras does not use the word *rhoga*) after they had been 'curtailed' by Isaac I Komnenos: Oikonomides, 'Title and income', 207–8, 211. Magdalino, citing a comment of Theodore Balsamon, considered that these changes went as far back as the reign of Constantine X Doukas: P. Magdalino, 'The Byzantine army and the land: from *stratiotikon ktema* to military *pronoia*', in K. Tsiknakis (ed.), *To empolemo Vyzantio: 9.–12. ai. / Byzantium at War (9th–12th c.)* (Athens, 1997), 15–36 at 30 and n. 53. My thanks to Robert Jordan and the late Ruth Macrides for assistance with the texts concerning *rhogai*.

an increased demand for coin to pay mercenaries in the eleventh century at a time of serious debasement, although this has been disputed – important questions are raised by the increase in grants of key imperial resources from the end of the century onwards.[102] Were the Komnenoi beginning a process of 'selling off the family silver' which fatally weakened the financial resource-base of the empire and, perhaps more significantly, irrevocably damaged the relationship between landholding elites and the emperor, to the detriment of the latter's power? Or should we see these new forms of reward as practical and effective responses to the military crisis in which the imperial power found itself by 1100 and which worsened in the following centuries?

It is important to distinguish between those forms of recognition and reward which had long been granted to favoured individuals and institutions and those which appear for the first time in the second half of the eleventh century. In the former category must be placed the remission or diversion of land taxes (logisimon; solemnion) or of supplementary charges and corvées (exkousseia) made as an imperial gift which the Marcian Treatise indicates were known before the reign of Emperor Leo VI (886–912).[103] Mark Bartusis has argued that these early privileges were only granted to religious institutions, but this interpretation turns on a tricky point of translation, and it may be that some laymen were also similarly favoured.[104] In addition, the imperial 'gift' of paroikoi, whereby monastic houses (we have no surviving early evidence for laymen) were granted exemptions from secondary taxes on a certain number of peasants already working their lands or were allowed to settle a certain number

---

[102] Oikonomides, 'Title and income', 207. For the decline in the precious metal content of the gold nomisma (87% fine under Constantine IX Monomachos; 70% fine under Romanos IV Diogenes; and 11% fine in the early years of Alexios I Komnenos) and the silver miliaresion (from 91%–71% fine under Romanos IV and 45% fine under Nikephoros III Botaneiates): LPIB, 115.

[103] For the Marcian Treatise: F. Dölger, Beiträge zur Geschichte der byzantinischen Finanzverwaltung: besonders des 10. und 11. Jahrhunderts (Leipzig, 1927), 113–23 (Greek); Brand, 'Two Byzantine treatises', 48–57 (English tr.). For a discussion of its date, which must be after 912, as Leo VI is referred to as deceased: LPIB, 33. It has been variously dated to the tenth, eleventh and even the twelfth centuries. The earliest surviving text of an exkousseia grant is Actes du Prôtaton, ed. D. Papachryssanthou, 2 vols (Paris, 1975), no. 1 (934).

[104] LPIB, 73–86, but see R. Morris, 'Monastic exemptions in tenth- and eleventh-century Byzantium', in W. Davies and P. Fouracre (eds), Property and Power in the Early Middle Ages (Cambridge, 1995), 200–20 at 205. The passage concerned (ed. Dölger, Beiträge zur Geschichte der byzantinischen Finanzverwaltung, 117; tr. Brand, 'Two Byzantine treatises', 50) reads, in Brand's translation: '[...] such and such an emperor ordered that the public revenues of properties belonging to such and such a hostel or old-people's home or monastery or church or someone else be not collected [...]'. Bartusis suggests that we should read 'something else', thus meaning that all the institutions concerned were ecclesiastical or charitable. The Greek could mean either.

of peasant families who would be free from such taxes, was well in evidence by the tenth century.[105]

By the mid-eleventh century, however, not only had such grants become more widespread and, without doubt, were also being given to laymen, but other types of imperial resources were being given out. As we have seen, between 1071 and 1078 Andronikos Doukas was granted estates previously forming part of an imperial *episkepsis* in western Asia Minor.[106] He was also allowed an *exkousseia* on certain charges. So too were Michael Attaleiates, for his properties at Rhaidestos and Constantinople (1074); Gregory Pakourianos (1083), who received grants of imperial land and privileges in Europe in compensation for lands lost to the Turks in Asia Minor; and Leo Kephalas, rewarded for his sterling efforts in combating the Normans in the Balkans by two extensive chrysobulls from Alexios I Komnenos granting him estates and exemptions at Tadrinou (1082) and Mesolimna (1084). The latter, interestingly, was land which the emperor had previously confiscated from two rebels, Othon and Leo Vaasprakhanites.[107]

Dearth of surviving evidence concerning grants to laymen (as against monasteries) makes it hard to adjudge how much of a departure these eleventh-century examples were. Nonetheless, one gains a distinct impression that they *had* become more widespread, along with the practice of granting the revenues of imperial *sekreta* (financial institutions) to favoured individuals. Constantine IX Monomachos made over the revenues of the *sekreton* of the Tropaiophoron to his mistress, Maria Skleraina; Nikephoros III Botaneiates granted revenues of three *sekreta* to Eudocia Makrembolitissa, the widow of his predecessor, Romanos IV Diogenes; and Alexios I Komnenos granted those of the *sekreton* of the Myrelaion to his mother, Anna Dalassene.[108] This may have been a specific method of rewarding elite females, debarred by their sex (and possibly their position as imperial or quasi-imperial) from being easily able to manage or defend large estates distant from Constantinople but certainly more than able to enjoy their revenues.[109]

Komnenian family government, whereby blood- or marriage-ties to the ruling house became the most important signifier of elite power at the end of the eleventh century, also had a part to play in this new system of rewards. Alexios I Komnenos created what Bartusis has termed a 'new aristocracy' by granting land and fiscal rights to close relatives. His brother-in-law Nikephoros Melissenos (d. 1104) was possibly granted

---

[105] For 'gifts' of *paroikoi* to monastic houses: *MLIB*, 186–8 (Table 1).
[106] See p. 423 and n. 58.   [107] *LPIB*, 86–7, 123–5, 128, 139–45; *MLIB*, 287–8.
[108] *LPIB*, 117.   [109] See pp. 21–3. These individuals were of topmost status in the elite.

the tax revenues of Thessaloniki; his brother Adrian Komnenos (d. 1105) was certainly granted those of the peninsula of Kassandra in the Chalkidike; and his brother-in-law John Doukas gained property and rights in the Strymon Valley. The properties and rights given to Alexios' brother Isaac Komnenos, also in the Chalkidike, were made up to a considerable extent from lands confiscated from two great monasteries of the region, the Athonite houses of Lavra and Iviron. The confiscations came after rigorous inspections by fiscal officials in the early years of Alexios' reign had found that the houses held considerable surpluses of land in relation to the taxes they were actually paying: another reminder of the role of imperial confiscation in the making – and breaking – of elite landed power.[110]

As Bartusis succinctly puts it, from the 1080s onwards, 'cash grants were out, land and tax revenues were in'.[111] But were these resources irrevocably lost to the fisc? Some were, such as the lands and privileges granted to Gregory Pakourianos which he then passed on to his monastic foundation at Bachkovo. But others were limited to the lifetime of the holder and could, indeed, be revoked at the emperor's whim.[112] These limitations were also true of the grants of fortresses (*kastra*) made to individuals in the late eleventh and twelfth centuries. Only the rubric of a *novella* of Michael VII Doukas (1071–8) on this subject survives. But it makes clear that such assigning of the maintenance and defence of fortresses was to be temporary – though, interestingly, now *kastra* also figured amongst donations to monasteries, and they, presumably, *did* hold onto them.[113] Thus the defence of the empire remained an imperial prerogative. So, far more importantly, did the administration of justice. At no time did Byzantine emperors willingly allow local seigneurial defensive and judicial rights and immunities to exist or expand. There is a contrast here with rulers in the Latin west.[114]

---

[110] *LPIB*, 132, 147; Oikonomides, 'Title and income', 211.   [111] *LPIB*, 150.

[112] For Gregory Pakourianos' monastic endowment: p. 431 n. 98.

[113] N. Oikonomides, 'The donation of castles in the last quarter of the eleventh century', in P. Wirth (ed.), *Polychronion: Festschrift Franz Dölger zum 75. Geburtstag* (Heidelberg, 1966), 413–17; repr. in his *Documents et études sur les institutions de Byzance* (London, 1976), no. 14; *LPIB*, 159–60. For the donation of *kastra* by Gregory Pakourianos to Bachkovo and the grant by Alexios Komnenos to Christodoulos of Patmos of the right to build fortresses on Patmos against the attacks of Turkish pirates, see Cheynet, 'Byzantine aristocracy', 36, and for later 'private' fortifications, see K. Smyrlis, 'Estate fortifications in late Byzantine Macedonia: the Athonite evidence', in F. Daim and J. Drauschke (eds), *Hinter den Mauern und auf dem offenen Land: Leben im byzantinischen Reich* (Mainz, 2016), 189–205.

[114] Cheynet, 'Byzantine aristocracy', 31–40; for the pluralistic jurisdictions and variant modes of dispute settlement in the west: pp. 145–8, 150–2, 165–9, 384–5, 400–4, 408–9; for methods of funding Islamic states: pp. 471–2.

The twelfth century saw the continuation by the Komnenian emperors both of the system of allocating swathes of land to be administered by their relatives and the granting of lands and revenues to third parties by way of confirming their loyalty and service to the empire. The historian John Kinnamos reported that John II Komnenos (1118–43) had planned to grant the administration (and presumably also the revenues) of Cilicia, Antioch, Attaleia and Cyprus to his son, the future emperor Manuel I Komnenos; the plan was overtaken by John's death.[115] Manuel himself took the process of granting land, exemption from secondary taxes and dues, and 'gifts' of *paroikoi* a stage further by granting them to those entered on the military rolls – Byzantines and foreign mercenaries alike. This not only regularised the system of grants known as *pronoiai* but also widened the social mix of those participating in this system of maintenance and reward. This development had certain advantages: it could encourage loyalty to the state and commitment to service in the army – and this at a time of major military challenge to the empire – and might well have been a more efficient means of supporting an increased military establishment off what the land could directly produce, rather than from diminishing imperial stocks of cash.[116] But it meant that what had, in previous centuries, been a means of strengthening elite privilege now became much more widespread. While such concessions only ran for the lifetime of any individual holder, were inalienable and were only granted (and re-granted) by imperial authority, little damage was done to imperial prerogatives. However, as Cheynet has pointed out, this was dependent on a strong, centralised imperial power and on the efficiency of its administration.[117]

The End of the 'Old Regime'

By the end of the twelfth century, the Komnenian system of family government had begun to unravel. This was partly because of the devolution of large areas of the empire to the governance of members of the family and the resentments this caused amongst other aristocrats outside the 'magic circle'. But greatest damage was done by the in-fighting amongst the Komnenos clan for the imperial power. All of them had come to regard this as part of a family patrimony in which even minor branches of the house had a stake. The family ties and personal

---

[115] John Kinnamos, *The Deeds of John and Manuel Comnenus*, tr. C. M. Brand (New York, 1976), 26–7.
[116] *LPIB*, 64, 95–7, 111–12, 170–2.   [117] Cheynet, 'Byzantine aristocracy', 29–30.

connections making up the Komnenian power system were proving disruptive to the workings of the state's formal institutions. The increasing tendency of the imperial members of the family to marry into foreign aristocratic families, particularly in the west, added a dangerous new dimension to the toxic competition.[118] The marginalisation and subsequent murder of the young Alexios II Komnenos (1180–3) by his cousin Andronikos I Komnenos (1183–5) was the spark which ignited the powder-keg of simmering resentment amongst other members of the kin. Andronikos himself was overthrown by the descendants of Alexios I Komnenos' daughter Theodora and her husband – the Angeloi – whose own internecine feuds and the appeal to the forces of their western relatives to intervene in them led directly to the diversion of most of the Fourth Crusaders to Constantinople.[119]

The fragmentation of power amongst the very highest echelons of the power elite had immediate consequences for the nature of imperial power. Separatist tendencies, always a latent threat in such a vast empire, came to the fore as local dynasts, often enlisting the help of urban elites, took advantage of dysfunctional imperial rule in Constantinople.[120] This was not a wholly new phenomenon. In the mid-eleventh century, the *archon* Nikoulitzes Delphinas had led a rebellion in Larissa against an increase in taxation ordered by Constantine X Doukas, and in 1077 the usurper Nikephoros Bryennios sought the support of the *archontes* of Adrianople before embarking on a march upon Constantinople. But the later alliances of urban leaders with elements of the citizenry were much more serious propositions; they were longer lasting, for one thing, and in many towns they marked the moment when the balance of power and authority slipped from the hands of loyal representatives of the emperor into those of more local interests. Around 1188, Theodore Mankaphas, a leading citizen, proclaimed himself emperor, minted coinage and set up a quasi-independent state centred on Philadelphia in western Asia Minor which lasted until 1206.[121] There are signs of urban elites trying to do their bit to maintain order, forming assemblies and councils, especially in Constantinople itself. These developments might eventually have worked to the advantage of the imperial order, but events overtook them, the

---

[118] Magdalino, 'Empire of the Komnenoi', 627, 657–8.

[119] For the Byzantine background to the Fourth Crusade: M. Angold, *The Fourth Crusade: Event and Context* (Harlow, 2003); J. Phillips, *The Fourth Crusade and the Sack of Constantinople* (London, 2005).

[120] For geography and centrifugal tendencies: pp. 180–2, 202.

[121] J.-C. Cheynet, 'Philadelphie, un quart de siècle de dissidence, 1182–1206', in H. Ahrweiler (ed.), *Philadelphie et autres études* (Paris, 1984), 39–54; repr. in *TBAMF*, no. 9. Kaldellis, *Byzantine Republic*, 118–64 sees these rebellions as expressions of 'the extra-legal sovereignty of the people'.

consequences of Komnenian in-fighting and, above all, the onset of the Fourth Crusade.[122] Leo Sgouros, son of an imperial tax official in Nauplia, seized power in Corinth and, in the chaos following 1204, attacked and burned the lower city of Athens, whilst its archbishop, Michael Choniates, defended the Acropolis on behalf of the emperor.[123] Isaac Komnenos, a brother of the emperor Manuel I, had seized power in Cyprus in 1184 and ruled the island until its conquest by Richard the Lionheart in 1191.[124] These centrifugal tendencies were exacerbated after the Latin conquest, when the scions of what had been the imperial family 'went local' in Epiros, Trebizond and Nicaea, girding themselves with imperial trappings but nonetheless heavily reliant on the support of local elites.[125] Even before 1204, questions could be legitimately asked about where imperial power actually lay. Centralised state service was no longer the unquestioned route to prestige and wealth: loyalty and adherence to imperial rule, wherever based, was now more a matter of strategic choice.[126]

Cataclysm or Continuity? 1204 and Beyond

While it is tempting to conclude that nothing was ever the same after 1204, many aspects of Byzantine elite power and its articulation persisted right up until the fall of Constantinople in 1453 and, indeed, beyond.[127] Elite groups of types familiar from earlier centuries can still be discerned: a few powerful family groupings at the top, such as the Palaiologoi, the Kantakouzenoi, the Tornikes, the Philes and the Angeloi, defined by their ability to claim at least one Komnenian ancestor; those who made their way up via the army or bureaucratic service, such as the *mesazon* (chief minister) Nikephoros Choumnos (1250/5–1327), who cemented his position by marrying his daughter to a son of Emperor Andronikos II Palaiologos (1282–1328); local *dynatoi* or landowners, both monastic and lay, and, increasingly, the holders of *pronoiai* and those referred to as *archontes*, whom Nevra Necipoğlu has defined as 'local office-holders who dominated civic

---

[122] D. Kyritses, 'The imperial council and the tradition of consultative decision-making in Byzantium (eleventh-fourteenth centuries)', in D. Angelov and M. Saxby (eds), *Power and Subversion in Byzantium* (Farnham, 2010), 57–69.
[123] Page, *Being Byzantine*, 86.
[124] Short survey in P. Stephenson, 'Political history (1025–1204)', in J. Harris (ed.), *Palgrave Advances in Byzantine History* (Basingstoke, 2005), 39–57.
[125] J. Shepard, 'General introduction', in *CHBE*, 2–75 at 43. See p. 415.
[126] See pp. 186–90.
[127] For arguments about continuity, especially of ideology: pp. 201–11, 292–5, 321–9.

life'.[128] To these should be added leading members of the increasingly important urban-based trading and banking groups.[129]

A major change, however, was that political fragmentation led to a shrinking in the scale of imperial power and its physical re-location. Late Byzantine history is essentially a history of regions, and each of the successor states – Nicaea, Trebizond and Epiros – constructed its own forms of ruler–elite relationships, as did other regimes, whether Frankish, Slav or Turkish operating in former Byzantine space.[130] Even when Byzantine rule was restored in Constantinople in 1261 this made little difference. The erstwhile capital of a single empire was now just one capital amongst many empires and statelets within the territory once constituting the Byzantine empire, some of which were not even ruled by 'Romans' at all.[131] Indeed, as Angeliki Laiou argued, the recovery of the city of Constantinople 'forced the empire into diplomatic and ideological positions which were often untenable',[132] as successive rulers attempted to cope with the challenges of reconciling imperial theory with harsh reality.

This harsh reality, of a much diminished territory under Greek rule, meant that dealing with the enemy – whether Latins, Turks or, increasingly, Serbs – was a major preoccupation both for those who considered themselves 'imperial', such as the scions of the Komnenian family who ruled in the successor states, and also for those who considered themselves important, if not influential, on a more local level.[133] The emperors of Nicaea and Trebizond, for example, saw no need to have any truck with the Latin conquerors of Constantinople; those who ruled in Epiros and, later, in the despotate of Morea had, of necessity, to do business with the Frankish lords who were now their masters or neighbours. On the other hand, reaction – whether in the form of hostility or of accommodation and compromise – to the Turks of western Asia Minor and, from the mid-

---

[128] Discussion of terminology in *BATEFC*, 7–74; A. E. Laiou, 'The Byzantine aristocracy in the Palaiologan period: a story of arrested development', *Viator* 4 (1973), 131–52; repr. in her *Gender, Society and Economic Life in Byzantium* (Aldershot, 1992), no. 6; N. Necipoğlu, 'The aristocracy in late Byzantine Thessaloniki: a case study of the city's *archontes* (late 14th–early 15th centuries)', *DOP* 57 (2003), 133–51 at 135 and n. 5; *BBOL*, 56–83.

[129] General surveys: K.-P. Matschke, 'Late Byzantine urban economy, thirteenth–fifteenth centuries', in *EHB*, ii:463–95; *idem*, 'Commerce, trade, markets and money, thirteenth–fifteenth centuries', in *EHB*, ii:771–806.

[130] J. Harris, 'Political history (1204–1453)', in Harris (ed.), *Palgrave Advances in Byzantine History*, 58–67 at 61.

[131] See pp. 188–9.   [132] Laiou, 'Palaiologoi and the world', 804.

[133] For the fragmentation of the Komnene kinship group: Magdalino, 'Empire of the Komenoi', 662.

fourteenth century onwards, the Balkans became an increasingly pressing challenge for all.[134]

'Sleeping with the Enemy'?

In the lands taken by the Latins after 1204, the problem of whether to collaborate with the new Frankish or Venetian rulers immediately presented itself to the Greek *archontes*. Teresa Shawcross has revealed a much more nuanced range of reactions than previous presentations of 'heroic resistance and non-cooperation' suggested. Although the Greek version of the *Chronicle of Morea*, the only detailed source for our Greek lands in the thirteenth century, mentions few 'collaborators' in the immediate aftermath of the Fourth Crusade, the letters of Michael Choniates, the erstwhile archbishop of Athens, take a more pragmatic approach. 'You would do well', he wrote to the *hegoumenos* of the monastery of Kaisariane, near Athens, 'to serve your present lords and carry out that which they deem agreeable'.[135] Some did precisely that, including Choniates' nephew, another Michael, who took service with the Frankish de la Roche family. Many, particularly clerics who could not leave their flocks, such as Euthymios Tornikes in Chalkis, seem to have kept their heads down whilst secretly keeping contact with fellow orthodox. Others, while gaining a reputation for collaboration, such as the *archon* Gabriel Larynx, deemed 'a supporter of the Franks' by Demetrios Chomatenos, archbishop of Ohrid (1216/17–c.1236), was also in active contact with officials in the successor state of Epiros.[136] But others again, especially as time went on and the Latin occupation showed no signs of ending, took more radical and decisive action. Choniates wrote of the *pansebastos* Chalkoutzes from Euboia, who, around 1214, 'abandoned his homeland, his estates, his children and his entire wealth and fortune' and fled to the court of the emperor Theodore I Laskaris (1205–21) in Nicaea. Theodore Komnenos Doukas, Despot of Epiros (c.1215–30), complained that his court was 'swarming with Peloponnesians'.[137] In general, however, in Greece at least, as the *Chronicle of Morea* reveals, many Greek landowners came to a rapprochement with their Frankish overlords, who, in their turn,

[134] For a general survey: *BBOL*, 3–17.
[135] T. Shawcross, 'The lost generation (c.1204–c.1222): political allegiance and local interests under the impact of the Fourth Crusade', in J. Herrin and G. Saint-Guillain (eds), *Identities and Allegiances in the Eastern Mediterranean after 1204* (Farnham, 2011), 9–46 at 21; for an older view of 'orthodox patriotism': N. Oikonomides, *Hommes d'affaires grecs et latins à Constantinople (XIIIe–XVe siècles)* (Montreal, 1979), 26–7, 32.
[136] Shawcross, 'Lost generation', 23–4.   [137] Shawcross, 'Lost generation', 27–8.

allowed them to retain their property, their 'Roman' ways of life (including inheritance customs) and, crucially, their church. In Adrianople, the Venetians claimed suzerainty over the city but left it autonomous under its *capitaneus* (governor), the caesar Theodore Branas, who swore loyalty to them and undertook to provide 500 cavalry when requested.[138] In Crete, on the other hand, the victorious Venetians confiscated considerable amounts of land and redistributed it to their own followers.[139]

Facing up to the Turks brought more serious disruption. By the mid-fourteenth century, most of Asia Minor had been lost; by the end of the century, the Balkans had also fallen.[140] As the Ottomans advanced, many of the Byzantine aristocrats who had regrouped around the Laskarid rulers of the empire of Nicaea moved their centre of operations westwards.[141] This was due partly to the regaining of property in and around Constantinople after the city was recaptured from the Franks in 1261 but also to the increasing acquisition of grants of land in the western themes after 1260.[142] The Philanthropenoi gained *pronoiai* in Thrace, the Choumnoi gained *pronoiai* in Macedonia and the Kantakouzenoi, whose wealth originally came from their estates in Asia Minor were, by the mid-fourteenth century, based around the city of Serres in Macedonia.[143] Demetrios Kyritses has characterised the 'high aristocracy' as 'rootless', gaining lands and privileges where they could, though still viewing Constantinople as their base. But some consolidation can been seen on a slightly lower social level: landholding in Thrace, for example, was dominated by court officials, such as the *protostrator* Theodore Synadenos, who had residences in Adrianople and Bizye and whose *oikeioi* controlled the latter town in 1321.[144]

The inexorable advance of the Turks had two serious consequences for the Byzantine landholding elite, both lay and ecclesiastical: loss of lands and the wealth they produced had somehow to be compensated for; and, on the wider political plane, the reduction of the power of the emperor – eventually himself a mere vassal of the Ottomans – precipitated a profound re-assessment of where the sources of power and influence now lay.[145] The Monastery of St John Prodromos on Mount Menoikeion

[138] M. Angold, 'Archons and dynasts: local aristocracies and the cities of the later Byzantine empire', in *TBA*, 236–53 at 244.
[139] Page, *Being Byzantine*, 182–93.
[140] General survey in Laiou, 'Palaiologoi and the world', 806–9, 829.
[141] *BATEFC*, 80.
[142] For the reclaiming of property in Constantinople in 1261 and the attribution of unclaimed assets to the caesar Alexios Strategopoulos: *BATEFC*, 84.
[143] Laiou, 'Byzantine aristocracy in the Palaiologan period', 142.   [144] *BATEFC*, 102–3.
[145] By *c.*1372 Emperor John V Palaiologos (1341–91) was a vassal of the Ottomans, and his son, the future Manuel II, was sent to the court of Murad I at Edirne (Adrianople). The

near Serres (founded *c.*1332) was first under the protection of Simonis, a daughter of Andronikos II and wife of the Serbian ruler, Stefan Uroš II Milutin (1282–1321), then under that of the future emperor John VI Kantakouzenos (1347–54). In 1345, it obtained from Stefan Uroš IV Dušan (1331–55) a chrysobull protecting its lands and subsequently received from the Turkish sultans Murad I (1362–89) and Mehmed I (1413–21) *fermans* exempting its property from taxes.[146] The process by which the Athonite monasteries, major landholders in Thrace and Macedonia, managed to negotiate new relationships with first Serbian and then Ottoman overlords in the region in the fourteenth and fifteenth centuries provides striking examples of this kind of institutional re-orientation. In 1423–4, a delegation of Athonites travelled to Edirne to give obeisance to Sultan Murad II (1421–51), but they had already tapped into the generally protective attitude of the Ottoman rulers to consolidate their property-holdings at the expense of less fortunate landowners.[147] In one notable episode, the Athonite monasteries of Koutloumousiou, Chilandar and Esphigmenou competed to buy up the lands of the impoverished Thessalonikan Monastery of Akapniou in the early 1390s; Esphigmenou won.[148]

Such re-orientation was imitated by the manoeuvrings of local lay landowners, fellow members of the general elite. Many kept their lands under the Serbs and Turks or received rewards for their support. In Thessaloniki and its hinterland, the Ottomans, who possessed the city from 1387–1403 and finally conquered it in 1430, tried to assure the loyalty of the local *archontes* by promising them high posts and granting them lands. The fate of the unfortunate Monastery of Akapniou was sealed by the granting of their lands at Achinos in the Strymon valley by the Turkish general and vizier Hayreddin Pasha to one Makarios Bryennios during the siege of Thessaloniki in 1383–7; by 1393 other lands in the same village had been granted to Demetrios Bryennios Laskaris as '*pronoia*' (possibly an early *timar* or fief) by either Murad I or his successor, Bayezid (1389–1402).

relationship of submission to the Ottoman sultan and payment of tribute to him remained until the fall of Constantinople in 1453. For a discussion of Byzantine elites' 'accomodation' with the Turks: T. Papademetriou, *Render unto the Sultan: Power, Authority, and the Greek Orthodox Church in the Early Ottoman Centuries* (Oxford, 2015), 179–213.
[146] '*Typikon* of Joachim, Metropolitan of Zichna, for the Monastery of St John the Forerunner on Mount Menoikeion near Serres', tr. T. Miller, in *BMFD*, iv:1579–1612.
[147] For a short introduction: E. A. Zachariadou, '"A safe and holy mountain": early Ottoman Athos', in A. Bryer and M. Cunningham (eds), *Mount Athos and Byzantine Monasticism* (Aldershot, 1996), 127–32; for longer studies: E. A. Zachariadou, 'Mount Athos and the Ottomans *c.* 1350–1550', in *CHC* 5, 154–68; Papademetriou, *Render unto the Sultan*, 88–101.
[148] *BBOL*, 92–4, 114.

These Bryennioi were not from Thessaloniki but from Serres, further to the east and in territory firmly under Ottoman control. In the city itself, Alexios Angelos Philanthropenos, the caesar of Thessaly, was reported to have 'made arrangements' with the Ottomans, with the consequence that, after they entered Thessaloniki in 1387, he was allowed to keep his small monastery of St Photis and other immoveable property.[149] Indeed, during the 1420s, when the city was under much-resented Venetian rule, Archbishop Symeon of Thessaloniki maintained that, although 'hoarding their wealth and exalting themselves', many of the Greek *archontes* would have 'preferred to be governed by the Turks'.[150]

Civil War and Its Beneficiaries

The military threats from Latins, Serbians and Turks defined the political climate in which emperors had to operate in the period after 1204. But within the higher echelons of the Byzantine elite, civil war also provided both challenges and opportunities. The first period of civil war in the 1320s can perhaps be interpreted as an 'old style' family conflict between the supporters of Andronikos II Palaiologos and those of his grandson Andronikos III (1328–41); the second civil war of 1341–7 was complicated by the issue of the minority of the young emperor John V Palaiologos (1341–91) and hostility to his regent, the future emperor John VI Kantakouzenos.[151] In both cases, the various protagonists rewarded their followers with money and lands and assigned them important military and administrative posts. John VI Kantakouzenos himself recorded in his *History* (written about 1355) how Andronikos II gave 'honours and benefactions to senators and mercenary soldiers'; the historian Nikephoros Gregoras (*c*.1290/1 or 1293/4–1358/61), describing the end of the second civil war in 1347, reported that John VI Kantakouzenos distributed 'the rest of the imperial *choria*' to his followers, implying that there was now little imperial land left to give.[152] Others were granted positions from which they could make a profit: the *mesazon* Alexios Apokaukos (d. 1345) was placed in charge of the fleet by Andronikos III and was also granted a 'private' fortress at Epibatai outside Constantinople. The *protokynegos* John Vatatzes was granted a fortress at Teribasis in Thrace. Particularly sought-after seem to have

---

[149] *BBOL*, 88–90. For the succession of *timar* to *pronoia*: *LPIB*, 579–613; Papademetriou, *Render unto the Sultan*, 55–6.
[150] Necipoğlu, 'Aristocracy in late Byzantine Thessalonike', 136.
[151] *BATEFC*, 333–90; *LPIB*, 528.
[152] Nikephoros Gregoras, *Byzantina historia*, ed. L. Schopen and I. Bekker, 3 vols, *CSHB* (Bonn, 1829–55), ii:818; *LPIB*, 329–32.

been posts as a *kephale* (imperial governor) of a town or theme, positions
which, in the urban context at least, allowed the holder to buy grain and
other supplies at imposed low prices, ostensibly to provide for the defence
of the city but in reality facilitating profitable speculation. Gregoras
reported that, in 1321, John Kantakouzenos sought a governorship in
Thrace and paid money to 'those holding power alongside the emperor'
(*paradounasteuontes*) to obtain it; John Vatatzes bought the post of *kephale*
of Thessaloniki in 1343, but the grant was cancelled before he could take
it up and given to a son of Alexios Apokaukos instead.[153] At the very
highest level, the Komnenian system of granting out of the resources of
whole regions to imperial relatives was taken a stage further by what has
been termed the first Byzantine apanage: the granting to John
Kantakouzenos' cousin, John Angelos, of a large tract of Thessaly in
1342/3. He was to rule it until his death, and it was then to be passed to
his successor on the same terms as he had held it – that is, simply in return
for military assistance west of Constantinople. He presumably retained
such monetary taxes and other resources as he could collect from the
area.[154]

Such gains could, however, be transient, as power swung back and
forth between the warring factions. Confiscation was used as a political
tool just as often as grant and donation. Although contemporaries
lamented the dire state of the imperial coffers, there were still vital, if
not overly rich, pickings to be had from the imperial table.[155] This was
still the case in the last century of Byzantine rule, despite endemic
Palaiologan in-fighting: as long as some territory remained and revenues
trickled in, it was worth aspiring to control them. During the seemingly
endless wars in this period, two things stand out. First, the price of
aristocratic support to any side was usually land, strongholds or revenues
granted initially to Greek allies and, increasingly to potential supporters
amongst the Ottomans or amongst a motley crew of Latin princelings,
trading interests and mercenaries. Second, no one save members of the
Palaiologos family aspired to the imperial throne.[156] Long gone were the
days when ambitious aristocrats dreamed of it; their strategies were now

---

[153] Nikephoros Gregoras, *Byzantina historia*, ed. Schopen and Bekker, i:302; ii:741; *BATEFC*, 194–5.

[154] *BATEFC*, 357, 378. On Capetian apanages held by cadet lines: p. 383; see also pp. 152–3.

[155] Imperial revenues in the 1320s have been estimated to be 200,000–300,000 *hyperpera* a year, compared to 12,000 *hyperpera* for a single – albeit rich – monastery (the Great Lavra on Athos) in the same period: *LPIB*, 529.

[156] For the last century of Byzantine rule: J. Harris, *The End of Byzantium* (New Haven, 2012), 47; M. Angold, *The Fall of Constantinople to the Ottomans: Context and Consequences* (Harlow, 2012), 25–61. For detail on the Morea: *BBOL*, 235–84.

much more locally expressed, focusing on short-term gain rather than long-term aspiration. But, crucially, what was never abdicated by the holders of the imperial power was the legal right to bestow, confirm and confiscate.[157] The continuing familiar process of issuing chrysobulls and privileges, as well as, more significantly, continual requests for their confirmation and re-confirmation, indicate that this right was still theoretically accepted by all parties. What both secular and ecclesiastical elites increasingly sought, however, were income streams and assets to survive the vagaries of political fortune and the granting of lands, rights and privileges to last, it could be hoped, for more than a lifetime. State service was not quite what it had been.

The Creation of Permanent Elite Privilege

It is on the local level that the all-important shift from temporary rights to permanent privilege can best be seen. While the allocation of *pronoia* estates remained an imperial prerogative, its potential to turn into a heritable grant meant that its very nature changed. Whilst in the twelfth and early thirteenth centuries *pronoia* land could be described as 'eternally under the hand of the fisc', usually returning to the state upon the death of the holder, by the fourteenth century increasing numbers of *pronoiai* grants included the concession of hereditary rights.[158] Many such rights were given to members of the higher aristocracy, especially in the aftermath of the civil wars. But since *pronoiai* had always been granted to those of a much lower social status – cavalry soldiers provide a good example, but administrators and even ecclesiastics could hold them – the potential for all such grants to become completely alienated from the state and for their holders to use them to build up their own permanent portfolio of lands and fiscal privileges had long been in existence. Bartusis has estimated that, in the thirteenth century, some 25 per cent of the empire's arable land was held by pronoiars holding lands of from 70 to 80 *hyperpera* per annum value; he also suggests that, by the fourteenth century, the Byzantine state received no tax revenue 'from the overwhelming majority of agrarian properties'.[159] Given that the grant of *pronoiai* seems to have been practised throughout the successor states as well as in the core lands of Constantinople-based rulers, two developments are worthy of note: firstly, imperial rights of receiving taxation and dues both from landholders and their peasant workforce had

---

[157] For parallels to the prestige without hard power of the Capetians: p. 408; on 'empire' more generally, especially in the later middle ages: pp. 65–6, 155–6, 177; on the continuing prestige of the Abbasids after the tenth century: p. 352.

[158] *LPIB*, 182, 192, 235, 274–5, 400–5.   [159] *LPIB*, 198, 430, 522, 611

now passed into local hands; secondly, it was no longer the case that such privileges were the sole preserve of the power elite; the general elite frequently enjoyed them, too.[160]

Just as the institution of the *pronoia* system was an attempt to ensure the defence of the empire was carried through on a local and more widespread level by those who had literally been granted a stake in its resources, so, too, can the ever more frequent granting of privileges to townsmen – known as 'common chrysobulls' since they were given to groups rather than individuals – be seen as an attempt to devolve defence to a more local sphere as well as ensuring loyalty to the imperial power or, increasingly frequently, one of the rivals for it. But they, too, contributed to the trend towards the permanent alienation of imperial rights. From the first half of the thirteenth century, in the Greek lands remaining to the empire and in its successor states, 'common chrysobulls' could be found in such cities as Thessaloniki, Berroia, Athens, Ioannina and Monemvasia.[161] Their terms usually included freedom from the *kommerkion* (imperial sales tax); the right to hand on patrimonial possessions (*gonikia*) without any taxes and charges; and the right for *epoikoi* (residents) to choose their own judges and follow 'local' penal customs.[162] This did not mean that Byzantine towns evolved into corporate entities like their contemporary western counterparts. But it *did* mean that the *epoikoi* (however defined) obtained important concessions which would greatly assist them both in building up wealth and, more importantly, handing it on to their heirs.[163] Nonetheless, as with the necessity to renew *pronoia* grants, the fact that the common chrysobulls were, in many cases, reissued by later rulers

---

[160] On the geographical distribution of *pronoiai*: *LPIB*, 499–513. As Bartusis freely admits, however, we are mainly dependent for this information on a few surviving sources, particularly the monastic archives of Athos, Patmos and the Virgin Lembiotissa Monastery near Smyrna. Note that far from all *pronoiai* granted by the late Byzantine state proved irrevocable: K. Smyrlis, 'The state, the land, and private property: confiscating monastic and church properties in the Palaiologan period', in D. G. Angelov (ed.), *Church and Society in Late Byzantium* (Kalamazoo, MI, 2009), 58–87.

[161] D. Kyritses, 'The "common chrysobulls" of cities and the notion of property in late Byzantium', *Symmeikta* 13 (1999), 229–45; E. Patlagean, 'L'immunité des Thessaloniciens', in M. Balard *et al.* (eds), *Eupsychia: mélanges offerts à Hélène Ahrweiler*, 2 vols (Paris, 1998), ii:591–601; A. E. Laiou-Thomadakis, 'The Byzantine economy in the Mediterranean trade system: thirteenth-fifteenth centuries', *DOP* 34–5 (1980–1), 177–222 at 206–9; repr. in her *Gender, Society and Economic Life in Byzantium*, no. 7.

[162] Patlagean, 'L'immunité des Thessaloniciens', 592–5; on the implications of inheritance *kata logon gonikotetos*: *LPIB*, 317–19; on the recognition of local tribunals and the authority of custom: Angold, 'Archons and dynasts', 244–5; see also pp. 326–7.

[163] For western counterparts: pp. 161–2, 383–4. Patlagean, 'L'immunité des Thessaloniciens', 597, distinguishes the *epoikoi* from the *archontes* (according to her the holders of imperial jobs or titles), but this seems rather too narrow a distinction. One group could well include the other.

seems to indicate the persistence of the notion that they remained in the gift of the imperial power and could be revoked, at least in theory.[164]

The fact that they never were and, moreover, that the rights originally granted to citizens on their home turf began to be granted to those of a specific urban origin now resident in other parts of the empire is one of the strongest indicators of the growing importance of their enterprises. In 1328, Andronikos III renewed the privilege granted by his predecessor to Monemvasiotes settled in Pegai on the southern shore of the Sea of Marmara by which they were to pay *kommerkion* of only 2 per cent in Constantinople and a series of towns on the coast of Thrace. He was thus encouraging Greek mercantile communities both in their home ports and in the new locations in which they had found themselves after 1204.[165]

Survival Techniques in an Age of Uncertainty

Diversification was the key to elite survival in the last hundred years of the empire, and, as the amount of land controlled by Byzantines shrank, it was to commerce and trading ventures that elites hitherto dependent on landholding and state office turned. Nowhere is this clearer than the case of the Notaras family, who rose in two generations from being provincial *archontes* in Monemvasia to positions of immense wealth and influence in the remains of the empire.[166] The first significant member of the family, George Notaras, came to Constantinople between 1340 and 1350 and, as so many before him, gained his first foot on the ladder at the imperial court. His post reflected the world in which emperors now had to operate: he was *diermeneutes* (interpreter; presumably in Greek, Latin and Italian) to Andronikos IV Palaiologos (1376–9). His son Nicholas (d. 1423) is described in Italian documents as a *burgensis* (burgher) of the Genoese enclave of Pera on the north shore of the Golden Horn, and, more significantly, as *Ianuensis*, that is a Genoese citizen. He became a Venetian citizen in 1397. But he is also described in Greek documents as 'senatorial' and as a *sympentheros* (father-in-law) and *gambros* of the emperor; both his sons married imperial relatives. Thus old-style definitions of elite status in terms of the imperial court and family were combined with new, more realistic identities. A citizen of cities whose

---

[164] In 1284 Andronikos II renewed the chrysobull issued by Michael VIII to Monemvasia; that of John III Vatatzes of Nicaea (1221–54) for Thessaloniki in 1246 included a reference to 'earlier rights'.

[165] Laiou-Thomadakis, 'Byzantine economy', 206.

[166] K.-P. Matschke, 'The Notaras family and its Italian connections', *DOP* 49 (1995), 59–72; T. Ganchou, 'Le rachat des Notaras après la chute de Constantinople ou les relations "etrangères" de l'élite byzantine au XVe siècle', in M. Balard and A. Ducellier (eds), *Migrations et diasporas méditerranéennes (Xe–XVIe siècles)* (Paris, 2002), 149–229.

merchants had long enjoyed preferential conditions of trade in Byzantium, Nicholas enjoyed access both to beneficial trading arrangements and, most importantly, to the financial institutions of the two great Italian cities. By 1391, he had opened two banking accounts in Genoa at the Banco di San Georgio. Nicholas' elder son, John, had the emperor as his godfather and was killed fighting against the Turks in 1411, an indication that he had entered into the remnants of the military aristocracy. Loukas, Nicholas' younger son, was the member of the family who gained most eminence, rising to the position of *mesazon* under John VIII Palaiologos (1425–48) and Constantine XI Palaiologos (1449–53). Painstaking research by Thierry Ganchou has established that, while Loukas seems not to have drawn upon his grandfather's Italian funds, nor yet added to them, he was still able to spend considerable sums on the marriages of his three eldest daughters: 60,000 *hyperpera* each as dowry and 20,000 *hyperpera* each on the celebrations themselves. The money left in Genoa was perhaps an insurance policy; after the fall of Constantinople in 1453 and the execution of Loukas and his sons by the Ottomans, the family agent in Genoa, Pelegro di Promontorio, went to extraordinary lengths to ransom the surviving Notaras women and transmit resources to them.[167]

The Notaras were by no means the only family to use trading and financial activity as a means of acquiring and preserving wealth: even John VII employed members of the Notaras and Goudeles families as intermediaries in trading ventures with Genoese merchants.[168] As the two main cities of the empire – Constantinople and Thessaloniki – shrank in size and were ever more beleaguered, it was towns and cities which could tap into the Italian trading routes which maintained, and, in some cases even increased, their prosperity. Some, like the coastal cities of the Peloponnese and those on Crete and Cyprus, were already under foreign rule; others, such as Adrianople, Kilia and the Thracian ports of Ainos and Rhaidestos, formed part of both local and international trading networks. In such places, there was money to be made through overt and enthusiastic participation in trade.[169] Again, however, a lack of surviving evidence may give a partial view, as only Italian-based archival sources have survived in any quantity.[170]

Even so, Italian sources like the *Libro dei conti* ('Account Book') of the Venetian merchant Giacomo Badoer, resident in Constantinople from

---

[167] Ganchou, 'Rachat des Notaras', 158–67; for women as elements in comparative political culture: p. 23.
[168] *BBOL*, 128.   [169] Laiou, 'Palaiologoi and the world', 818.
[170] A point forcibly made in Oikonomides, *Hommes d'affaires grecs*, 54. On the loss of nearly all archival sources from Byzantium: p. 89.

1436–40, reveals that the numbers of Greek merchants Badoer dealt with was considerable, and his volume of business with them was some 27 per cent of his associations.[171] Some very big names feature: Palaiologos, Kantakouzenos, Doukas and Argyros. Badoer noted the commercial company set up by Constantine Palaiologos, *kephale* of Agathopolis on the Black Sea (Ahtopol in modern Bulgaria), and Demetrios Notaras, son of Loukas and a *kommerkiarios* in Constantinople, in order to trade in grain, honey and cloth; the '*kyr* [lord] Todoro Ralli', whom he mentions as having commercial contacts as far away as Sicily, may well be the Theodore Rhalles who was a Byzantine envoy to the west in the early years of the fifteenth century. The surviving contracts of the Genoese notary Antonio di Ponzo, trading out of Kilia in the Danube Delta in 1360–1, reveal that, of fifty-seven ships listed, seventeen were partly or wholly owned by Greeks; two such investors, 'Jane Francopoulo' (John Phrangopoulos) and 'Jane Fassilico' (John Basilikos), originally from Adrianople, had some 2,000 *hyperpera* available to lend to Greek merchants and sea captains; the loans and the interest on them were to be collected in Pera.[172] Greek mercantile elites also become much more visible in such cities as Thessaloniki (participating in trade with Crete and the Peloponnese), Philadelphia, Monemvasia and Ioannina. The successful became integrated into the Italian trading networks in the eastern Mediterranean and even those leading to the west: members of the Laskaris family emerged in Bruges after 1453, and the wine-importer 'George of Constantinople' was to be found in London in 1445/6.[173]

As Klaus-Peter Matschke has pointed out, the last two centuries of the empire saw the final dismantling of the 'mental barriers that Byzantine society had erected against business involving goods and money'. Whether or not one accepts that 'aristocratic entrepreneurs' were a 'novelty' in the late Byzantine period, it is undeniable that their activities became much more overt, making up, to some extent at least, for the losses to their landed wealth. As the scholar John Argyropoulos (*c*.1393/4–1487) remarked in a speech to Constantine XI, the mint and the ship's deck were now more important to the survival of Byzantium than farmland or the battlefield.[174] This sea-change left its mark. Grand palaces were still built and displays of piety and high culture laid on by the Palaiologoi installed at Mistra in the Morea, prospering from their commercial and marriage-ties with Italy.

---

[171] *Il libro dei conti di Giacomo Badoer (Constantinopoli 1436–1440)*, ed. U. Dorini and T. Bertelè (Rome, 1956). For Greek merchants associated with Badoer: *BBOL*, 299–303 (Appendix III). However, on the problems of using Badoer's work, especially in respect of the downward social percolation of many once aristocratic surnames: T. Ganchou, 'Giacomo Badoer et kyr Théodôros Batatzès, "chomerchier di pesi" à Constantinople (flor. 1401–1449)', *REB* 61 (2003), 49–95.
[172] Matschke, 'Commerce, trade', 792.   [173] Matschke, 'Commerce, trade', 795–8.
[174] Matschke, 'Commerce, trade', 804.

And Theodore Palaiologos Kantakouzenos could still commission a palace in Constantinople in the early fifteenth century.[175] But by then the personal wealth of the imperial family was spiralling into debt.[176] The patriarchal court heard frequent cases concerning the likes of Michael Bouzenos, an *oikeios* of the emperor Manuel II Palaiologos who, probably in 1401, asked permission to sell houses which had formed part of his wife's dowry to one 'Argyropoulos'.[177] Those who had assets found it increasingly necessary to liquefy them. The imperial court and its offices were no longer a source of wealth, for all the kudos it still emitted. As the Turkish stranglehold around Constantinople tightened, it was those who could control the supply of vital foodstuffs or disposed of ready cash who were most able to survive. John Goudeles was a particularly successful profiteer, running the Turkish blockade with his own ships during Bayezid's siege of 1402 and bribing Genoese customs officials in order to bring supplies of wheat from Chios via their enclave on the other side of the Golden Horn in Pera: Goudeles sold it at the astronomical price of 31 *hyperpera* per measure.

Realignment and Reinvention

When the moment of truth finally arrived in Constantinople on 29 May 1453, the most pressing issue for those remaining in the City was how to avoid death or slavery. As ever in such circumstances, money could speak volumes. Anecdotal evidence reported a 'wealthy minority' who would not even transport weapons to the walls without payment and later pleaded for their freedom with the Turks bearing 'dishes full of coin'. Of those Greeks who managed to escape on Italian ships, many, such as the members of the Notaras, Palaiologos, Kantakouzenos and Laskaris families, had trading connections with Venetians or Genoese and Italian citizenship. They could thus claim some protection, and it is clear that they had ready cash or valuables to hand to aid them in their flight. Here the strategy of moving monetary assets out of Byzantium while the going was good clearly paid off.[178]

[175] S. Runciman, *Mistra: Byzantine Capital of the Peloponnese* (London, 1980), 94–108; Angold, *Fall of Constantinople*, 36; K.-P. Matschke, 'Builders and building in late Byzantine Constantinople', in Necipoğlu (ed.), *Byzantine Constantinople*, 315–28.
[176] Michael Angold suggests that the imperial power owed a total of *c.*19,275,000 *hyperpera* in 1453, of which some 585,000 was due to the Venetian government alone: Review of *The End of Byzantium* (review no. 1030), www.history.ac.uk/reviews/review/1030 (accessed 19 February 2020).
[177] *BBOL*, 157–9, 163.
[178] For Greek refugees in Italy after 1453: *BBOL*, 226–8 and 305–6 (Appendix V). Harris, *End of Byzantium*, 210, points out that the vast majority of the escapees on Italian ships (*c.*6,000) were Venetian or Genoese.

Many members of aristocratic families ended up in Italy after 1453; some became Latin Christians. In this they were following a form of reinvention already demonstrated by numerous members of the Byzantine intellectual elite in the course of the fifteenth century. They seldom found the confessional divide unbridgeable, and the ancient Greek language, learning and science were much in vogue. Thus the monk Bessarion (1399/1400–72), a star of the Byzantine delegation to the Council of Ferrara-Florence (1438–9), was offered a pension of 300 florins by Pope Eugenius IV (1431–47) to reside at the papal curia and, after becoming a Latin Christian, was made a cardinal in 1439. After a brief return to Constantinople, he spent the rest of his life in Italy, as did John Argyropoulos, who left Constantinople in 1456 to take up the chair of Greek at the University of Florence, where he lectured on Aristotle.[179]

For less intellectually talented individuals, other opportunities presented themselves. The early Ottoman regime was welcoming to those members of the power elite willing to enter its service. As early as 1398, George, the last Byzantine *kephale* of Kanina near Avlona in southern Albania, 'turned Turk'; according to Anthony Bryer, his family retained their office until 1943.[180] The fate of the three nephews of the last emperor, Constantine XI, is also suggestive. They re-emerged as, respectively, Mesih Pasha, by 1470 admiral of the Ottoman fleet and governor of the province of Gallipoli, later Grand Vizier; Hass Murad Pasha, governor of the Balkans by 1472; and, possibly, Gedik Ahmed Pasha, Grand Vizier in 1473, though the latter may, in fact, been of Serbian extraction. Of fifteen Grand Viziers who served (sometimes more than once) in the years 1453–1516, possibly seven originated from the Greek, Serbian, Bosnian or Albanian Christian nobilities.[181] For women, too, there were opportunities: of those wives or consorts who produced successors to the Ottoman sultans in the fourteenth and fifteenth centuries, five out of eight were of Christian origin.[182]

As Jonathan Harris has warned, it is a mistake to see the choices made by members of the Byzantine elites during the fourteenth and fifteenth centuries in terms of 'loyalty' or 'betrayal' or of a conscious desire to throw in their lot with either 'east', in the form of the Ottomans, or 'west', in the form of the Latin states of the west.[183] By 1453, so many of the power elite had established relationships – whether of blood, partnership

---

[179] Harris, *End of Byzantium*, 140, 250.
[180] A. Bryer, 'The Roman orthodox world (1393–1492)', in *CHBE*, 852–80 at 861–2.
[181] H. W. Lowry, *The Nature of the Early Ottoman State* (Albany, NY, 2003), 115–30 at 115–16. For the origins of the Grand Viziers: *ibid.*, 120–22 (table 7.1), 128.
[182] Lowry, *Nature of the Early Ottoman State*, 153–4 (Appendix 3).
[183] Harris, *End of Byzantium*, 196, 228–55.

or protection – with Italians, Serbs or, indeed, Ottomans that any sense of a purely Greek and orthodox upper crust had long since vanished. Indeed, in the early years of the Ottoman state, it is a moot point whether remaining Christian was a serious drawback; the mother and brother of Mahmud Pasha (Grand Vizier 1453–68; 1472–4), a member of the Serbian (and perhaps Byzantine) noble family of Angelovič, both came to Constantinople, and both remained Christian. She, indeed, was granted the 'Monastery of Prodromos Petros in Konstantiniye' by Mehmed II in 1472.[184] What was now of paramount importance, as direct Byzantine control over land diminished, was to preserve durable power or moveable wealth and manoeuvre into posts or businesses that would ensure this. The period from 1204 to 1500 demonstrates members of the Byzantine power or local elites exercising the kind of social, economic and, indeed, religious flexibility which allowed them to do this.

Plus ça change?

The early Ottoman years provide a useful standpoint to review the changing nature and fortunes of the Byzantine elite over the previous centuries – or more precisely elites, as one of the most striking aspects of the long-term perspective is the way in which a variety of privileged and powerful groups appeared at both the imperial and local levels. It is, of course, of the higher echelons that we know most. In a very real sense, nothing much changed for them in 1453; the emperors were replaced by the sultans (who initially styled themselves caesar, *basileus,* emperors of Constantinople and emperors of the Romans) and who distributed titles, offices, and the lands and revenues that went with them very much as their predecessors had done.[185] Kinship with the ruling house was still of importance, as it had been since the end of the eleventh century, though polygamy and the politics of the seraglio added further complexities. But fortunes could still be made – or preserved – by traditional means: entry into the Ottoman administrative elite for some, especially those whose high birth in the ancien regime meant that their new loyalty could encourage others to transfer their allegiance.[186] The intellectual elite also found the Ottomans welcoming; Michael Kritoboulos (d. *c.*1470), who had negotiated the surrender of the islands of Imbros, Lemnos and Thasos in 1453 and was rewarded with the governorship of Imbros (1456–66), wrote a history of the period from 1451 to 1467, giving Mehmed II the

[184] Lowry, *Nature of the Early Ottoman State,* 124.
[185] For the sultan's titles: Lowry, *Nature of the Early Ottoman State,* 119.
[186] For the successes of Greek *archontes* under Ottoman rule: Papademetriou, *Render unto the Sultan,* 189–202.

traditional place of the *basileus* at the centre of the narrative.[187] As the imperial power became ever more impoverished, the last centuries of Byzantium had seen an increasing tendency for service to the emperor to be based on family and personal loyalty rather than on wealth and status from office. Now loyalty had to be shown to a new and, to many, unfamiliar master, and the delicate network of marriage and personal alliances and loyalties had to be reconstructed.

Of all the power elites, it was those holding power in the church who avoided the religious realignment which became increasingly necessary in order to prosper, rather than merely survive, in the Ottoman state. Although much ecclesiastical land, both monastic and belonging to the secular church, was confiscated and many churches were converted into mosques, the Ottomans were careful to preserve the orthodox hierarchy, thus leaving the Greek Christian *millet* (community) with leaders and representatives and eventually providing themselves, it would seem, with tax-farmers.[188] As the survival to the present day of the monastic communities on Athos, Meteora and Patmos demonstrates, with trad-itional displays of subservience and by employing the careful long-term strategies of negotiation and consolidation with which they had long been familiar, monastic elites could also survive, providing, of course, that they could continue to attract the levels of patronage which could assure the payment of their tax liabilities, the maintenance of their buildings and the cultivation of their lands.[189] Here the initiative passed to the states of the old Byzantine Commonwealth: Serbia, Bulgaria, Romania and Russia.[190]

As the Ottoman reorganisation and redistribution of lands progressed, local Greek landowning elites were, in many cases, subject to displace-ment. The village of Radolibos, donated to the Athonite monastery of Iviron at the end of the eleventh century, was by 1465 held as a *timar* by one Ocak Beğ; other examples of villages previously held as monastic lands and subsequently transformed into *timar*s have been plotted in the Chalkidike peninsula from the time of Sultan Bayezid onwards.[191] But

---

[187] *BBOL*, 10–11. For Ottoman rulers adjusting – or being fitted in – to the Byzantine mould: pp. 82, 122–3, 124, 193.

[188] E. A. Zachariadou, 'The Great Church in captivity', in *CHC* 5, 169–86. The process of formation of the *millet* system was slower and more uneven than earlier historiography has supposed: Papademetriou, *Render unto the Sultan*, 10, 20–62

[189] See p. 442 and n. 147 for Athos; D. M. Nicol, *Meteora: The Rock Monasteries of Thessaly*, rev. edn (London, 1975). Difficult circumstances and their resolution are discussed in E. Kermeli, 'The confiscation and repossession of monastic properties in Mount Athos and Patmos monasteries, 1568–1570', *Bulgarian Historical Review / Revue bulgare d'histoire* 3–4 (2000), 39–53.

[190] On the Commonwealth, see p. 190.

[191] H. W. Lowry, 'Changes in fifteenth-century Ottoman peasant taxation: the case study of Radilofo (Radolibos)', in A. Bryer and H. W. Lowry (eds), *Continuity and Change in Late*

the picture seems to have been slightly different in the region of Trebizond, which fell to the Ottomans in 1461; here there is evidence for Christian *timar* holders assuring the defence of the region until the sixteenth century.[192] Much depended on the demographic character of a given region; where Christians remained in the majority, their traditional local *archontes* still had a role, if a somewhat reduced one, to play in the early Ottoman state.

In the larger towns and cities too, demographic change was sometimes slow to take place. The Ottoman tax survey (*defter*) of Thessaloniki (1478) reported a Muslim population of 4,320 heads of household but a Christian total of 6,094; by 1500 the Muslim total was 8,575 and the Christian 7,986, with a new element of some 3,770 Jews, many of them recent migrants from the Iberian peninsula. Whilst the administration and fiscal power now lay in Muslim hands, it seems clear that, both here and in Constantinople, Greek trading elites, particularly those with pre-existing Ottoman and Italian trading connections, could restore, or indeed increase, their fortunes.[193]

At the end of this survey, it is worthwhile returning to the vocabulary used by Byzantines to describe elite members. When all is said and done, the divisions which modern historians have tried to impose – high, middle and lesser aristocracy; power and local elites and so on – can often be subsumed under the commonly used Byzantine terms *dynatoi* (powerful) and *archontes* (rulers or leading men). And this perhaps justifies the amount of attention we have paid to the period after 1204. For all the dramatic denouements and displacements, and the growth of new sources of wealth, many features and dynamics of our power game that are visible often only in outline for the Middle Byzantine period emerge more clearly and fully for the better-documented Palaiologan era.[194] If we ask what made these individuals and groups powerful in the first place and helped to maintain their power, a number of answers spring to mind. First is the use of patronage: the power of one 'imperial' individual to influence the fortunes of another, or those of an institution, manifesting itself in the award of titles, offices, land, gifts and revenues. Second, kinship (whether blood or ritual) both defined influential groups and provided mechanisms for admitting 'outsiders' into them. Third is the possession of wealth or

Byzantine and Early Ottoman Society (Washington, DC, and Birmingham, 1986), 23–35 at 27; V. Dimitriades, 'Ottoman Chalkidki: an area in transition', in *ibid.*, 39–50.

[192] A. Bryer, 'Rural society in Matzouka', in Bryer and Lowry (eds), *Continuity and Change*, 53–95 at 75.

[193] Bryer, 'Roman orthodox world', 859; M. Mazower, *Salonica, City of Ghosts: Christians, Muslims and Jews 1430–1950* (London, 2005).

[194] For the distortion inherent in the formatting of our main narratives and the value of non-Byzantine sources: pp. 80–3.

the means to generate it, whether by land cultivation, by trading or by the extraction of fiscal revenues. Finally, particularly on the local level, is the ability to organise political and economic life in the interests of particular regional groups rather than looking to imperial imperatives. Ultimately, however, it was the existence of the concept of autocracy, underpinned by codified law, that enabled such levers of power to be created and, more importantly, maintained. When Byzantine elites wanted to record, maintain or renew their power, more often than not they used legal documents to do so. The emperor, as the 'fountain of law', stood therefore as the ultimate guarantor of rights and privileges; by the fifteenth century, this could well be described as 'the shadow of power', but it was power nonetheless.[195]

---

[195] See pp. 295–7. On approaches to preservation of title deeds to property and possessions in the Islamic world, as against in Byzantium and polities of the Latin west: p. 127.

15 The Islamic World
Nomads, Urban Elites and Courts in Competition

Andrew Marsham, Eric Hanne and Jo Van Steenbergen

Hard and (Relatively) Soft Power in Early Islam: Warriors, Tax Systems and Scholars

Political culture in the formative era of Islam is best understood in imperial terms:[1] our period begins with the continued expansion of what was at that time the largest empire in history by land area. However, military reach should not be mistaken for highly centralised administrative structures: indeed, it seems that the development of a more centralised administration actually coincided with the beginning of the fragmentation of the empire. The administrative structures that had only developed relatively recently at the old imperial centre were then replicated in the various emerging successor states of the tenth century. Nor should imperial success be mistaken for stability in imperial elites: as we have seen (pp. 237–8), the shifting composition of the military elite in this period is particularly striking, as is the emergence of new elites, notably the court scribes (*kuttab, wuzara'*) and the religious scholars (*'ulama', fuqaha'*). What persists with remarkable resilience is the hereditary origin of the caliphs at the imperial centre: after the *bouleversement* of the Abbasid Revolution, the same ruling family would reside in Iraq as the notional head of most of the Islamic world for 508 years. After the tenth century, the Abbasids had major rivals for the title of caliph on the Iberian peninsula and North Africa, but these opponents were also relatives: both lines claimed descent from the same group of seventh-century Meccans as the Abbasids themselves.

By the middle of the tenth century, then, Abbasid power was almost entirely ideological but no less real for that: the Abbasids were the figure-heads of Sunni Islam, necessary for the legitimisation of other political structures and too sacred to depose. However, for most of the early period, down to the crisis of the 860s and to some extent until the final disasters of the 920s, the caliphs had also been able to call upon formidable imperial

---

[1] See pp. 215–18.

Figure 15.1 Frontispiece from the *Maqamat al-Hariri* (1334/AH 734, also known as the *Vienna Maqamat*) showing a Mamluk prince on his throne with attendants and entertainers; reproduced by kind permission of the Österreichische Nationalbibliothek, Vienna; A.F.9, fol. 1 r

military power. Hence, the first part of this discussion of political practice and organisation will examine the changing foundations of Umayyad and Abbasid military power before glancing at the military forces of the early tenth-century successor states. Behind the military power of a ruling elite there are always the economic, fiscal and administrative structures that support the armies, and the changing taxation and administrative structures of the Islamic world in the formative period are the subject of the second part of this chapter's early Islamic section. Finally, the third part will examine the religious and clerical classes – the '*ulama*' – who established and elaborated ideological structures that long outlasted the first Muslim empires.

The Foundations of Umayyad and Abbasid Military Power

The military foundations of the Muslim empire changed very substantially at least three times during the 230 or so years between 711 and 945.[2] Under the Syrian Umayyads, the caliphs depended upon the Syrian army, composed primarily of the Arabic-speaking tribes of the Syrian desert, supplemented by tribesmen from the Arabian peninsula who had settled in post-Roman Syria after the conquests. In addition, there were the provincial conquest armies, garrisoned in the new cities of the provinces and still fighting an expansionist war on the frontiers of the empire. These armies often incorporated some local military power, notably Berber tribesmen in North Africa and the Iberian peninsula and local, Persian-speaking Khurasanians in north-east Iran and northern Afghanistan. And in a way the Syrian army itself followed the same pattern as these other frontiers, seeing that the bulk of the soldiers were recruited from what had been Roman Syria and had joined the armies of the new polity in the wake of the conquests. The Umayyad caliphs were unable to rely on the loyalty of the provincial armies and often used their Syrian following to enforce submission to their authority where it was not given willingly.

The Abbasid Revolution of 750 saw parts of the Khurasanian frontier army and new recruits from the villages of Khurasan overthrow Syrian forces that had already been weakened by a series of campaigns against rebels and a disastrously bloody civil war within the Umayyad elite and their Syrian soldiers. The result was that a new, Khurasanian, military elite was garrisoned at al-Hashimiyya, near Kufa, in Iraq, and then at

---

[2] For this pattern: *SOH*. For the prominent role of arms-bearers in the west: pp. 156–8, 376–9; in Byzantium, in contrast, arms-bearing was essentially the preserve of the army: pp. 316–18.

Baghdad. Khurasanian generals and their military followings were also sometimes posted to the provinces, where the local provincial armies were combined with these new troops. The descendants of the revolutionary soldiers who formed the backbone of early Abbasid military power from the 770s were known as the *abna' al-dawla* (Sons of the Revolution). What loosened the grip of the *abna'* on the resources of empire was the aligning of tensions within the ruling elite with tensions between the centre and the provinces. After the death of Harun al-Rashid (786–809), civil war broke out between the Iraqi centre and the Khurasanian periphery. Once again, Khurasan won.

After an experiment in ruling the Muslim empire from Merv, in Khurasan itself, the caliphal capital was returned to Iraq again in 819. However, a new imperial military elite was now composed of groups like the Tahirids, who had been the leading generals for the victorious side in the civil war, as well as other 'new' Khurasanians and Transoxianans, such as Harthama b. al-Nadr al-Khuttali and al-Afshin. A fourth military elite was introduced within less than a generation – again, as a consequence of tensions within the ruling political elite. Turkish slave soldiers were instrumental to the success of al-Mu'tasim in ousting his nephew al-Abbas in 833 and in seeing off an attempt to reinstall him in 838. After 836 a new capital of Samarra was constructed on the Tigris, about 100 kilometres north of Baghdad. The new and growing Turkish military cavalry force was garrisoned at Samarra, alongside troops of various other backgrounds, which reflects the complex history of the Muslim imperial military by this point. The new Transoxianan and Turkish soldiers of the ninth century also brought about a military revolution, introducing tactically manoeuvrable mounted archers as a mainstay of the Muslim armies. Earlier armies had relied heavily on infantry, using horses primarily for strategic mobility and for cavalry armed with lances, not bows. Had the ninth-century caliphate remained united and solvent, it would have remained a very effective military power.[3]

However, when the caliphs became unable to pay the military in the 920s, they were reduced to recognising warlords as legitimate authorities in Iraq in return for protection. The title of *amir al-umara'* (Commander of Commanders) was conferred on various potentates before Buyid adventurers from Daylam – originally supporters of the non-Muslim rebellion of

---

[3] On imperial elites and the army: H. Kennedy, *The Armies of the Caliphs: Military and Society in the Early Islamic State* (London, 2001); *idem, The Prophet and the Age of the Caliphates: The Islamic Near East from the Sixth to the Eleventh Centuries*, 3rd edn (Abingdon and New York, 2016); P. Crone, *From Arabian Tribes to Islamic Empire: Army, State and Society in the Near East, c.600–850* (Aldershot, 2008); on the armies and the politics of succession: *RIM*.

Mardavij – seized it in 945. This period of Abbasid *fainéance* coincided with the declaration of rival caliphates in North Africa, in 909, and in Spain twenty years later. The former, Fatimid, caliphate arose from a young revolutionary movement, not unlike the Abbasid Revolution. Its military support came primarily from the Kutama branch of the Sanhaja Berbers of Ifriqiya and then from slave soldiers, both 'Roman' (*Rum*) and 'Black' (*Sudan*). In contrast, the Umayyads had ruled the Iberian peninsula as an independent emirate for over 170 years by the time they declared their caliphate in 929. Their armies were composed primarily of the descendants of the Berber settlers in Spain and slave soldiers, both Black African (*'abid*) and Slavic (*saqaliba*). In the far east of the former caliphate, the Samanid rulers of Samarqand and Bukhara pointed to the future of the Islamic east, with their reliance on free nomad Turks and Turkish slave soldiers in their cavalry armies.[4]

Taxation and Administrative Structures

What had underpinned the military power of the imperial caliphate of the later seventh, eighth and ninth centuries was a taxation system that exploited the enormous agricultural wealth of the territories conquered by the Muslims in order to pay the armies. The monetary economy of the early Islamic world remained based on a precious metal coinage of gold dinars and silver dirhams, adapted respectively from the Roman *solidus* and Sasanian *drachm*. In addition, there was a copper coinage for smaller transactions. The bullion already in circulation in the post-Roman and post-Sasanian world – the gold and silver available in tribute payments and loot from Sub-Saharan Africa, Armenia and Transoxiana and from the extensive trade networks of North Africa, the Mediterranean, Armenia, Iran and the Indian Ocean – maintained supplies of the necessary metal. The caliphs and their provincial governors retained a monopoly on the production of precious metal coins: to strike coins that deviated from the caliphal designs was a declaration of rebellion throughout this period, as it had been in much of western Eurasia before Islam. They extracted the surplus agricultural wealth from their subjects, predominantly in the form of cash payments; these payments, made in coins that had been struck at the centres of the imperial administration, would then circulate back into the provinces via the army payroll.[5]

---

[4] On the tenth-century successor polities: pp. 107–9, 220–1.

[5] For the early Islamic coinage system and economy: H. Kennedy, 'The financing of the military in the early Islamic state', in A. Cameron (ed.), *The Byzantine and Islamic Near East, III: States, Resources and Armies* (Princeton, 1995), 361–78; *idem*, ' Military pay and the economy of the early Islamic state', *Historical Research* 75 (2002), 155–69; J. Haldon

The Arabian conquerors of the seventh and eighth centuries had taken over most of the provinces of what remained of the Roman empire and all of the Sasanian empire without causing serious damage to their provincial administrative infrastructures. The use of *diwan*s (army lists) already in the time of Umar I (634–44) had ensured that tax revenues were used to support armies that were garrisoned in new settlements and not, for the most part, on the conquered land. As a result, the conquerors inherited and maintained two venerable and effective taxation structures and their supporting resources. Both tax systems generated revenue in coin for the payment of armies. Within each of the two former empires there had been significant regional variation, and these regional variations appear to have persisted into early Islam. However, modifications to the tax system were made from the beginning. Changes are manifest in the documentary evidence: papyri from Egypt show the decline of Greek as an administrative language and the growth of Arabic alongside Coptic; certain parallels of practice in Umayyad Egypt and Afghanistan can be found in the papyri and parchment documents from the two regions.[6]

It seems likely that the bulk of tax revenues in the Umayyad period remained in the provinces where they were collected: governors returned little to the imperial centre but rather used the resources to pay the army in their province. At the same time, a governorship was enormously personally rewarding, and former governors were assumed to have extracted huge amounts of personal wealth as a result of their position, which their replacements often sought to extract from them. Despite this regional fiscal and military autonomy, gubernatorial appointments did remain the gift of the caliph in theory, and in practice provincial governors were replaced quite regularly, albeit from a small pool of tribal leaders and military commanders whom the caliphs were obliged to patronise. Indeed, the difficulty of balancing the competing interests of groups within the Arab-Muslim military contributed to the fall of the Umayyad

---

(ed.), *Money, Power and Politics in Early Islamic Syria: A Review of Current Debates* (Farnham, 2010); F. Bessard and H. Kennedy (eds), *Merchants and Trading Communities in Early Islam, 800–1000* (Oxford, forthcoming).

[6] On the administration in Egypt: P. Sijpesteijn, *Shaping a Muslim State: The World of a Mid-Eighth-Century Egyptian Official* (Oxford, 2013); for documents from Khurasan: G. Khan, *Arabic Documents from Early Islamic Khurasan* (London, 2007). That scribal and administrative practices developed early, and with Arabian roots, is illustrated by the very early appearance of Arabic-language documents in the conquered provinces that use distinctive vocabulary and calendars. See e.g. the famous tax receipt from Egypt, dated to April 643: A. Grohmann, *From the World of Arabic Papyri* (Cairo, 1952), 113–14; Sijpesteijn, *Shaping a Muslim State*, 68. For a discussion of some of the implications of the distinctive formulas: G. Khan, 'The pre-Islamic background of Muslim legal formularies', *Aram* 6 (1994), 193–224; *idem*, 'The opening formula and witness clauses in Arabic legal documents from the early Islamic period', *JAOS* 139 (2019), 23–40.

dynasty; once tribal factions aligned themselves with different members of the ruling Umayyad house in the 740s, Syrian unity was torn apart.

By the early eighth century, both the provinces and the Syrian centre had developed administrative networks to support their rule. Early historians such as Khalifa b. Khayyat (d. 854) list the various appointments to governorships and the leading administrative roles in the caliphate quite carefully, although, when this evidence is compared with the numismatic, documentary and sigillographic material, it is clear that the later historical record is not always precisely accurate. Where more local historiography is preserved, as in the work of Ibn Abd al-Hakam (d. 871) for Egypt and North Africa, some of the structures of provincial administration can also be reconstructed, and for Egypt they can be expanded by the records of the papyri as well as the coins. The governance structure was military and imperial, with an *amir* (commander, governor) ruling from the main garrison and administrative centre, with the assistance of sub-commanders (also called *amir*s). A chief of the guard (*sahib al-shurta*) assisted the *amir* with policing and justice and was often his deputy and commander of his bodyguard. A market official (*amil al-suq*, later the *muhtasib*) was responsible for policing the markets. There were also senior tax officials and scribes, managing taxation and communications. This 'imperial' administration interacted with the local elites who managed the conquered, tax-paying populations; during the eighth and ninth centuries, the use of Arabic and the employment of Muslim officials directly beholden to the administrative centre penetrated ever deeper into local levels of society.[7]

Some of these administrative structures and practices appear to have their origins in the earliest west Arabian community and so also very likely in pre-Islamic Arabian practices, as well as in decisions made under the leadership of Abu Bakr and Umar in the 630s and 640s.[8] However, the influence of the administrative cultures of the former Roman and Iranian provinces was also significant, even at the uppermost level of the administration of the empire. Scribes and administrators drawn from groups of pre-conquest heritage are prominent in the sources. In Syria, Sarjun

---

[7] On Khalifa and his history: T. Andersson, *Early Sunni Historiography: A Study of the Tarikh of Khalifa b. Khayyat* (Leiden, 2019); on Ibn Abd al-Hakam: E. Zygowicz-Coghill, *Conquests of Egypt: Making History in Abbasid Egypt* (unpublished DPhil thesis, University of Oxford, 2017); on the administrative offices in the province of Egypt and the evidence of the papyri: Sijpesteijn, *Shaping a Muslim State*; on the *muhtasib*: R. P. Buckley, 'The *Muhtasib*', *Arabica* 39 (1992), 59–117; on the *sahib al-shurta*: A. M. Rashid, *The Role of the Shurta in Early Islam* (unpublished PhD thesis, University of Edinburgh, 1983); M. Ebstein, '*Shurta* chiefs in Basra in the Umayyad period: a prosopographical study', *Al-Qantara* 31 (2010), 103–47. See also p. 126.

[8] See n. 6.

b. Mansur al-Rumi ('Sergius the Roman', fl. *c*.660–700) and Ubayd Allah b. Aws al-Ghassani ('the Ghassanid', fl. *c*.660–83) served the later Sufyanids and early Marwanids in Syria.[9] In Iraq, Zadhanfarrukh (fl. *c*.660–701) served the Umayyad governors of the same period in the same capacity.[10] Some of the first extant long prose texts produced for leading members of the Umayyad elite date from the 730s and 740s; they appear to reflect the recruitment of scribes of Iraqi heritage, such as Salim Abu al-Ala and Abd al-Hamid, into the imperial administration.[11]

After the Abbasid Revolution, the scribal and administrative classes grew in size and political importance, and the scribes (*kuttab*) and ministers (*wuzara'*) became significant players in court politics at Baghdad and al-Raqqa. Under al-Mansur (754–75) the title of *mawla amir al-mu'minin* (Client of the Commander of the Faithful) was granted to some administrators and advisers, who appear to have been deliberately selected for their dependence upon personal loyalty to the caliph for their position. The most important modification to the administration of the caliphate came from the centralisation of many of its functions under senior officials with extensive responsibilities over large sections of the empire; these appointments were often made in association with heirs to the throne appointed over multiple provinces. At the imperial centre, the post of vizier, or chief minister, became the most senior position. Although of Persian origin, it developed during the early centuries of Islam; the term itself derives from the Arabic word *wazir*, whose root meaning refers to one who has taken up a burden. The vizier had wide-ranging powers and access to enormous resources – and hence also influence over the army. Other very senior posts at the caliphal court included that of chamberlain (*hajib*), master of the prayer mat (*sahib al-musalla*), chief of the chancery (*sahib diwan al-rasa'il*) and private secretary (*katib al-sirr*). Dynasties of scribes tended to hold these offices, competing with one another for influence and power and often focusing their ambitions on the caliphal succession, with destructive consequences.[12]

During the early Abbasid administration, the tax system appears to have become more effective and centralised, with annual imperial

[9] A. Marsham, 'The architecture of allegiance in early Islamic late antiquity: the accession of Mu'awiya in Jerusalem, ca. 661 CE', in A. Beihammer *et al.* (eds), *Court Ceremonies and Rituals of Power in Byzantium and the Medieval Mediterranean: Comparative Perspectives* (Leiden, 2013), 87–112 at 103.

[10] M. G. Morony, *Iraq after the Muslim Conquests* (Princeton, 1984), 53.

[11] See pp. 236–7, 341.

[12] On developments in the early Abbasid period: Kennedy, *Prophet*; *RIM*. Byzantium inherited an effective central administration from imperial Rome: pp. 198, 318–19, 320, 413; few polities in the west could boast such bureaucracies until the later middle ages: pp. 68–70, 282–4.

revenues estimated to have amounted to nearly half a billion dirhams. However, during the ninth century, imperial revenues went into decline: they seem to have fallen by nearly 40 per cent by the 850s and by over 50 per cent by the beginning of the tenth century. The initial cause of this decline was probably the destructive civil war fought in and around Baghdad in 811–19, which appears to have damaged the city and its hinterland, including the fertile Sawad of Lower Iraq, whose agricultural produce was a major source of revenue for the caliphs. This same region suffered further severe damage in the civil war of the 860s and the revolt of agricultural slaves that took place between 868 and 883: one estimate has the Sawad's yield falling by 80 per cent during the ninth century. Civil wars also contributed to the loss of revenue from the provinces: caliphs lost the ability to appoint and remove governors at will, and in some cases provinces stopped paying tax to the centre and even ceased acknowledging Abbasid suzerainty. The loss of caliphal revenue meant that *iqta*'s (land grants) and tax-farming agreements became necessary to support an over-mighty military and bureaucracy, who now treated the caliphs as their puppets and the resources of the caliphate as their private domain. The historian Ibn Miskawayh (d. 1030) has a scribe advise his vizier in 908:

For God's sake do not appoint to the post another man who knows the house of one, the fortune of another, the gardens of a third, the slave-girl of a fourth, the estate of a fifth and the horse of a sixth; not one who has contacts among the people, has had experience of politics, is worldly wise and has made calculations of people's fortunes.[13]

Almost thirty years later, in 936, when the warlord Ibn Ra'iq was recognised as *amir al-umara*', the caliphs had ceased to be an effective imperial military power. The great military powers of the Muslim world were now centred on Cordoba, al-Mahdiyya and Bukhara.[14]

The Status and Role of the 'Ulama'

The most important form of power in Islamic society – besides the monarchical, military and administrative – was ideological. Although all the three elites discussed thus far also had some ideological power, religious authority was never controlled exclusively or even predominantly by the caliphs but was always diffuse and contested. The formation and even

---

[13] Ibn Miskawayh, *Tajarib al-umam: The Eclipse of the Abbasid Caliphate*, ed. H. F. Amedroz, tr. D. S. Margliouth, 6 vols (Oxford, 1920–1), i:3.
[14] On the Abbasid tax system and its collapse: H. Kennedy, 'The decline and fall of the first Muslim empire', *Der Islam* 81 (2004), 3–30.

the role of religious elites in early Islam is still quite poorly understood, but it is clear that the emergent sodality of the *'ulama'* was where much ideological power came to reside in the eighth and ninth centuries. Where this ideological power coincided with kinship to the Prophet, these religious leaders could prove particularly threatening to the caliphs; this combination of sources of religious authority led to both the Abbasid Revolution and the emergence of various forms of Shi'ism in the ninth and tenth centuries. Indeed, in some ways the Abbasid caliphs found themselves caught between emerging Shi'i and Sunni Islam; as we have seen, the crisis of caliphal power in the ninth century coincided with the failure of the caliphs and their allies within the scholarly elite to impose their interpretation of Islam on the empire by means of the *mihna* of 833–c.847.

That the *mihna* pitted two groups of scholars against one another – broadly the *ahl al-ray* (speculative rationalists) against the *ahl al-hadith* (tradition-minded folk) – is one indication of why it is very difficult to treat them as a group. The scriptural and ideological foundations of Islam were still very fluid in this period. The Qur'an itself had only recently been compiled, in the mid-to-late seventh century, and it had yet to achieve the fully vocalised forms in which we now know it. Furthermore, the Qur'an's exact status as law still appears to have been in significant flux, as was the status of the Prophet as a legal and spiritual archetype, not to mention the status of his 'successors', the caliphs and imams. The importance of the *hadith*, which would eventually come to be seen in Sunni Islam as a scripture equal to the Qur'an, remained in dispute, and 'canonical' collections of these texts had yet to be arrived at. Indeed, the idea of authoritative *written* collections, as opposed to orally transmitted traditions, was anathema for much of this period. Some of what became the principles of 'classical' Sunni Islamic law were systematically formulated by al-Shafi'i around 800, but these ideas also took some time to begin to become normative. The relevance of the scriptures and philosophies of non-Muslims also had yet to be agreed upon. One should note that the full impact of the Greek philosophical tradition was only just beginning to be felt during the ninth and early tenth centuries.[15]

The economic and social status of the *'ulama'* also varied greatly, as did their role in society and their relationship to imperial state structures. It is difficult to generalise about the social backgrounds of the religious scholars, beyond the general trend noted already: in the seventh and early eighth centuries, the religious and legal authorities were Arabians

---

[15] For a useful outline of these developments: T. Bernheimer and A. Rippin, *Muslims: Their Religious Beliefs and Practices*, 5th edn (London, 2019).

from Medina in the Hijaz and from the Iraqi garrison towns of Kufa and Basra; after the mid-eighth century, increasing numbers of non-Arabs joined their ranks, often in Baghdad, and then in the growing urban centres at the frontiers, notably in Khurasan. It is also clear that the emergence of this group must be related to the economic boom of early Muslim society, since significant wealth is needed to support the educa-tion of youths and men who would otherwise be contributing their labour to support their families. Nonetheless, from as early as the clerical elites can be seen in the sources, many of them appear to have held ambivalent opinions about having close association with the state. This is the case even though some of the same figures were in fact closely involved with caliphal or gubernatorial courts.[16]

The education of the scholarly elites had yet to take the somewhat more institutional forms that it began to acquire in the tenth and eleventh centuries: the *madrasa* did not yet exist, nor did formal Sufi orders. It is likely that the first antecedents to these institutions developed in the eastern Islamic lands in the later ninth and early tenth centuries. For most of this period, religious scholars trained at mosques and in the private houses of other clerics. Leading scholars acquired circles (*halqas*) of followers who learned to recite the Qur'an and traditions from them. From this pattern of the transmission of knowledge, informal networks of jurisprudence and theology developed, and these promoted rival approaches to scriptural and legal interpretation.

Private wealth certainly made studying in such an environment much easier. Abu Hanifa (d. 767), whose name would later be given to one of the main Sunni schools of law, the Hanafis, was the wealthy son of a silk merchant. Al-Tabari (d. 923), who is perhaps best known for his *History* but was in fact a leading interpreter of the Qur'an and legal theorist, after whom the (ultimately less successful) Jariri school of law was named, had a relatively modest private income from land in Tabaristan, south of the Caspian. This enabled him to remain independent from the caliphal court for much of his career even after he moved to Baghdad in the 850s. However, other scholars appear to have come from relatively humble backgrounds; where they were Arabs – such as Malik b. Anas (d. 796) and al-Shafi'i (d. 820) – they may have benefited from the stipends their families received from the army payroll and wealth acquired in the conquests.

The dynamism of Khurasanian Islam in the tenth and eleventh centur-ies may be related to the growth in the production of cotton planted on previously uncultivated land there: only uncultivated land was open to

---

[16] See pp. 331–2, 340–1.

Muslim occupation. It has been argued that the wealth generated by this economic boom led to the exponential growth of the cities in Khurasan after the ninth century, and the cities of north-east Iran were certainly growing rapidly in this period.[17] However, in considering the development of Islamic thought, it should also be noted that there were many other important urban centres. In the ninth and tenth centuries, Baghdad and Basra were two of the main centres of intellectual activity, and they remained important in later centuries too. Other cities in the Muslim world also expanded as quickly as those in Iran: Baghdad's population probably reached a million in this period; Cordoba is thought to have had a population of around 100,000 in the tenth century; and in the eleventh century, Cairo would quickly expand to rival Baghdad.[18]

Administering from Fixed Power Centres for Buyids and Seljuks

The decline of Baghdad's pre-eminent status and the loss of the Abbasid caliph's freedom in the tenth century heralded a 'medieval' era in which the Abbasid imperial system of organisation – the caliph, his vizier and his military *amir*s – was no longer viable; it was replaced in Muslim western Asia by a new tripartite system – the *amir*, the secretary-vizier and the caliph. The caliph remained but was now denuded of any vizierate of his own and was supported through *iqta'*s from the Buyids. These new players did not recreate the system from the ground up but rather reorganised them along new lines:

Old institutions, despite their powerlessness, do not disappear quickly, especially in a traditional society. There is a gradual shift in which old concepts take on a new functions and added power, adapting to reality while leaving the illusion of the old ideology intact.[19]

What follows is a brief overview of the ways in which the ruling powers of the tenth to thirteenth centuries organised and administered their lands, focusing on the Buyid and Seljuk eras. After outlining the structures of the ruling systems, we will consider the position of the vizier and the other offices that gained increasing political influence (such as the *shihna* and

---

[17] R. Bulliet, *Cotton, Climate and Camels in Early Islamic Iran: A Moment in World History* (New York, 2009).

[18] R. Bulliet, *Islam: The View from the Edge* (Columbia, 1994). These cities were also the chief administrative centres and locations of key law-courts and schools. The outlook of top administrators and *'ulama'* had something in common with that of Constantinople's bureaucratic elite and the likes of Psellos: pp. 95, 96–7, 309–11, 318–20. Plausible counterparts only begin to appear in the west from the twelfth century on: pp. 271–2, 406.

[19] *BDI*, 131.

atabeg), before sketching some suggestions for further study.[20] Many of the former Abbasid organisational system's functions remained intact: the need to maintain discipline, organise the revenue system and oversee the routine administration were the order of the day, regardless of who was nominally in power.[21]

The Buyid viziers took on the same administrative burdens as their Abbasid predecessors.[22] The vizier remained in charge of numerous ministries covering every aspect of society, and he was assisted by a large number of deputies, being responsible for the chancellery, the treasury and the land tax, among other matters. An increasingly bloated bureaucracy oversaw the markets, military pay, postal system (*diwan al-barid*) and non-religious courts (*diwan al-mazalim*). The Buyids did make a few changes, particularly to do with taxation: the *diwan al-wazir* was associated with the chief vizier and determined the nature and extent of the tax-farming system, which expanded during this period.[23] The viziers of the Buyid age were just as 'foreign' to the population as the Buyid emirs themselves. New families took over the positions of the vizierate in the tenth and eleventh centuries, bringing with them ideologies that were often markedly different from those they governed. The Muʿtazilite bias of many members of the governing elite helped create a widening gap between the people and the Buyid administration:

> In a sense the new bureaucracy was even more rootless than the old, because its power was based unsteadily on the favor of individual amirs and the support of a privileged army, and because it bore an unfamiliar face to the population it sought to content and control.[24]

When added on to the generally unstable nature of Buyid rule, based as it was on a system of family confederations, a volatile system was made all the more ineffective.

The Seljuks continued to widen this gap between the elites and the general population. We find accounts in which Seljuk sultans and their lieutenants needed translators when meeting the officials of lands they had recently conquered, a problem the Buyids had also faced at the start of their reign. Much like the Arabian Muslim conquerors of the seventh

[20] H. Busse, *Chalif und Grosskönig: die Buyiden im Iraq (945–1055)* (Beirut, 1969); *BDI*; C. E. Bosworth, 'The political and dynastic history of the Iranian world (AD 1000–1217)', in *CHI* 5, 1–202; A. K. S. Lambton, 'The internal structure of the Saljuq empire', in *CHI* 5, 203–82.

[21] For a detailed narrative of Buyid bureaucracy during their earlier years of power: *BDI*, 131–91.

[22] D. Sourdel, *Le Vizirat Abbaside de 749 à 936 (132 à 324 de l'Hégire)*, 2 vols (Damascus, 1959–60); E. Tyan, *Institutions du droit public musulman*, 2 vols (Paris, 1954–7); M. M. Bravmann, 'The etymology of Arabic *wazir*', *Der Islam* 37 (1961), 260–3.

[23] *BDI*, 144.   [24] *BDI*, 191.

century, the Buyids and Seljuks soon realised that it was much easier to take a city than it was to govern one. However, the Seljuks had a number of factors in their favour. Many of them were Sunnis, to start with, although the significance of this ideological affiliation should not be overblown: the Seljuks tended to favour the Hanafi *madhhab* rather than the Shafi'i or Hanbali schools that many of their officials followed.[25] What helped the Seljuks adjust to their new position as regional rulers was their ability to adapt their tribal ways to the ideological and administrative traditions they inherited. As in the case of the Buyids, the Seljuks used the standard vizieral system when they came to power. The Seljuk administration can be seen as part of a continuum, in which old institutions took on new meaning, and the vizierate was broken down into four major categories under the chief vizier: the chancellery *(divan-i al-rasa'il)*; taxation *(divan-i istifa-yi mamalik)*; the auditor of finances *(divan-i ishraf-i mamalik)*; and the military *(divan-i ard)*.[26] Recent scholarship has expanded our understanding of socio-political change during the Seljuk era, in both geographical scope and cultural traditions.[27]

The Role of Officials in the Sultan's Absence   The Seljuks at their height had the knack of employing superlative administrators, capable of acting as intermediaries with their subject peoples. Nizam al-Mulk (d. 1092) was one such.[28] As vizier for Alp Arslan (d. 1072) and then Malikshah (d. 1092), he has often been viewed as the heart and soul of government in the eleventh century – the true ruler of the Seljuk lands. After triumphing in a power struggle for the vizierate with his rival al-Kunduri, Nizam al-Mulk would dominate the ideological and administrative arenas for twenty years, on occasion influencing military matters, too. He is frequently credited with championing the rise and spread of the educational infrastructure of the *madrasa*.[29] His success at establishing

---

[25] Their profession of piety can be seen in the addition of *din* (religion) to their honourific titles.

[26] Lambton, 'Internal structure of the Saljuq empire', 257: the Persian terminology is reflective both of many of those who staffed these ministries and of those who wrote about them.

[27] E.g. C. Lange and S. Mecit (eds), *The Seljuqs: Politics, Society and Culture* (Edinburgh, 2011); E. Herzig and S. Stewart (eds), *The Age of the Seljuqs* (London, 2015). See also *GSE*.

[28] H. Bowen [C. E. Bosworth], *EI²* s.v. 'Nizam al-Mulk'; see also Bosworth, 'Political and dynastic history of the Iranian world'; Lambton, 'Internal structure of the Saljuq empire'; and for coverage of the Persian sources: J. S. Meisami, *Persian Historiography to the End of the Twelfth Century* (Edinburgh, 1999).

[29] For the medieval Islamic education system and its ideological and societal ramifications, see the works of George Makdisi, especially *Rise of Colleges: Institutions of Learning in Islam and the West* (Edinburgh, 1981).

a competent and loyal entourage (*nizamiyya*) together with his most famous work on statecraft, the *Siyasat-nameh* ('Rules for Kings'),[30] ensured his political and ideological legacy immediately after his death and well into the modern period. However, one should beware seeing him as the linchpin that held the Seljuk system together: this would be to take too much away from the accomplishments of his fellow viziers and, more importantly, the dynamism embodied in the sultans for whom Nizam al-Mulk worked. Rather, they operated in parallel power networks of people and resources, the one Turkish and the other Persian. Their initial cooperation and then mounting discord and fragmentation helps to explain the vicissitudes of Seljuk history.[31]

Beyond the highest administrative echelons, the Seljuks used the *shihna* to liaise with the Abbasid caliphate in Baghdad. This quasi-military/diplomatic figure was essential, especially following the revitalisation of the caliphate in the late eleventh and early twelfth centuries. Like the Buyids before them, the Seljuks did not have a permanent base in Baghdad, and the *shihna* became their eyes and ears there. Eminently practical in principle, in reality this office added to the complexity of the ruling system, since those filling the role tended to become implicated in any political intrigues. The same goes for another office adopted by the Seljuks to control their own dynasty – the *atabegate*. Both the *atabeg* and the *tughra* – a stylised monogram chosen by each sultan as sign of his rule – were 'new political symbols and practices which originated on the steppe'.[32] The term *atabeg* can be loosely translated as 'Father-Lord' and describes the military leaders who helped to educate and train Seljuk children. *Atabeg*s were often sent off with young Seljuk princes to assist them as they learned to govern a province on their own. As with the *shihna*, the *atabeg* system appeared quite practical on the surface. Difficulties arose when these *atabeg*s began to act in a more autonomous fashion or encouraged their wards to rebel. By the mid-twelfth century, when the sultan Sanjar's power was waning, the *atabeg* system had gained in influence, and this further exacerbated Seljuk woes.[33]

While we can learn much about the systems used by the Buyids and Seljuks to maintain and expand their lands, we must always remember

[30] M. Simidchieva, 'Kingship and legitimacy in the Nizam al-Mulk's *Siyasatnama*', in B. Gruendler and L. Marlow (eds), *Writers and Rulers: Perspectives on Their Relationship from the Abbasid and Safavid Times* (Wiesbaden, 2004), 97–131. See also pp. 110–11.

[31] D. Durand-Guédy, 'New trends in the political history of Iran under the Great Saljuqs (11th–12th centuries)', *History Compass* 13 (2015), 321–37, esp. 327–30.

[32] *GSE*, 3.

[33] For an introduction to the Eldiguzid *atabegate*: K. A. Luther, *The Political Transformation of the Saljuq Sultanate of Iraq and Western Iran, 1152–1187* (unpublished PhD thesis, Princeton University, 1964).

that they were not working in a vacuum. To Buyid and Seljuk officials this was quite clear. With the plethora of smaller kingdoms and emirates, and even the revitalisation of the caliphate, came additional administrative systems. We should not think of these as parallel administrations with no interconnections, particularly so far as the officials who worked for them are concerned. For example, the new Buyid emir Mu'izz al-Dawla kept on the previous chief emir's financial administrator, Ibn Shirzad, since he knew the ins and outs of the financial system; Ibn Shirzad had other plans, however, and soon began working for the neighbouring Hamdanids.[34] While the personal nature of the governing system allowed rulers to hire and fire at will, it also allowed viziers and other officials to change their employers. The 'early medieval' period saw a greater number of coexisting administrations than either pre-Buyid or post-Mongol times did, and it would be interesting to look into the level of real or perceived interaction and changing allegiances.

Taxes – and Fields for Fresh Research   Marriage alliances could also affect the organisation of the political arena. Both the Buyids and Seljuks intermarried with the Abbasid family and other powers, whether to increase their influence in the region or to ease tension among rival polities. Each party knew what was at stake in such alliances and understood the need to balance immediate concerns with the long-term effects of these unions. By studying such 'reproductive politics', we can gain a better understanding of how household politics worked, if only at elite level.[35] Further study should also shine light on the myriad roles that medieval elite women could – and did – play in medieval Islam.[36]

One area where a lot of research has already been undertaken for this period is in its financial history. Each of the post-tenth-century powers was well aware of the need to secure sufficient revenue to pay for their military and administrative systems. In addition to the monies acquired from the taxes sanctioned by *shari'a*,[37] the Buyids and the Seljuks

---

[34] *BDI*, 136–7.

[35] 'Reproductive politics' is a term coined and popularised by Leslie Peirce in her work on the Ottoman court system: *The Imperial Harem: Women and Sovereignty in the Ottoman Empire* (Oxford, 1993).

[36] For a variety of approaches that can help 'render women visible' in medieval Islam: G. R. G. Hambly (ed.), *Women in the Medieval Islamic World* (New York, 1998); E. J. Hanne, 'Women, power, and the eleventh and twelfth century Abbasid court', *Hawwa* 3(1) (2005), 80–105. For the visibility and agency of women in our other two spheres: pp. 502–4.

[37] These were *jizya* (a poll-tax on non-Muslims); *zakat* (an alms tax only imposed on Muslims); *kharaj* (a tax on agricultural land, initially only imposed on non-Muslims but soon extended to include Muslims as well); and *ushr* (a tax on harvests, imposed under Umar I).

regularly imposed separate taxes (*mukus*). These could take the form of tolls, taxes in the marketplace, and customs duties for local or long-distance trade. Merchants and citizens alike considered these onerous, grumbling when they were imposed and lauding the ruler who lifted them. The charges were, however, a ubiquitous feature of the post-tenth-century world, and they had a corps of administrators to oversee their collection and dispensation. We currently have a healthy under-standing of the land grant system (*iqta'*),[38] and material and textual evidence has helped expand our knowledge of the monetary system as a whole.[39]

Practices of Power and Politics of Violence in a Polycentric World

Archipelagos of Power between North Africa and Central Asia   In 1469–70 the Timurid sultan Husayn Bayqara succeeded, after many years of trying, in ousting his rival kinsmen from Herat and establishing himself as ruler of Khurasan. He achieved this in a manner that was not substantially different from that of Buyid, Seljuk and Turkmen strong-men several centuries earlier, with a small yet tried and tested military host of followers and allies, amidst the regional and trans-regional rival-ries, warfare and upheavals that had defined Iran, Khurasan and Transoxiana since the conquests made by his great-great-grandfather Temür (1370–1405). We have already noted the instability of Timurid power and its limited, ad hoc reach; its centres have been likened to an 'archipelago within a sea of semi-independent regions', where 'control

---

[38] C. Cahen, *EI²*, s.v. 'Ikta''; A. K. S. Lambton, 'Reflections on the *iqta*'', in G. Makdisi (ed.), *Arabic and Islamic Studies in Honor of H. A. R. Gibb* (Cambridge, 1965), 358–76; see also T. Sato, *State and Rural Society in Medieval Islam: Sultans, Muqta's and Fallahun* (Leiden, 1997). Grants of land-rights in return for loyalty and military service were fundamental to politico-military formations in the west in the central middle ages: pp. 74, 150, 376–7, 380, 400–1. Imperial grants were more circumscribed in Byzantium, at least until the later Palaiologan era: pp. 324, 435–6, 439, 441, 444–7.

[39] Notably the work of Andrew Ehrenkreutz on Egypt and the monetary systems in the pre-Crusade era: 'Contributions to the knowledge of the fiscal administration of Egypt in the middle ages', *BSOAS* 16 (1954), 502–14; idem, 'The crisis of the *dinar* in the Egypt of Saladin', *JAOS* 72 (1956), 178–84; idem, 'Monetary aspects of medieval Near Eastern history', in M. A. Cook (ed.), *Studies in the Economic History of the Middle East* (London, 1970), 37–50; idem, 'Studies in the monetary history of the Near East in the middle ages, 2: The standard of fineness of western and eastern *dinars* before the Crusades', *JESHO* 6 (1963), 243–77. In addition, light has been shed on the postal system of this era (*barid*): A. J. Silverstein, *Postal Systems in the Pre-Modern Islamic World* (Cambridge, 2007); and on the conceptualisation and practice of justice: C. Lange, *Justice, Punishment and the Medieval Muslim Imagination* (Cambridge, 2008).

was a matter of luck, alliance and an occasional punitive expedition'.[40] This could equally well apply to all the polycentric landscapes in Islamic western Asia and North Africa between the mid-thirteenth and early sixteenth centuries. The relationships of power, agency and violence linking up the leaderships of this era – whether Mongol, post-Mongol, Turkmen, Turco-Mongol or Arabo-Berber – with local and regional political practices that had undergone severe disruption or partial trans-formation were complex and many: multidirectional and highly fluid, they never settled easily into any one centralising mould.

Nevertheless, organisational frameworks do seem to have emerged at particular moments, forming around particular centres of trans-regional authority, and this sporadic process of stabilisation seems to culminate – in hindsight at least – in the rise of the early modern empires of the Islamic world.[41] These were highly centralised great powers that put an end to centuries of political instability and fragmentation. This tendency can be seen in the case of Husayn Bayqara's reign over Khurasan: although starting off with a great deal of violence and disruption, Husayn soon adopted, and adapted to, long-standing traditions of organisation, even-tually even investing in ancient Islamic religious institutions and authority structures to help develop Khurasan's rural economy. All of this resulted in more than three decades of relative political order, until Sultan Husayn died a natural death in 1506.[42]

In this and many similar cases, however, warfare, rivalry and violence were ever on the political horizon, and the metaphor of an archipelago remains valid. In Khurasan, we see this from the military campaigns that were pursued against late Timurid peers and rivals. Sultan Husayn's own sons rebelled repeatedly, and, shortly after his death in 1506, Herat was seized from them by the Uzbek khan Muhammad Shaybani (1500–10). It even emerges from the process of stabilisation itself and from the attempted transformation of this particular Timurid archipelago into a more solid, integrated political whole. The resulting tensions among Khurasan's elites culminated in 1494 with the murder of one of the main architects of this

---

[40] Above p. 246; B. Manz, *Power, Politics and Religion in Timurid Iran* (Cambridge, 2007), 2. On this point in general: J. Van Steenbergen, 'From Temür to Selim: trajectories of Turko-Mongol state formation in Islamic West-Asia's long fifteenth century', in J. Van Steenbergen (ed.), *Trajectories of State Formation across Fifteenth-Century Islamic West-Asia: Eurasian Parallels, Connections and Divergences* (Leiden, 2020), 27–87 [hereafter FTTS].

[41] These were the empires of the Ottomans in the west, the Safavids in Iran, the Mughals in India and the Uzbeks in Central Asia. The later middle ages saw a comparable contra-dictory pattern in the west, with some political structures firming up against a background of shifting alliances, local rivalries and religious contention: pp. 165–70, 383–5, 401–2, 408–9.

[42] *TIT*.

drive towards centralisation: Sultan Husayn's Persian chief administrator, Majd al-Din Muhammad Khwafi. More than anything else, violent rivalries continued to determine the organisation of power relationships: from the mid-thirteenth century, when Mongol and Christian armies turned Iraq in the east and southern al-Andalus in the west into unstable frontier zones, until the rise of the early modern empires.

In fact, between the two extremes of rapid change and longer-term stability, a politics of violence held sway across the entire late medieval Islamic world, in direct continuation with the political realities faced by Buyids, Fatimids, Seljuks, and their supporters and rivals. The relationships between dynastic rulers, military strongmen, expert administrators, tribal chiefs and a multitude of other local leaders in this polycentric landscape were interlinked yet competitive and often combative. As we shall see, these dynamics are discernible in the processes of disruption and stabilisation, at the heart of which lay the struggle for resources. Access to resources was bitterly fought over and keeping hold of them an ever-present concern, even in the more stable polities such as Khurasan under Sultan Husayn. The circumscribed, ad hoc nature of most of the leaderships meant that their impact was quite limited, and this went hand in hand with violent competition. But these constraints and pressures on a ruler should not be seen as just a negative by-product of the endemic instability, polycentrism, internecine warfare and destructive violence. As in any other pre-modern context, elites did not seek power in order to govern – as we understand the concept in a modern sense – but to ensure their own preservation, to eliminate their rivals, to protect their clients and supporters, and to accumulate sufficient resources to achieve these ends. The politics of violence were central to the pursuit of these narrow aims. Yet however many material, social and symbolic resources a ruler might manage to accumulate, they were never quite enough to counter the destabilising dynamics of these politics.

Warband Leadership and Elite Formations   Once the Mongols had swept through western Asia in the mid-thirteenth century, renewing and intensifying – after the Seljuk Turks and Oghuz Turkmen – Inner Asian traditions of charismatic leadership, family rule, personal power networks and blood-soaked modes of succession, these set the tone, in various adapted forms, of how elites operated. Central to leadership and the organisation of power was the ruler's entourage: even when more complex systems developed, this remained highly militarised and essentially strung around personal contacts. In Sultan Husayn's case, the foundations of his power and long reign in Khurasan were shaped in the decade or so before he seized Herat in 1469–70. Over the years he had made several attempts on the city and on Khurasan more generally, but without lasting success: Husayn and his followers were left to roam the inhospitable lands to the north and north-west of the region. But this not only allowed him to evade his rivals and await better times; it also let him rally trusty warriors around him, hardened by life on the road and buoyed up by booty from incessant raiding and looting. Later renderings of this heroic time suggest that Husayn's entourage was fluid, waxing and waning according to his success – or failure – as a brigand and Timurid contender, but that it would grow from a few dozen loyal supporters to over a thousand fighting men. When he finally took Herat and Khurasan, these men, the bonds they had forged and experiences they had undergone shaped Husayn's rule: his royal household and court were constructed out of ties of loyalty and reward; and his alliances – including matrimonial ones – were with the local leaders who had supported his struggle for power in the 1460s.[43]

Many of the great rulers of this period had similar backstories: the *mamluk* sultan Baybars (1260–77) in Syria in the 1250s; Osman (d. 1324) in western Asia Minor; and, in Transoxiana and Khurasan, Temür (in the 1360s) and his great-great-great grandson Babur (in the early sixteenth century). All are depicted as undergoing similar trials of their own abilities and their followers' loyalties, while being harried by rivals on the peripheries (geographical or social) of Mongol, post-Mongol, Turco-Mongol and also Arabo-Berber power. And most importantly, in each case these shared experiences led to the forming of a tightly knit warband which, in various guises – tribal group, military household or princely court – would lie at whatever centres of power and rule emerged.[44]

Thus close-knit groups of elites and their followers, bound by personal ties of kinship or mutual loyalties, were the key components of power throughout the region and the period. The fluidity of Sultan Husayn's entourage in the 1460s shows how mutable such groups could be. One of the most persistent, violent and yet mercurial forms to appear on the peripheries of the Islamic world were the peripatetic warbands of military leaders or tribal chiefs and their retinues. At the opposite extreme were the urbanised, highly structured entourages of sultans, Ilkhans, emirs and princes, with their sometimes extensive ranks of personal bodyguards, women, children, courtiers, servants and administrators.[45] Most lay

---

[43] *TIT*, 43–73.

[44] J. Gommans, 'The warband in the making of Eurasian empires', in M. van Berkel and J. Duindam (eds), *Prince, Pen, and Sword: Eurasian Perspectives* (Leiden, 2018), 297–383.

[45] FTTS; see also J. Van Steenbergen, 'The Mamluk sultanate as a military patronage state: household politics and the case of the Qalawunid *bayt* (1279–1382)', *JESHO* 56 (2013), 189–217; M. Eychenne, 'Le bayt à l'époque mamlouke: une entité sociale à revisiter',

somewhere between these two ends of the spectrum, and only a handful managed either to achieve or to maintain a high degree of organisational complexity. Those few that did mutated and stabilised with varying degrees of success into the centrally organised and centralising courts at Cairo, Tabriz and Sultaniyya, Bursa and Constantinople, and Herat and Samarqand (as well as at Tunis, Tlemcen, Fez and Granada).[46]

The success of these leaders and their entourages – whether orderly court or roving warband – was a highly personal matter, in fact one of life and death. Rulers such as Sultan Husayn and his great-great-grandfather Temür, or Ghazan of the Ilkhans (1295–1304), the Ottomans' Bayezid I (1389–1402) and Bayezid II (1481–1512) and the sultan Qalawun (1279–90) had constantly to fight for their survival, as did their many peers, descendants and rivals. Political order was a widely shared but highly volatile construction, under continuous pressures, including from within these close-knit power groups.[47] In fact nomadic traditions such as the family confederation, which had spread westwards with the Seljuks from the eleventh century on, continued to determine how power, status and resources were distributed within these close-knit groups. These widely shared practices led to rivalry and fragmentation, obstructing attempts to give structure to, let alone to bureaucratise, relationships of power and create orderly ladders of promotion. Elites considered themselves entitled to privileges, and to succeed to status, wealth and power, yet clear-cut hierarchies of individual rights, priorities and obligations were lacking. Since such benefits originated from intense competition and violence, and since agnatic kinship and dynastic seniority were only one asset among many, personal qualities – such as ambition, charisma and political acumen – and resources continued to prove more important historical determinants. In this context of regular dynastic fragmentation

Annales islamologiques 42 (2008), 275–95; J. Loiseau, *Reconstruire la maison du sultan, 1350–1450: ruine et recomposition de l'ordre urbain au Caire* (Cairo, 2010); C. Melville, 'The *Keshig* in Iran: the survival of the royal Mongol household', in L. Komaroff (ed.), *Beyond the Legacy of Genghis Khan* (Leiden, 2006), 135–64; T. T. Allsen, 'Guard and government in the reign of the Grand Qan Möngke, 1251–59', *Harvard Journal of Asiatic Studies* 46(2) (1986), 495–521; *TIT*, 18–24.

[46] Other power constellations that did not connect, or connected only indirectly, with these included the networks around intellectuals, Sufi masters and messianic figures, as well as commercial entrepreneurs, and combinations thereof: see e.g. I. E. Binbaş, 'Did the Hurufis mint coins? Articulation of sacral kingship in an Aqquyunlu coin hoard from Erzincan', in A. C. S. Peacock and S. N. Yıldız (eds), *Islamic Literature and Intellectual Life in Fourteenth- and Fifteenth-Century Anatolia* (Würzburg, 2016), 137–70; *INTI*; J. Van Steenbergen, 'Revisiting the Mamluk empire: political action, relationships of power, entangled networks, and the sultanate of Cairo in late medieval Syro-Egypt', in R. Amitai and S. Conermann (eds), *The Mamluk Sultanate from the Perspective of Regional and World History* (Bonn and Göttingen, 2019), 77–107.

[47] *FTTS*.

and violent succession, political participation was a matter not just of birth or choice but also of social survival and necessity. Elites everywhere had no option but to engage actively and unceasingly in the political arena, where the individual expertise and personal clout of successful military leaders were all-important.[48]

Such violent forms of leadership undoubtedly saw their most extreme form in Temür's politics of conquest between 1370 and 1405. Through raiding and looting on a trans-regional scale, this Turco-Mongol ruler from Transoxiana created a new elite of commanders and their men. He severed them from local – especially tribal Chaghadai – relationships and interests by constant campaigning elsewhere, and he bound them to the new political order that was being forged.[49] Similar elite formation can be seen in the thirteenth-century Jingizid-Mongol conquests and the violent transformation of the political landscape all the way between the Bosphoros and Indus. This is particularly true for the Jingizid–Ilkhanid polity that formed across most of that region after ten years or so of violent campaigning: the integration of allies and supporters and utter elimination of Jingizid and other rivals marked the Mongol ruler Hülegü's rise to power in the 1250s and 1260s. We see similar strategies of conquest, destruction and elite formation elsewhere: from post-Ilkhanid fourteenth-century western Asia and the early Ottomans in the far west to certain Timurid, late Ottoman and 'Turkish' contexts, which experienced regular periods of violence and internecine warfare, survival, conquest and restoration. These include Sultan Husayn's rise to power, as well as those of the Ottoman Mehmed I (1413–21) and his son Murad I (1421–51) and of the sultans al-Mu'ayyad Shaykh (1412–21), Barsbay (1422–38) and Jaqmaq (1438–53) in Cairo.

Organising towards Stabilisation of Regimes   Some polities managed to check – to a degree – the disruptive consequences of these leadership practices in Islamic western Asia: the Ottoman sultanate in the north-west, its 'Turkish' counterpart in the Syro-Egyptian south, and, more patchily, the Timurids in fifteenth-century Khurasan and Transoxiana. Here we see processes of stabilisation underway: the gradual appearance of a more coherent central apparatus of power and the corresponding sense of a sovereign Islamic political order upheld by it – whether Ottoman, 'Turkish' or Timurid. Various centripetal strategies

---

[48] FTTS. Greater participation in political life is also characteristic of western elites and groups of various types in this period: pp. 156–63, 277–80, 283–5, 401–2. There are glimmerings of such tendencies in late Byzantium: pp. 324, 326–7, 437–8, 446–7.

[49] See B. Manz, *The Rise and Rule of Tamerlane* (Cambridge, 1999).

tried to contain the violence and fragmentation that continued to plague moments of succession and transition in Bursa and Constantinople, in Cairo, and in Herat and Samarqand. The same goes for the various Arabicised dynasties that dominated North Africa, al-Andalus and Yemen between the mid-thirteenth and mid-sixteenth centuries. On the peripheries of these dynastic power centres, a few of the Turkmen, Turco-Mongol, and other nomadic, semi-nomadic and charismatic leaderships even managed some form of dynastic continuity, structure and stability, especially from the mid-fourteenth century on. Yet other groupings with trans-regional ambitions did not. The evaporation of the Ilkhanids and Timurids in Anatolia, Azerbaijan, Iraq and western Iran is a case in point. The series of Turkmen clans which overran and ruled these territories in the later fifteenth century had as much to do with Ilkhanid and Timurid leadership practices, their endemic internecine warfare and their lack of dynastic structures as with the Turkmen's own martial qualities.

The stabilising polities adopted many administrative techniques from their Abbasid and Seljuk predecessors, but they fused them with Mongol, post-Mongol and Turco-Mongol warband traditions (and, in the west, with Arabo-Berber and Islamo-Christian ones). The politics of the military household became ever more vital to rulership, with leading roles at court defined in terminology drawn from the warbands. Even when these courts came to be dominated by freedmen and slaves of very different ancestry – as was the case at Cairo and eventually at the Ottoman court – their titles reflected Mongol or Turkish elite origins. Membership of the household was no longer limited to a ruler's relatives and servants: military commanders, whether related or not, were an important component, their value and strength being rewarded above all by the number of men they could muster. Regardless of the extent of the polity, men tended to be organised in units of ideal sizes, such as the Mongol *tümen* of 10,000 or the regiments in Syria and Egypt of five, ten, forty or a hundred *mamluk*s led by *amir*s who were appointed by the sultan. This combination of leadership, manpower, martial identity and a more regular command structure gave rulers unmatched military muscle that could be effectively controlled and easily deployed – particularly in the shape of the formidable Mongol and Turkish mounted archers. These martial qualities and ideals of military organisation were picked up by ambitious military commanders elsewhere in western Asia. In the ever-recurring vacuums of central authority, a mixed bag of Turkish, Turkmen, Arab, Kurdish, Mongol, Iranian and other tribal chiefs adopted them in their bids to control the various territories and resources.

Such power vacuums were many and no one regime was ever absolute, capable of total control over local groups and communities. This would have required an enormous, sustained and impracticable investment of men and resources; more importantly, it would have defeated the main priorities of all rulers: protecting their own, eliminating their rivals and ensuring their line. Many rulers invested in communication technologies that substantially reduced the distances between them and their agents. Most obviously they restored or installed relay postal systems, although these were primarily geared to military intelligence-gathering and were always highly vulnerable to local or regional violence, warfare and dynastic transformation. In these conditions, the diverse and dynamic ranks of Mongol, post-Mongol and Turco-Mongol trans-regional military elites had to keep working with local urban and rural leaderships, constantly negotiating and sharing their power with very many others. This was even true of more stable, centralised polities such as the Ottomans, Ilkhanids, Timurids, Turkmen and the Syro-Egyptian 'Turks'.[50]

As we have seen, to the north and east, long-standing Persianate administrative, intellectual, cultural – and military – elites survived the Mongol onslaught of the thirteenth century without too much lasting disruption. They continued to serve as the organisational backbone to the Ilkhanid, post-Ilkhanid, Timurid and Turkmen political formations that came and went. In Syria and Egypt, similar administrative and religious elites continued to be favoured and employed by military leaders and their entourages, acquiring local power and substantial wealth in the process. Cairo and Damascus emerged as affluent, renowned centres of Arabo-Islamic learning and Sunni religious authority, attracting not only extensive patronage from rulers and their military elites but also scholars and students from all over the Islamic world, including North Africa, al-Andalus, Turkish Asia Minor and the Persian east. At the same time, resources circulated around and were amassed in these urban centres through skillful management by local Syrian and Egyptian families of administrators, many of whom were of Arabicised – and occasionally Islamised – Christian origin. Employed, and also empowered, in the service of the different households of military commanders and sultans who succeeded one another at the top of the sultanate's volatile political order, most of these families shared their patrons' often violent fates, especially in the fourteenth century.

These non-military elites from the later sultanate have left sets of detailed Arabic texts describing the performance and structure – both idealised and actual – of the elaborate military and administrative

---

[50] Comparable dynamics, but with different characters and scales, are discernible in the west: pp. 141–5, 153–6, 407–8, 409. For the interplay of formal and informal power, albeit on a different plane, in Byzantium: pp. 198–200, 203.

apparatuses of power. These include regularly copied and updated lists of office-holders. Serving as virtual *Who's Who*s, they offer unique insight into the organisation of the court in Cairo and its ties with other power centres in the sultanate. They are immensely complex, revealing a continuity of titles and organisation with long past dynasties, as well as with contemporary ones, and they show how the sultanate's administrative expertise and precedents were at least supposed to be structured and connected. A good example may be found in an early fourteenth-century panegyric chronicle taking up nine volumes. Its list of the sultanate's agents and hierarchies of power in 1335 is situated within a much broader survey of the period's West Asian political landscapes:

The caliph is the *imam* al-Mustakfi bi-llah Abu l-Rabi' Sulayman, Commander of the Faithful, and our lord the most powerful sultan, al-Malik al-Naṣir [Muhammad b. Qalawun, 1293–4/1299–1309/1310–41], is the sultan of Islam – may God prolong his days until the end of time [. . .].

The *amir* chamberlain is the *amir* Badr al-Din Amir Mas'ud b. Khatir – may God be good to him and may He augment his beneficence towards him –, his brother the *amir* Sharaf al-Din Mahmud being a chamberlain, just as the *amir* Sayf al-Din Jarik; the *amir* of the adjutants is the *amir* Shihab al-Din Saruja, and the speaker for issues of the vizierate that concern the collection of funds from the departmental bureaus is the *amir* Sayf al-Din Alakuz al-Naṣiri, with the assistance of Badr al-Din Lu'lu'; and the *amir* Rukn al-Din al-Ahmadi is an *amir* of the armour bearers, just as the amir Sayf al-Din Urum Bugha and the *amir* Sayf al-Din Balaban al-Hasani; the *amir* Sayf al-Din Aqbugha 'Abd al-Wahid is a major-domo, with the command over the sultanic *mamluk*s – may God almighty bless them – being joined to him after the dismissal of the eunuch 'Anbar al-Sahrati; and the controller in the victorious departmental bureau for the victorious armies is the *qadi* Makin al-Din b. Qarwina.

The viceroys in Syria are the *amir* Sayf al-Din Tankiz, the lord of the *amir*s, in well-protected Damascus [. . .]; the *amir* 'Ala' al-Din Altunbugha in Aleppo, the *amir* Jamal al-Din Aqush Na'ib al-Karak in Tripoli, the *amir* Sayf al-Din *al-hajj* Aruqtay in Safed, and the *amir* Sayf al-Din Taynal in Gaza.

The rulers of the different regions are, in Mecca [. . .] and the lord of Medina [. . .] and the lord of Yemen [. . .] and the lord of Mardin [. . .] and the lord of Hama [. . .] and the lord of the region from Iraq up to Khurasan is the king [Ilkhan] Abu Sa'id [1316–35] [. . .] and the lord of the lands of Barka [of the Mongol-Jingizid Golden Horde] is the king Uzbak [1312–41] [. . .] and the other kings of the Mongols are as they and their names have been mentioned for the preceding years.[51]

---

[51] Ibn Aybak al-Dawadari (fl. 1309–35), *Kanz al-durar wa-jami' al-ghurar, IX: al-Durr al-fakhir fi sirat al-Malik al-Nasir*, ed. H. R. Roemer (Cairo 1960), 379–80; J. Van Steenbergen, '"Mamlukisation" between social theory and social practice: an essay on reflexivity, state formation, and the late medieval sultanate of Cairo' (*ASK Working Paper* 22) (Bonn, 2015), 14.

Many such lists can be found in Arabic chronicles and manuals of court protocol, and they all describe a similar sort of organisation of the sultan's royal household, his court and his wider representation of the body politic. In the early sixteenth century, a list from a contemporary Arabic chronicle of Syro-Egyptian history distinguishes even more explicitly between the different groups and the hierarchies of power they represent. It, too, begins with 'the caliph of the time' and 'the sultan of Egypt' and then presents 'the four lord *qadi*s' who were the chief justices of the four Sunni schools of law active in the realm. This is followed by the military leaders, starting with 'the *amir* commanders, their number on that day being twenty-six *amir* commanders of 1,000, including six holders of court office'. Their ranks turn out to include one of the sultan's sons, who was '*amir* of the horse', and one of his nephews, 'as grand *amir* executive secretary, combining the grand executive sec-retaryship with the grand major-domoship, and as grand inspector of the provinces'. It continues with 'the viceroys in southern Syria and Aleppo' and a detailed list of 'the *amir*s of forty[52] who were holders of office', and it concludes with the comment that 'the *amir*s who were heads of the guards [. . .] were many and we will not detail them here for fear of length'. The other groups that are then identified are 'the holders of office from the leading officials and turban-wearers' and 'the notables from among the eunuchs'.[53] The long fragment finishes with some comments from the author on the organisation of the sultan's household and court:

During this year the sultan's private retinue grew to about 1,200 favourites, [chosen] from among his purchased [*mamluk*s]; a large contingent from them were established as holders of offices, including as executive secretary assistants, as arms-bearers, as armourers, as equerries, as cup-bearers and in all kinds of similar offices. During this year the number of *amir*s of forty and of ten grew beyond that of 300 *amir*s. The army had grown, but the regular income from fiscal tribute was low.[54]

The different titles, groups and the organisational complexity they repre-sent are not just emblematic of how disparate and unstable sets of agents became mainstays of regimes in Cairo and elsewhere. They also remind us of the functional distinctions that were drawn consistently, irrespective of the variations in polities and elites, whether they were military ones – the

---

[52] The *amir*s of forty each had that number of mounted slave-warriors (*mamluk*s) under his command.

[53] Ibn Iyas (1448–c.1524), *Bada'i' al-zuhur fi waqa'i' al-duhur*, ed. M. Sobernheim *et al.*, *Die Chronik des Ibn Ijâs: Fünfter Teil AH 922–928/AD 1516–1522* [= *Bibliotheca Islamica* 5e] (Leipzig and Istanbul, 1932), 2–5; Van Steenbergen, '"Mamlukisation"', 14–15.

[54] Ibn Iyas, *Bada'i' al-zuhur*, 5; Van Steenbergen, '"Mamlukisation"', 15.

Mongols or Turks – or the other elites involved in dynastic politics.[55] These distinctions go back to bureaucratic traditions of long standing, yet these continued to be effective for bringing order to militarised power of the Mongol, post-Mongol and Turco-Mongol polities (as they did for Arabo-Berber ones, too). Contemporary descriptions dub them the 'men of the sword', 'men of the turbans', and 'men of the pen', and they exercised power in, respectively, the fields of physical violence (military force); symbolic violence (religious and dynastic legal practice); and resources and communications.[56]

As both our lists suggest, whereas the men of the turbans were organised along the lines of the four schools of Sunni law (the *madhhabs*), as was the case in previous eras, the ubiquitous men of the pen were divided into bureaus (*diwans*; Persian *divan*). These managed, and often controlled access to, particular sets of symbolic and material resources, ranging from royal chancelleries and treasuries to military and fiscal registries. As mentioned before, supervising access to these records and resources was crucial in pre-modern court- and gift-based economies. At the heart of the matter lay exchange: of loyalty and service for direct or indirect shares in the resources of the dynastic centre. These resources might come in the form of gifts (whether of cash, horses, clothing or food), favours and privileges, booty, tribute and fiscal exemptions, or appointments to posts of conspicuous honour and entitlement. Access to material resources was particularly key for those who were, or wished to be, related to the dynastic centre. For the more successful and stable polities, where relationships of power were more structured, the management and control of resources was one of the chief routes to power, and this led to active engagement in the political arena by, as well as fierce competition among, these men of the pen, their families and their own entourages. In Ilkhanid Tabriz, 'Turkish' Cairo, Ottoman Bursa and Constantinople, and Timurid Herat, and also at the courts of North Africa and al-Andalus, the boundaries that marked these men of the pen out from those of the sword or the turban often became blurred, and quite a few bureaucrats rose to prominence, riches and power – with all the violence and dangers this involved.[57]

---

[55] These other elites were often referred to as Persianate Tadjiks in the east, Arabo-Sunni elites or Arabo-Christian families in Syria and Egypt; they were gradually replaced by specially trained and Turkified palace slaves by the Ottomans.

[56] M. van Berkel, 'The people of the pen: self-perceptions of status and role in the administration of empires and polities', in van Berkel and Duindam (eds), *Prince, Pen, and Sword*, 384–451.

[57] J. Van Steenbergen and W. Flinterman, 'Al-Nasir Muhammad and the formation of the Qalawunid state', in A. S. Landau (ed.), *Pearls on a String: Artists, Patrons, and Poets at the Great Islamic Courts* (Baltimore, MD, 2015), 87–113; and also *TIT*, 74–102; Manz, *Power, Politics and Religion*, 79–110; D. Kastritsis, 'Tales of viziers and wine: interpreting early

Resource Wars and Infrastructures The manpower and other material resources available to the various military leaderships and their administrators – and occasionally to their competitors – were another defining component of the distinctive leadership practices of this time and area. Since the tenth and eleventh centuries, the diverse, rich and long-standing agricultural economies of western Asia and North Africa had been forced to accommodate repeated influxes of nomadic groupings – and the often destructive changes these brought. This went on up to the sixteenth century, and they had also had to absorb the impact of the Black Death in the mid-fourteenth century and other, less catastrophic, cycles of pestilence, plague and depopulation. Transhumant nomads were prominent throughout the region – Arabs, Kurds, Turkmen, Amazigh (Berbers) and many other tribal affiliations – sharing it with mostly small-scale farmers and with ever more active mercantile networks connecting many established, densely populated towns and cities. Yet the trans-regional economy proved resilient enough to the political realities of endless warfare, elite formation and transformation, to maintain a reasonable level of surpluses, tax revenues and supplies.[58]

What defined a ruler's relationship with these local economies and their assets seems to have been their distance from his dynastic centre and the degree of control he could attain. In times of political rivalry, war and conquest, resources such as harvests, livestock, and non-Muslim men, women and children were invariably seized and distributed among campaigners and their followers as booty. Yet in practice local leaderships were often able to strike agreements with the marauders in an effort to forestall or mitigate such economic and political damage. Exchanges of precious gifts and pledges of tribute in cash or kind would then confirm such deals, generating alternative, more controlled, mechanisms to provide a return on the investment that was needed for military campaigning. Such ad hoc deals struck between local and central elites could metamorphose into more lasting and comprehensive arrangements, assuming they could be enforced; these involved forms of what was essentially tax farming. In the politically stabler areas, such as Ottoman western Anatolia, 'Turkish' Syro-Egypt, Ilkhanid Azerbaijan and Iran, or Timurid Khurasan and Transoxiana (and, for that matter, the hinterlands of Hafsid Tunis and Qayrawan, or the Marinid Maghreb), and in

Ottoman narratives of state centralization', in J. Van Steenbergen (ed.), *Trajectories of State Formation across Fifteenth-Century Islamic West-Asia: Eurasian Parallels, Connections and Divergences* (Leiden, 2020), 224–54; B. Manz, 'Iranian elites under the Timurids', in *ibid.*, 257–82; M. Ballan, *The Scribe of the Alhambra: Lisan al-Din Ibn al-Khatib, Sovereignty and History in Nasrid Granada* (unpublished PhD thesis, University of Chicago, 2019).
[58] In general: FTTS.

the catchment areas of powerful leaders such as Temür's son Shah Rukh, Jahan Shah of the Black Sheep Turkmen and Uzun Hasan of the White Sheep Turkmen, more direct forms of taxation tended to complement or even displace tax-farming and tributary arrangements. Each of these power centres operated very similar rural and urban tax regimes, often on the lines of long-standing local and regional fiscal traditions, thus drawing taxpayers, beneficiaries and administrators alike more closely into the central political and economic mesh. These more direct tax regimes combined traditional Islamic taxes – most importantly the land tax (*kharaj*) and, with the exception of the non-Muslim Ilkhanids, the poll tax (*jizya*) – with a motley array of customs duties, urban taxes and forced payments in cash, kind or services that did not enjoy the sanction of Muslim scripture.[59]

Land redistribution and tenure among dynastic elites was also rooted in precedent. Most direct tax regimes involved lands and rights that were legally (or at least theoretically) deemed to belong to the ruler, as personifying the sovereign political order or state. They were intended to be parcelled out in fiscal concessions and exemptions to members of his household, courtiers and military leaders, along with other beneficiaries, in return for their loyalty and service.[60] Such prebendal systems were a normative way of organising the political economy around successful trans-regional leaders, power elites, and their administrators. Although stretched to the outer limits – social and territorial – of these leaders' effective reach, they never completely turned into 'feudal' hierarchies of benefit and service, western-style. They intersected and had to compete with well-established fiscal regulations, local tax farming and tributary arrangements, and alternative land tenure provisions, notably those made for the religious endowments (*waqf*).[61]

A mechanism of long standing, the *waqf* became ever more prominent throughout the Islamic world, especially from the early fourteenth

---

[59] FTTS; P. Jackson, *The Mongols and the Islamic World: From Conquest to Conversion* (New Haven, CT, 2017), 111–13, 250–57, 301–3.

[60] These were known by many terms, including *timar* (Turkish), *iqta'* (Arabic) and *soyurghal* (Mongolian).

[61] Termed *waqf* (Arabic); *vaqf* (Persian); *vaqıf* (Turkish); and, in North Africa and al-Andalus, *hubus*. On this point in general: FTTS; also Manz, *Power, Politics and Religion*; *TIT*, 148–228; H. Inalcik, 'Autonomous enclaves in Islamic states: *temlik*s, *soyurghal*s, *yurdluk-ocaklık*s, *malikane-mukata'a*s and *awqaf*', in J. Pfeiffer and S. A. Quinn (eds), *History and Historiography of Post-Mongol Central Asia and the Middle East: Studies in Honor of John E. Woods* (Wiesbaden, 2006), 112–34. See also pp. 23, 500–1. The role of charitable and pious institutions or foundations in consolidating elites' hold, yet also binding society horizontally, is characteristic of Byzantium and western societies, too: pp. 88, 90, 99, 184, 203–5, 425–6, 264, 266, 275, 276–7.

century onwards. An effective counterweight to the effects of disintegrating dynasties, shifting elites and the violent play of household politics, this mechanism enabled dynasts and military commanders to align a wide variety of religio-cultural communities with their claims to authority. They could do so through patronising and promoting their culture, knowledge and infrastructures (for example, mosques, *madrasa*s and *khanqah*s). In theory, at least, the *waqf* provided a legal and socio-economic means of protecting the integrity and autonomy of elite families and households, allowing them to pass on their assets and interests down through the generations irrespective of what happened to individual family members or their patrons. Most *waqf* endowments were fairly circumscribed estates comprising farms, workshops and other commercial assets, whose expenditure was for specific religious and communal purposes as prescribed by Islamic scripture and the law. They offered unusually stable socio-economic bases from which various elite groups could engage in the constant, mostly violent rounds of negotiating local and regional relationships, balancing property and power.

The restrictive, self-governing, non-taxable and inalienable nature of *waqf*s made them a useful instrument in the hands of western Asian power elites, especially in the fifteenth century. By then it could work in opposite directions. *Waqf* endowments could be enlisted to serve centrifugal ends, but they could also act as stabilisers in the contest for power around central courts, dynastic households, and their many military and civilian agents. In fact, some of the larger endowments, especially those established by Ilkhanid viziers and Ottoman, Timurid and 'Turkish' sultans and *amir*s, became merged or clumsily linked up with these rulers' own resources. In Egypt and Khurasan, various rulers and their entourages (including Sultan Husayn) began trying to re-integrate the *waqf*s and tap their rich assets to fund and stabilise their regimes in Cairo and Herat.[62] In later fifteenth-century Anatolia, the Ottomans tried a comparable strategy, although using another set of tactics altogether: they seized – or at least changed the legal status of – the rural properties and the charitable and religious endowments of ever more elite groups and families throughout western, central and, eventually, even eastern Anatolia. This brought about a transformation in the Anatolian pattern of landholding, placing far more of the region directly under Ottoman control. It was, in fact, part and parcel of the drive towards centralisation following

---

[62] In general: FTTS; also D. Igarashi, *Land Tenure and Mamluk Waqfs* (Bonn, 2014); B. Hoffmann, *Waqf im mongolischen Iran. Rašiduddins Sorge um Nachruhm und Seelenheil* (Stuttgart, 2000); *TIT*, esp. ch.5: 'Piety and pragmatism: the role of the Islamic endowment' (148–91); R. D. McChesney, *Waqf in Central Asia: Four Hundred Years in the History of a Muslim Shrine, 1480–1889* (Princeton, 1991), 21–70.

Sultan Mehmed's conquest of Constantinople in 1453. The private estates and *waqf* lands of many local Anatolian elites now became Ottoman state lands (*miri*). In this way they were made the property of the Ottoman sultan in his role as embodiment of an increasingly stable political order, and many estates were now parcelled out as new prebendal grants to the sultan's cavalry leaders.[63] The resultant transformations in these regions' political economies would culminate in the rise of the early modern empires of the world of Islam, from the Ottomans' sway over the Balkans and the eastern Mediterranean to the Mughals in India, along with Muhammad Shaybani and the Uzbeks in Central Asia.

[63] H. Inalcik, 'Land possession outside the *miri* system', in H. Inalcik and D. Quataert (eds), *An Economic and Social History of the Ottoman Empire, 1300–1914, I: 1300–1600* (Cambridge, 1994), 126–131; Inalcik, 'Autonomous enclaves', 118, 124.

Part V

Conclusions

16   Comparisons, Connections and Conclusions

Jonathan Shepard

If, as Harold Lasswell maintains, political power-play consists of 'who gets what, when and how', one might conclude that the Ottomans were overall winners by the time our survey ends, knocking out the Byzantines while menacing a Christian west riven by internal divides. Like other leading Islamic powers, the Safavids in Iran and the Mughals in India, the Ottomans had brought from the steppes a talent for self-discipline, having at their head a charismatic clan that was capable of accommodating ruthless meritocracy whilst envisaging universal dominion.[1] Classical Persian and Hellenic precepts concerning a ruler's duties fused with modern firepower, enabling Ottoman artillery to blast the Roman-built walls of Constantinople in 1453 and subsequently aim for Vienna's. The two surviving spheres now confronted one another, nurturing in the west a sense of cultural antithesis and Orientalism.[2] Although in the sixteenth and seventeenth centuries western vessels shipped ever greater quantities of goods around the world and technical skills passed between the spheres, there was an intellectual parting of ways.[3] Political precepts

---

[1] See pp. 121–3, 230–2, 245–6.

[2] Not that some such sense was lacking in previous periods as, for example, when Christians sought or suffered death at Muslim hands in northern Syria, Egypt and al-Andalus and gave rise to cults of martyrs. However, these cults are characteristic of the earlier centuries of Muslim rule and, even in al-Andalus, 'the cults of the new martyrs seem to have petered out during the tenth century and beyond': C. C. Sahner, *Christian Martyrs under Islam: Religious Violence and the Making of the Muslim World* (Princeton, 2018), 247. And despite occasional invective from Muslim writers, substantial numbers of non-Muslim officials were still in the employ of the Mamluks into the fourteenth century: L. B. Yarbrough, *Friends of the Emir: Non-Muslim State Officials in Premodern Islamic Thought* (Cambridge, 2019). For Muslims in the service of Latin Christian rulers: pp. 129, 138, 386; for the Moorish lifestyle of a fifteenth-century king of Castile: pp. 138–9. The First Crusade itself can be seen as an offshoot of the Gregorian papacy's ambitions for the reordering of Christendom, rather than the elimination of Islam: p. 379.

[3] French diplomacy found opportunities to align with the Ottomans against the western emperor, and, unsurprisingly, news and rumours travelled between Istanbul and the west through many channels, written and oral: N. Malcolm, *Useful Enemies: Islam and the Ottoman Empire in Western Political Thought, 1450–1750* (Oxford, 2019), 110–19, 131–2; J.-P. Ghobrial, *The Whispers of Cities: Information Flows in Istanbul, London, and Paris in the Age of William Trumbull* (Oxford, 2013), 102–21, 159–63. However, the Humanists' image of the Turks as barbarous destroyers, 'the ruin of Greece', became engrained in

and philosophy from antiquity were engrained in the dominant elites'
bureaucracies, but their intellectual armouries were now self-sufficient,
no longer looking to one another for scraps of ancient knowledge.[4] At the
same time, members of our spheres were, in different ways, disseminating
monotheism across the world, thereby providing justification for our
singling out their political cultures. Islamic worship and culture prevailed
in such Sub-Saharan realms as Mali (whose ruler's pilgrimage to Mecca
in 1324 won Ibn Khaldun's admiration)[5] and had spread around the
Indian Ocean by the time westerners sailed in and set about weaving
commercial and colonial networks to straddle the globe and, often in
Christ's name, overturning civilisations.[6] Meantime a vigorous offshoot
of the Byzantine sphere was sponsoring predatory commercial ventures
which would, in 1638, take Lieutenant Moskvitin and his band of
Cossacks to the Pacific coast, leading to the establishment of the fort of
Okhotsk a few years later.[7]

Our objective in this book, though, is neither to pick winners nor to
explain why some formations lasted longer than others – nor even systematically to expound contrasts between the spheres. What we offer is
merely an outline of how their foremost monarchical formations developed, along with sidelights on alternative structures, noting change over
time and attempting to chart the rhythms of competition, conflict and
consensus that drive any multi-part political culture. We have identified
the main dynamics of power (and the forms that gaining and justifying it
took) within each sphere, presenting them in such a way as to facilitate
comparisons but without embarking on such an exercise ourselves or
going on to explore the patterns of interaction between spheres.[8] Four
vital elements of politics highlighted by Stephen Humphreys[9] – religion,

western thinking at many levels: N. Bisaha, *Creating East and West: Renaissance Humanists and the Ottoman Turks* (Philadelphia, 2004), 174–84.

[4] For external regimes' interest in materials from Byzantium, especially in the earlier middle ages: p. 191.

[5] Ibn Khaldun, *Muqaddima*, in *Corpus of Early Arabic Sources for West African History*, ed. and tr. N. Levtzion and J. F. P. Hopkins (Cambridge, 1981), 334; C. El Hamel, *Black Morocco: A History of Slavery, Race, and Islam* (Cambridge, 2013), 126. See also M. N. Pearson, 'The Indian Ocean and the Red Sea', in N. Levtzion and R. L. Pouwels (eds), *The History of Islam in Africa* (Athens, OH, 2000), 37–59; N. Levtzion, 'Islam in the Bilad al-Sudan to 1800', in *ibid.*, 63–91; J. Spaulding, 'Pre-colonial Islam in the Eastern Sudan', in *ibid.*, 117–29.

[6] P. Beaujard, *The Worlds of the Indian Ocean: A Global History*, tr. T. Loring *et al.*, 2 vols (Cambridge, 2019), ii:229–41, 341–53, 477–95, 492–512, 550–4.

[7] J. Forsyth, *History of the Peoples of Siberia: Russia's North Asian Colony, 1581–1990* (Cambridge, 1992), 81.

[8] Precisely because of their importance and profusion, the interconnections deserve a volume to themselves. See p. 16.

[9] See p. 19.

war, property, and women – provide a useful set of litmus tests; but the disparate, even kaleidoscopic, nature of the source materials, along with differing historiographical approaches, makes it difficult to treat these benchmarks systematically. They do, however, constitute a subtext, and bearing them in mind can help answer a fundamental question: what was different and what was new about the workings of the spheres' political cultures around 1500, as against 700? No less important is the need for alertness to *trompe l'oeil* played by our surviving sources. The impression of sophisticated administration and literatures in the west could, after all, merely reflect more documents surviving from 500 years ago as against 1,300. Likewise with the Latin west's tendency towards fragmentation, better documented for the fourteenth and fifteenth centuries than the earlier middle ages. And might not the Islamic sphere look at least as diffuse and variegated as the west had more archival documents and local chronicles survived? Further, the differences in scale between spheres, already vast, looked set to sharpen around 1500: the Latin west perched on Eurasia's western peninsulas, with the Islamic sphere, under self-proclaimed Ottoman headship, taking over much of the Byzantine sphere and impinging on the west's.

Nonetheless, change in the west's literacy levels was real and extensive. By 1500, far more business transactions, tax-liabilities and court-rulings were being set down in writing than in, say, the twelfth century, let alone the eighth.[10] Such a pattern of change is less obvious in what little was left of Byzantium by 1453 or in the Islamic sphere by around 1500. To some extent this simply reflects lower rates of source survival, and literacy was certainly widespread in these spheres' cities, if not the countryside. But the contrast also reflects a different approach in the Islamic world: not over the uses of writing for administrative, commercial or everyday purposes, but as to whether the written word should determine property-ownership and other rights and agreements.[11] Although Islamic rulers had outstanding religio-ethical status and took responsibility for life, limb and welfare of the members of the *umma*, interpreting *shariʿa* and adjudicating many types of dispute was something for the schools of jurists and the *qadi*s.[12] Scholarly bureaucrats were to hand, their knowledge of tax-

---

[10] See pp. 162–3, 276–82, 287, 377–8, 383–5, 388, 402–4.   [11] See pp. 126–7, 465.
[12] See pp. 104–5; P. Crone and M. Hinds, *God's Caliph: Religious Authority in the First Centuries of Islam* (Cambridge, 1986), 96–110; *Cal*, 116–17, 181–2, 205–6, 257–9. On the methods of formulating and reconciling the various doctrines and judgements of members of the main schools, and on the extent of their practical application: W. B. Hallaq, *Authority, Continuity and Change in Islamic Law* (Cambridge, 2001); B. Weiss, 'The Madhhab in Islamic legal theory', in P. Bearman *et al.* (eds), *The Islamic School of Law: Evolution, Devolution, and Progress* (Cambridge, MA, 2005), 1–9; D. Ephrat, 'Madhab and madrasa in eleventh-century Baghdad', in *ibid.*, 77–93.

files and suchlike records making them indispensable.[13] But they were neither closely involved with law-courts nor bound up with questions of 'who gets what, when, and how' in the manner of lawyers-cum-administrators of the Byzantine and western spheres. There, landowner-ship and inheritance overlapped with issues of taxation, military service and dispute settlement in general. The product was the legal literacy of the later medieval west, a swarm of lawyers who might make their living in the law-courts, join the administrations of kings or princes, or even, in Byzantium's case, end up as patriarch.[14]

Far from necessarily making for harmoniousness, such versatility could articulate resistance to policy or hinder the workings of government. Yet the interplay between making exactions and demanding service from subjects and, on the other hand, offering legal apparatus for effective resolution of disputes and securing of possessions could consolidate a polity and give an edge to rulers managing to hold the balance. And while a significant speed-up in communications lay far in the future, technical advances were making warfare costlier, advantaging those well-resourced enough to field cavalry and deploy artillery to pulverise any fortification. The obvious beneficiaries were rulers of quite finite realms like the French, English, Castilian and Aragonese, rather than little city states or magnates reliant mainly on revenues from their landholdings.[15] Such realms tended to combine – with local variations – the raising of revenues with extensive jurisdictions operated by government agents or proxies; regardless of the proportion of income raised directly from law cases and fines, the effect was to channel rivalries and focus interest-groups' attention on a single political arena. Moreover, as and when general taxes were levied with the assent of important payers in countries like England, the mechanisms for law-making and adjudication could serve this purpose: parliament's own origins stemmed from a royal court.[16] The linking-up of fiscal records with matters of property-holding and the law is discernible in Byzantium, too, and the fourteenth century saw signs of councils convening to discuss general affairs and even taxation.[17] These did not, however, turn into anything like the western assemblies. It was an Islamic power that excelled in linking fiscal matters with the operations of law-courts and dispute settlement. Not wholly coincidentally, this came to full fruition after the Ottomans captured Constantinople: they began to develop elaborate tax-registers, besides

[13] See pp. 234–5, 241, 340, 456, 458, 461–3, 468–71.
[14] For legal literacy: pp. 282–4; also pp. 159, 170, 388; and on a lawyer becoming patriarch of Constantinople: pp. 96–7, 318–19.
[15] See pp. 147–8, 169–70.   [16] See pp. 69–70, 154, 158, 160–1, 382, 402–3, 409.
[17] See pp. 85, 92, 93, 97, 326, 327–8.

starting up records of proceedings in the *qadis*' courts and themselves applying the law with the aid of the muftis they appointed.[18]

Through marshalling resources meticulously whilst 'harvesting' subject populations' talent in the form of the janissaries, the Ottomans made themselves the most formidable of the gunpowder empires. Their rule went virtually unchallenged across their far-flung lands in the sixteenth century.[19] Yet they sought to enlist the interests of local elites, whilst leaving a fair degree of autonomy to non-Muslim communities.[20] Thus even the most authoritarian of leaderships sought cooperativeness from its heterogeneous subjects. Western rulers still stood in need of cooperation in the later middle ages, being effectively locked into partnership with regional and local elites and their oft competing jurisdictions. In part this reflected the rustic economy of vast swathes of the west and the importance of the land. But even cities like London and Nuremberg were best left to manage their own affairs, and potentates taking over urbanised regions directly were apt to stifle commerce – and diminish revenues.[21] Rulers permitting the autonomy of cities such as Nuremberg and the Hanseatic towns could preside over vast and loose-knit polities, as the emperor did over the German-speaking lands, or they could direct fairly compact realms, like England. What emerges is the miscellany of societies underpinning them, with their cellular components detachable yet also capable of coalescing into impressive assemblages. If this put limitations on what a ruler could expect of his subjects – often with vociferous contestation – it entailed certain rhythms, and, although dynastic alliances could still involve drastic reconfiguration of territories, a matrix of realms held in the early sixteenth century.[22] If this scarcely adds up to centripetalism, it was not runaway fragmentation, and – with one fateful exception – the dynamics of legal literacy fit comfortably enough within the coordinates of royal courts, miscellaneous assemblies and *noblesse oblige*. No less strikingly, the later middle ages in the west saw participation in political discourse by broader bands of actors, amidst currents of thought amounting to public opinion.[23] This is not to deny such a term to the other two spheres, especially the more urbanised sectors of the Nile-to-Oxus region and the city of Constantinople.[24] But the debates among late Byzantine intellectuals concerning policy and

---

[18] G. Burak, 'The second formation of Islamic law: the post-Mongol context of the Ottoman adoption of a School of Law', *Comparative Studies in Society and History*, 55 (2013), 579–602 at 584–5, 589–99. See also pp. 123, 124, 362, 484, 452.
[19] See pp. 231–2, 246.   [20] See pp. 451, 453–4, 477–8.
[21] See pp. 62–3, 71–4, 170, 391.   [22] See pp. 147–8, 169–70, 373, 374, 376, 397–8.
[23] See pp. 156–7, 161–3.
[24] See pp. 107, 110–11, 121, 247–8, 354, 361–2, 467, 481–2, 324–7.

reform were no more grounded in the empire's foundations than were
their counterparts' concerning political order in the Islamic sphere. Only
in the west was public life geared to differences and conflict, 'an ongoing
argument'.[25]

This is not to claim that politico-cultural or religious pluralism could
flourish only on western soil. On the contrary, the Islamic world accommodated highly literate urban elites along with powerholders espousing
an explicitly warrior ethos.[26] And soldierly qualities, often held in esteem
in Byzantium, could place a man on the throne despite the empire's
ideological professions of 'peace', while the question of the emperor's
relationship to the law, sacred or profane, remained opaque.[27] Still more
open to debate were points of law in the Islamic world, especially since
law-making was not a prerogative of caliphs or sultans. There were four
main schools of law among the Sunnis, and shades of opinion across
a broad spectrum of topics were facts of everyday life.[28] And despite the
polemics among and between Shi'i and Sunni scholars and messianic
movements triggering upheavals and bloodshed, sectarian divergences
and even differences in faith did not preclude peaceful coexistence.
Thus one finds Shi'i leaders such as the Buyids ruling over predominantly
Sunni citizens in Baghdad, while the inhabitants of the Egyptian cities
under the Shi'i Fatimids were mostly Sunni.[29] Variations in legal positions alongside innovative concepts about rulership recur under the
Seljuks, Qalawunids and Timurids; indeed, although al-Tabari's brand
of Sunni legal thought was long gone, his vision, outlined in his 'History',
of the *umma* united by humane values lived on under the Turco-Mongol
warlords.[30]

The Islamic world's accommodation of legal and authority-related
positions without any single determinant stands, at first sight, in contrast
with what is on offer in the Christian spheres. Byzantium's imperial and
ecclesiastical leaderships were, despite occasional rifts, at one over doctrine and the need for *symphonia* in day-to-day affairs. Two hierarchies
were in play, and disputes turned on which should take responsibility for
what.[31] Still more hierarchical was the west's spiritual regimen: the papacy's organisation and resources made it, by the later middle ages,
a power in its own right, representing the church in antithesis to 'the

[25] See p. 167.   [26] See pp. 25–6, 110, 242, 339, 481–2.
[27] See pp. 198, 201, 291, 294, 295, 312, 316–29, 419–21.
[28] See pp. 104, 105, 112–13, 342–3, 347, 348–9, 361, 362.
[29] See pp. 109, 220–1, 224–5, 242–3, 332, 335–6. See now C. D. Baker, *Medieval Islamic Sectarianism* (Leeds, 2019), 37–75. Egypt was also home to sizeable Jewish and Christian populations throughout these centuries.
[30] See pp. 106–7, 118–21, 222, 353–5, 360–3. See also pp. 19–20.
[31] See pp. 91, 291–2, 297–8, 311–13.

state'.[32] With its law-courts, operating through canon law and pronouncing upon doctrine, the papacy drew the finest intellects from the universities into its service to refine theology but also conduct inquisitions, extirpating heresy.[33] Through performing royal coronations, prelates formatted ideology in terms akin to their ninth-century predecessors but now throughout the Latin west.[34]

From this perspective, the west offers a steelier, articulated mechanism for defining spiritual experience and regulating religious life in general, sharper than anything available in the Islamic world. However, the secular lawyers whose legal literacy skills were honed by its universities alongside young clerics could help kings to rebut papal demands and criticise church wealth and power. Indeed, as Len Scales notes, university teachers could launch heresies, not least Martin Luther;[35] their teachings struck home among laypersons, even before printing began to broadcast alternative visions. Once their numbers rose, the cellular structures that had served as safety-valves and alternatives to overbearing landed elites could foster hotbeds of dissent.[36] For example free cities in the German-speaking lands were among the first to rally to Luther's cause. What had long been an envelope for containing conflict came apart over questions of access to God, not sheer material self-interest.

Thus the Latin west fractured along fine yet irreparable lines in a manner unknown to the other spheres (including Byzantium's Muscovite offshoot), and notwithstanding the roles eventually espoused by the Ottomans and Safavids, respectively champions of Sunni and Shi'i Islam. This brings us to one of the key elements in political culture: religion. Its teachings bore on matters of life, marriage and death, and a ruler flouted them at their peril.[37] By the same token, a potentate gained immeasurably from endorsement by clerics. In all three of our spheres' versions of monotheism, the concept of transcendentalism privileged those who could key in to benefits from an omnipotent and unearthly power.[38] And here the west is distinctive for the role taken by its priesthood in channelling access to the divine. Its centrality to the inauguration-ritual of rulers was particularly prominent. Clerics played next to no part in the rites of accession for caliphs or sultans, whose legitimacy flowed from other sources.[39] In Byzantium the performance of coronation by the patriarch of Constantinople and also, eventually, of unction became indispensable for

---

[32] See pp. 175–6.   [33] See pp. 386–9, 399–400.
[34] See pp. 56–9, 66, 173, 255–60, 279, 394.   [35] See pp. 170–1.
[36] See pp. 175–6, 283–4, 288–9.   [37] See pp. 21, 312, 387–8, 399.
[38] A. Strathern, *Unearthly Powers: Religious and Political Change in World history* (Cambridge, 2019), esp. 3–10, 47–80, 109–24, 131–53.
[39] See pp. 333–4, 339–40.

affirming sovereign status. But Byzantine coronations lacked the constitutive force of their western counterparts, and the *basileus* was not held to an oath.[40] This reflected differences in conceptions of the holy and appropriate means of accessing it. In the Islamic sphere, a host of sages, scholars and law-schools studied and sought to heed the Will of God with the help of the Prophet's word, partaking of rightful guidance along with the caliph and other worthy successors of Muhammad. Eastern Christendom reserved the sacraments and religious offices for ordained clergy, deemed a class apart from the laity. Nonetheless, avenues to the spirit world remained multiple. Individual monks, in particular, were held in esteem, chapels in private households being not uncommon, and laypersons could feel personal access to a saint through the icon kept in their homes.[41]

In the west, in contrast, the *sacerdotium*'s monopoly of access to divine Grace was axiomatic. The clergy in tandem with duly tonsured orders of monks laid claim to the superiority of the 'spiritual sword'. And from the eleventh century onwards, the papacy set about proclaiming its right actively to lead the world to ecclesiastical discipline and salvation, using spiritual weaponry.[42] The corollary, a subaltern role for the laity, jarred with participation in political debate and also with rising literacy-levels. These tensions, long simmering, led to outright challenge of the clergy's monopolisation of mediation with the divine. If the sale of indulgences was the target of Luther's 95 Theses, the ecclesiology underlying them was in the line of fire.[43] The next few years would see Wars of Religion beginning to tear the socio-political fabric apart.

The other two spheres did not see warfare on quite such a scale between fellow-believers over devotional practices and issues of religious authority. Bitter and bloody as the Isma'ili 'Carmathians' (*Qaramita*) and other such messianic movements following or awaiting a Mahdi could be, and profound as the Sunni–Shi'i rift eventually became, this did not generate such thorough-going attempts at extirpation. Views as to religious correctness varied, without any single ruler, set of clerics or school of law laying claim convincingly to unique divine guidance.[44] Warfare, though, features prominently in our chapters devoted to the Islamic and, indeed, Byzantine spheres. The former, after all, grew out of jihad, and Ottoman writers would style their heroes as *ghazi*s.[45] War-faring loomed as a prospect, quite often a reality, on Byzantium's borders. Even so, conducting military operations was a specialised affair and not for the majority of the empire's taxpayers.[46] Likewise in the Islamic

[40] See p. 297. [41] See pp. 184, 207–9, 301, 315–16, 328–9, 424, 426.
[42] For the 'spiritual sword': p. 52; also pp. 145, 166–7, 387–8, 399. [43] See p. 51.
[44] See pp. 109, 116–18, 219–20, 243, 247, 335, 346–9, 469, 476. [45] See pp. 125, 359.
[46] See pp. 198, 298–9, 316–18, 418–19, 436.

world, arms-bearing was far from habitual for inhabitants of the urban-ised regions between the North African deserts and the Eurasian steppes. Specialisation between elites was customary, summed up by the categorisation of 'men of the pen', 'men of the turbans' and 'men of the sword'. Common in the Turco-Mongol polities, such terms go back to Islam's early centuries, underlining the importance of warriors to anyone aiming for supra-regional authority.[47] These elites differed markedly in lifestyles and over priorities of political order. Yet these very differences made them interdependent for the sake of the *umma* and also to maintain prosperity and keep tax revenues flowing. In any case, religious authority was spread too widely between caliphs, *'ulama'* and others for any clerical monopoly redolent of the papal theory of 'Two Swords' to gain momentum.[48] Besides, congregational mosques gave men access to the Friday prayer, supplementing private devotions and, to that extent, few could feel debarred from significant religious experience.

In the west, the *sacerdotium*'s claim to monopolise mediation with the divine was upheld by lay elites from kings down to local landholders. For lengthy periods this made for a series of checks and balances, the ecclesi-astical elite interlocking with the secular elite. Bishops also networked with one another and, from their sees, oversaw extensive landed estates and helped keep order; some held offices under kings and princes. On that level, this-worldly concerns blended with clerical ones more intensively than in any other sphere. Bishops' administrative duties could extend to military organisation and commands, as witnessed on a bishop of Durham's seal, showing him charging in armour.[49] Warfare grew more expensive in the later middle ages, not least from equipping armoured cavalry. But combat readiness denoted general elite membership, along with codes of chivalry. Even those grown rich from trade would buy rural residences and engage in jousting, hunting and other pursuits formerly betokening higher noble or royal status.[50] These belligerent postures were not purely for show. What emerges from our chapters is how menaces, property damage and violence remained an option for resolving multifari-ous disputes and rivalries in the political culture of urban communities as

[47] M. Van Berkel, 'The people of the pen: self-perceptions of status and role in the administration of empires and polities', in M. van Berkel and J. Duindam (eds), *Prince, Pen, and Sword: Eurasian Perspectives* (Leiden, 2018), 384–451 at 384–5, 397–405, 414–17; see also pp. 231, 245, 340, 473–9, 481–2.
[48] See pp. 464–8, 52–3.   [49] See pp. 148–9, 152, 159–60, 171–4, 264, 386–8, 398–9.
[50] See pp. 56, 157–9, 169, 267–8. On hunting and rulership: T. T. Allsen, *The Royal Hunt in Eurasian History* (Philadelphia, 2006), esp. 7–10.

well as agrarian societies.[51] Given the west's multiple cellular structures and the 'entrenched disunity' of pope and emperor,[52] this is scarcely surprising. But if the readiness of members of local elites to fend for themselves amounted to a self-regulating mechanism, the weapons and fortifications at their disposal facilitated and perpetuated conflict, once ecclesiastical guarantees of personal salvation rang hollow, and landowners and urban elites found alternative pathways to God. Wars of Religion were the outcome.

If organised religion was, like waging war, essentially men's business in our three spheres, so was the protection of property or, at least, landed property, another of Stephen Humphreys' vital elements. Landownership and the right to allocate land and its fruits more or less at will brought status to a family and to the individuals heading it. This is seen in Middle Byzantium, and landed estates were also sought after in populous Muslim polities such as Egypt.[53] But the link between landed possessions, standing and power was particularly close in the Latin west, at least in its intensively cultivated parts. There, surpluses of agrarian goods were still a basic source of wealth around 1500, and this made the amassing of permanent – non-perishable – valuables difficult, although not impossible. Regular exaction of such surpluses went hand-in-hand with force majeure or at least the threat of it, well-worn by custom. Arms-bearers played a key part in this, holding the land, protecting the means of production and, quite simply, consuming the produce. The upshot was that land and power were widely diffused, with leverage resting with the local and regional elites and those families which cooperated well enough to forge marriage-ties, accumulate territories, and maintain principalities or even royal dynasties.[54] A king might confer military commands on his loyal or formidable supporters, together with rights to land, but even in the late middle ages few rulers found themselves in a position to levy direct taxes or pay out sizable salaries to many officials and supporters. Besides, if general taxes were to be raised, this needed assent from the self-same local elites through representative assemblies. And until around this

---

[51] See pp. 33, 150–1, 154–5, 157, 159, 163, 166, 174, 375, 376–80, 406–7, 409. Urban violence is less well-attested in Byzantium, although upheavals could occur in times of civil war and central government's enfeeblement: pp. 326–7. 'Ritual cities' such as Constantinople and Cairo were less given to endemic armed clashes but other conurbations in the Islamic sphere, especially those such as Damascus in border-zones, saw ready recourse to violence by contending interest-groups: P. Sanders, *Ritual, Politics, and the City in Fatimid Cairo* (Albany, NY, 1994); P. Lantschner, 'Fragmented cities in the later middle ages: Italy and the Near East compared', *EHR* 130 (2015), 546–82; M. Brett, *The Fatimid Empire* (Edinburgh, 2017), 96–102.
[52] See p. 167.   [53] See pp. 421–3.   [54] See pp. 149, 152–3, 154–5, 160, 371, 375.

time most holders of top offices were clerics, with limited scope for power politics.[55]

In the other two spheres, however, the fiscal apparatus inherited from ancient Rome and Iran went on working. The political leaderships long proved able to monopolise coin-striking, in Byzantium's case virtually until the end, while the 'single market' between the Islamic urban centres throve long after the demise of the Abbasids who had fostered it. For those able to operate the apparatus's levers, great wealth was literally to hand and trans-ferrable into huge armies of salaried warriors in ninth- and earlier tenth-century Baghdad, or into Byzantium's vast diplomatic web, constantly rewoven through pay-outs of many kinds.[56] No one of substantial property in Byzantium could safely stand aloof from this apparatus, and regional landowners with middling estates found it prudent to seek court-titles and other links with the capital.[57] Until 1204, the mechanism was run by the bureaucracy based in Constantinople. Although the armed forces could throw up top players in power politics, their only means of staying on the throne was through cooperation with the capital's other elites, including the clerical establishment; and commitment to the empire's survival was axio-matic among the officer classes.[58] Comparable traditions and incentives kept the wheels of government turning in the Islamic sphere, different from Byzantium though the interplay was between the men of the pen and the men of the sword. Massive material resources went to whichever military commanders could gain the administrators' collaboration along with accept-ance from the 'ulama', bolstering their legitimacy through reverence for caliphs and protection of holy places.[59] With their extensive clans and warbands of horsemen protecting rather than preying on urbanised and populous zones and caravan-routes, they could safeguard agriculture and tax-collection. Indeed, the very differences between their skills and those of the urban elites could bring them together to mutual advantage.

This form of 'fiscal coexistence' is in sharp contrast with the imperial-ecclesiastical complex of Byzantium and with the balance struck between arms-bearers and clerics in the west. Landed property was much sought after, and, of course, the sheer immensity of the Islamic sphere accom-modated local elites that drew their resources mainly from agriculture and stock-raising and upheld their own customs, especially in the less access-ible terrains. And the land-grants (iqta's) doled out by sultans and emirs in return for military service could turn into lasting – hereditable – arrangements. Yet for all the centripetal possibilities they opened up,

[55] See pp. 69–70, 150–1, 159, 382, 402.   [56] See pp. 219, 237, 462–3, 182, 193–4, 206.
[57] See pp. 413–14, 415–16, 419, 421–2, 427.   [58] See pp. 198–9, 201, 298–9, 316–18.
[59] See pp. 109–11, 114, 116–17, 222–3, 225–6, 238–41, 246–7, 340–1, 344–6, 357–8, 479–84.

such grants did not necessarily make for dissipation of the grantor's authority, and, so long as commerce and fiscal operations carried on, the constraints on a grantee's leeway remained quite strong. The *iqta'* was more a means of allocating tax revenues and suchlike than of overall lordship extending to jurisdiction. In this respect, it was more akin to the Byzantine emperor's granting of *pronoia* estates.[60] For the highly ambitious, some kind of active service on behalf of the ruler held out the best prospect of fast-tracking to the apex of the system for amassing wealth and thus power – and of staying at the top. Equally, for members of the 'general' or regional elites outside the circles of the power elite, displays of deference and obligingness towards representatives of the emperor, caliph or sultan remained the surest means of holding onto their status and possessions in a region, if not acquiring new ones.[61] This did not preclude a family's accumulation of landed and other forms of property or testaments to bequeath them. But such property-empires did not in themselves generate political weight, and they were open to confiscation.[62] Full security of ownership lay with those at the controls of the fiscal apparatus, or near them. This holds true of Byzantium, whose concepts of property-rights derived from Roman law, and still more so of the Islamic world, where inheritance of property and kindred issues were for adjudication by the *'ulama'* but anyone falling foul of a sultan could not count on his estates surviving intact.

If overweening material resources and force majeure accruing around a power elite and capped by a sumptuous court set the tone for political culture in these spheres, things were different in the west. There, as our chapters show, a family's claims to the surpluses from – and general lordship over – the land and its workers were prime sources of wealth, standing and power, and challenges to its rights were met by force of arms. But other means of securing property-rights were available, whether by invoking custom or law in some court of law or vesting them in a pious or charitable foundation. The latter course did not necessarily rule out usufruct from, say, a monastery's estates, and founders and donors gained influence and other incalculable benefits from their show of largesse.[63] Comparably mixed motives underlay the patronage of *waqf*s in the Islamic world. These grew more prominent in the fourteenth century, often bolstering the prospects of ambitious emirs and dynasts. Yet they could also serve to consolidate a regime and stabilise socio-political

---

[60] See pp. 241, 464, 467–8, 471–2, 484, 200–2, 432–3, 436, 445–7.
[61] See pp. 410, 413–14, 422–5. For counterparts in the Islamic world: pp. 338–9, 344–5, 356, 361–2.
[62] For celebrated Byzantine examples: p. 423.
[63] For the assumptions and shrewd provisos of donors: pp. 381, 46, 425–6.

order.[64] In fact, many *waqf*s were the product of local initiatives, from women alongside men. Indeed, quite humble members of society made contributions to *waqf*s, by way of assuring themselves of support if and when illness struck, or old age, as well as for maintaining the *umma*.[65]

Elitist though pious and charitable foundations often were by origin, those in the Islamic and western spheres proliferated in the late middle ages and formed a kind of material underlay to the teaching about assistance for the poor and weak that the norms of all three spheres propound. Even allowing for the self-interestedness of donors, certain features stand out. Firstly, all three spheres saw a fair degree of alignment between ruling elites' nostrums, their religion's basic precepts and the foundations purporting to provide for all social strata in this world and the next. Secondly, this charitable work carried on more or less regardless of the main political arena, individual men and women sometimes setting the standard for political leaderships. Thirdly, some foundations were set up in light of 'demand' coming from the needy, especially in relatively urbanised contexts. Thus they exemplify the ways in which the political culture of the elites – often the political leadership in uneasy tandem with other hierarchies or property-holders – could take account of the unprivileged. And, finally, one may note how meticulous care was taken by Charlemagne to survey the shrines of the Holy Land and fund building works there, enhancing his leadership of Latin Christendom. This illustrates the rivalry between our spheres, with pious foundations constituting Charlemagne's stake in places sacred to all three.[66] No other configuration of cultures, religions and polities quite matches this weave, whether in China and Japan, South Asia, Sub-Saharan Africa or Mesoamerica.

Women constitute another element in Stephen Humphreys' formulation. Seeing that war and patriarchal religion remained the stuff of political culture, women were seldom at the forefront of power-play around 1500. Playing the part of royal widows or regents on behalf of minors, they were sometimes significant decision-makers in the west and Byzantium. The latter assigned the *augusta* and her ladies-in-waiting a role in court-ritual already during her husband's lifetime, highlighting her importance in palace affairs. Yet few empresses or queens regent can be said to have stayed in charge for long; and – with due allowance for

---

[64] See pp. 484–5.

[65] R. Peters *et al.*, *EI*² s.v. 'Wakf'; M. Borgolte, *Weltgeschichte als Stiftungsgeschichte: von 3000 v.u.Z. bis 1500 u.Z.* (Darmstadt, 2017), 266–98, 558–65; for the Ottomans' patronage of mosques and *waqf*s: *ibid.*, 311–14; above pp. 485–6.

[66] M. McCormick, *Charlemagne's Survey of the Holy Land: Wealth, Personnel, and Buildings of a Mediterranean Church between Antiquity and the Middle Ages* (Washington, DC, 2011), esp. 159–65, 177–81, 191–6.

figures such as Sitt al-Mulk, who, upon the disappearance of her half-brother, the Fatimid caliph al-Hakim, secured the succession for her nephew – sultanas regent are rarer still.[67] And, at least in the west, those failing to give birth to an heir were liable to be set aside for failing in a basic duty. Even so, one should not underestimate what women could do just beyond the spotlight of contestation for the throne. This holds true of power-play in Byzantium, too, at least in the era of the Komnenoi.[68] In the west, women could accumulate resources and exercise power more decisively at the level of principalities and lordships below the royal cockpit. This is perhaps surprising, given all the coverage of churchmen and warriors by our narrative and more discursive sources. But perhaps this goes to show how distorting their formatting can be. Away from the spotlight and the manly ideology it projected, in the records of cellular structures making up the socio-political fabric, women can be seen managing affairs and acquiring estates by means of marriage-ties or purchases. This is clear from well-known scenarios, such as the upwardly mobile Pastons of East Anglia under their matriarch, Margaret. Robust and a prolific letter-author, seeing many of her plans through to fruition, Margaret was almost the contemporary of Joan of Arc.[69]

Such figures from the fifteenth century raise the question whether women's talents now enjoyed more outlets in their respective spheres' political cultures, or whether the period's relative abundance of documents creates a false impression of increasing recourse to the written word. Propertied women really were gaining the means to communicate and have their way, as Margaret Paston illustrates, and printed materials could open households up to new ideas. One should, however, beware of seeing households in the west as offering an open door to literate women for management and free-thinking. They were far from being housebound in the manner of their counterparts in, for example, Muscovy.

---

[67] See p. 312; also pp. 203–4, 307, 232 n. 51, 397–8. Sitt al-Mulk's spell in power from 1021 to 1023 was vigorous and effective, as witness (*inter alia*) a petition addressed to her: M. Rustow, 'A petition to a woman at the Fatimid court (413–414 AH/1022–23 CE)', *BSOAS* 77 (2010), 1–27 at 9–14; Brett, *Fatimid Empire*, 157–8.

[68] See pp. 200–1, 311. Even after taking the nun's veil, top Komnenian women would strike seals giving their status as ladies-in-waiting, including one who styled herself as the emperor's mother: J.-C. Cheynet, 'Le bullaire monastique à Byzance', in O. Delouis and K. Smyrlis (eds), *Lire les Archives de l'Athos* [=*TM* 19/2] (Paris, 2019), 243–85 at 271–3.

[69] The letters were drafted by clerks: C. Richmond, 'Paston family (*per. c.* 1420–1504)', *ODNB*; H. Castor 'Paston, Sir John (1442–1479)', *ODNB*. See also pp. 68–9, 72 n. 132, 375 and, for a comparable instance of elite widows astutely taking advantage of Welsh and English law to secure their dowers (in the form of land) in the thirteenth century: E. Cavell, 'Widows, Native law and the long shadow of England in thirteenth-century Wales', *EHR* 133 (2018), 1387–1419.

There the book of *Domostroi* ('Household Management') presupposed an upper-class woman's seclusion while expecting her to 'keep a tight rein on her household', monitoring every servant.[70] But even in England as late as 1960, at the trial of those held responsible for an allegedly obscene publication, the prosecutor could ask the jury whether it was 'a book that you would even wish your wife or your servants to read'.[71] And if the literacy of non-elite English women – as of men – was on the rise, their opportunities for reading may have plateaued, if not declined, after the Reformation.[72] Nor was the tone of leading Protestant thinkers necessarily encouraging, as witness John Knox's abhorrence 'that a woman shall reign and have empire above man'.[73]

The regiment of Catholic queens arousing Knox's wrath registers the continuing awe for a hierarchy of crown, dynasty and gradations of subjects: this framework had enough support (and not only from elites) to allow a woman to occupy its apex for purposes of conserving God-given order. In other words, she was valued as an expedient prop to the system rather than in her own right. Attitudes towards a woman's rule over an entire realm were no more positive in the Islamic sphere. The wives of thirteenth-century Mongol leaders exercised considerable influence to secure the succession of particular khans; and women could effectively hold the reins of power, if not the throne itself, in newly won territories, as, for example, in Ilkhanid Iran.[74] But this tendency appears to have slackened when the leadership began to attune to Islamic norms. And if the Ottomans co-opted women of status in local, non-Islamic, elites to support the order they were imposing,[75] they took for granted women's unfitness for supreme rule. At the same time, the meritocratic assumptions of the power elites in early Ottoman Istanbul, that only the fittest of the sultan's offspring should mount the throne, gave ample scope for manoeuvring by the ablest or most pitiless of mothers in the harem.[76] A pattern of ups-and-downs in female rulership is discernible across the spheres, with, for example, Princess Olga (Helga) taking control of the

[70] *The Domostroi* ch. 29, tr. C. J. Pouncy (Ithaca, NY, 1994), 126

[71] The novel by D. H. Lawrence, *Lady Chatterley's Lover*, had been published in France in 1929 but only gained widespread circulation in England in 1960, upon publication by Penguin Books. For the proceedings: *The Trial of Lady Chatterley: Regina v. Penguin Books Limited*, ed. and intro C. H. Rolph (repr. London, 1990), 17; x (foreword).

[72] E. Duffy, *The Stripping of the Altars: Traditional Religion in England, c.1400–c.1580*, 2nd edn (New Haven, CT, 2005), 77–87, 209–65.

[73] John Knox (published anonymously), *The First Blast of the Trumpet against the Monstrous Regiment of Women* (Geneva, 1558), pp. 3v–4r.

[74] B. de Nicola, *Women in Mongol Iran: The Khatuns, 1206–1335* (Edinburgh, 2017), 90–100, 104–14. See also A. F. Broadbridge, *Women and the Making of the Mongol Empire* (Cambridge, 2018).

[75] See pp. 451, 452.   [76] See p. 471.

Rus polity on behalf of her infant son; Theophano and Adelheid, respectively the mother and grandmother of the young Otto III, directing the western empire's affairs capably later on in the tenth century; and the Norman-born Queen Emma making her mark on the cultural and political life of eleventh-century England.[77] Also of note, two generations later, is Matilda, the widow of the leading territorial prince Godfrey of Lotharingia. By tapping her estates' resources and leading armies to victory, she tipped the balance in Popes Gregory VII and Urban II's favour in their struggle with Emperor Henry IV.[78] Ironically, the ultimate outcome was sharper delimitation by the *sacerdotium* of the roles of man and woman in ecclesiastical and even temporal affairs, not to the latter's advantage. Capable women feature as war-leaders in the Islamic sphere, too, notably Shajar al-Durr. She became the sultana after the death in 1249 of her husband, al-Salih, the last Ayyubid ruler of Egypt, and went on to run the country effectively for several years. One should, however, note that this former slave-girl was of Qipchaq Turkish origins, and this will have given her useful affinities with the Turkish-born slave soldiers (*mamluks*) who eventually took over.[79] Once established in power, the sultan Baybars and his successors showed no appetite for female rulership.

In light of such cross-currents and paradoxes, charting the progress of women in political culture in lineal terms is hazardous. Tracing ebbs and flows makes better sense: sovereign rule would elude most women's grasp until religion, war and landed property ceased to frame answers to Harold Lasswell's question of 'who gets what, when, and how'. On the other hand, power was still widely diffused in the west around 1500, even in the more compact polities, while the gunpowder empires looked to local elites for collaboration. The fiscal and judicial down-reach of the French and English kings and other such rulers was extending, but they were far from exercising – or even wanting – a monopoly of violence or of resolving local disputes. The building-blocks of socio-political order remained agrarian estates or holdings, over which lords presided with greater or lesser

---

[77] For Olga's initiatives: *Russian Primary Chronicle*, tr. S. H. Cross and O. P. Sherbowitz-Wetzor (Cambridge, MA, 1953), 78–84; on Theophano and Adelheid acting on Otto III's behalf: see S. MacLean, *Ottonian Queenship* (Oxford, 2017), 150–79. For Emma: p. 55.

[78] D. Hay, *The Military Leadership of Mathilda of Canossa, 1046–1115* (Manchester, 2008), 239–47.

[79] A. Levanoni, 'The Mamluks in Egypt and Syria: the Turkish Mamluk sultanate (648–784/1250–1382) and the Circassian Mamluk sultanate (784–923/1382–1517)', in *NCHI* 2, 237–84 at 237–8. See also A. Levanoni, 'Šaǧar ad-Durr: a case of female sultanate in medieval Islam', in U. Vermeulen and J. Van Steenbergen (eds), *Egypt and Syria in the Fatimid, Ayyubid and Mamluk Eras III* (Leuven, 2001), 209–18.

intensity. And the local elites themselves functioned ultimately by way of households. *In*formal power was still the order of the day. Few persons had the time, resources or connections to participate in affairs outside their locality, limiting the pool of contenders for the very top. Indeed those polities predicated on cellular structures gave, around 1500, promise of long-term viability notwithstanding rivalries and grievances, notably the empire's German-speaking lands and the Polish-Lithuanian Commonwealth.[80] Equally, there was no guarantee that the personal union of Aragon and Castile would survive Queen Isabella and King Ferdinand, and Wars of Religion would soon splinter the realm of France almost irreparably. As already noted, the future looked brighter for those gunpowder empires where authoritarianism and military regimentation went with a fair degree of religious toleration, day-to-day responsibilities being devolved to community-leaders of the various non-Muslim subject populations. Foremost among these practitioners of what might be termed religiously liberal autocracy or militarism were the Ottomans.[81] Their concern for the functioning of law-courts and, in the sixteenth century, careful revisions of tax-registers helped their empire outlast the Safavids and Mughals, right into the twentieth century. In prioritising these functions, they were reprising the ways of their predecessor, the Byzantines, if not the totality of their political culture.

---

[80] J. Whaley, *Germany and the Holy Roman Empire*, 2 vols (Oxford, 2012), i:25–57, 122–42; R. I. Frost, *The Oxford History of Poland-Lithuania, I: The Making of the Polish-Lithuanian Union, 1385–1569* (Oxford, 2015), 286–323, 344–65. See also J. H. Elliott, 'A Europe of composite monarchies', *P&P* 137 (1992), 48–71 at 56.

[81] Some Shi'i sects and groupings in Anatolia, in contrast, did not enjoy nearly so relaxed an approach from the government: Y. Küçükdağ, 'Measures taken by the Ottoman state against Shah Ismail's attempts to convert Anatolia to Shia', *Gaziantep University Journal of Social Sciences* 7 (2008), 1–17 at 13–16; V. Nasr, *The Shia Revival: How Conflicts within Islam Will Shape the Future*, rev. edn (New York, 2016), 65–6.

Appendix

Over 100 scholars have been involved in our informal, self-funded network Political Culture in Three Spheres: Byzantium, Islam and the West, $c.700–c.1450$,[1] and we would like to thank all of them for their stimulating contributions. Many have gone on to publish elsewhere, some directly referencing the project and others – we would like to think – drawing inspiration from it.[2] It began in 2005 with a series of thematically linked sessions at the Leeds International Medieval Congress (IMC) which ran until 2012, comparing aspects of medieval political culture in the Latin west, Byzantium and the Islamic world. Gradually the subject started to take on a life of its own, with members of the network organising a series of events: 2010 saw a workshop on ideology in Cambridge organised by Nora Berend and a conference on court ceremonial and rituals of power in Cyprus organised by Alexander Beihammer.[3] The following year a Table Ronde on 'Political Cultures in Constantinople, the Provinces and Beyond' was held at the 22nd International Congress of Byzantine Studies in Sofia. By 2008, the Leeds IMC sessions had inspired us to run a dedicated workshop comparing the three spheres; held in Aberystwyth,[4] it was followed by further workshops in Oxford and York. To focus discussion, we produced a working definition of political culture and a checklist of 'dumb questions' which all participants were asked to address. These proved useful prompts as we sought to construct initial coordinates for the subject of political culture in three spheres and as we each attempted to make our own sphere comprehensible to scholars from the other two. This volume, focusing on the internal dynamics of each

---

[1] See www.aber.ac.uk/en/history/research/research-projects/political-culture/ (accessed 30 January 2020).
[2] A. Metcalfe, 'Orientation in three spheres: Medieval Mediterranean boundary clauses in Latin, Greek and Arabic', *TRHS* 6th series 22 (2012), 37–55; D. Tor, *The 'Abbasid and Carolingian Empires: Studies in Civilizational Formation* (Leiden, 2017).
[3] A. Beihammer *et al.* (eds), *Court Ceremonies and Rituals of Power in Byzantium and the Medieval Mediterranean* (Leiden, 2013).
[4] See http://users.aber.ac.uk/bkw/rulership2008/ (accessed 30 January 2020).

sphere, is the result, and we hope that it will form an important first stage in a wider project to identify and explain comparisons and connections between spheres. Useful though the questions were, we did not insist on slavish adherence to them from our contributors: the spheres and their geopolitics are simply too different in terms of historical events; rates of source survival vary significantly; and these differences are reflected in the modern historiography. However, given the importance of our working definition and the dumb questions to the genesis and development of this study, and to make our collaborative working methods clear to readers, we include both in this appendix.

Defining Political Culture; Themes and Rationale of the Project

Political culture encompasses both the ideology and the practice of hegemonial groups. It involves the self-definition (expressed verbally, visually or symbolically) and the actual practices, customs, and working assumptions of groups of individuals aspiring to large-scale, long-term hegemony, be it internally (within a given community) or externally (against its neighbours or rivals).

Political culture results from individual actors trying to define and achieve their goals within an agreed set of values, expectations and rules of behaviour. Those rising to or inheriting prominence in this arena make up the political elite of any given society, as do non-players of high birth, substantial means or other forms of leverage who retain the capacity to intervene or obstruct. These elites, furthermore, often sought to transcend and regulate local communities, affiliations and regions; they invoked universal values in vindication of their use of force, role as arbitrator and exaction of resources. Empires, overseeing a wide variety of regions, local elites and interests, are prime candidates for a study of this kind of political culture. But so are smaller polities governing heterogeneous regions, including kingdoms, principalities, bishoprics, city states, despotates, governorships, emirates and sultanates.

The political cultures of such entities were often informed partly by their historical genesis and by the earlier stages of their ascendancy; by their application of force; and by their adaptation to changing circumstances over time. Their internal workings – such as justice, administration and tax-collecting – are obviously relevant, as are the identity, weighting and interplay of political players, but these ought to be viewed alongside the question of how a ruling elite explained and justified its ascendancy and of how their subjects, peers and rivals responded to these claims. In addition, attention ought to be given to the branding of a polity by its rulers and by others (including outsiders): political cultures often define themselves in apposition to other political cultures, deemed either superior and advanced or heterodox and deviant. The dynamics of the interplay between all these elements, the penumbra thrown up by a specific polity's, institution's or movement's kudos, is the essence of what, in the present context, is meant by political culture. Concrete features include, for example, endemic tensions and essential religious coordinates; ideology and propaganda; dynamics of political power and the interaction between public authority and loci of real power.

Our aim is to start filling a gap in the historiography and to identify long-term trends, mechanisms and processes in the interplay between the political cultures of Byzantium, the Islamic world and the Latin west. Through the identification of key themes for future meetings and projects, we may take first steps towards reconstructing the *longue durée* of these political cultures' development and towards understanding the divergences and convergences in their paths from common origins in late antiquity to overt confrontation in early modernity.

Historical Context: What/Who Are We Talking About?

How would you define your sphere chronologically and geographically?

What political formations within your sphere do you consider relevant (regimes, dynasties, institutions [...]) and how do they (not) fit in?

What social groups are/become politically involved in these formations (military, bureaucrats, clergy, nobility, commoners, townspeople, women [...]), and how are they involved (as groups including families/households, as individuals, active or passive [...])?

What are these formations' endemic tensions, fluctuations or paradoxes that affect their political process (inclusivity vs. exclusivity, blood vs. merit, family rule vs. monarchic rule, centre vs. periphery, public vs. private domain [...])?

What are the essential religious coordinates in your sphere and/or formation?

Ideology and Propaganda: How Do Elites/Would-Be Elites Explain Their Hegemony?

What are the vital ingredients of political ideology in your sphere (in general and in particular within each formation)?

To what extent were there conflicting ideologies/ideas/concepts at work in your sphere and/or formation?

What types of power and authority did these ideologies underscore (autocracy, oligarchy, monarchy, regional, universal, centralised, decentralised, communal, imperialist, hegemonic, pragmatic, spiritual, secular, dynastic, hierarchic, egalitarian, charismatic, tribal, patriarchal, patrimonial, legislative, soft [...]), and (how) did they change over time?

How did formations support/enhance these ideologies through propaganda (verbal and non-verbal, including literature, historiography, rituals, ceremonials, art and architecture), and (how) did this change over time?

How do the essential religious coordinates (as identified above) influence political culture and ideology in your sphere?

Practice and organisation: How do elites attain and maintain political power?

What are the practical sources for your formation's elite's hegemony (monopoly of violence, of economic resources, of religious authority, of knowledge and interpretation, of symbols [...]) and (how) did these change over time?

To what extent was political power publicly organised in your formation (administration, economy, justice, security, religion, ritual, law) and (how) did it change over time?

To what extent was political power devolved to the private domain (household politics), and (how) did this change over time?

How important is the geographical setting to your formation's political culture?

How is the continuation of an elite's hegemony built into the political practice of your formation?

What is the role of peace-keeping and violence (internal and external) in your formation's political practice?

Glossary

al-Andalus (A)[1] geographical term, in the Islamic world up to the end of the middle ages, denoting the Iberian peninsula

amir al-umara ' (A) chief emir, supreme commander of the army; in reality emirs became virtual rulers while the caliphs' power waned

archon (s.), *archontes* (pl.) (G) ruler (other than the *basileus*); holder of imperial title or office; provincial landholding elite which dominated the towns

Arianism heresy (named after its main proponent, the third-century theologian Arius) which denied the full divinity of Jesus Christ

atabeg ('guardian') system (Turkish) Seljuk system of government which made young princes the wards of powerful Turkish former-slave generals (*atabeg*s) who acted as their regents, often intermarrying with the princely family; these family ties gradually eroded, with a large number of disconnected, often hostile dynasties competing to rule

augustus (m.), *augusta* (f.) (L.) senior emperor within a group of co-emperors or within a single family; honorary title usually bestowed on the wife of the reigning emperor

basileus (m.), *basilissa* (f.) (G) main formal designation of the Byzantine emperor from the seventh century on

bay 'a (A) reciprocal oath of mutual loyalty and assistance made between an Islamic ruler and his followers

Berbers the name given by outsiders for the inhabitants of the region from the Egyptian frontier to the Atlantic and the great bend of the Niger, who speak – or used to speak before Arabicisation – variants of a single language, Berber (Imazighen, s. Amazigh)

---

[1] A: Arabic; G: Greek; L: Latin.

Bilad al-Sham (A) Greater Syria: in early Islamic usage, *bilad al-Sham* covered modern Syria, Lebanon, Jordan, Israel and the West Bank of Palestine, spreading north into the modern Turkish provinces of Hatay, Gaziantep and Diyarbakr

Cathars dualist Christian sect which flourished in twelfth- and thirteenth-century western Europe, holding that the material world is evil; comparable views were held in the Balkans and the Middle East by the Bogomils and Paulicians

Chalcedonianism belief that there are two, inseparably joined natures (*physeis*) in Christ, the human and the divine; named after the council of Chalcedon (451)

chirograph (from G: *cheir* ['hand'] *graphe* ['writing']) a deed written out two or three times on parchment with the word CHIROGRAPHUM between, enabling it to be cut through the word so that each party had a copy that could be authenticated; the third (bottom) portion was often filed with the king's court as a public record

chrism a mixture of olive oil and balsam, consecrated by a bishop and used for anointing at baptism, confirmation, ordination and other sacraments in the Latin church; mixed with other aromatic ingredients, including wine, nuts and gum, and consecrated by the patriarch in orthodox churches

commendam, in (L) term used of a benefice which had been given in charge ('commended') to a qualified clerk or layman, to hold until a suitable incumbent was found; later, the practice of bestowing a benefice upon a layman or secular ecclesiastic with the right to its revenues for life

cortes (Spanish) a representative assembly, or parliament, of the medieval Iberian kingdoms from the thirteenth century onwards (if not earlier)

dar al-Islam (A) 'the land of Islam'; the territory in which Islamic law obtains

denier tournois (French) originally a base silver penny (denier) struck by the abbots of St Martin of Tours; later a similar coin struck by the kings of France and in several Frankish states in Greece after the Fourth Crusade

devshirme (Turkish) 'recruitment': a 'child levy' which took Christians for training in the Ottoman administration and, especially, in the 'new army' (Turkish *yeni cheri*; English janissary). Girls could aspire to the harem

dynatoi (G: 'the powerful'; pl. of *dynatos*) term for prominent office- or title-holders capable of using their positions to better themselves at the expense of weaker neighbours

family confederation a system of tribal, nomadic organisation where territories were assigned to the foremost member of the leading family

gaon (Hebrew: 'excellency'; pl. geonim) the title of Jewish spiritual leaders and scholars who headed Talmudic academies in Babylonia and Palestine between the seventh and thirteenth centuries

ghazi (A) fighter for the (Muslim) faith; later a title of honour reserved for those distinguishing themselves in such battles

hadith (A) the reported saying(s) of the Prophet

hajj (A) the annual pilgrimage to Mecca, required of all Muslims once in their life, if possible; one of the five 'pillars' (*arkan*) of Islam

Hanafi (A) one of the four religious Sunni schools of jurisprudence (*fiqh*)

Hashimite any of the Arab descendants of the Prophet Muhammad; members of Muhammad's wider tribal group of Hashim

Hegira (A: *hidjra*) Muhammad's flight from Mecca to Medina in September 622; year zero in the Muslim calendar, with dates normally given using the initials AH (*anno hegirae*)

Ifriqiya the eastern part of the Mahgreb (modern-day Tunisia), sometimes confused with the whole of the Mahgreb, since usage varied according to context and period

Imami Shi'i (A) [Imamiyya, Twelver Shi'i or Ithna Ashari] the main Shi'i group recognising supreme spiritual authority in a line of imams reaching back to Ali, the Prophet's son-in-law; since the twelfth imam is believed to have disappeared (in the later ninth century), great authority rests with those scholars who are representatives of the 'hidden imam'

Isma'ili Shi'i (A) second-largest branch of the Shi'i; they took their name from Isma'il, who did not succeed his father Ja'far al-Sadiq upon the imam's death in 148/765. The movement branched away from the main group, the Imamiyya, and in the late ninth century rallied round a supposed descendant of Isma'il (although one group argued in favour of awaiting Isma'il's return)

iqta' (A) assignment of the right to raise revenues from a piece of land (ranging from a field or village to an entire province); in return for this 'salary', the *iqta'*-holder had to provide men for military service; in theory the *iqta'* could be removed by the ruler at any time, although in practice it was a means for weaker rulers to pay their troops and collect taxes

jihad (A) struggle, or striving, but often understood as warfare against infidels

Ka'ba (A) the most sacred site in Islam, situated at the centre of the Great Mosque in Mecca

khalifa (A) 'caliph': 'deputy' or 'successor' of the Prophet Muhammad and so head of the *umma* or of the Islamic state

khanqah (Persian) originally a place of spiritual retreat for Muslim mystics, sometimes likened to a 'monastery'

Kharijites (A) radical Islamic religious sect who rebelled in the seventh century, in the belief that anyone with the necessary piety and moral purity could be elected caliph, and who contested the claims of the Quraysh clan to the caliphate

khatib (A; pl. *khutaba*) originally the spokesman who extolled his tribe's deeds and qualities; from the time of the Abbasids on, delivered the sermon at divine services

khil'a (A) robe of honour

khutba (A) weekly sermon preceding the communal Friday prayer, often delivered in an Islamic ruler's name and therefore an important medium for claims to legitimate sovereignty

laqab (A; pl. *alqab*) honorific title

leidang (Old Norse: *leiðangr*) medieval Scandinavian raising of fleets for seasonal excursions and in defence of the realm; later, a public levy of free farmers

madhhab (A) 'a way of acting'; 'a doctrine'; 'school of law'; used to describe the four legal systems recognised as orthodox by Sunni Muslims (Hanafi, Maliki, Shafi'i and Hanbali)

Maghreb (A: *al-Maghrib*) the name given by Arab writers to that part of North Africa which includes Tripolitania, Tunisia, Algeria and Morocco

Mahdi (A: *al-mahdi*, 'God guided') term with messianic overtones for a leader who could bring in a new era of truly Islamic government; claimed by some later caliphs, notably the Shi'ite Fatimid caliphs of Egypt (969–1171)

mallus (L) a convention or assembly among the Anglo-Saxons and other Germanic peoples

mamluk (A: 'thing possessed') slave, especially used in the sense of military slave and coming to replace the term *ghulam* from the eleventh century on

Mamluk sultanate modern, somewhat controversial, term for the medieval realm spanning Egypt, the Levant and Hijaz that established itself as a caliphate and lasted from the overthrow of the Ayyubid dynasty until the Ottoman conquest of Egypt in 1517; variously known as the sultanate of Egypt and Syria, the Cairo Sultanate, or the 'Turkish' sultanate

miliaresion (s.), *miliaresia* (pl.) (G) the basic Byzantine silver coin, introduced by Leo III and worth 12 to the *nomisma*; characteristic of the eighth to eleventh centuries

miri (Turkish) (shortened form of *amiri*) literally 'pertaining to the commander or governor, the amir'; under the Ottomans, used to mean government lands, the land tax levied from such lands and more generally the public treasury

monotheletism (G: *monos* 'one' and *thelein* 'to will') doctrine recognising that in Christ there was only one 'will' but two natures; condemned by the Sixth Ecumenical Council in Constantinople (680/81)

muluk al-tawa'if (A) 'the kings of the territorial divisions': used by Muslim historians to describe the rulers of some forty principalities (*taifa*s) which sprang up in al-Andalus after the collapse of the Umayyad emirate there

Mu'tazili (A) 'those who withdraw, or stand apart'; by the tenth century, referred to an Islamic school of speculative theology that flourished in Basra and Baghdad from the eighth to tenth centuries

nomisma (s.), *nomismata* (pl.) (G) (L: *solidus*): gold coin struck at 72 to the pound of gold, valued at 12 miliaresia or 288 folleis; from *c.*1092 onwards, Alexios I's new version was generally known as a *hyperperon*

novella (s.), *novellae* (pl.) [L] 'new'; Byzantine imperial legislation

paroikos (s.), *paroikoi* (pl.) (G) peasant tenant on private or state land, paying rent as well as tax; from the thirteenth century onwards, most peasants seem to have been *paroikoi*

Paulicians a dualistic Christian sect perhaps originating in Armenia in the mid-seventh century

Persianate a society based on, or strongly influenced by, Persian language and culture

Persianising that which takes on or produces Persian characteristics or attributes

pronoia (s.), *pronoiai* (pl.) (G) assignment of taxes and other revenues from state-owned land or other specified properties, usually in return for military or other forms of service; introduced from the late eleventh century, it eventually became inheritable

protostrator (G) head groom in charge of the emperor's private stable; commander of the troops and one of the highest Palaiologan dignitaries

purple-born (G: *porphyrogennetos/a*) born in the Porphyra, a chamber of the Great Palace in Constantinople which had walls of porphyry (a deep red or purple stone), normally signifying birth to a reigning empress

qadi (A) judge at a *shari'a* court

Qur'an (A) the Muslim scripture, containing the revelations recited by Muhammad and preserved in a fixed, written form

rhoga (s), *rhogai* (pl.) (G) stipend paid to Byzantine title-holders, senior officials and soldiers annually

shari'a (A) the legal and ethical rules guiding the life of a Muslim, established through *fiqh* (jurisprudence)

Shi'i (A) (lit. 'group', 'party') Muslims who, against the Sunni view, insist that the fourth caliph, Ali (656–61), was the legitimate successor to the Prophet Muhammad, along with the line of Ali's male descendants by his wife Fatima

signoria (I) 'lordship': characteristic form of government in the Italian city states from the mid-thirteenth to early sixteenth centuries, which was run by a *signore* (lord, or despot) and which replaced republican institutions

sikka (A) granting the right to be named on the coinage

strator (s.), *stratores* (pl.) (L) 'groom': official in the imperial stables

Sufism that aspect of Islamic life based on the mystical

Sunni mainstream branch of Islam which recognises the first four caliphs as the Prophet Muhammad's rightful successors; its teachings follow the Qur'an, the *hadith*s and the four schools of law (Hanafi, Hanbali, Maliki and Shafii)

theme in the Middle Byzantine era, the district where soldiers were quartered and from which they were recruited; an administrative unit; the army based in such a region

Thing (*Þing*) (Old Norse) an assembly of free men in Scandinavian society

Twelver (Imami) Shi'i; see Imami Shi'i

'ulama' (s: *alim*) (A) (s.) a learned man, particularly in Islamic religious and legal studies; (pl.) the guardians, transmitters and interpreters of religious knowledge, of Islamic doctrine and law

umma (A) 'people, community'; generally means the community of Muslim believers as a whole, which is thought to possess final authority (under God) with respect to overseeing the leadership of the Muslims

urbarium (L) register of fief ownership, including the rights and benefits that the fief holder has over his serfs and peasants

villa (s.), ***villae*** (pl.) (L) substantial agrarian estate of the late Roman period

waqf (A) in Islamic law, the act of founding a charitable trust, and hence the trust itself; the essential elements are that a person, with the intention of committing a pious deed, declares part of his or her property to be henceforth unalienable and designates persons or public utilities as beneficiaries of its yields; the resultant foundation, providing for religious and educational needs and for general welfare

Zaydi Shi'i (Zaydiyya, Fivers) (A) radical branch of the Shi'i arising out of the abortive revolt against the Umayyad caliphate by Zayd b. Ali, who was the great-grandson of the fourth caliph Ali and was martyred outside Kufa in 740

Index

NOTE: locators in italic type denote illustrations.

143; Romano-German ideology, 65, 143; succession, 371, 394–5, 396; universalism, 135, 155, 156, 372–3; *see also individual polities and topics and* Carolingian empire; Charlemagne; Hapsburg, house of; Ottonian dynasty
Wettin dynasty of Anhalt, 288
White Sheep Turkmen (Aq Qoyunlu), *Map 9f*, 121, 230, 232, 234, 351, 483–4; *see also* Uzun Hasan
William I, the Conqueror, king of England, *251*, 379, 395
William I, the Lion, king of Scotland, 396–7
William Marshal, 378, 406
William of Newburgh, 138
wills, Byzantine, 45, 295; *see also* Gregory Pakourianos; Kale-Maria Pakourianos
Wipo; *Gesta Chuonradi imperatoris*, 251–2; contents, 53, 252, 255–9, 272, 287; context, 53, 259–70
women, 19, 21–4, 27, 490–1, 501–4; attitudes towards rule, 22, 55–6, 503; family, and influence, 23, 24, 37, 222–3, 471; misogyny, 22–3; patronage, 23, 44–5, 200–1; property, 24, 420–1, 502; religious attitudes to, 22, 503, 504; resource and household management, 23, 37; in Russia, 208, 502–4; succession by female line, 23, 300, 395–6, 397
   BYZANTIUM: and court, 204, 311, 407; holy, 208; imperial titles and offices, 204, 420–1; patronage and networks, 200–1; political influence, 200–1, 203–4, 311, 501, 502; property, 420–1, 434; regents, 204, 312–13, 501; trade and commerce, 430
   ISLAMIC WORLD, 21–2; family,

and political power, 23, 222–3, 471; local elites, hold office, 503; Ottomans and, 246, 451, 452, 503; regency of Sitt al-Mulk, 501–2; rule by, 503
   LATIN WEST, 502–3; political participation, 164; power in principalities, 375, 502; previous studies, 21; property, 24, 502; regents, 501–2, 504; religious attitudes to, 22, 503, 504; royal consorts, 45, 407; rulers, 55–6, 397–8, 504; and written culture, 44–5, 502–3
   see also marriage alliances, dynastic world, medieval concepts of, 134–5
Worms, *Map 5*; Concordat, 399
writs, English chancery, 48, 50
written culture, 9; in Islam, 9, 126–7; and judicial testimony, 46, 47, 97, 126–7, 492–3; in Latin west, 44–50, 285, 409, 502–3; *see also* book culture; libraries; literacy
Wulfstan of York; *Institutes of Polity*, 259, 263

yasa, Jingiz Khan's laws of the, 362
Yazd, *Map 7*, 354
Yolanda-Eirene, Byzantine empress, 325

Zadhanfarrukh, Umayyad administrator, 462–3
Zanj revolt, 219, 464
Zayyanids of Tlemcen, 228
Zengids, *Maps 8c, 10c*, 228
Ziyarids, *Map 10b*, 223
Zoe, Byzantine empress, 204, 307, 312
Zubayda, wife of Harun al-Rashid, 106

For EU product safety concerns, contact us at Calle de José Abascal, 56–1°, 28003 Madrid, Spain or eugpsr@cambridge.org.

www.ingramcontent.com/pod-product-compliance
Ingram Content Group UK Ltd.
Pitfield, Milton Keynes, MK11 3LW, UK
UKHW020404140625
459647UK00020B/2643